Psychosocial Adaptation To Chronic Illness and Disability

Hanoch Livneh, PhD

Professor of Rehabilitation Counseling
Coordinator, Rehabilitation Counseling Program
Department of Special and Counselor Education
Portland State University
Portland, Oregon

Richard F. Antonak, EdD

Professor of Research and Applied Statistics
Department of Educational Leadership, Research, and Technology
Associate Dean for Faculty Development, Research, and Technology
College of Education
The University of North Carolina at Charlotte
Charlotte, North Carolina

An Aspen Publication

Aspen Publishers, Inc.
Gaithersburg, Maryland
1997

Aspen Publishers, Inc., is not affiliated with the American Society of Parenteral and Enteral Nutrition.

Library of Congress Cataloging-in-Publication Data

Livneh, Hanoch.
Psychosocial adaptation to chronic illness and disability/Hanoch Livneh, Richard F. Antonak.
p. cm.
Includes bibliographical references and index.
ISBN 0-8342-0967-5
1. Chronic diseases—Psychological aspects. 2. Chronic diseases—Social aspects. 3. Catastrophic illness—Psychological aspects. 4. Catastrophic illness—Social aspects. 5. Physically handicapped.
6. Adjustment (Psychology) I. Antonak, Richard F. II. Title.
RC108.L59   1997
616′.001′9—dc21   97-14138
CIP

Orders: (800) 638-8437
Customer Service: (800) 234-1660

About Aspen Publishers • For more than 35 years, Aspen has been a leading professional publisher in a variety of disciplines. Aspen's vast information resources are available in both print and electronic formats. We are committed to providing the highest quality information available in the most appropriate format for our customers. Visit Aspen's Internet site for more information resources, directories, articles, and a searchable version of Aspen's full catalog, including the most recent publications: **http://www.aspenpub.com**
    Aspen Publishers, Inc. • The hallmark of quality in publishing
        Member of the worldwide Wolters Kluwer group.

Editorial Resources: Greg Balas
Library of Congress Catalog Card Number: 97-14138
ISBN: 0-8342-0967-5

Printed in the United States of America

1 2 3 4 5

Table of Contents

Foreword

Livneh and Antonak have produced an impressive text in which they focus mainly on recent developments in the area of chronic illness and disability by reviewing, discussing, and evaluating research carried out in the preceding 15 years. It is instructive to supplement their contemporaneous approach by examining how the authors' encyclopedic venture reconciles two opposing and historically important ways of thinking about the topic they address.

In 1962 Garrett and Levine published an authoritative text, *Psychological Practices With the Physically Disabled*. Their edited volume contained 13 chapters. Each was about a different form of illness or disability, and each was written by an authority on the condition covered by the chapter. It seems likely that the organization of Garrett and Levine's book was influenced by the then prevalent idea that different kinds of chronic illnesses or disabilities produce correspondingly different kinds of psychological problems for the persons who have them.

This idea constituted the somatopsychological variant of the then dominant psychosomatic *specificity* hypothesis. That hypothesis asserted that certain personality traits or complexes produce particular physical disorders (eg, peptic ulcers). According to the somatopsychological variant, every chronic illness or disability generates its own psychology. Persons with hearing impairments were expected to differ psychologically from persons with visual impairments, cerebral palsy, multiple sclerosis, or other physical disorders.

The somatopsychological specificity hypothesis had staying power. As late as 1977, I noted that two assumptions regarding the relationship between disability or illness and personality were generally accepted. One was that specific forms of somatic disorder are associated with specific personality characteristics. The other was that some types or degrees of disorders of the body are sufficient to cause psychological maladjustment.

A different way of looking at the influence of disabilities was available, although it was less generally accepted at the time. Wright's book, *Physical Disability—A Psychological Approach*, had expressed this different point of view two years before the appearance of Garrett and Levine's volume. Wright's book spelled out a set of psychological principles that accounted for the processes by which people manage all forms of misfortune. The idea behind these principles is that body states are embedded within a broader context of meanings or values, and these determine how people deal with physical states or conditions.

In 1973 Garrett and Levine produced a second volume, *Rehabilitation Practices With the Physically Disabled*. It also contained 13 chapters on specific forms of disability or illness, and each was written by a different authority. Unlike its predecessor, however, this book contained a chapter by W. Gellman, titled "Fundamentals of Rehabilitation," and a chapter by E. Lynton, titled "The Physically Handicapped Citizen: A Human Rights Issue." These chapters are notable because they did not discuss specific body conditions but issues that concern persons with chronic illness or disabilities of almost any kind. Their inclusion in Garrett and Levine's book suggested movement toward recognizing that certain principles and issues are not specific to medical diagnoses and conditions but cut across diagnostic categories.

Particularly important is the fact that one issue involved human rights, or values. In the second edition of her book, published in 1983, Wright made it clear that her approach concerns values. The very first of the "value-laden" principles, upon which her theories were based, merits reexamination: "Every individual needs respect and encouragement; the presence of a disability, no matter how severe, does not alter these fundamental rights" (p. xi, preface to second ed.).

Though consistent in emphasizing values as the matrix from which human actions emerge, Wright's view had undergone a slight shift. The shift was reflected in the change in the title of her book, from "Physical Disability—A Psychological Approach," in the first edition to "Physical Disability—A Psychosocial Approach" in the second edition. The later title expresses Wright's preference of understanding the individual in terms of interpersonal relationships and the social environment, rather than in terms of psychodynamics, such as denial, or intrapsychic structures, such as body image.

The book by Livneh and Antonak may appear at first glance to follow the tradition of Garrett and Levine. For one thing, they commit each of 18 chapters in Parts II through V to reviews of the literature on specific disabilities or health disorders. For another, they devote one chapter in Part I to critiques of eight measures of adaptation to specific chronic illnesses or disabilities. However, it is no accident that the word psychosocial is prominent in the title of this new work, because its approach is closer to Wright's than to Garrett and Levine's.

Part I of Livneh and Antonak's book describes an inclusive psychosocial approach and advocates theory building and testing using psychometrically sound instruments. Part VI offers a comprehensive conceptual framework for the study of psychosocial adaptation to chronic illness and disability. It also provides recommendations for future research. All these discussions deal with issues that are important, whatever a client's diagnosis or physical state. Livneh and Antonak recognized the need to provide an overall perspective, showing readers both the forest and the trees.

An additional feature is that all chapters are written by the same authors, who have evidently worked closely together throughout the project. This lends the writing a coherence not found in most edited volumes. The exhaustive reviews of recent scientific literature are written by the same persons, and this enhances their value. Also the emphasis on methodology that characterizes much of the text is commendable, and, again, continuity of authorship makes it coherent and consistent.

From a purely personal perspective, I would wish for only one addition to these volumes. It would be to include more discussion of the need to study individuals as such.

In collaborative research with individuals, the flow of events that produces outcomes is the main focus of concern. For example, whether a treatment is successful or unsuccessful, this type of research yields insights into the interplay of events, conditions, and experiences from which the outcome emerges. Because rehabilitation is predominantly a matter of intervention, systematic studies of individuals are ideally suited for conducting rehabilitation-relevant programmatic research that will have both practical and theoretic value. Research with individuals should supplement, rather than substitute, for research on groups. But studies of persons can provide a unique understanding of underlying processes, and that is the ultimate goal of scientific explanation.

This final observation is merely a quibble, and I have only good things to say about Livneh and Antonak's text. I expect this comprehensive treatise to become the next classic in its field.

Dr Franklin C. Shontz
Professor Emeritus, Rehabilitation Psychology
University of Kansas
Lawrence, Kansas

REFERENCES

Garrett, J. F., & Levine, E. S. (1962). *Psychological practices with the physically disabled.* New York: Columbia University Press.

Garrett, J. F., & Levine, E. S. (1973). *Rehabilitation practices with the physically disabled.* New York: Columbia University Press.

Shontz, F. C. (1977). Physical disability and personality: Theory and recent research. In R. P. Marinelli and A. E. Dell Orto (Eds.), *The psychological and social impact of physical disability* (pp. 105–129). New York: Springer.

Wright, B. A. (1960). *Physical disability—a psychological approach.* New York: Harper & Row.

Wright, B. A. (1983). *Physical disability—a psychosocial approach* (2nd ed.). New York: Harper & Row.

Preface

Clinicians and researchers alike have demonstrated increased interest in the psychological and social reactions evinced by persons who experience traumatic or sudden onset disabilities, disease-related health disorders, sensory impairments, and chronic neurological and neuromuscular disorders. To account for these reactions, theorists have posited the construct of psychosocial adaptation to illness and disability. Viewed as a special case of coping with a traumatic life event, psychosocial adaptation is thought to entail the gradual process of assimilation of changes in the individual's body, body image, ego, self-concept, and person-environment interactions. Experts agree that the individual's response to rehabilitation opportunities will be limited if he or she has not made a successful adaptation to these changes. Consequently, determination of the individual's psychosocial needs must precede the prescription of an appropriate intervention strategy designed to help the individual with a chronic illness or disability to live and work in typical community settings.

But a number of unanswered questions remain in this domain of inquiry. How are persons with various chronic illnesses and disabilities affected by their conditions? How do they react to and cope with these imposed conditions? What disability- or illness-related, sociodemographic, personality, and environmental factors are linked to successful psychosocial adaptation? This book was written as an attempt to address these and other questions pertinent to the topic of psychosocial adaptation to chronic illness and disability.

This book is divided into six parts. Part I of the book consists of three chapters that provide an introduction to the theory of psychosocial adaptation to chronic illness and disability and to the methods available for the measurement of the construct. Chapter 1 introduces the construct of psychosocial adaptation to illness and disability, provides definitions of key terms related to the construct, and includes a brief historic overview of research in this domain, including a review of theoretical models to account for the nature, structure, and temporal ordering of psychosocial reactions to chronic illness and disability. The chapter concludes with a discussion of the distinction between psychosocial adaptation associated with a chronic illness and psychosocial adaptation associated with a traumatic event.

The purpose of Chapters 2 and 3 is to provide information for clinicians and researchers in the fields of health and disability studies on the availability and suitability of 21 instruments for measuring psychosocial adaptation to chronic illness and disability. Chapter 2 presents reviews of 10 general measures of this construct. Chapter 3 presents reviews of 11 instruments developed to investigate the psychosocial adaptation of individuals with eight specific chronic illnesses and disabilities: namely, cancer, diabetes mellitus, epilepsy, hearing impairment, rheumatoid arthritis, spinal cord injury, traumatic brain injury, and visual impairment.

In Parts II, III, IV, and V we provide reviews of the research literature on psychosocial adaptation to 18 specific chronic illnesses and disabilities. In particular, Part II concerns 4 traumatic or sudden onset disabilities: Chapter 4—cardiovascular diseases; Chapter 5—spinal cord injury; Chapter 6—traumatic brain injury; and Chapter 7—amputation. Part III concerns 3 disease-related health disorders: Chapter 8—cancer; Chapter 9—diabetes mellitus; and Chapter 10—rheumatoid arthritis. Part IV concerns 2 sensory impairments: Chapter 11—blindness and visual impairments; and Chapter 12—deafness and hearing impairments. Part V concerns 9 neurologic and neuromuscular disabilities: Chapter 13—epilepsy; Chapter 14—multiple sclerosis; Chapter 15—cerebral palsy; Chapter 16—amyotrophic lateral sclerosis; Chapter 17—muscular dystrophy; Chapter 18—myasthenia gravis; Chapter 19—neurofibromatosis; Chapter 20—Parkinson's disease; and Chapter 21—spina bifida.

In each of these chapters we begin with a synopsis of available information on the nature, cause, and course of the chronic illness or disability. This is followed by a review of the research literature focusing on the research conducted in the last 15 years. The third section summarizes information on the sociodemographic characteristics, personality factors, illness- or disability-related variables, and environmental circumstances associated with psychosocial adaptation to the chronic illness or disability. Each chapter ends with tentative conclusions derived from the findings reported in the literature reviewed.

Part VI provides an opportunity for us to reflect upon the findings reported in our reviews of the research literature in Chapters 4 to 21. Our goal for Chapter 22 is to provide the clinician with insights into the application of the research findings to counseling interventions. The chapter begins with an overview of theoretical models that have been used to support clinical interventions. Examples are provided of intervention strategies designed to reduce clients' maladaptive psychosocial reactions, teach them appropriate coping skills and problem-solving methods, and provide them with emotional, cognitive, and behavioral support during the process of adaptation. The chapter concludes with an examination of the small but growing number of well-designed empirical studies to assess the effectiveness of various psychosocial interventions with people with a chronic illness or disability.

Our goal for Chapter 23 is to provide the theoretician with a framework for conceptualizing the study of this important construct. The chapter begins with a review of ecological models of psychosocial adaptation to the onset of life crises and transition that have been proposed by researchers and clinicians. Building upon these models and insights gained from the reviews of the research literature, a conceptual framework for the study of psychosocial adaptation to illness and disability is proposed. We argue that to successfully investigate the nature and process of psychosocial adaptation to chronic illness and disability, four broad classes of variables must be considered. These classes of variables and their interactions are illustrated with examples from the research literature. The chapter provides examples of the application of this framework to both research and clinical practice for groups of persons with diverse chronic illnesses and disabilities. The chapter concludes with an introduction to several innovative statistical methods that can assist researchers concerned with the validation of the proposed conceptual framework.

Our goal for Chapter 24 is to provide the researcher with recommendations for improving the quality of future research in this domain of inquiry. On the basis of our reviews of the literature on psychosocial adaptation to the 18 chronic illnesses and disabilities considered in this book, we present a listing of significant research problems that limit the usefulness and generalizability of the available information, together with recommendations for future research, organized into five areas: research conceptualization, study design, sampling, measurement, and data analysis. Modest recommendations to overcome or circumvent these problems in future research investigations are proposed when possible.

The idea for the structure and content of this book was not formed as a whole, but rather evolved out of a series of previous successful research collaborations and joint writing ventures. In June 1991, Hanoch Livneh was invited by Ernest J. Henley, editor of *CRC Critical Reviews in Physical and Rehabilitation Medicine*, to prepare and submit a manuscript presenting a critical review of the research literature on psychosocial reactions to disability. Hanoch responded that he would be pleased to undertake such a writing project provided that he could invite Richard Antonak to participate as a joint author. At that time we had coauthored a book on the measurement of attitudes toward persons with disabilities (Antonak & Livneh, 1988) and had just finished the psychometric work necessary to create the Reactions to Impairment and Disability Inventory (RIDI). Information on the development and validation of the RIDI was published in a series of research articles (Antonak & Livneh, 1991; Livneh & Antonak, 1990; Livneh & Antonak, 1991a; Livneh & Antonak, 1991b). Two other joint writing projects were under way in 1991, a review of the literature on psychosocial adaptation to epilepsy and another on psychosocial adaptation to traumatic brain injury. The first effort led to the publication of an article in the *Journal of Epilepsy* (Antonak & Livneh, 1992) edited by Allen R. Wyler. The second effort led to the publication of an article, with Chris Antonak as the third author, published in *The Journal of Head Trauma Rehabilitation* (Antonak, Livneh, & Antonak, 1993) edited by Mitchell Rosenthal.

The invited monograph that was eventually published in *CRC Critical Reviews in Physical and Rehabilitation Medicine* (Livneh & Antonak, 1994a) included five sections: a general introduction to the theory and research literature in this area; a description of a collection of measures of adjustment to illness, impairment, and disability; reviews of the research literature on psychosocial reactions to spinal cord injury, traumatic brain injury, myocardial infarction, multiple sclerosis, cancer, blindness, epilepsy, and spina bifida; an overview of psychosocial intervention strategies; and a concluding section presenting recommendations for research in this area. A table was included in the monograph that presented information on the availability and suitability of 15 instruments to measure psychosocial adjustment to disability. Portions of the published reviews of the research literature concerning epilepsy and traumatic brain injury were incorporated into the third section of this monograph.

In a conversation with Douglas Strohmer about a new journal that he and H. Thompson Prout were coediting entitled *Assessment in Rehabilitation and Exceptionality*, Richard mentioned the second section of the soon-to-be-published CRC monograph that concerned the 16 measures of adjustment to illness, impairment, and disability. With the permission of CRC monograph editor E. J. Henley, this section was subsequently revised, updated, expanded, and published as a set of two articles on measures of psychosocial adaptation to chronic illness and disability that appeared in series in the Strohmer and Prout-edited journal (Antonak & Livneh, 1994a; Antonak & Livneh, 1994b). The table that had appeared in the CRC monograph was split and appeared as two tables, one in each of the two articles.

The portion of the CRC monograph concerning psychosocial adaptation to multiple sclerosis was updated, expanded, and submitted as the literature review section of a proposal to the National Institutes of Health for a research investigation using the RIDI with a stratified national sample of persons with this disease. The research proposal was not funded, but a review article based in part on this literature review later appeared in *Social Science and Medicine* (Antonak & Livneh, 1995), edited by Peter McEwan.

In June 1993, we responded to a call for articles to appear in a special issue of the *Journal of Social Behavior and Personality* on psychosocial perspectives on disability that was to be edited by Dana Dunn. We proposed to undertake a review of the research literature on psychosocial reactions to seven neuromuscular disabilities: cerebral palsy, muscular dystrophy, Parkinson's disease, amyotrophic lateral sclerosis, myasthenia gravis, neurofibromatosis, and spina bifida. Our proposal was accepted, but our efforts to review this literature led to a manuscript that was more than twice the length indicated in the guidelines for articles to appear in the special issue. So we cut the manuscript in half and published one half (reviews of the literature on cerebral palsy, muscular dystrophy, and Parkinson's disease) in the *Journal of Social Behavior and Personality* (Livneh & Antonak, 1994c) and the other half (reviews of the literature on amyotrophic lateral sclerosis, myasthenia gravis, neurofibromatosis, and spina bifida) as a second article in the *Journal of Rehabilitation Sciences* (Livneh & Antonak, 1994b), edited by Hans Bussman.

At that point in 1993 it was apparent to both of us that we had the nucleus of a book on psychosocial adaptation to chronic illness and disability scattered across the CRC monograph and the eight published or in-press journal articles. While attending a meeting of the Society for Disability Studies in Seattle, Washington, we organized our collection of previously published work and laid out what became the table of contents of the present book. Although portions of our nine previously published works would appear in part in various chapters of this book, we knew that all of these reviews would require substantial updating, expansion, and revision to match a common format and structure. To make the book a comprehensive treatment of the research literature, we also decided to add chapters that would review psychosocial adaptation to a number of other chronic illnesses and disabilities (eg, the chapters on amputation, cancer, deafness, rheumatoid arthritis). The eventual total reached 18 commonly encountered chronic illnesses and disabilities. Chapters on theories of psychosocial adaptation, on methods of studying the construct, and on counseling intervention strategies were planned, and a concluding chapter that would present our recommendations for future research in this area was envisioned.

Two and a half years of sustained effort since that time have resulted in this book. It remains up to you, the reader, to decide whether we were successful in meeting our goal of providing an up-to-date source of information on the nature, phases, correlates, and individual variability in the process of psychosocial adaptation to chronic illness and disability.

We thank Ms Peggy Wright and Ms Mary Deschler for their research and secretarial assistance. And we acknowledge with deep appreciation the support and understanding of our families, friends, and colleagues throughout the time this book has been our preoccupation.

REFERENCES

Antonak, R. F., & Livneh, H. (1988). *The measurement of attitudes toward people with disabilities: Methods, psychometrics, and scales*. Springfield, IL: C C Thomas.

Antonak, R. F., & Livneh, H. (1991). A hierarchy of reactions to disability. *International Journal of Rehabilitation Research, 14*, 13–24.

Antonak, R. F., & Livneh, H. (1992). A review of research on psychosocial adjustment to impairment among persons with epilepsy. *Journal of Epilepsy, 5*, 194–205.

Antonak, R. F., & Livneh, H. (1994a). Instruments to measure psychosocial adjustment to illness and impairment: Part I. General measures. *Assessment in Rehabilitation and Exceptionality, 1*, 125–161.

Antonak, R. F., & Livneh, H. (1994b). Instruments to measure psychosocial adjustment to illness and impairment: Part II. Specific illness and impairment measures. *Assessment in Rehabilitation and Exceptionality, 1*, 175–202.

Antonak, R. F., & Livneh, H. (1995). Adaptation to disability and its investigation among persons with multiple sclerosis. *Social Science and Medicine, 40*, 1099–1108.

Antonak, R. F., Livneh, H., & Antonak, C. (1993). A review of research on psychosocial adjustment to impairment among persons with traumatic brain injury. *Journal of Head Trauma Rehabilitation, 8*(4), 89–102.

Livneh, H., & Antonak, R. F. (1990). Reactions to disability: An empirical investigation of their nature and structure. *Journal of Applied Rehabilitation Counseling, 21*(4), 13–21.

Livneh, H., & Antonak, R. F. (1991a). The development of a scale to measure reactions to disability: The Reactions to Impairment and Disability Inventory (RIDI). In G. Kiger & S. C. Hey (Eds.), *Research in disability studies: Vol 3. The social organization of disability experiences* (pp. 103–108). Salem, OR: Willamette University Press.

Livneh, H., & Antonak, R. F. (1991b). Temporal structure of adaptation to disability. *Rehabilitation Counseling Bulletin, 34*, 298–319.

Livneh, H., & Antonak, R. F. (1994a). Reactions to disability: A review and critique of the literature. *Critical Reviews in Physical and Rehabilitation Medicine, 6*, 1–100.

Livneh, H., & Antonak, R. F. (1994b). Review of research on psychosocial adaptation to neuromuscular disorders: Amyotrophic lateral sclerosis, myasthenia gravis, neurofibromatosis, and spina bifida. *Journal of Rehabilitation Sciences, 7*, 66–79.

Livneh, H., & Antonak, R. F. (1994c). Review of research on psychosocial adaptation to neuromuscular disorders: I. Cerebral palsy, muscular dystrophy, and Parkinson's disease. *Journal of Social Behavior and Personality, 9*, 201–230.

About the Authors

HANOCH LIVNEH, PhD, received his BA degree in psychology from the Hebrew University, Jerusalem, Israel (1971), and his MA (1973) and PhD (1976) degrees in Rehabilitation Counseling Psychology from the University of Wisconsin—Madison. In 1973, while doing his practicum and internship at the Division of Vocational Rehabilitation and the Dane County Mental Health Center, he counseled clients with both physical and psychiatric disabilities. Also during his doctoral studies he supervised graduate students enrolled in rehabilitation counseling practicum courses. He joined the faculty of the Rhode Island College Counselor Education Department (later restructured and renamed the Department of Counseling and Educational Psychology) in 1977 as the Assistant Director of the Rehabilitation Counseling Program. In 1979 he became the director of the program and in 1980 led it to national accreditation by the Council on Rehabilitation Education (CORE). In 1988 Dr Livneh joined the Counselor Education Program at Portland State University and established its Rehabilitation Counseling Specialization. The specialization achieved national accreditation by CORE in 1993. He is currently a Professor of Rehabilitation and Counselor Education, the Coordinator of the Rehabilitation Counseling Specialization, and Acting Chairperson of the Counselor Education Program at Portland State University.

Dr Livneh's research interests are in attitude formation and measurement, adjustment to and coping with disability, psychiatric rehabilitation, and counseling and personality theories. He has authored theoretical and research articles and book chapters on attitude origination and measurement, adjustment to disability, the structure of anxiety and death anxiety, coping with stress, functional limitations, and rehabilitation models. He serves as a vocational expert for the Office of Hearings and Appeals, Social Security Administration. He served as a consultant to various public and private rehabilitation agencies and as a grant reviewer to the Rehabilitation Services Administration and the US Department of Education.

Dr Livneh serves as a reviewer for three journals, the *Journal of Applied Rehabilitation Counseling, Rehabilitation Counseling Bulletin*, and *Rehabilitation Education*. He is a Certified Rehabilitation Counselor, National Certified Counselor, and Licensed Professional Counselor in the State of Oregon.

Dr Livneh and Dr Antonak were the recipients of the American Rehabilitation Counseling Association's Annual Research Award in 1991 and again in 1995.

RICHARD F. ANTONAK received the AB degree in mathematics from Rutgers College (1969) and the MEd (1970) and EdD (1975) degrees in special education from Temple University. His first professional experience with persons with disabilities was as a teacher of adolescents with mental retardation at the Woods Schools in Langhorne, Pennsylvania. From 1970 to 1973 he was a special education teacher at Penncrest High School in Media, Pennsylvania. While completing graduate study he supervised teachers of exceptional children and taught special education courses at the Delaware Valley Campus of The Pennsylvania State University. He joined the faculty of the education department at The University of New Hampshire in 1975, where he served as coordinator of special education programs continuously until 1990. In 1990 he joined the faculty of the Department of Teaching Specialties in the College of Education at The University of North Carolina at Charlotte as a professor of research methods, measurement, and applied statistics. In 1994 he became the Associate Dean for Faculty Development, Research, and Technology in the College of Education. In this role he also directed the work of the Office of Educational Research and Evaluation. In July of 1997, he was appointed Dean of School of Education, Indiana State University, Terra Haute, Indiana.

Dr Antonak's research specialties are in attitude measurement, disability studies, psychometrics, and applied multivariate statistics. He has published more than a dozen research instruments to measure attitudes toward persons with disabilities. He has authored research articles, reviews, monographs and book chapters on topics in attitude measurement, psychometrics, psychosocial adaptation to chronic illness and disability, and applied statistical methods, including 26 publications coauthored with Hanoch Livneh.

Dr Antonak was elected to Phi Beta Kappa and Pi Mu Epsilon (the National Honorary Mathematics Society) while at Rutgers and was advanced to Fellow of the American Association on Mental Retardation in 1983. He is a member of the American Academy on Mental Retardation, the Society for Disability Studies, the American Statistical Association, the American Rehabilitation Counseling Association, and the American Educational Research Association.

Theory and Methods

Part I of the book consists of three chapters. Chapter 1 begins with an introduction to the construct of psychosocial adaptation to chronic illness and disability, including the definition of key terms (eg, impairment, disability, handicap), a historical overview of research in this domain of disability studies, and an exegesis of the relationships of the construct to related constructs (eg, coping, body image, grief). The chapter continues with an examination of several theoretical models that have been propounded to account for the nature, structure, and temporal ordering of the psychological reactions that are thought to constitute phases of a process of psychosocial adaptation. This examination provides definitions of eight psychological reactions that are most often identified in the research literature (ie, shock, anxiety, denial, depression, internalized anger, externalized hostility, acknowledgment, and adjustment) and addresses the question of whether a process of psychosocial adaptation exists. Chapter 1 concludes with a discussion of the distinction between psychosocial adaptation associated with a chronic illness, such as multiple sclerosis, and psychosocial adaptation associated with a disability, such as a spinal cord injury.

The purpose of the next two chapters in Part I is to address an important methodologic issue in the study of psychosocial adaptation to chronic illness and disability. Our reviews of the literature revealed that a significant weakness of most of the descriptive and experimental research, even some of the best designed and best executed research, was the selection of a psychometrically inadequate instrument to operationalize the construct of psychosocial adaptation. An inadequate instrument will yield inadequate data, data that are of little value for theory building and theory testing. In these two chapters we provide information for clinicians and researchers in the fields of health and disability studies on the availability and suitability of 21 instruments for measuring psychosocial adaptation. Chapter 2 presents reviews and critiques of 10 general measures of this construct organized into three categories: (1) measures of psychosocial adaptation to chronic illness (five instruments), (2) unidimensional measures of psychosocial adaptation to disability (three instruments), and (3) multidimensional measures of psychosocial adaptation to disability (two instruments). Chapter 3 presents reviews and critiques of 11 instruments developed to investigate the psychosocial adaptation of individuals with eight specific chronic illnesses and disabilities: cancer, diabetes mellitus, hearing impairment (two instruments), rheumatoid arthritis, seizure disorders (two instruments), spinal cord injury, traumatic brain injury (two instruments), and visual impairment.

We will focus our attention on the application of the theory and methods associated with psychosocial adaptation in Part VI of this book. Following our reviews of the research literature on psychosocial adaptation to 18 chronic illnesses and disabilities in Parts II, III, IV, and V, we review counseling interventions (Chapter 22) and present a framework for studying adaptation to chronic illness and disability (Chapter 23). The last chapter of the book (Chapter 24) lists significant research problems together with recommendations for future research.

CHAPTER 1

Psychosocial Adaptation to Chronic Illness and Disability

INTRODUCTION

Chronic illnesses and disability are common experiences in the lives of many individuals. They affect the physical, psychological, social, vocational, and economic functioning of those affected and that of their families. It is estimated that currently more than 35 million Americans have some form of chronic illness or a disabling condition that interferes with their daily lives (Eisenberg, Glueckauf, & Zaretsky, 1993). Many of these conditions are physical in nature, permanent, and considered severe.

Estimates also indicate that

- Eight of the 10 most common causes of death in the United States are linked to chronic illness, including the three leading causes of death: cardiovascular diseases, cancer, and cerebrovascular diseases (Stachnik, Stoffelmayr, & Hoppe, 1983).
- The typical American will spend nearly 12 years in a state of "limited functioning" because of both acute and chronic medical conditions (Eisenberg et al., 1993).
- Costs of annual medical care and income support provided by the US government to persons with disabilities have reached $60 billion, or approximately 7% of the gross national product (Eisenberg et al., 1993).

The prolonged course of treatment, the often uncertain prognosis, the constant and intense psychosocial stress, the gradually increasing interference with the performance of daily activities and life roles, and the associated impact on family and friends all combine to create a profound effect on the lives of persons with chronic illnesses and disabilities.

3

Chronic illnesses and disabilities come in many forms. Some are congenital while others are adventitious and may be acquired during infancy, adolescence, adulthood, or old age. There are, however, substantial psychological differences between persons with congenital physical disabilities and those who acquire them following physical trauma or disease (Grzesiak & Hicok, 1994; Wright, 1983). For example, children with congenital physical disabilities are only familiar with their already impaired bodies. Furthermore, the process of their body image, ego, and self-identity development is likely to follow similar psychological and social routes as that of children without disabilities (Lussier, 1980). The quality of psychosocial adaptation among these children is, therefore, closely linked to early parental and social issues of shame, pity, guilt, stigma, and ridicule (Grzesiak & Hicok, 1994; Wright, 1983). Persons with adventitious disabilities, on the other hand, often experience an acute sense of loss and grief. Among persons with sudden onset disabilities or gradually progressive diseases, shock and anxiety are common reactions at the initial recognition of the condition. These feelings are typically followed by depression and anger when the condition's magnitude and consequences are fully appreciated.

Disabilities of sudden onset, such as those caused by an accident or injury, are more apt to be viewed as a crisis situation (Moos & Schaefer, 1984). However, unlike life crises that are normally time limited and reversible, chronic illnesses and injury-triggered disabilities constitute prolonged crises of extended duration and may result in permanent changes to the lives of the affected individual and his or her family. Persons with certain types of chronic illnesses and disabilities (eg, myocardial infarction, spinal cord injury) may attain a level of medical and functional stability following initial trauma or disease onset, while the lives of persons with other conditions (eg, cancer, multiple sclerosis, rheumatoid arthritis) may be marked by an unstable disease or disability course with periods of exacerbation and remission. These two broad types of conditions trigger different kinds of psychosocial reactions and experiences. They may also require different coping patterns and time periods to progress toward successful psychosocial adaptation.

Indeed, it is often assumed that aside from the variable medical and functional involvement, persons with chronic illnesses and disabilities also vary greatly along more subjective dimensions, such as premorbid and postmorbid personality attributes, coping abilities, degree of psychosocial adaptation, and perceived social support. How are persons with chronic illnesses and disabilities affected by their conditions? How do they cope with these imposed conditions? What disability- or illness-related sociodemographic, personality, and environmental factors are linked to successful psychosocial adaptation? This book seeks to address these and other questions pertinent to the topic of psychosocial adaptation to chronic illness and disability.

TERMS RELATED TO PSYCHOSOCIAL ADAPTATION

Before proceeding with the reviews of the research that attempt to answer these questions, we will present a brief description of the terms most commonly encountered in the literature on psychosocial adaptation to chronic illness and disability and in the literature on models of adaptation to crisis, illness, and disability.

Impairment, Disability, and Handicap

Although the terms impairment, disability, and handicap are often used interchangeably in the literature, they refer to different levels of functional limitations and should be distinguished (World Health Organization, 1980).

Impairment

Impairment is defined as "any loss or abnormality of the psychological, physiological, or anatomic structure or function" (World Health Organization, 1980, p. 47). As such, impairment reflects disturbances at the body organ, or system level (eg, back, leg, brain). Impairments, therefore, reflect the residual effects of disease or injury and as such are prolonged (but not necessarily permanent) clinical conditions that disrupt average physical, cognitive, or affective functioning (Livneh, 1987; World Health Organization, 1980).

Disability

Disability is defined as "any restriction or lack of ability to perform an activity in the manner or within the range considered normal for a human being" (World Health Organization, 1980, p. 143). Disability, therefore, reflects disturbances at the person level or self-system. Put differently, disability relates to those deficiencies in normally anticipated function, behavior, or performance (eg, inability to walk, inability to sit for an extended period of time, limited ability to retain knowledge). Disabilities, then, result from impairments and convey restrictions of the integrated activities expected of the whole person. They are long-term conditions and can be reversible, stable, or progressive (Livneh, 1987; World Health Organization, 1980).

Handicap

Handicap is defined as "a disadvantage for a given individual, resulting from an impairment or disability that limits or prevents the fulfillment of a role that is normal (depending on age, sex, and social and cultural factors) for that individual" (World Health Organization, 1980, p. 183). Handicap, accordingly, reflects the sociocultural, economic, and environmental consequences (ie, exterio self-system) that result from impairment or disability. As such, handicap represents disadvantage in the successful fulfillment of an individual's social and occupational roles (ie, disadvantages of social and occupational integration and of economic self-sufficiency). Handicaps are measured against norms and policies of a particular environment, society, or culture. They are generally irreversible conditions of prolonged duration because of well-entrenched societal belief and value systems (Livneh, 1987; World Health Organization, 1980).

Adjustment and Adaptation

The concepts of psychosocial adjustment and psychosocial adaptation share much. In fact, their use is often indistinguishable in the literature on disability and coping with crisis situations. Before their differentiating and overlapping features are addressed, a brief historical review of these concepts will be provided.

In one of the earliest efforts to analyze psychosocial adjustment to disability, Dembo, Leviton, and Wright (1956) equated successful adjustment with a "coping" framework. In contrast, the inability to achieve successful adjustment was regarded as a reflection of a "succumbing" framework. The coping framework was predicated upon the following characteristics: (1) emphasizing what the person can do, (2) assuming an active role in shaping one's life, (3) recognizing personal accomplishments, (4) successfully managing negative life experiences, (5) reducing limitations through changes in the physical and social environments, and (6) participating in and enjoying valued activities.

Expanding on earlier writings, Wright (1983) paralleled acceptance of disability with psychosocial adjustment as evidenced in the domain of one's value system. Acceptance, or adjustment, was equated with the ability to minimize actual or perceived losses that stem from a disabling condition and the ability to retain the value of existing abilities (Keany & Glueckauf, 1993). Wright (1983), accordingly, proposed four revaluation changes that limit devaluation of self and broaden acceptance of loss. These changes included (1) enlargement of the scope of values, or the recognition of the existence of values other than those directly affected by the disability; (2) subordination of physique relative to other values, or decreasing the relative importance of physical appearance in comparison to other personal abilities and values; (3) containment of disability effects, or limiting the deleterious impact of disability spread to nonaffected areas; and (4) transformation of comparative-status values to asset values, or replacing external-based (ie, standard, normative) abilities and qualities with internal-based (ie, inherent, intrinsic) values and qualities.

Other theorists have suggested models of adjustment to chronic illness or disability from clinical observations or research data. For example, Hamburg and

Adams (1967), in discussing the coping behaviors manifested by persons with severe physical disabilities, observed the following behaviors as indicative of successful psychosocial functioning: (1) keeping distress within manageable limits, (2) maintaining a sense of personal worth, (3) restoring relationships with significant others, (4) increasing opportunities for recovery of physical functioning, and (5) increasing likelihood of achieving personally valued and socially acceptable life goals.

Shontz (1975) perceived psychological adjustment as a final stage in his temporal model of response to disability. He further argued that adjustment was a function of the congruence between the subjective world of the person and the external environment. The better the fit between the psychological framework and the external reality, the better the degree of adjustment. Successful adjustment, therefore, necessitated two separate processes. On the one hand, internal perceptions led to actions that maximized available environmental opportunities. On the other hand, the environment must be adapted to facilitate efficacious behaviors. Adaptation was viewed by Shontz (1975) as that dynamic, mutual accommodation of both subjective experience and external environment. The evolving process of adaptation required the individual to show sensitivity to the environment as typically evidenced by one's internal mental state, knowledge of available resources, and interpersonal skills.

Roessler and Bolton (1978) regarded adjustment to disability both as a state or a goal and as a process consisting of a succession of situations requiring specific solutions. Based on their review of the existing models of adjustment to disability, they advocated a comprehensive, synthesized model that they called a "behavioral coping" model, which incorporated such elements as survival ability, potential assets, person-environment congruence, and positive striving. According to this model, maladjustment was regarded as failure to resolve problems in living, while successful adjustment reflected the ability to manage one's environment and efficiently use problem-solving skills. DeLoach and Greer (1981), in a similar manner, argued that adjustment comprised self-acceptance, responsible behavior, appropriate social techniques, and successful coping strategies. They offered no insight into the interrelationships among these domains, nor did they discuss the specific psychosocial and coping efforts associated with successful adjustment to disability.

Clinicians and researchers writing more recently (see, for example, Jacobson et al., 1990; Pollock, 1986) also failed to draw a distinction between the concepts of adjustment and adaptation. Pollock (1986), for instance, perceived adaptation to chronic illness and disability as a complex process involving both internal and external factors. Ultimately, however, she asserted that adaptation refers to the degree to which the person adjusts (ie, functions successfully) physiologically, psychologically, and socially to the chronic condition. Jacobson et al. (1990)

offered a more comprehensive definition of adjustment to chronic illness. They viewed adjustment as referring to those affective and behavioral changes made in response to the immediate external environment, to developmental stages, and to long-term life situations. They further suggested that adjustment could be measured by variables, including (1) self-esteem, (2) psychological symptoms, (3) behavioral problems, (4) demonstrated skills in educational and social situations, and (5) attitudes regarding the chronic illness.

In concert with these theoretical formulations, we regard psychosocial adaptation to chronic illness and disability as an evolving, dynamic, general process through which the individual gradually approaches an optimal state of person-environment congruence manifested by (1) active participation in social, vocational, and avocational pursuits; (2) successful negotiation of the physical environment; and (3) awareness of remaining strengths and assets as well as existing functional limitations. Adjustment, on the other hand, will refer more specifically to a particular phase (ie, set of experiences and reactions) of the psychosocial adaptation process. As such, adjustment is the clinically and phenomenologically hypothesized final phase—elusive as it may be—of the unfolding process of adaptation to crisis situations including the onset of chronic illness and disability. It is alternatively expressed by terms such as (1) reaching and maintaining psychosocial equilibrium; (2) achieving a state of reintegration; (3) positively striving to reach life goals; (4) demonstrating positive self-esteem, self-concept, self-regard, and the like; and (5) experiencing positive attitudes toward oneself, others, and the disability (Jacobson et al., 1990; Livneh, 1986; Roessler & Bolton, 1978; Wright, 1983).

As is evident from this cursory discussion, psychosocial adaptation will be manifested differently depending on the type of chronic illness or disability and its long-term implications. For example, adaptation in the case of more stable, non–life-threatening conditions, such as amputation, is vastly different from that associated with unstable conditions, such as multiple sclerosis, or deteriorating, life-threatening conditions, such as cancer of the liver. We will return to this point in Chapter 23.

Coping with Stress, Crisis, and Disability

The investigation of how persons cope with a variety of stressful life events and crisis situations has generated a plethora of theoretical perspectives and clinical observations, lists of coping strategies, and numerous measurement scales. The coping literature, however, has resulted in a fragmented body of knowledge and often inconsistent, even contradictory, findings (see, for example, Carver, Scheier, & Weintraub, 1989; Tobin, Holroyd, Reynolds, & Wigal, 1989).

Clinicians and researchers who have conceptualized the process of coping as consisting of intrapsychic mechanisms often draw a distinction between maladaptive (ie, negative, rigid, emotion-focused, neurotic) and adaptive (ie, positive, flexible, problem-focused, reality-based) coping strategies (Haan, 1977; Zeitlin, 1980). The research team of Lazarus and Folkman (Folkman, 1984; Lazarus, 1966; Lazarus & Folkman, 1984) suggested one of the earliest multifaceted models in which coping with stress was composed of four interactive dimensions. These included (1) the *functions* of coping, consisting of the reduction of noxious environmental conditions or problem solving, and regulation of emotions, or the maintenance of positive self-esteem; (2) the *determinants* of coping, including personal factors (eg, beliefs, skills) and situational factors (eg, available resources, type of stress); (3) the *appraisal* of coping, including both primary cognitive assessments (ie, appraisal of an event's significance for one's well-being) and secondary cognitive assessments (ie, appraisal of available resources, options, and imposed constraints); and (4) the actual *coping modes* of direct action, information seeking, action inhibition, intrapsychic and cognitive strategies, and turning to others.

Similar models of coping with life stresses were advanced by Pearlin and Schooler (1978) and by Billings and Moos (1981; 1984). The former team of researchers suggested a tripartite model of coping strategies that included responses directed at controlling negative affect, responses that alter the meaning or appraisal of the event, and responses directed at altering the situation itself. The latter team of researchers, on the other hand, posited a two-facet model. The first facet, the *focus of coping*, was seen to be composed of three elements: (1) appraisal focusing (eg, logical analysis, cognitive redefinition, avoidance, denial); (2) problem focusing (eg, seeking information and support, taking action, identifying alternative rewards); and (3) emotion focusing (eg, affective regulation, emotional discharge, resigned acceptance). The second facet, the *method of coping*, was seen to be composed of three elements: active-cognitive, active-behavioral, and avoidance.

In addition to these conceptual models of coping with crisis and stress, many specific coping strategies have been proposed or can be identified in the literature (Aldwin & Revenson, 1987; Carver et al., 1989; McCrae, 1984; Tobin et al., 1989). Much of this research uses empirically derived scales that posit the operation of coping modes such as (1) avoidance or escapism, (2) problem solving or instrumental action, (3) denial or minimization, (4) seeking social support, (5) seeking meaning, (6) blaming or criticizing oneself, (7) planning, (8) acceptance of a situation, (9) turning to religion or wishful thinking, (10) disengaging from a situation, (11) negotiating or bargaining (eg, with God, medical experts), and (12) ventilating feelings.

Investigation of the patterns of coping displayed by persons with sudden onset and chronic physical disabilities has gradually captured the interest of researchers in the past decade. Three of the more commonly investigated disabilities in this area of research have been spinal cord injury, myocardial infarction (heart attack), and cancer. Feifel, Strack, and Nagy (1987), for example, examined the relationships between the selection of coping strategies by persons with a chronic illness and several disability-related and personality variables. Their findings showed that (1) use of acceptance-resignation coping modes was associated with negative self-esteem, lower expectations of chances of recovery, longer duration of chronic illness, and expression of negative affect; (2) use of avoidance was linked to negative self-esteem and to reduced self-directed life orientation; and (3) survivors of myocardial infarction coped more successfully with their disability when they minimized the use of both acceptance-resignation and avoidance coping modes.

Dunkel-Schetter, Feinstein, Taylor, and Falke (1992) studied the relationships between coping patterns and a number of medical and psychological variables among persons with cancer. Findings suggested that (1) focusing on the positive was the most frequently adopted coping mode among the younger individuals and those in remission; (2) using social support was linked to greater perceived stress from cancer and having more functional limitations; and (3) cognitive and behavioral escape-avoidance modes were associated with recurrent treatment for cancer, having more functional limitations, and living alone.

Finally, Hanson, Buckelew, Hewett, and O'Neal (1993) investigated the relationship between coping modalities and psychosocial adaptation among persons with a spinal cord injury. Results of this longitudinal study indicated that (1) persons with a spinal cord injury strongly endorsed the use of three coping modes over time: namely, threat minimization, information seeking, and cognitive restructuring; and (2) two coping strategies were associated with acceptance of disability at that time but not with vocational or medical status: namely, using cognitive restructuring and not using wish-fulfilling fantasy.

The findings from these and other investigations (eg, Frank et al., 1987; Keckeisen & Nyamathi, 1990; Nolan & Wielgosz, 1991; Pegler & Borgen, 1984) strongly suggest that the adoption of more active, problem-focused, information-seeking, and social support-seeking coping strategies (regarded clinically as adaptive coping) results in better psychosocial adaptation to physically disabling conditions. In contrast, the use of more passive, emotion-focused, self-blame, avoidance-escape coping modalities (typically regarded as maladaptive) generally results in poorer psychosocial adaptation and increased psychological distress. It is conceivable, however, that different patterns of coping strategies may have phase-specific and function-specific properties. For example, problem-focused, information-seeking strategies may be more adaptive early in the process of disablement or when expectancy of recovery is high. Emotion-focused avoidance strategies (eg, emotion regulation, ventilation of feelings), on the other hand, may become more useful later in the process when ambiguity is high or when chances for recovery are poor.

Body Image

The concept of body image has intrigued researchers for many years. Schilder (1950), inspired by the earlier work of Head (1920), viewed body image as the mental representation or schema of one's own body. This mental picture reflects a three-dimensional image that incorporates personal, interpersonal, environmental, and temporal factors. Schilder asserted further that body image evolved gradually as a result of multiple sensory inputs, including visual, auditory, tactile, proprioceptive, and kinesthetic. In addition to these early sensory inputs, body image was thought to be influenced by societal attitudes and reactions to others (Lambert & Lambert, 1979; McDaniel, 1976). Jourard (1963), in a similar vein, perceived body image as composed of those perceptions, beliefs, and values the person attaches to his or her body, physical appearance, structure, state of health, function, and physical boundaries.

Two of the most thorough researchers of the concept of body image, Fisher and Cleveland (Fisher, 1970; Fisher & Cleveland, 1968), devoted considerable time to investigating the relationship between body experience (ie, body image, body concept) and personality. They argued that body experience is associated with three important psychological operations. These included (1) dampening and magnification—body experiences may be minimized or completely avoided from consciousness or intensified to be the sole focus of consciousness; (2) creating boundaries between the self and the environment—differentiating body or self from the external environment; and (3) distributing attention to important body regions, based on both functional, personal, or symbolic significance.

Another important figure in body image research is Shontz (1975), who viewed body experience as occurring at four separate levels, ranging from those most dependent to those least dependent upon immediate sensory input. The four levels included:

1. *Body schemata*, composed of topographic and spatial localization of body parts and hedonic distinction between painful and pleasurable stimulation
2. *Body self*, where boundaries between self and environment are established, personal space is developed, and evaluative judgment of body experience is gained
3. *Body fantasy*, which refers to those elaborate fantasies, of symbolic nature, about one's body and related wishes and impulses

4. *Body concept*, where accumulated knowledge results in labeling and partial cognitive control of body parts, functions, and actions.

As can be observed from this cursory discussion, body image—and its related concept of body experience—serves as a standard of much significance when persons relate to themselves, to others, and to the external environment (Bramble, 1995). It is intimately tied to, and is often perceived to be at the root of, one's self-concept, self-esteem, and, in general, one's personal and interpersonal identity. Body image is typically regarded as a developmental or dynamic concept and is thought to evolve and change throughout one's life cycle. As such, it affects not only one's perceptions, emotions, cognitions, attitudes, and functional abilities, but also the reactions of others toward oneself (Bramble, 1995; Jourard, 1963; McDaniel, 1976).

Chronic illness and disability are believed to alter (some argue to distort) one's body image and self-concept because the imposed physical changes must be accommodated by the individual (Falvo, 1991). Problems associated with the onset of a disability, such as physical (eg, aesthetic, visible) disfigurement, functional limitations (eg, loss of a body part, reduced physical capacity), and pain, all threaten the stability of one's body image and may result in significant changes to the body image (Bramble, 1995). When the disability results in distortions of body image, these changes may be traced to disruption of perceptual processes (McDaniel, 1976). This may further reflect a deficiency in processing feedback about the imposed bodily changes and an inability to accurately assess and organize perceptions and information. Many of the experienced body image changes that result from a chronic illness or disability may, indeed, be partially due to restricted mobility, sensory isolation, social restriction, and cognitive distortion (McDaniel, 1976). The hallmark of successful psychosocial adaptation to a chronic illness or disability is the integration of imposed physical changes into one's reconstructed body image and self-perception. Unsuccessful adaptation, on the other hand, is marked by experiences of physical and psychiatric symptoms that may include psychogenic pain, chronic fatigue, anxiety, depression, social withdrawal, and anger (Bramble, 1995; Falvo, 1991).

Clinical and empirical research efforts regarding the impact of physical disability on body image have yielded conflicting results. Fisher (1970) concluded from an early yet extensive review of the literature on disability and body image that severe physical disability apparently exerts only minor impact upon measured body image. This conclusion, however, must remain tentative in light of Fisher's failure to consider that (1) most measures of body image lack psychometric soundness and may be insensitive to the complexity of the measured concept; (2) the affected individual will frequently deny the resultant body changes because these are often too threatening and anxiety-provoking to assimilate; and

(3) changes in body image usually follow a prolonged process of intrapsychic accommodations and interpersonal interactions, thus rendering early postdisablement measures inaccurate and even misleading. In situations where shifts in body image occurred following disability, Fisher (1970) observed the following patterns: (1) denying and shutting out the existence of one's body, (2) searching for an illusory restoration of the lost body part or function, (3) focusing attention on a nonimpaired part of one's body as a means to deny impairment to the affected part, and (4) undergoing a period of crisis and defense mobilization followed by a gradual acceptance and assimilation of an altered body.

Loss, Grief, Depression, and Sorrow

The onset of traumatic or insidious disability constitutes a crisis in the life of the affected person. As such it triggers a mourning process for the lost body part or function that is often evidenced by feelings of grief and despair. Although most writers define mourning as a time-limited, depressive period, the nature and dynamics of the mourning process and the ensuing feelings of depression that follow the onset of disability have never been satisfactorily unraveled. In fact, considerable disagreement exists in the literature concerning the necessity of mourning for achieving a successful psychosocial adaptation to a chronic illness or disability. Whereas some writers (eg, Shontz, 1975; Wright, 1983) perceive the experiences of depression and mourning as necessary for psychological growth to occur and for acceptance of permanent loss to be internalized, others (eg, Trieschmann, 1988; Wortman & Silver, 1987; 1989) disagree with this deterministic perspective. The latter writers argue that no convincing empirical data currently exist to support claims of the inevitable occurrence of depression following physical loss or of its necessity for successful psychosocial adjustment. More recently, however, substantial evidence has accumulated that suggests a much higher prevalence rate of depression among persons with physical disability than in the general population (Friedland & McColl, 1992; Turner & Wood, 1985).

In a series of studies, Turner and colleagues (Friedland & McColl, 1992; Turner & Beiser, 1990; Turner & McLean, 1989; Turner & Noh, 1988; Turner & Wood, 1985) demonstrated convincingly that a strong link existed between the onset of a physical disability and depressive symptomatology. Turner and Wood (1985) found that in a Canadian sample of nearly 1,000 persons with physical disabilities encompassing a wide range of disorders (eg, musculoskeletal, circulatory, neurological, respiratory), the prevalence rate of depression (as measured by the Center for Epidemiological Studies Depression scale) was approximately twice that found in the general population. Turner and Noh (1988), using the Center for Epidemiological Studies Depression scale in a two-wave longitudinal research design with samples of community-based persons who reported a variety of physical disabilities (n = 967 at time 1; n = 730 at time 2 four years later), concluded that this group was at greater risk for experiencing depressive symptomatology. In fact, over one third of the samples exhibited clinically significant levels of depression at both times 1 and 2. These results held true regardless of sex, age, educational level, marital status, and level of income. Finally Turner and Beiser (1990) showed that as compared to a large sample of persons without disabilities (n = 850), individuals with physical disabilities (n = 727) were more than three times as likely (37% versus 12%) to report an episode of major depression within the six-month period preceding the data collection interview. Again, these results were consistent across both sexes and all age-based groupings. It may be further argued that the prevalence rate of depression reported by these community-based samples of persons with a disability underestimated the true prevalence rate of depression since persons in institutions, who typically experience more severe, prolonged, and life-threatening disabilities, were excluded from these studies.

Although the data provided by Turner and colleagues and by other researchers (Rodin & Voshart, 1986) do not support the inevitability of depression following loss and disability, they do strongly support, contrary to the views of Trieschmann (1988) and of Wortman and Silver (1987; 1989), the existence of highly elevated prevalence rates of depressive symptomatology among persons who experience a physical disability. It should also be noted that whereas the bulk of the research that Wortman and Silver (1987; 1989) reviewed dealt with losses generated by death of family members, the research of Turner and colleagues and that of Rodin and Voshart (1986) relied extensively on losses triggered by disabling conditions or losses of body parts and functions (eg, Friedland & McColl, 1992).

More recently several researchers (Burke, Hainsworth, Eakes, & Lindgren, 1992; Davis, 1987) have taken what appears to be a "middle-of-the-road" position and argued that the term "chronic sorrow" (a term originally coined by Olshansky, 1962) may be the most appropriate to describe the grief experienced by persons with a disability. Davis (1987), for example, argued that individuals who become disabled experience grief differently. This is because permanent disabilities or chronic illnesses require extended and unpredictable periods of mourning. She claimed further that traditional stage theories of adaptation to loss distort the grief experienced by persons who must live continuously with their disability. Because the mourning process that follows the onset of a physical disability is cyclical and prolonged, the person with a disability must gradually come to terms with an altered and suffering self. This constitutes the chronic sorrow experience.

Burke et al. (1992), in a similar vein, perceived chronic sorrow as a form of grief for a loss of normality. The presence of a disability and its chronicity serve as constant reminders of the loss. Chronic sorrow does not culminate in the predictable and time-limited resolutions referred to as acceptance and adjustment. But unlike pathological grief, which often results in continuous feelings of sadness, guilt, and anger, chronic sorrow does not prevent the affected individual from staying highly functional and focused despite the constant reminder of the permanent loss.

The antecedents of chronic sorrow have been identified by Teel (1991) as (1) disruption of a relationship of attachment, (2) a negative and permanent disparity between past and present conditions, and (3) the existence of trigger events that result in recognition of this disparity. Lindgren, Burke, Hainsworth, and Eakes (1992) elaborated on what they perceived to be the critical attributes of chronic sorrow. These included (1) a perception of sorrow over time with no predictable end, (2) sadness that is recurrent or cyclic, (3) sadness that is triggered either externally or internally and reawakens one's losses and fears, and (4) sadness that is progressive and that can increase long after the initial loss.

Denial

One of the most controversial components of the process of psychosocial adaptation to chronic illness and disability is that of denial. Denial has been regarded by researchers and theoreticians as either (1) a specific stage, or phase, in the adaptation or mourning process triggered by the onset of traumatic loss (eg, death, disability); or (2) a defense mechanism to ward off anxiety and other distressing emotions. In this second conceptualization, denial is viewed as an unrelenting process by which one protects the ego from being engulfed by painful reminders of an altered external reality (eg, the disabling condition) and emotional flooding (Horowitz, 1986). Denial of terminal illness implies different psychosocial processes than denial of a non–life-threatening disability. The former is manifested in patterns such as denial of the existence of the terminal disease, denial of the future risks imposed by the illness, and, finally, denial of impending death (Stewart, 1994). The latter is more typically reflected in denial of the extent and severity of the disability, its functional limitations, and its permanence.

Several models of denial have been proposed in the literature. Over 40 years ago, Weinstein and Kahn (1955) argued that denial of a disability or chronic illness may be expressed in five general patterns. These include:

1. complete denial, in which the person totally denies any signs of illness;
2. denial of major disability, in which the individual denies major limitations but stresses some less threatening aspect of the disability;

3. minimization of the disability or the attribution of difficulties to some other benign cause;
4. projection of disability outside one's body, or attribution of its ownership to others; and
5. temporal displacement of the disability, in which the person admits disability in the past but claims recovery in the present.

In what might be the most thorough analysis of denial, Breznitz (1983) postulated the existence of seven types of denial. Each type referred to a different level of processing threatening information. The seven forms of denial included:

1. denial of personal relevance, or maximizing the perceived differences between oneself and others involved in the threatening situation;
2. denial of urgency, or using methods to perceive the situation as less pressing in the present;
3. denial of vulnerability, or maximizing perceived personal strengths and control over the situation;
4. denial of affect, or using methods to reduce the emotional impact of the threatening situation;
5. denial of affect relevance, or construing the emotion in terms of other, unrelated causes (ie, diverting attention to secondary issues);
6. denial of threatening information, or using selective inattention to, or only partial awareness of, the threatening situation; and
7. denial of all information, or creating a barrier between one's psyche and the external environment.

Denial has been viewed historically from a psychoanalytic perspective as a defense mechanism that operates unconsciously (Fenichel, 1945; A. Freud, 1966; S. Freud, 1936). It is, therefore, inaccessible to immediate insight. Others have argued that it is at least partially under conscious control. Wright (1983), for instance, suggested that, during the earliest phases of adaptation to a disability, the person attempts to conceal his or her disability. This concealment ("as if" behavior) stems from the belief that being disabled renders the individual less desirable and valuable as a person.

Denial may be an adaptive strategy that is important to survival when it counters stress and extreme anxiety engendered by various life crises, including chronic illness and disability (Hackett & Weisman, 1969; Levine et al., 1987; Meyerowitz, 1980). This is particularly true during the earliest phases of the adaptation process. During these early periods denial serves to protect the self from confronting and being overwhelmed by the deleterious implications of the injury or illness (ie, loss of function). It allows, therefore, for gradual assimilation of the altered reality while maintaining a cohesive sense of the self (Langer,

1994; Stewart, 1978). However, denial loses its initial useful function and is termed pathological when it continues to operate, when it interferes with processing of therapeutic information and procedures, or when it results in self-harming behaviors (Langer, 1994; White, 1974).

MODELS OF PSYCHOSOCIAL ADAPTATION TO ILLNESS AND DISABILITY

The onset of a physical disability invariably triggers a chain of psychological reactions in the affected individual, viewed as a special case of coping with a traumatic life event. Clinicians and researchers have posited several theoretical models to account for the nature, structure, and temporal ordering of the observed reactions. In this section of the chapter we will turn our attention to an investigation of these models.

Conceptual Issues

The literature on psychosocial adaptation to chronic illness and disability (Brooks & Matson, 1982; Drudge, Rosen, Peyser, & Pieniadz, 1986; Frank, Van-Valin, & Elliott, 1987; Gottesman & Lewis, 1982; Kerr & Thompson, 1972; Lawrence & Lawrence, 1979; Levin, Banks, & Berg, 1988; Lipowski, 1970; Shontz, 1975; Whalley-Hammell, 1992; Wright, 1983) contains valuable theoretical discussions and the results of clinical studies with diverse populations. Examination of this literature shows, however, that there is little agreement on the nature of the concept (Livneh & Antonak, 1994a). Most authors (Bray, 1978; Dunn, 1975; Falek & Britton, 1974; Frank, Corcoran, & Wonderlich, 1987; Johnson & Morse, 1990; Katz & Florian, 1986–1987; Livneh & Antonak, 1990; Pepper, 1977; Weller & Miller, 1977) have posited models in which adaptation is conceptualized as a process of change in reactions triggered by functional limitations associated with external environmental antecedents (eg, injuries, accidents, traumas) or internal pathogenic conditions (eg, diseases). From a methodologic perspective, the adaptation process suggests an unfolding paradigm in which the individual's reactions to his or her chronic illness or disability follow a stable sequence of phases (ie, partially overlapping and nonexclusive psychosocial reactions), or stages (ie, discrete and categorically exclusive psychosocial reactions) that can be temporally and hierarchically ordered. Others (Caplan & Shechter, 1987; Frank, Elliott, Corcoran, & Wonderlich, 1987; Silver, Boon, & Stones, 1983; Silver & Wortman, 1980; Trieschmann, 1988; Westbrook & Viney, 1982; Wortman & Silver, 1987; Wortman & Silver, 1989) view psychosocial adaptation to chronic illness and disability as one of a set of independent and nonsequential patterns of human behavior.

Proponents of phase models contend that human adaptation to the onset of a chronic disease or sudden physical disability involves a gradual process of psychological assimilation of the resultant changes in body, self-concept, and person-environment interaction. To support their argument of a linear adaptation process, they typically identify common reactions (eg, anxiety, depression, anger) in the population under observation. The order of emergence of these reactions is assumed to be invariant within this population or even across populations coping with similar physical, medical, and environmental problems. Furthermore, the emergence of more distal adaptation phases is predicated upon the person's successful negotiation of the more proximal phases linked to the onset of the disabling condition.

In contrast, opponents of phase models of adaptation to chronic illness and disability—and of coping with loss in general—have argued three points. First, reactions to chronic illness or disability are not universally experienced. For example, these researchers have tried to demonstrate that the experience of depression is not a necessary reaction to a chronic illness or disability. Put differently, grieving for the functional loss or impaired body part is not viewed as a required concomitant of the so-called adaptation process, nor is it seen as necessary to be experienced to abandon one's old self and adopt a new self-image (Caplan & Shechter, 1987; Silver & Wortman, 1980; Trieschmann, 1988; Wortman & Silver, 1989). Second, a state of final adjustment (alternatively referred to as resolution, acceptance, assimilation, reorganization, reintegration) is not always achieved by persons with chronic illnesses and disabilities (Frank et al., 1987; Silver et al., 1983; Wortman & Silver, 1987). And finally, based on the available clinical and empirical evidence, they argue that psychological recovery does not follow an orderly sequence of reaction phases (Silver & Wortman, 1980; Wortman & Silver, 1989).

Before addressing these issues specifically, it is necessary to outline the assumptions shared by most phase model adherents and to briefly discuss the phases ostensibly experienced by individuals beset by sudden-onset physical disabilities, disease-related health disabilities, or chronic neurological disorders.

Assumptions Common to Phase Models

The assumptions inherent in all phase models of adaptation to a chronic illness or disability include the following:

- For an adaptation process to be initiated, a chronic illness or traumatic physical disability must result in permanent and significant changes in the body's appearance and functional capabilities. These changes are typically followed by changes in body image and self-concept.

- Adaptation implies a dynamic and unfolding process punctuated by a gradual shift from earlier experiences of distress (eg, feelings of anxiety and depression) to subsequent reconciliation and assimilation of loss.
- The onset of symptoms of a chronic illness or a sudden physical disability results in temporary loss of psychological equilibrium. Gaining renewed equilibrium involves a gradual process of reintegration and adaptation to the perceived misfortune.
- The initiation, progression, and sequencing of the phases of adaptation to a chronic illness or disability appear to be mainly internally determined, but external events or direct interventions (eg, counseling, environmental changes) are capable of modifying the structure and pace of the experienced reactions.
- Successful transition through the phases of adaptation produces increased psychological growth and maturity.
- The sequence of experienced reactions to a chronic illness or disability is not universal. Human uniqueness and variability strongly influence the presumed temporal ordering of these adaptation phases.
- The process of adaptation is not irreversible. Individuals who experience a chronic illness or sustain a permanent disability may regress to an earlier phase or skip one or more phases of psychosocial adaptation.
- Phases of adaptation comprise nondiscrete and categorically overlapping reactions. These reactions may fluctuate and blend with one another, providing for the experience of more than one reaction at a time.
- Attempts to specify the duration of each phase, or of the entire adaptation process, are futile at best. The length of time each reaction is experienced is multiply determined by factors such as age at onset of symptoms, premorbid personality, prior exposure to crisis situations, nature and severity of the illness or disability, extent of social support network, and available human and financial resources.
- Not all individuals with a chronic illness or disability successfully reach the theoretical endpoint of the adaptation process; some fixate at an earlier nonadaptive phase.

Phases of Adaptation to a Chronic Illness or Disability

Reviews of research concerning psychosocial adaptation to various chronic illnesses and disabilities (Antonak & Livneh, 1992; Antonak & Livneh, 1995; Antonak, Livneh, & Antonak, 1993; Bray, 1978; Devins & Seland, 1987; Dunn, 1975; Krueger, 1981–1982; Livneh, 1986; Livneh & Antonak, 1994a; Livneh & Antonak, 1994b; Livneh & Antonak, 1994c; Livneh, Antonak, & Maron, 1995; Rigoni, 1977; Russell, 1981; Shontz, 1965; Siller, 1976; Weller & Miller, 1977) have most often identified the reaction phases of shock, anxiety, denial, depression, internalized anger, externalized hostility, acknowledgment, and final adjustment. More generic models of adaptation to crisis and loss have been proposed by Kübler-Ross (1969) to describe acceptance and adaptation to death and dying, by Bowlby (1973; 1980) and Parkes (1972; 1975) to describe mourning and adaptation to grief and bereavement following personal loss, and by Horowitz (1985; 1986) to describe the phases of adaptation to catastrophic life events. These authors have also identified phases such as shock/numbness, yearning/pining, denial, depression, anger/resentment, and final recovery/completion (ie, acceptance, reorganization, resolution). In this section we will briefly describe each of these reactions associated with psychosocial adaptation to chronic illness and disability.

Shock

Shock is generally perceived as the individual's initial or emergency reaction to the onset of a sudden and severe physical injury (eg, spinal cord injury, amputation) or psychological trauma (eg, diagnosis of a life-threatening disease or neurological disorder). It is a reaction resulting from the impact of an overwhelming experience characterized by psychic numbness, depersonalization, cognitive disorganization, and often dramatically decreased mobility and speech.

Anxiety

Anxiety is viewed as a panic-stricken reaction upon initial sensing of the magnitude of the physically or psychologically traumatic event. This statelike reaction is signified by confused thinking, cognitive flooding, numerous physiological correlates (eg, breathing problems, rapid pulse rate), and purposeless overactivity. It should not be confused with anxiety as a traitlike character concept. Anxiety in persons with a chronic illness is often associated with waiting for results of medical tests, learning about life-threatening diagnoses, anticipating invasive procedures, experiencing side effects of certain treatment modalities, contemplating changes in lifestyle (eg, vocational, social, sexual activities), fear of recurrence of symptoms, uncertainty about the future, and possible medical complications (Lambert & Lambert, 1979; Thompson, Webster, Cordle, & Sutton, 1987; Welch-McCaffrey, 1985).

Denial

Denial, considered a more problematic reaction to verify due to its subtle and often conflicting aspects, is regarded as a defensive mobilization (ie, psychological retreat) against painful realization of the extent, duration, and future implications of the chronic illness or disability. It involves negation or minimization of the chronicity of the condition because of its psychological implications (Naugle,

1988). It often includes a wishful and unrealistic expectancy of recovery. The denying person is often described as aloof, indifferent, and selectively attentive. He or she appears to employ selective attention to the surroundings, accepting those facts that appear to support a self-imposed, distorted picture of reality but minimizing and avoiding any reminder of the unacceptable reality.

Depression

Depression, a reaction often observed among adventitiously impaired persons, is considered to be the typical reaction upon initial realization of disease sympto- matology or the loss of prior body integrity stemming from a sustained bodily insult and realization of ensuing physical, social, and behavioral limitations. It is regarded as a reactive response of bereavement for the lost body part or function or of impending death and suffering. Feelings of helplessness, hopelessness, despair, isolation, self-depreciation, and distress have been frequently observed among persons with a chronic illness or disability. Reviewers of the literature in this area (eg, Rodin, Craven, & Littlefield, 1991; Taylor & Aspinwell, 1990) have noted that depression is variously accounted for by (1) premorbid propen- sity (eg, family history, predisability personality); (2) reactions to stressors (eg, damaged self-esteem, loss of social roles) associated with the onset of disease symptoms or the disabling condition; or (3) manifestations of biological and neu- rochemical changes attributable to disease or disability.

Internalized Anger

Internalized anger is perceived to be a manifestation of self-directed resent- ment and bitterness, often associated with feelings of self-blame. Feelings of guilt are observed, and they usually center on issues such as attribution of respon- sibility to one's behavior and health practices regarding the onset of the illness or disability, the extent of the loss, or the failure to improve medically and the like. The physical disability or life-threatening disease is often believed by the indi- vidual to be causally linked to past transgressions. Self-injurious acts and suicidal ideation may follow. This reaction should be most evident in persons who realize their impairment is a chronic condition (Levin & Grossman, 1978).

Externalized Hostility

Externalized hostility, viewed as an attempt at retaliation against imposed functional limitations, is hostility directed at other persons, objects, or aspects of the environment believed to be associated with the onset of the disease or disabil- ity or with the obstacles encountered during the rehabilitation process. Aggres- sive acts, other-blaming verbalizations and behaviors, feelings of antagonism, demanding and critical attitudes, abusive accusations, and passive-aggressive modes of obstructing treatment are usually manifest during this phase. Externalized hostility should be particularly evident with increasing passage of time from the onset of disease symptoms or physical impairment (ie, chronicity; Brooks, 1988).

Acknowledgment

Acknowledgment is regarded as the first indication that the person has cognitively reconciled with (eg, recognized) or accepted the permanency of the condition and the future implications stemming from the chronic illness or disability. The individual reaches a state of cognitive reorganization and reorientation toward the self and the external environment typified by the integration of the functional limitations associated with the condition into his or her self-concept. More specifically, during this state the individual (1) accepts himself or herself as a person with a disability, (2) gains a new sense of self-concept, (3) reappraises life values, and (4) seeks new meanings and goals.

Adjustment

Adjustment, theoretically conceptualized as the final phase of the adaptation process, is considered to reflect both an affective internalization (ie, emotional acceptance) of the functional limitations imposed by the chronic illness or disability into one's self-concept and a sociobehavioral reintegration into the newly perceived life situation. During this period the person fully assimilates the functional limitations associated with the disease or disability into a new, cohesive self and, more important, is fully capable of successfully adjusting to the outside world. The person who reaches this state (1) reestablishes a positive self-worth, (2) realizes the existence of remaining and newly discovered potentialities, (3) actively pursues and implements social and vocational goals, and (4) successfully overcomes obstacles encountered during the course of pursuing these goals.

Does a Process of Adaptation to a Chronic Illness or Disability Exist?

To show that adaptation to a chronic illness or disability is a temporally ordered, hierarchical process, it is necessary to identify a sequence of reaction phases for a population under study (Carpenter & Strauss, 1977; Coombs & Smith, 1973). While overlap may exist among the intervals associated with temporally juxtaposed phases, the order of emergence of the phases should remain invariant. The researcher may observe the behavior of a small sample of persons (the cohort) at different times to study time-ordered associations. An illustration of this longitudinal research design is the work of Lezak and colleagues (Lezak, 1987; Lezak & O'Brien, 1988), who collected data at one-year intervals up to five years posttrauma from persons with traumatic brain injuries. Three patterns of change were observed: (1) continuing psychosocial dysfunction over time, (2) gradual and variable improvement over time, and (3) a curvilinear pattern in which gains were observed within the second half of the first year after injury (ie, anxiety and depression decreased) but then were lost in subsequent years.

Longitudinal investigations may yield rich data, but they are generally time-consuming and expensive endeavors. An alternative is to obtain data from a cross section of the population at one time with the hope that the characteristics of the persons sampled will represent each of the phases of the process being investigated. Data-analytic procedures, such as scalogram analysis (Guttman, 1944), unfolding theory (Coombs, 1964), and ordering theory (Krus, Bart, & Airasian, 1975), are then used to test the hypothesized phase sequence. This design, although unable to delineate the exact timing of acquired and deleted phases, may reveal a time-ordered sequence of the process studied. Cross-sectional studies are useful for the identification and isolation of salient variables and relationships that can be studied in detail with longitudinal designs.

The controversy surrounding the existence of an orderly process composed of phases of adaptation to chronic illness and disability has been raging for many years in the field of disability studies. Although no solution to this dispute is proposed here, a few comments can be made in response to the criticisms of phase models raised previously. First, it would be foolhardy to argue that a universal process of adaptation to misfortune exists, considering the wide range of human misfortune experienced (eg, traumatic injuries, insidious chronic illnesses, stressful situations, the death of loved ones, loss of property). To argue against the existence of a structured process of adaptation to loss, insisting that the existence of an orderly universal structure or precise time of recovery must first be demonstrated by empirical findings (see Silver & Wortman, 1980; Trieschmann, 1988), is tantamount to ignoring the intricate nature and diversity of human losses. The sequencing and duration of the adaptation process are intimately linked to the nature of the crisis encountered, dooming to failure any search for a universal process across all crisis situations.

Second, because most proponents of a phase model concede that the adaptation process might be reversed or elements of the process skipped altogether, the lack of emotional distress (ie, experienced depression or internalized anger) in some individuals who experience a chronic illness or sustain a disability can be explained on the grounds that grief is not mandatory for transition to more distal phases of the adaptation process. Finally, the inability of some persons who suffered physical or psychological loss to reach a state of acceptance, resolution, or adjustment is explained in similar terms. Not all individuals are capable of cognitively assimilating or accepting their loss (ie, a phase of acknowledgment) let alone emotionally reintegrating the loss into their body image or self-concept (ie, a phase of final adjustment). Moreover, even when such a state is achieved, future life crises or repeated environmental obstacles can result in regressive behaviors that signify a reversal of the adaptation process.

Although empirical investigation of the process of adaptation to chronic illness and disability is in its infancy, several interesting findings have emerged in the past two decades. For example, Bracken, Shepard, and Webb (1981) examined several psychosocial reactions (eg, anxiety, depression, denial, anger) for persons with a spinal cord injury. Although no temporal changes in these reactions were explored, the authors reported that at the time of hospital discharge, respondents' scores on their measures of anxiety, depression, and anger demonstrated only moderate intercorrelations (ranging from 0.35 to 0.60). Scores on the denial measure, on the other hand, were independent of the other three measures, highlighting the importance of viewing reactions to disability from a multidimensional perspective.

Westbrook and Viney (1982) investigated psychosocial reactions (eg, anxiety, depression, anger, helplessness, positive feelings) to various chronic illnesses using content analysis of respondents' verbal responses. The pattern of reactions of the persons with chronic illnesses differed considerably from that of persons without illnesses, lending support to the psychological distress of the former group. Again, these results suggested the existence of a multifaceted constellation of psychosocial reactions to chronic illness. Ferguson, Dodds, Craig, Flannigan, and Yates (1994) investigated psychosocial adaptation to sight loss using a longitudinal research design (before and after a rehabilitation training program) and linear structural modeling statistical techniques. Their findings indicated the existence of temporal changes in anxiety and depression (both decreased) and in acceptance and self-esteem (both increased) over time.

Livneh and Antonak (1991) investigated a hypothesized temporal order of phases of psychosocial adaptation to disability in a cross-sectional sample of persons with various physical disabilities using unfolding-theoretic analysis (Davison, 1977). The results obtained revealed a phase ordering that did not coincide with the hypothesized ordering (ie, shock, anxiety, denial, depression, internalized anger, externalized hostility, acknowledgment, and adjustment). A set of five nonadaptive reactions (ie, depression, internalized anger, shock, anxiety, and externalized hostility) preceded and was distinguishable from a set of two adaptive reactions (ie, acknowledgment and adjustment), with the reaction of denial intermediate to these two polar sets.

Suspecting that the failure to recover the hypothesized order was an artifact of examining the process with a linear analytic technique, this research team subsequently investigated the relationships among the eight reaction phases using ordering theory, a nonlinear analytic technique, with data from a sample of persons with noncongenital physical impairments (Antonak & Livneh, 1991). Acknowledgment and adjustment were seen as distinct final phases, suggesting that the individual may acknowledge his or her disability but fail to achieve full adjustment to it. Reaching one of these adaptive phases was dependent upon passing through prerequisite phases of anxiety, depression, internalized anger, and externalized hostility. Experiencing shock was apparently prerequisite to experiencing depression and internalized anger, whereas denial was independent of the other reactions. While the authors cautioned that the obtained reaction phase hierarchy was not universal and needed to be cross-validated with other samples, their results demonstrated the fruitfulness of conceptualizing psychosocial adaptation to chronic illness and disability as a nonlinear, multidimensional, hierarchical process.

DIFFERENCES IN ADAPTATION TO A CHRONIC ILLNESS AND ADAPTATION TO A DISABILITY

As previously suggested, it is important to distinguish between psychosocial adaptation to congenital and adventitious disabilities. It is likewise useful to make a distinction between psychosocial adaptation to a chronic illness, such as multiple sclerosis, and psychosocial adaptation to a disability associated with a traumatic event, such as a spinal cord injury. With a traumatic event, the onset of disability is sudden, with physical stability achieved more or less soon afterward. The onset of a chronic illness is typically gradual and insidious. The course of the illness is often uncertain and is marred by periods of deterioration and remission. The distinction between these two conditions, although only occasionally intimated in the literature (Cassileth et al., 1984; Dakoff & Mendelsohn, 1986; Viney & Westbrook, 1981), is of theoretical importance when conceptualizing the unfolding nature of adaptation to life crises generally and to medical conditions specifically.

The reaction of shock, for example, will generally be experienced following the onset of a traumatic condition (eg, amputation, spinal cord injury, head injury, myocardial infarction), but it may have a more narrow psychic focus when the person is confronted with the diagnosis of a life-threatening or end-stage disease (eg, cancer, amyotrophic lateral sclerosis, acquired immune deficiency syndrome [AIDS]). Shock may not be experienced at all, however, by persons with a gradually deteriorating and uncertain medical condition (eg, rheumatoid arthritis, Parkinson's disease, diabetes mellitus, deafness in old age). Similarly, the reactions of anxiety and depression may be manifest in a variety of clinical forms, depending upon the disabling condition. When a chronic illness is involved, anxiety and depression, which often share common ingredients, are manifest as fear of body damage, fear of an uncertain future, and even fear of death (Brown & MacCarthy, 1990; Viney & Westbrook, 1982). Following a sudden, traumatic, physical disability, however, anxiety and depression typically include grieving for a lost body part or function and psychomotor retardation (Parkes, 1975). In other words, whereas chronic illness related anxiety and depression appear to be future oriented (eg, fear of the unknown, feelings of hopelessness), traumatic event related anxiety and depression appear to be more past oriented (eg, grieving for the loss of an intact physical or cognitive ability).

As a final example, the reactions of acknowledgment and adjustment are likely to take different forms depending on whether the disability is related to a chronic illness or a traumatic event. When a chronic, especially a life-threatening, illness is the condition, acknowledgment and acceptance would constitute some form of recognition or internalization that the condition is likely to worsen or that death is imminent. Psychosocial adaptation under such conditions is almost inconceivable. Following a traumatic event, however, psychosocial adaptation to a permanent and relatively stable loss or alteration of function implies reconstruction of one's life followed by efforts to successfully reintegrate oneself into society.

It is noted, however, that the study of psychosocial adaptation to either a chronic illness or to a traumatic disability is complicated by many intervening and mediating factors. These include cognitive impairments associated with the impairment or illness (eg, central nervous system versus peripheral system involvement), age at onset, chronicity, premorbid coping mechanisms and skills (eg, level of successful coping with previous life crises), severity of the resultant functional limitations, and the availability of a supportive family network and social resources (Cassileth et al., 1984; Livneh, 1986; Viney & Westbrook, 1981; Viney & Westbrook, 1982). We will return to a discussion of these and related issues in Chapter 23.

CONCLUSION

Chronic illnesses and disabilities are common experiences in the lives of many individuals. They profoundly influence the physical, psychological, social, vocational, and economic functioning of those affected and that of their families. How, precisely, are persons with chronic illnesses and disabilities affected by their conditions? How do they cope with these imposed conditions? What psychological reactions do they typically manifest? Do these reactions constitute a process of adaptation to the chronic illness or disability? If so, can this process be ordered both temporally and hierarchically? What disability- or illness-related, sociodemographic, personality, and environmental factors are linked to successful psychosocial adaptation? This book seeks to address these and other questions pertinent to the topic of psychosocial adaptation to chronic illness and disability.

This first chapter began with a presentation and brief description of the terms most commonly encountered in the literature on psychosocial adaptation to chronic illness and disability and the literature on models of coping with crisis, illness, and disability. In particular, this chapter (1) differentiated and defined the terms impairment, disability, and handicap; (2) compared psychosocial adjustment to psychosocial adaptation; (3) examined the concept of coping with stressful life events and crisis situations and discussed different coping strategies that have been proposed; (4) discussed the concept of body image; (5) examined the constructs of loss, grief, and sorrow and compared them to the construct of depression; and (6) differentiated between denial as a phase in the process of adaptation and as a defense mechanism and examined models of denial of loss. In the process of these discussions, the chapter also provided a succinct historical review of efforts to analyze psychosocial adaptation to chronic illness and disability and efforts to create conceptual models of coping with crisis and stress.

The next section of the chapter presented an overview of theoretical models that attempt to account for the nature, structure, and temporal ordering of psychological reactions triggered by functional limitations associated with external environmental antecedents (eg, injuries, accidents, traumas) or internal pathogenic conditions (eg, diseases). Two types of models were distinguished: namely, those models in which adaptation is conceptualized as an unfolding of these psychosocial reactions in a stable sequence of phases (ie, partially overlapping and nonexclusive psychosocial reactions) or stages (ie, discrete and categorically exclusive psychosocial reactions) that can be temporally and hierarchically ordered, and those models in which adaptation is viewed as just one of a set of independent and nonsequential patterns of human behavior. A set of 10 assumptions inherent in phase models of psychosocial adaptation to a chronic illness or disability were presented and discussed. This was followed by a description of the reaction phases most commonly encountered in the literature: shock, anxiety, denial, depression, internalized anger, externalized hostility, acknowledgment, and final adjustment.

The next section of the chapter described requisite research designs and introduced data-analytic methods for investigators seeking to examine the question of whether an orderly process of adaptation to a chronic illness or disability exists. The results of several recent research investigations were presented to illustrate the potential benefits for theory building and theory testing in this area of inquiry. The chapter concluded with a discussion of the differences that distinguish psychosocial adaptation to a chronic illness and psychosocial adaptation to a disability associated with a traumatic event.

The next two chapters in this first part of the book are concerned with a description and critique of measures of psychosocial adaptation to illness and disability commonly used by clinicians and researchers in the fields of health and disability studies. Chapter 2 provides information on the availability and suitability of general instruments for measuring psychosocial adaptation to illness and disability organized into three categories: (1) measures of adaptation to illness,

(2) unidimensional measures of adaptation to disability, and (3) multidimensional measures of adaptation to disability. Chapter 3 provides information on the availability and suitability of instruments for measuring psychosocial adaptation to specific illnesses and disabilities, namely, cancer, diabetes mellitus, hearing impairment, rheumatoid arthritis, seizure disorders, spinal cord injury, traumatic brain injury, and visual impairment.

REFERENCES

Aldwin, C. M., & Revenson, T. A. (1987). Does coping help: A reexamination of the relation between coping and mental health. *Journal of Personality and Social Psychology, 53,* 337–348.

Antonak, R. F., & Livneh, H. (1991). A hierarchy of reactions to disability. *International Journal of Rehabilitation Research, 14,* 13–24.

Antonak, R. F., & Livneh, H. (1992). A review of research on psychosocial adjustment to impairment among persons with epilepsy. *Journal of Epilepsy, 5,* 194–205.

Antonak, R. F., & Livneh, H. (1995). Adaptation to disability and its investigation among persons with multiple sclerosis. *Social Science and Medicine, 40,* 1099–1108.

Antonak, R. F., Livneh, H., & Antonak, C. (1993). A review of research on psychosocial adjustment to impairment among persons with traumatic brain injury. *Journal of Head Trauma Rehabilitation, 8*(4), 89–102.

Billings, A. G., & Moos, R. H. (1981). The role of coping responses and social resources in attenuating the stress of life events. *Journal of Behavioral Medicine, 4,* 139–157.

Billings, A. G., & Moos, R. H. (1984). Coping, stress and social resources among adults with unipolar depression. *Journal of Personality and Social Psychology, 46,* 877–891.

Bowlby, J. (1973). *Attachment and loss: Vol. 2. Separation: Anxiety and anger.* New York: Basic Books.

Bowlby, J. (1980). *Attachment and loss: Vol. 3. Loss, sadness and depression.* New York: Basic Books.

Bracken, M. B., Shepard, M. J., & Webb, S. B. (1981). Psychosocial response to acute spinal cord injury: An epidemiological study. *Paraplegia, 19,* 271–283.

Bramble, K. (1995). Body image. In I. M. Lubkin (Ed.), *Chronic illness: Impact and interventions* (3rd ed.) (pp. 285–299). Boston: Jones and Bartlett.

Bray, G. P. (1978). Rehabilitation of spinal cord injured: A family approach. *Journal of Applied Rehabilitation Counseling, 9,* 70–78.

Breznitz, S. (1983). The seven kinds of denial. In Breznitz (Ed.), *The denial of stress* (pp. 257–280). New York: International Universities Press.

Brooks, N. (1988). Behavioural abnormalities in head injured patients. *Scandinavian Journal of Rehabilitation Medicine Supplement, 17,* 41–46.

Brooks, N. A., & Matson, R. R. (1982). Social-psychological adjustment to multiple sclerosis. *Social Science and Medicine, 16,* 2129–2135.

Brown, R. G., & MacCarthy, B. (1990). Psychiatric morbidity in patients with Parkinson's disease. *Psychological Medicine, 20,* 77–87.

Burke, M. L., Hainsworth, M. A., Eakes, G. G., & Lindgren, C. L. (1992). Current knowledge and research on chronic sorrow: A foundation for inquiry. *Death Studies, 16,* 231–245.

Caplan, B., & Shechter, J. (1987). Denial and depression in disabling illness. In B. Caplan (Ed.), *Rehabilitation psychology desk reference* (pp. 133–170). Rockville, MD: Aspen.

Carpenter, W. T., & Strauss, J. S. (1977). Methodological issues in the study of outcome. In J. S. Strauss, H. M. Babigian, & M. Roff (Eds.), *The origin and course of psychopathology* (pp. 345–367). New York: Plenum Press.

Carver, C. S., Scheier, M. F., & Weintraub, J. K. (1989). Assessing coping strategies: A theoretically based approach. *Journal of Personality and Social Psychology, 56,* 267–283.

Cassileth, B. R., Lusk, E. J., Strouse, T. B., Miller, D. S., Brown, L. L., Cross, P. A., & Tenaglia, A. N. (1984). Psychosocial status in chronic illness: A comparative analysis of six diagnostic groups. *New England Journal of Medicine, 311*(8), 506–511.

Coombs, C. H. (1964). *A theory of data.* New York: John Wiley & Sons.

Coombs, C. H., & Smith, J. E. (1973). On detection of structure in attitude and developmental processes. *Psychological Review, 80,* 337–351.

Dakoff, G. A., & Mendelsohn, G. A. (1986). Parkinson's disease: The psychological aspects of a chronic illness. *Psychological Bulletin, 99,* 375–387.

Davis, B. H. (1987). Disability and grief. *Social Casework, 68,* 352–357.

Davison, M. L. (1977). On a metric, unidimensional unfolding model for attitudinal and developmental data. *Psychometrika, 42,* 523–548.

DeLoach, C., & Greer, B. G. (1981). *Adjustment to severe physical disability: A metamorphosis.* New York: McGraw-Hill.

Dembo, T., Leviton, G. L., & Wright, B. A. (1956). Adjustment to misfortune—A problem of social-psychological rehabilitation. *Artificial Limbs, 3*(2), 4–62.

Devins, G. M., & Seland, T. P. (1987). Emotional impact of multiple sclerosis: Recent findings and suggestions for future research. *Psychological Bulletin, 101,* 363–375.

Drudge, O. W., Rosen, J. C., Peyser, J. M., & Pieniadz, J. (1986). Behavioral and emotional problems and treatment in chronically brain-impaired adults. *Annals of Behavioral Medicine, 8*(1), 9–14.

Dunkel-Schetter, C., Feinstein, L. G., Taylor, S. E., & Falke, R. L. (1992). Patterns of coping with cancer. *Health Psychology, 11,* 79–87.

Dunn, M. E. (1975). Psychological intervention in a spinal cord injury center: An introduction. *Rehabilitation Psychology, 22,* 165–178.

Eisenberg, M. G., Glueckauf, R. L., & Zaretsky, H. H. (Eds.). (1993). *Medical aspects of disability: A handbook for the rehabilitation professional.* New York: Springer.

Falek, A., & Britton, S. (1974). Phases in coping: The hypothesis and its implications. *Social Biology, 21,* 1–7.

Falvo, D. R. (1991). *Medical and psychosocial aspects of chronic illness and disability.* Gaithersburg, MD: Aspen.

Feifel, H., Strack, S., & Nagy, V. T. (1987). Degree of life-threat and differential use of coping modes. *Journal of Psychosomatic Research, 31,* 91–99.

Fenichel, O. (1945). *The psychoanalytic theory of neuroses.* New York: W. W. Norton.

Ferguson, E., Dodds, A., Craig, D., Flannigan, H., & Yates, L. (1994). The changing face of adjustment to sight: A longitudinal evaluation of rehabilitation. *Journal of Social Behavior and Personality, 9,* 287–306.

Fisher, S. (1970). *Body experience in fantasy and behavior.* New York: Appleton-Century-Crofts.

Fisher, S., & Cleveland, S. E. (1968). *Body image and personality* (2nd ed.). New York: Dover.

Folkman, S. (1984). Personal control and stress and coping processes: A theoretical analysis. *Journal of Personality and Social Psychology, 46,* 839–852.

Frank, R. G., Elliott, T. R., Corcoran, J. R., & Wonderlich, S. A. (1987). Depression after spinal cord injury: Is it necessary? *Clinical Psychology Review, 7,* 611–630.

Frank, R. G., Umlauf, R. L., Wonderlich, S. A., Askanazi, G. S., Buckelew, S. P., & Elliott, T. R. (1987). Differences in coping styles among persons with spinal cord injury: A cluster analytic approach. *Journal of Consulting and Clinical Psychology, 55,* 727–731.

Frank, R. G., VanValin, P. H., & Elliott, T. R. (1987). Adjustment to spinal cord injury: A review of empirical and nonempirical studies. *Journal of Rehabilitation, 53,* 43–48.

Freud, A. (1966). *The ego and the mechanisms of defense* (Rev. ed.). New York: International Universities Press.

Freud, S. (1936). *The problem of anxiety.* New York: Psychoanalytic Quarterly Press.

Friedland, J., & McColl, M. (1992). Disability and depression: Some etiological considerations. *Social Science and Medicine, 34,* 395–403.

Gottesman, D., & Lewis, M. C. (1982). Differences in crisis reactions among cancer and surgery patients. *Journal of Consulting and Clinical Psychology, 50,* 381–388.

Grzesiak, R. C., & Hicok, D. A. (1994). A brief history of psychotherapy and physical disability. *American Journal of Psychotherapy, 48,* 240–250.

Guttman, L. (1944). A basis for scaling qualitative data. *American Sociological Review, 9,* 139–150.

Haan, N. (1977). *Coping and defending.* New York: Academic Press.

Hackett, T. P., & Weisman, A. D. (1969). Denial as a factor in patients with heart disease and cancer. *Annals of the New York Academy of Sciences, 164,* 802–817.

Hamburg, D. A., & Adams, J. E. (1967). A perspective on coping behavior: Seeking and utilizing information in major transitions. *Archives of General Psychiatry, 17,* 277–284.

Hanson, S., Buckelew, S. P., Hewett, J., & O'Neal, G. (1993). The relationship between coping and adjustment after spinal cord injury: A 5-year follow-up study. *Rehabilitation Psychology, 38,* 41–52.

Head, H. (1920). *Studies in Neurology, Vol. II.* London: Oxford University Press.

Horowitz, M. J. (1985). Disasters and psychological responses to stress. *Psychiatric Annals, 15*(3), 161–167.

Horowitz, M. J. (1986). *Stress response syndromes* (2nd ed.). New York: Jason Aronson.

Jacobson, A. M., Hauser, S. T., Lavori, P., Wolfsdorf, J. I., Herskowitz, R. D., Milley, J. E., Bliss, R., Gelfand, E., Wertlieb, D., & Stein, J. (1990). Adherence among children and adolescents with insulin-dependent diabetes mellitus over a four-year longitudinal follow-up: I. The influence of patient coping and adjustment. *Journal of Pediatric Psychology, 15,* 511–526.

Johnson, J. L., & Morse, J. M. (1990). Regaining control: The process of adjustment after myocardial infarction. *Heart and Lung, 19,* 126–135.

Jourard, S. M. (1963). *Personal adjustment: An approach through the study of healthy personality.* New York: Macmillan.

Katz, S., & Florian, V. (1986–1987). A comprehensive theoretical model of psychological reaction to loss. *International Journal of Psychiatry in Medicine, 16,* 325–345.

Keany, K. C., & Glueckauf, R. L. (1993). Disability and value changes: An overview and analysis of acceptance of loss theory. *Rehabilitation Psychology, 38,* 199–210.

Keckeisen, M. E., & Nyamathi, A. M. (1990). Coping and adjustment to illness in the acute myocardial infarction patient. *Journal of Cardiovascular Nursing, 5*, 25–33.

Kerr, W. G., & Thompson, M. A. (1972). Acceptance of disability of sudden onset in paraplegia. *Paraplegia, 10*, 94–102.

Krueger, D. W. (1981–1982). Emotional rehabilitation of the physical rehabilitation patient. *International Journal of Psychiatry in Medicine, 11*, 183–191.

Krus, D. J., Bart, W. M., & Airasian, P. W. (1975). *Ordering theory and methods.* Los Angeles: Theta Press.

Kübler-Ross, E. (1969). *On death and dying.* New York: Macmillan.

Lambert, V. A., & Lambert, C. E. (1979). *The impact of physical illness and related mental health concepts.* Englewood Cliffs, NJ: Prentice Hall.

Langer, K. G. (1994). Depression and denial in psychotherapy of persons with disabilities. *American Journal of Psychotherapy, 48*, 181–194.

Lawrence, S. A., & Lawrence, R. M. (1979). A model of adaptation to the stress of chronic illness. *Nursing Forum, 18*, 33–42.

Lazarus, R. A. (1966). *Psychological stress and the coping process.* New York: McGraw-Hill.

Lazarus, R. S., & Folkman, S. (1984). Coping and adaptation. In W. D. Gentry (Ed.), *Handbook of behavioral medicine* (pp. 282–325). New York: Guilford Press.

Levin, H. S., & Grossman, R. G. (1978). Behavioral sequelae of closed head injury. *Archives of Neurology, 35*, 720–727.

Levin, R., Banks, S., & Berg, B. (1988). Psychosocial dimensions of epilepsy: A review of the literature. *Epilepsia, 29*, 805–816.

Levine, J., Warrenburg, S., Kerns, R., Schwartz, G., Delaney, R., Fontana, A., Gradman, A., Smith, S., Allen, S., & Cascione, R. (1987). The role of denial in recovery from coronary heart disease. *Journal of Psychosomatic Medicine, 49*, 109–117.

Lezak, M. D. (1987). Relationship between personality disorders, social disturbance, and physical disability following traumatic brain injury. *Journal of Head Trauma Rehabilitation, 2*(1), 57–59.

Lezak, M. D., & O'Brien, K. P. (1988). Longitudinal study of emotional, social, and physical changes after traumatic brain injury. *Journal of Learning Disabilities, 21*, 456–463.

Lindgren, C. L., Burke, M. L., Hainsworth, M. A., & Eakes, G. G. (1992). Chronic sorrow: A lifespan concept. *Scholarly Inquiry for Nursing Practice: An International Journal, 6*, 27–40.

Lipowski, Z. J. (1970). Physical illness, the individual and the coping process. *International Journal of Psychiatry in Medicine, 1*, 91–102.

Livneh, H. (1986). A unified approach to existing models of adaptation to disability—II. Intervention strategies. *Journal of Applied Rehabilitation Counseling, 17*(2), 6–10.

Livneh, H. (1987). Person-environment congruence: A rehabilitation perspective. *International Journal of Rehabilitation Research, 10*, 3–19.

Livneh, H., & Antonak, R. F. (1990). Reactions to disability: An empirical investigation of their nature and structure. *Journal of Applied Rehabilitation Counseling, 21*(4), 13–21.

Livneh, H., & Antonak, R. F. (1991). Temporal structure of adaptation to disability. *Rehabilitation Counseling Bulletin, 34*, 298–319.

Livneh, H., & Antonak, R. F. (1994a). Reactions to disability: A review and critique of the literature. *Critical Reviews in Physical and Rehabilitation Medicine, 6*, 1–100.

Livneh, H., & Antonak, R. F. (1994b). Review of research on psychosocial adaptation to neuromuscular disorders: Amyotrophic lateral sclerosis, myasthenia gravis, neurofibromatosis, and spina bifida. *Journal of Rehabilitation Sciences, 7,* 66–79.

Livneh, H., & Antonak, R. F. (1994c). Review of research on psychosocial adaptation to neuromuscular disorders: I. Cerebral palsy, muscular dystrophy, and Parkinson's disease. *Journal of Social Behavior and Personality, 9,* 201–230.

Livneh, H., Antonak, R. F., & Maron, S. (1995). Progeria: Medical aspects, psychosocial perspectives, and intervention guidelines. *Death Studies, 19,* 433–452.

Lussier, A. (1980). The physical handicap and the body ego. *International Journal of Psychoanalysis, 61,* 179–185.

McCrae, R. R. (1984). Situational determinants of coping responses: Loss, threat, and challenge. *Journal of Personality and Social Psychology, 46,* 919–928.

McDaniel, J. W. (1976). *Physical disability and human behavior* (2nd ed.). New York: Pergamon Press.

Meyerowitz, B. E. (1980). Psychosocial correlates of breast cancer and its treatments. *Psychological Bulletin, 87,* 108–131.

Moos, R. H., & Schaefer, J. A. (1984). The crisis of physical illness. In R. H. Moos (Ed.), *Coping with physical illness. Vol. 2: New perspectives* (pp. 3–31). New York: Plenum Press.

Naugle, R. I. (1988). Denial in rehabilitation: Its genesis, consequences, and clinical management. *Rehabilitation Counseling Bulletin, 31,* 218–231.

Nolan, R. P., & Wielgosz, A. T. (1991). Assessing adaptive and maladaptive coping in the early phase of acute myocardial infarction. *Journal of Behavioral Medicine, 14,* 111–124.

Olshansky, S. (1962). Chronic sorrow: A response to having a mentally defective child. *Social Casework, 43,* 191–193.

Parkes, C. M. (1972). Components of the reaction to loss of a limb, spouse or home. *Journal of Psychosomatic Research, 16,* 343–349.

Parkes, C. M. (1975). Psychosocial transitions: Comparison between reactions to loss of a limb and loss of a spouse. *British Journal of Psychiatry, 127,* 204–210.

Pearlin, L. I., & Schooler, C. (1978). The structure of coping. *Journal of Health and Social Behavior, 19,* 2–21.

Pegler, M., & Borgen, F. H. (1984). The defense mechanisms of coronary patients. *Journal of Clinical Psychology, 40,* 669–679.

Pepper, G. A. (1977). The person with a spinal cord injury: Psychological care. *American Journal of Nursing, 77,* 1330–1336.

Pollock, S. E. (1986). Human response to chronic illness: Physiologic and psychosocial adaptation. *Nursing Research, 35*(2), 90–95.

Rigoni, H. C. (1977). Psychological coping in the patient with spinal cord injury. In D. P. Pierce & V. H. Nickel (Eds.), *The total care of spinal cord injuries* (pp. 229–307). Boston: Little, Brown.

Rodin, G., Craven, J., & Littlefield, C. (1991). *Depression in the medically ill: An integrated approach.* New York: Brunner/Mazel.

Rodin, G., & Voshart, K. (1986). Depression in the medically ill: An overview. *American Journal of Psychiatry, 143,* 696–705.

Roessler, R., & Bolton, B. (1978). *Psychosocial adjustment to disability.* Baltimore: University Park Press.

Russell, R. A. (1981). Concepts of adjustment to disability: An overview. *Rehabilitation Literature,* *42,* 330–338.

Schilder, P. (1950). *The image and appearance of the human body.* New York: John Wiley & Sons.

Shontz, F. C. (1965). Reactions to crisis. *Volta Review, 67,* 364–370.

Shontz, F. C. (1975). *The psychological aspects of physical illness and disability.* New York: Macmillan.

Siller, J. (1976). Psychological aspects of physical disability. In J. Meislin (Ed.), *Rehabilitation medicine and psychiatry* (pp. 455–484). Springfield, IL: C C Thomas.

Silver, R. L., Boon, C., & Stones, M. H. (1983). Searching for meaning in misfortune: Making sense of incest. *Journal of Social Issues, 39,* 81–102.

Silver, R. L., & Wortman, C. B. (1980). Coping with undesirable life events. In J. Garber & M. E. P. Seligman (Eds.), *Human helplessness: Theory and applications* (pp. 279–340). New York: Academic Press.

Stachnik, T., Stoffelmayr, B., & Hoppe, R. B. (1983). Prevention, behavior change, and chronic disease. In T. G. Burish & L. A. Bradley (Eds.), *Coping with chronic disease: Research and applications* (pp. 447–473). New York: Academic Press.

Stewart, J. R. (1994). Denial of disabling conditions and specific interventions in the rehabilitation counseling setting. *Journal of Applied Rehabilitation Counseling, 25*(3), 7–15.

Stewart, T. D. (1978). Coping behavior and the moratorium following spinal cord injury. *Paraplegia, 15,* 338–342.

Taylor, S. E., & Aspinwell, L. G. (1990). Psychosocial aspects of chronic illness. In P. T. Costa & G. R. VandenBox (Eds.), *Psychological aspects of serious illness: Chronic conditions, fatal diseases, and clinical care* (pp. 7–60). Washington, DC: American Psychological Association.

Teel, C. S. (1991). Chronic sorrow: Analysis of the concept. *Journal of Advanced Nursing, 16,* 1311–1319.

Thompson, D. R., Webster, R. A., Cordle, C. J., & Sutton, T. W. (1987). Specific sources and patterns of anxiety in male patients with first myocardial infarction. *British Journal of Medical Psychology, 60,* 343–348.

Tobin, D. L., Holroyd, K. A., Reynolds, R. V., & Wigal, J. K. (1989). The hierarchical factor structure of the Coping Strategies Inventory. *Cognitive Therapy and Research, 13,* 343–361.

Trieschmann, R. B. (Ed.). (1988). *Spinal cord injuries: Psychological, social, and vocational rehabilitation* (2nd ed.). New York: Demos.

Turner, R. J., & Beiser, M. (1990). Major depression and depressive symptomatology among the physically disabled: Assessing the role of chronic stress. *Journal of Nervous and Mental Diseases, 178,* 343–350.

Turner, R. J., & McLean, P. D. (1989). Physical disability and psychological distress. *Rehabilitation Psychology, 34,* 225–243.

Turner, R. J., & Noh, S. (1988). Physical disability and depression: A longitudinal analysis. *Journal of Health and Social Behavior, 29,* 23–37.

Turner, R. J., & Wood, D. W. (1985). Depression and disability: The stress process in a chronically strained population. In J. R. Greenley (Ed.), *Research in community and mental health: Vol. 5* (pp. 77–109). Greenwich, CT: JAI Press.

Viney, L. L., & Westbrook, M. T. (1981). Psychological reactions to chronic illness-related disability as a function of its severity and type. *Journal of Psychosomatic Research, 25,* 513–523.

Viney, L. L., & Westbrook, M. T. (1982). Patterns of anxiety in the chronically ill. *British Journal of Medical Psychology, 55*, 87–95.

Weinstein, E. A., & Kahn, R. L. (1955). *Denial of illness: Symbolic and physiological aspects.* Springfield, IL: C C Thomas.

Welch-McCaffrey, S. (1985). Cancer, anxiety, and quality of life. *Cancer Nursing, 8*, 151–158.

Weller, D. J., & Miller, P. M. (1977). Emotional reactions of patient, family, and staff in acute-care period of spinal cord injury: Part I. *Social Work in Health Care, 2*, 369–377.

Westbrook, M. T., & Viney, L. L. (1982). Psychological reactions to the onset of chronic illness. *Social Science and Medicine, 16*, 899–905.

Whalley-Hammell, K. R. (1992). Psychological and sociological theories concerning adjustment to traumatic spinal cord injury: The implications for rehabilitation. *Paraplegia, 30*, 317–326.

White, R. W. (1974). Strategies of adaptation: An attempt at systematic description. In G. V. Coelho, D. A. Hamburgh, & J. E. Adams (Eds.), *Coping and adaptation* (pp. 47–68). New York: Basic Books.

World Health Organization. (1980). *International classification of impairments, disabilities, and handicaps: A manual of classification relating to the consequences of disease.* Geneva, Switzerland: Author.

Wortman, C. B., & Silver, R. C. (1987). Coping with irrevocable loss. In G. R. Vanden Bos & B. K. Bryant (Eds.), *Cataclysms, crises and catastrophes: Psychology in action* (pp. 189–235). Washington, DC: American Psychological Association.

Wortman, C. B., & Silver, R. C. (1989). The myth of coping with loss. *Journal of Consulting and Clinical Psychology, 57*, 349–357.

Wright, B. A. (1983). *Physical disability—A psychosocial approach* (2nd ed.). New York: Harper & Row.

Zeitlin, S. (1980). Assessing coping behavior. *American Journal of Orthopsychiatry, 50*, 139–144.

CHAPTER 2

General Measures of Psychosocial Adaptation to Chronic Illness and Disability

INTRODUCTION

The study of psychosocial adaptation of individuals with chronic illnesses and disabilities is an enterprise that historically has been based on clinical observations, anecdotal impressions, speculation, and surmise rather than on empirical data. Even well-designed and well-executed research will have limited value for theory building and theory testing if the data analyzed are substandard. The quality of these data, in turn, is dependent upon the quality of the instrument selected to operationalize psychosocial adaptation. Without assurances of the psychometric soundness of the instrument, confidence in the accuracy and applicability of the conclusions drawn from research may be unjustified.

Our reviews of the research concerning the psychosocial adaptation of individuals with diverse physical, cognitive, disease-related, sensory, and chronic neurological and health impairments do not support a sanguine view of the psychometric adequacy of available measuring instruments. The small number of published reviews of this type have focused primarily on the measurement of psychopathology or general personality traits of persons with chronic illnesses or disabilities (Eber, 1976); of the respondent's health status, functioning, and well-being (Balinsky & Berger, 1975; Brook et al., 1979; Stewart & Ware, 1992; Ware, 1976); or of coping reactions manifest in general medical populations (Burish & Bradley, 1983; Lipowski, 1970). We were unable to locate any articles that presented reviews of a comprehensive set of instruments concerned with psychosocial adaptation to chronic illness and physical disability.

This chapter is concerned with a description and critique of 10 general measures of psychosocial adaptation to chronic illness and disability commonly used by clinicians and researchers in the fields of health and disability studies. The 10 instruments reviewed are organized into three categories: (1) five measures of adaptation to general medical and psychiatric illness: two distinct versions of the General Health Questionnaire, the Millon Behavioral Health Inventory, the Psychosocial Adjustment to Illness Scale, and the Sickness Impact Profile; (2) three unidimensional measures of adaptation to disability: the Acceptance of Disability scale, the Acceptance of Loss scale, and the Bell Disability Scale of Adjustment; and (3) two multidimensional measures of adaptation to disability: the Heinemann and Shontz Q-Sort, and the Reactions to Impairment and Disability Inventory.

Summary information on these 10 instruments is provided in Table 2–1. It should be noted that the instruments within each section are arranged in alphabetical order. The reader should not infer a judgment of the overall psychometric quality of an instrument from its order of appearance in this chapter.

MEASURES OF ADAPTATION TO ILLNESS

In this section we review five instruments that purport to provide information on psychosocial adaptation to general medical and psychiatric illness. The first— the 60-item version of the General Health Questionnaire—is a unidimensional instrument to screen psychiatric health from psychiatric illness, while the second—the 28-item version of the General Health Questionnaire—is a multidimensional instrument designed for the same purpose. The remaining three instruments—the Millon Behavioral Health Inventory, the Psychosocial Adjustment to Illness Scale, and the Sickness Impact Profile—are multidimensional measures of the impact of medical illness on the individual.

General Health Questionnaire

The General Health Questionnaire (GHQ) is a self-report questionnaire designed in England for differentiating psychiatric sickness from psychiatric health among individuals in community settings (Goldberg, 1972; Goldberg & Blackwell, 1970); that is, the GHQ was developed to screen for nonpsychotic mental disorders and not to measure particular personality traits or to diagnose psychiatric disorders. The original version of the questionnaire comprised 60 questions concerning typical functioning of persons without impairments (eg, "Felt that you were playing a useful part in things?" "Been managing to keep yourself busy and occupied?" "Been able to enjoy your normal day-to-day activities?") and the appearance of new and distressing phenomena related to general health and mental status (eg, "Been getting pains in your head?" "Felt constantly under strain?" "Been thinking of yourself as a worthless person?"). Respondents were asked to compare their recent state with their usual state by indicating whether these 60 symptoms or behaviors were experienced "Less than usual,"

TABLE 2-1 A Summary of Information on the Availability and Suitability of General Measures of Psychosocial Adaptation to Chronic Illness and Disability

Measure	Type	Intended Use	Scores	Strengths	Weaknesses
General Measures of Psychosocial Adaptation to Chronic Illness					
General Health Questionnaire—60	60-item self-report questionnaire concerning normal healthy functioning and appearance of new symptoms	To screen respondents for nonpsychotic mental disorders (ie, to distinguish psychiatric health from psychiatric illness)	Global general health index score	Reported to have adequate sensitivity, specificity, reliability, and homogeneity values. Concurrent validity reported to be adequate. Translated into many languages and widely used. 30-, 20-, and 12-item versions available (eg, to reduce time to administer).	Reliability, sensitivity, and specificity decrease with fewer-item GHQ versions. Factorial structure unclear. Response bias influences not investigated carefully.
General Health Questionnaire—28	28-item self-report questionnaire	To create a patient profile of psychiatric illness for in-depth evaluation	Four domain scores: • Somatic symptoms • Anxiety and insomnia • Social dysfunction • Severe depression	Derived from GHQ—60 using sound psychometric criteria. Sensitivity and specificity reported to be adequate.	Subscales may not be unique and should not be used for differential diagnosis.

Millon Behavioral Health Inventory	150-item self-report questionnaire	To characterize the psychological makeup of patients in rehabilitation and general medical settings, to study its impact on the course of a disease, and to formulate a psychological intervention	A total of 20 scale scores organized in four domains:
			• Coping styles
			  ** Introversive
			  ** Inhibited
			  ** Cooperative
			  ** Sociable
			  ** Confident
			  ** Forceful
			  ** Respectful
			  ** Sensitive
				Constructed through sequential psychometric process. Reliability and construct validity reported to be adequate. Utility for planning interventions reported to be adequate. Used in a variety of medical and rehabilitation settings.	Factor analysis results have not matched inventory's hypothesized structure. Respondent bias and reactivity influences not investigated.

continues

TABLE 2–1 continued

Measure	Type	Intended Use	Scores	Strengths	Weaknesses

			• Psychogenic attitudes
			  •• Chronic tension
			  •• Recent stress
			  •• Premorbid pessimism
			  •• Future despair
			  •• Social alienation
			  •• Somatic anxiety
			• Psychosomatic complaints
			  •• Allergic inclination
			  •• Gastrointestinal susceptibility
			  •• Cardiovascular tendency
			• Prognostic index
			  •• Pain treatment responsivity
			  •• Life-threat reactivity
			  •• Emotional vulnerability
					Response bias influences not investigated. Norms to date based on small and somewhat nonrepresentative samples.

Psychosocial Adjustment to Illness Scale	46-item semistructured psychiatric interview (PAIS) or 46-item self-report questionnaire (PAIS-SR)	To measure the respondent's psychosocial adjustment within the last 30 days to a medical illness and its residual effects	An overall adjustment score and scores on seven a priori defined subscales with tables to convert scale scores to norms for distinct illnesses (lung cancer, renal disease, burns, hypertension, heart disease): • Health care orientation • Vocational environment • Domestic environment • Sexual relationships • Extended family relationships • Social environment • Psychological distress	Subscales reported to be reasonably specific, independent, reliable, and homogenous. Construct validity of the subscales reported to be reasonable. Factor structure approximates a priori subscale structure. Concurrent validity reported to be reasonable. Modification can yield an informant-report version. Goal is to develop a library of norms for the full range of illness and impairments.	

Measure	Type	Intended Use	Scores	Strengths	Weaknesses
Sickness Impact Profile	Respondents select from among 136 descriptors of sickness-related and behavioral dysfunction that apply to them.	To measure the impact of sickness as perceived by the patient using a general purpose health status index in order to evaluate health care services	A total score and 12 subscale scores. The first three subscales combine to yield a Physical dimension score and the next four subscales combine to yield a Psychosocial dimension score: (Physical dimension) • Ambulation • Mobility • Body care and movement (Psychosocial dimension) • Social interaction • Alertness behavior • Emotional behavior • Communication (Other) • Sleep and rest • Eating • Work • Home management • Recreational pastimes	Comprehensive and rigorous psychometric development. Scored as percentage of total possible for interscale comparison purposes. Reliability, construct validity, and concurrent validity reported to be adequate. Widely used with patients with a variety of health and physical disorders. Spanish language version available.	Factor structure unclear. May be susceptible to a defensiveness response bias. Sensitivity to patient changes may be less than ideal.

Unidimensional Measures of Psychosocial Adaptation to Disability

Measure	Type	Intended Use	Scores	Strengths	Weaknesses
Acceptance of Disability Scale	50-item self-report summated rating scale	To measure the respondent's degree of acceptance of a disability	A single score representing acceptance of disability	Reliability reported to be adequate, but data are limited.	Construct validity may be suspect due to contradictory data. Factor structure not fully investigated. Response bias not investigated. Based on a unidimensional concept of acceptance of disability, limiting usefulness in research.

continues

TABLE 2-1 continued

Measure	Type	Intended Use	Scores	Strengths	Weaknesses
Acceptance of Loss Scale	29-item self-report summated rating scale	To measure the respondent's reaction to a physical disability as a factor influencing psychological and social behavior	A single score measuring level of acceptance of loss resulting from a physical disability	Initial reports of reliability and construct validity are reasonable, but data are limited.	Factor structure unclear. Response bias influences not investigated. Based on a unidimensional concept of acceptance of loss, limiting usefulness in research. Meager criterion-referenced validity data.
Bell Disability Scale of Adjustment	40-item self-report summated rating scale	To measure the respondent's degree of acceptance of a traumatic orthopaedic disability (spinal cord injury)	A single score measuring level of acceptance of disability	Preliminary construct validity data are reasonable.	Factor structure not investigated. Response bias influences not investigated. No reliability data reported.
Multidimensional Measures of Psychosocial Adaptation to Disability					
Heinemann and Shontz Q-Sort	48 items that respondents sort into sets descriptive of their typical and ideal selves	To evaluate a four-stage model of reaction to a physical disability	Sortings of the items representative of four stages of reactions to a physical disability: • Shock • Defensive retreat • Acknowledgment • Adaptation	Derived from a unique multidimensional psychometric methodology (Stephenson's Q-methodology).	Not used by researchers other than the developers. Limited validity data.

Measure	Type	Intended Use	Scores	Strengths	Weaknesses
Reactions to Impairment and Disability Inventory	90-item self-report summated rating scale	To investigate the multidimensional structure of the respondent's psychosocial reactions to the onset of a disability or chronic impairment	Eight psychosocial reaction scores: • Shock • Anxiety • Denial • Depression • Internalized anger • Externalized hostility • Acknowledgment • Adjustment	Comprehensive psychometric development. Preliminary data on specificity, homogeneity, independence, and reliability of subscales are adequate. Multidimensional structure supported by factor analyses. Preliminary construct validity data are adequate. Useful for studying nonlinear hierarchical reaction process.	Meager concurrent validity data available to date. Factor structure needs clarification. Response bias influences not investigated.

"No more than usual," "Rather more than usual," or "Much more than usual." Goldberg scored the first two of these responses as 0 and the last two as 1 and then summed these dichotomous scores to obtain an overall index of general health with higher scores indicating poorer health. Goldberg experimented with several different response scoring keys, including summated rating scales with response values from 1 to 4, but selected the 0, 0, 1, 1 system, arguing that it broke a response selection set (eg, selecting only the intermediate or only the extreme response alternatives) and yielded a global index that efficiently accomplished the purpose of the instrument.

Of an original scale development sample of 553 individuals who were either psychiatrically disturbed or not psychiatrically disturbed, 200 were also interviewed by a psychiatrist using Goldberg's Clinical Interview Schedule (Goldberg, Cooper, Eastwood, Kedward, & Shepherd, 1970) to determine whether they were a "case" or a "noncase." The sensitivity (ie, the proportion of "cases" correctly identified) of the GHQ—60 was found to be 0.96 and the specificity (the proportion of "noncases" correctly identified) to be 0.88. Similar results with other samples led Goldberg to conclude that the GHQ—60 was a reliable and valid measure of general physical and mental health (Goldberg, 1972).

Goldberg derived a 30-item version of the GHQ by omitting those items that concerned only physical illness and deleting those remaining items that showed the least power to discriminate persons who were severely ill from persons who were mildly ill and from the persons who were not mentally ill. The sensitivity and specificity values of the GHQ—30 were reported to be 0.86 and 0.77, respectively (Goldberg, Rickels, Downing, & Hesbacher, 1976). Using psychometric criteria of item discrimination and scale reliability and accuracy (ie, the proportion of the total sample correctly identified as a "case" or a "noncase"), a 20-item version and a 12-item version were derived from the GHQ—30 for quick screening purposes.

Burvill and Knuiman's (1983) review of the literature concerning the 60-, 30-, 20-, and 12-item versions of the GHQ, together with analyses of their own data from a sample of more than 2,000 individuals in Australia, led them to conclude that reliability, validity, sensitivity, specificity, and accuracy values decreased and standard errors increased gradually with the fewer-item GHQ versions. Psychometric characteristics for even the short GHQ versions, however, have been found to be remarkably high. For example, Malt (1989) reported homogeneity coefficients and stability reliabilities for the GHQ—20 to be 0.86 and 0.86 at 6 to 9 months, and 0.91 and 0.81 at an average of 28 months posthospitalization. Because the only advantage of the shorter versions of the GHQ is reduced time to administer the questionnaire, Burvill and Knuiman (1983) recommended that the GHQ—60 be used in all cases unless time is an important factor.

Factor analysis of the data from the original sample of respondents disclosed a single factor accounting for 45% of the variance that was interpreted to be the hypothesized construct of general health (Goldberg, 1972). A subsequent factor analysis with a sample of 523 respondents attending a general medical practice clinic, however, supported the retention and interpretation of four factors that were named somatic symptoms, anxiety and insomnia, social dysfunction, and severe depression (Goldberg & Hillier, 1979). By selecting the seven items with the highest loadings above 0.50 on each factor, a 28-item "scaled" version of the GHQ was derived (14 items on the GHQ—28 do not appear on the GHQ—30). Reanalyses of the rescored protocols showed that these four factors accounted for 59% of the total variance in the sample data.

Factor analyses of GHQ—28 data from two additional samples of 552 and 4,247 persons attending a general medical practice replicated the four-factor solution, with 26 of the 28 items correctly loading on the predicted factors (Goldberg & Hillier, 1979). The sensitivity and specificity of the GHQ—28 in the original data were reported to be 0.88 and 0.84 with an accuracy of 86%. Similar values were found in a subsequent investigation (Bridges & Goldberg, 1986). Goldberg and Hillier (1979) noted that because a general factor accounted for 35% of the variance in the unrotated GHQ—28 item response matrix, the four empirically derived scales may not be specific measures of distinct components of health (intercorrelations ranged from 0.33 to 0.61 with a median of 0.55). The authors cautioned against their clinical use for the study of components of adaptation or for differential diagnosis of psychiatric disorders. Rather, profiles of the four scale scores could be used to identify individuals using psychiatric interviews and suitable diagnostic instruments as candidates for in-depth evaluation.

Some researchers have factor analyzed one or more of the various versions of the GHQ with results suggesting a similar four-factor structure (Burvill, Knuiman, & Finlay-Jones, 1984; Graetz, 1991), while others have argued for a more parsimonious three-factor solution (Hobbs, Ballinger, Greenwood, Martin, & McClure, 1984; Worsley & Gribbin, 1977). It is also noteworthy that some factor analytic solutions have placed the anxiety and depression items on one factor (Goldberg et al., 1976), while others have found them to load on distinct factors (Huppert, Walters, Day, & Elliott, 1989).

The validity and factorial structure of the GHQ have been more carefully investigated than the potentially biasing influences of respondent sensitization, reactivity, faking, and response styles. In the only study of these influences that was located, Parkes (1980) reported that, in a sample of 101 female nursing students enrolled in an introductory training course, the GHQ was somewhat affected by social desirability responding. This effect, however, was limited to the Social Dysfunction scale. Noting the unique research setting and character of her sample, Parkes nevertheless concluded that neither defensiveness nor social desirability should unduly bias responses to the GHQ.

The GHQ is one of the most widely used instruments of its kind and has been translated into at least 16 languages, including Chinese (Chan, 1985), Italian (Fontanesi, Gobetti, Zimmerman-Tansella, & Tansella, 1985), Japanese (Iwata, Okuyama, Kawakami, & Saito, 1988), Portuguese (Mari & Williams, 1984), Spanish (Munoz, Vazques, Pastrana, Rodriquez, & Oneca, 1978), and Yoruba (Oduwole & Ogunyemi, 1989). The GHQ has been selected to operationalize adaptation to chronic illness and disability in persons with rheumatoid arthritis (Chandarana, Eals, Steingart, Bellamy, & Allen, 1987; Gardiner, 1980), bronchitis (Morgan, Peck, Buchanan, & McHurdy, 1983; Rutter, 1977), cancer (Hughson, Cooper, McArdle, & Smith, 1988), cerebral palsy (Andrews, Platt, Quinn, & Nielson, 1977), dermatological disorders (Lewis & Wessely, 1990), drug and alcohol abuse (Ross & Glaser, 1989), epilepsy (Hermann, Whitman, Wyler, Anton, & Vanderzwagg, 1990; Hermann, Wyler, & Somes, 1992; Hoare & Kerley, 1991; Kogeorgos, Fonagy, & Scott, 1982; Roy, 1979), chronic fatigue syndrome (Blakely et al., 1991), hearing impairments (Singerman, Riedner, & Folstein, 1980), heart disease (Prince, Frasure-Smith, & Rolicz-Woloszyk, 1982), hip fracture (Billig, Ahmed, Kenmore, Amaral, & Shakhashiri, 1986), hypertension (Mann, 1977), gastroenteritis (Morris & Goldberg, 1989), kidney disease (Livesley, 1981), multiple sclerosis (Dalos, Rabins, Brooks, & O'Donnell, 1983; Rabins & Brooks, 1981; Rabins et al., 1986; Warren, Warren, & Cockerill, 1991), chronic neurological disorders (DePaulo, Folstein, & Gordon, 1980), chronic obstructive airway disease (Williams & Bury, 1989), chronic pain (Poulsen, Hansen, Langemark, Olesen, & Bech, 1987), stroke (Ebrahim, Barer, & Nouri, 1987; Robinson & Price, 1982), traumatic brain injury (Kinsella, Ford, & Moran, 1989; Kinsella, Moran, Ford, & Ponsford, 1988), and visual impairment (Dodds, Bailey, Pearson, & Yates, 1991).

There has been some dispute, evident in the research, concerning the sensitivity of the GHQ in certain population subsets, such as females (Benjamin, Decalmer, & Haran, 1982) or persons with chronic psychiatric disorders (Goodchild & Duncan-Jones, 1985). Attempts to resolve this dispute (Aldrich & Van Schoubroeck, 1989; Duncan-Jones, Grayson, & Moran, 1986) have involved proposing alternative scoring methods, including one derived from Rasch's latent-trait analysis. While these investigations have not yet led to a scoring system that is unequivocally superior to Goldberg's original (Newman, Bland, & Orn, 1988), they do illustrate the vitality of interest in the GHQ more than 25 years after its original publication.

Millon Behavioral Health Inventory

Millon and associates (Millon, Green, & Meagher, 1979) recognized a need for psychologists in rehabilitation and general medical settings to (1) characterize the psychological make-up of persons served by general medical practices; (2) study the impact of emotional needs, motivation, and coping style on the course of a disease; and (3) formulate a comprehensive intervention plan to mitigate negative psychological influences. Arguing that this need could not be met with existing psychiatric instruments (eg, the Minnesota Multiphasic Personality Inventory, the 16 Personality Factors test), they set out to develop a brief, valid, multidimensional, behavior-oriented self-report inventory relevant to medical and rehabilitation issues.

The instrument was constructed through a sequential psychometric process of content specification, item preparation and analysis, and scale discrimination and reliability analyses (Millon, Green, & Meagher, 1981; Millon, Green, & Meagher, 1982). The Millon Behavioral Health Inventory (MBHI) comprises 150 true or false items organized into 20 clinical scales in four domains as follows: (1) Coping styles—enduring interpersonal and broad personality patterns (introversive, inhibited, cooperative, sociable, confident, forceful, respectful, sensitive); (2) Psychogenic attitudes—specific stressful influences or pathological dimensions of personality that may precipitate or exacerbate physical illness (chronic tension, recent stress, premorbid pessimism, future despair, social alienation, somatic anxiety); (3) Psychosomatic complaints—empirically derived correlates differentiating major disease syndromes (allergic inclination, gastrointestinal susceptibility, cardiovascular tendency); and (4) Prognostic index—empirically derived psychological indices of future problems that may influence the course of the individual's disability or the efficacy of a treatment (pain treatment responsivity, life-threat reactivity, emotional vulnerability).

The initial report on the MBHI (Millon et al., 1979) reported homogeneity reliability indices of the 20 scales ranging from 0.66 to 0.90 with a median value of 0.82. Stability reliability values for data from a sample of 89 respondents over a period of one to eight months ranged from 0.72 to 0.90 with a median value of 0.83. Initial validity coefficients concerning the relationships of various scales to the Minnesota Multiphasic Personality Inventory and other instruments (eg, Beck Depression Inventory, Symptoms Check List—90, California Psychological Inventory) supported the construct validity of the instrument. Factor analytic study of the scales (Millon et al., 1981) suggested that four factors accounted for the majority of the variance in the data. A similar four-factor solution, accounting for 84% of the common variance, was derived in a study involving a heterogeneous sample of 63 persons (Murphy, Tosi, Sharratt Wise, & Eshbaugh, 1987). These factors were labeled: I—Inhibition, Oversensitivity, and Emotional Distress; II—Emotional Instability and Somatic Distress; III—Agitation and Negative Affect; and IV—Anxiety and Rumination Over Somatic Functioning.

A number of investigations have used the MBHI to evaluate treatments with diverse populations in assorted settings, generating additional data concerning the construct and predictive validities of the instrument. For example, the MBHI has proven to be useful for discriminating among groups of respondents and, thereby, modifying rehabilitation plans to meet the unique needs of persons with chronic pain (Duefton, 1990; Gatchel, Deckel, Weinberg, & Smith, 1985; Gatchel, Mayer, Capra, Barnett, & Diamond, 1986; Green, Meagher, & Millon, 1983; Labbé, Goldberg, Fishbain, Rosomoff, & Steele-Rosomoff, 1989; Murphy, Sperr, & Sperr, 1986; Sweet, Breuer, Hazlewood, Toye, & Pawl, 1985), coronary bypass surgery (Green et al., 1983), cancer (Antoni & Goodkin, 1989; Goodkin, Antoni, & Blaney, 1986; Jensen, 1987; Rozensky, Nonor, Tovian, Herz, & Holland, 1985; van Komen & Redd, 1985), kidney disease (Weisberg & Page, 1988), impotence (Camic, 1983; Segraves, 1987), agoraphobia (Norton & Allen, 1985), weight problems (Clifford, Tan, & Gorsuch, 1991), depression (Amori & Lenox, 1989), and digestive disorders (Richter, Obrecht, Bradley, Young, & Anderson, 1986).

The data on the reliability, specificity, validity, sensitivity, and utility of the MBHI support its usefulness as a tool for the diagnosis, treatment, and prognosis of physiological conditions, health impairments, and psychosomatic disorders in a variety of medical and rehabilitation settings. Investigation of potential respondent bias and reactivity influences needs to be undertaken.

Psychosocial Adjustment to Illness Scale

The Psychosocial Adjustment to Illness Scale (PAIS) is a 46-item instrument designed to measure a respondent's psychosocial adjustment to a medical illness and its residual effects (Derogatis, 1976; Derogatis, 1977; Derogatis & Lopez, 1983). It can be administered as a semistructured psychiatric interview by a trained clinician or as a self-report questionnaire (PAIS-SR). The respondent is directed to answer each question about his or her current functioning (eg, "How adequately do you do your job now?" "Do you depend on the members of your family for any help or assistance, particularly since your illness?") with reference to "the past 30 days including today" on a four-point scale (the response anchors vary for each item).

In addition to an overall adjustment score, the PAIS yields scores on seven subscales defined a priori to represent domains most commonly considered by clinicians when evaluating the impact of illness and the outcome of treatment (Derogatis, 1986; Morrow, Chiarello, & Derogatis, 1978). Six scales concern general life functioning: (1) Health Care Orientation (expectations about treatment and clinicians, information on the medical disorder, adjustment to illness), (2) Vocational Environment (effects of medical illness on employment, changes in performance, expectations, and goals), (3) Domestic Environment (changes in domestic functioning, communication with others in the household, others' reactions to the illness, fiscal impact), (4) Sexual Relationships (changes in sexual behavior and satisfaction), (5) Extended Family Relationships (impact on the extended family and family members' interactions with the respondent and each other), and (6) Social Environment (impact on social and leisure activities). A seventh dimension, entitled Psychological Distress, includes items indicative of the psychological reactions of anxiety, depression, guilt, and hostility and of the respondent's self-esteem and body image. With slight modification to the wording of the items and format of the questionnaire, the PAIS can be administered to the parents, spouses, children, or other relatives of the respondent.

After reversing the responses for the negatively worded items, the responses are summed and then converted to standard normal scores using tables provided in the manual for individuals with distinct illnesses (eg, lung cancer, renal disease, acute burns, hypertension, heart disease). Higher scores are indicative of greater impairment. It should be noted that the norms available to date were constructed from relatively small and nonrepresentative samples of respondents. The authors' stated goal is to create a library of norm tables for the full range of illness and disability categories.

Psychometric investigations of the PAIS (Derogatis, 1986; Morrow et al., 1978) suggested that the subscales were reasonably specific and independent (subscale intercorrelation ranged from 0.00 to 0.70, Median (Mdn) = 0.22), reliable (interrater reliability values ranged from 0.33 to 0.86, Mdn = 0.71), homogeneous (alpha coefficients ranged from 0.12 to 0.93, Mdn = 0.82), and construct valid (subscale-to-total correlations ranged from 0.08 to 0.83, Mdn = 0.53). Interrater reliability for the total scale score was 0.83. Test-retest reliability data have not been reported by the authors. A recent homogeneity analysis of the PAIS subscales with data from 215 respondents attending cancer, gastroenterology, and rheumatology clinics reported coefficient alpha values ranging from 0.63 (Health Care Orientation) to 0.81 (Vocational Environment), with a median value of 0.79 (Browne, Arpin, Corey, Fitch, & Gafni, 1990).

A confirmatory principal components analysis for a sample of 120 individuals with lung cancer (Derogatis, 1986) produced seven factors accounting for 63% of the variance that replicated with reasonable accuracy the theoretically defined PAIS scales. Factor I (accounting for 18% of the common variance) recovered all six items from the Social Environment scale as well as five other items; Factor II (10%) recovered all six items of the Vocational Environment scale; Factor III (9%) recovered all six items of the Sexual Relationships scale; Factor IV (8%) recovered six of the eight Health Care Orientation items; Factor V (8%) combined two Health Care Orientation items and three Extended Family items; Factor VI (8%) recovered six of the seven Psychological Distress items; and Factor VII (5%) recovered five of the eight Domestic Environment items.

Scores on the Psychological Distress subscale correlated significantly in the predicted direction with scores on the State-Trait Anxiety Inventory, the Symptoms Check List—90-Revised, the Affect Balance Scale, and the Beck Depression Inventory (Derogatis, 1986; Morrow et al., 1978). Additional support for the concurrent validity of the PAIS has been reported in studies using the Symptoms Check List—90-R (Conrady, Wish, Agre, Rodriquez, & Sperling, 1989), the Coping Response Styles questionnaire (Roberts et al., 1987), the Arthritis Impact Measurement Scales (Lerner et al., 1991), the Hamilton Depression and Hamilton Anxiety scales (Cain et al., 1983), and the Sickness Impact Profile (Sugarbaker, Barofsky, Rosenberg, & Gianola, 1982).

The discriminant and predictive validities of the PAIS have been demonstrated in studies investigating psychosocial adaptation of persons with amputation (Lerner et al., 1991), rheumatoid arthritis (Engle, Callahan, Pincus, & Hochberg, 1990; Hochberg & Sutton, 1988; Lerner et al., 1991), burns (Browne et al., 1985; Roberts et al., 1987), cancer (Baider, Amikam, & Kaplan De-Nour, 1984; Carpenter, Morrow, & Schmale, 1989; Cella, Mahon, & Donovan, 1990; Friedman, Baer, Lewy, Lane, & Smith, 1988; Northouse, 1988; Northouse & Swain, 1987; Sugarbaker et al., 1982; Wolberg, Tanner, Romsaus, Trump, & Malic, 1987), gastroenteritis (Arpin, Fitch, Browne, & Corey, 1990), heart disease (Folks, Blake, Fluse, Sokol, & Freeman, 1986; Gundle, Reeves, Tate, Raft, & McLaurin, 1980; Langeluddecke, Fulcher, Baird, Hughes, & Tennant, 1989; Raft, McKee, Popio, & Haggerty, 1985), hypertension (DeVon & Powers, 1984; Powers, 1987), kidney disease (Binik, 1983; Goodwin, 1988; Kaplan De-Nour, 1982; Kaye, Bray, Gracely, & Levison, 1989; Soskolne & Kaplan De-Nour, 1989), and poliomyelitis (Conrady et al., 1989).

The PAIS and PAIS-SR appear to be promising scales for the assessment of psychosocial adaptation to illness (Swassing, 1987; Weissman, Sholomskas, & John, 1981). As with the GHQ and the MBHI, there is a need to investigate the potentially biasing influences of respondent sensitization, reactivity, faking, and response styles. Confidence in the validity and utility of the scale should increase as more researchers use the PAIS to evaluate psychosocial adaptation and treatment outcomes with larger and more representative samples of individuals.

Sickness Impact Profile

The Sickness Impact Profile (SIP) was developed to meet a need to evaluate health care services using a general purpose outcome measure of health status (Bergner et al., 1976; Carter, Bobbitt, Bergner, & Gilson, 1976; Gilson et al., 1975). The impact of sickness as perceived by the respondent is measured on this instrument by directing respondents to select descriptors of sickness-related behavioral dysfunction that apply to them today.

A pool of more than 1,250 statements was obtained from a review of other instruments and from medical patients, health care professionals, and individuals without impairments who were asked to describe sickness-related changes in behavior. Examination and editing of these statements led to a set of 312 unique statements that were sorted into 14 categories: social interaction, ambulation, sleep and rest, taking nutrition, usual daily work, household management, mobility, body movement, communication, leisure and recreational activities, intellectual functioning, interaction with family members, personal hygiene, and emotions and sensations. Edwards' (1957) equal-appearing interval scale discrimination method was then used to derive scale values for the items. A group of 25 judges was asked to rate each item on an 11-point scale representing the extent to which the item described a sickness-related behavioral dysfunction and again a second time on a 15-point scale from most to least dysfunctional. Stable scale values were obtained for 284 items that were then field tested with a sample of 246 individuals attending a group medical practice. Four different scoring methods were tested before settling on the percentage of total possible score (ie, summing the scale values of all the items checked, dividing that sum by the sum of the values of all the SIP items, and multiplying the quotient by 100%).

Revisions to the SIP were based on subsequent investigations of the instrument's reliability, validity, and utility (Bergner, Bobbitt, Carter, & Gilson, 1981; Bergner, Bobbitt, Pollard, Martin, & Gilson, 1976). The final form of the SIP comprises 136 items that yield a global score and scores on 12 subscales, with higher scores indicating greater dysfunction. Three scales can be combined to yield a physical dimension score (ambulation, mobility, and body care and movement); four scales can be combined to obtain a psychosocial dimension score (social interaction, alertness behavior, emotional behavior, and communication); and the remaining five scales represent general independent categories that may be scored separately (sleep and rest, eating, work, home management, and recreation and pastimes). The SIP has been translated into Spanish (Gilson et al., 1980; Hendricson et al., 1989).

Test-retest reliability values have been reported to be 0.97 for interviewer-administered data and 0.87 for self-administered data from a sample of 53 respondents in a group medical practice over 24 hours (Bergner et al., 1981); 0.88 for the Total scores collected over 24 hours from 119 respondents with physical disabilities (Pollard, Bobbitt, Bergner, Martin, & Gilson, 1976); 0.91 for Total, 0.95 for Physical, and 0.79 for Psychosocial scores collected over six months from 23 respondents with rheumatoid arthritis (Deyo, Inui, Leininger, & Overman, 1983); 0.85 for Total, 0.94 for Physical, and 0.63 for Psychosocial scores collected over six months from 80 respondents attending a low-back pain clinic (Deyo & Diehl, 1983); and 0.88 for a modified version of the scale (deleting the Work scale) for a group of 35 homebound and terminally ill respondents over three months (McCusker & Stoddard, 1984).

Concurrent and construct validity analyses have entailed the investigation of the relationship of SIP data with data obtained from other instruments, including the Profile of Mood States (Greenwald, 1987; Subramanian & Rose, 1988), the Arthritis Impact Measurement Scales (Hendricson et al., 1989), the Psychosocial Adjustment to Illness Scale (Sugarbaker et al., 1982), the Carroll Depression Rating Scale (Brooks, Jordan, Divine, Smith, & Neelon, 1990), the Minnesota Multiphasic Personality Inventory (Brooks et al., 1990: Follick, Smith, & Ahern, 1985), the McGill Pain Questionnaire (Greenwald, 1987), the Mood Adjective Check List (Ahlmén, Bengtsson, Sullivan, & Bjelle, 1990), Katz's Activities of Daily Living Index (Bergner, Bobbitt, Pollard, Gilson, & Morris, 1976), and the National Health Interview Survey Index of Activity Limitations, Work Loss, and Bed Days (Bergner et al., 1981). In all cases the relationships have been in the reported direction, although the magnitudes of the coefficients have varied considerably.

Only a single study was located that factor analyzed SIP data. Results obtained for the responses of 221 respondents hospitalized for either medical or psychiatric problems showed the four Psychosocial Dimension scales loaded on a single factor and the three Physical Dimension scales, together with the Home Management scale, loaded on a second factor (Brooks et al., 1990). When the SIP data were factor analyzed together with responses to the Carroll Depression Rating Scale and Minnesota Multiphasic Personality Inventory data, the same structure was obtained with the Minnesota Multiphasic Personality Inventory Depression and Anxiety scales and the Carroll Depression Rating Scale loading on Factor I. The Carroll Depression Rating Scale and the Minnesota Multiphasic Personality Inventory accounted for 62% of the variance in predicted SIP Psychosocial Dimension scores.

The SIP has been used to investigate adaptation in respondents with various health and physical disabilities, providing information concerning the discriminant and predictive validity of the instrument. Included in these studies have been individuals with rheumatoid arthritis (Deyo & Inui, 1984; Deyo, Inui, Leininger, & Overman, 1982; Stuifbergen, 1988; Sullivan, Ahlmén, & Bjelle, 1990), cancer (Greenwald, 1987; Sugarbaker et al., 1982), chronic pain (Deyo & Diehl, 1983; Follick et al., 1985; Roland & Morris, 1983; Subramanian & Rose, 1988), diabetes mellitus (Littlefield, Rodin, Murray, & Craven, 1990; Stuifbergen, 1988), heart disease (Bergner, Hallstrom, Bergner, Eisenberg, & Cobb, 1985; Munro, Creamer, Haggerty, & Cooper, 1988; Ott et al., 1983; Stuifbergen, 1988), hyperthyroidism (Rockey & Griep, 1980), multiple sclerosis (Devins, Seland, Klein, Edworthy, & Saary, 1993; Rao et al., 1991; Stuifbergen, 1988; Zeldow & Pavlou, 1988), spinal osteoporosis (Effinger et al., 1988), and traumatic brain injury (Fraser, Dikmen, McLean, Miller, & Temkin, 1988; Klonoff, Costa, & Snow, 1986; Klonoff, Snow,

& Costa, 1986; Lysaght & Bodenhamer, 1990; Temkin, Dikmen, Machamer, & McLean, 1989; Temkin, McLean, Dikmen, & Machamer, 1988).

Two psychometric concerns about the SIP have been raised recently in the research literature. In a study with 332 individuals with medical and psychiatric disorders, the correlations between the Minnesota Multiphasic Personality Inventory L and K scales and the Total and Psychosocial dimension scores suggested that the SIP may be susceptible to a defensiveness response bias (Brooks et al., 1990). The second concern is the sensitivity of the SIP to detect changes in medical and surgical patients' reactions to their conditions in prospective longitudinal research (MacKenzie, Charlson, DiGioia, & Kelley, 1986). A total of 43 individuals were administered the SIP within 24 hours of hospital admission and again at one, two, four, and six weeks postdischarge. Physicians' diagnostic information and ratings of illness were also collected. Analyses of change scores showed that the SIP was less accurate in detecting positive than negative change as measured by the physicians' ratings of patient status.

The comprehensiveness and rigor of the psychometric techniques used to develop the SIP are impressive. The subscales appear to demonstrate sufficient homogeneity, reliability, and specificity to be of use for respondent profile analysis. The total scale score and the two dimension scores also demonstrate acceptable reliability, and available evidence is supportive of construct and concurrent validity. The SIP should provide data that practitioners and researchers can use to plan as well as evaluate the effectiveness of health interventions. Additional investigations of the factorial structure and of the sensitivity of the SIP are warranted.

UNIDIMENSIONAL MEASURES OF ADAPTATION TO DISABILITY

In this section we review three instruments that purport to provide information on psychosocial adaptation of persons with physical disabilities where adaptation is conceived as a unidimenstional construct (ie, a single score is obtained placing the individual on a continuum of psychosocial adaptation). The first two—the Acceptance of Disability scale and the Acceptance of Loss scale—were developed from Dembo, Leviton, and Wright's (1956) theory of shifts in the value system of the person with a disability. The third instrument—the Bell Disability Scale of Adjustment—was based on the concept of the individual's acceptance of his or her dependency needs.

Acceptance of Disability Scale

Linkowski's (1969) Acceptance of Disability (AD) scale was developed from a theory of acceptance of loss emphasizing subjective meaning of disability to the individual with an impairment (Dembo et al., 1956). The theory posits a process of value shifts in four domains: (1) enlargement of the scope of values from those that the individual has lost to those that do not conflict with the disability, (2) subordination of physique to other attributes such as personality and social relationships with concomitant de-emphasis of physical aspects of the self, (3) containment of disability effects to the area of actual physical limitation to prevent inadequacy in one domain from predominating self-evaluation, and (4) transformation of self-evaluation based upon comparative values to self-evaluation based upon asset values. It was hypothesized that "people who were more accepting of their disabilities would be more open to information about their disabilities and their ability to function than would those who were less accepting. Also, they would 'suffer' less in their interactions with people who did not have disabilities" (Linkowski, 1989, p. 3).

A total of 50 items representing the four value shift domains was written and randomly arranged to constitute the AD scale (Linkowski, 1971). The participant's responses to the items on 6-point rating scales were summed to yield a single score representing the degree of acceptance of the physical disability. The instrument was administered to a sample of 46 persons with physical disabilities, and the Spearman-Brown corrected split-half reliability index was calculated to be 0.93. Factor analysis yielded a single factor accounting for 48% of the common variance, suggesting that the items constituted a homogeneous measure of a single construct. What that construct may be, however, is not altogether clear.

There is evidence to suggest that the AD scale does measure the construct implied by its title. For example, scores on the Attitudes Toward Disabled Persons Scale—Form B (Yuker, Block, & Younng, 1966), a measure of accepting attitudes toward persons with a disability as a group, correlated 0.81 with scores on the AD scale (Linkowski, 1971). In a subsequent study (Linkowski & Dunn, 1974), AD scale scores for a sample of 76 university students with a physical disability were found to be positively and significantly correlated with scores on two measures of self-concept. Starr and Heiserman (1977) modified the AD items by replacing the word disability with the word cleft and found that the resultant scale reliably discriminated self-esteem among a sample of 72 teenagers with oral-facial clefts. Poll and Kaplan De-Nour (1980) modified the AD scale by changing the referent from disability to disease to study the relationship between locus of control and acceptance of disability in chronic hemodialysis patients. As predicted, respondents with an internal locus of control were found to be significantly more accepting of their disability than were respondents with an external locus of control. Finally, Patrick (1984) found that a group of novice and veteran wheelchair athletes differed on mean AD scores in the predicted direction.

Other research, by failing to confirm predictions about the relationship of the construct measured to certain other sociodemographic and disability-related variables, has raised questions about the construct validity of the AD scale. For example, the results of a mail survey of 51 persons with amputations (Thomas, Davis, & Hochman, 1976) revealed that AD scores were not related to age, cause of amputation, age at time of amputation, time since amputation, years of work experience, income before amputation, current income, secondary disability, employment status, and marital status. Contrary to the expectations of Poll and Kaplan De-Nour (1980), AD scores were not correlated with respondents' ages or number of years on hemodialysis but were positively correlated with number of years of education. Analyses of data from a sample of 251 individuals with a spinal cord injury (Woodrich & Patterson, 1983) revealed no relationship of AD scores to marital status or extent of paralysis, but females were found to score higher than males. Curiously, AD scores were found to be positively related to chronicity after the influence of age was partialled out but negatively related to age after the influence of chronicity was partialled out. In a study using a Hebrew version of the scale with a sample of persons with amputations (Almagor, Jaffee, & Lomranz, 1978), the AD was found to correlate with a Hebrew version of the Attitude Toward Disabled Persons scale, but AD scores did not discriminate individuals who differed on a measure of the phantom limb phenomenon. In a study of 103 consecutive respondents with a spinal cord injury who were attending a rehabilitation institute over a 28-month period (Heinemann, Goranson, Ginsburg, & Schnoll, 1989), AD scores were found to be higher for females than for males. But, contrary to expectations, they were not related to age or chronicity of disability, and they were not a significant predictor of alcohol use, alcohol drinking activity patterns, or family history of alcohol use.

Data from the use of the AD scale in a small collection of other studies provides additional information on the validity of the scale for measuring psychosocial adaptation to disability. For example, when the AD scale was administered together with measures of anxiety and hope to a sample of 48 young adults with disabilities (Boone, Roessler, & Cooper, 1978), curvilinear relationships were discovered, suggesting that moderate levels of hope and anxiety were most conducive to acceptance of disability. A positive relationship between AD scores and measures of assertiveness in samples of individuals with physical disabilities has been found in two nonequivalent control group quasi-experimental studies (Glueckauf, Horley, Poushinsky, & Vogel, 1984; Starke, 1987). AD scale score means, however, did not differ between groups of persons with epilepsy who did and did not receive a two-day specialized training program designed to provide medical education and psychosocial counseling (Helgeson, Mittan, Tan, & Chayasirisobhon, 1990). A recent study (Heinemann & Hawkins, 1995) examined the relationships among substance abuse and medical complications of spinal cord injury and the variables of depression and acceptance of disability as measured by the AD scale. Use of illicit drugs and prescription medication was unrelated to both depression and disability acceptance at three time periods, but severity of drinking problems was directly related to depression and inversely related to disability acceptance within the first six months after a spinal cord injury.

It is interesting that AD scores were found to be positively and significantly correlated with years of education in a sample of chronic hemodialysis patients (Poll & Kaplan De-Nour, 1980), a sample of persons with amputation (Thomas et al., 1976), and a sample of persons with spinal cord injury (Woodrich & Patterson, 1983). Although the most plausible explanation is that years of education was confounded in these samples with other sociodemographic variables, such as age and socioeconomic status, it is conceivable that this observation may be related to difficulty reading and interpreting the 50 items on the scale or to the biasing influences of respondent sensitization and social desirability responding. No research was located that investigated the salience of these two threats to the validity of the AD scale, nor the related threats of faking and response style influences.

It would seem reasonable that a large sample psychometric reanalysis and revalidation of the AD scale should be conducted in view of the AD scale's age, growing disfavor in recent years with the theory on which it was based, the paucity of reliability and factor analytic data, and the inconsistency of available validity data. The unidimensional conception of acceptance of disability represented by the AD scale may limit its utility to a narrow range of research investigations.

Acceptance of Loss Scale

Osuji (1975) designed the Acceptance of Loss (AL) scale to measure the presumed intervening variable of reaction to disability as a factor influencing psychological and social behaviors of persons with physical impairments. Similar to Linkowski, Osuji based the development of the AL scale on the value system change model described previously (Dembo et al., 1956). A set of 45 items, together with a definition of the construct of acceptance of loss and a description of the value change domains, was written and submitted to a panel of eight experts in rehabilitation in England. The experts were asked to sort the items into groups representing favorable and unfavorable acceptance of loss and to identify any ambiguous or defective items. The 37 items that achieved 100% classification agreement were then written as summated rating items with five categories (strongly agree, agree, undecided, disagree, and strongly disagree). A total of 72 individuals receiving the services of an industrial rehabilitation unit responded to the prototype scale (Osuji, 1975). Item analytic results led to the elimination of eight items.

The AL scale was scored by totaling a participant's responses to the 29 remaining statements, resulting in a single score ostensibly measuring one's level of acceptance of loss resulting from a physical disability. The corrected split-half reliability of the scale was found to be 0.92 (Osuji, 1975). Factor analysis (type not identified) of the data from the 72 respondents yielded 10 first-order factors accounting for 92% of the variance. Eigenvalues were, however, unreported, so it is unclear how many of these factors were meaningful. Two of the factors represented unique items, two others represented only two items each, and two others represented only three items.

The initial scale development study also did not report any data concerning the validity of the scale for measuring adaptation to disability. Two subsequent studies (Osuji, 1985; Osuji, 1987) did provide preliminary construct validity data. In the first of these two studies (Osuji, 1985) the scale, together with Ravens Progressive Matrices and the Maudsley Personality Inventory, was administered twice five weeks apart to a nonrandom sample of 330 consecutive persons with a physical disability who were admitted to a rehabilitation program in England. AL scale difference scores were calculated and divided into thirds to classify participants as either good, average, or poor accepters of their disabilities. Those in the good accepters of loss group scored highest on the extroversion scale of the personality measure and lowest on the neuroticism scale. Those in the poor accepters of loss group showed the greater AL scale score gains as a result of the rehabilitation intervention. In the second study (Osuji, 1987) analyses of data collected from a nonrandom sample of 414 individuals attending a rehabilitation program revealed that those with the lowest AL scale scores were more likely to be late for training sessions, absent from the program, and noncompleters of the program. AL scale scores were also associated with rehabilitation success as indicated by an employability rating obtained from a rehabilitation clinician.

Although the homogeneity data are encouraging, no reliability data on stability over time have been reported, and the scale's factorial structure has not been adequately determined. It is also unknown whether the scale is susceptible to response bias influences. As noted in the discussion of the AD scale, growing disfavor in recent years with Dembo's unidimensional acceptance of loss theory on which the AL scale was based would also suggest that an investigation of the scale's content validity is warranted. The lack of psychometric data from researchers other than the developer of the instrument and the meager construct and criterion-related validity data suggest that clinicians should be cautious in their use and interpretation of this scale.

Bell Disability Scale of Adjustment

The Bell Disability Scale of Adjustment (BDSA) was developed to measure a person's degree of acceptance of a traumatic orthopaedic impairment based on an assumption that all individuals seek need-dependency gratification (Bell, 1967).

Adaptive adjustment was thought to be reflected in the behavior and attitude of a person with a disability when he or she achieved acceptance of dependency needs. The BDSA consists of 40 items describing acceptance attitudes and behaviors derived from the author's clinical experience as a psychologist and from introspection about his own disability. Each item is rated on a six-point scale and summed to yield a total score, with high scores signifying a less accepting attitude.

The scale was administered, together with the Attitudes Toward Disabled Persons scale and a measure of cognitive ability, to a sample of persons with orthopaedic impairments. Additionally data were collected concerning age at onset of disability, chronicity, and type of disability. No significant relationship was found between BDSA scores and the measure of cognitive ability. The relationship between the BDSA and the Attitudes Toward Disabled Persons scale scores was in the predicted direction, with respondents least accepting of their disabilities manifesting a perception of persons with disabilities as different from the population of persons without disabilities. In addition, a comparison of the BDSA score means of those individuals who were hospitalized with those who were living in the community revealed that the hospitalized individuals were least accepting of their disabilities. BDSA scores were also found to be related in the predicted direction to both age at onset of disability (ie, those who were impaired at a younger age were more accepting) and chronicity of disability (ie, those who were impaired longer were more accepting).

Bell implied that the scale could be used for persons with a physical disability to differentiate acceptance, perceived to range on a univariate continuum from passive rejection (nonacceptance of disability and low motivation for activity), through active rejection (nonacceptance of disability but high motivation for activity) and passive acceptance (acceptance but low motivation to activity), to active acceptance (acceptance and high motivation to activity). No information was provided, however, on how to convert derived BDSA scores to measure these phases of adjustment.

Although Bell called for further reliability and validity studies of the BDSA, only one other research investigation was located that has used the instrument. In a recent study by Wassem (1992), the BDSA was administered to a nonrandom sample of 62 persons with multiple sclerosis as a measure of psychosocial adaptation to disability. No reliability data were reported. It was discovered that 72% of the variance in BDSA scores was accounted for by a self-report measure of the individual's confidence in performing activities related to self-care and disease management (eg, taking medications) and a measure of disability severity.

The more than reasonable initial validity data would suggest that a psychometric investigation of an updated version of the instrument might yield a satisfactory, albeit unidimensional, measure of adaptation to disability. A combined investigation of the first three instruments—the AD scale, the AL scale, and the BDSA—may yield a more satisfactory and contemporary multidimensional instrument with adequate construct and predictive validity.

MULTIDIMENSIONAL MEASURES OF ADAPTATION TO DISABILITY

In this section we review two instruments that purport to provide information on psychosocial adaptation of persons with physical disabilities where adaptation is conceived as a multidimensional construct (ie, a set of scores is obtained representing related but distinct aspects of the individual's psychosocial adaptation). The first measure—the Heinemann and Shontz Q-Sort—was developed to test Fink's (1967) four-stage theoretical model of reaction to crisis following a physical disability, namely shock, defensive retreat, acknowledgment, and adaptation. This measure is distinct from the other nine instruments reviewed in this chapter, as it is based upon a qualitative measurement technique known as Q-methodology (Stephenson, 1953). The second instrument—the Reactions to Impairment and Disability Inventory—enables the researcher to study different patterns of adaptation to disability through the examination of subscale scores representing eight psychosocial reaction categories: shock, anxiety, denial, depression, internalized anger, externalized hostility, acknowledgment, and adjustment.

Heinemann and Shontz Q-Sort

Arguing that the complex process of adaptation to disability following a life-disrupting disability may be unique and heterarchically organized for different individuals, Heinemann and Shontz (1984; 1985) used a person-centered qualitative measurement technique known as Q-methodology in place of a conventional quantitative strategy. Q-methodology, an advanced rank-ordering methodology developed by Stephenson (1953), requires the respondent to sort cards presenting statements about a referent into an ordered collection of piles according to a researcher-defined criterion, such as favorability, intensity of agreement, or self-descriptiveness. The number of cards is typically large (100 or more), and the number of piles and the number of statements the respondent can place in each pile are fixed by the researcher in advance. For example, the respondent may be asked to sort 100 cards into 9 piles with 4, 8, 13, 16, 18, 16, 13, 8, and 4 items in each pile. The respondent is told to order the piles from least to most descriptive of his or her concept of ideal self.

The item arrangements are tabulated and clusters of respondents with similar orderings are identified. The content of the most frequently occurring items in each pile for a cluster of respondents is examined and constructs are proposed to characterize these respondents, that is, samples of respondents are clustered and interpreted rather than samples of items, as in principal components or factor analysis. Several applications of the Q-sort results are available for rehabilitation clinicians. The clinician may attempt to assign a new client to one of a set of previously identified respondent clusters by examining his or her sort of the items, thereby increasing the likelihood of selecting the most appropriate rehabilitation intervention. The item clusterings of a group of clients may also be examined before and after an intervention to evaluate the success of the procedure for accomplishing hypothesized changes.

Q-methodology may also be used to answer research questions. If the items to be sorted can be written to represent a particular theoretical perspective, the sorting requirement can be arranged to test that theory. For example, Barker (1964) used Q-methodology to test a theoretical model concerning the grouping of disability labels. Finally, changes over time in the sortings of a group of individuals may be examined to validate a developmental process for a psychological construct presumed to underlie the sorting. An early review of investigations using Q-methodology in psychiatric research is provided by Block (1961).

Heinemann and Shontz (1984) developed a set of 48 items divided into four groups to test Fink's (1967) theoretical model of reaction to crisis following a physical disability that posited four stages: shock, defensive retreat, acknowledgment, and adaptation. An original pool of 64 items representing the four stages was written and submitted to a panel of five judges who were familiar with the model. Items were retained and assigned to a group representing one of the reaction stages if at least four of the five judges agreed in their classification of the item. Two 24-year-old individuals who had spinal cord injuries were subsequently asked to sort the 48 items into sets descriptive of their typical and ideal selves at each of four times keyed to the four reaction stages: shortly after injury during hospitalization (shock); postinjury, when life seemed to lack purpose (defensive retreat); postinjury, when hope for the future was high (acknowledgment); and the present (adaptation). It was hypothesized that progression through the four stages would be signified by different sortings for the four times. The sortings for the two individuals were interpreted to illustrate two courses of adaptation, one of which confirmed the hypothesized stage model (but not in the expected order) whereas the other did not, showing little change across time. The authors suggested that the results of their work confirm their view that clinicians should modify interventions to meet the needs of different individuals understood as complex wholes rather than as mere behavers who react to unique environmental events and disability-related crises.

Heinemann and Shontz (1985) have acknowledged, however, that adaptation must be examined prospectively in longitudinal research to validate developmental processes. They denigrated the claim that respondent reactivity may have biased the results of their earlier investigation and limited the generalizability of the findings to other respondents, arguing instead that the individual was the focus of interest in their research and the construction of group profiles was irrelevant. It would seem possible to combine a person-centered clinical application of the methodology (ie, to determine the counseling needs of the individual who is confronting a life-altering disability) together with the group-centered statistical application of the methodology (ie, to identify the characteristics of clusters of individuals as they react to their disabilities). Investigating changes in these cluster profiles longitudinally could provide the data needed to validate psychosocial adaptation as a developmental process.

Reactions to Impairment and Disability Inventory

The unidimensional conception of adaptation to disability evident in the three instruments reviewed in the previous section of this chapter ignores the fact that psychosocial adaptation has multiple antecedents and that reactions experienced by persons with disabilities have multiple facets. The recently introduced Reactions to Impairment and Disability Inventory (RIDI) may furnish researchers with a more useful multidimensional measurement device to explore this construct (Livneh & Antonak, 1990).

Using interviews with rehabilitation experts and an examination of published instruments and various texts, research reports, and handbooks, over 300 statements were written operationalizing psychological reactions to a disabling condition or major life crisis. A review of the items eliminated those deemed redundant, ambiguous, or highly specific reactions manifested only by certain disability groups. A list of slightly more than 200 items was then sorted into one of eight a priori specified reaction categories: shock, anxiety, denial, depression, internalized anger, externalized hostility, acknowledgment, and adjustment. Items that did not clearly belong to any of the categories or that were judged to belong to more than one category were reworded or discarded. These procedures yielded a set of 143 items.

The items were then submitted to a panel of 15 experts in psychology, counseling, and related disciplines who were requested to (1) specify, for each item, if it belonged, belonged only marginally, or definitely did not belong to its assigned reaction category; and (2) comment on the items portraying these reaction categories and add any not included in the list presented. The list of items was reduced to 95 based on the responses and suggestions made by the panel of experts. The items were pilot tested in personal interviews with a small number of individuals with various physically disabling conditions, and the set was reduced to 90 items that were then arranged in a random order as a summated rating inventory comprising eight scales. Approximately half the items in each set were worded positively and half negatively to break an acquiescence response set. The scales, in their hypothesized temporal order, were Shock (8 items), Anxiety (11 items), Denial (10 items), Depression (14 items), Internalized Anger (8 items), Externalized Hostility (12 items), Acknowledgment (12 items), and Adjustment (15 items). The directions asked respondents to rate the extent to which they experienced each reaction on a 4-point scale, ranging from 1—Never, through 2—Rarely (The reaction is seldom experienced; less than 4 times per month.), and 3—Sometimes (The reaction is occasionally experienced; approximately 5 to 10 times per month.), to 4—Often (The reaction is frequently experienced; more than 10 times per month.). Responses to the items within each of the eight scales were summed to yield a score for each scale.

The inventory was administered to a sample of 214 individuals with various physical disabilities and chronic health and neurological disabilities (eg, spinal cord injury, stroke, multiple sclerosis, myocardial infarction) in both inpatient and outpatient rehabilitation programs in southern New England. Analyses of these data (Livneh & Antonak, 1990) revealed that the eight scales were reasonably specific, independent, and reliable, with Cronbach coefficient alpha values of 0.79, 0.83, 0.64, 0.88, 0.81, 0.84, 0.78, and 0.89, respectively. Factor analytic study provided support for the multidimensional structure of the RIDI, yielding seven factors accounting for 44% of the variance in the data. These factors appeared to recover the essence of the Acknowledgment, Adjustment, Depression, Internalized Anger, Externalized Hostility, and Denial scales, although the empirical assignment of items to scales did not completely coincide with the theoretical assignment. No consistent relationships were found between the RIDI scale scores and the respondent variables of sex, age, or educational attainment. A composite of the Anxiety, Internalized Anger, and Externalized Hostility scales was found to differentiate respondents grouped according to age at onset of disability. The correlation between scores on Linkowski's AD scale and a composite of the items on the Acknowledgment and Adjustment scales for a subsample of individuals with duration of disability of at least three years was found to be 0.68.

In an investigation of the temporal structure of the process of adaptation to disability (Livneh & Antonak, 1991), respondents were asked to rate each RIDI item twice, indicating the extent to which they experienced each reaction in the Past (defined as "any time during the period immediately following the onset of the impairment or disability until recently, but not including the past month") and in the Present (defined as "during only the last month"). Data for 185 participants included the eight Past and eight Present RIDI scale scores, sociodemographic characteristics (ie, sex, age, ethnicity, marital status, and educational attainment), and disability-related variables (ie, type of disability, its cause, age at onset of disability, and chronicity of disability). As predicted, all the correlations between chronicity and the first six nonadaptive reactions in both the past and the present were negative, and both of the chronicity-Adjustment scale correlations were positive. The Past data were found to discriminate reliably between two groups containing individuals with the shortest and the longest chronicity of disability. A similar analysis for the Present data yielded a similar result. A multivariate analysis of variance yielded a main effect for time (Past versus Present) with Shock, Anxiety, Depression, Internalized Anger, and Externalized Hostility experienced more often in the past than in the present, while the reverse was true for Acknowledgment and Adjustment. Denial scores did not differ between the two times. The most salient predictor of respondents' scores on the Past Adjustment scale was score on the Past Acknowledgment scale, the scale most closely related, both conceptually and temporally, to final adaptation to disability. Other significant predictors were scores on the Past Depression and Denial scales. The only sociodemographic variable that contributed to the prediction equation was chronicity of disability. Combined, these four variables explained 75% of the variance in the Past Adjustment scale scores.

Unfolding-theoretic analysis (Davison, 1977) was used in this study to explore the validity of a hypothesized temporal structure of the eight Present and Past psychosocial reactions. The obtained linear orderings did not coincide with the hypothesized temporal ordering of the reaction phases. A graphic presentation showed that in both cases a set of five nonadaptive reactions (Depression, Internalized Anger, Shock, Anxiety, and Externalized Hostility) was distinguishable from a set of two adaptive reactions (Acknowledgment and Adjustment). The reaction of Denial was intermediate to these two polar sets.

One explanation for this distortion of the hypothesized latent continuum concerned the psychometric purity of the RIDI scales. Although analyses of the item and scale data demonstrated adequate item characteristics and scale reliabilities, the homogeneity and specificity of the eight scales were considered less than optimal. A second explanation centered on the heterogeneity of the sample of individuals who provided data for the analyses. Specifically, individuals with congenital disabilities as well as adventitious losses resulting from traumatic or degenerative conditions experienced later in life were part of the sample. A third explanation involved the unfolding-theoretic statistical procedure used to analyze the data, that is, the failure to recover exactly the hypothesized order of the reactions might have been an artifact of examining a nonlinear phenomenon with a linear analytic procedure. To overcome these limitations, another investigation with data from a sample of 118 individuals with adventitious physical disabilities was undertaken to refine the RIDI with analyses of data from a more homogeneous sample of respondents (Antonak & Livneh, 1991). In addition, ordering-theoretic data analyses (Krus, Bart, & Airasian, 1975) were used to investigate the nonlinear, multidimensional, hierarchical relationships among the eight reactions.

On the basis of iterative item, scale, and factor analytic analyses, the original 90-item RIDI was reduced to the current 60-item version with the same eight scales: Shock (7 items), Anxiety (8 items), Denial (7 items), Depression (8 items), Internalized Anger (7 items), Externalized Hostility (8 items), Acknowledgment (7 items), and Adjustment (8 items). Results of reliability and specificity analyses supported the conclusion that the scales were not only homogeneous (Cronbach coefficient alpha values of 0.75, 0.73, 0.69, 0.78, 0.74, 0.79, 0.77, and 0.85, respectively) but also specific measures of reactions. Multiple regression analyses revealed that chronicity was the best predictor for each of the first five (nonadaptive) reactions. The predictive efficiency increased significantly only when educational attainment was added to these equations. Full-model predictive efficiencies ranged from a low of 8% for the Denial scale to 15% for the Internalized Anger scale. For the last two (adaptive) scales, the only significant predictor was educational attainment, accounting for 4% of the variance in the Acknowledgment scale scores and 3% of the variance in the Adjustment scale scores. Full model efficiencies were 7% and 6%, respectively.

Alpha factor analysis supported the retention and interpretation of five factors accounting for 49% of the variance in the data. One factor recovered the Denial scale completely; a second combined all the items of the Acknowledgment and Adjustment scales; a third factor included all the Anxiety items; a fourth factor included all the Externalized Hostility items; and a fifth factor combined five of the seven Shock, four of the seven Internalized Anger, and five of the eight Depression items. The remaining Shock, Internalized Anger, and Depression items were scattered between the third and fourth factors.

In contrast to the results of the unfolding-theoretic analysis, the hierarchy obtained from the ordering-theoretic analysis depicted a set of five nonadaptive reactions not only distinguishable from, but also prerequisite to, a set of two adaptive reactions. The reaction of denial was not intermediate to but rather independent of these two sets of reactions. The positions of acknowledgment and adjustment suggested that these could be viewed conceptually as distinct reaction patterns, with anxiety, depression, internalized anger, and externalized hostility all prerequisite to reaching a final state of adaptation. Experiencing these nonadaptive reactions, however, did not occur in any prerequisite sequence; that is, they were independent. The positions of shock, anxiety, and externalized hostility in the ordering suggested that they were experienced concurrently, but that shock was apparently prerequisite to experiencing depression and internalized anger and, subsequently, acknowledgment or adjustment.

Taken together, these results provide preliminary documentation of the RIDI's homogeneity, specificity, and content and construct validities and supportive evidence for the multidimensional structure of the inventory. Reliability data concerning stability over time for the scales have not yet been collected. The inventory's factorial structure requires further exploration considering the discrepancy noted between the theoretical and empirically derived structures. The self-report format of the inventory will require verification of respondent data by other independent methods, such as significant others' reports or behavioral observations by independent judges, to determine whether the RIDI is free from the confounding and biasing effects of reactivity, socially desirable responding, and faking. One of the advantages of the RIDI is its multidimensional format that enables the study of different patterns of adaptation to disability concurrently. In its present form, however, the RIDI is strictly an experimental tool for researchers. Attempts to use it as a clinical or diagnostic instrument are clearly unwarranted until it undergoes further conceptual elaborations and psychometric investigations.

CONCLUSION

The purpose of this chapter was to provide information on the availability and suitability of 10 general instruments for measuring psychosocial adaptation to illness and disability. In Chapter 24 of this book we will present a listing of some of the problems surrounding the measurement of psychosocial adjustment to chronic illness and disability that we identified in the reviews of the 10 instruments in this chapter. Recommendations for the solution of these problems will also be provided at that time.

One observation revealed by our reviews of the 10 instruments in this chapter that is worth making here is the considerable variability in the theoretical orientations of the developers of these instruments and the concomitant variation in the operational definitions of psychosocial adaptation to chronic illness and disability. For instance, psychosocial adaptation (or maladaptation) has been operationalized as: (1) presence of new and distressing physical, behavioral, and psychosomatic complaints (GHQ, MBHI, SIP); (2) alteration of vocational and avocational productivity (PAIS); (3) reduction in performance of domestic or activities of daily living skills (PAIS, SIP); (4) coping style (MBHI); (5) degree of disability acceptance (AD scale, AL scale, BDSA); (6) pathological dimensions of personality that influence the course of disability or the efficacy of treatment (MBHI); (7) impact on interpersonal relations, communication, and sexual behavior (PAIS, SIP); and (8) emotional and psychological distress, as manifested by the reactions of anxiety, shock, guilt, depression, anger, hostility, and denial (Heinemann and Shontz Q-Sort, RIDI).

Regardless of how the researcher defines the construct, it is necessary to select a psychometrically sound instrument to answer questions concerning the nature and process of psychosocial adaptation, and subsequently the prescription and evaluation of intervention strategies for persons with diverse physical, mental, disease-related, sensory, and chronic neurological and health impairments. The 10 instruments reviewed in this chapter should be among those considered by researchers who are seeking to answer these important questions.

Chapter 3, the last chapter in this first part of the book, will present reviews of 11 instruments that have been developed to investigate the psychosocial adaptation of individuals with eight specific chronic illnesses and disabilities: namely, cancer, diabetes mellitus, hearing impairment, rheumatoid arthritis, seizure disorders, spinal cord injury, traumatic brain injury, and visual impairment.

REFERENCES

Ahlmén, E. M., Bengtsson, C. B., Sullivan, B. M., & Bjelle, A. (1990). A comparison of overall health between patients with rheumatoid arthritis and a population with and without rheumatoid arthritis. *Scandinavian Journal of Rheumatology, 19*, 413–421.

Aldrich, D., & Van Schoubroeck, L. (1989). The General Health Questionnaire: A psychometric analysis using latent trait theory. *Psychological Medicine, 19*, 469–485.

Almagor, M., Jaffee, Y., & Lomranz, J. (1978). The relation between limb dominance, acceptance of disability, and the phantom limb phenomenon. *Journal of Abnormal Psychology, 87*, 377–379.

Amori, G., & Lenox, R. H. (1989). Do volunteer subjects bias clinical trials? *Journal of Clinical Psychopharmacology, 9*, 321–327.

Andrews, G., Platt, L. J., Quinn, P. T., & Nielson, P. D. (1977). An assessment of the status of adults with cerebral palsy. *Developmental Medicine and Child Neurology, 19*, 803–810.

Antonak, R. F., & Livneh, H. (1991). A hierarchy of reactions to disability. *International Journal of Rehabilitation Research, 14*, 13–24.

Antoni, M. H., & Goodkin, K. (1989). Host moderator variables in the promotion of cervical neoplasia—II. Dimensions of life stress. *Journal of Psychosomatic Research, 33*, 457–467.

Arpin, K., Fitch, M., Browne, G. B., & Corey, P. (1990). Prevalence and correlates of family dysfunction and poor adjustment to chronic illness in specialty clinics. *Journal of Clinical Epidemiology, 43*, 373–383.

Baider, L., Amikam, J. L., & Kaplan De-Nour, A. (1984). Time-limited thematic group therapy with post-mastectomy patients. *Journal of Psychosomatic Research, 28*, 323–330.

Balinsky, W., & Berger, R. (1975). A review of research on general health status indexes. *Medical Care, 13*, 283–293.

Barker, D. G. (1964). Concepts of disabilities. *Personnel and Guidance Journal, 43*, 371–374.

Bell, A. H. (1967). Measure for adjustment of the physically disabled. *Psychological Reports, 21*, 773–778.

Benjamin S., Decalmer. P., & Haran, D. (1982). Community screening for mental illness: A validity study of the General Health Questionnaire. *British Journal of Psychiatry, 140*, 174–180.

Bergner, L., Hallstrom, A. P., Bergner, M., Eisenberg, M. S., & Cobb, L. A. (1985). Health status of survivors of cardiac arrest and of myocardial infarction controls. *American Journal of Public Health, 75*, 1321–1323.

Bergner, M., Bobbitt, R. A., Carter, W. B., & Gilson, B. S. (1981). The Sickness Impact Profile: Development and final revision of a health status measure. *Medical Care, 19*, 787–805.

Bergner, M., Bobbitt, R. A., Kressel, S., Pollard, W. E., Gilson, B. S., & Morris, J. R. (1976). The Sickness Impact Profile: Conceptual formulation and methodology for the development of a health status measure. *International Journal of Health Services, 6*, 393–415.

Bergner, M., Bobbitt, R. A., Pollard, W. E., Martin, D. P., & Gilson, B. S. (1976). The Sickness Impact Profile: Validation of a health status measure. *Medical Care, 14*, 57–67.

Billig, N., Ahmed, S. W., Kenmore, P., Amaral, D., & Shakhashiri, M. Z. (1986). Assessment of depression and cognitive impairment after hip fractures. *Journal of the American Geriatrics Society, 34*, 499–503.

Binik, Y. M. (1983). Coping with chronic life-threatening illness: Psychosocial perspectives on end stage renal disease. *Canadian Journal of Behavioural Sciences, 15*, 373–391.

Blakely, A. A., Howard, R. C., Socich, R. M., Murdoch, J. C., Menkes, D. B., & Spears, G. F. S. (1991). Psychiatric symptoms, personality and ways of coping in chronic fatigue syndrome. *Psychological Medicine, 21*, 347–362.

Block, J. (1961). *The Q-sort method in personality assessment and psychiatric research.* Springfield, IL: C C Thomas.

Boone, S. E., Roessler, R. T., & Cooper, P. G. (1978). Hope and manifest anxiety: Motivational dynamics of acceptance of disability. *Journal of Counseling Psychology, 25*, 551–556.

Bridges, K. W., & Goldberg, D. P. (1986). The validation of the GHQ-28 and the use of the MMSE in neurological inpatients. *British Journal of Psychiatry, 148*, 548–553.

Brook, R. H., Ware, J. E., Davies-Avery, A., Stewart, A. L., Donald, C. A., Rodgers, W. H., Williams, K. N., & Johnston, S. A. (1979). Overview of adult health status measures fielded in Rand's Health Insurance Study. *Medical Care, 17*(9 Suppl), 1–131.

Brooks, N. B., Jordan, J. S., Divine, G. W., Smith. K. S., & Neelon, F. A. (1990). The impact of psychologic factors on measurement of functional status: Assessment of the Sickness Impact Profile. *Medical Care, 28*, 793–804.

Browne, G., Byrne, C., Brown, B., Pennock, M., Streiner, D., Roberts, R., Eyler, P., Truscott, D., & Dabbs, R. (1985). Psychosocial adjustment of burn survivors. *Burns, 12*, 28–35.

Browne, G. B., Arpin, K., Corey, P., Fitch, M., & Gafni, A. (1990). Individual correlates of health service utilization and the cost of poor adjustment to chronic illness. *Medical Care, 28*, 43–58.

Burish, T. G., & Bradley, L. A. (Eds.). (1983). *Coping with chronic disease.* New York: Academic Press.

Burvill, P. W., & Knuiman, M. W. (1983). Which version of the General Health Questionnaire should be used in community studies? *Australian and New Zealand Journal of Psychiatry, 17*, 237–242.

Burvill, P. W., Knuiman, M. W., & Finlay-Jones, R. A. (1984). A factor analytic study of the 60-item General Health Questionnaire in Australian community and general practice settings. *Australian and New Zealand Journal of Psychiatry, 18*, 256–262.

Cain, E. N., Kohorn, E. I., Quinlan, D. M., Schwartz, P. E., Latimer, K., & Rogers, L. (1983). Psychosocial reactions to the diagnosis of gynecologic cancer. *Obstetrics and Gynecology, 62*, 635–641.

Camic, P. M. (1983). Differentiating organic and psychogenic erectile dysfunction with the Millon Behavioral Health Inventory. *Sexuality and Disability, 6*, 145–149.

Carpenter, P. J., Morrow, G. R., & Schmale, A. H. (1989). The psychosocial status of cancer patients after cessation of treatment. *Journal of Psychosocial Oncology, 7*(1), 95–103.

Carter, W. B., Bobbitt, R. A., Bergner, M., & Gilson, B. S. (1976). Validation of an interval scaling: The Sickness Impact Profile. *Health Services Research, 11*, 516–528.

Cella, D. F., Mahon, S. M., & Donovan, M. I. (1990). Cancer recurrence as a traumatic event. *Behavioral Medicine, 16*(1), 15–22.

Chan, D. W. (1985). The Chinese version of the General Health Questionnaire: Does language make a difference? *Psychological Medicine, 15,* 147–155.

Chandarana, P. C., Eals, M., Steingart, A. B., Bellamy, N., & Allen. S. (1987). The detection of psychiatric morbidity and associated factors in patients with rheumatoid arthritis. *Canadian Journal of Psychiatry, 32,* 356–361.

Clifford, P. A., Tan, S.-Y., & Gorsuch, R. L. (1991). Efficacy of a self-directed behavioral health change program: Weight, body composition, cardiovascular fitness, blood pressure, health risk, and psychosocial mediating variables. *Journal of Behavioral Medicine, 14,* 303–323.

Conrady, L. J., Wish, J. R., Agre, J. C., Rodriquez, A. A., & Sperling, K. B. (1989). Psychologic characteristics of polio survivors: A preliminary report. *Archives of Physical Medicine and Rehabilitation, 70,* 458–463.

Dalos, N. P., Rabins, P. V., Brooks, B. R., & O'Donnell, P. (1983). Disease activity and emotional state in multiple sclerosis. *Annals of Neurology, 13,* 573–577.

Davison, M. L. (1977). On a metric, unidimensional unfolding model for attitudinal and developmental data. *Psychometrika, 42,* 523–548.

Dembo, T., Leviton, G. L., & Wright, B. A. (1956). Adjustment to misfortune—A problem of social-psychological rehabilitation. *Artificial Limbs, 3*(2), 4–62.

DePaulo, J. R., Folstein, M. F., & Gordon, B. (1980). Psychiatric screening on a neurological ward. *Psychological Medicine, 10,* 125–132.

Derogatis, L. R. (1976). *Scoring and procedures manual for the PAIS.* Baltimore: Clinical Psychometric Research.

Derogatis, L. R. (1977). *Psychological Adjustment to Illness Scale.* Baltimore: Clinical Psychometric Research.

Derogatis, L. R. (1986). The Psychosocial Adjustment to Illness Scale (PAIS). *Journal of Psychosomatic Research, 30,* 77–91.

Derogatis, L. R., & Lopez, M. (1983). *Psychosocial Adjustment to Illness Scale (PAIS & PAIS-SR): Scoring, procedures, and administration manual.* Baltimore: Clinical Psychometric Research.

Devins, G. M., Seland, T. P., Klein, G. M., Edworthy, S. M., & Saary, M. J. (1993). Stability and determinants of psychosocial well-being in multiple sclerosis. *Rehabilitation Psychology, 38,* 11–26.

DeVon, H. A., & Powers, M. J. (1984). Health beliefs, adjustment to illness, and control of hypertension. *Research in Nursing and Health, 7,* 10–16.

Deyo, R. A., & Diehl, A. K. (1983). Measuring physical and psychosocial functioning in patients with low-back pain. *Spine, 8,* 635–642.

Deyo, R. A., & Inui, T. S. (1984). Toward clinical applications of health status measures: Sensitivity of scales to clinically important changes. *Health Services Research, 19,* 277–289.

Deyo, R. A., Inui, T. S., Leininger, J. D., & Overman, S. (1982). Physical and psychosocial function in rheumatoid arthritis: Clinical use of a self-administered health status instrument. *Archives of Internal Medicine, 142,* 879–882.

Deyo, R. A., Inui T. S., Leininger, J. D., & Overman, S. (1983). Measuring functional outcomes in chronic disease: A comparison of traditional scales and a self-administered health status questionnaire in patients with rheumatoid arthritis. *Medical Care, 21,* 180–192.

Dodds, A. G., Bailey, P., Pearson, A., & Yates, L. (1991). Psychological factors in acquired visual impairment: The development of a scale of adjustment. *Journal of Visual Impairment and Blindness, 85,* 306–310.

Duefton, B. D. (1990). Depression and the medication of chronic pain. *Journal of Clinical Psychiatry, 51,* 248–250.

Duncan-Jones, P., Grayson, D. A., & Moran, P. A. (1986). The utility of latent trait models in psychiatric epidemiology. *Psychological Medicine, 16,* 391–405.

Eber, H. W. (1976). Personality and psychopathology inventories. In B. Bolton (Ed.), *Handbook of measurement and evaluation in rehabilitation* (pp. 101–116). Baltimore: University Park Press.

Ebrahim, S., Barer, D., & Nouri, F. (1987). Affective illness after stroke. *British Journal of Psychiatry, 151,* 52–56.

Edwards, A. L. (1957). *Techniques of attitude scale construction.* New York: Appleton-Century-Crofts.

Effinger, B., Block, J. E., Smith, R., Cummings, S. R., Harris, S. T., & Genant, H. K. (1988). An examination of the association between vertebral deformities, physical disabilities and psychological problems. *Maturitas, 10,* 283–296.

Engle, E. W., Callahan, L. F., Pincus, T., & Hochberg, M. S. (1990). Learned helplessness in systemic lupus erythematosus: Analysis using the Rheumatology Attitudes Index. *Arthritis and Rheumatism, 33,* 281–286.

Fink, S. L. (1967). Crisis and motivation: A theoretical model. *Archives of Physical Medicine and Rehabilitation, 48,* 592–597.

Folks, D. G., Blake, D. J., Fluse, L., Sokol, R. S., & Freeman, A. M., III. (1986). Quality of life six months after coronary artery bypass surgery: A preliminary report. *Southern Medical Journal, 79,* 397–399.

Follick, M. J., Smith, T. W., & Ahern, D. K. (1985). The Sickness Impact Profile: A global measure of disability in chronic low back pain. *Pain, 21,* 67–76.

Fontanesi, F., Gobetti, C., Zimmerman-Tansella, C. H., & Tansella, T. (1985). Validation of the Italian version of the General Health Questionnaire in a general practice setting. *Psychological Medicine, 15,* 411–415.

Fraser, R., Dikmen, S., McLean, A. J., Miller, B., & Temkin, N. (1988). Employability of head injured survivors: First year post-injury. *Rehabilitation Counseling Bulletin, 31,* 276–288.

Friedman, L. C., Baer, P. E., Lewy, A., Lane, M., & Smith, F. E. (1988). Predictors of psychosocial adjustment to breast cancer. *Journal of Psychosocial Oncology, 6*(1), 75–94.

Gardiner, B. M. (1980). Psychological aspects of rheumatoid arthritis. *Psychological Medicine, 10,* 159–163.

Gatchel, R. J., Deckel, A. W., Weinberg, N., & Smith. J. E. (1985). The utility of the Millon Behavioral Health Inventory in the study of chronic headaches. *Headache, 25,* 49–54.

Gatchel, R. J., Mayer, T. G., Capra, P., Barnett, J., & Diamond, R. (1986). Millon Behavioral Health Inventory: Its utility in predicting physical function in patients with low back pain. *Archives of Physical Medicine and Rehabilitation, 67,* 878–882.

Gilson, B. S., Erickson, D., Chavez, C. T., Bobbitt, R. A., Bergner, M., & Carter, W. B. (1980). A Chicano version of the Sickness Impact Profile (SIP). *Culture, Medicine and Psychiatry, 4,* 137–150.

Gilson, B. S., Gilson, J. S., Bergner, M., Bobbitt, R. A., Kressel, S., Pollard, W. E., & Vesselago, M. (1975). The Sickness Impact Profile: Development of an outcome measure of health care. *American Journal of Public Health, 65,* 1304–1310.

Glueckauf, R. L., Horley, J., Poushinsky, M. F., & Vogel, R. (1984). Assertiveness training for disabled individuals in wheelchairs: Preliminary findings. *International Journal of Rehabilitation Research, 7*, 441–443.

Goldberg, D. P. (1972). *The detection of psychiatric illness by questionnaire.* London: Oxford University Press.

Goldberg, D. P., & Blackwell, B. (1970). Psychiatric illness in general practice. A detailed study using a new method of case identification. *British Medical Journal, ii*, 439–443.

Goldberg, D. P., Cooper, B., Eastwood, M. R., Kedward, H. B., & Shepherd, M. (1970). A standardised psychiatric interview suitable for use in community surveys. *British Journal of Preventive and Social Medicine, 24*, 18–23.

Goldberg, D. P., & Hillier V. F. (1979). A scaled version of the General Health Questionnaire. *Psychological Medicine, 9*, 139–145.

Goldberg, D. P., Rickels, K., Downing, R., & Hesbacher, P. (1976). A comparison of two psychiatric screening tests. *British Journal of Psychiatry, 129*, 61–67.

Goodchild, M. E., & Duncan-Jones, P. (1985). Chronicity and the General Health Questionnaire. *British Journal of Psychiatry, 146*, 55–61.

Goodkin, K., Antoni, M. H., & Blaney, P. H. (1986). Stress and hopelessness in the promotion of cervical intraepithelial neoplasia to invasive squamous cell carcinoma of the cervix. *Journal of Psychosomatic Research, 30*, 67–76.

Goodwin, S. D. (1988). Hardiness and psychosocial adjustment in hemodialysis clients. *ANNA Journal, 15*, 211–215.

Graetz, B. (1991). Multidimensional properties of the General Health Questionnaire. *Social Psychiatry and Psychiatric Epidemiology, 26*, 132–138.

Green, C. J., Meagher, R. B., Jr., & Millon, T. (1983). The MBHI: Its utilization in assessment and management of the coronary bypass surgery patient. *Psychotherapy and Psychosomatics, 39*, 112–121.

Greenwald, H. P. (1987). The specificity of quality-of-life measures among the seriously ill. *Medical Care, 25*, 642–651.

Gundle, M. J., Reeves, B. R., Tate, S., Raft, D., & McLaurin, L. P. (1980). Psychosocial outcome after coronary artery surgery. *American Journal of Psychiatry, 137*, 1591–1594.

Heinemann, A. W., Goranson, N., Ginsburg, K., & Schnoll, S. (1989). Alcohol use and activity patterns following spinal cord injury. *Rehabilitation Psychology, 34*, 191–205.

Heinemann, A. W., & Hawkins, D. (1995). Substance abuse and medical complications following spinal cord injury. *Rehabilitation Psychology, 40*, 125–140.

Heinemann, A. W., & Shontz, F. C. (1984). Adjustment following disability: Representative cases. *Rehabilitation Counseling Bulletin, 28*, 3–14.

Heinemann, A. W., & Shontz, F. C. (1985). Methods of studying persons. *Counseling Psychologist, 13*, 111–125.

Helgeson, D. C., Mittan, R., Tan, S.-Y., & Chayasirisobhon, S. (1990). Sepulveda Epilepsy Education: The efficacy of a psychoeducational treatment program in treating medical and psychosocial aspects of epilepsy. *Epilepsia, 31*, 75–82.

Hendricson, W. D., Russell, I. J., Prihoda, T. J., Jacobson, J. M., Rogan, A., & Bishop, C. D. (1989). An approach to developing a valid Spanish language translation of a health-status questionnaire. *Medical Care, 27*, 959–966.

Hermann, B. P., Whitman, S., Wyler, A. R., Anton, M. T., & Vanderzwagg, R. (1990). Psychosocial predictors of psychopathology in epilepsy. *British Journal of Psychiatry, 156*, 98–105.

Hermann, B. P., Wyler, A. R., & Somes, G. (1992). Preoperative psychological adjustment and surgical outcome are determinants of psychosocial status after anterior temporal lobectomy. *Journal of Neurology, Neurosurgery, and Psychiatry, 55*, 491–496.

Hoare, P., & Kerley, S. (1991). Psychosocial adjustment of children with chronic epilepsy and their families. *Developmental Medicine and Child Neurology, 33*, 201–215.

Hobbs, P., Ballinger, C. B., Greenwood, C., Martin, B., & McClure, A. (1984). Factor analysis and validation of the General Health Questionnaire in men: A general practice survey. *British Journal of Psychiatry, 144*, 270–275.

Hochberg, M. C., & Sutton, J. D. (1988). Physical disability and psychosocial dysfunction in systemic lupus erythematosus. *Journal of Rheumatology, 15*, 959–964.

Hughson, A. V. M., Cooper, A. F., McArdle, C. S., & Smith, D. C. (1988). Validity of the General Health Questionnaire and its subscales in patients receiving chemotherapy for early breast cancer. *Journal of Psychosomatic Research, 32*, 393–402.

Huppert, F. A., Walters, D. E., Day, N. E., & Elliott, B. J. (1989). The factor structure of the General Health Questionnaire (GHQ-30). *British Journal of Psychiatry, 155*, 178–185.

Iwata, N., Okuyama, Y., Kawakami, Y., & Saito, K. (1988). Psychiatric symptoms and related factors in a sample of Japanese workers. *Psychological Medicine, 18*, 659–663.

Jensen, M. R. (1987). Psychobiological factors predicting the course of breast cancer. *Journal of Personality, 55*, 317–342.

Kaplan De-Nour, A. (1982). Psychosocial Adjustment to Illness Scale (PAIS): A study of chronic hemodialysis. *Journal of Psychosomatic Research, 26*, 11–22.

Kaye, J., Bray, S., Gracely, E. J., & Levison, S. (1989). Psychosocial adjustment to illness and family environment in dialysis patients. *Family Systems Medicine, 7*, 77–89.

Kinsella, G., Ford, B., & Moran, C. (1989). Survival of social relationships following head injury. *International Disability Studies, 11*, 9–14.

Kinsella, G., Moran, C., Ford, B., & Ponsford, J. (1988). Emotional disorder and its assessment within the severe head injured population. *Psychological Medicine, 18*, 57–63.

Klonoff, P. S., Costa, L. D., & Snow, W. G. (1986). Predictors and indicators of quality of life in patients with closed-head injury. *Journal of Clinical and Experimental Neuropsychology, 8*, 469–485.

Klonoff, P. S., Snow, W. G., & Costa, L. D. (1986). Quality of life in patients 2 to 4 years after closed head injury. *Neurosurgery, 19*, 735–743.

Kogeorgos, J., Fonagy, P., & Scott, D. F. (1982). Psychiatric symptom patterns of chronic epileptics attending a neurological clinic: A controlled investigation. *British Journal of Psychiatry, 140*, 236–243.

Krus, D. J., Bart, W. M., & Airasian, P. W. (1975). *Ordering theory and methods*. Los Angeles: Theta Press.

Labbé, E. E., Goldberg, M., Fishbain, D., Rosomoff, H., & Steele-Rosomoff, R. (1989). Millon Behavioral Health Inventory norms for chronic pain patients. *Journal of Clinical Psychology, 45*, 383–390.

Langeluddecke, P. M., Fulcher, G., Baird, D., Hughes, C., & Tennant, C. (1989). A prospective evaluation of the psychosocial effects of coronary artery bypass surgery. *Journal of Psychosomatic Research, 33*, 37–45.

Lerner, R. K., Esterhai, J. L., Polomono, R. C., Cheatle, M. C., Heppenstall, R. B., & Brighton, C. T. (1991). Psychosocial, functional, and quality of life assessment of patients with posttraumatic fracture nonunion, chronic refractory osteomyelitis, and lower extremity amputation. *Archives of Physical Medicine and Rehabilitation, 72,* 122–126.

Lewis, G., & Wessely, S. (1990). Comparison of the General Health Questionnaire and the Hospital Anxiety and Depression Scale. *British Journal of Psychiatry, 157,* 860–864.

Linkowski, D. C. (1969). *A study of the relationship between acceptance of disability and response to rehabilitation.* Unpublished doctoral dissertation, State University of New York at Buffalo, Buffalo, NY.

Linkowski, D. C. (1971). A scale to measure acceptance of disability. *Rehabilitation Counseling Bulletin, 14,* 236–244.

Linkowski, D. C. (1989). *A cross-cultural study of aging and acceptance of disability: Taiwan and USA.* Unpublished report, The George Washington University, Washington, DC.

Linkowski, D. C., & Dunn, M. A. (1974). Self-concept and acceptance of disability. *Rehabilitation Counseling Bulletin, 18,* 28–32.

Lipowski, Z. J. (1970). Physical illness, the individual and the coping process. *International Journal of Psychiatry in Medicine, 1,* 91–102.

Littlefield, C. H., Rodin, G. M., Murray, M. A., & Craven, J. L. (1990). Influence of functional impairment and social support on depressive symptoms in persons with diabetes. *Health Psychology, 9,* 737–749.

Livesley, W. J. (1981). Factors associated with psychiatric symptoms in patients undergoing chronic hemodialysis. *Canadian Journal of Psychiatry, 26,* 562–566.

Livneh, H., & Antonak, R. F. (1990). Reactions to disability: An empirical investigation of their nature and structure. *Journal of Applied Rehabilitation Counseling, 21*(4), 13–21.

Livneh, H., & Antonak, R. F. (1991). Temporal structure of adaptation to disability. *Rehabilitation Counseling Bulletin, 34,* 298–319.

Lysaght, R., & Bodenhamer, E. (1990). The use of relaxation training to enhance functional outcomes in adults with traumatic head injuries. *American Journal of Occupational Therapy, 44,* 797–802.

MacKenzie, C. R., Charlson, M. E., DiGioia, D., & Kelley, K. (1986). Can the Sickness Impact Profile measure change? An example of scale assessment. *Journal of Chronic Diseases, 39,* 429–438.

Malt, U. F. (1989). The validity of the General Health Questionnaire in a sample of accidentally injured adults. *Acta Psychiatrica Scandinavica Supplementum, 355,* 103–112.

Mann, A. H. (1977). Psychiatric morbidity and hostility in hypertension. *Psychological Medicine, 7,* 653–659.

Mari, J. J., & Williams, P. (1984). Minor psychiatric disorders in primary care in Brazil: A pilot study. *Psychological Medicine, 14,* 223–227.

McCusker, J., & Stoddard, A. M. (1984). Use of a surrogate for the Sickness Impact Profile. *Medical Care, 22,* 789–795.

Millon, T., Green, C. J., & Meagher, R. B., Jr. (1979). The MBHI: A new inventory for the psychodiagnostician in medical settings. *Professional Psychology, 10,* 529–539.

Millon, T., Green, C. J., & Meagher. R. B. (1981). *The Millon Behavioral Health Inventory Manual.* Minneapolis, MN: National Computer Systems.

Millon, T., Green, C. J., & Meagher, R. B., Jr. (1982). A new psychodiagnostic tool for clients in rehabilitation settings: The MBHI. *Rehabilitation Psychology, 27,* 23–35.

Morgan, A. D., Peck, D. F., Buchanan, D., & McHurdy, G. J. R. (1983). Psychological factors contributing to disproportionate disability in chronic bronchitis. *Journal of Psychosomatic Research, 27*, 259–263.

Morris, P. L. P., & Goldberg, R. J. (1989). Validity of the 28-item General Health Questionnaire in hospitalized gastroenterology patients. *Psychosomatics, 30*, 290–295.

Morrow, G. R., Chiarello, R. J., & Derogatis, L. R. (1978). A new scale for assessing patients' psychosocial adjustment to medical illness. *Psychological Medicine, 8*, 605–610.

Munoz, P. E., Vazques, J. L., Pastrana, E., Rodriquez, F., & Oneca, C. (1978). Study of the validity of Goldberg's 60-item GHQ in its Spanish version. *Social Psychiatry, 13*, 99–104.

Munro, B. H., Creamer, A. M., Haggerty, M. R., & Cooper, F. S. (1988). Effect of relaxation therapy on post-myocardial infarction patients' rehabilitation. *Nursing Research, 37*, 231–235.

Murphy, J. K., Sperr, E. V., & Sperr, S. J. (1986). Chronic pain: An investigation of assessment instruments. *Journal of Psychosomatic Research, 30*, 289–296.

Murphy, M. A., Tosi, D. J., Sharratt Wise, P., & Eshbaugh, D. M. (1987). Note on the factor structure of the Millon Behavioral Health Inventory. *Psychological Reports, 66*, 699–802.

Newman, S. C., Bland, R. C., & Orn, H. (1988). A comparison of methods of scoring the General Health Questionnaire. *Comprehensive Psychiatry, 29*, 402–408.

Northouse, L. L. (1988). Social support in patients' and husbands' adjustment to breast cancer. *Nursing Research, 37*, 91–95.

Northouse, L. L., & Swain, M. A. (1987). Adjustment of patients and husbands to the initial impact of breast cancer. *Nursing Research, 36*, 221–225.

Norton, G. R., & Allen, G. E. (1985). Predicting treatment preferences for agoraphobia. *Behavior Research and Therapy, 23*, 699–701.

Oduwole, O. O., & Ogunyemi, A. O. (1989). Validity of the GHQ-30 in a Nigerian medical outpatient clinic. *Canadian Journal of Psychiatry, 34*, 20–23.

Osuji, O. N. (1975). 'Acceptance of loss'—Quantification of the concept. *Rehabilitation Digest, 6*, 3–8.

Osuji, O. N. (1985). Personality factors in acceptance of loss among the physically disabled. *Psychological Record, 35*, 23–28.

Osuji, O. N. (1987). 'Acceptance of loss' and industrial rehabilitation: An empirical study. *International Journal of Rehabilitation Research, 10*, 21–27.

Ott, C. R., Sivarajan, E. S., Newton, K. M., Almer, M. J., Bruce, R. A., Bergner, M., & Gilson, B. S. (1983). A controlled randomized study of early cardiac rehabilitation: The Sickness Impact Profile as an assessment tool. *Heart and Lung, 12*, 162–170.

Parkes, K. R. (1980). Social desirability, defensiveness and self-report psychiatric inventory scores. *Psychological Medicine, 10*, 735–742.

Patrick, G. D. (1984). Comparison of novice and veteran wheelchair athletes' self-concept and acceptance of disability. *Rehabilitation Counseling Bulletin, 27*, 186–188.

Poll, I. B., & Kaplan De-Nour, A. (1980). Locus of control and adjustment to chronic hemodialysis. *Psychological Medicine, 10*, 153–157.

Pollard, W. E., Bobbitt, R. A., Bergner, M., Martin, D. P., & Gilson, B. S. (1976). The Sickness Impact Profile: Reliability of a health status measure. *Medical Care, 14*, 146–155.

Poulsen, D. L., Hansen, H. J., Langemark, M., Olesen, J., & Bech, P. (1987). Discomfort or disability in patients with chronic pain syndrome. *Psychotherapy and Psychosomatics, 48*, 60–62.

Powers, M. J. (1987). Profile of the well-controlled, well-adjusted hypertensive patient. *Nursing Research, 36*, 106–110.

Prince, R., Frasure-Smith, N., & Rolicz-Woloszyk, E. (1982). Life stress, denial and outcome in ischemic heart disease patients. *Journal of Psychosomatic Research, 26*, 23–31.

Rabins, P. V., & Brooks, B. R. (1981). Emotional disturbance in multiple sclerosis patients: Validity of the General Health Questionnaire (GHQ). *Psychological Medicine, 11*, 425–427.

Rabins, P. V., Brooks, B. R., O'Donnell, P., Pearlson, G. D., Moberg, P., Jubelt, B., Coyle, P., Dalos, N., & Folstein, M. F. (1986). Structured brain correlates of emotional disorders in multiple sclerosis. *Brain, 109*, 585–597.

Raft, D., McKee, D. C., Popio, K. A., & Haggerty, J. J. (1985). Life adaptation after percutaneous transluminal coronary angioplasty and coronary artery bypass grafting. *American Journal of Cardiology, 56*, 395–398.

Rao, S. M., Leo, G. L., Ellington, L., Nauertz, T., Bernardin, L., & Unverzagt, F. (1991). Cognitive dysfunction in multiple sclerosis: II. Impact on employment and social functioning. *Neurology, 41*, 692–696.

Richter, J. E., Obrecht, W. F., Bradley, L. A., Young, L. D., & Anderson, K. O. (1986). Psychological comparison of patients with nutcracker esophagus and irritable bowel syndrome. *Digestive Diseases and Sciences, 31*, 131–138.

Roberts, R., Browne, G., Streiner, D., Byrne, C., Brown, B., & Love, B. (1987). Analyses of coping responses and adjustment: Stability of conclusions. *Nursing Research, 36*, 94–97.

Robinson, R. G., & Price, T. R. (1982). Post-stroke depressive disorders: A follow-up study of 103 patients. *Stroke, 13*, 635–641.

Rockey, P. H., & Griep, R. J. (1980). Behavioral dysfunction in hyperthyroidism: Improvement with treatment. *Archives of Internal Medicine, 140*, 1194–1197.

Roland, M., & Morris, R. (1983). A study of the natural history of back pain: Part I. Development of a reliable and sensitive measure of disability in low-back pain. *Spine, 8*, 141–144.

Ross, H. E., & Glaser, F. B. (1989). Psychiatric screening of alcohol and drug patients: The validity of the GHQ—60. *American Journal of Drug and Alcohol Abuse, 15*, 429–442.

Roy, A. (1979). Some determinants of affective symptoms in epileptics. *Canadian Journal of Psychiatry, 24*, 554–556.

Rozensky, R. H., Nonor, L. F., Tovian, S. M., Herz, G., & Holland, M. A. (1985). Tolerance of pain by cancer patients in hyperthermia treatment. *Journal of Psychosocial Oncology, 3*, 75–82.

Rutter, B. M. (1977). Some psychological concomitants of chronic bronchitis. *Psychological Medicine, 7*, 459–464.

Segraves, R. T. (1987). Discrimination between psychogenic and biogenic impotence utilizing psychometric instruments. *Sexuality and Disability, 8*, 138–142.

Singerman, B., Riedner, E., & Folstein, M. (1980). Emotional disturbance in hearing clinic patients. *British Journal of Psychiatry, 137*, 58–62.

Soskolne, V., & Kaplan De-Nour, A. (1989). The psychosocial adjustment of patients and spouses to dialysis treatment. *Social Science and Medicine, 29*, 497–502.

Starke, M. C. (1987). Enhancing social skills and self-perceptions of physically disabled young adults. *Behavior Modification, 11*, 3–16.

Starr, P., & Heiserman, K. (1977). Acceptance of disability by teenagers with oral-facial clefts. *Rehabilitation Counseling Bulletin, 20*, 198–201.

Stephenson, W. (1953). *The study of behavior: Q-technique and its methodology.* Chicago: University of Chicago Press.

Stewart, A. L., & Ware, J. E., Jr. (Eds.). (1992). *Measuring functioning and well being: The Medical Outcomes Study approach.* Durham, NC: Duke University Press.

Stuifbergen, A. K. (1988). *Chronic physical illness and family functioning: An analysis of the impact of spouses' perceptions of severity of illness and consensus between spouses on dimensions of family functioning.* Unpublished doctoral dissertation, University of Texas at Austin, Austin, TX.

Subramanian, K., & Rose, S. D. (1988). Social work and the treatment of chronic pain. *Health and Social Work, 13,* 49–60.

Sugarbaker, P. H., Barofsky, I., Rosenberg, S. A., & Gianola, F. J. (1982). Quality of life assessment of patients in extremity sarcoma clinical trials. *Surgery, 91,* 17–23.

Sullivan, M., Ahlmén, M., & Bjelle, A. (1990). Health status assessment in rheumatoid arthritis. I. Further work on the validity of the Sickness Impact Profile. *Journal of Rheumatology, 17,* 439–447.

Swassing, C. S. (1987). Review of the Psychosocial Adjustment to Illness Scale. In J. V. Mitchell, Jr. (Ed.), *The tenth mental measurements yearbook* (pp. 670–671). Lincoln, NE: Buros Institute on Mental Measurement.

Sweet, J. J., Breuer, S. R., Hazlewood, L. A., Toye, R., & Pawl, R. P. (1985). The Millon Behavioral Health Inventory: Concurrent and predictive validity in a pain treatment center. *Journal of Behavioral Medicine, 8,* 215–226.

Temkin, N. R., Dikmen, S., Machamer, J., & McLean, A. (1989). General versus disease-specific measures: Further work with the Sickness Impact Profile for head injury. *Medical Care, 27*(3 Suppl.), S44–S53.

Temkin, N. R., McLean, A., Dikmen, S., & Machamer, J. (1988). Development and evaluation of modifications to the Sickness Impact Profile for head injury. *Journal of Clinical Epidemiology, 41,* 47–57.

Thomas, K. R., Davis, R. M., & Hochman, M. E. (1976). Correlates of disability acceptance in amputees. *Rehabilitation Counseling Bulletin, 19,* 508–511.

van Komen, R. W., & Redd, W. H. (1985). Personality factors associated with anticipatory nausea/vomiting in patients receiving cancer chemotherapy. *Health Psychology, 4,* 189–202.

Ware, J. E. (1976). Scales for measuring general health perceptions. *Health Services Research, 11,* 396–415.

Warren, S., Warren, K. G., & Cockerill, R. (1991). Emotional stress coping in multiple sclerosis (MS) exacerbation. *Journal of Psychosomatic Research, 35,* 37–47.

Wassem, R. (1992). Self-efficacy as a predictor of adjustment to multiple sclerosis. *Journal of Neuroscience Nursing, 24,* 224–229.

Weisberg, M. B., & Page, S. (1988). Millon Behavioral Health Inventory and perceived efficacy of home and hospital dialysis. *Journal of Social and Clinical Psychology, 6,* 408–422.

Weissman, M. M., Sholomskas, D., & John, K. (1981). The assessment of social adjustment: An update. *Archives of General Psychiatry, 38,* 1250–1258.

Williams, S. J., & Bury, M. R. (1989). Impairment, disability and handicap in chronic respiratory illness. *Social Science and Medicine, 29,* 609–616.

Wolberg, W. H., Tanner, M. A., Romsaus, E. P., Trump, D. L., & Malic, J. F. (1987). Factors influencing options in primary breast cancer treatment. *Journal of Clinical Oncology, 5,* 68–74.

Woodrich, F., & Patterson, J. B. (1983). Variables related to acceptance of disability in persons with spinal cord injuries. *Journal of Rehabilitation, 49*(3), 26–30.

Worsley, A., & Gribbin, C. C. (1977). A factor analytic study of the twelve item General Health Questionnaire. *Australian and New Zealand Journal of Psychiatry, 11*, 269–272.

Yuker, H. E., Block, J. R., & Younng, J. H. (1966). *The measurement of attitudes toward disabled persons* (Human Resources Study No. 7). Albertson, NY: Human Resources Center.

Zeldow, P. B., & Pavlou, M. (1988). Physical and psychosocial functioning in multiple sclerosis: Descriptions, correlations, and a tentative typology. *British Journal of Medical Psychology, 61*, 185–195.

CHAPTER 3

Measures of Psychosocial Adaptation to Specific Chronic Illnesses and Disabilities

INTRODUCTION

The 11 instruments to be reviewed in this chapter concern the measurement of psychosocial adaptation of persons with eight specific chronic illnesses and disabilities: (1) cancer—the Mental Adjustment to Cancer scale, (2) diabetes mellitus—the Diabetic Adjustment Scale, (3) hearing impairment—the Communication Profile for the Hearing Impaired and the Social-Emotional Assessment Inventory for Deaf and Hearing-Impaired Students, (4) rheumatoid arthritis—the Arthritis Impact Measurement Scales, (5) seizure disorders—the Washington Psychosocial Seizure Inventory and Adolescent Psychosocial Seizure Inventory, (6) spinal cord injury—the Psychosocial Questionnaire for Spinal Cord-Injured Persons, (7) traumatic brain injury—the Glasgow Assessment Schedule and the Portland Adaptability Inventory, and (8) visual impairment—the Nottingham Adjustment Scale.

Summary information on the 11 instruments reviewed in this chapter is provided in Table 3–1. It should be noted that the instruments in Table 3–1 are presented in alphabetical order. This is also true for the order of appearance of the chronic illness and disability categories in this article and for the instruments within a category if there are more than one. The reader should not infer a judgment of the overall psychometric quality of an instrument by its order of appearance in this chapter or in Table 3–1.

CANCER

Mental Adjustment to Cancer Scale

The Mental Adjustment to Cancer (MAC) scale (Watson et al., 1988) was developed as a self-report screening device to investigate a respondent's psychological reactions to the diagnosis of cancer. The authors sought a reliable measure

Table 3-1 Availability and Suitability of Measures of Psychosocial Adaptation to Specific Chronic Illnesses and Disabilities

Measure	Type	Intended Use	Scores	Strengths	Weaknesses
Adolescent Psychosocial Seizure Inventory	139-item self-report summated rating scale	To measure the psychological and social concerns of adolescents (CA 12 to 19 years) with epilepsy	Scores on nine scales. Three additional validity scales are included to check for faking and response sensitization: • Family background • Emotional adjustment • Interpersonal adjustment • Vocational outlook • School adjustment • Adjustment to seizures • Medicine and medical management • Antisocial activity • Overall psychosocial functioning	Multidimensional index. Inclusion of MMPI-like validity scales to investigate respondent biases. Translated into at least three foreign languages. English language version widely used throughout the world. Computerized scoring available.	Overall psychosocial functioning scored with items from other scales yielding redundant information. Items selected and scaled by professional ratings introducing a potential rater expectancy bias. Validity not checked with factor analytic methods. Meager data on homogeneity, specificity, and construct validity of the scales. No data available on the reliability, sensitivity, or predictive validity of the profile norms.
Arthritis Impact Measurement Scales	Self-reported ratings of functioning with the item-response format varying with the domain	To provide a multidimensional index of health status in persons with arthritis by combining indices of physical status with measures of psychosocial adjustment and pain	Nine scale scores: • Mobility • Physical activity • Social activity • Household activities • Anxiety • Depression • Activities of daily living • Pain • Dexterity	Reliability, homogeneity, sensitivity, specificity, and independence of scales reasonable, as are construct and criterion-related validity. Translated into several languages. Computer scoring yields health status summary report. Juvenile, Geriatric, Short-form, and Anglicized versions available.	Response bias influences not investigated.

Measure	Type	Intended Use	Scores	Strengths	Weaknesses
Communication Profile for the Hearing Impaired	145-item self-report summated rating scale	To measure the communicative performance skills of persons with hearing impairments and their psychosocial reactions to the effects of hearing impairment	25 scale scores organized into four communication domains: • Performance (6 scales) • Importance (3 scales) • Environment (4 scales) • Strategies (3 scales) and a fifth domain of: • Personal adjustment, with 63 items on 9 scales: •• Self-acceptance •• Acceptance of loss •• Anger •• Displacement of responsibility •• Exaggeration of responsibility •• Discouragement •• Stress •• Withdrawal •• Denial	Reliability, specificity, homogeneity, and independence of scales reasonable. Construct and criterion-related validity reported to be adequate.	Response bias influences not investigated.
Diabetic Adjustment Scale	29 true-false item self-report questionnaire	To measure potential problems in adolescent girls' attitudes about and adjustment to living with diabetes	Overall adjustment score and scores on six factor analytically derived scales: • Dependence-independence issues • Body image concerns • Peer relationships • Family relationships • Attitudes toward health and diabetes • School adjustment	Criterion-related validity of the overall adjustment score may be adequate. Brief and easy to administer. Multidimensional index.	Instrument developed with adolescent girls in a unique environment. No data on reliability of overall score or scores on six subscales. Specificity and homogeneity data suggest subscales may not be measures of distinct components of adjustment. Construct validity data are meager. Response bias influences not investigated. Included in this listing for information purposes only.

continues

Table 3–1 continued

Measure	Type	Intended Use	Scores	Strengths	Weaknesses
Glasgow Assessment Schedule	Assessment from clinical evidence and informant reports	A rehabilitation assessment and outcome evaluation measure for persons with a traumatic brain injury	The individual is rated as normal, moderate, or severe (impairment) in six domains: • Personality changes • Subjective complaints • Occupational functioning • Cognitive functioning • Physical examination • Activities of daily living	Interrater reliability and criterion-related validity reported to be adequate. Brief and easy to administer. Multidimensional index.	Meager information on specificity, homogeneity, independence, and construct validity of the six domain scales.
Mental Adjustment to Cancer Scale	50-item self-report summated rating scale	To screen the respondent's psychosocial reactions to the diagnosis of cancer and to study the relationship of reactions to coping and survival	Scores on four a priori defined scales: • Fighting spirit • Denial • Stoic acceptance • Helpless/hopeless	Reliability and homogeneity of scales reported to be adequate. Criterion-related validity reported to be adequate. Multidimensional index.	Factor analysis results do not support a priori structure of scales. Specificity of the four scales may be less than adequate. Meager construct and predictive validity data. Response bias influences not investigated.
Nottingham Adjustment Scale	43-item self-report summated rating scale	Prototype experimental instrument to measure adjustment to the loss of sight in persons with an acquired visual impairment	Scores on five empirically derived subscales: • Hopelessness • Acceptance • Self-efficacy • Anxiety • Attitudes	Multidimensional index. Preliminary data on construct validity are promising.	Meager data on reliability, homogeneity, and specificity of the five subscales. Using subscale scores for profile development is not recommended. Response bias influences not investigated. Included in this listing for informational purposes only.
Portland Adaptability Inventory	24-item informant-report summated rating scale	To measure, by informant reports, the individual's adjustment to traumatic brain injury	Scores on three scales: • Temperament and emotionality • Activities of social behavior • Physical capabilities	Multidimensional index. Easy to administer and score.	Meager reliability and validity data to date.

Measure	Type	Intended Use	Scores	Strengths	Weaknesses
Psychosocial Questionnaire for Spinal Cord-Injured Persons	35-item self-report summated rating scale	To measure the respondent's psychosocial adjustment to spinal cord injury for rehabilitation planning	Scores on four scales: • Anxiety • Depression • Social discomfort • Positive outlook	Multidimensional index.	No psychometric data are currently published concerning this instrument. Included in this listing for informational purposes only.
Social-Emotional Assessment Inventory for Deaf and Hearing-Impaired Students	58-item (school-aged) or 49-item (preschool) informant-report summated rating scale	To assist teachers and administrators to identify preschoolers, children, and adolescents with hearing impairments who may be at risk for psychosocial maladaptation	School-aged version has three factor analytically derived scales: • Social adjustment • Self-image • Emotional adjustment Preschool version has four factor analytically derived scales: • Sociable, communicative behaviors • Impulsive, dominating behaviors • Developmental lags • Anxious, compulsive behaviors	Constructed through comprehensive psychometric process. Multidimensional index. Homogeneity and reliability reported to be adequate. Preliminary data support criterion-related and construct validity of the overall score (both versions).	Response bias influences not investigated. No data on specificity, independence, or construct validity of the scales on each version.
Washington Psychosocial Seizure Inventory	132-item self-report summated rating scale	To measure the psychological and social concerns of adults (CA 19 years and up) with epilepsy	Scores on eight scales. Three additional validity scales are included to check for faking and response sensitization: • Family background • Emotional adjustment • Interpersonal adjustment • Vocational adjustment • Financial status • Adjustment to seizures • Medicine and medical management • Overall psychosocial functioning	Multidimensional index. Inclusion of MMPI-like validity scales to investigate respondent biases. Translated into at least three foreign languages. English language version widely used throughout the world. Computerized scoring available.	Overall psychosocial functioning scored with items from other scales yielding redundant information. Items selected and scaled by professional ratings introducing a potential rater expectancy bias. Validity not checked with factor analytic methods. Meager data on homogeneity, specificity, and construct validity of the scales. No data available on the reliability, sensitivity, or predictive validity of the profile norms.

of reactions to cancer for research on the relationship between psychosocial distress and levels of coping and to explore the possibility that the individual's psychological reactions may affect survival.

A group of 58 items, derived from analyses of the responses drawn from structured clinical interviews of individuals with cancer, was sorted into four a priori specified categories: fighting spirit, denial, stoic acceptance, and helpless/hopeless. Four responses were provided to each item, ranging from 1, to signify "Definitely does not apply to me," to 4, to signify "Definitely applies to me." The prototype scale was administered to 235 individuals diagnosed with 25 different types of cancer at two hospitals in Great Britain. The first 100 individuals also completed the Hospital Anxiety and Depression scale (Zigmond & Snaith, 1983), a measure designed for use with general medical and surgical patients. A second random sample of 34 individuals completed the MAC a second time, an average of 24 days later, so that stability of responses could be investigated. Finally, for 24 randomly selected respondents, the spouse or partner was asked to complete a spouse's version of the questionnaire independently with reference to the individual.

A principal components analysis of these MAC data extracted four factors (eigenvalues and factor loadings were not reported), but the factors did not coincide with the a priori categorizations of the items. Although the first was a bipolar factor combining fighting spirit (positive) with helpless/hopeless (negative), the authors decided to regain these two as inversely related distinct subscales on the final version of the MAC. The items loading on the second factor related to anxious preoccupation with the disease, while the third factor contained items relating to stoic acceptance, but was renamed fatalism. A fourth factor included only one significant item. This factor was thought to represent extreme avoidance (ie, "I don't really believe I have cancer."). The respondent-spouse correlation coefficients for the Fighting Spirit, Helpless/Hopeless, Anxious Preoccupation, and Fatalism scales were reported to be 0.76, 0.66, 0.63, and 0.63, respectively. The coefficient alpha internal consistency estimates for the four scales were reported to be 0.84, 0.79, 0.65, and 0.65, while the stability coefficients for the scales were 0.52, 0.65, 0.56, and 0.38, respectively.

A subsequent validation study (Greer, Moorey, & Watson, 1989) involved the investigation of the relationship between MAC scores and clinical ratings of psychosocial adaptation of a consecutive series of 52 individuals with cancer referred for psychiatric consultation. A categorization of the individual's adaptation into one of four types (fighting spirit, helpless/hopeless, anxious preoccupation, fatalism) was made independently by two psychiatrists based on responses to specific questions in a structured interview. Interrater agreement was found to be 0.85, with disagreements occurring exclusively in the classification of individuals in the fatalism type. The respondent's MAC scores were standardized, and the respondent was classified into that category that produced the largest standard normal score. MAC and clinical ratings were found to agree for 79% of the cases (Cohen's Kappa statistic = 0.72), with lowest agreement in the fatalism category (7 of 10 respondents classified in this category by MAC scores were classified in this category by the clinicians).

Validity data for the MAC were obtained in a subsequent investigation (Watson, Greer, Pruyn, & Van Den Borne, 1990) in which 57 individuals with cancer responded to the MAC, the Hospital Anxiety and Depression Scale, and the Courtauld Emotional Control Scale (Watson & Greer, 1983). The last two instruments measure the individual's emotional control of feelings of anger, anxiety, and depression. Results showed that Fighting Spirit scores on the MAC were significantly positively related to scores measuring internal control over the course of the illness as predicted. MAC Anxious Preoccupation scores were significantly positively related to scores on the Courtauld Emotional Control Scale measuring internal cause of the illness (eg, "Becoming ill had something to do with my personality."), and MAC Fatalism scores were significantly related to scores on the Courtauld Emotional Control Scale measuring religious control of the disease (eg, "I became ill partly because God decided so."). In addition, MAC Fighting Spirit scores were inversely related to disease stage, and MAC Fatalism scores were directly related to age.

Available data have revealed, however, a lack of specificity of the four MAC subscales. In the original study (Watson et al., 1988), scores on the Fighting Spirit and Helpless/Hopeless subscales were significantly negatively related, as expected from the results of the principal components analysis. The Helpless/ Hopeless subscale, however, was found to be significantly positively related to the Anxious Preoccupation and Fatalism subscales. In addition, the Anxious Preoccupation, Fatalism, and Helpless/Hopeless subscales of the MAC were significantly positively related to the depression subscale of the Hospital Anxiety and Depression Scale, and the Anxious Preoccupation subscale of the MAC was significantly positively related to the Hospital Anxiety and Depression Scale. In a later study of the relationship between adaptation to cancer as measured by the MAC (Watson et al., 1991), emotional control as measured by the Courtauld Emotional Control Scale, and levels of depression and anxiety as measured by the Hospital Anxiety and Depression Scale in 359 women recently diagnosed with breast cancer, it was confirmed that Anxious Preoccupation, Fatalism, and Helpless/Hopeless scales on the MAC were significantly positively interrelated, and all three were significantly positively related to both anxiety and depression as measured by the Hospital Anxiety and Depression Scale. In addition, MAC Fatalism scores were significantly positively related to the tendency to control the reactions of anger, anxiety, and depression, and MAC Helpless/Hopeless scores were significantly positively related to control of anger and anxiety.

The results of analyses of MAC data to date suggest (as the authors themselves have speculated) that the four hypothesized subscales of the MAC may be more correctly viewed as measuring positive (or adaptive) responses (fighting spirit) and negative (or nonadaptive) responses (anxious preoccupation, fatalism, help-less/hopeless) of a general bipolar process of adaptation to cancer. Additional psychometric investigation of the specificity of the MAC subscales and factor analyses of data from diverse samples is warranted to investigate this possibility. Data concerning the construct and predictive validity of the instrument are also needed before it can be concluded that the MAC, as the authors proposed, can be used in research studying the relationship between psychosocial distress and levels of coping in individuals with cancer.

DIABETES MELLITUS

Diabetic Adjustment Scale

Sullivan (1979a) lamented the paucity of data in the literature concerning the psychological concomitants of juvenile diabetes. She suggested that this was partly due to the lack of a scale to measure potential problems in individuals' adjustment to living with diabetes. The Diabetic Adjustment Scale (DAS) was designed specifically to meet this measurement need with adolescent girls with diabetes.

The final set of 37 true-false items concerning adolescent girls' attitudes and thoughts about diabetes was selected by a team of clinicians from an initial group of 86 generated from a review of the available literature on psychosocial adaptation to chronic illness and disability and was supplemented with items generated from interviews with adolescents with diabetes, their parents, physicians and clinicians, and from persons who lived with them. The number and characteristics of the clinicians who selected the items were not specified, nor were the rules they used for item selection. A total of eight items were deleted following a review because they "sought direct information and did not assess adjustment" (p. 120).

A team of specialists in pediatrics and psychiatry determined whether each item measured positive or negative adjustment, using as reference "clinical experience and judgment as well as knowledge of ego strengths, coping, and stress" (p. 120). Agreement with a negative adjustment item was scored 2, whereas disagreement was scored 1; agreement with a positive adjustment item was scored 1, whereas disagreement was scored 2. These item scores were then summed for the total set of items on the scale. Consequently, a higher score represented greater risk of psychological maladjustment.

The scale was administered to a nonrandom sample of 105 female adolescents between 12 and 16 years of age with diabetes who were attending a medically oriented summer camp for girls in Massachusetts. The mean age for the sample was 13.8 years, and the mean chronicity was 7.1 years (range six months to 16 years). The girls who consented to respond were told that the researchers were interested in gathering information about how girls their age feel about themselves and their diabetes. In addition to the DAS, all of the respondents were administered the Beck Depression Inventory and the Rosenberg Self-Esteem Scale. All responses were anonymous and confidential.

No data were provided on the reliability of the DAS. A set of six subscales was derived from a factor analysis of the data (type of extraction and rotation procedures were not specified, nor were statistical indices provided): Dependence-Independence Issues, Body Image Concerns, Peer Relationships, Family Relationships, Attitudes Toward Health and Diabetes, and School Adjustment. Apparently all of the 29 items were retained, but the assignment of items to factors and their loadings were not reported. In addition, no data were provided on the reliability of these subscales.

Scores on each of the six subscales were correlated with total scale scores and with scores on all the other subscales. Correlations between the six subscales and the total scale were reported to range from 0.41 (Body Image) to 0.95 (Attitudes Toward Health and Diabetes), with a mean of 0.65 for these six correlations. Subscale intercorrelations ranged from 0.01 (Body Image Concerns—Family Relationships) to 0.75 (Attitudes Toward Health and Diabetes—Peer Relationships), with the mean of 0.33 for the 15 intercorrelations. A total of 11 of these intercorrelations were found to be significant for a sample of size 105, suggesting that the six factor analytically derived subscales may not be specific measures of distinct components of adjustment to diabetes as Sullivan proposed.

In a subsequent report (Sullivan, 1979b) the author reported the results of analyses of the relationships among the scores of the 105 girls in the sample on the DAS, the Beck Depression Inventory, and the Rosenberg Self-Esteem Scale. Sullivan reported a number of analyses of the resultant data; however, most of these analyses were statistically and psychometrically questionable. For example, the respondents were sorted into "good" and "poor" categories on the total DAS and on each of the six subscales. How this was accomplished was not specified. A total of 11 significant results were reported out of a series of 14 *t*-tests comparing the mean self-esteem and depression scores of the two groups. No attempt was made to control for an inflated Type I error rate with a Bonferroni procedure. In another series of analyses, the self-esteem scores were apparently used to create groups of respondents referred to as "excellent" and "moderate." The mean scores of these two groups were then compared on the DAS, all six subscales, and four "types" of depression (ie, vital depression, self-debasement, pessimism-suicide, and indecision-inhibition). It does appear as though scores on the total DAS correlated in the expected direction with scores measuring depression and self-esteem, lending a modicum of support to the validity of the DAS for measuring the construct of psychological adjustment of adolescent girls to living with diabetes.

The DAS was used in a recent study of the relationship between severity of diabetic sequelae and a collection of measures of psychosocial adaptation in a sample of 37 adolescents with diabetes mellitus (Smith, Mauseth, Palmer, Pecoraro, & Wenet, 1991). Reliability data were not provided by the authors. No relationships were found to be significant between DAS scores and the variables of age, sex, or chronicity of the disease. Scores on all six DAS scales were related in the expected direction with self-reports of negative life events, but these scores were not related to self-reports of positive life events. It was noted and convincingly explained that better diabetic control was related to DAS scores that represented independence conflicts and poorer family relationships (eg, issues of overprotectiveness or overinvolvement in their child's life).

It should be noted that the instrument was developed with a sample of adolescent girls attending a camp for adolescents with diabetes mellitus. The results of analyses of DAS data to date from samples of adolescent girls have not conclusively established the specificity or reliability of the six factor analytically derived subscales nor the reliability of the overall instrument. The meager data do not establish the validity of the DAS for the measurement of the constructs the author purports it measures. Psychometric investigations of the reliability of the construct and predictive validity of the DAS using data from diverse samples are warranted before it can be concluded that the DAS can be used in research that attempts to elucidate the construct of psychological adjustment to juvenile diabetes.

HEARING IMPAIRMENT

Communication Profile for the Hearing Impaired

The Communication Profile for the Hearing Impaired (CPHI) (Demorest & Erdman, 1986; Demorest & Erdman, 1987) was developed at the Walter Reed Army Medical Center to measure not only communication performance skills of persons with hearing impairments but also their reactions to "the environmental, behavioral, emotional, and attitudinal factors that enhance or detract from communication effectiveness" (Demorest & Erdman, 1987, p. 129). Development of the instrument proceeded in three phases: (1) content definition and item writing, (2) pilot testing and psychometric analyses, and (3) final testing with psychometric analyses of scales and subscales. A total of 827 individuals provided data for these three phases. These individuals were active-duty and retired military personnel (96% male) of heterogeneous rank and occupation who ranged in age from 20 to 70 years (mean age 39.1 years).

The content domain for the CPHI was derived from an examination of clinical records and anecdotal reports of the effects of hearing impairment from a large number of individuals served by the Army's Aural Rehabilitation Program, supplemented by the suggestions of experts in aural rehabilitation. One of the most common recurrent themes was emotional factors in coping with the effects of the hearing impairment. Consequently, a major section of the CPHI was devoted to the measurement of the individual's adjustment to his or her hearing impairment. The CPHI includes a Denial scale to assess the respondent's denial of personal adjustment problems and thereby provides a means to determine response bias in the data.

A total of 215 items was assigned to two parallel forms of a pilot instrument and administered to 394 individuals over a 14-month period. Depending on the item content, the respondent was asked to report either (1) the extent of his or her agreement with the item, ranging from 1 to signify Strongly Disagree to 5 to signify Strongly Agree; or (2) how frequently the item was true, ranging from 1 to signify Rarely or Almost Never to 5 to signify Usually or Almost Always. The direction of scoring was selected so that a low score was indicative of psychosocial risk and need for intervention. Item, item characteristic, scale, subscale, and factor analyses were performed to refine the items and to create two alternate forms of a psychometrically sound instrument composed of 155 items arranged on five scales and 19 subscales. This second version of the CPHI was administered to a second sample of 433 individuals over a 15-month period. A similar set of statistical analyses was applied to these data to obtain the final version of the CPHI (Demorest & Erdman, 1986). The CPHI contains 145 items and provides a total of 25 scores. A set of 22 scales constitutes the communication profile that is organized into five areas: (1) Communication Performance (6 scales), (2) Communication Importance (3 scales), (3) Communication Environment (4 scales), (4) Communication Strategies (3 scales), and (5) Personal Adjustment (9 scales). The CPHI has been translated into Swedish for use in measuring coping with deafness and hearing impairments (Hallberg, Eriksson-Mangold, & Carlsson, 1992).

The nine scales in the Personal Adjustment area are the ones of concern to researchers investigating acceptance of and adjustment to deafness and hearing impairment and will be the focus of the remainder of this review. A total of 63 items are arranged on the nine scales in the area of personal adjustment. All of the items are written to present negative or undesirable emotional reactions or feelings. The scales are Self-acceptance—8 items (eg, "Feel foolish when misunderstand," "Hearing loss makes me feel incompetent"); Acceptance of Loss—9 items (eg, "Try to hide hearing problem," "Can't talk to people about hearing loss"); Anger—6 items (eg, "My hearing loss makes me mad," "Really get annoyed when people shout"); Displacement of Responsibility—5 items ("People should be more patient when talking to me," "It's up to others to speak more clearly"); Exaggeration of Responsibility—6 items (eg, "Hearing loss is my problem; hate to bother others," "Don't like to ask others for help"); Discouragement—6 items (eg, "Feel depressed as result of hearing loss," "I let my hearing problems get me down"); Stress—8 items (eg, "Feel threatened by communication situations," "Get tense because of hearing loss"); Withdrawal—7 items (eg, "Feel left out of conversations," "Don't enjoy going places with friends"); and Denial—8 items (eg, "Sometimes feel left out when I can't follow," "Sometimes get angry at myself when I can't hear"). Coefficient alpha reliability values ranged from 0.70 (Displacement of Responsibility) to 0.89 (Stress), with a mean of 0.82. The average of the item intercorrelations was reported to be 0.30 (excluding the Denial items), while the average of the scale intercorrelations was reported to be 0.56. It is important to note that the Denial scale measures denial *of* emotional reactions rather than denial *as* an emotional reaction. It was included in the CPHI as a means of determining whether an individual's responses to the items on the Personal Adjustment scales are influenced by response bias. Scores on this scale can provide the clinician with an empirical measure of the degree of confidence that can be placed in the individual's self-assessment responses.

A total of 101 active duty military personnel who received aural rehabilitation at Walter Reed were tested before and retested four to six weeks after the program was terminated (Demorest & Erdman, 1988). The values of the reliability coefficients indicating stability over time for the nine Personal Adjustment scales ranged from 0.58 (Exaggeration of Responsibility) to 0.78 (Self-acceptance) with a mean of 0.70. The scores on the Self-acceptance scale increased significantly, and the scores on the Withdrawal scale decreased significantly from pretest to posttest, contributing some evidence to the validity of these two scales for the measurement of psychosocial adjustment to hearing impairment. An exploratory factor analysis of data from 1,226 military personnel yielded a five-factor solution that accounted for 68% of the variance in the CPHI data. Factor I, labeled Adjustment, accounted for 29% of the total variance and comprised all nine of the Personal Adjustment scales as well as five additional scales from other domains: (1) Attitudes of Others, (2) Behaviors of Others, (3) Maladaptive Behaviors, (4) Denial, and (5) Problem Awareness.

A canonical correlation analysis of data from 919 military personnel revealed that the CPHI Personal Adjustment scales were significantly related in orderly and predictable ways to the scales in the Communication Performance, Communication Environment, and Communication Strategies domains (Demorest & Erdman, 1989). The researchers interpreted these patterns of relationships as providing empirical support for the construct validity of the Personal Adjustment scales. Decreased stress, decreased maladaptive coping behaviors, decreased feelings of isolation and withdrawal, and decreased anxiety were all related to increased effectiveness of communication, increased feelings of self-acceptance and adequacy, and increased perceptions of attitudes and acceptance by others.

Additional validity evidence comes from a study by Knutson and Lansing (1990) who related data from the CPHI to data from the Beck Depression Inventory (Beck, 1978), the UCLA Loneliness Scale (Russell, Peplau, & Cutrona, 1980), the Social Anxiety and Distress Scale (Watson & Friend, 1969), the Rathus Assertiveness Scale (Rathus, 1982), and the Depression, Paranoia, and Social Introversion scales of the Minnesota Multiphasic Personality Inventory. The Personal Adjustment scale scores were related in the predicted direction to the scores on the UCLA Loneliness Scale, the Social Anxiety and Distress Scale, and the Rathus Assertiveness Scale. Depression scores on the Beck Depression Inventory were significantly related to the CPHI Personal Adjustment scale scores but not to Depression scores on the Minnesota Multiphasic Personality Inventory.

Although these initial results are promising, other studies are needed to contribute additional data concerning the reliability, specificity, sensitivity, and validity of the CPHI Personal Adjustment scales for the measurement of psychosocial adaptation to deafness and hearing impairments. The authors of the CPHI cautioned that the instrument, while useful for research purposes, required additional psychometric investigations. Moreover, they stressed that the subscales should not be used for differential diagnosis of psychosocial adaptation problems, but could be used as one element in a comprehensive battery of information to yield a profile for an individual that a clinician could address with suitable counseling interventions.

Social-Emotional Assessment Inventory for Deaf and Hearing-Impaired Students

Following the passage in 1975 of federal legislation mandating individualized educational planning for students with special needs, a group of researchers associated with Gallaudet College sought to investigate the impact of this policy on the social and emotional adjustment of children aged 7 to 21 years with hearing impairments. These researchers soon discovered that no instrument existed that had been validated for this specific measurement purpose. Consequently they undertook to develop an instrument through extensive psychometric research, primarily with students enrolled at the Kendall Demonstration Elementary School operated by Gallaudet College. The instrument was published as the Meadow-Kendall Social-Emotional Assessment Inventory for Deaf and Hearing-Impaired Students (SEAI; Meadow, Karchmer, Petersen, & Rudner, 1980). The purpose of the SEAI is to assist teachers and administrators to identify children with hearing impairments who may be at risk for psychosocial maladaptation and who may need assistance to achieve mature social and emotional development.

The SEAI is intended for use by informants (eg, teachers, parents) who have extensive opportunities to observe the target child's social and emotional behaviors in natural settings. Items were developed in consultation with the teachers in the Kendall Demonstration Elementary School and reviewed by a national panel of experts in deafness and deaf education. Extensive psychometric analyses of data collected from samples of children with hearing impairments at various sites across the United States led to the retention of the final set of items (Meadow et al., 1980). The school-aged version of the SEAI comprises 58 items on three factor analytically derived scales: Social Adjustment, Self-Image, and Emotional Adjustment. The observer-informant is asked to read each statement carefully and to decide if it describes the observable behavior of the target child. The reference for each statement is "all children of the same age, whether they have a hearing loss or not." For the statements unique to children with a hearing impairment (eg, those concerning hearing aid use), the reference group is all children with hearing impairments. A four-point rating scale is provided, ranging from Very True ("Statement gives a very good description of this child as she or he behaves most of the time") to True ("Statement describes this child's behavior some of the time"), False ("Statement is not a good description of this child's behavior"), and Very False ("This child would never—or almost never—be described in this way"). A fifth option is also provided for each item ("Cannot rate—not enough opportunities for observation—or does not apply to this child's situation").

An extension of this instrument for use with preschoolers aged three to six years with hearing impairments was subsequently developed through a similar psychometric process and made available to the research community (Meadow, 1983). The preschool version of the SEAI comprises 49 items on four factor analytically derived scales: (1) Sociable, Communicative Behaviors (SC); (2) Impulsive, Dominating Behaviors (ID); (3) Developmental Lags (DL); and (4) Anxious, Compulsive Behaviors (AC). A set of additional items is included that relates specifically to deafness (eg, "Accepts hearing aid without complaint"). SEAI norms are available for various ages and for each sex. The SEAI has also been translated into Danish under Meadow's direction and used to compare the social and emotional adaptation of children with hearing impairments in these two cultures (Meadow & Dyssegaard, 1983a; Meadow & Dyssegaard, 1983b).

Kluwin, Blennerhassett, and Sweet (1990) reported Cronbach coefficient alpha values of 0.95, 0.91, and 0.81 for the Social Adjustment, Self-Image, and Emotional Adjustment scales, respectively, from a sample of 324 high school aged students with hearing impairments. Meadow (1983) reported interrater reliability coefficients ranging from 0.75 to 0.90 and test-retest reliability coefficients that ranged from 0.70 to 0.90 for the four scales of the preschool version of the SEAI.

Preliminary data supporting the validity of the SEAI for the measurement of psychosocial adaptation among persons with hearing impairments are available from a small number of empirical studies. Using the SEAI, Powers, Elliott, Fairbank, and Monaghan (1988) confirmed the significant social and emotional problems of children with severe and profound hearing impairments in a residential school for students who are deaf who had been identified by their teachers and speech therapists as displaying significant behavior problems. In addition, the SEAI scores identified an additional group of students with significant problems who had not been identified by the raters, suggesting that the SEAI may be a sensitive screening device. In contrast, Kluwin et al. (1990) found no significant associations among scores on the three SEAI scales and scores on a measure of 12 dimensions of coping in a sample of 324 high school students with hearing impairments. In an investigation of the effectiveness of 50-minute psychodrama sessions one day per week for 12 weeks for 35 adolescents with hearing impairments who were living in a residential school (Barrett, 1987), it was reported that mean SEAI scores for the 19 individuals in the experimental group were significantly greater than those for the 16 adolescents in the control group who did not receive the experimental treatment.

In a study of the relationship of previous elementary educational placement (ie, residential school for students who are deaf, special day school for students who are deaf, total communication special services in a typical school, oral-only special services in a typical school) to social and emotional adaptation of adolescents with hearing impairments (Lytle, Feinstein, & Jonas, 1987), it was discovered that low SEAI scores from parent informants were significantly related to the likelihood of referral for mental health services after placement in a model residential secondary school program for the deaf. Cartledge, Paul, Jackson, and Cochran (1991) reported that SEAI scores for a group of 76 adolescents with moderate to severe hearing impairments in a residential setting were significantly related to scores on the teacher-informant form of the Social Skills Rating Scale (Gresham & Elliott, 1990). Meadow (1984), using teacher-informant SEAI data for a total of 262 preschool-aged children, showed that, as predicted, the presence of an impairment in addition to a hearing impairment (eg, cerebral palsy, learning disability) was a significant psychosocial risk factor. The children with a hearing impairment and no other impairment did not differ from their peers without any impairment on the four SEAI scales of social and emotional adaptation. Compared to these two groups of children, the multiply handicapped children, with and without a hearing impairment, scored lower on the SC scale and higher on the ID and AC scales. The multiply handicapped children with a hearing impairment scored lower than the children in the other three groups on the DL scale. Finally, in an investigation of the relationship between self-concept and psychosocial adaptation in 35 children aged 9 to 19 years with moderate to profound hearing impairments in a residential school for students who are deaf, Chovan and Roberts (1993) reported significant correlations between SEAI scores and scores on a questionnaire measuring both academic and nonacademic self-concept.

Although the SEAI has been available for more than 15 years, it has not received the extensive use and detailed psychometric scrutiny that instruments measuring psychosocial adaptation to other chronic illnesses or disabilities have received. This is perhaps a function of the relatively small size of this low-incidence population and the small number of researchers who are pursuing empirical investigations of this construct.

RHEUMATOID ARTHRITIS

Arthritis Impact Measurement Scales

The Arthritis Impact Measurement Scales (AIMS) were developed to provide a reliable, valid, practical, and comprehensive multidimensional respondent self-report index of health status in persons with rheumatoid arthritis (Meenan, 1986; Meenan, Gertman, & Mason, 1980). Accepting the World Health Organization definition of health as comprising physical, mental, and social well-being, the AIMS combined indices of physical status in key areas with measures of psychosocial adaptation and pain status (Meenan, 1982).

Two previously published health status measures were incorporated in large part into the AIMS. Items for the scales of Mobility (ability to move about in the community), Physical Activity (lower extremity function), Social Activity (interactions with friends and family), Household Activities (routine household tasks), Anxieties (feelings of tension or nervousness), and Depression (feelings of despair or lack of enjoyment) were adapted from the Rand Health Insurance Study batteries (Brook et al., 1979) and from Bush's Index of Well-Being (Patrick, Bush, & Chen, 1973). New scales measuring Activities of Daily Living (basic self-care tasks), Pain (degree of physical discomfort), and Dexterity (hand function) were included to yield a more arthritis-specific measure. The original number of items composed for each scale in the order listed was 5, 5, 9, 8, 6, 7, 5, 5, and 5. The items on the Mobility, Physical Activity, and Dexterity scales required Yes or No responses; those on the Household Activities and Activities of Daily Living scales required the respondent to rate level of difficulty accomplishing various tasks on 3-point scales ranging from No Difficulty to Cannot Do. Items on the remaining scales required ratings of occurrence from Always to Never. Item responses were summed to create scale scores and were also standardized to a 0 to 10 range to allow profile construction.

A nonrandom sample of 104 consecutive individuals in two large rheumatology practices were given the AIMS at the time of their clinic visit and either completed it then or mailed it back to the researchers (Meenan et al., 1980). Individuals also provided responses to eight sociodemographic items, four items requesting information on their general health status, four items concerning perceptions of their susceptibility to illnesses, and three items requesting estimates of their functional status and disease severity. Each respondent's physician also provided information on functional level, recent disease activity, and the number of affected joints. Initial data analyses involved attempts to generate item groups meeting the criteria for reliable and homogeneous scales. A total of nine items were dropped to obtain the final scales. The number of items in the Mobility, Physical Activity, Social Activity, Household Activities, Activities of Daily Living, Pain, Depression, Anxiety, and Dexterity scales was 4, 5, 5, 7, 4, 4, 5, 6, and 6, respectively. The coefficient alpha homogeneity indices reported for these nine scales were 0.85, 0.76, 0.63, 0.85, 0.70, 0.85, 0.84, 0.88, and 0.88, respectively. All nine scales were significantly correlated in the predicted direction with a composite measure of the respondents' health status perceptions and with the physicians' ratings of their physical status. In addition, the Mobility, Physical Activity, Social Activity, Household Activities, and Pain scales were significantly correlated with respondents' ages.

In a subsequent investigation (Meenan, Gertman, Mason, & Dunaif, 1982) the AIMS was completed by 625 individuals at 15 arthritis clinics in 10 states. The mean stability reliability correlation (time interval not specified) for a subsample of 100 respondents for the nine scales was found to be 0.87. Coefficient alpha indices for the nine scales ranged from 0.71 (Activities of Daily Living and Shock) to 0.90 (Anxiety). Significant correlations for all scales were obtained with physicians' ratings of health status and with the composite report of respondents' overall health status. Intrascale factor analyses showed all the scales, with the exception of Household Activities, to be specific measures of single constructs. Multiple regression analysis showed that the nine scales accounted for more than 60% of the variance in physicians' and respondents' reports of health status. Similar reliability and validity results were obtained for subsets of respondents diagnosed with one of four major arthritis disease types. Interscale factor analysis supported a three-factor solution as the most parsimonious. The first factor was entitled Physical Function and comprised the Mobility, Physical Activity, Dexterity, Household Activities, and Activities of Daily Living scales with loading ranging from 0.42 to 0.81. The second factor, Psychological Status, included the Anxiety and Depression scales with loadings of 0.77 and 0.89. Pain was the final factor identified with the AIMS Pain scale with a loading of 0.86. The Social Activity scale loadings on the three factors were 0.28, 0.20, and 0.23, but this scale was assigned to the Physical Function factor for theoretical reasons.

This three-factor structure of the AIMS was replicated in a study involving data from 48 individuals with arthritis (Brown et al., 1984). Moreover, a factor analysis of these AIMS data combined with data from the 21-item, nine-scale Health Assessment Questionnaire (Fries, Spitz, Kraines, & Holman, 1980) revealed three noteworthy factors: the Physical Health scale of the AIMS and the Physical scales (ie, arising, dressing and grooming, activities, eating, walking, reaching, personal hygiene, and grip and grasp) of the Health Assessment Questionnaire loaded on a single factor; the Pain scale of the AIMS and the Pain scales of the Health Assessment Questionnaire loaded on a second factor; and the Psychological Dimension scales of the AIMS loaded on a third factor. Analyses of data in a different investigation collected from 360 individuals with arthritis (Mason, Anderson, & Meenan, 1988), however, revealed that the Dexterity scale failed to load on any factor, and the Social Activity scale seemed to constitute a distinct factor.

Other studies have contributed additional data concerning the reliability, specificity, and validity of the AIMS. A study of 124 individuals with arthritis who were administered the AIMS twice, six months apart (Kazis, Meenan, & Anderson, 1983), reported stability reliabilities of 0.53, 0.80, and 0.62 for the Physical, Psychological, and Pain subsets of scales, respectively. Test-retest reliability index values for the nine scales were reported to range from 0.63 to 0.89 for a group of 227 individuals administered the AIMS twice three weeks apart (Burckhart, Woods, Schultz, & Ziebarth, 1989). Similar reliability and factor analysis results were found in the data obtained from three samples of 112 white, 105 black, and 100 Hispanic respondents (Coulton, Hyduk, & Chow, 1989). Although no significant differences were found between a group of 108 individuals with chronic arthritis and a group of 313 individuals with recent-onset arthritis (onset less than one year prior), significant differences were found on the three subsets of scales between the individuals with arthritis and a group of 188 friends and relatives without impairments (Meenan, Kazis, Anthony, & Wallin, 1991). Finally, Potts and Brandt's (1987) data suggested that the Household Activities scale was a more appropriate measure for females than for males and that the Activities of Daily Living scale was most useful for those individuals with the most severe impairments.

A recent investigation (Weinberger, Samsa, Tierney, Belyea, & Hiner, 1992) compared the AIMS, a specific measure of health status in persons with rheumatoid arthritis, with the Sickness Impact Profile (SIP; see Chapter 2), a generic measure of health status in persons with chronic illnesses. Data from the two instruments were collected from a random sample of 150 persons with rheumatoid arthritis attending a clinic over a 1-year period (time one), and then again 6 months later ($n = 134$, time two) and 12 months later ($n = 132$, time three). Complete data at all three times were obtained from 115 respondents. It was reported that changes over time in total scores for the two instruments were similar, with consistency reliability values for the SIP ranging from 0.65 to 0.82 and for the AIMS ranging from 0.78 to 0.81. The intercorrelations for the AIMS and SIP physical subscales ranged from 0.75 to 0.76; for the psychological subscales, from 0.37 to 0.45; and for the total scales, from 0.70 to 0.73. The authors interpreted the low values for the psychological subscales to reflect different definitions of psychological health that are operationalized by the two instruments. The authors argued that the generic instrument (the SIP) was a reasonable one to use to measure global health status in persons with rheumatoid arthritis, but that the specific instrument (the AIMS) was superior if the researcher was interested in measuring psychosocial adjustment to the disease.

Investigations have provided data to support the sensitivity of the AIMS for the measurement of treatment effects. In one of the earliest studies (Meenan, 1982), changes in AIMS scale scores were related to changes over six months for individuals receiving both standard clinical treatment and individuals receiving the active drug in a blind drug protocol. In a 21-week, double-blind trial of two treatments and a placebo in 121 individuals at 10 university rheumatology centers (Meenan et al., 1984), the AIMS was related to previously validated health status scales and clinician measures of arthritis effects (eg, joint counts, grip strength) and was able to detect clinically meaningful differences between the drug treatments.

Versions of the AIMS have been created for special purposes, including a juvenile version (Coulton, Zborowsky, Lipton, & Newman, 1987), a geriatric version (Hughes, Edelman, Chang, Singer, & Schuette, 1991), and a short version (Wallston, Brown, Stein, & Dobbins, 1989). In addition, the AIMS has been translated into Dutch (Taal, Jacobs, Seydel, Wiegman, & Rasker, 1989; van der Heijde, van Riel, & van de Putte, 1990), French (Sampalis et al., 1990), German (Jaeckel, Cziske, Schochat, & Jacobi, 1987), Spanish (Hendricson et al., 1989), and an Anglicized version for British respondents (Hill, Bird, Lawton, & Wright, 1990). The AIMS can also be scored by computer, and a health status summary for the respondent can be generated for use by the physician (Kazis, Callahan, Meenan, & Pincus, 1990).

Other investigations have confirmed that the AIMS is useful for research exploring determinants and correlates of health status perceptions and health behaviors in individuals with rheumatoid arthritis who live in diverse settings (Allaire, Meenan, & Anderson, 1991; Anderson, Firschein, & Meenan, 1989; Beckham, Keefe, Caldwell, & Roodman, 1991; Hawley & Wolfe, 1988; Kazis, Anderson, & Meenan, 1989; Kazis, Anderson, & Meenan, 1990; Kazis et al., 1983; Keefe et al., 1987; Koestner, Ramey, Kelner, Meenan, & McClelland, 1989; Liang, Cullen, & Larson, 1983; Parker et al., 1984; Weinberger, Tierney, Booher, & Hiner, 1990) and for the comparison of psychosocial adaptation across groups of individuals with various chronic illnesses (Dailey, Bishop, Russell, & Fletcher, 1990; Goeppinger, Doyle, Charlton, & Loriz, 1988; Liang, Fossel, & Larson, 1990; Mason, Weener, Gertman, & Meenan, 1983). The AIMS appears to meet the authors' goals of establishing a practical, simple, dependable, and multidimensional index of health status that is useful for evaluating the success of a variety of interventions in individuals with rheumatoid arthritis.

SEIZURE DISORDERS

Washington Psychosocial Seizure Inventory and the Adolescent Psychosocial Seizure Inventory

Recognizing the limitations of projective methods developed to investigate psychopathology in nonimpaired populations and the need for a measure of psychosocial problems of adaptation specific to persons with epilepsy, Dodrill and colleagues (Dodrill, Batzel, Queisser, & Temkin, 1980) developed the Washington Psychosocial Seizure Inventory (WPSI), a 132-item questionnaire that purports to measure psychological and social concerns of adults with epilepsy. The Adolescent Psychosocial Seizure Inventory (APSI) is a 139-item questionnaire that purports to measure similar concerns among persons from 12 to 19 years of age with epilepsy (Batzel et al., 1991).

The eight scales on the WPSI are: (1) Family Background, to identify "problems in one's upbringing that were of an interpersonal nature and that might well result in psychological difficulties later in life," including parent and peer interaction and school adjustment; (2) Emotional Adjustment, to evaluate "depression, tension, anxiety, worry, inability to think clearly, nonspecific somatic concerns, oversensitivity, poor self-image, and generalized dissatisfaction with life" as well as "a few items suggestive of psychotic disorders"; (3) Interpersonal Adjustment, to investigate characteristics such as meeting people, ease in social situations, and having close friends; (4) Vocational Adjustment, to survey the vocational status and needs of the person; (5) Financial Status, to appraise the felt security and perceived financial status of the person; (6) Adjustment to Seizures, to analyze the person's reactions to his or her seizures, including fear, resentment, and insecurity; (7) Medicine and Medical Management, to evaluate the person's views of the medical treatment received and reactions to the medication regimen; and (8) Overall Psychosocial Functioning, purporting to be "a single global index of overall psychosocial adjustment," that does not include distinct items but rather is composed of items from the other seven scales "with an especially strong representation from [the] Emotional Adjustment [scale]." Similar to the Minnesota Multiphasic Personality Inventory (Graham, 1987), three additional validity scales are composed of items that assist the examiner in eliminating a respondent's protocol because of faking or response sensitization (Dodrill et al., 1980, pp. 124–125).

The APSI items are scored on nine scales, five of which are also on the WPSI: (1) Family Background, (2) Emotional Adjustment, (3) Interpersonal Adjustment, (4) Adjustment to Seizures, and (5) Medicine and Medical Management. School Adjustment appears in place of Financial Status, and Vocational Outlook is included rather than Vocational Adjustment. A scale unique to the APSI is Antisocial Activity, which includes questions concerning the adolescent's association with an antisocial peer group and substance abuse. As with the WPSI, an Overall Psychosocial Functioning scale, with items taken from the other eight scales, purports to indicate the adolescent's global degree of psychosocial adaptation.

Since its introduction, the WPSI has been used in a variety of investigations of the psychosocial adaptation of persons with epilepsy, both in this country and around the world (Alvarado et al., 1992; Beran & Flanagan, 1985; Beran & Flanagan, 1987; Dodrill, 1986; Dodrill et al., 1984; Dodrill, Beyer, Diamond, Dubinsky, & Geary, 1984; Flanagan & Beran, 1985; Helgeson, Mittan, Tan, & Chayasirisobhon, 1990; Hermann, Whitman, Wyler, Anton, & Vanderzwagg, 1990; Tan, 1986; Tellier, Adams, Walker, & Rourke, 1990; Trostle, Hauser, & Sharbrough, 1989). In addition to its use in English-speaking countries, the WPSI has been translated for use in Japan (Hosokawa, 1986; Wang, Nakashima, & Takahashi, 1993). The inventory has also been modified, grammatically, to be used in investigations of psychosocial adaptation in populations with chronic neurological impairments, including closed-head injury (Tellier et al., 1990) and multiple sclerosis (Tan, 1986).

Dodrill and his colleagues stated that the scales of the WPSI and the APSI and the specific items they comprise were selected using a two-part model similar to that used for the development of the Minnesota Multiphasic Personality Inventory. The domains to be represented on each inventory and appropriate items for each were prepared in advance. For the WPSI, either "a social worker or a psychologist" (these individuals were unspecified) interviewed 127 persons with epilepsy who were consecutive, self-selected outpatients at the epilepsy clinic at the University of Washington (a "reasonably representative" sample). The individuals also responded to a pool of items on a prototype version of the WPSI. Using a specially designed Psychosocial Rating Sheet, a panel of judges (the number and qualifications of the judges are unclear) then rated the adaptation of the individuals from a tape recording of the clinical interview. Apparently the raters were not unaware of the individuals' diagnosis of epilepsy and associated disabilities, nor of their attendance at the clinic, and may even have been involved in the diagnosis and treatment of the individuals.

The rating sheet consisted of 25 items divided into the seven a priori domains (eg, Family Background had two questions, Interpersonal Adjustment had six questions), with the rater assigning a value from 1 = "Definitely yes," to 3 = "Possibly," to 5 = "Definitely not." Higher rating values indicated "greater certainty of problems" as well as "greater intensity and number of difficulties," but how the raters were expected to operationalize these constructs is unclear. An eighth area asked the raters to rate (1) Overall Psychosocial Functioning of the person from 0 = "No impairment in any aspect of psychosocial functioning" to 10 = "Completely impaired in every aspect of psychosocial functioning"; and (2) anticipated need in the next two years for "professional help in the psychosocial area" (eg, social, psychological, vocational services) from 0 = "Expect that no professional help will be needed" to 10 = "Expect nearly continual help will be needed in nearly every area" (Dodrill et al., 1980, pp. 127, 128).

The decision to retain an item and the assignment of the item to a WPSI scale were based on examination of the bivariate correlations between the item responses of 100 of the 127 individuals and the judges' ratings of the individuals in the eight domains. To investigate the content validity of the devised scales, scale scores were calculated and correlated with ratings in each domain. The data for the remaining 27 individuals were similarly correlated as a cross-validation procedure. Rather than develop standard score norms for the scales, the authors chose to create a profile form for recording the individuals' scale scores, with "four regions of profile elevation." These regions represented "(1) no significant problems; (2) possible problems, but of limited significance; (3) distinct difficulties with definite adjustmental significance; and (4) severe problems having a striking impact upon adjustment" (Dodrill et al., 1980, p. 128).

The nine APSI scales and profile form with the same four regions were developed "following the model of the WPSI." Interviews with 120 adolescents and their parents in five North American metropolitan areas were conducted. The taped interviews were rated in the nine areas, and these data were correlated with the adolescents' responses to the items on the prototype APSI. It should be noted, however, that Batzel et al. (1991) explicitly stated that the interview raters were "L.W.B. or C.B.D." (Batzel or Dodrill), a procedure compromising the validity of the APSI by introducing reactive effects operating on the raters (ie, the expectancy phenomenon; Batzel et al., 1991, pp. 204, 205).

While the decision by Dodrill and colleagues to eschew a factor analytic approach for the development of the two inventories in favor of their professional ratings approach may have been theoretically defensible, it did not obviate the use of multivariate analyses available to psychometricians (eg, principal components, cluster, and latent partition analyses) to test the homogeneity, specificity, and construct validity of their resultant scales. In particular, the data presented concerning the specificity of the first seven WPSI and the first eight APSI scales suggest that the scales do not measure independent clinical characteristics as the authors suggested. For the WPSI, the median intercorrelation of the seven scales was 0.46, ranging from 0.27 for Medicine and Medical Management, and Financial Status to 0.76 for Interpersonal Adjustment and Emotional Adjustment. For the APSI, the median intercorrelation was 0.50, ranging from 0.03 for Antisocial Activity and Adjustment to Seizures to 0.70 for Emotional Adjustment and either School Adjustment or Vocational Outlook.

Another troubling aspect of these inventories is the use of the individual's profile of scale scores for "making judgments as to the absolute level of problems in any area." The statistical process used was explained as follows: "The actual placement of scores on the profile corresponded to the best prediction of the professional rating that could be made for each area based upon the simple linear regression of the rating on the inventory scale." While this may explain why a Family Background scale score of 8 corresponds to a professional rating of 4.0, it does not explain why a Family Background scale score of 8 or more is in profile elevation region 4. Using graphic interpolation, region 4 appears to correspond to ratings from 4.1 to 5.0, region 3 to ratings from 2.9 to 4.0, region 2 to ratings from 2.3 to 2.8, and region 1 to ratings from 1.0 to 2.2. Because the same region boundaries appear on the APSI, the authors apparently used some consistent procedure, but that procedure was not explained and could not be determined. No data were provided in any publication reviewed to date to document the reliability, sensitivity, or predictive validity of these norms. Until these psychometric characteristics are assured, clinicians should refrain from using the WPSI and APSI profiles for differential assessment of the psychosocial reactions of persons with epilepsy (Dodrill et al., 1980. p. 129).

A most troubling issue is the measurement of Overall Psychosocial Functioning on either inventory by scoring for a second time items already scored on one of the other scales, an approach that is indefensible on both psychometric and conceptual grounds. Psychometrically, the scoring of items on one of the scales as well as the overall scale yields redundant information as seen in the spuriously high interscale correlations. For the WPSI, the median correlation for the Overall Psychosocial Functioning scale with the other seven scales is 0.69, with a range from 0.48 with Financial Status to 0.93 with Emotional Adjustment. For the APSI the median correlation is 0.76 with a range from 0.47 with Antisocial Activity to 0.90 with Emotional Adjustment.

Although acknowledging the need for a multidimensional instrument specific to epilepsy, a review of these two inventories suggests that their utility for the investigation of psychosocial reactions may be limited. Specific concerns center on (1) biases introduced during inventory development and (2) the paucity of data concerning the psychometric characteristics and intended multidimensional structure of the instruments. Conceptually, Dodrill et al. (1980) and Batzel et al.

(1991) set out to create inventories "which would permit a comprehensive, systematic, and objective assessment of psychosocial problems" (Dodrill et al., 1980, p. 124). Throughout their papers introducing the two inventories, they referred to the construct to be assessed in the plural (eg, "psychological and emotional problems," "behavioral problems," "adjustmental problems," "psychological and social difficulties," "psychiatric, psychological, and behavioral difficulties"). It is contradictory to conceptualize adaptation as a multidimensional construct and to operationalize the construct with seven or eight scales "as independent of each other as possible," and then to offer a scale purporting to be a "single global index of overall psychosocial adjustment" (Dodrill et al., 1980, p. 125, 133). Moreover, a unidimensional conception of adaptation to epilepsy ignores the multiple antecedents of psychosocial reactions and the multiplicity of behaviors in which they may be manifest. The WPSI and APSI overall adaptation score cannot be used to investigate psychosocial adaptation as a multidimensional, hierarchical, and temporally ordered process.

SPINAL CORD INJURY

Psychosocial Questionnaire for Spinal Cord Injured Persons

Arguing that psychosocial adaptation to a spinal cord injury is a significant factor influencing the individual's total rehabilitation success, Bodenhamer, Achterberg-Lawlis, Kevorkian, Belanus, and Cofer (1983) developed the Psychosocial Questionnaire for Spinal Cord Injured Persons (PQ for SCIP). On the basis of a review of previously published scales, a total of 35 items were organized into four domains: anxiety (5 items), depression (5 items), social discomfort (20 items), and positive outlook (5 items). Respondents were asked to indicate their agreement with each statement on 5-point rating scales ranging from 1, to signify "Not at all," to 5, to signify "Very much." Responses were summed to derive four subscale scores for each respondent.

From two rehabilitation programs in Texas, a nonrandom sample of 46 individuals with a spinal cord injury responded to the questionnaire. Curiously no psychometric data whatsoever were provided in the only published report on the PQ for SCIP. Significant associations were found, however, between Depression subscale scores and the number of hospital admissions ($r = 0.48$) and occupational level ($r = -0.26$).

Similar to the Nottingham Adjustment Scale to be reviewed in a later section, the PQ for SCIP has been included in this article with the hope that other researchers may undertake to investigate the psychometric adequacy and utility of this measure of psychosocial adaptation of persons with a spinal cord injury.

TRAUMATIC BRAIN INJURY

Glasgow Assessment Schedule

The Glasgow Assessment Schedule (GAS) has been proposed by Livingston and colleagues (Livingston & Livingston, 1985; Livingston & McCabe, 1990) as a comprehensive measure for rehabilitation assessment and outcome evaluation of persons with a traumatic brain injury. The GAS was developed to supplement Jennett and Bond's (1975) Glasgow Outcome Scale, a unidimensional measure useful for categorizing, by global level of dependence (ie, good outcome, moderate dependency, severe dependency), individuals with a traumatic brain injury but not for providing information on individuals' abilities in different domains of functioning. The items were derived from previous instruments and the review of clinical data in order to focus on both physical functioning and psychosocial problem solving.

Using clinical documentation and informant reports, the individual with a traumatic brain injury is rated as 0 (normal), 1 (moderate), or 2 (severe) in six domains, the first two of which have particular value for the assessment of psychological, psychiatric, and social consequences of traumatic brain injury. The domains and their component scales are (1) Personality Changes (ie, emotional lability, irritability, aggressiveness, other behavior change), (2) Subjective complaints (ie, sleep disturbance, incontinence, family stress, financial problems, sexual problems, alcohol abuse, reduced leisure activities, headache, dizziness, paraesthesia, reduced sense of smell, reduced hearing, reduced vision), (3) Occupational Functioning (ie, at work at same job, similar job, less skilled job; not at work but employable; unemployable), (4) Cognitive Functioning (ie, immediate recall and two-minute recall of name, address, telephone number; attention and concentration; orientation to time, place, and person; general mental ability), (5) Physical Examination (ie, dysphasia, dysarthria, muscle tone in all limbs, walking, cranial nerve deficits, seizures), and (6) Activities of Daily Living (ie, cooking, domestic tasks, shopping, traveling, personal hygiene, feeding, dressing, mobility).

Interrater reliabilities (Cohen's Kappa statistic) from two raters of 26 individuals evaluated in their homes ranged from 0.71 to 1.00. Each scale was also found to discriminate between a group of 41 males with a minor head injury and 42 males with a severe head injury seen three months postinjury. Level of severity of injury was measured by the Glasgow Coma Scale (Teasdale & Jennett, 1974). Assessments at 3, 6, and 12 months postinjury for a sample of 57 men with a severe head injury indicated the GAS could be used to report trends in functioning in all the areas evaluated.

The GAS scores for the 57 persons with a severe injury were totaled to yield a global score that was related to each individual's Glasgow Outcome Scale global-dependency rating. Analysis of variance showed that the mean GAS scores for the sample differed significantly in the predicted directions for the three Glasgow Outcome Scale categories at 3, 6, and 12 months postinjury. While this result indicated that the GAS combined score gives a valid measure of global dependency, this did not provide any information on the validity of the subscales. In fact, the analysis contradicts the purpose for which the GAS was developed (ie, to provide a multidimensional measure of outcome). A more appropriate analysis would have involved the multivariate multiple regression of Glasgow Outcome Scale outcome category on the GAS subscales.

Although the GAS appears to be a reliable and easy-to-administer measure of traumatic brain injury outcome, the lack of information on the specificity and construct validity of the six subscales would suggest that researchers and clinicians apply the results of the instrument with some caution. Because there are several other widely used instruments measuring functioning in each of the six domains, it should be easy to obtain the data necessary to examine further the concurrent validity of the measure.

Portland Adaptability Inventory

The Portland Adaptability Inventory (PAI) is a 24-item questionnaire designed by Lezak (1987) to collect information on the difficulties experienced by individuals with a traumatic brain injury in three areas: temperament and emotionality (7 items), activities of social behavior (11 items), and physical capabilities (6 items). An informant is asked to rate the individual with a traumatic brain injury on each PAI item on a 4-point scale, ranging from 0 (the characteristic is not present or no impairment or disturbance is noted in this area) through 1, 2, and 3 to signify mild, moderate, or severe degrees of impairment or disturbance, respectively. The temperament and emotionality subscale purports to measure constructs that are associated with adaptation to disability. The seven items on the temperament and emotionality subscale include irritability to aggression, anxiety to agitation, indifference (analogous to denial), depression, delusions and hallucinations, paranoia, and initiative.

Only a single study of the reliability of the PAI has been reported in the literature. Kaplan (1988) collected data for the PAI from the case records of 25 persons who had been referred to the rehabilitation psychology service of a midwestern community hospital. Kaplan reported an internal consistency coefficient of 0.94 for the PAI, with coefficients of 0.90, 0.89, and 0.79 for the Temperament and Emotionality, Activities of Social Behavior, and Physical Capabilities subscales, respectively. Items that demonstrated the lowest correlations with the total PAI score were Activities of Social Behavior #8 (Law violation), Activities of Social Behavior #9 (Alcohol abuse), Activities of Social Behavior #10 (Drug abuse), Physical Capabilities #3 (Sensory status—audition), and Physical Capabilities #4

(Sensory status—vision). The mean interitem correlation for the seven Temperament and Emotionality items was 0.53 (range 0.23 to 0.85). Presumably because of the small sample, no attempt was made to recover the hypothesized subscale structure of the PAI with factor analytic methods.

Two investigations were located that have reported the analyses of data using the PAI. Kaplan (1993) collected PAI data one, three, and five years postinjury from informants of a sample of 25 individuals with a severe traumatic brain injury who were consecutive referrals to a rehabilitation psychology service of a large hospital. Results showed that the individuals with a traumatic brain injury evinced an overall trend toward continuing improvement in psychosocial adaptation but evidence of persistent mild to moderate social and emotional difficulties. Kaplan concluded that the PAI was a useful instrument for tracking changes in psychosocial adaptation over time in persons with a traumatic brain injury.

Malec, Smigielski, and DePompolo (1991) used the PAI to operationalize rehabilitation success for a group of 12 individuals with a traumatic brain injury who were participating in an experimental program. The PAI was completed for the individuals at the time of initial evaluation for program participation, at program completion, and a third time at 2 to 10 months postprogram. In addition, work outcome for each individual at the program's end was rated from 1 (unemployed) to 5 (competitively employed), and living outcome was rated from 1 (needs 24-hour supervision) to 3 (lives independently). It was found that both initial and postprogram PAI scores were lower (ie, fewer problems were reported) for those individuals whose work and living outcomes were rated higher compared to those rated lower, but initial PAI scores did not reliably discriminate program dropouts from successful program completers. While these results seem to substantiate the validity of the PAI, it must be noted that those operating the program were the informants for the PAI each time, introducing a compromising expectancy effect. Moreover, the statistical treatment of the data was inappropriate given the size of the sample and the experimental design (ie, a repeated measure with unequal intervals between measurements).

Given the increased awareness of traumatic brain injury as a seriously disabling impairment and the growing number of postacute rehabilitation programs operating in the United States, there is a significant need for a reliable and valid multidimensional measure of psychosocial adaptation of individuals with a traumatic brain injury that can be used to select intervention strategies and to evaluate treatment outcomes. The PAI appears to be a reasonable first attempt to provide that needed instrument, but additional information on the psychometric characteristics of the PAI is needed. A logical approach would be to compare data from the Glasgow Assessment Schedule and the PAI for a representative sample of individuals with a traumatic brain injury and to relate both of these sets of scores to other measures of personality, activities of daily living skills, and social and physical functioning.

VISUAL IMPAIRMENT

Nottingham Adjustment Scale

The Nottingham Adjustment Scale (NAS) is an experimental instrument (Dodds, Bailey, Pearson, & Yates, 1991) developed for rehabilitation counselors to measure adaptation to the loss of sight in persons with an acquired visual impairment. Dodds et al. (1991) argued that measurement of this variable would clarify the psychological processes involved and permit the specification of a rehabilitation program to meet the needs of the individual and the evaluation of the effectiveness of the intervention. Their review of the theoretical literature, however, uncovered considerable controversy among rehabilitation specialists over the definition and nature of adaptation to visual impairment. Rejecting traditional metaphoric accounts of adaptation to visual impairment as similar to grieving over loss, they selected coping and stress as a defensible theoretical framework (Ferguson, Dodds, Craig, Flannigan, & Yates, 1994). They identified seven cognitive and emotional variables they thought were particularly relevant to the construct and undertook to discover to what extent they overlapped.

The seven variables and the measures they selected to assess them (Dodds et al., 1991) were (1) anxiety/depression, the General Health Questionnaire—28 (Goldberg & Hillier, 1979); (2) acceptance of disability, the Acceptance of Disability scale (Linkowski, 1971); (3) self-efficacy (ie, the feeling that one can be effective in bringing about change in one's circumstances), Sherer Self-Efficacy Questionnaire (Sherer et al., 1982); (4) locus of control, the Recovery Locus of Control Questionnaire (Partridge & Johnson, 1989); (5) self-esteem, the Rosenberg Self-Esteem Questionnaire (Rosenberg, 1965); (6) attitudes to blindness, a modification of the Attitudes Toward Disabled Persons scale—Form O (Yuker, Block, & Campbell, 1960), with a change of referent in the statements from "disabled" to "blind"; and (7) attributional style (ie, the way in which one ascribes internal or external causes to events in one's life), an adaptation of the Attributional Style Questionnaire (Peterson et al., 1982) designed for this investigation. Data were collected from 50 individuals in England who were participating in a vocational training program for persons with a visual impairment.

In an attempt to increase the homogeneity of the scales, the researchers examined the item-to-total scale correlations for each scale separately and eliminated items that failed to meet a minimum value. The number of items remaining on each scale at the end of this iterative process was 12, 9, 8, 4, 9, 7, and 6, respectively. Scores on the shortened versions of the scales were recalculated, and interscale analyses were performed. The results of a cluster analysis revealed two clusters: one comprised general mental health and self-esteem, and the other comprised self-efficacy and locus of control. The attitude and acceptance variables did not belong to either cluster but were significantly intercorrelated, and the attributional style variable was not related to any of the other six variables.

Scores from an augmented sample of 200 persons on the seven shortened scales were collected and intercorrelated. These results confirmed the independence of the attributional style measure from the other six and led the researcher to drop this variable from the subsequent principal components analysis. Discarding items that loaded on none or more than one component led to the prototype version of a 43-item composite instrument titled the Nottingham Adjustment Scale. The five components were named (1) hopelessness (13% of the variance, 14 items), (2) acceptance (12% of the variance, 11 items), (3) self-efficacy (10% of the variance, 8 items), (4) anxiety (8% of the variance, 5 items), and (5) attitudes (6% of the variance, 5 items). A second-order principal components analysis of the respondents' five factor scores yielded a single component that was thought to be the hypothesized construct of adaptation to visual impairment. The authors defined this construct empirically as low levels of anxiety and depression together with high self-esteem and self-efficacy and sense of responsibility for recovery.

Curiously no subscale homogeneity coefficients were provided in this report, and the authors failed to investigate the specificity of the subscales. The authors stated, however, that they were currently collecting additional data to determine whether the NAS was a reliable measure that was valid for the purposes for which it was created. Their suggestion that a profile of subscale scores may be helpful for identifying persons with a visual impairment who are in need of special counseling services is premature. They also fail to make clear whether a subscale is one of the six shortened scales or one of the five principal components derived from the six scales. Data from additional samples of persons with a visual impairment must be provided confirming the sensitivity of the inventory for identifying "cases" in need of additional help.

In a subsequent validation study (Dodds, Flannigan, & Ng, 1993), NAS data obtained from a total of 425 rehabilitation participants were subjected to a principal components analysis. An orthogonally rotated seven-component solution accounted for 53% of the variance. The names assigned to these components and the percentages of the total variance that each accounted for were anxiety (7%), hopelessness-depression (8%), self-efficacy (8%), acceptance (11%), attitudes (6%), self-esteem (8%), and attributions (5%). Retest data from a group of 100 of the participants following a 10-week vocational and social rehabilitation program showed significant changes in the predicted direction for the anxiety, self-esteem, acceptance, self-efficacy, and hopelessness-depression measures. Once again, no homogeneity or reliability data were reported and no specificity analyses were conducted to confirm that the subscales measured separate dimensions of a construct of psychosocial adaptation to blindness and visual impairment.

A study to examine whether a training program was successful in increasing vocational abilities and independence of adults with recently acquired sight loss (Ferguson et al., 1994) provided data on the usefulness of the NAS for the measurement of adaptation to visual impairment. A total of 469 individuals at a national rehabilitation center in England were assessed upon entry. Of these, 126 completed the training program and were assessed a second time. These 126 individuals did not differ significantly from the 323 individuals who dropped out on the variables age or sex. Instruments included the same seven instruments as in the earlier investigation (Dodds et al., 1991). Because of ethical reasons, a control group of individuals who did not receive the training could not be created. To circumvent some of the serious limitations of a one-group pretest-posttest design, the researchers analyzed their data with LISREL, a structural modeling statistical procedure. The results indicated that participants in the training program showed significant improvements in the expected directions on all NAS subscales except attributional style, on which no change was detected. Of course, in the absence of a suitable control group, these results cannot be interpreted to mean that the training program was responsible for these improvements in psychosocial adaptation.

In a separate publication (Dodds et al., 1994), the authors reported these reliability coefficients for the data from the 469 individuals in the Ferguson et al. (1994) study: anxiety-depression, 0.62; attitudes to blindness, 0.38; locus of control, 0.29; acceptance of disability, 0.51; self-efficacy, 0.53; and attributional style, 0.27. Interscale correlations ranged from 0.12 (anxiety-depression with attributional style) to 0.62 (attitudes to blindness with acceptance of disability), with a mean value of 0.37.

This description of the scale has been included in this chapter to encourage other researchers to accept the challenge issued at the end of the Ferguson et al. (1994) report: namely, to investigate the psychometric adequacy and utility of the NAS for measuring the psychosocial adaptation of persons with blindness and visual impairments.

CONCLUSION

Our review of 11 instruments to measure psychosocial adaptation to eight specific chronic illnesses and disabilities in this chapter, together with our review of 10 instruments to measure general psychosocial adjustment to chronic illness and disability in Chapter 2, revealed significant problems surrounding this important measurement task. We will defer our consideration of these methodological problems, however, until Chapter 24. As part of our presentation of recommendations for future research in this area, we will identify problems surrounding the measurement of the construct. Modest suggestions for the potential solution of these measurement problems will also be provided at that time.

The next four parts of this book provide reviews of the research literature on psychosocial adaptation to 18 specific chronic illnesses and disabilities. In Part II we consider four traumatic or sudden onset disabilities—cardiovascular disorders, spinal cord injury, traumatic brain injury, and amputation; in Part III we consider three disease-related chronic health disorders—cancer, diabetes mellitus, and rheumatoid arthritis; in Part IV we consider two sensory impairments— blindness and visual impairments and deafness and hearing impairments; in Part V we consider nine neurological or neuromotor disabilities—epilepsy, multiple sclerosis, cerebral palsy, amyotrophic lateral sclerosis, muscular dystrophy, myasthenia gravis, neurofibromatosis, Parkinson's disease, and spina bifida.

REFERENCES

Allaire, S. H., Meenan, R. F., & Anderson, J. J. (1991). The impact of rheumatoid arthritis on the household work performance of women. *Arthritis and Rheumatism, 34,* 669–678.

Alvarado, L., Ivanovic-Zuvic, F., Candia, X., Méndez, M., Ibarra, X., & Alarcón, J. (1992). Psychosocial evaluation of adults with epilepsy in Chile. *Epilepsia, 33,* 651–656.

Anderson, J. J., Firschein, H. E., & Meenan, R. F. (1989). Sensitivity of a health status measure to short-term clinical changes in arthritis. *Arthritis and Rheumatism, 32,* 844–850.

Barrett, M. E. (1987). Self-image and social adjustment change in deaf adolescents participating in a social living class. *Journal of Group Psychotherapy, Psychodrama, and Sociometry, 39,* 3–11.

Batzel, L. W., Dodrill, C. B., Dubinsky, B. L., Ziegler, R. G., Connolly, J. E., Freeman, R. D., Farwell, J. R., & Vining, E. P. G. (1991). An objective method for the assessment of psychosocial problems in adolescents with epilepsy. *Epilepsia, 32,* 202–211.

Beck, A. T. (1978). *Depression inventory.* Philadelphia: Center for Cognitive Therapy.

Beckham, J. C., Keefe, F. J., Caldwell, D. S., & Roodman, A. A. (1991). Pain coping strategies in rheumatoid arthritis: Relationships to pain, disability, depression, and daily hassles. *Behaviour Therapy, 22,* 113–124.

Beran, R. G., & Flanagan, P. J. (1985). Examination of the problems confronting those with epilepsy. *Clinical and Experimental Neurology, 21,* 183–188.

Beran, R. G., & Flanagan, P. J. (1987). Psychosocial sequelae of epilepsy: The role of associated cerebral pathology. *Epilepsia, 28,* 107–110.

Bodenhamer, E., Achterberg-Lawlis, J., Kevorkian, G., Belanus, A., & Cofer, J. (1983). Staff and patient perceptions of the psychosocial concerns of spinal cord injured persons. *American Journal of Physical Medicine, 62,* 182–193.

Brook, R. H., Ware, J. E., Davies-Avery, A., Stewart, A. L., Donald, C. A., Rodgers, W. H., Williams, K. N., & Johnston. S. A. (1979). Overview of adult health status measures fielded in Rand's Health Insurance Study. *Medical Care, 17*(9 Suppl), 1–131.

Brown, J. H., Kazis, L. E., Spitz, P. W., Gertman, P., Fries, J. F., & Meenan, R. F. (1984). The dimensions of health outcome: A cross-validated examination of health status measurement. *American Journal of Public Health, 74,* 159–161.

Burckhart, C. S., Woods, S. L., Schultz, A. A., & Ziebarth, D. M. (1989). Quality of life of adults with chronic illness: A psychometric study. *Research in Nursing and Health, 12,* 347–354.

Cartledge, G., Paul, P. V., Jackson, D., & Cochran, L. L. (1991). Teachers' perceptions of the social skills of adolescents with hearing impairments in residential and public school settings. *Remedial and Special Education, 12*(2), 34–39, 47.

Chovan, W. L., & Roberts, K. (1993). Deaf students' self-appraisals, achievement outcomes, and teachers' inferences about social-emotional adjustment in academic settings. *Perceptual and Motor Skills, 77,* 1021–1022.

Coulton, C. J., Hyduk, C. M., & Chow, J. L. (1989). An assessment of the Arthritis Impact Measurement Scales in three ethnic groups. *Journal of Rheumatology, 16,* 1110–1115.

Coulton, C. J., Zborowsky, R., Lipton, J., & Newman, A. J. (1987). Assessment of the reliability and validity of the Arthritis Impact Measurement Scales for children with juvenile arthritis. *Arthritis and Rheumatism, 30,* 819–824.

Dailey, P. A., Bishop, G. D., Russell, I. J., & Fletcher, E. M. (1990). Psychological stress and the fibrositis/fibromyalgia syndrome. *Journal of Rheumatology, 17,* 1380–1385.

Demorest, M. E., & Erdman, S. A. (1986). Scale composition and item analysis of the Communication Profile for the Hearing Impaired. *Journal of Speech and Hearing Research, 29,* 515–535.

Demorest, M. E., & Erdman, S. A. (1987). Development of the Communication Profile for the Hearing Impaired. *Journal of Speech and Hearing Disorders, 52,* 129–143.

Demorest, M. E., & Erdman, S. A. (1988). Retest stability of the Communication Profile for the Hearing Impaired. *Ear and Hearing, 9,* 237–242.

Demorest, M. E., & Erdman, S. E. (1989). Relationships among behavioral, environmental, and affective communication variables: A canonical analysis of the CPHI. *Journal of Speech and Hearing Disorders, 54,* 180–188.

Dodds, A. G., Bailey, P., Pearson, A., & Yates, L. (1991). Psychological factors in acquired visual impairment: The development of a scale of adjustment. *Journal of Visual Impairment and Blindness, 85,* 306–310.

Dodds, A. G., Ferguson, E., Ng, L., Flannigan, H., Hawes, G., & Yates, L. (1994). The concept of adjustment: A structural model. *Journal of Visual Impairment and Blindness, 88,* 487–497.

Dodds, A. G., Flannigan, H., & Ng, L. (1993). The Nottingham Adjustment Scale: A validation study. *International Journal of Rehabilitation Research, 16,* 177–184.

Dodrill, C. B. (1986). Correlates of generalized tonic-clonic seizures with intellectual, neuropsychological, emotional, and social function in patients with epilepsy. *Epilepsia, 27,* 399–411.

Dodrill, C. B., Batzel, L. W., Queisser, H. R., & Temkin, N. R. (1980). An objective method for the assessment of psychological and social problems among epileptics. *Epilepsia, 21,* 123–135.

Dodrill, C. B., Beier, R., Kasparick, M., Tacke, I., Tacke, U., & Tan, S.-Y. (1984). Psychosocial problems in adults with epilepsy: Comparison of findings from four countries. *Epilepsia, 25,* 176–183.

Dodrill, C. B., Beyer, D. N., Diamond, M. B., Dubinsky, B. L., & Geary, B. B. (1984). Psychosocial problems among adults with epilepsy. *Epilepsia, 25,* 168–175.

Ferguson, E., Dodds, A., Craig, D., Flannigan, H., & Yates, L. (1994). The changing face of adjustment to sight: A longitudinal evaluation of rehabilitation. *Journal of Social Behavior and Personality, 9,* 287–306.

Flanagan, P. J., & Beran, R. G. (1985). A simple and validated tool for the clinician to assess psychosocial status when conducting anticonvulsant drug trials. *Clinical and Experimental Neurology, 21,* 189–194.

Fries, J. F., Spitz, P. W., Kraines, R. G., & Holman, H. R. (1980). Measurement of patient outcome in arthritis. *Arthritis and Rheumatism, 23,* 137–145.

Goeppinger, J., Doyle, M. A. T., Charlton, S. L., & Loriz, K. (1988). A nursing perspective on the assessment of function in persons with arthritis. *Research in Nursing and Health, 11,* 321–331.

Goldberg, D. P., & Hillier, V. F. (1979). A scaled version of the General Health Questionnaire. *Psychological Medicine, 9,* 139–145.

Graham, J. R. (1987). *The MMPI: A practical guide* (2nd ed.). New York: Oxford University Press.

Greer, S., Moorey, S., & Watson, M. (1989). Patients' adjustment to cancer: The Mental Adjustment to Cancer (MAC) scale vs. clinical ratings. *Journal of Psychosomatic Research, 33,* 373–377.

Gresham, F., & Elliott, S. (1990). *Social skills rating system manual.* Circle Pines, MN: American Guidance Services.

Hallberg, L. R.-M., Eriksson-Mangold, M., & Carlsson, S. G. (1992). Psychometric evaluation of a Swedish version of the Communication Strategies scale of the Communication Profile for the Hearing Impaired. *Journal of Speech and Hearing Research, 35,* 666–674.

Hawley, D. J., & Wolfe, F. (1988). Anxiety and depression in patients with rheumatoid arthritis: A prospective study of 400 patients. *Journal of Rheumatology, 15,* 932–941.

Helgeson, D. C., Mittan, R., Tan, S.-Y., & Chayasirisobhon, S. (1990). Sepulveda Epilepsy Education: The efficacy of a psychoeducational treatment program in treating medical and psychosocial aspects of epilepsy. *Epilepsia, 31,* 75–82.

Hendricson, W. D., Russell, I. J., Prihoda, T. J., Jacobson, J. M., Rogan, A., & Bishop, C. D. (1989). An approach to developing a valid Spanish language translation of a health-status questionnaire. *Medical Care, 27,* 959–966.

Hermann, B. P., Whitman, S., Wyler, A. R., Anton, M. T., & Vanderzwagg, R. (1990). Psychosocial predictors of psychopathology in epilepsy. *British Journal of Psychiatry, 156,* 98–105.

Hill, J., Bird, H. A., Lawton, C. W., & Wright, V. (1990). The Arthritis Impact Measurement Scales: An anglicized version to assess the outcome of British patients with rheumatoid arthritis. *British Journal of Rheumatology, 29,* 193–196.

Hosokawa, K. (1986). Washington Psychosocial Seizure Inventory (WPSI)—introduction to Japan and its exploration. *Journal of the Japanese Epilepsy Society, 4,* 171–178.

Hughes, S. L., Edelman, P., Chang, R. W., Singer, R. H., & Schuette, P. (1991). The GERI-AIMS: Reliability and validity of the Arthritis Impact Measurement Scales adapted for elderly patients. *Arthritis and Rheumatism, 34,* 856–865.

Jaeckel, W. H., Cziske, R., Schochat, T., & Jacobi, E. (1987). Assessing health status after inpatient rehabilitation in rheumatoid arthritis. *International Rehabilitation Medicine, 8,* 54–59.

Jennett, B., & Bond, M. (1975). Assessment of outcome after severe brain damage. *Lancet, 1,* 480–484.

Kaplan, S. P. (1988). Adaptation following serious brain injury: An assessment after one year. *Journal of Applied Rehabilitation Counseling, 19*(3), 3–8.

Kaplan, S. P. (1993). Five-year tracking of psychosocial changes in people with severe traumatic brain injury. *Rehabilitation Counseling Bulletin, 36,* 151–159.

Kazis, L. E., Anderson, J. J., & Meenan, R. F. (1989). Effect sizes for interpreting changes in health status. *Medical Care, 27*(3 Suppl), S178–S189.

Kazis, L. E., Anderson, J. J., & Meenan, R. F. (1990). Health status as a predictor of mortality in rheumatoid arthritis: A five-year study. *Journal of Rheumatology, 17*, 609–613.

Kazis, L. E., Callahan, L. F., Meenan, R. F., & Pincus, T. (1990). Health status reports in the care of patients with rheumatoid arthritis. *Journal of Clinical Epidemiology, 43*, 1243–1253.

Kazis, L. E., Meenan, R. F., & Anderson, J. T. (1983). Pain in the rheumatic diseases: Investigation of a key health status component. *Arthritis and Rheumatism, 26*, 1017–1022.

Keefe, F. J., Caldwell, D. S., Queen, K. T., Gil, K. M., Martinez, S., Crisson, J. E., Ogden, W., & Numley, J. (1987). Pain coping strategies in osteoarthritis patients. *Journal of Consulting and Clinical Psychology, 55*, 208–212.

Kluwin, T., Blennerhassett, L., & Sweet, C. (1990). The revision of an instrument to measure the capacity of hearing-impaired adolescents to cope. *Volta Review, 92*, 283–291.

Knutson, J. F., & Lansing, C. R. (1990). The relationship between communication problems and psychological difficulties in persons with profound acquired hearing loss. *Journal of Speech and Hearing Disorders, 55*, 656–664.

Koestner, R., Ramey, A., Kelner, S., Meenan, R., & McClelland, P. (1989). Indirectly expressed motivational deficits among arthritic adults. *Motivation and Emotion, 13*, 21–29.

Lezak, M. D. (1987). Relationship between personality disorders, social disturbance, and physical disability following traumatic brain injury. *Journal of Head Trauma Rehabilitation, 2*(1), 57–59.

Liang, M. H., Cullen, K. E., & Larson, M. G. (1983). Measuring function and health status in rheumatic disease clinical trials. *Clinics in Rheumatic Diseases, 9*, 531–539.

Liang, M. H., Fossel, A. H., & Larson, M. G. (1990). Comparisons of five health status instruments for orthopedic evaluation. *Medical Care, 28*, 632–642.

Linkowski, D. C. (1971). A scale to measure acceptance of disability. *Rehabilitation Counseling Bulletin, 14*, 236–244.

Livingston, M. G., & Livingston, H. M. (1985). The Glasgow Assessment Schedule: Clinical and research assessment of head injury outcome. *International Rehabilitation Medicine, 7*, 145–149.

Livingston, M. G., & McCabe, R. J. R. (1990). Psychosocial consequences of head injury in children and adolescents: Implications for rehabilitation. *Pediatrician, 17*, 255–261.

Lytle, R. R., Feinstein, C., & Jonas, B. (1987). Social and emotional adjustment in deaf adolescents after transfer to a residential school for the deaf. *Journal of the American Academy of Child and Adolescent Psychology, 26*, 237–241.

Malec, J. F., Smigielski, J. S., & DePompolo, R. W. (1991). Goal attainment scaling and outcome measurement in postacute brain injury rehabilitation. *Archives of Physical Medicine and Rehabilitation, 72*, 138–143.

Mason, J. H., Anderson, J. J., & Meenan, R. F. (1988). A model of health status for rheumatoid arthritis: A factor analysis of the Arthritis Impact Measurement Scales. *Arthritis and Rheumatism, 31*, 714–720.

Mason, J. H., Weener, J. L., Gertman, P. M., & Meenan, R. F. (1983). Health status in chronic disease: A comparative study of rheumatoid arthritis. *Journal of Rheumatology, 10*, 763–768.

Meadow, K. P. (1983). An instrument for assessment of social-emotional adjustment in hearing-impaired preschoolers. *American Annals of the Deaf, 128*, 826–834.

Meadow, K. P. (1984). Social adjustment of preschool children: Deaf and hearing, with and without other handicaps. *Topics in Early Childhood Special Education, 3*(4), 27–40.

Meadow, K. P., & Dyssegaard, B. (1983a). Social-emotional adjustment of deaf students. Teachers' ratings of deaf children: An American-Danish comparison. *International Journal of Rehabilitation Research, 6,* 345–348.

Meadow, K. P., & Dyssegaard, B. (1983b). Teachers' ratings of deaf children: An American-Danish comparison. *American Annals of the Deaf, 128,* 900–908.

Meadow, K. P., Karchmer, M. A., Petersen, L. M., & Rudner, L. (1980). *Meadow/Kendall Social-Emotional Assessment Inventory for Deaf Students: Manual.* Washington, DC: Gallaudet College, Pre-College Programs.

Meenan, R. F. (1982). The AIMS approach to health status measurement: Conceptual background and measurement properties. *Journal of Rheumatology, 9,* 785–788.

Meenan, R. F. (1986). New approaches to outcome assessment: The AIMS questionnaire for arthritis. *Advances in Internal Medicine, 31,* 167–185.

Meenan, R. F., Anderson, J. J., Kazis, L. E., Egger, M. J., Altz-Smith, M., Samuelson, C. O., Jr., Willkens, R. F., Solsky, M. A., Hayes, S. P., Blocka, K. L., Weinstein, A., Guttadauria, M., Kaplan, S. B., & Klippel, J. (1984). Outcome assessment in clinical trials: Evidence for the sensitivity of a health status measure. *Arthritis and Rheumatism, 27,* 1344–1352.

Meenan, R. F., Gertman, P. M., & Mason, J. H. (1980). Measuring health status in arthritis: The Arthritis Impact Measurement Scales. *Arthritis and Rheumatism, 23,* 146–152.

Meenan, R. F., Gertman, P. M., Mason, J. H., & Dunaif, R. (1982). The Arthritis Impact Measurement Scales: Further investigation of a health status measure. *Arthritis and Rheumatism, 25,* 1048–1053.

Meenan, R. F., Kazis, L. E., Anthony, J. M., & Wallin, B. A. (1991). The clinical and health status of patients with recent-onset rheumatoid arthritis. *Arthritis and Rheumatism, 34,* 761–765.

Parker, J. L., Singsen, B. H., Hewett, J. E., Walker, S. E., Hazelwood, S. E., Hall, P. J., Holsten, D. J., & Rodon, C. M. (1984). Educating patients with rheumatoid arthritis: A prospective analysis. *Archives of Physical Medicine and Rehabilitation, 65,* 771–774.

Partridge, C., & Johnson, M. (1989). Perceived control of recovery from physical disability: Measurement and prediction. *British Journal of Clinical Psychology, 28,* 53–58.

Patrick, D. L., Bush, J. W., & Chen, M. M. (1973). Toward an operational definition of health. *Journal of Health and Social Behavior, 14*(3), 6–23.

Peterson, C., Semmel, A., von Baeyer, C., Abramson, L. Y., Metalsky, G. I., & Seligman, M. E. P. (1982). The Attributional Style Questionnaire. *Cognitive Therapy and Research, 6,* 287–300.

Potts, M. K., & Brandt, K. D. (1987). Evidence of the validity of the Arthritis Impact Measurement Scales. *Arthritis and Rheumatism, 30,* 93–96.

Powers, A., Elliott, R., Fairbank, D., & Monaghan, C. (1988). The dilemma of identifying hearing disabled and hearing impaired students. *Volta Review, 90,* 209–218.

Rathus, D. (1982). A 30-item schedule for assessing assertive behavior. *Behavior Therapy, 4,* 398–406.

Rosenberg, M. (1965). *Society and the adolescent self-image.* Princeton, NJ: Princeton University Press.

Russell, D., Peplau, L. A., & Cutrona, C. E. (1980). The revised UCLA Loneliness Scale: Concurrent and discriminant validity evidence. *Journal of Personality and Social Psychology, 39,* 472–480.

Sampalis, J. S., Pouchot, J., Beaudet, F., Carette, S., Gutkowski, A., Harth, M., Myhal, D., Senécal, J.-L., Yeadon, C., Williams, J. I., & Esdaile, J. M. (1990). Arthritis Impact Measurement Scales:

Reliability of a French version and validity in Adult Still's Disease. *Journal of Rheumatology, 17*, 1657–1661.

Sherer, M., Maddux, J. E., Mercadante, B., Prentice-Dunn, S., Jacobs, B., & Rogers, R. W. (1982). The self-efficacy scale: Construction and validation. *Psychological Reports, 51*, 663–671.

Smith, M. S., Mauseth, R., Palmer, J. P., Pecoraro, R., & Wenet, G. (1991). Glycosylated hemoglobin and psychological adjustment in adolescents with diabetes. *Adolescence, 26*, 31–40.

Sullivan, B. J. (1979a). Adjustment in diabetic adolescent girls: I. Development of the diabetic adjustment scale. *Psychosomatic Medicine, 41*, 119–126.

Sullivan, B. J. (1979b). Adjustment in diabetic adolescent girls: II. Adjustment, self-esteem, and depression in diabetic adolescent girls. *Psychosomatic Medicine, 41*, 127–128.

Taal, E., Jacobs, J. W., Seydel, E. R., Wiegman, B., & Rasker, J. J. (1989). Evaluation of the Dutch Arthritis Impact Measurement Scales (DUTCH-AIMS) in patients with rheumatoid arthritis. *British Journal of Rheumatology, 28*, 487–491.

Tan, S.-Y. (1986). Psychosocial functioning of adult epileptic and MS patients and adult normal controls on the WPSI. *Journal of Clinical Psychology, 42*, 528–534.

Teasdale, G., & Jennett, B. (1974). Assessment of coma and impaired consciousness. *Lancet, 2*, 81–84.

Tellier, A., Adams, K. M., Walker, A. E., & Rourke, B. P. (1990). Long-term effects of severe penetrating head injury on psychosocial adjustment. *Journal of Consulting and Clinical Psychology, 58*, 531–537.

Trostle, J. A., Hauser, W. A., & Sharbrough, F. W. (1989). Psychologic and social adjustment to epilepsy in Rochester, Minnesota. *Neurology, 39*, 633–637.

van der Heijde, D. M. F. M., van Riel, P. L. C. M., & van de Putte, L. B. A. (1990). Sensitivity of a Dutch health assessment questionnaire in a trial comparing hydroxychloroquine vs. sulphasalzine. *Scandinavian Journal of Rheumatology, 19*, 407–412.

Wallston, K. A., Brown, G. K., Stein, M. J., & Dobbins, C. J. (1989). Comparing the short and long versions of the Arthritis Impact Measurement Scales. *Journal of Rheumatology, 16*, 1105–1109.

Wang, Y., Nakashima, K., & Takahashi, T. (1993). The application of the WPSI to epilepsy patients. *Japanese Journal of Psychiatry and Neurology, 47*, 537–539.

Watson, D., & Friend, R. (1969). Measurement of social-evaluative anxiety. *Journal of Consulting and Clinical Psychology, 33*, 448–457.

Watson, M., & Greer, S. (1983). Development of a questionnaire measure of emotional control. *Journal of Psychosomatic Research, 27*, 299–305.

Watson, M., Greer, S., Pruyn, J., & Van Den Borne, B. (1990). Locus of control and adjustment to cancer. *Psychological Reports, 66*, 39–48.

Watson, M., Greer, S., Rowden, L., Gorman, C., Robertson, B., Bliss, J. M., & Tunmore, R. (1991). Relationships between emotional control, adjustment to cancer and depression and anxiety in breast cancer patients. *Psychological Medicine, 21*, 51–57.

Watson, M., Greer, S., Young, J., Inayat, Q., Burgess, C., & Robertson, B. (1988). Development of a questionnaire measure of adjustment to cancer: The MAC scale. *Psychological Medicine, 18*, 203–209.

Weinberger, M., Samsa, G. P., Tierney, W. M., Belyea, M. J., & Hiner, S. L. (1992). Generic versus disease specific health status measures: Comparing the Sickness Impact Profile and the Arthritis Impact Measurement Scales. *Journal of Rheumatology, 19*, 543–546.

Weinberger, M., Tierney, W. M., Booher, P., & Hiner, S. L. (1990). Social support, stress, and functional status in patients with osteoarthritis. *Social Science and Medicine, 30,* 503–508.

Yuker, H. E., Block, J. R., & Campbell, W. J. (1960). *A scale to measure attitudes toward disabled persons* (Human Resources Study No. 5). Albertson, NY: Human Resources Center.

Zigmond, A. S., & Snaith, R. P. (1983). The Hospital Anxiety and Depression Scale. *Acta Psychiatrica Scandinavica, 67,* 361–370.

Psychosocial Adaptation to Traumatic or Sudden Onset Disabilities

Part I of this book presented an overview of the theory associated with the study of psychosocial adaptation to chronic illness and disability and a review and critique of 21 instruments for the measurement of this construct. In Part II we provide the first 4 of a total of 18 reviews of the research literature on psychosocial adaptation to specific chronic illnesses and disabilities. Part II concerns four traumatic or sudden onset disabilities: Chapter 4—cardiovascular diseases, Chapter 5—spinal cord injury, Chapter 6—traumatic brain injury, and Chapter 7—amputation.

These traumatic, or sudden onset, disabilities share several common features. They (1) are caused by a traumatic event; (2) normally affect a specific body part (eg, myocardial infarction—the heart, traumatic brain injury—the brain); (3) are irreversible; and (4) normally become medically stable with appropriate treatment. These disabilities, however, differ along other dimensions. They (1) result in different types and degrees of functional limitations (eg, spinal cord injury and amputation commonly involve mobility, manipulation, pain, and fatigue limitations, while myocardial infarction normally results in fatigue-related restrictions); (2) pose variable degrees of lethality to the individual; (3) typically occur in different age groups (eg, spinal cord and traumatic brain injuries at late adolescence and early childhood, myocardial infarction among older individuals); and (4) involve different degrees of visibility (eg, spinal cord injury is highly visible, whereas myocardial infarction is mostly invisible).

Our review of the literature for each of these disabilities will follow the same format. We begin each chapter with a brief description of the disability, including a synopsis of available information on incidence and prevalence, causal factors, signs and symptoms, complications, course, and prognosis. This is followed by a review of the research literature on psychosocial adaptation to the disability, focusing on the research conducted in the last 15 years. The third section of each chapter summarizes the available information on characteristics associated with psychosocial adaptation to the disability. This section is organized into three areas: sociodemographic characteristics (eg, age at time of injury or disease onset, chronicity, sex, educational level, socioeconomic status), personality factors (eg, premorbid personality, ego strength, attribution of blame, perception of disability, locus of control), and disability-related variables (eg, neuropathology, severity of impairment, type of treatment). If it is available, information on environmental factors (eg, degree of family or peer support, level of independence, modifiability of the work environment) that are thought to be related to psychosocial adaptation to the disability also appears in this section. Each chapter ends with a presentation of tentative conclusions concerning psychosocial adaptation to the disability derived from the findings reported in the literature reviewed.

CHAPTER 4

Cardiovascular Diseases

DESCRIPTION

Cardiovascular diseases are the leading cause of death among American adults. It is estimated that over 10% of the American population has some form of heart and blood vessel disease (Houd, 1978). Approximately 1 to 1.5 million heart attacks occur each year in the United States. About 50% of those who experienced heart attacks survived them (Johnson & Getzen, 1992; Passamani, Frommer, & Levy, 1984). Annually 25% of all deaths in the United States are caused by heart attacks, a figure that rises to 35% of all deaths when attention is restricted to men between 35 and 50 years of age (Berkow, 1992; Rey, 1993).

Some of the common clinical types of cardiovascular disease include the following:

- *Valvular heart disease.* This condition often results from early rheumatic fever (usually during childhood), causing damage to the heart valves, including the mitral and aortic valves. The valves may become insufficient, stenotic (constricted), or both (Berkow, 1992; Johnson & Getzen, 1992).
- *Myocardiopathy.* This condition involves inflammation causing weakness of the heart muscle (myocardium). It is usually secondary to viral infections, exposure to chemical or toxic agents, alcoholism, diabetes, hypertension, or coronary heart disease (Johnson & Getzen, 1992: Rey, 1993).
- *Angina pectoris.* This clinical syndrome is due to myocardial ischemia (an imbalance between oxygen demand and oxygen supply). It is characterized by episodes of chest discomfort, pressure, or pain. The experience is typically precipitated by physical exertion (Berkow, 1992; Rey, 1993).
- *Hypertensive heart disease.* This condition is commonly associated with elevated blood (especially diastolic) pressure. It can be either primary in nature ("essential"), meaning with no known specific cause, or secondary to

other disorders such as kidney disease, endocrine abnormalities, or vascular abnormalities (Berkow, 1992; Johnson & Getzen, 1992).

- *Myocardial infarction.* This condition, commonly known as heart attack, usually results from abrupt and total cessation of coronary blood flow to a segment of the myocardium, lasting for 30 minutes or longer, and resulting in damage to the affected segment. Myocardial infarction occurs when an acute thrombus (blood clot) occludes the coronary artery that was previously completely or partially obstructed by atherosclerotic plaque (eg, an accumulation of cholesterol; Johnson & Getzen, 1992). Myocardial infarction invariably results in a damaged heart muscle often leading to congestive heart failure (Falvo, 1991).

- *Congestive heart failure.* This condition usually signifies the end stage of most gradually deteriorating cardiovascular diseases. The condition is characterized by cardiac hypertrophy (enlarged heart chambers) and thick muscle walls. Symptoms most frequently include dyspnea (shortness of breath), edema (swelling due to fluid retention) in lower extremities, fatigue, and weakness (Johnson & Getzen, 1992; Rey, 1993).

The present chapter focuses primarily on psychosocial adaptation to myocardial infarction. In certain instances references are made to other forms of cardiovascular disease, especially those associated with complications of myocardial infarction. Survivors of myocardial infarction encounter numerous physical, vocational, financial, and environmental concerns, both during their hospitalization and upon discharge. These include chest pains, shortness of breath, weakness, reduced activity level, fatigue, and sleep disturbance, all of which necessitate modifications of the individual's lifestyle. Psychosocial concerns range from uncertainty about resuming physical, sexual, and work activities to depression, anxiety over recurrence of myocardial infarction, and fear of death (Krantz & Deckel, 1983).

PSYCHOSOCIAL ADAPTATION TO MYOCARDIAL INFARCTION

The individual's reactions to myocardial infarction have been postulated (Bell, Bell, & Lewis, 1987; Hackett & Cassem, 1984; Krantz & Deckel, 1983) to include the following phases: (1) psychic shock, or the fear of impending death; (2) anxiety about one's present and future situation; (3) denial, including the repression of one's feelings and minimization of the seriousness of the condition; (4) depression, including feelings of helplessness, reduced self-esteem, and dependency on others; (5) anger and resentment, especially against society and the ensuing medical treatment; and (6) recognition or acceptance of the condition. Wiklund, Sanne, Vedin, and Wilhelmsson (1985) viewed the process of adaptation to myocardial infarction as a derivative of the more general process of coping with crisis. Accordingly, they suggested a four-phase model:

1. *Shock phase*, lasting from 0 to 3 days, noted for its reactions of disbelief, confusion, and adaptive behaviors of denial and dependency;
2. *Reaction phase*, lasting up to 2 months, with anxiety, depression, and irritability reactions and adaptive behaviors of grief and ventilation of emotions;
3. *Reconstruction phase*, lasting from 2 to 12 months, where reactions of anxiety, depression, and irritability are still experienced but at a lower level, and adaptive behaviors of assuming gradual control and responsibility, and striving for independence become increasingly more prevalent; and
4. *Reorientation phase*, lasting from 12 months on, noted for its gradual emotional stability and behaviors that reflect acceptance of reality, independence, control, responsibility, and self-confidence.

A somewhat different temporal model of adaptation was recently proposed by Johnson and Morse (1990), who viewed adaptation to myocardial infarction in the context of a struggle to regain control. Four stages were postulated: (1) defending oneself (reminiscent of anxiety and denial reactions); (2) coming to terms (similar to recognition and acknowledgment of one's mortality and limitations); (3) learning to live; and (4) living again. The last two of these stages further define final adjustment and reestablishment of control and mastery over one's life.

The course and duration of the process of adaptation to disability in persons who experience myocardial infarction are variable, determined by many medical, familial, and environmental factors (Croog, Levine, & Lurie, 1968; Faller, 1990; Goldberg, 1982; Gray, Reinhardt, & Ward, 1969; Whitehouse, 1960). Considerable clinical and empirical data have been obtained on the incidence and nature of anxiety, denial, and depression. Anxiety among myocardial infarction survivors is associated with the threat of impending death and with worries about employability, financial status, and sexual activity (Cay, Vetter, Philip, & Dugard, 1972b; Hackett & Cassem, 1974). The incidence of anxiety immediately following myocardial infarction was reported to be as high as 50% to 75% (Stern, Plionis, & Kaslow, 1984; Waltz, Badura, Pfaff, & Schott, 1988). Cay et al. (1972b) reported that 65% of their sample evinced emotional upset (anxiety and depression) during convalescence. Whereas 55% experienced anxiety after the first myocardial infarction, only 42% experienced this reaction following subsequent myocardial infarctions. In contrast, depression was experienced by 37% of the individuals after the first myocardial infarction but rose to 58% in individuals with subsequent myocardial infarctions.

Cassem and Hackett (1971; 1973) studied the occurrence of anxiety and depression reactions evinced among patients in cardiac care units and concluded that, although a certain temporal overlap existed, anxiety typically peaked during the first two days of hospitalization, while denial followed it and was observed mainly in the second day. Depression, in contrast, appeared to peak during the third through fifth days of hospital stay. Buchanan, Cowan, Burr, Waldron, and Kogan (1993) reported that, unlike those of depression, denial, and anger, state anxiety scores were elevated among their sample of postacute myocardial infarction patients during each of the first four days following myocardial infarction. At a six-month follow-up, however, all scores were within the average range. Other reports have confirmed the existence of only moderate levels of anxiety two to three weeks and three months after myocardial infarction (Terry, 1992). Most researchers, however, have reported findings suggesting that approximately one third of myocardial infarction survivors experience anxiety long after their convalescence period (Brown & Munford, 1983–1984; Conn, Taylor, & Wiman, 1991; Nickel, Brown, & Smith, 1990). Although most researchers suggest that anxiety peaks either early (Cassem & Hackett, 1973) or late (Trelawney-Ross & Russell, 1987) in the adaptation process, others (Dellipiani et al., 1976; Dobson, Tattersfield, Adler, & McNicol, 1971; Philip, Cay, Vetter, & Stuckey, 1979) have reported what may be considered a two-wave anxiety syndrome. The first occurrence is immediately after the onset of myocardial infarction (within one or two days), and a later occurrence is experienced toward the end of the hospitalization or immediately after hospital discharge.

Short-term fluctuations in anxiety may not always be reliably measured by self-rating anxiety scales. For example, Thompson, Webster, Cordle, and Sutton (1987) followed individuals who experienced myocardial infarction over a one-year postacute period and reported different anxiety trajectories for scores obtained from the State-Trait Anxiety Inventory than for scores obtained from a specially designed self-rating scale for individuals who experience myocardial infarction. Byrne (1979; 1980), however, explored the relationship between measures of state and trait anxiety among myocardial infarction survivors and found significant positive correlations between the two. The uniqueness of each anxiety reaction is supported by findings revealing that, although state anxiety may be higher among myocardial infarction survivors than among individuals who experience chest pain only (Byrne, 1979; Byrne, 1980), no relationship appears to exist between anxiety level and severity of myocardial infarction (Cay, Vetter, Philip, & Dugard, 1972a; Cay et al., 1972b; Dellipiani et al., 1976; Stern, Pascale, & McLoone, 1976). When compared to two other groups of individuals with traumatic impairments (stroke and spinal cord injury), depressed myocardial infarction survivors were found to report lower levels of generalized anxiety than those reported by depressed individuals who experienced a stroke but similar levels of anxiety to those of depressed individuals with a spinal cord injury (Fedoroff et al., 1991). It is likely that various medical correlates, personality attributes, and socioenvironmental factors play a major role in determining the nature and course of the individual's anxiety reaction.

Researchers have recently postulated that symptoms of posttraumatic stress disorder could be experienced in the aftermath of myocardial infarction (Doerfler, Pbert, & DeCosimo, 1994; Kutz, Garb, & David, 1988). These experiences are typically associated with feelings of intense fear (eg, fear of death), a sense of loss of control, nightmares, impairment in concentration, reexperiencing the traumatic event, and increased autonomic arousal. Using the Diagnostic and Statistical Manual—III and III—R criteria for posttraumatic stress disorder, the Symptom Checklist—90, and a battery of specific self-report measures (eg, depression, trait anxiety, anger, social adjustment), Doerfler et al. (1994) concluded that (1) only low levels of psychosocial distress were reported in their sample 6 to 12 months postincident; (2) only a small number of myocardial infarction survivors (approximately 8% to 10%) reported symptoms of (ie, met the Diagnostic and Statistical Manual—III-R criteria for) posttraumatic stress disorder 6 to 12 months after the coronary event; and (3) the posttraumatic stress disorder symptoms, despite their relatively low frequency in these samples, correlated strongly with the measures of depression, anxiety, anger, and the Symptom Checklist—90-based measure of global psychopathology.

Depression in myocardial infarction survivors has been reported to range from 20% to 75% (Block, Boyer, & Imes, 1984; Cay et al., 1972a; Cay et al., 1972b; Dovenmuehle & Verwoerdt, 1962; Forrester et al., 1992; Garcia, Valdes, Jodar, Riesco, & de Flores, 1994; Legault, Joffe, & Armstrong, 1992; Nickel et al., 1990; Schleifer et al., 1989; Silverstone, 1987). Depression is often regarded as a grief reaction to the recognition of loss of health, physical prowess, anticipated pain and discomfort, deprivation of prior habits, job uncertainty, and concern with death (Gentry & Haney, 1975; Hackett & Cassem, 1984; Levenson & Friedel, 1985). Unlike endogenous depression, depression in the wake of myocardial infarction is termed exogenous or reactive and is typically first evident on the third day of cardiac care unit stay (Hackett & Cassem, 1974). Myocardial infarction-triggered depression has not been found to be related to severity of cardiac disease (Cay et al., 1972b; Schleifer et al., 1989), although it was positively related to chronicity and number of hospitalizations (Dovenmuehle & Verwoerdt, 1963; Fielding, 1991).

In a study of 100 consecutive myocardial infarction cases, Lloyd and Cawley (1982) reported that, one week past admission, 35% of the individuals were identified as having significant psychiatric morbidity, mainly depression and anxiety. However, in approximately one half of these individuals the psychiatric illness dated back to the time of the myocardial infarction. In the remaining one half, symptoms were apparently precipitated by the mycardial infarction and appeared to be more transient in nature. Individuals with a history of myocardial infarction were also found to have more episodes of depression and more total symptoms of depression when compared to individuals with diabetes mellitus or individuals with hypertension when followed over a two-year period (Wells, Rogers, Burnam, & Camp, 1993). They were also found to have a higher rate of depression, during early hospitalization, when compared to individuals with angina only and individuals with noncardiac chest pain (Legault et al., 1992).

Longitudinal studies of change in the nature of depression are scarce. Results of one study in which individuals who experienced myocardial infarction were followed over one year showed that, compared to two months postmyocardial infarction, individuals observed at one year postmyocardial infarction showed reduced feelings of depression, anxiety, and restlessness. Irritability, however, increased mildly during this period (Wiklund, Sanne, Vedin, & Wilhelmsson, 1984). In another study, Trelawney-Ross and Russell (1987) followed individuals over six months and found few changes in indices of depression over time. It is likely, however, that the data obtained in these studies were compromised not only by the nature of the measures used (eg, self-report scales, clinician's observation) but also by a unique constellation of premorbid personality attributes and medical, social, and environmental factors affecting the individual at a particular time.

Partial reduction of the often deleterious effects of anxiety and depression on the lives of myocardial infarction survivors can be attributed to early onset of another psychosocial reaction—denial. As previously outlined, denial is a complex defense strategy to ward off negative affect. It may assume various forms, including denial of facts, denial of feelings stemming from these facts, and denial of future implications of the disease and its related functional limitations. It may also range from temporary and partial denial to permanent and complete denial (Caplan & Shechter, 1987; Hackett & Cassem, 1974). The incidence of denial among early-stage myocardial infarction survivors has been estimated at 20% to 25% (Croog & Levine, 1977; Esteve, Valdes, Riesco, Jodar, & De Flores, 1992; Stern et al., 1984).

Areas in which denial is most evident among individuals who experience myocardial infarction include smoking cessation, return to work, avoiding emotional turmoil, weight control and dieting, and engaging in physical activity (Croog, Shapiro, & Levine, 1971). Results concerning the role of denial in lowering anxiety, depression, or even reducing chest pain and increasing survival are equivocal (Billing, Lindell, Sederholm, & Theorell, 1980; Dimsdale & Hackett, 1982; Froese, Hackett, Cassem, & Silverberg, 1974; Gentry, Foster, & Haney, 1972; Hackett & Cassem, 1974; Krantz & Deckel, 1983). It has been suggested (Esteve et al., 1992; Krantz & Deckel, 1983; Miller & Rosenfeld, 1975; Nolan & Wielgosz, 1991; Soloff, 1977–1978; Soloff & Bartel, 1979) that denial may initially mitigate anxiety, but in the long run it may hamper recovery and endanger the rehabilitation process. In a longitudinal study of postmyocardial infarction males, Esteve et al. (1992) found that although deniers, as compared to nondeniers, reported lower levels of anxiety and depression at the coronary unit (in addition to presenting less psychopathology on the Clinical Interview Schedule), these differences were somewhat diminished one month later. At a one-year postdischarge evaluation, no differences were found between deniers and nondeniers on these measures. Despite the early success of denial in alleviating negative emotional reactions to myocardial infarction, denial showed no relationship to measures of cardiologic functioning during the same time period.

Three recent empirical studies investigated denial in individuals recovering from myocardial infarction. Levine et al. (1987) used their semistructured interview protocol, called the Levine Denial of Illness Scale, to follow males who were hospitalized after myocardial infarction or coronary bypass surgery. The follow-up period extended for one year postdischarge. No relationships were found between severity of disease or risk factors and scores on the Levine Denial of Illness Scale. High deniers manifested fewer cardiac symptoms during their hospitalization when compared to low deniers, but during the one-year follow-up, high deniers were rehospitalized for longer duration and were more noncompliant with the prescribed medical regimen.

Warrenberg et al. (1989) also found that denial (as measured by the Levine Denial of Illness Scale) had short-term beneficial effects as measured by lowered anxiety levels and reduced systolic blood pressures. These findings lend support to the notion that denial is adaptive early, during emergency situations, but gradually becomes maladaptive because of its continuous deleterious effect on one's affective and cognitive processes, resulting in erosion of coping skills and limited use of problem-solving behaviors. Finally, Jacobsen and Lowery (1992) sought to investigate the factorial structure of the Levine Denial of Illness Scale among a sample of 152 hospitalized individuals who survived myocardial infarction. A five-factor solution was obtained that included these factors: (1) cognitive denial of illness, (2) denial of impact on the future, (3) denial of need of care, (4) affective denial, and (5) a less usable factor termed "unrealistic expectations for care." As expected, a negative correlation was found between several of these denial factors, especially affective denial and a summated denial score, and measures of state anxiety and depression. These denial of illness factors, however, were not found to be related to measures of functional limitations or to sociodemographic status of the individuals.

In a large prospective study with Norwegian myocardial infarction survivors, Havik and Maeland (1988) examined the association among three different types of verbal denial assessed during hospitalization and medical and psychosocial outcome measures obtained during six-month and three- to five-year follow-ups. First, denial of illness, defined as "a verbal repudiation of the illness and of need for treatment," was related to having fewer problems after resuming work and fewer interruptions of sexual and physical activities. Individuals who denied their illness also had a lower mortality rate. Second, denial of impact, composed of items measuring denial of anxiety and denial of secondary consequences, was found to be moderately and positively associated with less emotional disturbance (ie, less reported anxiety, depression, and irritability) in the hospital. Higher scores on denial of impact were associated, but not significantly, with increased mortality rate. The third and final measure, suppression, defined as "a conscious effort to avoid thinking about the illness or of trying to forget it," was also related to reduced self-reported anxiety, depression, and irritability. Denial of fear and anxiety associated with the myocardial infarction, but not its reality, may act to ward off emotional distress, but it may also be associated with increased mortality among myocardial infarction survivors. Surprisingly, no significant relationships were found between any of the denial measures and resumption of physical, sexual, or work activities.

Despite the frequency with which reactions of anxiety, denial, depression, and irritability are observed among myocardial infarction survivors, individual patterns of these and other psychosocial reactions vary widely (Doehrman, 1977; Garrity, 1981). Further support for the variability of these reactions among individuals who experience myocardial infarction was obtained from three cluster analytic studies purporting to classify myocardial infarction survivors according to illness behavior dimensions (Byrne, Whyte, & Lance, 1978–1979), emotional reactions (Havik & Maeland, 1990), and self-reported psychological symptoms (Hagen, 1991). Byrne et al. (1978–1979) administered the Illness Behavior Questionnaire (Pilowsky & Spence, 1975), designed to assess individuals' feelings and attitudes toward the illness and how they view their psychosocial condition, to 120 myocardial infarction survivors. The four-cluster solution obtained consisted of individuals who (1) showed high levels of somatic awareness and concern; increased tension, depression, and anxiety; and concomitant disruption of interpersonal relations and acceptance of the sick role; (2) recognized and accepted their illness and its role in their lives but who experienced marked affective disruption; (3) recognized and accepted their illness but who scored lower on affective disruption, possibly suggesting better coping ability; and (4) scored lower on all the scales except affective inhibition, suggesting denial of the illness and its consequences. Unfortunately the use of a static design in this study did not allow for investigation of temporal changes in these reaction patterns.

In their cluster analytic study, Havik and Maeland (1990) identified six subgroups of individuals who experienced myocardial infarction based on state-derived measures of anxiety, depression, and irritability administered at six times: twice during hospital stay and four times thereafter, ranging from one week to five years. Two of the subgroups failed to achieve long-term emotional adaptation. One subgroup had high levels of emotional disruption at all times, while the other showed increased emotional disturbance six months after discharge. Two additional subgroups had intermediate levels of long-term emotional adaptation. The first showed initial low levels of emotional disturbance that gradually increased over time, while the other showed average in-hospital emotional disturbance that peaked immediately after discharge and then gradually decreased. The last two subgroups showed little emotional disturbance at follow-up. Individuals in one group had no elevated scores from initial assessment to final follow-up, while individuals in the other group showed moderate levels of emotional disturbance after discharge that gradually dissipated. The researchers concluded that for some individuals, emotional recovery followed a linear progression, while for others it followed a more complex course of recovery partially determined by the individual's age, premorbid personality traits, presence of chest pain, degree of marital conflicts, and occupational status.

Hagen (1991) classified individuals recovering from coronary bypass surgery one to two years postdischarge using the Symptoms Check List—90-R. The cluster analytic solution yielded three groups: (1) low distress (below the 53rd percentile on all symptom dimensions), (2) moderate distress (from the 77th to the 90th percentile on all dimensions), and (3) high distress (above the 96th percentile on all but one dimension). Unfortunately, as in Byrne et al.'s (1978–1979) study, no longitudinal data were provided on these clusters of individuals, thus precluding any possibility of studying temporal changes in emotional reactions among respondents.

In the past decade clinicians and researchers have shown an increasing interest in the defensive and coping strategies used by individuals who experience myocardial infarction. Pegler and Borgen (1984) studied the efficacy of defensive mechanisms, as measured by the Defense Mechanism Inventory, in mitigating anxiety and their relationships to perception of health and survival rate among individuals who experienced myocardial infarction. Principalization (ie, approaching a conflict intellectually by separating content and affect and repressing the latter) was found to be the most successful defense. It correlated positively with both perception of health and survival while being negatively correlated with measures of state and trait anxiety. Projection (ie, blaming an external object or another person for one's weaknesses or problems) was the least successful defense, correlating negatively with perception of health and survival at three months and positively with anxiety.

The concept of coping strategies as psychosocial correlates of adaptation to medical illness was also investigated by Feifel, Strack, and Nagy (1987) among individuals representing three groups of medical diagnoses: (1) myocardial infarction, (2) cancer, and (3) non-life-threatening disabilities (eg, rheumatoid arthritis, orthopaedic impairments). Using a series of multiple regression analyses, these authors reported that in this sample (1) acceptance-resignation (as a coping mode) was best predicted by negative self-esteem, less hope for recovery, gloomy outlook of future, longer illness, negative affectivity, and external locus of control; (2) confrontation or assertiveness was best predicted by high extroversion, perception of illness as being serious, and having a life-threatening illness (myocardial infarction and cancer); (3) avoidance or denial was best predicted by low socioeconomic status group membership, negative self-perception, having a less self-directed life orientation, and external locus of control; and (4) survivors of myocardial infarction tended to cope well and adapt more successfully when they minimized the use of both acceptance-resignation and avoidance coping strategies.

Keckeisen and Nyamathi (1990) studied the differential use of problem-focused and emotional-focused coping strategies, as measured by the Jalowiec Coping Scale, among myocardial infarction survivors and their relationships to three adaptation outcome variables: (1) psychological, as measured by the Psychological Distress subscale of the Psychosocial Adjustment to Illness Scale; (2) social, as measured by the Social Environment subscale of the Psychosocial Adjustment to Illness Scale; and (3) physiological, as measured by the Physiologic Symptoms subscale of the Spousal Coping Instrument. Individuals who relied more on problem-focused coping were better adjusted psychologically and socially than those using more emotional-focused coping. These findings suggest that gaining information and actively discussing and trying to change the situation may be instrumental in gaining control over one's illness, thereby increasing psychosocial adaptation.

Nolan and Wielgosz (1991) identified two groups based on their responses to several psychological and behavioral measures. The adaptive group scored higher on behavioral compensation for stress, suggesting the use of more active and direct coping strategies. The maladaptive group had a profile with elevated hostility and internalized anger, suggesting their inability to constructively cope with stress. In addition, they reported using more distraction and ignoring of symptoms and were more concerned with reoccurrence of myocardial infarction.

Martin and Lee (1992) investigated several sociodemographic variables, personality attributes, and environmental or life events associated with active (eg, problem-solving) versus passive (eg, evasion, denial) coping modes among myocardial infarction survivors. Their results indicated that, in general, a large number of previously experienced life events (as a measure of premyocardial infarction degree of stress) and perceived family support predicted the use of active coping. On the other hand, lower socioeconomic status and feelings of insecurity were found to be the best predictors of passive coping and feeling threatened by the myocardial infarction, respectively.

Finally, Terry (1992), who distinguished between emotion-focused (eg, ventilating feelings, avoidance) and problem-focused (ie, behavioral, cognitive efforts to manage stress) coping modes, reported that use of the former modes was associated with high levels of psychological symptoms (eg, state anxiety), disruption of social and recreational activities, and poor self-rated coping effectiveness among individuals who experienced myocardial infarction. Use of problem-focused coping strategies, unexpectedly, was not related to any of the measures selected by the author to represent psychosocial adaptation to myocardial infarction.

CHARACTERISTICS ASSOCIATED WITH ADAPTATION TO MYOCARDIAL INFARCTION

A review of studies investigating the relationships between sociodemographic variables and psychosocial adaptation to myocardial infarction demonstrated rather surprisingly that the majority of these variables (eg, age, age at onset, sex, marital status, socioeconomic status) bear only little relationship to adaptation to myocardial infarction (Stern et al., 1976). There is some evidence that adaptation is related to earlier resumption of work (Garrity, 1981; Kjoller, 1976; Shapiro, Weinblatt, & Frank, 1972) and that myocardial infarction occurring at a younger age may be associated with failure to reach long-term emotional adaptation (Havik & Maeland, 1990). Only limited data exist that suggest that female survivors of myocardial infarction exhibit more long-term depression and anxiety than male survivors (Nickel et al., 1990). Higher socioeconomic status and economic security have also been linked to decreased levels of anxiety and depression post-myocardial infarction (Nickel et al., 1990; Terry, 1992; Waltz et al., 1988), to higher self-rated health (Winefield & Martin, 1981–1982), and to successful return to work, with white collar workers tending to resume work with greater frequency than blue collar workers (Shapiro et al., 1972; Weinstock & Haft, 1974).

Among illness-related variables, persistent angina pectoris, dyspnea, fatigue (prior to myocardial infarction), presence of other major health problems or somatic illnesses, and the number of hospitalizations due to heart disease have been found to be related to poorer psychosocial adaptation (Havik & Maeland, 1990; Legault et al., 1992; Lloyd & Cawley, 1982; Nickel et al., 1990; Waltz et al., 1988; Zyzanski, Stanton, Jenkins, & Klein, 1981), depression (Ladwig, Lehmacher, Roth, & Breithardt, 1992; Legault et al., 1992), life dissatisfaction at one year postmyocardial infarction (Wiklund et al., 1984), and lower rates of resumption of work, leisure pursuits, and sexual activities (Kjoller, 1976; Legault et al., 1992; Lloyd & Cawley, 1982; Trelawney-Ross & Russell, 1987). No relationships were found by some researchers between depression and infarction size or severity (Ladwig et al., 1992) or between anxiety, depression, and heart rate variability (a measure of autonomic nervous system control of the heart indicating degree of physiological-cardiac functioning) (Buchanan et al., 1993). Other researchers, in contrast, reported significant correlations between severity (ie, size) of myocardial infarction and measure of mood disorder (depression and anxiety) as well as between severity of functional physical impairment (ie, degree of independence of daily living activities) and mood disorder (Forrester et al., 1992).

Researchers have also investigated the relationship between a number of personality characteristics of individuals who experienced myocardial infarction and several groups of outcome measures, including medical (eg, rates of mortality, recurrence of myocardial infarction, chronicity of heart disease), vocational (eg, return to work), and mental status. Variables found to be positively linked to higher rates of mortality or recurrence of myocardial infarction include higher levels of depression prior to myocardial infarction (Bruhn, Chandler, & Wolf, 1969; Kimball, 1969), poorer emotional adaptation (eg, higher levels of postmyocardial infarction depression, anxiety, and hostility) during the acute phase or following myocardial infarction (Affleck, Tennen, Croog, & Levine, 1987; Forrester et al., 1992; Garrity & Klein, 1975; Mumford, Schlesinger, & Glass, 1982; Obier, MacPherson, & Haywood, 1977; Silverstone, 1987; Tennant & Langeluddecke, 1985), failure to perceive benefits early in the adaptation process (Affleck et al., 1987), blaming others after myocardial infarction (Affleck et al., 1987), and Type A behavior pattern (Jenkins, Zyzanski, Rosenman, & Cleveland, 1971; Zyzanski et al., 1981). Variables that have been suggested as predictors of return to work include experiencing lower levels of depression and anxiety (Cay, Vetter, Philip, & Dugard, 1973; Doehrman, 1977; Maeland & Havik, 1987; Nagle, Gangola, & Picton-Robinson, 1971; Schleifer et al., 1989; Trelawney-Ross & Russell, 1987), premyocardial infarction successful social adaptation (Mayou, 1984), personal resources as estimated by professional helpers (Philip, Cay, Stuckey, & Vetter, 1981), acceptance of sick role or recognition of the presence of an illness at a later stage of recuperation (Byrne, 1982; Byrne, Whyte, & Butler, 1981), and early denial of negative affect (Stern, Pascale, & Ackerman, 1977; Stern et al., 1976).

With regard to psychiatric status, history of depression and anxiety, but especially increased depression and anxiety within six months postmyocardial infarction have been suggested as significant predictors of later depression, anxiety, and distress (Byrne, 1982; Forrester et al., 1992; Garcia et al., 1994; Havik & Maeland, 1990; Legault et al., 1992; Lloyd & Cawley, 1982; Nickel et al., 1990; Nir & Neumann, 1990; Stern, Pascale, & Ackerman, 1977; Terry, 1992; Wiklund et al., 1984). High initial (ie, during convalescence) degrees of depression, helplessness, and pessimism, in particular, have been linked to future passivity, social withdrawal, and life dissatisfaction (Legault et al., 1992; Wiklund et al., 1984; Winefield & Martin, 1981–1982). Concurrent levels of depression were also found to account for most of the variability in perceived quality of life and self-care behaviors (eg, exercise, diet, medication use) among older survivors of myocardial infarction (Conn et al., 1991). Two additional variables that may be associated with poor future mental status and psychiatric morbidity are psychological vulnerability, or a high probability of developing psychological symptoms under stress conditions (Mayou, 1979), and use of avoidant coping strategies (Garcia et al., 1994). Type A behavior patterns have also been linked to poorer adaptation to myocardial infarction (Garcia et al., 1994; Waltz et al., 1988; Zyzanski et al., 1981).

On the other hand, higher self-esteem and self-efficacy were found to be associated with postmyocardial infarction adaptation and lower psychological symptoms following myocardial infarction by Ben-Sira and Eliezer (1990), by Nir and Neumann (1990), and by Terry (1992). Similarly, the individual's available personality resources, as judged by a psychiatrist, were found to predict successful adaptation to myocardial infarction (Philip et al., 1981; Terry, 1992). Positive perception of one's health has been suggested as related to higher morale and life satisfaction among myocardial infarction survivors (Brown, Rawlinson, & Hilles, 1981; Garrity, 1973; Nolan & Wielgosz, 1991). Two recently explored personality attributes—agency (a tendency to be self-assertive and self-protective) and hardiness (a tendency to be committed and to exert personal control and challenge oneself)—have shown promise in predicting positive adaptation following myocardial infarction (Drory & Florian, 1991; Nir & Neumann, 1990).

Among environmental factors suggested as predictors of psychosocial adaptation to myocardial infarction (eg, lower depression and anxiety), the one to emerge consistently has been social or family support, both prior to illness and during the convalescence period (Ben-Sira & Eliezer, 1990; Forrester et al., 1992; Havik & Maeland, 1990; Mayou, 1979; Mayou, 1984; Obier et al., 1977). Two longitudinal studies investigated the role of marital and social support systems on psychosocial adaptation to myocardial infarction. In the first study Waltz et al. (1988) collected data on various marital, medical status, and health perception variables from a sample of German males who experienced myocardial infarction and their spouses. Data were collected at five time periods (ie, during hospitalization and at approximately 6 months, 12 months, $3\frac{1}{2}$ years, and 5 years). The psychosocial response to illness measures included scales of anxiety and depression. Participants from marriages marked by low intimacy, high spousal conflict, and chronic role strain assessed their illness situation more negatively and reported greater depressed and anxious moods at later time periods. The inverse relation found between marital support and depressed mood may indicate the often assumed buffering effect of intimate, supportive relationships when coping with adverse life events.

In the second longitudinal study, Fontana, Kerns, Rosenberg, and Colonese (1989) measured levels of support, psychological distress, and cardiac symptoms among male myocardial infarction and coronary artery bypass surgery patients. Measures were obtained at hospitalization, and at 3, 6, and 12 months postdischarge. Results indicated that intimacy at hospitalization ameliorated threat, distress, and symptoms of dyspnea during the first six months, but its influence faded over the following six months. The authors conjectured that this decline in causal relationship over time may have resulted from support being perceived as onerous when provided over an extended time period.

Family support and quality of family relations have also been linked to decreased levels of psychological symptoms (Terry, 1992); to increased coping effectiveness (Terry, 1992); to more frequent resumption of work, social, and physical activities (Terry, 1992; Trelawney-Ross & Russell, 1987); and to lower mortality rate (Obier et al., 1977). One study was located (Drory & Florian, 1991), however, that failed to find any relationship between family cohesion and adaptation to myocardial infarction.

CONCLUSION

The literature on psychosocial adaptation to myocardial infarction strongly suggests that postmyocardial infarction survivors commonly experience temporary reactions of anxiety, depression, denial, and, to a lesser degree, irritability and anger. Denial appears to be associated with early positive adaptation but in the long run exerts a negative effect on psychosocial and medical outcomes. Poor long-term psychosocial adaptation to myocardial infarction and unsuccessful coping with the emotional reactions to it appear to be associated with the use of more passive and emotion-based coping strategies, while successful long-term adaptation to the ensuing trauma is generally linked to the use of more direct and active (eg, problem-focused, task-oriented) coping strategies.

Of all the variables investigated, personality variables and family variables appear to play the most prominent role in predicting psychosocial adaptation to myocardial infarction and the resumption of work and physical activities. Most prominent among these two classes of variables are (1) degree of premyocardial infarction and acute-phase reactions of anxiety and depression, (2) Type A behavior, (3) self-esteem and self-efficacy, and (4) social and family support. Severity of myocardial infarction and sociodemographic variables, such as age and occupational status, show widely variable power to predict future psychosocial adaptation, and that may be restricted to narrow outcomes such as resumption of employment.

The results of studies of psychosocial adaptation to myocardial infarction are limited by conceptual and methodological problems. These include (1) the investigation of heterogeneous outcomes ranging in scope from those assessing present mental or emotional status to those focusing on social, leisure, and work-related activities to those directed at assessment of physical capabilities and medical status; (2) attrition in cross-sectional and longitudinal studies due to progressive mortality among individuals who experience myocardial infarction; and (3) attempting to study personal and social characteristics and experiences with retrospective self-report research designs hampered by recall problems of individuals who experience myocardial infarction and confounded by the nature and extent of the traumatic event.

REFERENCES

Affleck, G., Tennen, H., Croog, S., & Levine, S. (1987). Causal attribution, perceived benefits, and morbidity after a heart attack: An 8 year study. *Journal of Consulting and Clinical Psychology, 55,* 29–35.

Bell, D. B., Bell, B. W., & Lewis, F. D. (1987). Psychological aspects of heart disease. In A. B. Cobb (Ed.), *Medical and psychological aspects of disability* (pp. 37–70). Springfield, IL: C C Thomas.

Ben-Sira, Z., & Eliezer, R. (1990). The structure of adjustment after heart attack. *Social Science and Medicine, 30,* 523–536.

Berkow, R. (Ed.). (1992). *The Merck manual of diagnosis and therapy* (16th ed.). Rahway, NJ: Merck Research Laboratories.

Billing, E., Lindell, B., Sederholm, M., & Theorell, T. (1980). Denial, anxiety, and depression following myocardial infarction. *Psychosomatics, 21,* 639–645.

Block, A. R., Boyer, S. L., & Imes, C. (1984). Personal impact of myocardial infarction: A model for coping with physical disability in middle age. In M. G. Eisenbert, L. C. Sutkin, & M. A. Jansen (Eds.), *Chronic illness and disability through the life span* (pp. 209–221). New York: Springer.

Brown, J. S., Rawlinson, M. E., & Hilles, N. C. (1981). Life satisfaction and chronic disease: Exploration of a theoretical model. *Medical Care, 19,* 1136–1146.

Brown, M. A., & Munford, A. (1983–1984). Rehabilitation of post MI depression and psychological invalidism: A pilot study. *International Journal of Psychiatry in Medicine, 13,* 291–297.

Bruhn, J. G., Chandler, B., & Wolf, S. (1969). A psychological study of survivors and nonsurvivors of myocardial infarction. *Psychosomatic Medicine, 31,* 8–19.

Buchanan, L. M., Cowan, M., Burr, R., Waldron, C., & Kogan, H. (1993). Measurement of recovery from myocardial infarction using heart rate variability and psychological outcomes. *Nursing Research, 42,* 74–78.

Byrne, D. G. (1979). Anxiety as state and trait following survived myocardial infarction. *British Journal of Social and Clinical Psychology, 18,* 417–423.

Byrne, D. G. (1980). Attributed responsibility for life events in survivors of myocardial infarction. *Psychotherapy and Psychosomatics, 33,* 7–13.

Byrne, D. G. (1982). Psychological responses to illness and outcome after survived myocardial infarction: A long-term follow-up. *Journal of Psychosomatic Research, 26,* 105–112.

Byrne, D. G., Whyte, H. M., & Butler, K. L. (1981). Illness behavior and outcome following survived myocardial infarction: A prospective study. *Journal of Psychosomatic Research, 25,* 97–107.

Byrne, D. G., Whyte, H. M., & Lance, G. N. (1978–1979). A typology of responses to illness in survivors of myocardial infarction. *International Journal of Psychiatry in Medicine, 9,* 135–144.

Caplan, B., & Shechter, J. (1987). Denial and depression in disabling illness. In B. Caplan (Ed.), *Rehabilitation psychology desk reference* (pp. 133–170). Rockville, MD: Aspen.

Cassem, N. H., & Hackett, T. P. (1971). Psychiatric consultation in a coronary care unit. *Annals of Internal Medicine, 75,* 9–14.

Cassem, N. H., & Hackett, T. P. (1973). Psychological rehabilitation of myocardial infarction patients in the acute phase. *Heart and Lung, 2,* 382–388.

Cay, E. L., Vetter, N., Philip, A., & Dugard, P. (1972a). Psychological reaction to a coronary care unit. *Journal of Psychosomatic Research, 16,* 437–447.

Cay, E. L., Vetter, N., Philip, A., & Dugard, P. (1972b). Psychological status during recovery from an acute heart attack. *Journal of Psychosomatic Research, 16,* 425–435.

Cay, E. L., Vetter, N., Philip, A., & Dugard, P. (1973). Return to work after a heart attack. *Journal of Psychosomatic Research, 17,* 231–243.

Conn, V. S., Taylor, S. G., & Wiman, P. (1991). Anxiety, depression, quality of life, and self-care among survivors of myocardial infarction. *Issues in Mental Health Nursing, 12,* 321–331.

Croog, S. H., & Levine, S. (1977). *The heart patient recovers.* New York: Human Sciences Press.

Croog, S. H., Levine, S., & Lurie, Z. (1968). The heart patient and the recovery process. *Social Science and Medicine, 2,* 111–164.

Croog, S. H., Shapiro, D. S., & Levine, S. (1971). Denial among male heart patients: An empirical study. *Psychosomatic Medicine, 33,* 385–397.

Dellipiani, A. W., Cay, E. L., Philip, A. E., Vetter, N. J., Colling, W. A., Donaldson, R. J., & McCormack, P. (1976). Anxiety after a heart attack. *British Heart Journal, 38,* 752–757.

Dimsdale, J. E., & Hackett, T. P. (1982). Effect of denial on cardiac health and psychological assessment. *American Journal of Psychiatry, 139,* 1477–1480.

Dobson, M., Tattersfield, A. E., Adler, M. W., & McNicol, M. W. (1971). Attitudes and long-term adjustment of patients surviving cardiac arrest. *British Medical Journal, 3,* 207–212.

Doehrman, S. R. (1977). Psychosocial aspects of recovery from coronary heart disease: A review. *Social Science and Medicine, 11,* 199–218.

Doerfler, L. A., Pbert, L., & DeCosimo, D. (1994). Symptoms of posttraumatic stress disorder following myocardial infarction and coronary artery bypass surgery. *General Hospital Psychiatry, 16,* 193–199.

Dovenmuehle, R. H., & Verwoerdt, A. (1962). Physical illness and depressive symptomatology. I. Incidence of depressive symptoms in hospitalized cardiac patients. *Journal of the American Geriatrics Society, 10,* 932–948.

Dovenmuehle, R. H., & Verwoerdt, A. (1963). Physical illness and depressive symptomatology. II. Factors of length and severity of illness and frequency of hospitalization. *Journal of Gerontology, 18,* 260–266.

Drory, Y., & Florian, V. (1991). Long-term psychosocial adjustment to coronary artery disease. *Archives of Physical Medicine and Rehabilitation, 72,* 326–331.

Esteve, L. G., Valdes, M., Riesco, N., Jodar, I., & de Flores, T. (1992). Denial mechanisms in myocardial infarction: Their relations with psychological variables and short-term outcome. *Journal of Psychosomatic Research, 36,* 491–496.

Faller, H. (1990). Coping with myocardial infarction: A cognitive-emotional perspective. *Psychotherapy and Psychosomatics, 54,* 8–17.

Falvo, D. R. (1991). *Medical and psychosocial aspects of chronic illness and disability*. Gaithersburg, MD: Aspen.

Fedoroff, J. P., Lipsey, J. R., Starkstein, S. E., Forrester, A., Price, T. R., & Robinson, R. G. (1991). Phenomenological comparisons of major depression following stroke, myocardial infarction or spinal cord lesions. *Journal of Affective Disorders, 22*, 83–89.

Feifel, H., Strack, S., & Nagy, V. T. (1987). Coping strategies and associated features of medically ill patients. *Psychosomatic Medicine, 49*, 616–625.

Fielding, R. (1991). Depression and acute myocardial infarction: A review and reinterpretation. *Social Science and Medicine, 32*, 1017–1027.

Fontana, A. F., Kerns, R. D., Rosenberg, R. L., & Colonese, K. L. (1989). Support, stress, and recovery from coronary heart disease: A longitudinal causal model. *Health Psychology, 8*, 175–193.

Forrester, A. W., Lipsey, J. R., Teitelbaum, M. L., DePaulo, J. R., Andrzejewski, P. L., & Robinson, R. G. (1992). Depression following myocardial infarction. *International Journal of Psychiatry in Medicine, 22*, 33–46.

Froese, A., Hackett, T. P., Cassem, N. H., & Silverberg, E. L. (1974). Trajectories of anxiety and depression in denying and nondenying acute myocardial infarction patients during hospitalization. *Journal of Psychosomatic Research, 18*, 413–420.

Garcia, L., Valdes, M., Jodar, I., Riesco, N., & de Flores, T. (1994). Psychological factors and vulnerability to psychiatric morbidity after myocardial infarction. *Psychotherapy and Psychosomatics, 61*, 187–194.

Garrity, T. F. (1973). Social involvement and activeness as predictors of mortality six months after first myocardial infarction. *Social Science and Medicine, 7*, 199–207.

Garrity, T. F. (1981). Behavioral adjustment after myocardial infarction. In S. M. Weiss & J. A. Herd (Eds.), *Perspectives on behavioral medicine* (pp. 67–87). New York: Academic Press.

Garrity, T. F., & Klein, R. F. (1975). Emotional response and clinical severity as early determinants of six-month mortality after myocardial infarction. *Heart and Lung, 4*, 730–737.

Gentry, W. D., Foster, S., & Haney, T. (1972). Denial as a determinant of anxiety and perceived health status in the coronary care unit. *Psychosomatic Medicine, 34*, 39–44.

Gentry, W. D., & Haney, T. (1975). Emotional and behavioral reaction to acute myocardial infarction. *Heart and Lung, 4*, 738–745.

Goldberg, R. L. (1982). Psychologic sequelae of myocardial infarction. *Family Physician, 25*, 209–213.

Gray, R. M., Reinhardt, A. M., & Ward, J. R. (1969). Psychosocial factors involved in the rehabilitation of persons with cardiovascular diseases. *Rehabilitation Literature, 30*, 354–359, 362.

Hackett, T. P., & Cassem, N. H. (1974). Development of a quantitative rating scale to assess denial. *Journal of Psychosomatic Research, 18*, 93–100.

Hackett, T. P., & Cassem, N. H. (1984). Psychologic aspects of rehabilitation after myocardial infarction and coronary artery bypass surgery. In N. K. Wenger & H. K. Hellerstein (Eds.), *Rehabilitation of the coronary patient* (pp. 437–451). New York: John Wiley & Sons.

Hagen, J. W. (1991). Psychological adjustment following coronary artery bypass graft surgery. *Rehabilitation Counseling Bulletin, 35*, 97–104.

Havik, O. E., & Maeland, J. G. (1988). Verbal denial and outcome in myocardial infarction patients. *Journal of Psychosomatic Research, 32*, 145–157.

Havik, O. E., & Maeland, J. G. (1990). Patterns of emotional reactions after a myocardial infarction. *Journal of Psychosomatic Research, 34*, 271–285.

Houd, H. (1978). Cardiac disorders. In R. M. Goldenson (Ed.), *Disability and rehabilitation handbook* (pp. 318–330). New York: McGraw-Hill.

Jacobsen, B. S., & Lowery, B. J. (1992). Further analysis of the psychometric properties of the Levine Denial of Illness Scale. *Psychosomatic Medicine, 54*, 372–381.

Jenkins, C., Zyzanski, S., Rosenman, R., & Cleveland, G. (1971). Association of coronary-prone behavior scores with recurrence of coronary heart disease. *Journal of Chronic Diseases, 24*, 601–611.

Johnson, J., & Getzen, J. (1992). Cardiovascular disease. In M. G. Brodwin, F. A. Tellez, & S. K. Brodwin (Eds.), *Medical, psychosocial and vocational aspects of disability* (pp. 317–333). Athens, GA: Elliott & Fitzpatrick.

Johnson, J. L., & Morse, J. M. (1990). Regaining control: The process of adjustment after myocardial infarction. *Heart and Lung, 19*, 126–135.

Keckeisen, M. E., & Nyamathi, A. M. (1990). Coping and adjustment to illness in the acute myocardial infarction patient. *Journal of Cardiovascular Nursing, 5*, 25–33.

Kimball, C. P. (1969). Psychological responses to the experience of open-heart surgery. *American Journal of Psychiatry, 126*, 348–359.

Kjoller, E. (1976). Resumption of work after acute myocardial infarction. *Acta Medica Scandinavica, 199*, 379–385.

Krantz, D. S., & Deckel, A. W. (1983). Coping with coronary heart disease and stroke. In T. G. Burish & L. A. Bradley (Eds.), *Coping with chronic disease* (pp. 85–112). New York: Academic Press.

Kutz, I., Garb, R., & David, D. (1988). Post-traumatic stress disorder following myocardial infarction. *General Hospital Psychiatry, 19*, 169–176.

Ladwig, K. H., Lehmacher, W., Roth, R., & Breithardt, G. (1992). Factors which provoke post-infarction depression: Results from the post-infarction late potential study. *Journal of Psychosomatic Research, 36*, 723–729.

Legault, S. E., Joffe, R. T., & Armstrong, P. W. (1992). Psychiatric morbidity during the early phase of coronary care for myocardial infarction: Association with cardiac diagnosis and outcome. *Canadian Journal of Psychiatry, 37*, 316–325.

Levenson, J. L., & Friedel, R. O. (1985). Major depression in patients with cardiac disease: Diagnosis and somatic treatment. *Psychosomatics, 26*, 91–102.

Levine, J., Warrenburg, S., Kerns, R., Schwartz, G., Delaney, R., Fontana, A., Gradman, A., Smith, S., Allen, S., & Cascione, R. (1987). The role of denial in recovery from coronary heart disease. *Journal of Psychosomatic Medicine, 49*, 109–117.

Lloyd, G. G., & Cawley, R. H. (1982). Psychiatric morbidity after myocardial infarction. *Quarterly Journal of Medicine, 201*, 33–42.

Maeland, J. G., & Havik, O. E. (1987). Psychological predictions of return to work after a myocardial infarction. *Journal of Psychosomatic Research, 31*, 471–481.

Martin, P., & Lee, H. (1992). Indicators of active and passive coping in myocardial infarction victims. *Journal of Gerontology, 47*, P238–P241.

Mayou, R. (1979). The course and determinants of reactions to myocardial infarction. *British Journal of Psychiatry, 134*, 588–594.

Mayou, R. (1984). Prediction of emotional and social outcome after a heart attack. *Journal of Psychosomatic Research, 26*, 17–25.

Miller, W. B., & Rosenfeld, R. (1975). A psychophysiological study of denial following acute myocardial infarction. *Journal of Psychosomatic Research, 19*, 43–54.

Mumford, E., Schlesinger, H., & Glass, G. (1982). The effects of psychological intervention on recovery from surgery and heart attacks: An analysis of the literature. *American Journal of Public Health, 72*, 141–151.

Nagle, R., Gangola, R., & Picton-Robinson, I. (1971). Factors influencing return to work after myocardial infarction. *Lancet, 2*, 454–456.

Nickel, J. T., Brown, K. J., & Smith, B. A. (1990). Depression and anxiety among chronically ill heart patients: Age differences in risk and predictors. *Research in Nursing & Health, 13*, 87–97.

Nir, Z., & Neumann, L. (1990). Motivation patterns, self-esteem, and depression of patients after first myocardial infarction. *Behavioral Medicine, 16*, 62–66.

Nolan, R. P., & Wielgosz, A. T. (1991). Assessing adaptive and maladaptive coping in the early phase of acute myocardial infarction. *Journal of Behavioral Medicine, 14*, 111–124.

Obier, K., MacPherson, M., & Haywood, L. J. (1977). Predictive value of psychosocial profiles following acute myocardial infarction. *Journal of the National Medical Association, 69*, 59–61.

Passamani, E. R., Frommer, P. L., & Levy, R. I. (1984). Coronary heart disease: An overview. In N. K. Wenger & H. K. Hellerstein (Eds.), *Rehabilitation of the coronary patient* (2nd ed.) (pp. 1–15). New York: John Wiley & Sons.

Pegler, M., & Borgen, F. H. (1984). The defense mechanisms of coronary patients. *Journal of Clinical Psychology, 40*, 669–679.

Philip, A. E., Cay, E. L., Stuckey, N. A., & Vetter, N. J. (1981). Multiple predictors and multiple outcomes after myocardial infarction. *Journal of Psychosomatic Research, 25*, 137–141.

Philip, A. E., Cay, E. L., Vetter, N. J., & Stuckey, N. A. (1979). Short-term fluctuations in anxiety in patients with myocardial infarction. *Journal of Psychosomatic Research, 23*, 277–280.

Pilowsky, I., & Spence, N. D. (1975). Patterns of illness behaviour in patients with intractable pain. *Journal of Psychosomatic Research, 19*, 279–289.

Rey, M. J. (1993). Cardiovascular disorders. In M. G. Eisenberg, R. L. Glueckauf, & H. H. Zaretsky (Eds.), *Medical aspects of disability* (pp. 119–146). New York: Springer.

Schleifer, S. J., Macari-Hinson, M. M., Coyle, D. A., Slater, W. R., Kahn, M., Gorlin, R., & Zucker, H. D. (1989). The nature and course of depression following myocardial infarction. *Archives of Internal Medicine, 149*, 1785–1789.

Shapiro, S., Weinblatt, E., & Frank, C. (1972). Return to work after first myocardial infarction. *Archives of Environmental Health, 24*, 17–26.

Silverstone, P. H. (1987). Depression and outcome in acute myocardial infarction. *British Medical Journal, 294*, 219–220.

Soloff, P. H. (1977–1978). Denial and rehabilitation of the post-infarction patient. *International Journal of Psychiatry in Medicine, 8*, 125–132.

Soloff, P. H., & Bartel, A. G. (1979). Effects of denial on mood and performance in cardiovascular rehabilitation. *Journal of Chronic Diseases, 32*, 307–313.

Stern, M. J., Pascale, L., & Ackerman, A. (1977). Life adjustment postmyocardial infarction. *Archives of Internal Medicine, 137*, 1680–1685.

Stern, M. J., Pascale, L., & McLoone, J. B. (1976). Psychosocial adaptation following an acute myocardial infarction. *Journal of Chronic Diseases, 29*, 513–526.

Stern, M. J., Plionis, E., & Kaslow, L. (1984). Group process expectations and outcome with postmyocardial infarction patients. *General Hospital Psychiatry, 6*, 101–108.

Tennant, C. C., & Langeluddecke, P. M. (1985). Psychological correlates of coronary heart disease. *Psychological Medicine, 15*, 581–588.

Terry, D. J. (1992). Stress, coping and coping resources as correlates of adaptation in myocardial infarction patients. *British Journal of Clinical Psychology, 31*, 215–225.

Thompson, D. R., Webster, R. A., Cordle, C. J., & Sutton, T. W. (1987). Specific sources and patterns of anxiety in male patients with first myocardial infarction. *British Journal of Medical Psychology, 60*, 343–348.

Trelawney-Ross, C., & Russell, O. (1987). Social and psychological responses to myocardial infarction: Multiple determinants of outcome at six months. *Journal of Psychosomatic Research, 31*, 125–130.

Waltz, M., Badura, B., Pfaff, H., & Schott, T. (1988). Marriage and the psychological consequences of a heart attack: A longitudinal study of adaptation to chronic illness after 3 years. *Social Science and Medicine, 27*, 149–158.

Warrenburg, S., Levine, J., Schwartz, G. E., Fontana, A. F., Kerns, R. D., Delaney, R., & Mattson, R. (1989). Defensive coping and blood pressure reactivity in medical patients. *Journal of Behavioral Medicine, 12*, 407–424.

Weinstock, M., & Haft, J. (1974). The effect of illness on employment opportunities. *Archives of Environmental Health, 29*, 79–83.

Wells, K. B., Rogers, W., Burnam, M. A., & Camp, P. (1993). Course of depression in patients with hypertension, myocardial infarction, or insulin-dependent diabetes. *American Journal of Psychiatry, 150*, 632–638.

Whitehouse, F. A. (1960). Psychological factors influencing rehabilitation of the cardiac patient. *Journal of Rehabilitation, 26*, 4–7, 39.

Wiklund, I., Sanne, H., Vedin, A., & Wilhelmsson, C. (1984). Psychosocial outcome one year after a first myocardial infarction. *Journal of Psychosomatic Research, 28*, 309–321.

Wiklund, I., Sanne, H., Vedin, A., & Wilhelmsson, C. (1985). Coping with myocardial infarction: A model with clinical applications, a literature review. *International Journal of Rehabilitation Medicine, 7*, 167–175.

Winefield, H. R., & Martin, C. J. (1981–1982). Measurement and prediction of recovery after myocardial infarction. *International Journal of Psychiatry in Medicine, 11*, 145–154.

Zyzanski, S. J., Stanton, B. A., Jenkins, C. D., & Klein, M. D. (1981). Medical and psychosocial outcomes in survivors of major heart surgery. *Journal of Psychosomatic Research, 23*, 213–221.

CHAPTER 5

Spinal Cord Injury

DESCRIPTION

The onset of spinal cord injury disrupts a wide range of a person's life activities and future plans. This disruption is particularly devastating because over 50% of affected individuals are between 15 and 24 years of age. The leading causes of traumatic spinal cord injury include automobile accidents, falls, stab and gunshot wounds, and diving accidents (Britell & Hammond, 1994; Hu & Cressy, 1992). It is estimated by the National Spinal Cord Injury Data Research Center (Young, Burns, Bowen, & McCutchen, 1987) that over 150,000 Americans now have a spinal cord injury (both quadriplegia and paraplegia). Over 80% of persons with a spinal cord injury are male (Britell & Hammond, 1994). The incidence of spinal cord injury in the United States is approximately 8,000 to 10,000 new injuries per year (Donovan, 1981).

Foremost among the resultant functional limitations are those affecting mobility, sensation, object manipulation (ie, high-level spinal cord injury), sexuality, and vocational and avocational pursuits. Major complications resulting from spinal cord injury include (1) infections (eg, genitourinary and respiratory system infections); (2) sexual dysfunction, especially in males; (3) autonomic hyperreflexia (abnormal stimulation of the autonomic nervous system in persons with lesions about T7, resulting in headaches and sudden increase in blood pressure, decreased heart rate, sweating, nasal congestion, or blurred vision); (4) spasticity; (5) pain experienced as chronic, abnormal, noxious sensations below the injury level; and (6) pressure sores, or decubitus ulcers (Britell & Hammond, 1994; Hu & Cressy, 1992).

PSYCHOSOCIAL ADAPTATION TO SPINAL CORD INJURY

Despite the claims of a minority of clinicians and researchers that there is no evidence to support the existence of phases of psychosocial adaptation to spinal cord injury (Buckelew, Frank, Elliott, Chaney, & Hewett, 1991; Trieschmann, 1988), the majority of investigators have argued that a temporal sequence of reactions to spinal cord injury does exist (Bracken & Shepard, 1980; Bray, 1978; Dunn, 1975; Gunther, 1969; Hohmann, 1975; Kerr & Thompson, 1972; Peter, 1975; Rigoni, 1977; Siller, 1969; Singleton, 1985; Sword & Roberts, 1974; Weller & Miller, 1977). Typically the phases posited follow this order: (1) shock, (2) anxiety (at times termed partial recognition or initial realization), (3) denial (also called protection, defensive retreat, or bargaining), (4) depression (and internalized anger), (5) anger (also termed hostility), and (6) adaptation (also referred to as readjustment, acceptance, integration, reconstruction, recovery, resolution, or adaptation). Moreover, most authors suggest that not all phases are evident in each individual case and that the reactions may overlap, fluctuate back and forth, and appear in varying order. There is also growing recognition that the adaptation process is only partially determined by internal (or automatically triggered) mechanisms. Indeed, various factors have been suggested as exerting strong influence on the nature, structure, pace, and duration of this adaptation process. Among the most frequently mentioned factors are preinjury personality attributes (eg, self-concept, optimism, independence, motivation, locus of control, body image, problem-solving skills) and situational conditions (eg, socioeconomic status, financial resources, social support network, available medical treatment).

Only a scant number of empirical investigations of the process of adaptation to disability among persons with spinal cord injury have been reported in the literature. Most published research studies have used one-shot, static group designs to investigate a single reaction (eg, depression, anxiety) in this population. Among notable exceptions is the work of Bracken and associates (Bracken & Bernstein, 1980; Bracken, Shepard, & Webb, 1981), who explored several psychosocial reactions longitudinally in a four-year study of temporal adaptation to spinal cord injury that entailed interviewing individuals at discharge from the hospital and again one-year postinjury. Although only moderate shifts occurred in the affective reactions of anxiety, denial, depression, and anger among the persons with a spinal cord injury during this time, these shifts were generally in a positive direction (ie, reflecting less distress). Denial, however, showed a slight tendency to increase over the period. The results of their otherwise well-designed study (Bracken et al., 1981) are suspect, however, because of the use of one-item questions to measure affective reactions and, additionally, the use of a psychometrically untested adjective checklist to measure current feelings.

In a controlled study (Richards, 1986), individuals with spinal cord injury completed a battery of tests, including the Beck Depression Inventory, the Wiggins Hostility Scale, and the Handicap Problem Inventory at three weeks, three months, and one year postdischarge from the hospital. A group of respondents without disabilities completed the same battery of tests at similar time intervals. Results showed that immediately after discharge the spinal cord injury group scored moderately higher than the comparison group on the measures of depression and hostility. These differences, however, were virtually undetectable at the final datapoint. Moreover, the members of the spinal cord injury group demonstrated significantly lower levels of distress regarding their disability at the final follow-up as compared to their initial reactions.

In a similar investigation, Crewe and Krause (1990) used self-report measures to follow a group of persons with spinal cord injury. They reported that respondents rated themselves significantly higher on overall adaptation at follow-up than they had 11 years earlier. Despite the dubious psychometric quality of the self-report measures that were used and sampling flaws present in this study, the results suggest a gradual diminution of distress among persons with spinal cord injury over this extended time span.

In a series of longitudinal studies, Craig, Hancock and coworkers (Craig, Hancock, & Dickson, 1994a; Craig, Hancock, & Dickson, 1994b; Hancock, Craig, Dickson, Chang, & Martin, 1993) followed a sample of persons with spinal cord injury over a two-year period (the number of participants decreased from 41 to 31 over the course of these studies due to sample attrition). As compared to a matched group of able-bodied controls, a significantly greater percentage of individuals in the spinal cord injury group was found to be depressed (27% versus 3%) and anxious (25% versus 5%) across four separate time periods (ie, two to four months postinjury, six to eight months postinjury, approximately one year postinjury, and approximately two years postinjury). However, an examination of the mean group scores for both depression (as measured by the Beck Depression Inventory) and anxiety (as measured by Spielberger's Trait Anxiety Inventory) showed no significant decrease on either of these self-report measures. A trend suggesting decrease in both depression and anxiety was, however, noted during the first three assessment periods (ie, within the first year postinjury). Similarly, locus of control among this sample of persons with spinal cord injury did not change over time. Several limitations of these studies, however, may have marred the researchers' findings. These limitations include small sample sizes, exclusive reliance on single self-report measures, lack of direct behavioral observations of participants, use of a trait anxiety (rather than a state anxiety) measure, relatively short follow-up period (two years), and high participant attrition rate (approximately 25%).

The most widely researched of the psychosocial reactions to spinal cord injury has been depression (Frank, Elliott, Corcoran, & Wonderlich, 1987; Trieschmann, 1988), a reaction viewed by some clinicians and writers as a necessary phase in the adaptation process (Gunther, 1969; McDaniel, 1976; Siller, 1969; Tucker, 1980; Wright, 1960; Wright, 1983). The necessity of experienced depression as part of the mourning process associated with the loss of body integrity has, however, been challenged by several researchers (Cook, 1976; Frank et al., 1987; Wortman & Silver, 1989). Cook (1979) studied vocational rehabilitation participants who sustained a spinal cord injury and concluded that, based on participants' Mini-Mult (the abbreviated version of the Minnesota Multiphasic Personality Inventory) scores, depressive reactions were not evident (ie, most scores fell well within the average range). Similar results were obtained by Thompson and Dexter (1980) using scores from the Minnesota Multiphasic Personality Inventory. In this latter study, however, groups of respondents with paraplegia and quadriplegia scored approximately one standard deviation above the mean on the Depression scale normed for persons without a physical disability (mean scores ranged from 58 to 64). Moreover, female respondents tended to score somewhat higher on the Depression scale at three months postinjury as compared to one month postinjury. Nestoros, Demers-Desrosiers, and Dalcandro (1982) administered the Zung Self-Rating Scale for Depression to persons who sustained a spinal cord injury and found that the majority of their respondents scored within the average range. No significant differences were detected between the groups of individuals with more severe (quadriplegia) and less severe (paraplegia) disabilities.

On the other hand, Howell, Fullerton, Harvey, and Klein (1981) studied 22 persons with a spinal cord injury using the Schedule for Affective Disorders and Schizophrenia, a standardized interview form, and the Beck Depression Inventory. They concluded that 23% of their respondents manifested a diagnosable level of depression within six months of injury. In an expansion and follow-up of their original study (Fullerton, Harvey, Klein, & Howell, 1981) using identical measures and diagnostic criteria, the authors revised their conclusions and argued that although depression was not a universal phenomenon in persons with a spinal cord injury, it occurred in a significant minority of this population (33% to 50%). Malec and Neimeyer (1983), also using the Beck Depression Inventory in conjunction with the Symptoms Checklist—90 and the Minnesota Multiphasic Personality Inventory Depression scale, found that mean scores for their group showed only mild elevations compared to standardized norms. Scores on the Beck Depression Inventory alone, however, classified almost one half of the sample into mild (25%) and moderate to severe (18%) levels of depression.

Judd, Burrows, and Brown (1986) investigated the incidence of depression following spinal cord injury using the Hamilton Depression Rating Scale and the DSM—III criteria for depression. They concluded that 11% of respondents met the criteria for major affective disorder. In a later study (Judd, Stone, Webber, Brown, & Burrows, 1989) using similar criteria for depression and adding the Beck Depression Inventory to their test battery, these researchers concluded that 20% of the persons with a spinal cord injury who were studied met the criteria for major depressive disorder and that an additional 18% of the sample showed transient periods of depression. A more recent study (Judd, Brown, & Burrows, 1991) examined the frequency of psychiatric disorders among 227 consecutive admissions to a spinal cord injury rehabilitation unit. These authors concluded that 21% of the sample demonstrated discrete psychiatric disorders during their inpatient treatment and that of these, 75% had major depression.

In a study comparing two measures of depression in samples of 162 persons with a spinal cord injury treated as outpatients and 30 persons with a spinal cord injury treated as inpatients, Tate, Forchheimer, Maynard, Davidoff, and Dijkers (1993) reported frequencies of depression ranging from 21.6% (Zung Self-Rating Depression Scale) to 25.5% (Brief Symptom Inventory Depression Scale) among their combined samples.

MacDonald, Nielson, and Cameron (1987) investigated the incidence of depression among persons with a spinal cord injury who resided in the community using the Beck Depression Inventory and the Multiple Affect Adjective Check List. Time since injury ranged from 1 to 28 years. Clinical depression was evidenced in approximately 15% of their sample, with an additional 45% of the respondents manifesting mild levels of depression. No differences in level of depression were found between those with quadriplegia and those with paraplegia. (The authors' failure to report on the relationship between time since injury and level of depression makes it impossible to investigate how these variables may have covaried in this study.) Tate, Kewman, and Maynard (1990) studied persons having a spinal cord injury using the Brief Symptom Inventory, an abbreviated version of the Symptom Check List—90-Revised. The authors concluded that the respondents were significantly more distressed (ie, had higher scores on scales measuring depression, anxiety, and somatization) than the normative group. Similar results using the Symptom Check List—90-Revised were also reported by Hanson, Buckelew, Hewett, and O'Neal (1993), who concluded that 29% of their sample of persons with a spinal cord injury reported significant levels of distress five to six years postinjury.

The results of these studies suggest that depression is not a universal phenomenon among persons who sustain a spinal cord injury, a conclusion similar to that reached in other reviews of the research (Frank et al., 1987; Frank, VanValin, & Elliott, 1987). Nevertheless, there are many reports claiming that the incidence of depression among populations of persons with a spinal cord injury typically ranges from 12% to 50%, figures that are higher than the rates of 5% to 10% reported for the general population (Craig, Hancock, Dickson, Martin, & Chang, 1990; Judd et al., 1991). In addition, suicide rates have been found to be higher in groups of individuals with a spinal cord injury (DeVivo, Black, Scott-Richards, & Stover, 1991; Sakinofsky, 1980; Woodbury, 1978). Two additional factors cast some doubt on findings purportedly showing only infrequent occurrence of depression among persons with a spinal cord injury. First, the diagnostic criteria used to define depression lack consistency across studies. Must a reactive type of depression (ie, spinal cord injury-triggered) reach a clinical level of depression as defined by the DSM—III and DSM—III-R systems? Second, all of the studies reviewed measured depression at one time only. If depression in persons with a spinal cord injury is a transient phenomenon, then only longitudinal studies can document its existence.

The results of a study by Lawson (1978), although not directly reporting on incidence of depression among persons with a spinal cord injury, are of interest here. Using four measures of depressive affect (ie, self-report, hospital staff ratings, behavioral-verbal index, and an endocrine measure), Lawson studied persons hospitalized with a spinal cord injury five days a week for an average of almost four months. Although not a universal reaction during the early phase of rehabilitation, depression was prevalent in the hospital setting and was related to various personality variables (eg, hopeful perspective of the future) and environmental variables (eg, daily events). Another recent study (Lundqvist, Siosteen, Blomstrand, Lind, & Sullivan, 1991) also demonstrated convincingly that although mood states (depression and anxiety) of persons with a spinal cord injury did not differ appreciably across time from those of a general population comparison group, actual differences did exist when time since injury was controlled for. Specifically, more mood disturbances (ie, elevated levels of depression on the Multiple Affect Adjective Check List and the Hospital Anxiety and Depression Scale) were evident during the first four years postinjury than afterward. More recent studies (Alfano, Neilson, & Fink, 1993; Crisp, 1992) have also indicated that among persons with a spinal cord injury whose injury was of at least a five-year duration, responses to most measures of psychosocial adaptation (eg, life satisfaction, depression, anxiety) were within average range.

Denial as a defense maneuver or a phase of adaptation to a spinal cord injury has been regarded as exerting a positive impact on the adaptation process when occurring soon after the injury but has been viewed as an obstacle to successful adaptation when occurring later or when extended over a long period of time (Bracken & Shepard, 1980; Siller, 1969). Only a single empirical study was found, however, that explored this contention. Rosenstiel and Roth (1981) investigated the relationship between measures of anticipatory cognitive coping activities (eg, rationalization, denial, worrying, catastrophizing) and adaptation in four persons with a spinal cord injury. Their findings suggested that rationalization and denial were associated with less future anxiety and better adaptation. Avoiding catastrophizing and worrying about the future were also linked to less anxiety. The generalizability of the results of this study, however, is limited by the small sample size and unreported psychometric properties of the measures of cognitive coping strategies.

An attempt to classify coping styles among persons with a spinal cord injury was reported by Frank, Elliott, Corcoran, & Wonderlich (1987). These authors used cluster analysis to identify two clinical groups based on responses to the Ways of Coping questionnaire and the Multidimensional Health Locus of Control scale. Participants in one group used all coping strategies extensively (eg, wishful thinking, problem focus, threat minimization), attributed health status to external events, and reported elevated levels of depression. Participants in the second group relied less on coping methods, viewed health as an internal attribute, and were less emotionally distressed. The authors suggested that overuse of coping strategies, coupled with an external locus of control orientation, were associated with greater emotional distress in their sample of persons with a spinal cord injury.

More recently, Nieves, Charter, and Aspinall (1991) studied coping effectiveness among 40 individuals with a spinal cord injury using McNett's Coping Effectiveness Questionnaire. They found that level of coping effectiveness was positively related to time postinjury among persons with quadriplegia (but not paraplegia) and that coping effectiveness was also a good predictor of quality of life among all study participants. Hanson and coworkers (1993), in their follow-up study of 28 persons with a spinal cord injury, concluded that the use of three of the six subscales of the Ways of Coping—Revised Questionnaire, namely Threat Minimization, Information Seeking, and Cognitive Restructuring, increased over a five-year period. Moreover, the use of active and adaptive coping modes (eg, Cognitive Restructuring) has been associated with acceptance of disability (ie, better adaptation). The use of passive and maladaptive coping strategies (eg, Wish Fulfilling Fantasy), on the other hand, was found to be related to lack of disability acceptance. No other studies were located that researched affective, cognitive, and behavioral coping strategies among persons with a spinal cord injury.

CHARACTERISTICS ASSOCIATED WITH ADAPTATION TO SPINAL CORD INJURY

Several sociodemographic variables have been investigated as correlates of adaptation to spinal cord injury. The variables most frequently found to be associated with adaptation are age, chronicity, educational level, and socioeconomic status. Younger age has been frequently associated with better acceptance of disability (Woodrich & Patterson, 1983), better adaptation (Alfano et al., 1993; Heinemann, Bulka, & Smetak, 1988; Kerr & Thompson, 1972; Krause & Crewe, 1991), more positive self-concept (Green, Pratt, & Grigsby, 1984), greater level of perceived well-being (Schulz & Decker, 1985), and better occupational stability (Krause, 1992). Chronological age, however, was found in one investigation to have a curvilinear relationship with economic satisfaction and number of work hours (Krause & Crewe, 1991). People who were in youngest (18 to 35 years) or oldest (56 to 65 years) age cohorts reported less economic satisfaction and lower number of work hours than those in the middle-aged (36 to 55 years) group. It has been pointed out (Frank, Elliott, Buckelew, & Haut, 1988), however, that negative life stress acts as a moderator variable in these relationships, that is, when life stress was controlled for, the differences in distress as measured by the Symptom Check List—90-Revised between younger and older individuals were drastically reduced. This result has been confirmed by the same authors in a recent study (Buckelew et al., 1991).

Higher educational attainment among persons with a spinal cord injury has been linked to better adaptation (Alfano et al., 1993; Kerr & Thompson, 1972; Nickerson, 1981), better acceptance of disability (Woodrich & Patterson, 1983), more positive self-concept (Green et al., 1984), and better occupational stability (Krause, 1992). Similar results were obtained for financial security, employment (versus unemployment), and high socioeconomic status (Bodenhamer, Achter-berg-Lawlis, Kevorkian, Belanus, & Cofer, 1983; Crisp, 1992; Kerr & Thompson, 1972; Nickerson, 1981). These socioeconomic variables were all found to be positively correlated with better psychosocial adaptation (eg, greater life satisfaction, lower depression).

Among studies investigating the impact of injury-related variables on adaptation to a spinal cord injury, the three variables most often implicated are chronicity, severity of injury, and level of pain. Chronicity has been shown to be positively associated with better adaptation and coping ability (Heinemann et al., 1988; Krause & Crewe, 1991; Nieves et al., 1991; Sholomskas, Steil, & Plummer, 1990; Woodrich & Patterson, 1983), better economic stability, and higher satisfaction (Krause, 1992; Krause & Crewe, 1991). Research results on degree of severity have supported mixed conclusions. Whereas several authors (Craig et al., 1994b; Judd et al., 1989; Tucker, 1980; Woodrich & Patterson, 1983) argued that no relationship could be found between degree of injury (ie, quadriplegia versus paraplegia) and level of adaptation, others (Bracken & Bernstein, 1980; Bracken et al., 1981) found that greater neurological and motor dysfunction at hospital discharge was associated with more distress (ie, higher levels of anxiety, depression, and anger) one year postdischarge. Similarly, Alfano et al. (1993) found that higher anatomical injury level was significantly correlated with poorer overall psychosocial adaptation as measured by a composite score derived from the seven subscales comprising the Psychosocial Adjustment to Illness Scale. Finally, higher levels of (experienced) pain have been found in several investigations to be associated with higher depression scores (Craig et al., 1994a; Summers, Rapoff, Varghese, Porter, & Palmer, 1991).

Among the most widely investigated of the personality attributes thought to be linked to successful adaptation to a spinal cord injury are locus of control and self-blame/other-blame (for causation of injury). The research literature on locus of control (Craig et al., 1994a; Crisp, 1992; Dinardo, 1971; Frank & Elliott, 1989; Frank et al., 1987; Mazzulla, 1984; Schulz & Decker, 1985; Shadish, Hickman, & Arrick, 1981) suggests that individuals demonstrating an internal locus of control (ie, those perceiving personal control over most life events) are typically found to demonstrate less emotional distress and greater perceived well-being than those demonstrating an external locus of control (ie, those believing that chance and fatalism control most events). Perceived control was also found to be a predictor of vocational identity (ie, having a clear and stable view of one's goals, skills, and interests) among persons with a spinal cord injury (Crisp, 1992). Bulman and Wortman (1977) were among the first to suggest that the attribution of the cause of one's injury to others (other-blame) was associated with poor adaptation (ie, unsuccessful coping as rated by therapists), whereas self-blame was related to better adaptation. Later research designed to replicate this attribution of blame study, however, yielded equivocal findings. Schulz and Decker (1985) found only moderate correlations between measures of self-blame and adaptation. Van Den Bout, Van Son-Schoones, Schipper, and Groffen (1988) failed to detect any statistically significant relationships between attributional cognitions and measures of coping behavior or self-esteem. When studying the effect of chronicity on these results, these authors argued that the recency of injury exerted a strong influence on attributional cognitions, that is, among those who were recently injured, concern about the avoidability of the accident was associated with poor ratings of coping. Nielson and MacDonald (1988), in contrast, found that self-blaming was related to poorer coping as measured by various self-report instruments. Again, the argument was raised that attribution of blame may be differentially related to adaptation. Self-blame may be adaptive in the earlier phases of the adaptation process but may exert a maladaptive influence in later phases. Buckelew, Baumstark, Frank, and Hewett (1990) found self-blame to be positively related to psychological distress. Although chronicity was not directly associated with general psychological distress, the use of differential coping strategies by their research participants was associated with distress, suggesting that it may have confounded the relationship.

Researchers' lack of attention to intervening or moderating variables may partially explain the inability of other recent studies to detect consistent relationships between attributions of responsibility for the injury and measures of disability acceptance or coping modes (Heinemann et al., 1988; Sholomskas et al., 1990). Some preliminary data suggest, however, that the type of coping strategy used (eg, active, adaptive) and its effectiveness may be related to measures of psychosocial adaptation (eg, acceptance of disability, perceived quality of life) but not to measures of vocational or medical status (Hanson et al., 1993; Nieves et al., 1991). Another complicating factor may be the quality of the instruments used to measure coping, ranging from single-item ratings to self-report measures of varying degrees of psychometric soundness and complexity.

Several other personality variables have only infrequently been investigated. The greater the ego strength or ego resilience of the person with a spinal cord injury, the better he or she has coped with the disability and the less emotional distress he or she has reported (Bracken et al., 1981; Roberts, 1972). Carlson (1979) investigated repression-sensitization and reported that repressors held higher self-concept while sensitizers were more depressed. Krause and Dawis (1992) reported that lower dependency was positively related to general life satisfaction. Finally, conceptual abstractness (ie, the ability to experience openness, flexibility, and personal control) was found to correlate positively with higher life satisfaction following spinal cord injury (Krause & Dawis, 1992).

In a study by Krause (1992), employment status was used as a general measure of adjustment to life following spinal cord injury. When compared to participants who were never employed since injury or who were currently unemployed, those participants who were currently working reported (1) greater general and economic satisfaction, (2) self-perceptions of better adjustment, (3) fewer problems of emotional distress, (4) lower level of dependency, and (5) fewer health problems. This study, therefore, illustrates the importance that subjective components of psychosocial adaptation play in securing and maintaining employment among persons with a spinal cord injury.

Of the environmental variables implicated in successful adaptation to spinal cord injury, the two most often reported are interpersonal relationships and degree of independence. Greater and more stable social or family support has been consistently linked to better adaptation and coping (Bracken & Shepard, 1980; Crisp, 1992; Elliott, Herrick, Witty, Godshall, & Spruell, 1992; Harris, Patel, Greer, & Naughton, 1973; Kerr & Thompson, 1972; Rintala, Young, Hart, Clearman, & Fuhrer, 1992; Schulz & Decker, 1985). Physical independence, with medical, functional, and environmental components, was studied by Green et al. (1984), who found that both degree of perceived independence and the provision of one's own transportation were positively related to higher scores on the Tennessee Self-Concept Scale.

CONCLUSION

The literature on psychosocial adaptation to spinal cord injury indicates considerable disagreement among clinicians, researchers, and theoreticians concerning the nature and sequencing of the adaptation process. This disagreement focuses mainly on the notion of the existence of psychosocial phases (ordered reactions) to the trauma and the necessity of experienced depression during the adaptation process. Although reports of depression among persons who are recovering from a spinal cord injury appear to be widespread, the nature and severity of this reaction (eg, clinical depression versus typical reactive adjustment disorder) have not been fully explored. Moreover, perceptual discrepancies between the reactions of depression and social discomfort (often overestimated among staff) among persons with a spinal cord injury and among those of the medical staff may further confound this issue (Bodenhamer et al., 1983; Cushman & Dijkers, 1990; Ernst, 1987). An additional confounding factor, the overlapping symptoms of depression and the physical consequences of spinal cord injury (eg, low energy level, sleep problems, poor appetite), has only recently received some attention in the literature (Clay, Hagglund, Frank, Elliott, & Chaney, 1995; Rodevich & Wanlass, 1995).

Several characteristics that have been found to be empirically associated with successful psychosocial adaptation to spinal cord injury include younger age, increased time since injury, internal locus of control, ego resiliency and effective coping, and stable and positive social support. These tentative conclusions, however, are compromised because the definition and measurement of the concept of adaptation to spinal cord injury reveal wide variability. For instance, adaptation has been conceived as (1) degree of life satisfaction, (2) vocational or avocational productivity, (3) prevention of medical complications, (4) use of activities of daily living skills, (5) coping style, (6) degree of disability acceptance, and (7) degree of emotional distress. The measurement of adaptation in the research reviewed was approached through a diverse set of psychological instruments, including (1) the Symptom Check List—90-Revised, (2) the Millon Behavioral Health Inventory, (3) various depression scales (eg, the Beck Depression Inventory), (4) life satisfaction indices, (5) the Acceptance of Disability scale, and (6) expert ratings such as therapist ratings of coping or judges' Q-Sort ratings.

Despite the increasing efforts of researchers to investigate the psychosocial adaptation to spinal cord injury, we concur with a recent observation (Craig et al., 1990) that "there is a great need for controlled research in the area aimed at identifying which persons will experience problems. There is also a need for planned research isolating the determinants of favorable outcome or adjustment to spinal cord injury" (p. 424).

REFERENCES

Alfano, D. P., Neilson, P. M., & Fink, M. P. (1993). Long-term psychosocial adjustment following head or spinal cord injury. *Neuropsychiatry, Neuropsychology, and Behavioral Neurology, 6*, 117–125.

Bodenhamer, E., Achterberg-Lawlis, J., Kevorkian, G., Belanus, A., & Cofer, J. (1983). Staff and patient perceptions of the psychosocial concerns of spinal cord injured persons. *American Journal of Physical Medicine, 62*, 182–193.

Bracken, M. B., & Bernstein, M. B. (1980). Adaptation to disability one year after spinal cord injury: An epidemiological study. *Social Psychiatry, 15,* 33–41.

Bracken, M. B., & Shepard, M. J. (1980). Coping and adaptation following acute spinal cord injury: A theoretical analysis. *Paraplegia, 18,* 74–85.

Bracken, M. B., Shepard, M. J., & Webb, S. B. (1981). Psychosocial response to acute spinal cord injury: An epidemiological study. *Paraplegia, 19,* 271–283.

Bray, G. P. (1978). Rehabilitation of spinal cord injured: A family approach. *Journal of Applied Rehabilitation Counseling, 9,* 70–78.

Britell, C. W., & Hammond, M. C. (1994). Spinal cord injury. In R. M. Hays, G. H. Kraft, & W. C. Stolov (Eds.), *Chronic disease and disability: A contemporary rehabilitation approach to medical practice* (pp. 142–160). New York: Demos.

Buckelew, S. P., Baumstark, K. E., Frank, R. G., & Hewett, J. E. (1990). Adjustment following spinal cord injury. *Rehabilitation Psychology, 35,* 101–109.

Buckelew, S. P., Frank, R. G., Elliott, T. R., Chaney, J., & Hewett, J. (1991). Adjustment to spinal cord injury: Stage theory revisited. *Paraplegia, 29,* 125–130.

Bulman, R. J., & Wortman, C. B. (1977). Attributions of blame and coping in the "real world": Severe accident victims react to their lot. *Journal of Personality and Social Psychology, 35,* 351–363.

Carlson, C. E. (1979). Conceptual style and life satisfaction following spinal cord injury. *Archives of Physical Medicine and Rehabilitation, 60,* 346–352.

Clay, D. L., Hagglund, K. J., Frank, R. G., Elliott, T. R., & Chaney, J. M. (1995). Enhancing the accuracy of depression diagnosis in patients with spinal cord injury using Bayesian analysis. *Rehabilitation Psychology, 40,* 171–180.

Cook, D. W. (1976). Psychological aspects of spinal cord injury. *Rehabilitation Counseling Bulletin, 19,* 535–543.

Cook, D. W. (1979). Psychological adjustment to spinal cord injury: Incidence of denial, depression, and anxiety. *Rehabilitation Psychology, 26,* 97–104.

Craig, A. R., Hancock, K. M., & Dickson, H. G. (1994a). A longitudinal investigation into anxiety and depression in the first 2 years following a spinal cord injury. *Paraplegia, 32,* 675–679.

Craig, A. R., Hancock, K. M., & Dickson, H. G. (1994b). Spinal cord injury: A search for determinants of depression two years after the event. *British Journal of Clinical Psychology, 33,* 221–230.

Craig, A. R., Hancock, K. M., Dickson, H., Martin, J., & Chang, E. (1990). Psychological consequences of spinal injury: A review of the literature. *Australian and New Zealand Journal of Psychiatry, 24,* 418–425.

Crewe, N. M., & Krause, J. S. (1990). An eleven-year follow-up of adjustment to spinal cord injury. *Rehabilitation Psychology, 35,* 205–210.

Crisp, R. (1992). The long-term adjustment of 60 persons with spinal cord injury. *Australian Psychologist, 27,* 43–47.

Cushman, L. A., & Dijkers, M. (1990). Depressed mood in spinal cord injured patients: Staff perceptions and patient realities. *Archives of Physical Medicine and Rehabilitation, 71,* 191–196.

DeVivo, M. J., Black, K. J., Scott-Richards, J., & Stover, S. L. (1991). Suicide following spinal cord injury. *Paraplegia, 29,* 620–629.

Dinardo, Q. E. (1971). *Psychological adjustment to spinal cord injury.* Unpublished doctoral dissertation, University of Houston, Houston, TX.

Donovan, W. H. (1981). Spinal cord injury. In W. C. Stolov & M. R. Clowers (Eds.), *Handbook of severe disability* (pp. 65–82). Washington, DC: U. S. Department of Education.

Dunn, M. E. (1975). Psychological intervention in a spinal cord injury center: An introduction. *Rehabilitation Psychology, 22,* 165–178.

Elliott, T. R., Herrick, S. M., Witty, T. E., Godshall, F., & Spruell, M. (1992). Social support and depression following spinal cord injury. *Rehabilitation Psychology, 37,* 37–48.

Ernst, F. A. (1987). Contrasting perceptions of distress by research personnel and their spinal cord injured subjects. *American Journal of Physical Medicine, 66,* 182–193.

Frank, R. G., & Elliott, T. R. (1989). Spinal cord injury and health locus of control beliefs. *Paraplegia, 27,* 250–256.

Frank, R. G., Elliott, T. R., Buckelew, S. P., & Haut, A. E. (1988). Age as a factor in response to spinal cord injury. *American Journal of Physical Medicine and Rehabilitation, 67,* 128–131.

Frank, R. G., Elliott, T. R., Corcoran, J. R., & Wonderlich, S. A. (1987). Depression after spinal cord injury: Is it necessary? *Clinical Psychology Review, 7,* 611–630.

Frank, R. G., Umlauf, R. L., Wonderlich, S. A., Askanazi, G. S., Buckelew, S. P., & Elliott, T. R. (1987). Differences in coping styles among persons with spinal cord injury: A cluster analytic approach. *Journal of Consulting and Clinical Psychology, 55,* 727–731.

Frank, R. G., VanValin, P. H., & Elliott, T. R. (1987). Adjustment to spinal cord injury: A review of empirical and nonempirical studies. *Journal of Rehabilitation, 53,* 43–48.

Fullerton, D. T., Harvey, R. E., Klein, M. H., & Howell, T. (1981). Psychiatric disorders in patients with spinal cord injuries. *Archives of General Psychiatry, 38,* 1369–1371.

Green, B. C., Pratt, C. C., & Grigsby, T. E. (1984). Self-concept among persons with long-term spinal cord injury. *Archives of Physical Medicine and Rehabilitation, 65,* 751–754.

Gunther, M. (1969). Emotional aspects. In R. Reuge (Ed.), *Spinal cord injuries.* Springfield, IL: C C Thomas.

Hancock, K. M., Craig, A. R., Dickson, H. G., Chang, E., & Martin, J. (1993). Anxiety and depression over the first year of spinal cord injury: A longitudinal study. *Paraplegia, 31,* 349–357.

Hanson, S., Buckelew, S. P., Hewett, J., & O'Neal, G. (1993). The relationship between coping and adjustment after spinal cord injury: A 5-year follow-up study. *Rehabilitation Psychology, 38,* 41–52.

Harris, P., Patel, S. S., Greer, W., & Naughton, J. A. (1973). Psychological and social reactions to acute spinal paralysis. *Paraplegia, 11,* 132–136.

Heinemann, A. W., Bulka, M., & Smetak, S. (1988). Attributions and disability acceptance following traumatic injury: A replication and extension. *Rehabilitation Psychology, 33,* 195–205.

Hohmann, G. W. (1975). Psychological aspects of treatment and rehabilitation of the spinal cord injured person. *Clinical Orthopedics, 112,* 81–88.

Howell, T., Fullerton, D. T., Harvey, R. F., & Klein, M. (1981). Depression in spinal cord injured patients. *Paraplegia, 19,* 284–288.

Hu, S. S., & Cressy, J. M. (1992). Paraplegia and quadriplegia. In M. G. Brodwin, F. Tellez, & S. K. Brodwin (Eds.), *Medical, psychosocial and vocational aspects of disability* (pp. 369–391). Athens, GA: Elliott & Fitzpatrick.

Judd, F. K., Brown, D. J., & Burrows, G. D. (1991). Depression, disease and disability: Application to patients with traumatic spinal cord injury. *Paraplegia, 29,* 91–96.

Judd, F. K., Burrows, G. D., & Brown, D. J. (1986). Depression following acute spinal cord injury. *Paraplegia, 24,* 358–363.

Judd, F. K., Stone, J., Webber, J. E., Brown, D. J., & Burrows, G. D. (1989). Depression following spinal cord injury: A prospective in-patient study. *British Journal of Psychiatry, 154,* 668–671.

Kerr, W. G., & Thompson, M. A. (1972). Acceptance of disability of sudden onset in paraplegia. *Paraplegia, 10*, 94–102.

Krause, J. S. (1992). Adjustment to life after spinal cord injury: A comparison among three participant groups based on employment status. *Rehabilitation Counseling Bulletin, 35*, 218–229.

Krause, J. S., & Crewe, N. M. (1991). Chronologic age, time since injury, and time of measurement: Effect on adjustment after spinal cord injury. *Archives of Physical Medicine and Rehabilitation, 72*, 91–100.

Krause, J. S., & Dawis, R. V. (1992). Prediction of life satisfaction after spinal cord injury: A four-year longitudinal approach. *Rehabilitation Psychology, 37*, 49–59.

Lawson, N. C. (1978). Significant events in the rehabilitation process: The spinal cord patient's point of view. *Archives of Physical Medicine and Rehabilitation, 59*, 573–579.

Lundqvist, C., Siosteen, A., Blomstrand, C., Lind, B., & Sullivan, M. (1991). Spinal cord injuries: Clinical, functional, and emotional status. *Spine, 16*, 78–83.

MacDonald, M. R., Nielson, W. R., & Cameron, M. G. (1987). Depression and activity patterns of spinal cord injured persons living in the community. *Archives of Physical Medicine and Rehabilitation, 68*, 339–343.

Malec, J., & Neimeyer, R. (1983). Psychologic prediction of duration of inpatient spinal cord injury rehabilitation and performance of self-care. *Archives of Physical Medicine and Rehabilitation, 64*, 359–363.

Mazzulla, J. R. (1984). The relationship between locus of control expectancy and acceptance of acquired traumatic spinal cord injury. *American Archives of Rehabilitation Therapy, 10*, 10–13.

McDaniel, J. W. (1976). *Physical disability and human behavior* (2nd ed.). New York: Pergamon Press.

Nestoros, J. N., Demers-Desrosiers, L. A., & Dalicandro, L. A. (1982). Levels of anxiety and depression in spinal cord-injured patients. *Psychosomatics, 23*, 823–830.

Nickerson, E. T. (1981). Some correlates of adjustment by paraplegics. *Perceptual and Motor Skills, 32*, 11–23.

Nielson, W. R., & MacDonald, M. R. (1988). Attributions of blame and coping following spinal cord injury: Is self-blame adaptive? *Journal of Social and Clinical Psychology, 7*, 163–175.

Nieves, C. C., Charter, R. A., & Aspinall, M. J. (1991). Relationship between effective coping and perceived quality of life in spinal cord injured patients. *Rehabilitation Nursing, 16*, 129–132.

Peter, A. R. (1975). Psychosocial aspects of spinal cord injury. *Maryland State Medical Journal, 24*, 65–69.

Richards, J. S. (1986). Psychologic adjustment to spinal cord injury during first postdischarge year. *Archives of Physical Medicine and Rehabilitation, 67*, 362–365.

Rigoni, H. C. (1977). Psychological coping in the patient with spinal cord injury. In D. P. Pierce & V. H. Nickel (Eds.), *The total care of spinal cord injuries* (pp. 229–307). Boston: Little, Brown.

Rintala, D. H., Young, M. E., Hart, K. A., Clearman, R. R., & Fuhrer, M. J. (1992). Social support and the well-being of persons with spinal cord injury living in the community. *Rehabilitation Psychology, 37*, 155–163.

Roberts, A. H. (1972). Spinal cord injury: Some psychological considerations. *Minnesota Medicine, 55*, 1115–1117.

Rodevich, M. A., & Wanlass, R. L. (1995). The moderating effect of spinal cord injury on MMPI-2 profiles: A clinically derived T-score correction procedure. *Rehabilitation Psychology, 40*, 181–190.

Rosenstiel, A. K., & Roth, S. (1981). Relationship between cognitive activity and adjustment in four spinal cord-injured individuals: A longitudinal investigation. *Journal of Human Stress, 7*, 35–43.

Sakinofsky, I. (1980). Depression and suicide in the disabled. In D. Bishop (Ed.), *Behavioral problems and the disabled: Assessment and management* (pp. 17–51). Baltimore: Williams & Wilkins.

Schulz, R., & Decker, S. (1985). Long-term adjustment to physical disability: The role of social support, perceived control, and self-blame. *Journal of Personality and Social Psychology, 48,* 1162–1172.

Shadish, W. R., Hickman, D., & Arrick, M. C. (1981). Psychological problems of spinal cord injury patients: Emotional distress as a function of time and locus of control. *Journal of Consulting and Clinical Psychology, 49,* 297.

Sholomskas, D. E., Steil, J. M., & Plummer, J. K. (1990). The spinal cord injured revisited: The relationship between self-blame, other-blame and coping. *Journal of Applied Social Psychology, 20,* 548–574.

Siller, J. (1969). Psychological situation of the disabled with spinal cord injuries. *Rehabilitation Literature, 30,* 290–296.

Singleton, S. M. (1985). Crisis intervention with the spinal cord injured individual. *Emotional First Aid, 2,* 29–35.

Summers, J. D., Rapoff, M. A., Varghese, G., Porter, K., & Palmer, R. E. (1991). Psychosocial factors in chronic spinal cord injury pain. *Pain, 47,* 183–189.

Sword, S., & Roberts, M. M. (1974). The spinal cord injured patient. In R. E. Hardy & J. G. Cull (Eds.), *Severe disabilities: Social and rehabilitation approaches* (pp. 173–184). Springfield, IL: C C Thomas.

Tate, D. G., Forchheimer, M., Maynard, F., Davidoff, G., & Dijkers, M. (1993). Comparing two measures of depression in spinal cord injury. *Rehabilitation Psychology, 38,* 53–61.

Tate, D. G., Kewman, D. G., & Maynard, F. (1990). The Brief Symptom Inventory: Measuring psychological distress in spinal cord injury. *Rehabilitation Psychology, 35,* 211–216.

Thompson, D. D., & Dexter, W. R. (1980). Personality characteristics of spinal cord injury patients at injury and one-year follow-up. *SCI Digest, 2,* 9–15.

Trieschmann, R. B. (Ed.). (1988). *Spinal cord injuries: Psychological, social, and vocational rehabilitation* (2nd ed.). New York: Demos.

Tucker, S. J. (1980). The psychology of spinal cord injury: Patient-staff interaction. *Rehabilitation Literature, 41,* 114–121, 160.

Van Den Bout, J., Van Son-Schoones, N., Schipper, J., & Groffen, C. (1988). Attributional cognitions, coping behavior, and self-esteem in inpatients with severe spinal cord injuries. *Journal of Clinical Psychology, 44,* 17–22.

Weller, D. J., & Miller, P. M. (1977). Emotional reactions of patient, family, and staff in acute-care period of spinal cord injury: Part I. *Social Work in Health Care, 2,* 369–377.

Woodbury, B. (1978). Psychological adjustment to spinal cord injury: A literature review, 1950–1977. *Rehabilitation Psychology, 25,* 119–134.

Woodrich, F., & Patterson, J. B. (1983). Variables related to acceptance of disability in persons with spinal cord injuries. *Journal of Rehabilitation, 49*(3), 26–30.

Wortman, C. B., & Silver, R. C. (1989). The myth of coping with loss. *Journal of Consulting and Clinical Psychology, 57,* 349–357.

Wright, B. A. (1960). *Physical disability—A psychological approach.* New York: Harper & Row.

Wright, B. A. (1983). *Physical disability—A psychosocial approach* (2nd ed.). New York: Harper & Row.

Young, J. S., Burns, P. E., Bowen, A. M., & McCutchen, R. (1987). *Spinal cord injury statistics: Experience of the regional spinal cord injury systems.* Phoenix, AZ: Good Samaritan.

CHAPTER 6

Traumatic Brain Injury

DESCRIPTION

Traumatic brain injury is defined as acquired damage to the brain that results when the head is hit, strikes a stationary object, or is shaken violently (Noble, Conley, Laski, & Noble, 1990). Specifically excluded from the definition of traumatic brain injury is brain injury due to prenatal and perinatal factors (eg, genetic abnormalities, infections, birth trauma), degenerative diseases (eg, diabetes, Alzheimer's disease), infectious diseases, tumors, and stroke. Related terms include closed head injury, nonpenetrating head injury, and blunt head trauma.

Traumatic brain injury is the number one killer of people under the age of 34 years in the United States, and one of the leading causes of death and disability among children and adolescents (Martin, 1988; National Head Injury Foundation, nd; Worthington, 1989). Traumatic brain injury occurs most frequently between 15 and 24 years of age (Livingston & McCabe, 1990), with males four times more likely to sustain traumatic brain injury than females, primarily the result of motor vehicle (particularly motorcycle) accidents. Of the nearly 500,000 persons who sustain traumatic brain injury each year (Interagency Head Injury Task Force, 1989), approximately 95% survive due to aggressive treatment and sophisticated medical technology (Burke, 1988). The impact of traumatic brain injury on the individual can range from mild physical disability to a pervasive set of physical, behavioral, and cognitive deficits that severely affect functioning throughout the individual's lifetime.

Although comprehensive rehabilitation strategies have been proposed (Burke, 1988; Prigatano & others, 1986), more than 75% of the survivors of traumatic brain injury do not receive specialized rehabilitation (Trauma, 1989). It is estimated that the cost of lifelong treatment for an individual with traumatic brain injury may exceed $4.5 million. The cost of traumatic brain injury to society each year was estimated recently (Noble et al., 1990) to approach a staggering $5 billion for medical intervention, rehabilitation, residential care, and lost earnings and may be several times that amount if consideration is given to the costs incurred by family, friends, and neighbors.

PSYCHOSOCIAL ADAPTATION TO TRAUMATIC BRAIN INJURY

Psychosocial adaptation to the internal and external changes brought on by a traumatic physical injury requires on the part of the individual accurate perception of reality, flexibility in thinking, cognitive adjustment of self-image, awareness of situational demands, and adequate judgment (Florian, Katz, & Lahov, 1991). But it is precisely these traits that are most affected when the physical injury is to the brain. The emotional difficulties, psychological reactions, and personality changes that accompany the traumatic brain injury are the result of a complex interplay of neurological changes, premorbid behavior patterns, and alterations of social supports (Prigatano & others, 1986; Tellier, Adams, Walker, & Rourke, 1990; Virkkunen, Nuutila, & Huusko, 1976). It has been argued (Armstrong, 1991; Brooks, 1988; Lezak & O'Brien, 1988; Lishman, 1973; McClelland, 1988; Prigatano, 1986; Slagle, 1990) that these psychosocial consequences may be more handicapping than the residual cognitive and physical disabilities, especially for those with a mild head injury (Merskey & Woodforde, 1972; O'Shaughessy, Fowler, & Reid, 1984), and that the determination of psychosocial needs must precede the prescription of an appropriate, long-term rehabilitation plan.

Adaptation to traumatic brain injury has been a concern of researchers at least since the pioneering work of Strauss and Savitsky, who coined the term postconcussional syndrome in 1934 (Lidvall, Linderoth, & Norlin, 1974). One of the earliest groups of persons with traumatic brain injury to be systematically studied was that of persons who survived head wounds during World War II (Goldstein, 1942) and who have been followed periodically since then (Lishman, 1968; Tellier et al., 1990; Virkkunen et al., 1976). Veterans of the Vietnam War who sustained head wounds have recently been added to this study population (Black, 1974).

One problem in meeting the rehabilitation needs of persons with traumatic brain injury is significant gaps in the corpus of knowledge concerning psychosocial adaptation (Armstrong, 1991; Brooks, 1988; Kaplan, 1988). Research scientists are still in the process of elucidating the research problems, defining the relevant variables, exploring alternative research designs, developing psychometrically sound instruments, and selecting appropriate statistical analysis procedures. Most studies of the psychosocial reactions of persons with a traumatic

brain injury have relied on anecdotal and retrospective data derived from interviews and clinical case reports, relatives' reports of individuals' posttrauma
behavior change, or individuals' self-reports using behavioral or symptom checklists of dubious psychometric quality (Bergland & Thomas, 1991; Brooks,
Campsie, Symington, Beattie, & McKinlay, 1987; Caplan, Gibson, & Weiss,
1984; Dikmen, McLean, & Tempkin, 1986; Dodwell, 1988; Elsass & Kinsella,
1987; Fletcher, Ewing-Cobbs, Miner, Levin, & Eisenberg, 1990; Karpman,
Wolfe, & Vargo, 1986; Mahon & Elger, 1989; Newton & Johnson, 1985; Oddy,
Humphrey, & Uttley, 1978). Concerns over methodological weaknesses of these
studies limit the generalizability of their findings (Dicker, 1989; McKinlay &
Brooks, 1984). Other investigators (Black, 1974; Bornstein, Miller, & Van
Schoor, 1989; Bornstein, Miller, & van Schoor, 1988; Dikmen & Reitan, 1977;
Fordyce & Roueche, 1986; Klonoff, Costa, & Snow, 1986) have attempted to
construct traumatic brain injury personality profiles using data from clinical
instruments such as the Minnesota Multiphasic Personality Inventory, but no
clear and consistent profile has yet emerged.

Given the methodological weaknesses in this domain of research, the results of
more recent investigations do shed light on the psychosocial reactions manifest
by persons with a traumatic brain injury. Although some investigators (Lezak,
1986; Martin, 1988) have referred to "the shock of" traumatic brain injury for the
family, no research was found that operationalized shock as a psychosocial reaction and used it as the dependent variable in a study with persons with a traumatic
brain injury. Several investigations have shown an increased incidence of anxiety
as a clinical trait (Askenasy & Rahmani, 1988; Bornstein et al., 1988; Dikmen &
Reitan, 1977; Fordyce, Roueche, & Prigatano, 1983; Levin & Grossman, 1978;
McLean, Dikmen, & Temkin, 1993) but have been unable to demonstrate a clear
relationship to neurological disorder as measured by variables such as age at time
of injury, chronicity, lesion site, length of coma, or duration of posttraumatic
amnesia. Tyerman and Humphrey (1984) questioned a sample of 25 persons with
a traumatic brain injury 2 to 15 months postinjury and found that 44% reported
feeling anxious. Kay (1986) has argued that anxiety should be particularly acute
in those with a minor injury (ie, one that is essentially transparent to the individual) because disruptions to the predictability and order of life are unexpected and
inexplicable. The inability to accomplish for no apparent reason what were previously facile tasks in everyday life leads to profound self-doubt, worry, and anxiety when confronting new situations. Data to support this assertion are at present
unavailable.

Denial of neurological deficits has been reported to be common in individuals
with a traumatic brain injury, typically persisting for many years posttrauma
(Deaton, 1986; Kay, 1986; Prigatano, 1986). Although denial may have some
psychological utility as a defense mechanism (Florian et al., 1991), with specific

behaviors motivated by a need to keep cognitive, perceptual, and motor deficits out of awareness, it is thought to have an organic basis manifest as failure or inability to self-monitor, especially in those individuals with damage to the nondominant hemisphere (Armstrong, 1991).

Depression in persons with a traumatic brain injury is typically observed as self-reported feelings of helplessness, immobility, lethargy, listlessness, lack of motivation, and lack of initiative, as well as withdrawal from social situations and refusal to participate in rehabilitation programs (Levin & Grossman, 1978). More than 60% of Tyerman and Humphrey's (1984) sample of persons with a traumatic brain injury reported feeling depressed. Levin, Grossman, Rose, & Teasdale (1979) reported that the characteristics of anxiety and depression, as measured by the Brief Psychiatric Rating Scale, were present in 25% of a sample of 27 individuals with a severe traumatic brain injury. Fedoroff et al. (1991) collected psychiatric interview data from 66 persons with a traumatic brain injury who were consecutively admitted to a trauma center and discovered that 29% met DSM—III criteria for the diagnosis of major depressive mood, and an additional 3% met the diagnostic criteria for minor depressive mood (dysthymia). Garske and Thomas (1992) found that 42% of their sample of 47 persons with a traumatic brain injury experienced mild to moderate depression, as measured by the Beck Depression Inventory, and 13% experienced moderate to severe depression. Moreover, they found a significant negative correlation between depression and self-esteem.

Some researchers (Kay, 1986; Kumar & Finley, 1988; Merskey & Woodforde, 1972) have argued that depression is a natural consequence of the individual's appreciation of personal losses and repeated failures with tasks that were successfully accomplished previously. Others (Jeste, Lohr, & Goodwin, 1988; O'Shanick, 1986) have speculated, however, that depression may be biologically mediated by changes in amines and neuroreceptors consequent to the injury, particularly in individuals with lesions to the temporal and frontal lobes. As yet the data needed to resolve this controversy are unavailable.

The reaction of internalized anger should be most evident in persons with a traumatic brain injury who realize their disability is a chronic condition (Levin & Grossman, 1978; Lezak, 1978) and who are the victims of an injury for which they are at fault (eg, a failed suicide attempt). The data on the occurrence of this psychosocial reaction are minimal at present (Bergland & Thomas, 1991; Elsass & Kinsella, 1987; McLean et al., 1993) and rely exclusively on the reports of relatives, self-reports of individuals with traumatic brain injuries, or clinical case record reviews. For example, nearly 36% of Tyerman and Humphrey's (1984) sample of persons with a traumatic brain injury reported feelings of anger. Reports of increased behavioral disinhibition, irritability, aggressiveness, affective instability, impulsivity, and sexual aggression among persons with a traumatic brain injury are common (Bergland & Thomas, 1991; Bornstein, Miller, & van Schoor, 1989). McLean et al. (1993) found that 28% of their sample of 102 persons with a traumatic brain injury reported feelings of anger and 45% reported feelings of increased irritability.

Research suggests that minor traumatic brain injury may account for a disproportionate number of cases of what is called episodic dyscontrol syndrome (Elliott, 1984). Externalized hostility should be particularly evident with increasing chronicity (Brooks, 1988), especially when others are at fault for the individual's injury (eg, a pedestrian victim of a drunk driver). The proportion of a person's hostile or aggressive behavior that is attributable to neurochemical changes following the organic injury and the proportion that is attributable to psychosocial reactions as the individual attempts to cope with the loss of function and transformation of preinjury status cannot be determined from the existing literature (Lishman, 1968; Slagle, 1990).

Prigatano and colleagues (Fordyce & Roueche, 1986; Prigatano & Fordyce, 1986) argued that differences between the self-appraisal of disability by persons with a traumatic brain injury—what they term "one of the most highly integrated of all brain functions"—and the appraisals of relatives and of rehabilitation personnel may lead to family conflict, low level of participation in rehabilitation programs, and poor vocational outcome. To investigate self-appraisal of disability, Fordyce and Roueche (1986) collected data from 28 persons with a traumatic brain injury 3 to 28 months posttrauma using the Patient Competency Rating Scale (Roueche & Fordyce, 1983). This scale asks the individual to judge his or her competence to perform a variety of everyday activities (eg, preparing meals), instances of emotional control (eg, handling arguments with people), and instances of social reactions (eg, starting conversations in a group). A second form of the Patient Competency Rating Scale, with the same items but different pronouns, was administered to the participant's relatives and to rehabilitation personnel. Participant, staff, and relative competency ratings were compared, and differences in perspective were related to vocational outcomes and to Minnesota Multiphasic Personality Inventory profiles. As predicted, participants whose perspectives of their disability most closely matched those of relatives and staff experienced the most reduction in emotional distress and tended to make the most progress toward vocational success.

Hendryx (1989) collected data from 20 adults with a traumatic brain injury 1 to 7.5 years postinjury who were on a Veterans Administration hospital outpatient caseload and from 13 family members of these individuals. A specially designed questionnaire asked respondents to rate their perception of their own or their relative's changes from pretrauma to posttrauma in three areas: physical (eg, dizziness, headaches), emotional (eg, anxiety, impatience, depression), and cognitive (eg, memory or concentration loss). A control group of 20 adult staff volunteers also responded to the questionnaire reporting their current self-perceptions. As expected, the persons with a traumatic brain injury perceived themselves as worse in all three areas posttrauma, and their self-perceptions were significantly worse than those of the control respondents. Of interest was the finding that the relatives perceived the individuals with a traumatic brain injury as manifesting more emotional than cognitive or physical problems posttrauma, whereas the individuals with a traumatic brain injury perceived themselves as experiencing more cognitive and physical problems than emotional problems. The authors speculated that this may reflect the individuals' denial or lack of awareness in support of the view of Prigatano and Fordyce (1986). It should be noted, however, that the individuals with a traumatic brain injury questioned in Hendryx's (1989) study all had a good prognosis for recovery and, consequently, were more articulate, aware, and perceptive.

The results of a recent study by Godfrey, Partridge, and Knight (1993) suggest that persons with a traumatic brain injury may experience a condition that the authors referred to as posttraumatic insight disorder. Data were obtained from a nonrandom sample of 24 persons with a traumatic brain injury and from a nonrandom sample of 27 persons with an orthopaedic impairment on a variety of measures of neurological functioning, behavior, social skills, depression, anxiety, and self-esteem. Data were collected at four times—immediately postinjury, and six months, one year, and two to three years postinjury. Persons with a traumatic brain injury were significantly more impaired in all areas at all four times than were those persons with an orthopaedic impairment. But interview data also revealed that the persons with a traumatic brain injury underreported their social, behavioral, and cognitive problems and overestimated their abilities in these areas. Accuracy of insight (self-appraisal) increased with increasing time postinjury, but so too did the risk of emotional problems. The authors suggested that the inability of the persons with a traumatic brain injury to accurately appraise the extent and severity of their impairments and consequent psychosocial risk contributed to problems of maladaptation by delaying or reducing their participation in rehabilitation programs.

Findings of follow-up studies using a variety of instruments and informants reveal that seldom do persons with a traumatic brain injury attain satisfactory adaptation to their disability. For example, the results of a pair of studies in Toronto (Klonoff et al., 1986; Klonoff, Snow, & Costa, 1986) revealed significant residual psychosocial distress in a sample of 78 persons two to four years posttrauma. Merskey and Woodforde (1972) noted the persistence of symptoms of psychiatric disturbance in a review of the case records of 27 persons followed two to five years postinjury, particularly a blend of protracted depression and anxiety. Rivara and colleagues (Rivara et al., 1993; Rivara et al., 1994) found an increasing decline in social and psychological functioning in a sample of 94 children with a traumatic brain injury who were studied at three weeks, three months, and one year postinjury. Brooks et al. (1987), based on behavioral checklist data collected over seven years from participants and their relatives, noted that psychosocial problems were pervasive and persisted unabated. Brown and Nell's (1992) prospective longitudinal study of persons in South Africa with diffuse traumatic brain injury revealed that problems of psychosocial adaptation worsened over time. Data from a variety of measures (eg, Profile of Mood States, Bipolar Personality Adjective Scale) showed that over time the individuals became less happy, less energetic, ruder, more emotionally labile, less attentive, more tense and irritable, more forgetful, more aggressive, and more depressed. In a study of a nonrandom sample of 25 persons with a traumatic brain injury using the Portland Adaptability Inventory at one, three, and five years postinjury, Kaplan (1993) found that the individuals showed an overall trend toward increasing psychosocial adaptation, but that mild to moderate social, vocational, and emotional problems persisted. A total of 40% reported mild to moderate depression, 48% reported mild disruptions in their social relationships, and only 50% returned to school or work. Of those who were working competitively, 25% were working in jobs considerably below their premorbid level.

Thomsen's (1984) study of Danish persons 10 to 15 years posttrauma found that two thirds of 40 respondents reported permanent changes in emotionality, changes that were most pronounced in those who were most severely injured. A follow-up study 20 years postinjury (Thomsen, 1992) of 31 individuals in the original sample revealed that none escaped lifelong psychosocial sequelae and that psychosocial adaptation was widely variable. The most significant changes occurred in the areas of aggressiveness, violence, and inappropriate sexual behavior. Although 10 individuals had marked personality disorders, 7 were rated by the author as making "rather good" adjustment to their impairment. Thomsen's observations are consistent with those reported in a pair of investigations by Oddy and colleagues (Oddy, Coughlan, Tyerman, & Jenkins, 1985; Weddell, Oddy, & Jenkins, 1980) in which 44 young adults with severe head injuries were first observed at two years posttrauma and then 33 of the original 44 persons were observed at seven years posttrauma. Relatives reported more than 30 personality changes in their family members with traumatic brain injuries, with irritability, talkativeness, disinhibition, and childishness the most commonly reported characteristics. Significant reductions in their occupational status and social interactions at two years were noted. Results of the second evaluation revealed little change overall in neurophysical, cognitive, employment, or psychosocial status over the additional five years. Relatives continued to characterize their family members with traumatic brain injuries as childish, impatient, lacking initiative, quick to anger, and moody. These researchers concluded that the prognosis for improvement beyond two years was bleak and appeared to be limited to those who (1) were younger at the time of their injury, (2) sustained milder injuries and limited secondary disabilities, (3) found employment and a living situation in the community, and (4) maintained a social life.

Other reviewers of the follow-up literature (Bond, 1979; Brooks, 1988; Fahy, Irving, & Millac, 1967) have cautioned that although the psychosocial adaptation of persons with a traumatic brain injury, as a group, apparently worsens as chronicity increases, it is not yet possible to predict behavioral difficulties in specific individuals. In fact, the presumed linear relationship may be an artifact of the retrospective longitudinal methodology used to study it. Lezak and colleagues (Lezak, 1987; Lezak & O'Brien, 1988) examined data on psychosocial functioning collected on various subsets of 42 white male volunteers with a traumatic brain injury at one-year intervals up to five years postinjury using a prospective longitudinal design. Results supported the existence of three patterns of change: (1) continuing dysfunction over time, (2) gradual and variable improvement over time, and (3) a curvilinear pattern in which gains were observed within the second half of the first year after injury (ie, decreased anxiety and depression) but then were lost in subsequent years.

In a series of prospective longitudinal investigations designed to discover which psychosocial and cognitive changes are attributable to minor head injury, Rutter, Chadwick, and colleagues (Brown, Chadwick, Shaffer, Rutter, & Traub, 1981; Chadwick, Rutter, Groun, Shaffer, & Traub, 1981; Chadwick, Rutter, Shaffer, & Shrout, 1981; Rutter, Chadwick, Shaffer, & Brown, 1980) identified three groups of children: (1) 29 with mild injury (defined as posttraumatic amnesia duration between one hour and seven days), (2) 31 with severe injury (defined as posttraumatic amnesia duration longer than seven days), and (3) 28 controls matched for age and sex who were admitted to the same hospital for minor trauma other than traumatic brain injury (eg, fractures). Data were obtained from a battery of neuropsychological and behavioral instruments as well as from parent and teacher interviews at the time of admission, and then four months, one year, and two years postdischarge. Results revealed that both the frequency and intensity of cognitive and psychosocial difficulties were linked to the severity of the initial injury but did not vary with sex or age at time of injury. Regrettably developmental trends in these data were not analyzed.

The psychosocial adaptation of individuals with traumatic brain injury has been related to adaptation of individuals with a spinal cord injury (Caplan et al., 1984; Richards et al., 1991; Stambrook et al., 1991) and individuals with epilepsy (Beran & Flanagan, 1987). In a study involving 31 persons with a spinal cord injury and 15 persons with traumatic brain injury who responded to a mailed questionnaire asking them to recall stressful life events six months before and six months after their trauma (Caplan et al., 1984), it was discovered that both groups reported significant psychosocial alterations in their lives. Richards et al.

(1991) reported no significant differences in psychosocial adaptation when analyzing data from a battery of instruments. including the Sickness Impact Profile and the Minnesota Multiphasic Personality Inventory, from a set of 21 individuals with a spinal cord injury who were also rated by at least two of three neuropsychologists as manifesting traumatic brain injury and a set of 21 individuals with a spinal cord injury with no apparent traumatic brain injury and equivalent in age, education, and neurological disorder. It was noted, however, that the raters were unanimous only 29% of the time in their classification of individuals into the two categories.

In comparison, Stambrook et al. (1991) found that 17 individuals with a severe traumatic brain injury experienced greater overall psychosocial distress, depression, social dysfunction, and anxiety than did 31 individuals with a moderate traumatic brain injury, and both of these groups were at significantly more risk for psychosocial maladaptation than was a comparison group of 24 persons with a spinal cord injury who were matched for age, sex, income, and chronicity of impairment. The results of this investigation could not be widely generalized, however, as the persons in all three groups were married and significantly older (mean age 45 years) than typical persons with a traumatic brain injury or with a spinal cord injury. Beran and Flanagan (1987) reported a higher incidence of psychosocial maladaptation among their sample of Australian persons with a traumatic brain injury than among a sample of individuals with idiopathic epilepsy and attributed this difference to specific brain pathology instead of environmental or experiential factors.

The generalizability of the results of comparative investigations may be limited by sampling bias (ie, studying nonrandom samples of individuals who have sought specialized treatment or who have been hospitalized for psychiatric complaints), small sample sizes, confounding of sample characteristics (ie, the presence of psychiatric history in members of research samples obtained from outpatient clinics or of characteristics suggestive of maladaptation in the families of sample members), and instrumentation weaknesses (ie, using a nonvalidated self-report measure or an instrument validated for populations other than persons with traumatic brain injury). Additional comparative investigations using a prospective longitudinal design, sound sampling, and valid instruments to operationalize adaptation to disability are warranted.

CHARACTERISTICS ASSOCIATED WITH ADAPTATION TO TRAUMATIC BRAIN INJURY

Several investigators have analyzed data on sociodemographic (age, sex, race, marital status, socioeconomic status) and injury-related variables (eg, length of coma, posttraumatic amnesia duration, site of brain lesion, associated physical and sensory disorders, chronicity) in an effort to determine their relationship to psychosocial reactions. Kinsella, Moran, Ford, & Ponsford (1988) designed a study to investigate whether individuals who experience significant sensory or motor disorders as a result of their traumatic brain injury are most likely to manifest psychosocial distress. They found that the best predictor of adaptation to disability, as measured by the General Health Questionnaire, among 30 persons with a traumatic brain injury, was a rating of physical disability alone among a set of variables including age, posttraumatic amnesia duration, and chronicity. In a subsequent study (Kinsella, Ford, & Moran, 1989), these researchers found that a measure of motor and sensory disability was the only significant predictor of adaptation among a set of variables including chronicity, posttraumatic amnesia duration, and employment status. These results are similar to the findings of a study in which a composite index of motor dysfunction was found to be the best predictor of quality of life as measured by the Sickness Impact Profile, the Minnesota Multiphasic Personality Inventory, and self-reports of well-being and social role functioning (Klonoff, Costa, & Snow, 1986).

Although the severity of the traumatic brain injury, as measured by indices such as length of coma, posttraumatic amnesia duration, presence of a skull fracture, or onset of posttraumatic seizures, is generally thought to be related to the degree of emotional and behavioral alteration (Brooks, 1988; Chadwick, 1985; Dacey et al., 1991; Dikmen & Reitan, 1977; Kumar & Finley, 1988; Prigatano & Fordyce, 1986; Rutter, 1981), there is a notable lack of confirmatory objective evidence for this assertion. Brooks et al. (1987) found no relationship between severity of traumatic brain injury and severity of emotional symptoms when they analyzed behavioral checklist data from a sample of 134 individuals. Asarnow, Satz, and Light (1991) collected Child Behavior Check List data from the caregivers of 11 children with severe closed head injury and 120 children with mild closed head injury (severity was defined by length of coma and of posttraumatic amnesia) one to four years postinjury. They discovered no differences in subtest scores between the two groups and also found that both groups were experiencing severe behavior and emotional problems as compared to the norms for the instrument. Results similar to these were reported in studies by Bornstein et al. (1989), Garske and Thomas (1992), McLean, Dikmen, Temkin, Wyler, and Gale (1984), Rivara et al. (1994), and Thomsen (1992). These investigators found no consistent relationship between severity of injury and psychosocial functioning of persons with a traumatic brain injury.

On the other hand, results of several investigations have found a direct relationship between severity of injury and severity of emotional and behavioral problems (Brown & Nell, 1992; Levin & Grossman, 1978; McLean et al., 1993; Tate, Lulham, Broe, Strettles, & Pfaff, 1989). Oddy et al. (1978) collected data from a group of 49 individuals at the time of injury and six months posttrauma and found that disruptions in work status, leisure activities, independence, and social contacts were most pronounced among those sustaining the most severe injuries. Emotional withdrawal and affective disturbances, the predominant characteristics revealed in clinicians' ratings of 62 persons with a traumatic brain injury using the Brief Psychiatric Rating Scale, were both positively related to the severity of the injury as measured by length of coma (Levin & Grossman, 1978).

Tate et al. (1989) attempted to relate severity of head injury, as measured by the Glasgow Outcome Scale, with psychosocial disability using a protocol created specifically for this investigation to collect data from clinical records and informant interviews. From these data the researchers rated in three areas each of 87 persons with a traumatic brain injury who had been admitted to a rehabilitation hospital from three years four months to seven years nine months earlier: (1) vocational and avocational pursuits, from 1 (working) to 3 (no work, no avocational interests); (2) significant interpersonal relations, from 1 (able to form and maintain) to 3 (unable to form and maintain); and (3) independent living, from 1 (lives independently) to 3 (completely dependent). A total score of 3 was taken as indicative of good adaptation, a score from 4 to 6 was judged as substantially limited adaptation, and a score from 7 to 9 was judged as poor adaptation. Analyses of their data revealed a significant positive relationship between adaptation and severity of head injury, with 20 of the 45 individuals rated as good recovery on the Glasgow Outcome Scale rated as manifesting good adaptation, and all 16 of the individuals with a severe disability rated as manifesting poor adaptation.

The data concerning the relationship between age at time of injury and consequent psychosocial dysfunction are also equivocal (Garske & Thomas, 1992; Rutter, 1981), in large part due to confounding by variables such as location and severity of injury, premorbid personality characteristics, cognitive deficits that compromise the reliability of self-report data, and situational influences (eg, quality of medical care, emotional problems of parents that may contribute to child abuse or neglect, delay until the initiation of a rehabilitation program). There are, moreover, several different neurological processes at work that reduce the predictive validity of these data (ie, the immature brain is more susceptible to injury and consequent neurological dysfunction, but it is also more plastic and amenable to rehabilitation). For adolescents, traumatic brain injury recovery is thought to be particularly difficult due to the psychosocial turmoil of this development period (Mattsson, 1972; Worthington, 1989). Tracheotomy scars, reconstructive surgery scars, paralysis, tremors, and other physical symptoms of the traumatic brain injury are particularly difficult for adolescents to cope with as they are working through typical physical and emotional changes. The traumatic brain injury may increase their already negative self-image and feelings of insecurity. Emerging sexuality, sexual identity, and socialization with peers are increasingly important for adolescents, but traumatic brain injury may isolate the individual from crucial experiences, increasing withdrawal and heightening depression and suicidal ideation. Although the adolescent's stage of psychosexual development should be a significant determinant of the course of adaptation and the success of recovery, no empirical data are available to substantiate this contention.

Chronicity was a variable investigated by Bornstein and colleagues (Bornstein et al., 1988; Bornstein et al., 1989), who cluster analyzed Minnesota Multiphasic Personality Inventory profiles for a sample of 124 individuals with a work-related traumatic brain injury and identified four personality profiles. The clusters could not be distinguished by a set of traumatic brain injury related variables, including chronicity. A contradictory result concerning chronicity was found by Fordyce et al. (1983), who investigated the relationship of chronicity to emotional reactions in a group of 52 individuals at a rehabilitation hospital, 17 of whom were defined as acute (ie, less than six months posttrauma) and the remainder defined as chronic (ie, six months or greater posttrauma). Those in the chronic group were found to be more emotionally distressed, as measured by the Minnesota Multiphasic Personality Inventory, and were perceived as more distressed by a cohabiting relative who provided a Katz Adjustment Scale profile. This result was also found when posttraumatic amnesia duration was entered as a covariate to control for severity of injury. It is important to note, however, that sampling biases may limit the generalizability of these results. Individuals with a persistent or worsening psychosocial reaction are more likely to seek or be referred to a rehabilitation program for treatment, and no attempt was made to control for premorbid personality differences that may have contributed to the occurrence of injury in the individuals studied.

Data concerning the link between the site and extent of brain injury and the severity of psychiatric and behavioral sequelae are hard to collect and notoriously unreliable even in recent studies using the most advanced technology available, such as magnetic resonance imaging and positron emission tomographic scanning (Fedoroff et al., 1991; Rutter, 1981; Slagle, 1990). As a result, no definitive conclusions are now possible.

One finding deserving special attention was elucidated in the longitudinal investigations of the Rutter group (Brown et al., 1981; Chadwick, Rutter, Groun, et al., 1981; Chadwick, Rutter, Shaffer, et al., 1981; Rutter et al., 1980) discussed previously. Children with mild traumatic brain injuries were found to be predominantly boys of lower socioeconomic status who had manifest behavioral difficulties as reported by their parents and teachers prior to their hospital admission for traumatic brain injury. The difference in psychosocial adaptation between the children with and without mild traumatic brain injury did not increase over the two years of the study, whereas the psychosocial difficulties of the children with severe injury, who did not differ behaviorally from the control children premorbidly, were more than double those of the controls in frequency and intensity at two years postinjury. The observation that children and young adults with traumatic brain injuries may not represent the typical population has been alluded to by others (Chadwick, 1985; Craft, Shaw, & Cartlidge, 1972; Fahy et al., 1967; Fenton, McClelland, Montgomery, MacFlynn, & Rutherford, 1993; Kumar & Finley, 1988; Rutter, 1981), that is, preinjury social environment and premorbid behavior and personality characteristics of individuals who sustain traumatic brain injury might predispose them to engage in risky activities that have a high probability of resulting in head injury from accidents.

CONCLUSION

Determination of the psychosocial needs of persons with traumatic brain injuries must precede the prescription of appropriate intervention strategies designed to teach coping skills so the individual may live and work in typical community settings. Our review of the research literature in this area revealed that information concerning these needs has been derived in large part from investigators who have (1) relied almost exclusively on cross-sectional, case-control, matched designs of dubious experimental validity, (2) studied small and nonrepresentative samples, (3) differed in the selection and definition of independent variables, (4) operationalized the dependent variable with instruments of considerable diversity often without regard to standards of psychometric adequacy, and (5) analyzed data with univariate statistical procedures with negligible power to detect true differences. The verification of this clinical lore requires empirically based objective investigations of the ways that persons with traumatic brain injuries perceive, assess, and gradually assimilate various changes in body, self, and person-environment interactions. It is possible, however, to present several tentative conclusions concerning psychosocial adaptation to traumatic brain injury.

First, the emotional difficulties, psychological reactions, and personality changes that accompany a traumatic brain injury are the result of a complex interplay of changes in neurological structures, premorbid behavior patterns, and alterations of social supports. As a result, persons with a traumatic brain injury manifest extreme variability in psychosocial adaptation to their impairments. Research shows that as a group they display an increase in the clinical traits of anxiety, denial of impairment, depression, anger, and hostility. It is not possible at present to determine whether these traits are psychosocial reactions to the individual's appreciation of personal losses (ie, the inability to accomplish what were previously facile tasks in everyday life) or are biologically mediated by neurological changes consequent to the brain injury.

Second, persons with traumatic brain injuries display an apparent inability to accurately appraise the extent and severity of their impairments and consequent psychosocial risk. This characteristic has been evident in their underreporting of social, behavioral, and cognitive problems and in their overestimation of their abilities in these areas. Third, findings of follow-up studies reveal that persons with traumatic brain injuries seldom attain satisfactory adaptation to their disability. These studies note over time the persistence of symptoms of psychiatric disturbance (ie, protracted depression and anxiety); increased emotional lability, physical aggressiveness, and sexually inappropriate behavior; and declines in social and vocational functioning.

Fourth, there is a notable lack of confirmatory objective evidence for the assertions that either severity or chronicity of disability is directly related to severity of emotional and behavioral problems in persons with traumatic brain injuries. Although several investigations have documented the predicted relationships, others have found no such links. Fifth, the data concerning the relationship between age at time of injury and consequent psychosocial dysfunction are also equivocal. Our reviews of the literature in this and in other chapters concerning chronic health and neurological impairments suggest that the relationship may be curvilinear, with increased risk of psychosocial distress during the periods of adolescence and young adulthood. The traumatic brain injury may increase the negative self-image and feelings of insecurity associated with emerging sexuality, sexual identity, and peer socialization that are typical of individuals without an impairment during these developmental periods. No empirical data are available to substantiate this contention.

Finally, researchers are beginning to report the results of their study of the possible link between the site and extent of brain injury and the severity of psychiatric and behavioral sequelae using advanced scanning technology such as magnetic resonance imaging and positron emission tomography. This work is still in its infancy, and no definitive conclusions are possible at the present time.

REFERENCES

Armstrong, C. (1991). Emotional changes following brain injury: Psychological and neurological components of depression, denial, and anxiety. *Journal of Rehabilitation, 57*(2), 15–22.

Asarnow, R. F., Satz, P., & Light, R. (1991). Behavior problems and adaptive functioning in children with mild and severe closed head injury. *Journal of Pediatric Psychology, 16*, 543–555.

Askenasy, J. J. M., & Rahmani, L. (1988). Neuropsycho-social rehabilitation of head injury. *American Journal of Physical Medicine, 66*, 315–327.

Beran, R. G., & Flanagan, P. J. (1987). Psychosocial sequelae of epilepsy: The role of associated cerebral pathology. *Epilepsia, 28*, 107–110.

Bergland, M. M., & Thomas, K. R. (1991). Psychosocial issues following severe head injury in adolescence: Individual and family perceptions. *Rehabilitation Counseling Bulletin, 35*, 5–22.

Black, F. W. (1974). Use of the MMPI with patients with recent war-related head injuries. *Journal of Clinical Psychology, 30*, 571–573.

Bond, M. R. (1979). The stages of recovery from severe head injury with special reference to late outcome. *International Rehabilitation Medicine, 1*, 155–159.

Bornstein, R. A., Miller, H. B., & van Schoor, T. (1988). Emotional adjustment of compensated head injury patients. *Neurosurgery, 23*, 622–627.

Bornstein, R. A., Miller, H. B., & van Schoor, J. T. (1989). Neuropsychological deficits and emotional disturbance in head-injured patients. *Journal of Neurosurgery, 70*, 509–513.

Brooks, N. (1988). Behavioural abnormalities in head injured patients. *Scandinavian Journal of Rehabilitation Medicine Supplement, 17*, 41–46.

Brooks, N., Campsie, L., Symington, C., Beattie, A., & McKinlay, W. (1987). The effects of severe head injury on patient and relative within seven years of injury. *Journal of Head Trauma Rehabilitation, 2*(3), 1–13.

Brown, D. S. O., & Nell, V. (1992). Recovery from diffuse traumatic brain injury in Johannesburg: A concurrent prospective study. *Archives of Physical Medicine and Rehabilitation, 73*, 758–770.

Brown, G., Chadwick, O., Shaffer, D., Rutter, M., & Traub, M. (1981). A prospective study of children with head injuries: III. Psychiatric sequelae. *Psychological Medicine, 11*, 63–78.

Burke, W. H. (1988). *Head injury rehabilitation: An overview.* Houston, TX: HDI.

Caplan, B., Gibson, C. J., & Weiss, R. (1984). Stressful sequelae of disabling illness. *International Rehabilitation Medicine, 6*, 58–62.

Chadwick, O. (1985). Psychological sequelae of head injury in children. *Developmental Medicine and Child Neurology, 27*, 72–75.

Chadwick, O., Rutter, M., Groun, G., Shaffer, D., & Traub, M. (1981). A prospective study of children with head injuries: II. Cognitive sequelae. *Psychological Medicine, 11*, 49–61.

Chadwick, O., Rutter, M., Shaffer, D., & Shrout, P. E. (1981). A prospective study of children with head injuries: IV. Specific cognitive deficits. *Journal of Clinical Neuropsychology, 3*, 101–120.

Craft, A. W., Shaw, D. A., & Cartlidge, N. E. F. (1972). Head injuries in children. *British Medical Journal, 4*, 200–203.

Dacey, R., Dikmen, S., Temkin, N., McLean, A., Armsden, G., & Winn, H. R. (1991). Relative effects of brain and non-brain injuries on neuropsychological and psychosocial outcome. *Journal of Trauma, 31*, 217–222.

Deaton, A. V. (1986). Denial in the aftermath of traumatic head injury: Its manifestations, measurement, and treatment. *Rehabilitation Psychology, 31*, 231–240.

Dicker, B. G. (1989). Preinjury behavior and recovery after minor head injury: A review of the literature. *Journal of Head Trauma Rehabilitation, 4*(4), 73–81.

Dikmen, S., McLean, A., & Tempkin, N. (1986). Neuropsychological and psychosocial consequences of minor head injury. *Journal of Neurology, Neurosurgery, and Psychiatry, 49*, 1227–1232.

Dikmen, S., & Reitan, R. M. (1977). Emotional sequelae of head injury. *Annals of Neurology, 2*, 492–494.

Dodwell, D. (1988). The heterogeneity of social outcomes following head injury. *Journal of Neurology, Neurosurgery, and Psychiatry, 51*, 833–838.

Elliott, F. A. (1984). The episodic dyscontrol syndrome and aggression. *Neurologic Clinics of North America, 2*, 113–125.

Elsass, L., & Kinsella, G. (1987). Social interaction following closed head injury. *Psychological Medicine, 17*, 67–78.

Fahy, T. J., Irving, M. H., & Millac, P. (1967). Severe head injuries: A six-year follow-up. *Lancet, 2*, 475–479.

Fedoroff, J. P., Lipsey, J. R., Starkstein, S. E., Forrester, A., Price, T. R., & Robinson, R. G. (1991). Phenomenological comparisons of major depression following stroke, myocardial infarction or spinal cord lesions. *Journal of Affective Disorders, 22*, 83–89.

Fenton, G., McClelland, R., Montgomery, A., MacFlynn, G., & Rutherford, W. (1993). The postconcussional syndrome: Social antecedents and psychological sequelae. *British Journal of Psychiatry, 162*, 493–497.

Fletcher, J. M., Ewing-Cobbs, L., Miner, M. E., Levin, H. S., & Eisenberg, H. M. (1990). Behavioral changes after closed head injury in children. *Journal of Consulting and Clinical Psychology, 58*, 93–98.

Florian, V., Katz, S., & Lahov, V. (1991). Impact of traumatic brain damage on family dynamics and functioning: A review. *International Disability Studies, 13*, 150–157.

Fordyce, D. J., & Roueche, J. R. (1986). Changes in perspective of disability among patients, staff, and relatives during rehabilitation of brain injury. *Rehabilitation Psychology, 31*, 217–229.

Fordyce, D. J., Roueche, J. R., & Prigatano, G. P. (1983). Enhanced emotional reactions in chronic head trauma patients. *Journal of Neurology, Neurosurgery, and Psychiatry, 46*, 620–624.

Garske, G. G., & Thomas, K. R. (1992). Self-reported self-esteem and depression: Indexes of psychosocial adjustment following severe traumatic brain injury. *Rehabilitation Counseling Bulletin, 36*, 44–52.

Godfrey, H. P. D., Partridge, F. M., & Knight, R. G. (1993). Course of insight disorder and emotional dysfunction following closed head injury: A controlled cross-sectional follow-up study. *Journal of Clinical and Experimental Neuropsychology, 15*, 503–515.

Goldstein, K. (1942). *Aftereffects of brain injuries in war.* New York: Grune & Stratton.

Hendryx, P. M. (1989). Psychosocial changes perceived by close-head-injured adults and their families. *Archives of Physical Medicine and Rehabilitation, 70*, 526–530.

Interagency Head Injury Task Force. (1989). *Interagency Head Injury Task Force report.* Washington, DC: U. S. Department of Health and Human Services, Public Health Service.

Jeste, D. V., Lohr, J. B., & Goodwin, F. K. (1988). Neuroanatomical studies of major affective disorders: A review and suggestions for further research. *British Journal of Psychiatry, 153*, 444–459.

Kaplan, S. P. (1988). Adaptation following serious brain injury: An assessment after one year. *Journal of Applied Rehabilitation Counseling, 19*(3), 3–8.

Kaplan, S. P. (1993). Five-year tracking of psychosocial changes in people with severe traumatic brain injury. *Rehabilitation Counseling Bulletin, 36*, 151–159.

Karpman, T., Wolfe, S., & Vargo, J. W. (1986). The psychological adjustment of adult clients and their parents following closed head injury. *Journal of Applied Rehabilitation Counseling, 17*(1), 28–33.

Kay, T. (1986). *Minor head injury: An introduction for professionals.* Framingham, MA: National Head Injury Foundation.

Kinsella, G., Ford, B., & Moran, C. (1989). Survival of social relationships following head injury. *International Disability Studies, 11*, 9–14.

Kinsella, G., Moran, C., Ford, B., & Ponsford, J. (1988). Emotional disorder and its assessment within the severe head injured population. *Psychological Medicine, 18*, 57–63.

Klonoff, P. S., Costa, L. D., & Snow, W. G. (1986). Predictors and indicators of quality of life in patients with closed-head injury. *Journal of Clinical and Experimental Neuropsychology, 8,* 469–485.

Klonoff, P. S., Snow, W. G., & Costa, L. D. (1986). Quality of life in patients 2 to 4 years after closed head injury. *Neurosurgery, 19,* 735–743.

Kumar, H. V., & Finley, S. (1988). Psychological sequelae of head injury. *British Journal of Hospital Medicine, 39,* 522–527.

Levin, H. S., & Grossman, R. G. (1978). Behavioral sequelae of closed head injury. *Archives of Neurology, 35,* 720–727.

Levin, H. S., Grossman, R. G., Rose, J. E., & Teasdale, G. (1979). Long-term neuropsychological outcome of closed head injury. *Journal of Neurosurgery, 50,* 412–422.

Lezak, M. D. (1978). Living with the characterologically altered brain injured patient. *Journal of Clinical Psychiatry, 39,* 592–598.

Lezak, M. D. (1986). Psychological implications of traumatic brain injury for the patient's family. *Rehabilitation Psychology, 31,* 241–250.

Lezak, M. D. (1987). Relationship between personality disorders, social disturbance, and physical disability following traumatic brain injury. *Journal of Head Trauma Rehabilitation, 2*(1), 57–59.

Lezak, M. D., & O'Brien, K. P. (1988). Longitudinal study of emotional, social, and physical changes after traumatic brain injury. *Journal of Learning Disabilities, 21,* 456–463.

Lidvall, H. F., Linderoth, B., & Norlin, B. (1974). Causes of post-concussional syndrome. *Acta Neurologica Scandinavica, 50*(Suppl. 56), 3–141.

Lishman, W. A. (1968). Brain damage in relation to psychiatric disability after head injury. *British Journal of Psychiatry, 114,* 373–410.

Lishman, W. A. (1973). The psychiatric sequelae of head injury: A review. *Psychological Medicine, 3,* 304–318.

Livingston, M. G., & McCabe, R. J. R. (1990). Psychosocial consequences of head injury in children and adolescents: Implications for rehabilitation. *Pediatrician, 17,* 255–261.

Mahon, D., & Elger, C. (1989). Analysis of posttraumatic syndrome following a mild head injury. *Journal of Neuroscience Nursing, 21,* 382–384.

Martin, D. A. (1988). Children and adolescents with traumatic brain injury: Impact on the family. *Journal of Learning Disabilities, 21,* 464–470.

Mattsson, A. (1972). Long-term physical illness in childhood: A challenge to psychosocial adaptation. *Pediatrics, 5,* 801–811.

McClelland, R. J. (1988). Psychosocial sequelae of head injury—Anatomy of a relationship. *British Journal of Psychiatry, 153,* 141–146.

McKinlay, W. W., & Brooks, D. N. (1984). Methodological problems in assessing psychosocial recovery following severe head injury. *Journal of Clinical Neuropsychology, 6,* 87–99.

McLean, A., Dikmen, S., Temkin, N., Wyler, R., & Gale, J. L. (1984). Psychosocial functioning at 1 month after head injury. *Neurosurgery, 14,* 393–399.

McLean, A., Jr., Dikmen, S. S., & Temkin, N. R. (1993). Psychosocial recovery after head injury. *Archives of Physical Medicine and Rehabilitation, 74,* 1041–1046.

Merskey, H., & Woodforde, J. M. (1972). Psychiatric sequelae of minor head injury. *Brain, 95,* 521–528.

National Head Injury Foundation. (nd). *National Head Injury Foundation factsheet.* Southborough, MA: Author.

Newton, A., & Johnson, D. A. (1985). Social adjustment and interaction after severe head injury. *British Journal of Clinical Psychology, 24,* 225–234.

Noble, J. H., Jr., Conley, R. W., Laski, F., & Noble. M. A. (1990). Issues and problems in the treatment of traumatic brain injury. *Journal of Disability Policy Studies, 1*(2), 19–45.

O'Shanick, G. J. (1986). Neuropsychiatric complications in head injury. *Advances in Psychosomatic Medicine, 16,* 173–193.

O'Shaughnessy, E. J., Fowler, R. S., Jr., & Reid, V. (1984). Sequelae of mild closed head injuries. *Journal of Family Relations, 18,* 391–394.

Oddy, M., Coughlan, T., Tyerman, A., & Jenkins, O. (1985). Social adjustment after closed head injury: A further follow-up seven years after injury. *Journal of Neurology, Neurosurgery, and Psychiatry, 48,* 564–568.

Oddy, M., Humphrey, M., & Uttley, D. (1978). Subjective impairment and social recovery after closed head injury. *Journal of Neurology, Neurosurgery, and Psychiatry, 41,* 611–616.

Prigatano, G. P. (1986). Personality and psychosocial consequences of brain injury. In G. P. Prigatano & and others (Eds.), *Neuropsychological rehabilitation after brain injury* (pp. 29–50). Baltimore: Johns Hopkins University Press.

Prigatano, G. P., & Fordyce, D. J. (1986). Cognitive dysfunction and psychosocial adjustment after brain injury. In G. P. Prigatano & and others (Eds.), *Neuropsychological rehabilitation after brain injury* (pp. 1–17). Baltimore: Johns Hopkins University Press.

Prigatano, G. P., & others. (Eds.). (1986). *Neuropsychological rehabilitation after brain injury.* Baltimore: Johns Hopkins University Press.

Richards, J. S., Osuna, F. J., Jaworski, T. M., Novack, T. A., Leli, D. A., & Boll, T. J. (1991). The effectiveness of different methods of defining traumatic brain injury in predicting postdischarge adjustment in a spinal cord population. *Archives of Physical Medicine and Rehabilitation, 72,* 275–279.

Rivara, J. M. B., Jaffe, K. M., Fay, G. C., Polissar, N. L., Martin, K. M., Shurtleff, H. A., & Liao, S. (1993). Family functioning and injury severity as predictors of child functioning one year following traumatic brain injury. *Archives of Physical Medicine and Rehabilitation, 74,* 1047–1055.

Rivara, J. M. B., Jaffe, K. M., Polissar, N. L., Fay, G. C., Martin, K. M., Shurtleff, H. A., & Liao, S. (1994). Family functioning and children's academic performance and behavior problems in the year following traumatic brain injury. *Archives of Physical Medicine and Rehabilitation, 75,* 369–379.

Roueche, J. R., & Fordyce, D. J. (1983). Perceptions of deficits following brain injury and their impact on psychosocial adjustment. *Cognitive Rehabilitation, 1,* 4–7.

Rutter, M. (1981). Psychological sequelae of brain damage in children. *American Journal of Psychiatry, 138,* 1533–1544.

Rutter, M., Chadwick, O., Shaffer, D., & Brown, G. (1980). A prospective study of children with head injuries: I. Design and methods. *Psychological Medicine, 10,* 633–645.

Slagle, D. A. (1990). Psychiatric disorders following closed head injury: An overview of biophysical factors in their etiology and management. *International Journal of Psychiatry in Medicine, 20,* 1–35.

Stambrook, M., Moore, A. D., Peters, L. C., Zubek, E., McBeath, S., & Friesen, I. C. (1991). Head injury and spinal cord injury: Differential effects on psychosocial functioning. *Journal of Clinical and Experimental Neuropsychology, 13,* 521–530.

Tate, R. L., Lulham, J. M., Broe, G. A., Strettles, B., & Pfaff, A. (1989). Psychosocial outcome for the survivors of severe blunt head injury: The results from a consecutive series of 100 patients. *Journal of Neurology, Neurosurgery, and Psychiatry, 52*, 1128–1134.

Tellier, A., Adams, K. M., Walker, A. E., & Rourke, B. P. (1990). Long-term effects of severe penetrating head injury on psychosocial adjustment. *Journal of Consulting and Clinical Psychology, 58*, 531–537.

Thomsen, I. V. (1984). Late outcome of very severe blunt head trauma: A 10–15 year second follow up. *Journal of Neurology, Neurosurgery, and Psychiatry, 47*, 260–268.

Thomsen, I. V. (1992). Late psychosocial outcomes in severe traumatic brain injury. Preliminary results of a third follow-up study after 20 years. *Scandinavian Journal of Rehabilitation Medicine Supplement, 26*, 142–152.

Trauma of brain injury. (1989). *ASHA, 31*, 83–85.

Tyerman, A., & Humphrey, M. (1984). Changes in self-concept following severe head injury. *International Journal of Rehabilitation Research, 7*, 11–23.

Virkkunen, M., Nuutila, A., & Huusko, S. (1976). Effect of brain injury on social adaptability. *Acta Psychiatrica Scandinavica, 53*, 168–172.

Weddell, R., Oddy, M., & Jenkins, D. (1980). Social adjustment after rehabilitation: A two-year follow-up of patients with severe head injuries. *Psychological Medicine, 10*, 257–263.

Worthington, J. (1989). The impact of adolescent development on recovery from traumatic brain injury. *Rehabilitation Nursing, 14*, 118–122.

CHAPTER 7

Amputation

DESCRIPTION

Amputation refers to a loss of a portion of or an entire body part. Causes of amputation include (1) trauma related to injuries and accidents (eg, automobile accident, industrial accidents, gunshots); (2) vascular diseases or insufficiency (eg, diabetes related) that may result in the reduction or loss of blood supply to an extremity, often leading to gangrene; (3) chronic infections of the bones or joints; (4) tumors, both malignant and benign; and (5) congenital limb deformity, resulting in extensive loss of muscle strength or nerve supply (Dunham, 1978; Falvo, 1991; Williamson, Schulz, Bridges, & Behan, 1994).

There are approximately 400,000 persons with an amputation in the United States with approximately 43,000 to 50,000 new amputations performed each year (Bradway, Malone, Racy, Leal, & Poole, 1984; Frierson & Lippmann, 1987; Goldberg, 1984). Of these, approximately 90% involve a lower limb. Among persons with an amputation, the ratio of males to females is approximately 3 to 1 with over 75% of all amputations performed on persons over the age of 65 years (Goldberg, 1984; Williamson et al., 1994). Surgical amputations are typically described by the area of the loss, such as below the knee (BK), above the knee (AK), hip disarticulation (HD), below the elbow (BE), above the elbow (AE), and shoulder disarticulation (SD) (Dunham, 1978; Falvo, 1991). These amputations result in one of two functional limitations: mobility or manipulative limitations (Tyc, 1992).

Complications resulting from amputation generally involve (1) skin ulceration, (2) edema (swelling) of the stump, (3) contractures (chronic muscle contractions), (4) infections, (5) neuromas (bundles of nerve fibers) located at the stump's scar tissue and resulting in persistent pain, and (6) phantom limb pain (Falvo, 1991; Friedmann, 1981). Phantom limb pain, typically viewed as a persisting mental image of the lost limb, has been extensively researched (McDaniel, 1976; Parkes, 1972; Parkes, 1976; Sherman, Sherman, & Bruno, 1987), but a consideration of this construct is beyond the scope of the present discussion.

PSYCHOSOCIAL ADAPTATION TO AMPUTATION

The traumatic loss of a limb forces the individual to face a new reality and a new definition of his or her body and self (Kohl, 1984). The individual's sense of wholeness or intactness is likewise being lost (Kindon & Pearce, 1982). Several authors have argued that the ensuing feelings of body fragmentation result in distorted body image, lowered self-esteem, self-pity, increased social isolation, and increased dependence (Friedmann, 1981; Goldberg, 1984; Grossman, 1990). Furthermore, amputation may pose an additional psychosocial threat if the loss of a body part is viewed as symbolic of castration, punishment for sin, and even death (Block & Ventur, 1963; Fenichel, 1945; Freud, 1936; Goldberg, 1984).

Reactions of anxiety (concerns about future mutilation) and grief (varying from reactive depression to major depression) among persons with both upper and lower limb amputation have been consistently reported in the literature (Friedmann, 1981; Frierson & Lippmann, 1987; Grossman, 1990; Parkes, 1975; Pfefferbaum & Pasnau, 1976; Shukla, Sahu, Tripathi, & Gupta, 1982; Whylie, 1981). Frierson and Lippmann (1987), in a comprehensive study of 86 persons with an amputation (mean age 43 years, range 12 to 89 years), reviewed medical and psychiatric histories and interviewed both the persons with an amputation and their families during a 10-year period. These researchers reported that in this sample, major psychiatric diagnoses included grief (50%), adjustment disorders and life-circumstance problems (75%), and major depression (12%). Several persons with an amputation obtained multiple diagnoses. Among the specific symptoms noted were (1) despondency (55 to 60%), (2) anxiety (50%), (3) insomnia (40%), (4) suicidal ideation (20%), and (5) flashbacks (17%), especially early in the hospitalization process. Other experienced reactions included body image distortions, feelings of helplessness, denial (often exacerbated by phantom limb pain), anger, and guilt.

Most reactions to amputation, however, have been typically described as phases within a psychosocial process of adaptation to this traumatic event. Among the clinically observed models of adaptation to amputation, those advocated by Parkes (1972; 1975; 1976), Walters (1981), and Bradway and colleagues (Bradway et al., 1984) are most often mentioned. Based on extensive clinical observations, Parkes (1972; 1975; 1976) drew a parallel between psychosocial reactions to bereavement (eg, death of a spouse) and to amputation. He contended that these reactions could best be understood as a process of realization comprising the following phases:

- *Shock*, including a sense of numbness, was observed in about 40% to 50% of samples of persons with an amputation.
- *Denial* of affective reality that followed shock and was also observed in approximately one half of the persons with an amputation studied.
- *Anxiety* and *distress*, including separation anxiety, was observed in almost 60% of the persons with an amputation.
- *Depression* and *disorganization*, including feelings of pining for aspects of the world that was lost, tearfulness, tenseness, difficulties in concentration, social withdrawal, insomnia, and self-blame, were evident during the adaptation process in 25% to 63% of the persons with an amputation who were studied.
- *Reorganization* was conceptualized as the final adaptation phase in which the person with an amputation constructs a new view of him- or herself and the world.

Walters (1981) suggested a model of adaptation to loss of lower extremity that included these four phases: (1) *impact*, typified mainly by feelings of despair and discouragement; (2) *retreat*, upon recognition of new reality, where feelings of acute grief and anxiety are most notable; (3) *acknowledgment*, where most previous symptoms have been resolved but where some hostility and frustration, in addition to willingness to participate in rehabilitation activities, become apparent; and (4) *reconstruction*, in which the individual attempts to obtain maximum functional potential.

Finally, Bradway et al. (1984) suggested that medical and psychosocial adaptation to the loss of a limb can be divided into a preoperative phase and three postoperative phases. These four phases were described as (1) realization that the loss of the limb is imminent, including feelings of anticipated grief and concern about pain and future physical limitations; (2) early postoperative hospitalization, in which a wide range of responses is experienced, including grief, anxiety, and early acceptance; (3) in-hospital rehabilitation, in which denial (of existing reality) and even euphoric mood often prevail, but when these are unsuccessful, grief and depression may reoccur; and (4) home rehabilitation, where the individual must face the reality of the resultant disability, leading to either successful adaptation to the disability or to regression into denial and avoidance.

These and other reactions to the loss of a limb might assume different content, valence, and sequencing among children with congenital or early-life limb deficiencies because of either parental reactions of rejection or overprotection or the gradual realization of physical deviation from the norm (Friedmann, 1981; Siller, 1960). Siller (1960) studied 52 children with an amputation (27 with upper extremity and 25 with lower extremity amputation; age range $2\frac{1}{2}$ to 17 years). Following semistructured clinical interviews of the children and their parents, each participant was rated in four areas: (1) reactions to disability, (2) parental acceptance, (3) social sensitivity, and (4) general adjustment. Results indicated that avoidance reactions (eg, denial, withdrawal, depression), restitutive reactions (eg, compensation, independence), and insecurity reactions (eg, inferiority feelings, dependence) were the most frequently experienced reactions to disability among these children. Although the majority of parents appeared to accept their child's disability, others demonstrated feelings of guilt, rejection, and overprotection. Almost one half of the children experienced social sensitivity to their physical condition, and over one half of the children were rated as having obtained adequate to superior adjustment. Children with traumatic amputations showed a higher degree of feelings of inferiority and depression than children with congenital limb deformities.

Two other studies explored psychosocial adaptation among children and adolescents with an amputation. Boyle, Tebbi, Mindell, and Mettlin (1982) compared a group of youngsters who had undergone limb amputation for cancer treatment (27 adolescents and young adults ranging in age from 14 to 37 years; mean age 23 years) with a group who had sustained traumatic amputation (8 youngsters ranging in age from 16 to 22 years; mean age 19 years). Among the persons with cancer, more females than males reported experiencing social problems, although the majority of individuals (70%) reported no, or only minor, changes in social activities despite being self-conscious and having concerns about acceptance in social situations. The authors concluded that as a group, these youngsters demonstrated a high overall degree of adjustment, as measured by level of functional independence and by educational, occupational, and social achievements. These findings support earlier reports on the successful adaptation of pediatric cancer survivors (O'Malley, Foster, Koocher, & Slavin, 1980).

Additional support for the successful psychosocial adaptation of adolescents with an amputation was more recently provided by Tebbi and Mallon (1987). These researchers found that in a sample of 20 long-term survivors who had undergone amputation for cancer in their teens and early 20s, the majority made a successful adaptation on various measures of psychosocial, interpersonal, educational, and vocational domains and learned how to live successfully with their disability despite demonstrating a high degree of self-consciousness regarding impaired body image and having sexual concerns. Tyc (1992) similarly concluded from a recent review of the literature on psychosocial adaptation of children and adolescents with limb deficiencies that despite common concerns about body image, young persons with acquired limb loss do report positive psychosocial outcomes.

Researchers and clinicians have also observed feelings of anger, guilt, and other-blame among persons with an amputation. For example, Parkes (1972; 1976), Frierson and Lippmann (1987), and Monforton, Helmes, and Deathe (1993) reported feelings of anger and guilt among the individuals in these studies. These feelings were primarily evidenced through bitterness and anger toward others (often displaced toward family members and medical personnel), fate, and God.

Data obtained from empirical studies on the prevalence and severity of psychosocial reactions to traumatic amputations have generally yielded inconsistent results. Two studies were located that used Goldberg's General Health Questionnaire. In the first MacBride, Rogers, Whylie, and Freeman (1980) studied a sample of elderly inpatients with an amputation (mean age 64 years) and found that 74% of these individuals scored above 5, a score typically regarded as indicative of emotional distress requiring further psychiatric evaluation. At discharge 47% of the individuals still scored above that level. In contrast, Lindesay (1986) reported that in a sample of 35 persons with an amputation (mean age 55 years) with long-standing phantom and stump pain who underwent limb fitting, only 30% attained scores of 5 and above. In a study measuring general personality and cognitive aspects of amputation, Pinzur, Graham, and Osterman (1980) investigated personality traits (using Cattell's 26 Personality-Factor scale and the Minnesota Multiphasic Personality (MMPI) Inventory) and cognitive performance (using the WAIS, the Wechsler Memory Scale, and other tests specifically measuring mental functioning among elderly persons) of 60 men with lower extremity amputation (mean age 60 years.) Results indicated that 10% of the participants demonstrated cognitive deficits severe enough to limit their rehabilitation potential. An additional 13% of the participants demonstrated, according to the authors, "covert psychiatric illness" (p. 238).

Several studies have attempted to investigate the incidence of depression, anxiety, and other reactions among persons with amputations using symptom-specific, psychometrically sound instruments rather than general psychiatric and personality measures. The incidence of depression among persons with amputation has been reported to range from less than 10% among 55 individuals with lower limb amputations using the Inventory State of Anxiety and Depression (Stephen, 1982) to 35% among 65 individuals, most with lower limb amputation, using both the Beck Depression Inventory and DSM—III-based semistructured interviews (Kashani, Frank, Kashani, Wonderlich & Reid, 1983). Two other studies reported intermediate incidence of depression. Williamson et al. (1994) reported that 21% of their 160 older, mostly lower extremity outpatients with an amputation experienced depression, while Rybarczyk et al. (1992) found that 23% of their 89 persons with leg amputation reported depression. Finally, Frank et al. (1984), in a study comparing levels of depression between 33 younger (mean age 47 years) and 33 older (mean age 73 years) persons with amputation found that although the younger group scored somewhat higher on the Beck Depression Inventory than its older counterpart, mean scores for both groups fell below the cutoff score of 10 generally used to indicate depression. The median score of 10 for the total group, however, suggests that one half of this sample may have experienced some level of depression.

A study by Schubert, Burns, Paras, and Sioson (1992) compared rates of depression between 17 individuals postamputation (median age 63 years) and 14 individuals poststroke (median age 72 years), using the Geriatric Depression Scale, an instrument derived from Zung Depression Scale. The Geriatric Depression Scale was administered within one week of admission and again at discharge. At admission 35% of the individuals with amputation and 40% of those who sustained stroke were considered depressed (ie, obtained scale scores above 11). At discharge 12% of individuals with amputation and 20% of poststroke individuals were diagnosed as depressed, suggesting, again, no appreciable differences in frequency of depression between the two groups.

Three additional comparative studies by Weinstein (1985), Bhojak and Nathawat (1988), and Marshall, Helmes, and Deathe (1992) are worth mentioning. Weinstein (1985) compared a sample of 30 persons with lower extremity amputation (mean age 62 years) with a randomly selected group of 30 hospital visitors without a disability (mean age 54 years) on measures of assertiveness, anxiety, and personal discomfort. No differences were found between the two groups on the Rathus Assertiveness Schedule, Spielberger's State-Trait Anxiety Inventory, and the Discomfort Scale, a scale purporting to measure discomfort in interpersonal situations.

Bhojak and Nathawat (1988) compared a sample of 50 persons with a lower limb amputation selected from a rehabilitation center in India with a control group of 50 surgery patients matched on age, sex, education, and socioeconomic status. As a group the persons with an amputation scored significantly higher than their counterparts on measures of body image distortion (using Fisher's Body Image Questionnaire), hopelessness (using Beck's Hopelessness Scale), and Neuroticism (using Eysenck's Extroversion-Neuroticism-Psychoticism Inventory). Marshall et al. (1992) compared a group of 47 individuals who underwent lower extremity amputation (mean age 54 years) with a group of 47 individuals with chronic pain (mean age 41 years) using the Sickness Impact Profile and the Millon Clinical Multiaxial Inventory. Results showed that although no differences were found between the two groups on the Sickness Impact Profile total score, the persons with chronic pain scored higher than persons with an amputation on the Emotional Behavior and Social Interaction subscales. Interestingly, those individuals in the group of persons with an amputation who reported experiencing high levels of pain scored significantly higher than the low-pain group on the total Sickness Impact Profile score, with persons with chronic pain occupying an intermediate position. On the Millon Clinical Multiaxial Inventory, three scales (Anxiety, Dysthymia, and Somatoform) showed significant differences between the groups of persons with an amputation and with chronic pain. In each case the pain group reported a higher degree of symptomatology than the group of persons with an amputation. Frequency of occurrence of anxiety and dysthymia in the latter group was, however, high, reaching 40.4% and 27.7% in the two groups, respectively. Both groups (persons with an amputation and with chronic pain) also scored higher on the Sickness Impact Profile total score than a group of individuals with arthritis (Deyo, Inui, Leininger, & Overman, 1982) and general population norms.

CHARACTERISTICS ASSOCIATED WITH ADAPTATION TO AMPUTATION

Several researchers have attempted to investigate sociodemographic, disability-related, psychosocial, and environmental characteristics associated with adaptation to amputation. One of the sociodemographic variables most often explored has been age at time of amputation. Findings of age differences in psychosocial adaptation to amputation have been inconsistent. Whereas several researchers conclude that individuals who are older at the time of amputation tend to have more difficulties with social adjustment (Bradway et al., 1984; Parkes, 1975) and experience higher frequency of reactive depression (Nichols, 1971) than do younger persons, other studies have failed to replicate these findings (Rybarczyk et al., 1992; Varni, Rubenfeld, Talbot, & Setoguchi, 1989c) or have reported contradictory findings (Williamson et al., 1994).

Frank et al. (Frank et al., 1984), based on extensive testing of 66 persons with an amputation that included administration of the Symptoms Check List—90, Beck Depression Inventory, and a semistructured interview, concluded that older and younger persons with an amputation differed significantly on a number of Symptoms Check List—90 subscales, including Interpersonal Sensitivity, Depression, Anxiety, Hostility, Paranoid Ideation, Psychoticism, the Global Severity Index, and the Positive Symptom Distress Index. These results suggest that younger persons with an amputation, in general, demonstrate more psychopathology than older persons with an amputation. An unexpected interaction effect between age and time since amputation suggested that younger persons with an amputation reported more depression at a later time (following 18 months since amputation) while older persons with an amputation reported more depression at earlier time (prior to 18 months since amputation).

A few reports regarding marital status in the literature suggest that married individuals with an amputation experience fewer social adjustment difficulties than single individuals (Bradway et al., 1984; Parkes, 1975). Other sociodemographic variables that have failed to predict level of psychosocial adaptation to amputation include sex (Bradway et al., 1984; Rybarczyk et al., 1992; Siller, 1960) and socioeconomic status (Tyc, 1992). Boyle et al. (1982), however, reported poorer adjustment among lower socioeconomic status groups. Finally, stable work history among adults with an amputation has been shown to be associated with better psychosocial adjustment (Tyc, 1992).

The associations of several disability-related variables and psychosocial adaptation to amputation have been investigated. Schubert et al. (1992) reported a significant negative correlation between scores on the Barthel Functional Index (a measure of level of daily functioning) and change scores (from admission to discharge) on the Geriatric Depression Scale, suggesting that the greater the increase in functional ability, the greater the decrease in level of depression. Other studies investigating medically related variables have reported that (1) persons with a lower extremity amputation experience more social adjustment difficulties than persons with an upper extremity amputation (Bradway et al., 1984; Parkes, 1975); (2) activity restriction is a significant predictor of depression among persons with an amputation (Williamson et al., 1994); and (3) early prosthetic fitting, successful prosthetic functioning, and satisfaction with prosthesis result in more successful physical, psychological (eg, decreased depression), and vocational adjustment among persons with an amputation (Boyle et al., 1982; Bradway et al., 1984; Goldberg, 1984; Parkes, 1972). Perceived good health has also been found to be a predictor of decreased depression among persons with amputation (Rybarczyk, Nyenhuis, Nicholas, Cash, & Kaiser, 1995; Rybarczyk et al., 1992). Investigations concerning two other disability-related variables (extent of limb loss and time since amputation) reported inconclusive findings but in general failed to establish direct relationships between these variables and depression (Rybarczyk et al., 1992; Tyc, 1992; Williamson et al., 1994). More recently Rybarczyk et al. (1995) reported a significant association between time since amputation and quality of life among adults with leg amputation.

Two central psychosocial and experiential variables that have been reported to successfully predict adaptation to amputation include coping modes and social discomfort. Siller (Siller, 1960), in his study of children with an amputation, concluded that those children who were judged to be successfully adjusted, as measured on a 5-point scale of "general effectiveness of the amputee's personality in relating to personal, situational, and social aspects of the environment" (p. 111) following a semistructured interview, demonstrated more restitutive (eg, compensation, independence) and less avoiding (eg, denial, withdrawal) and aggressive responses. In a similar vein, Tyc (1992) and Varni and colleagues (Varni, Rubenfeld, Talbot, & Setoguchi, 1989b; Varni et al., 1989c) concluded that greater stress level (or the inability to cope with stress) was associated with greater degree of maladjustment among children with an amputation.

Social discomfort has been more recently investigated by Rybarczyk et al. (1992), who concluded from their study of adult and elderly individuals with lower extremity amputations that social discomfort (measured by a specifically constructed scale) is a significant predictor of depression. In their multiple regression analysis, these authors found that social discomfort significantly explained additional variance in depression over and above the variance initially explained by a set of sociodemographic and medical variables. More specifically, it was found that the three predictor variables that significantly correlated with depression (explaining a total of 36% of the variance) included high social discomfort, perceived poor health, and perceived low social support.

More recently, Rybarczyk et al. (1995) investigated the predictive power of two additional variables, namely, body image and perceived social stigma. These two predictor variables were measured by instruments specifically constructed for this investigation: the Amputation-Related Body Image Scale and the Perceived Social Stigma Scale, an instrument specifically designed for this investigation that contained items reflecting negative stereotypes about persons with disabilities. Using multiple regression analyses, the investigators discovered that in this sample of adults with leg amputation, body image independently predicted levels of depression, quality of life, and psychological adjustment and that perceived social stigma successfully predicted depression.

Finally, strong social support is the only environmental variable to be investigated that has yielded consistent association on adaptation to amputation (eg, decreased depression, positive self-esteem; Rybarczyk et al., 1995; Rybarczyk et al., 1992; Tyc, 1992; Varni, Rubenfeld, Talbot, & Setoguchi, 1989a; Varni et al., 1989b; Varni, Setoguchi, Rappaport, & Talbot, 1992; Williamson et al., 1994).

CONCLUSION

A review of the clinical literature indicates that reactions of depression (ranging from grief to clinical depression) and, to a lesser degree, anxiety often follow the traumatic experience of amputation. Moreover, it appears that these and other reactions (eg, initial shock, denial, acceptance, reorganization) may follow in a certain temporal sequencing, although no empirical investigation of these psychosocial phases has been undertaken by researchers.

The available literature on psychosocial adaptation does not provide definitive answers on short-term or long-term levels of adaptation to amputation. It appears, however, that children and adolescents often demonstrate remarkable resilience to this traumatic event (Tyc, 1992). Among adults and elderly persons with an amputation, findings are less consistent. The results of several studies have suggested the existence of emotional and cognitive distress (eg, increased depression, body image distortion) among persons with an amputation, although no clear pattern has emerged in studies that attempted to follow persons with an amputation over a period of time. The scant literature on comparative studies, using samples of other groups of persons with disabilities, does not allow us to draw definitive conclusions on the unique nature, extent, and degree of severity of emotional distress among persons with an amputation.

Finally, research on various characteristics associated with adaptation to amputation indicates that several sociodemographic, medical, psychosocial and environmental variables may be linked to poor (or positive) adaptation. Among the variables that appear to predict positive psychosocial adaptation, those receiving more consistent empirical support include (1) being married, (2) possessing higher functional ability (eg, better ambulation), (3) using successful stress-reducing coping modalities, and (4) having a supportive social network.

REFERENCES

Bhojak, M. M., & Nathawat, S. S. (1988). Body image, hopelessness, and personality dimensions in lower limb amputees. *Indian Journal of Psychiatry, 30,* 161–165.

Block, W. E., & Ventur, P. A. (1963). A study of the psychoanalytic concept of castration anxiety in symbolically castrated amputees. *Psychiatric Quarterly, 37,* 518–526.

Boyle, M., Tebbi, C. K., Mindell, E. R., & Mettlin, C. J. (1982). Adolescent adjustment to amputation. *Medical and Pediatric Oncology, 10,* 301–312.

Bradway, J. K., Malone, J. M., Racy, J., Leal, J. M., & Poole, J. (1984). Psychological adaptation to amputation: An overview. *Orthotics and Prosthetics, 38,* 46–50.

Deyo, R. A., Inui, T. S., Leininger, J., & Overman, S. (1982). Physical and psychosocial function in rheumatoid arthritis: Clinical use of a self-administered health status instrument. *Archives of Internal Medicine, 142,* 159–161.

Dunham, C. S. (1978). Amputations. In R. M. Goldenson (Ed.), *Disability and rehabilitation handbook* (pp. 219–223). New York: McGraw-Hill.

Falvo, D. R. (1991). *Medical and psychosocial aspects of chronic illness and disability.* Gaithersburg, MD: Aspen.

Fenichel, O. (1945). *The psychoanalytic theory of neuroses.* New York: W. W. Norton.

Frank, R. G., Kashani, J. H., Kashani, S. R., Wonderlich, S. A., Umlauf, R. L., & Ashkanazi, G. S. (1984). Psychological response to amputation as a function of age and time since amputation. *British Journal of Psychiatry, 144,* 493–497.

Freud, S. (1936). *The problem of anxiety.* New York: Psychoanalytic Quarterly Press.

Friedmann, L. W. (1981). Amputation. In W. C. Stolov & M. R. Clowers (Eds.), *Handbook of severe disability* (pp. 169–188). Washington, DC: U. S. Department of Education.

Frierson, R. L., & Lippmann, S. B. (1987). Psychiatric consultation for acute amputees. *Psychosomatics, 28,* 183–189.

Goldberg, R. T. (1984). New trends in the rehabilitation of lower extremity amputees. *Rehabilitation Literature, 45,* 2–11.

Grossman, E. F. (1990). The Gestalt approach to people with amputations. *Journal of Applied Rehabilitation Counseling, 21*(1), 16–19.

Kashani, J. H., Frank, R. G., Kashani, S. R., Wonderlich, S. A., & Reid, J. C. (1983). Depression among amputees. *Journal of Clinical Psychiatry, 44,* 256–258.

Kindon, D., & Pearce, T. (1982). Psychosocial assessment and management of the amputee. In S. Banerjee (Ed.), *Rehabilitation management of the amputees* (pp. 350–371). Baltimore: Williams & Wilkins.

Kohl, S. J. (1984). Emotional coping with amputation. In D. W. Krueger (Ed.), *Rehabilitation psychology: A comprehensive textbook* (pp. 273–282). Rockville, MD: Aspen.

Lindesay, J. (1986). Validity of the General Health Questionnaire (GHQ) in detecting psychiatric disturbance in amputees with phantom pain. *Journal of Psychosomatic Research, 30,* 277–281.

MacBride, A., Rogers, J., Whylie, B., & Freeman, S. J. (1980). Psychosocial factors in the rehabilitation of elderly amputees. *Psychosomatics, 21,* 258–265.

Marshall, M., Helmes, E., & Deathe, A. B. (1992). A comparison of psychosocial functioning and personality in amputee and chronic pain populations. *The Clinical Journal of Pain, 8,* 351–357.

McDaniel, J. W. (1976). *Physical disability and human behavior* (2nd ed.). New York: Pergamon Press.

Monforton, M., Helmes, E., & Deathe, A. B. (1993). Type A personality and marital intimacy in amputees. *British Journal of Medical Psychology, 66,* 275–280.

Nichols, A. J. (1971). Some problems in the rehabilitation of the severely disabled. *Proceedings of the Royal Society of Medicine, 64,* 349–353.

O'Malley, J. E., Foster, D., Koocher, G., & Slavin, L. (1980). Visible physical impairment and psychological adjustment among pediatric cancer survivors. *American Journal of Psychiatry, 137,* 94–96.

Parkes, C. M. (1972). Components of the reaction to loss of a limb, spouse or home. *Journal of Psychosomatic Research, 16,* 343–349.

Parkes, C. M. (1975). Psychosocial transitions: Comparison between reactions to loss of a limb and loss of a spouse. *British Journal of Psychiatry, 127,* 204–210.

Parkes, C. M. (1976). The psychological reaction to loss of a limb: The first year after amputation. In J. G. Howells (Ed.), *Modern perspectives in the psychiatric aspects of surgery* (pp. 515–532). New York: Brunner/Mazel.

Pfefferbaum, B., & Pasnau, R. O. (1976). Post-amputation grief. *Nursing Clinics of North America, 11,* 687–690.

Pinzur, M. S., Graham, G., & Osterman, H. (1980). Psychologic testing in amputation rehabilitation. *Clinical Orthopaedics, 229,* 236–240.

Rybarczyk, B. D., Nyenhuis, D. L., Nicholas, J. J., Cash, S. M., & Kaiser, J. (1995). Body image, perceived social stigma, and the prediction of psychosocial adjustment to leg amputation. *Rehabilitation Psychology, 40,* 95–110.

Rybarczyk, B. D., Nyenhuis, D. L., Nicholas, J. J., Schulz, R., Alioto, R. J., & Blair, C. (1992). Social discomfort and depression in a sample of adults with leg amputations. *Archives of Physical Medicine and Rehabilitation, 73,* 1169–1173.

Schubert, D. S., Burns, R., Paras, W., & Sioson, E. (1992). Decrease of depression during stroke and amputation rehabilitation. *General Hospital Psychiatry, 14,* 135–141.

Sherman, R. A., Sherman, C. J., & Bruno, G. M. (1987). Psychological factors influencing chronic phantom limb pain: An analysis of the literature. *Pain, 28*, 285–295.

Shukla, G. D., Sahu, S. C., Tripathi, R. P., & Gupta, D. K. (1982). A psychiatric study of amputees. *British Journal of Psychiatry, 141*, 50–53.

Siller, J. (1960). Psychological concomitants of amputation in children. *Child Development, 31*, 109–120.

Stephen, P. J. (1982). Psychiatric aspects of amputation. *British Journal of Psychiatry, 141*, 535–536.

Tebbi, C. K., & Mallon, J. C. (1987). Long-term psychosocial outcome among cancer amputees in adolescence and early adulthood. *Journal of Psychosocial Oncology, 6*, 69–82.

Tyc, V. L. (1992). Psychosocial adaptation of children and adolescents with limb deficiencies: A review. *Clinical Psychology Review, 12*, 275–291.

Varni, J. W., Rubenfeld, L. A., Talbot, D., & Setoguchi, Y. (1989a). Determinants of self-esteem in children with congenital/acquired limb deficiencies. *Developmental and Behavioral Pediatrics, 10*, 13–16.

Varni, J. W., Rubenfeld, L. A., Talbot, D., & Setoguchi, Y. (1989b). Family functioning, temperament, and psychological adaptation in children with congenital or acquired limb deficiencies. *Pediatrics, 84*, 323–330.

Varni, J. W., Rubenfeld, L. A., Talbot, D., & Setoguchi, Y. (1989c). Stress, social support, and depressive symptomatology with congenital/acquired limb deficiencies. *Journal of Pediatric Psychology, 14*, 515–530.

Varni, J. W., Setoguchi, Y., Rappaport, L. R., & Talbot, D. (1992). Psychological adjustment and perceived social support in children with congenital/acquired limb deficiencies. *Journal of Behavioral Medicine, 15*, 31–44.

Walters, J. (1981). Coping with a leg amputation. *American Journal of Nursing, 81*, 1349–1352.

Weinstein, C. L. (1985). Assertiveness, anxiety, and interpersonal discomfort among amputees: Implications for assertiveness training. *Archives of Physical Medicine and Rehabilitation, 66*, 687–689.

Whylie, B. (1981). Social and psychological problems of the adult amputee. In J. Kostiuk (Ed.), *Amputation, surgery and rehabilitation: The Toronto experience* (pp. 387–393). New York: Churchill Livingstone.

Williamson, G. M., Schulz, R., Bridges, M. W., & Behan, A. M. (1994). Social and psychological factors in adjustment to limb amputation. *Journal of Social Behavior and Personality, 9*, 249–268.

PART III

Psychosocial Adaptation to Disease-Related Health Disorders

Part II of this book presented reviews of the research literature on psychosocial adaptation to four traumatic, or sudden onset, disabilities: cardiovascular diseases, spinal cord injury, traumatic brain injury, and amputation. In Part III we provide reviews of the research literature on psychosocial adaptation to three disease-related health disorders: Chapter 8—cancer, Chapter 9—diabetes mellitus, and Chapter 10—rheumatoid arthritis.

These disease-related health disorders have the following aspects in common. They (1) are usually acquired later in life (with the exception of early onset diabetes mellitus), (2) are caused by a disease process of a gradual or insidious onset, (3) have a systemic effect on the body, (4) are generally progressive and result in gradual deterioration in the health of the person affected, and (5) are normally invisible. Several other features lend uniqueness to each of these disorders. These include (1) a wide range of disease-specific functional limitations that are greatly influenced by the disease duration, degree of body system involvement, and level of severity of symptoms; (2) differential degrees of lethality (eg, cancer versus rheumatoid arthritis); and (3) varying levels of complexity, extensiveness, and side effects of treatment procedures that are applied to the disease.

Each of these reviews will follow the same format as those in Part II. We begin with a brief description of the disease-related health disorder, including a synopsis of available information on incidence and prevalence, causal factors, signs and symptoms, complications, course, and prognosis. This is followed by a review of the research literature on psychosocial adaptation to the disorder, focusing on research conducted in the last 15 years. The third section of each chapter summarizes the available information on characteristics associated with psychosocial adaptation to the disorder. This section is organized into three areas: (1) sociodemographic characteristics (eg, age at time of injury or disease onset, chronicity, sex, educational level, socioeconomic status), (2) personality factors (eg, premorbid personality, ego strength, attribution of blame, perception of disability, locus of control), and (3) disease-related variables (eg, neuropathology, severity of impairment, type of treatment). If it is available, information on environmental factors (eg, degree of family or peer support, level of independence, modifiability of the work environment) that are thought to be related to psychosocial adaptation to the disorder is also included. Each chapter ends with a presentation of tentative conclusions concerning psychosocial adaptation to the disease-related health disorder derived from the findings reported in the literature reviewed.

CHAPTER 8

Cancer

DESCRIPTION

It is estimated that approximately 1 individual in 4 will, at some time in his or her life, contract cancer (Dunham, 1978). The number of new cancer cases in 1991 alone exceeded 1.1 million (American Cancer Society, 1991). Of those who were diagnosed with cancer that year, it was estimated that only 4 to 5 out of 10 would still be alive 5 years after the termination of treatment (Elmayan, 1992). Although certain types of cancer (eg, prostate, colon) peak in the period between ages 60 to 80 years, other types (eg, acute lymphoma, acute leukemia) are most prevalent in the period from infancy to 10 years of age (Freidenbergs & Kaplan, 1993). Nevertheless cancer is far more common among older than younger individuals (Healey & Zislis, 1981). Cancer also affects each sex differently. Whereas the leading type of cancer among women is breast cancer (32%), men most frequently contract prostate cancer (23%). Lung cancer, however, is the leading cause of death in both groups (Freidenbergs & Kaplan, 1993).

Cancer is not a single disease entity. There are over 100 different types of cancers or neoplastic diseases (Falvo, 1991). Still, all cancerous cellular masses comprise malignant tumors that are characterized by unregulated and uncontrolled growth and the spawning of new tumors at other sites in the body (a process known as metastasis) (Berkow, 1992; Elmayan, 1992). The known causes of cancer include (1) genetic factors, (2) environmental hazards of both chemical (eg, asbestos, coal tar) and physical agents (eg, ionizing radiation, ultraviolet radiation), and (3) social practices (eg, smoking, alcohol and tobacco consumption, diet) (Elmayan, 1992; Freidenbergs & Kaplan, 1993). Functional limitations resulting from cancer may range widely from those associated with restricted mobility, pain, fatigue, and limited endurance to those affecting communication, cognitive performance, and social relationships.

185

PSYCHOSOCIAL ADAPTATION TO CANCER

The diagnosis of cancer carries with it for the individual an immense level of anxiety. The many types of anxiety typically involve fears and concerns of loss of control, loss of independence, loss of bodily functions, loss of income, loss of privacy, family role difficulties, sexual dysfunction, mutilation, social isolation, somatic side effects, pain, unpredictable future, and death (Freidenbergs & Kaplan, 1993; Stam, Bultz, & Pittman, 1986). In addition to the often experienced feelings of anxiety, reactions to cancer also include depression, reduced self-esteem, impaired body image, guilt, denial, and anger.

Since the pioneering clinical work of Kübler-Ross (1969) on the psychosocial stages associated with dying, several models of psychosocial adaptation to life-threatening illnesses have been proposed. Francis (1969) observed that individuals faced with life-threatening illness first experienced denial of the illness or of its seriousness. Denial was found to be typically followed by anxiety (ie, feelings of nervousness and restless behavior), which in time gave way to regression (ie, dependence on others). The fourth stage observed was depression, characterized by low self-esteem and social withdrawal. Finally, realistic adaptation to the illness and its implications was achieved.

Cobb (1973) suggested that emotional response to the diagnosis of cancer follows three phases: (1) shock reaction (eg, feelings of depersonalization and disbelief), (2) short-term use of psychological defenses (eg, denial), and (3) long-term psychological patterns (eg, depression, changes in body image). Finally, Gullo, Cherico, and Shadick (1974), relying on a series of extensive clinical interviews with five persons with cancer and their family members, proposed a seven-stage model of common response patterns to cancer. The stages were (1) shock (which includes avoidance and denial), (2) anger ("Why me?"), (3) grief and depression, (4) bargaining (turning to God), (5) uncertainty (usually after recovering from surgery), (6) renewal and rebuilding (of life aspirations), and (7) integration of the experience into one's life. The latter two stages were observed only in those individuals whose prognosis was favorable following treatment.

Two of the most commonly observed psychological reactions in persons with cancer are anxiety and depression, so much so that they are regarded as natural concomitants of the diagnosis of cancer. Although these reactions have been observed by clinicians for many years, it is only in the past 25 years that efforts have been made to empirically validate their existence (Glanz & Lerman, 1992; Lewis & Bloom, 1978–1979). In one of the earliest attempts, Koenig, Levin, and Brennan (1967) collected Minnesota Multiphasic Personality Inventory data from persons with cancer and concluded that 25% of their sample reported symptoms of severe depression. As a group, however, the persons with cancer were less emotionally distressed than a group of persons hospitalized for depressive symptoms. In another early study Peck (1972) found that over 80% of persons with various types of cancer were diagnosed as having moderate to severe anxiety based on structured psychiatric interviews. Depression ranked second in frequency and was diagnosed in over 40% of the individuals in their sample. This study, however, suffered from three major methodological flaws: (1) the lack of a control or comparison group, (2) the high incidence (over 50%) of premorbidly diagnosed psychiatric disorders among the respondents, and (3) the author's reliance on interviewer-based diagnosis of psychological reactions.

Craig and Abeloff (1974) studied psychiatric symptoms among persons with cancer using the self-report Symptom Check List—90-Revised. More than 50% of the individuals reported moderate to high levels of depression, and 43% and 30% scored at similar levels on the Somatization and Anxiety scales, respectively. Nearly 25% of the individuals manifested overall symptom patterns similar to those observed in persons admitted to emergency psychiatric settings. No effort was made by the authors to control for various demographic, personality, or disease-related variables, nor was a control group used in the study.

In one of the earliest comparative research attempts, Plumb and Holland (1977) studied the prevalence of depression in three groups: (1) persons with advanced-stage cancer undergoing chemotherapy, (2) their relatives, and (3) persons without impairments who had attempted suicide. Using the Beck Depression Inventory, the authors concluded that although persons with cancer scored higher (were more depressed) than their immediate relatives, these differences were not statistically significant. Both groups scored significantly lower than the group of persons who had attempted suicide. Less than 25% of the persons with cancer scored in the moderate to severe depression range. Unfortunately no control group of persons who were not directly affected by the experience of cancer (personally or familiarly) was included in the study. Also, data on demographic, personality, or illness-related variables were not reported.

In a follow-up study, Plumb and Holland (1981) compared persons with cancer with a group of demographically matched persons without impairments who had attempted suicide. Using a semistructured interview protocol to assess psychiatric problems (the Current and Past Psychopathology scales), the authors noted that approximately 20% of the persons with cancer were diagnosed as being severely depressed at the time of the interview as compared to 50% of the persons who had attempted suicide. Also the persons with cancer were judged to be significantly less anxious. The percentage of persons with cancer exhibiting moderate to severe levels of anxiety was approximately 50%. Gottesman and Lewis (1982) compared women who underwent surgery for breast cancer with women who underwent surgery for non-life-threatening illnesses and with women without impairments. The authors found that individuals in the cancer group reported significantly more helplessness and depression than those in the other two groups. Individuals in the cancer group also scored higher on anxiety than those in the remaining groups, but the mean difference was not statistically significant. The authors concluded that persons with cancer consistently experienced the highest level of subjective distress when compared to demographically matched comparison groups.

Mendelsohn (1990) used extensive semistructured interviews and the Q-sort technique to classify interview material into psychosocial and functional categories with three groups of women treated for breast, gynecologic, and other types of cancer. The women demonstrated much variability in their psychosocial responses to their illnesses. Three main clusters of individuals were identified based on the available psychosocial data. These included (1) women in sound psychological condition (eg, optimistic, socially secure, successful in their roles); (2) women who resembled those in the first group, but who showed evidence of continued distress; and (3) women who showed both psychological and physical distress (eg, depression, pessimism, apprehension). Sites of cancer were not found to be differentially associated with these psychosocial-based groupings. Age and severity of illness, however, did discriminate among these groups. For example, degree of physical impairment and poor prognosis were more frequently observed among individuals in the third group. Recently, Nelson, Friedman, Baer, Lane and Smith (1994) used cluster analysis to classify the responses of persons with breast cancer to the Psychosocial Adjustment to Illness Scale. Four subtypes of psychosocial adjustment were identified. These included (1) persons with favorable adjustment, especially in the social, recreational, and domestic areas; (2) persons with poor adjustment and especially elevated emotional distress; (3) persons whose adjustment difficulties focus primarily on health care problems; and (4) persons with favorable health care but with some problems in the vocational, social, and sexual areas. Further analyses indicated that the first psychosocial adjustment subtype used significantly less avoidance coping than persons in the second and third subtypes. In addition, persons in the second subtype demonstrated the least fighting spirit attitude (as measured by the Cancer Adjustment Survey). In other words, the most globally maladjusted individuals (second subtype) resorted most often to avoidance coping and least often to fighting spirit, while the subtype demonstrating most successful adjustment (subtype one) resorted less often to avoidance coping.

In their study on psychiatric disorders among persons with cancer, Derogatis et al. (1983) randomly sampled persons with cancer newly admitted to three separate cancer centers. Individuals were assessed by both psychiatric interviews (leading to DSM—III diagnosis) and by standardized self-report psychological tests, including the Symptom Check List—90-Revised, the Raskin Depression Screen, and the Global Adjustment to Illness Scale. Results indicated that 47% of the individuals were assigned a DSM—III-based psychiatric diagnosis with two thirds of these adjustment disorders. Only 13% of the sample was diagnosed as having depression. A smaller number (4%) was diagnosed as having anxiety disorders. In total, approximately 85% of these individuals were diagnosed positively for a psychiatric disorder (or 40% of the total sample) and experienced reactive depression or anxiety as a central feature of their condition. A high concordance between depression and anxiety in persons with cancer was also reported by Cassileth, Lusk, Huter, Strouse, and Brown (1984).

Bukberg, Penman, and Holland (1984) studied persons hospitalized with cancer using both self-report measures (ie, the Beck Depression Inventory, Lubin's Adjective Check List) and interview-based rating scales leading to DSM—III diagnosis (ie, the Modified DSM—III Depression Scale, the Hamilton Depression Rating Scale). Results indicated that 42% of the sample met the criteria for major depression. An additional 14% demonstrated depression symptoms not meeting the criteria for major depression. Jenkins, May, and Hughes (1991) studied psychological morbidity among women who suffered recurrence of breast cancer using a structured interview format followed by completion of anxiety and depression rating scales. Results indicated that up to two years postsurgery, 45% of these women manifested symptoms of psychological disturbance as evidenced by high levels of clinical anxiety and depression.

Several studies used longitudinal research designs to investigate psychosocial adaptation to the diagnosis of cancer. Lewis, Gottesman, and Gutstein (1979) compared individuals undergoing surgery for cancer with individuals awaiting surgery for less serious illnesses using a battery of tests that included measures of anxiety (the State-Trait Anxiety Inventory), depression (the Wakefield Self-Assessment Depression Inventory), locus of control, self-concept, and a general measure of crisis (the Halpern Crisis Scale). A longitudinal research design was used in which participants were tested immediately prior to surgery and three times thereafter at three-week intervals. The cancer group reported significantly more anxiety (both state and trait) than the comparison group, both at the initial testing and over time. Similar results were noted regarding depression, with the cancer group reporting significantly higher levels of depression than the surgery group over the four testing periods. The results from the Halpern Crisis Scale confirmed that the persons with cancer experienced a significantly more intense crisis during the entire testing period in comparison to their counterparts.

Gottschalk and Hoigaard-Martin (1986) investigated the psychosocial adaptation of four groups of women at 1 to 3 months and 10 to 12 months postsurgery. The groups included (1) women who had undergone a mastectomy, (2) women who had undergone a biopsy with benign breast disease, (3) women who had undergone a cholecystectomy, and (4) a control group of women without impairments. Measures of adaptation included the Symptom Checklist—90, the Global Assessment Scale (a clinical, interviewer-rated psychiatric scale), and the

Gottschalk-Gleser Content Analysis Scales (Gottschalk, 1982). Women in the mastectomy group reported a greater degree of psychological distress than women in the other three groups on the scales measuring total anxiety, mutilation anxiety, death anxiety, denial, and hostility. These differences were also found at the 10 to 12 months postsurgery testing period. Women in the three surgery groups also had significantly lower emotional well-being scores than women in the control group. Again these differences were maintained at the second testing period. The women in the mastectomy group scored significantly higher on the scales measuring anxiety and depression than women in the remaining three groups at both time periods. Finally, among those in the mastectomy group, significant decreases in mean anxiety and shame scores occurred over the time period, coincident with increases in mean overt hostility scores and decreases in positive hope scores.

Malec, Wolberg, Romsaas, Trump, and Tanner (1988) compared persons with breast cancer and persons with benign biopsy using the Millon Clinical Multiaxial Inventory. The inventory was administered after initial clinic examination and again four or eight months later. Results indicated that compared to individuals in the benign biopsy group, individuals in the cancer group had a higher percentage of clinical profiles indicative of moderate to severe impairment. Among the persons with cancer, symptoms of anxiety, depression, and somatic concern were the most common. Approximately 30% of those with cancer experienced increased psychological distress at both periods. Data obtained in a later investigation by these authors (Wolberg, Romsaas, Tanner, & Malec, 1989) suggested that at a 16-month follow-up, most of these psychological symptoms were sufficiently alleviated for the persons with breast cancer. The authors also reported that (1) persons with cancer evidenced greater psychological disturbance at all times when compared to persons in a benign control group on most subscales of the Psychosocial Adjustment to Illness Scale; (2) at the first postsurgery (ie, mastectomy) assessment, persons with cancer as compared to those in the benign control group exhibited higher levels of distress on the Profile of Mood States scales of Tension/Anxiety, Depression/Dejection, and Fatigue; and (3) at the 16-month follow-up assessment, although still manifesting more distress than those in the control group on several scales, individuals in the mastectomy group did exhibit significant improvement on the above Profile of Mood States scales and also on the Psychosocial Adjustment to Illness Scale Psychological Distress subscale.

In an expertly designed and carried out longitudinal prospective study (Psychological Aspects of Breast Cancer Study Group, 1987), women treated for breast cancer were compared with (1) women treated for cholecystectomy following gallbladder disease, (2) women having biopsy for benign breast disease, and (3) women with no surgical treatment. A battery of psychosocial (eg, Brief Symptom Inventory, Body Image Scale, Self-Esteem, Symptoms Check List—

90) and physical and health rating scales were administered at four separate times (ie, 0 to 3, 4 to 6, 7 to 9, and 10 to 12 months postsurgery). Additional data were obtained from structured clinical interviews and content analysis of verbal samples. Results indicated that (1) women in the mastectomy group, in contrast to the other groups, scored higher on all psychosocial (eg, self-depreciation, irritability, anxiety, hostility) and somatic measures, thus indicating greater degree of distress; (2) women in the mastectomy group had higher denial scores than did women in any of the comparison groups; (3) psychosocial impairment scores, separation, death anxieties, and somatic distress declined over time among the women in the mastectomy group but still reflected a moderate degree of disturbance one year postsurgery; and (4) women with breast cancer showed greater degree of impairment in everyday functioning including social, domestic, and leisure-time role activities when compared to individuals in the other groups.

Ell and coworkers (Ell, Nishimoto, Morvay, Mantell, & Hamovitch, 1989) examined psychosocial adaptation among persons with cancer at three time points (T1 = 3 to 6 months, T2 = 9 to 12 months, and T3 = 2 or more years after initial diagnosis). For the entire sample, level of adaptation, as measured by the Mental Health Index (Veit & Ware, 1983), declined significantly over the two-year period, and this was particularly true for persons with lung and breast cancer. State of illness was not found to be associated with psychosocial adaptation. Initial psychosocial status was found to be the best predictor of subsequent psychosocial adaptation.

Finally, Vinokur and coworkers (Vinokur, Threatt, Caplan, & Zimmerman, 1989; Vinokur, Threatt, Vinokur-Kaplan, & Satariano, 1990) investigated psychosocial and physical adaptation to breast cancer over a one-year period, as part of a breast cancer detection demonstration project. Measures included a range of psychosocial and physical functioning indicators, including measures of psychological well-being (eg, anxiety, depression, somatic concerns, anger, irritation, self-esteem, locus of control), social functioning (eg, perceived roles, social contacts, relationship satisfaction), and physical and medical condition. As compared to matched pairs of women in a control group, the persons with cancer, as a group, demonstrated similar levels of quality of life and mental health and physical well-being. However, the recency of diagnosis adversely affected the emotional well-being of younger individuals more than it did that of the older individuals. In other words, younger women with breast cancer with a more recent diagnosis reflected a greater degree of mental health distress and poor psychosocial functioning as compared to older women with breast cancer. Additional findings indicated that in this group of women (1) significant increase occurred in anger and irritation during the same time period; (2) significant reduction occurred in the appraised threat of breast cancer and its experienced stress, from first assessment to follow-up; and (3) despite these decreases in perceived stress and threat, only minor improvements in mental health and well-being were reported.

Three conclusions can be tentatively drawn from these studies and from earlier reviews (Freidenbergs et al., 1981–1982) of the research on psychosocial adaptation to cancer. First, the rates of depression and anxiety are higher among persons with cancer (typically ranging from 20% to 50%) than among the general population. Second, as a group, persons with cancer appear to be less depressed than persons hospitalized for depression or suicidal symptoms. Third, persons with cancer experience elevated degrees of psychological distress when compared to persons without cancer or individuals without impairments, especially during the first year following diagnosis.

Review of the psychosocial adaptation to cancer literature also reveals an increasing interest in studying the coping strategies adopted by persons with cancer to alleviate feelings of depression and anxiety. In their definitive study of ego defenses among persons with cancer, Bahnson and Bahnson (1969) explored the hypothesis that persons with cancer more frequently adopt repressive and denying rather than projective defense mechanisms to cope with experiences associated with feelings of depression, anxiety, and hostility. A group of 30 men with cancer was administered adjective checklists purporting to measure present mood state (the Bahnson Adjective Check List) and projective tendencies (the Bahnson Projective Check List). Results suggested that the cancer group scored below a control group of normally functioning men on projection of anxiety, depression, guilt, and hostility, lending support to the authors' hypothesis.

A frequently used defense mechanism among persons with cancer is denial (Meyerowitz, 1980; Meyerowitz, 1983). Although it was identified as a universally used mechanism by persons with cancer in at least one study (O'Malley, Koocher, Foster, & Slavin, 1979), other researchers (Mastrovito, 1974) view denial as an effective but temporary and selective mechanism used to ward off stressful events during the early stages of the adaptation process. In a study of individuals who had undergone a mastectomy, Meyerowitz (1983) administered a comprehensive test battery to the participants that included measures of depression, anxiety, hostility (ie, the Multiple Affect Adjective Check List), and denial (ie, the Personal Opinion Survey to assess cancer-specific denial and the Survey of Concerns to assess cancer-specific as well as generalized denial). Results indicated that the two cancer-specific denial measures were the only variables to specifically predict emotional distress. The generalized denial measure was the only variable to successfully predict individuals' dissatisfaction with their levels of activity. Higher levels of denial were associated with lower levels of distress and dissatisfaction.

Similarly, Watson, Greer, Blake, and Shrapnell (1984) reported that persons with breast cancer who denied the implications of their diagnosis also were found to experience less mood disturbance during the first week of hospitalization, as measured by the Profile of Mood States, when compared to individuals who accepted their diagnosis. They also reported lower levels of state anxiety at that time, as measured by the Spielberger State-Trait Anxiety Inventory. However, findings that denial reduces psychological distress have been challenged. Quinn, Fontana and Reznikoff (1986), for example, in their study of men with lung cancer, reported that coping strategies, such as self-blaming denial, as measured by the Felton Coping Scale (Felton, Ravenson, & Hinrichsen, 1984), and wish-fulfilling fantasy, were associated with greater psychological distress. It is therefore possible that distortion of reality may ameliorate psychological distress under some personal, medical, or environmental conditions (eg, time since diagnosis, type of life-threatening event) but may actually exacerbate distress under different conditions.

Several studies have sought to compare coping strategies used by persons with cancer and those used by individuals with other disabling conditions (eg, cardiovascular disease). Levine and Zigler (1975) assessed the use of denial among persons with stroke, heart disease, and cancer, and a fourth group of individuals without impairments. On the basis of their measure of denial (a difference score between ideal and real self-image before and after onset of disease), the authors concluded that the persons with cancer displayed more denial than did persons with heart disease but less than that of persons who had suffered a stroke. Kneier and Temoshok (1984) studied repressive coping responses among persons with cancer and persons with heart disease. Repressive coping responses were operationally defined as a discrepancy between reported anxiety as measured by statements in an experimental setting and that measured physiologically through a skin conductance response. Other measures of repressive defensiveness were also employed (ie, Byrne's Repression-Sensitization Scale, Taylor's Manifest Anxiety Scale, the Marlowe-Crowne Social Desirability Scale). The persons with cancer were found to exhibit significantly more repressive behaviors than the individuals in the cardiovascular and disease-free control groups in the experimental procedure (ie, the physiological discrepancy scores) and more repressive behaviors on the psychological measure when compared to the persons with heart disease.

Researchers have demonstrated interest in studying and classifying other forms of coping strategies associated with cancer (Burgess, Morris, & Pettingale, 1988; Heim et al., 1987; Morris, Blake, & Buckley, 1985). Gotay (1984), for instance, used semistructured interviews with persons with early stage cervical cancer and their spouses, as well as persons with advanced-stage breast or gynecological cancer and their spouses. The most prevalent coping strategies for both cancer groups as well as the spouses of group members included those of action taking (ie, specific action-oriented responses) and self-talk (ie, positive thinking responses). Differences were noted between persons with early-stage and advanced-stage cancer in several of the coping strategies employed. Seeking more information, for example, was ranked higher by persons with early stage cancer, while praying/hoping was ranked higher by persons with advanced-stage cancer. Of interest is the finding that avoidance/denial was ranked last as a coping strategy among persons with early-stage cancer but was ranked fourth among persons with advanced-stage cancer. When responding directly to questions on specific mechanisms employed to deal with fear of cancer, participants showed a reversal in their tendency to deny. Termed "try to forget," this strategy was ranked second by persons with early-stage cancer but dropped to seventh place among persons with advanced-stage cancer. These seemingly contradictory findings suggested the operation of more than one denial mechanism among persons with cancer.

Adopting a dichotomous coping response classification based on a structured interview, Manuel, Roth, Keefe, and Brantley (1987) categorized persons with early-stage head and neck cancer into those using approach (moving toward the source of stress) or avoidance (moving away from the source of stress) strategies. An unexpected finding that emerged from this study was that persons adopting either high-approach/low-avoidance or low-approach/high-avoidance strategies scored significantly lower on a measure of distress (the Global Severity Index of the Symptom Check List—90-Revised). In other words, persons who used either approach or avoidance strategies to cope with cancer reported less emotional distress than persons using neither of these strategies. As suggested by this study, the use of approach or avoidance strategies was not mutually exclusive. The results of this study must be viewed cautiously due to the small sample size, the unknown effects of possible cognitive impairment in the persons with head cancer, and the subjective and dichotomous assessment of approach-avoidance coping strategies.

Feifel, Strack, and Nagy (1987a; 1987b) investigated coping strategies of persons facing life-threatening diseases (ie, cancer, myocardial infarction). Three factor-analytic–derived coping scales, termed Confrontation, Avoidance, and Acceptance-Resignation, were specifically constructed for this study. Results indicated that persons with cancer and persons with heart disease were significantly more confrontational than a comparison group composed of individuals with chronic non-life-threatening illnesses. No difference, however, was found between the groups of persons with cancer and persons with heart disease in the use of confrontation, and no differences were found among the three groups on the two remaining coping scales. The authors interpreted these findings as suggesting that persons who experience severe, life-threatening illnesses may resort to similar coping styles that transcend their specific diseases.

Lerman et al. (1990) found that higher scores on "blunting" (a coping tendency to use avoidance or distraction) were associated with lower degrees of anxiety and depression prior to chemotherapy treatment. Higher scores on "monitoring" (a coping tendency to use vigilance and information seeking) were related to higher degree of chemotherapy-associated psychological distress and more nausea prior to treatment. Friedman and associates (Friedman, Baer, Lewy, Lane, & Smith, 1988; Friedman, Nelson, Baer, Lane, & Smith, 1990; Nelson, Friedman, Baer, Lane, & Smith, 1989) sought to investigate the coping styles among women treated for breast cancer. Using Greer, Morris, and Pettingale's (1979) cancer-specific coping survey, they subjected participants' scores to principal components factor analysis and recovered four factors. These were labeled (1) Fighting Spirit, (2) Energy, (3) Information Seeking, and (4) Denial. When examining the relationships between these coping modes, coping modes derived from Billings and Moos' (1981) Coping Scale (ie, active-cognitive, active-behavioral, and avoidance), and several disease-related and personality-related variables, the authors found that (1) active coping strategies such as fighting spirit and active-cognitive coping were positively linked to psychosocial adjustment and inversely related to negative affect following diagnosis of cancer, (2) information seeking was positively linked to active behavioral coping, (3) avoidance was negatively linked to adjustment, and (4) denial was associated with prior adjustment in the domain of health care orientation (the individual's attitudes and knowledge regarding illness and its treatment) but not with measures of affect or coping modes (eg, active-behavioral, active-cognitive, avoidance).

Hilton (1989) investigated the relationship between a set of coping strategies (the Revised Ways of Coping Scale, Folkman, Lazarus, Dunkel-Schetter, DeLongis, & Gruen, 1986) and a set of psychosocial variables including perception of uncertainty, commitment, threat of reoccurrence appraisal, and perception of control of the course of disease among a group of women with breast cancer. Analyses of the data indicated that women with breast cancer who used escape-avoidance, who did not positively reappraise their situation, and who rejected responsibility for their situation also demonstrated low commitment, high uncertainty, and threat of disease recurrence and felt not in control of the cancer course. In addition, women who sought social support, used problem solving, positive reappraisal and self-control and who did not use escape-avoidance showed low threat of recurrence and a high perception of control of the cancer situation.

Dunkel-Schetter, Feinstein, Taylor, and Falke (1992), using the Ways of Coping-Cancer Version Questionnaire, extracted five factors of coping from their data obtained from a sample of 603 persons with cancer. The five factors were labeled (1) Seeking and Using Social Support, (2) Focusing on the Positive, (3) Distancing, (4) Cognitive Escape-Avoidance, and (5) Behavioral Escape-

Avoidance. Participants used distancing coping modes most frequently (26%), while behavioral escape-avoidance was used least frequently (11%). Each of the five coping patterns was regressed on a number of personal, environmental, medical, and emotional variables, and results suggested that (1) younger age was related to more social support seeking, more focusing on the positive, and more behavioral escape; (2) lower level of education was associated with more distancing and more cognitive escape; (3) religiosity (ie, spiritual belief) was linked to more cognitive escape and more focusing on the positive; (4) participation in support groups was associated with more use of social support and more focusing on the positive; (5) perceived stressfulness was related to social support seeking but also to both forms of escape-avoidance; (6) duration since cancer diagnosis was linked to more use of behavioral escape; and (7) less emotional distress was related to use of social support, focusing on the positive, distancing, and reduced use of both forms of escape-avoidance.

Finally, in a longitudinal study Stanton and Snider (1993) followed 117 women diagnosed with either breast cancer ($n = 36$) or benign tumors ($n = 81$) after biopsy. Both groups were administered a battery of tests that included, as predictors, measures of locus of control, dispositional optimism, cognitive appraisal (eg, threat, challenge), and coping. The latter was assessed with the revised 66-item Ways of Coping questionnaire (Folkman et al., 1986). Psychosocial adaptation was measured with the Profile of Mood States (McNair, Lorr, & Droppleman, 1971), an instrument that assesses both positive (the vigor scale) and negative (five scales measuring tension, depression, anger, fatigue, and confusion) affect. Measures were obtained before breast biopsy, immediately following diagnosis, and, for those diagnosed with cancer, also postsurgery. Results indicated that (1) distress and perceived threat were at their highest immediately following the diagnosis of cancer; (2) for women diagnosed with cancer, levels of tension, depression, and confusion decreased significantly following surgery, but levels of fatigue increased and vigor decreased; (3) women who were younger, more optimistic, more threatened, and engaged in more cognitive avoidance coping were more distressed prior to learning their diagnosis, while those who coped by focusing on the positive reported higher levels of vigor; (4) of the two prebiopsy coping modes that significantly predicted psychosocial adaptation, seeking social support predicted postbiopsy vigor while focusing on the positive predicted prebiopsy vigor, but these relationships did not persist postsurgery; and (5) engaging in cognitive avoidance coping significantly predicted greater psychosocial distress and reduced vigor at both postbiopsy and postsurgery.

In summary, although it appears there is a considerable variability in how they use coping modes (Heim et al., 1987), persons with cancer often resort to repressive or denying strategies, especially early in the adaptation process. These strategies, however, may be typical of coping with most life-threatening situations and not unique to coping with cancer. Mixed results have been obtained in investigations of the use of more confrontational, action-oriented coping strategies among persons with cancer.

CHARACTERISTICS ASSOCIATED WITH ADAPTATION TO CANCER

The most widely researched sociodemographic variables that have been implicated in successful (and unsuccessful) psychosocial adaptation to cancer are age at time of cancer diagnosis and age at time of surgery. Data typically suggest that older persons with cancer adapt more successfully to the illness (Ell, Nishimoto, Mantell, & Hamovitch, 1992; Fobair & Mages, 1981; Ganz, Schag, & Heinrich, 1985; Gotay, 1985; Jamison, Wellisch, & Pasnau, 1978; Maguire, 1975; Vinokur et al., 1989). However, the results of other studies have failed to substantiate these findings (Gottschalk & Hoigaard-Martin, 1986; Keyes, Bisno, Richardson, & Marston, 1987). Keyes et al. (1987) did find, however, differences in the use of coping strategies between their younger and older persons with colon cancer. Older persons used significantly less active behavioral coping strategies than did younger persons. Only modest support has been found for the assumption that the psychosocial adaptation process in persons with cancer is a linear one (Meyerowitz, 1980). In other words, the emotional distress of some persons with cancer may abate over time, but other individuals may continue to face myriad difficulties. Meyerowitz (1983), however, did find a significant negative correlation between time since surgery and level of emotional distress postmastectomy among persons with breast cancer.

Among the illness-related variables, stage or severity of illness, type of medical treatment, and physical condition have been frequently studied. Whereas some researchers have found no relationship between stage or severity of cancer and measures of psychosocial adaptation (Friedman et al., 1988; Friedman et al., 1990; Taylor et al., 1985), other studies have reported that time since diagnosis was related not only to accepting responsibility and problem solving but also to behavioral escape (Dunkel-Schetter et al., 1992; Hilton, 1989) and that more advanced disease was linked to greater psychosocial distress (Psychological Aspects of Breast Cancer Study Group, 1987; Taylor, Lichtman, & Wood, 1984; Vinokur et al., 1989). The results of the differential effects of chemotherapy, radiation therapy, and surgery on the psychosocial adaptation of persons with cancer have been equivocal (Meyerowitz, 1980). In contrast, some available data tentatively support a positive relationship between the physical condition of persons with cancer and emotional adaptation (Bukberg et al., 1984; Carey, 1974; Craig & Abeloff, 1974; Meyerowitz, 1980; Taylor et al., 1985). Degree of physical impairment and extent of surgery were also found to directly affect mental health among women with breast cancer (Vinokur et al., 1990). In a similar vein, the extent of one's health concerns was found to be positively correlated with emotional distress (Weisman & Worden, 1976–1977).

Although no clear relationships are yet evident between site or type of cancer and psychosocial adaptation (Meyerowitz, 1980; Pettingale, Burgess, & Greer, 1988), a few recent studies have suggested that types of surgery following cancer may result in differential psychosocial adaptation. Krouse and Krouse (1982) compared two groups of women cancer survivors (ie, breast and gynecological cancer) and a group of persons with a benign breast biopsy. Results indicated that the persons with gynecological cancer scored significantly higher (showed poorer adaptation) than those in the other two groups on the Beck Depression Inventory and on a measure of body image. In contrast to these two groups who showed rapid adaptation, the persons with gynecological cancer maintained these increased feelings of depression and lowered body image 20 months postsurgery.

Holmberg, Omne-Ponten, Burns, Adami, and Bergstrom (1989) found that among breast cancer survivors, these women who underwent breast-conserving surgery showed more favorable psychosocial adjustment (ie, lower symptoms of anxiety and depression and higher ratings on adjustment to social life, marriage, parent role, and work) than women who underwent modified radical mastectomy. In their earlier study Taylor et al. (1985) also reported that individuals with a lumpectomy were better psychosocially adjusted than individuals with a radical mastectomy. It appears that the perception of body disfigurement created by the more radical surgery, combined with feelings of reduced sexual and marital functioning, contributed to this poorer psychosocial adaptation (Sanger & Reznikoff, 1981; Taylor et al., 1985).

The relationship between several personality characteristics and psychosocial adaptation to cancer has also been explored. Among the most frequently investigated personality attributes are pessimistic (or apathetic) attitude, ego strength, degree of neuroticism, denial, and attribution of blame. Data generally suggest that pessimistic, passive, helpless, apathetic, fatalistic attitudes among persons with cancer are associated both with early death (Davis, Quinlan, McKegney, & Kimball, 1973) and poor adaptation (Achterberg & Lawlis, 1977; Achterberg & Lawlis, 1979; Burgess et al., 1988; Davis et al., 1973; Watson et al., 1991; Weisman & Worden, 1976–1977). Similarly, inability to express negative feelings, such as anxiety and depression, was found to be related to increased psychosocial disturbance among breast cancer survivors (Grassi & Molinari, 1988; Watson et al., 1984). However, expression of anger was found to be significantly linked to poor psychological adjustment (Friedman et al., 1988).

Degree of ego strength (typically measured by Barron's ego strength scale) was also found to correlate positively with better adaptation and problem resolution (Weisman & Worden, 1976–1977; Worden & Sobel, 1978). Degree of neurotic behavior, typically measured by the Minnesota Multiphasic Personality

Inventory, the Symptom Check List—90-Revised, or the Eysenck Personality Inventory, was also found to be linked to adaptation to cancer. Results obtained, however, present a mixed picture. Derogatis, Abeloff, and Melisaratos (1979) found that long-term survivors showed greater symptomatology on the Symptom Check List—90-Revised than did short-term survivors. More specifically, subjective distress, as evidenced by feelings of anxiety, alienation, dysphoric mood, and hostility, was associated with longer survival time. The authors hypothesized that these persons' abilities to externalize their negative feelings and underlying conflicts may have been the reason for the finding. Results of other investigations (Jamison et al., 1978; Morris, Greer, & White, 1977; Sobel & Worden, 1979; Weisman & Worden, 1976–1977), however, showed a positive relationship between early neurotic symptoms and distress. It should be noted, however, that the Derogatis et al. (1979) study addressed physical survival, whereas the latter studies focused mainly upon emotional adaptation.

Another personality variable that has been investigated with mixed results is denial of illness. (See also the section on coping strategies in Chapter 1.) Achterberg and Lawlis (1977) found that a high level of denial of illness was associated with poor disease prognosis, as measured by various blood chemistry studies. Meyerowitz (1983), on the other hand, found that a high level of cancer-specific denial was linked to low emotional distress. Similarly, Watson et al. (1984) reported that women with breast cancer with increased level of denial experienced less psychological distress following diagnosis than women reporting low level of denial. The results obtained from these studies are difficult to compare, since their authors adopted different definitions of denial of illness and used different outcome measures.

A personality construct that has been receiving increasing interest recently is the individual's attribution of blame for the onset of cancer. Taylor et al. (1984) reported findings suggesting that blaming others for the onset of the disease is associated with poorer adaptation. Attributions of cancer to oneself, to chance, or to the environment showed no relationship to psychosocial adaptation. Gotay (1985) also failed to find any relationship between attributional indicators and adaptation. A related construct, the belief in one's psychological (especially cognitive) control over cancer, was found to be related to better psychosocial adaptation (Ell et al., 1992; Ell et al., 1989; Lowery, Jacobsen, & DuCette, 1993; Taylor et al., 1984). In a similar vein, Timko and Janoff-Bulman (1985) reported that among women with breast cancer, feelings of invulnerability (to recurrence of cancer) and the belief of a cancer-free future were strongly associated with psychosocial adaptation. These authors found that whereas attributions of blame (for cancer onset) to one's own personality or to others were negatively related to good psychosocial adaptation, attributions to one's behavior were positively related to adaptation.

Somewhat different results were reported by Marks, Richardson, Graham, and Levine (1986). These researchers found that for a group of persons with hematologic malignancies, beliefs in self-control were strongly and negatively correlated with depression only for those who perceived their illness to be very severe. No relationship was noted between beliefs about control and depression among persons perceiving their illness to be less severe. Consistent with these findings, Watson, Greer, Pruyn, and Van Den Borne (1990) found that high perception of internal control over the course of cancer, as measured by their Cancer Locus of Control Scale, was associated with a Fighting Spirit attitude only among those persons whose disease was in its earlier stage. At the same time, strong belief in internal control over the course of cancer was related to Anxious Preoccupation with the illness for all persons regardless of disease progression. Locus of control was not associated with measures of psychological disturbance (ie, depression and anxiety).

Finally, three environment-related variables have been related to adaptation to cancer: (1) quality or extent of social support, (2) ability to return to work, and (3) daily hassles. The association between strong interpersonal relationships with significant others and psychosocial and behavioral adaptation has been frequently reported (Bloom, 1982; Bukberg et al., 1984; Carey, 1974; Cobliner, 1977; Ell et al., 1989; Irvine, Brown, Crooks, Roberts, & Browne, 1991; Jenkins, Linington, & Whittaker, 1991; Northouse, 1988; Quinn et al., 1986; Vinokur et al., 1990; Weisman & Worden, 1976–1977). Meyerowitz (1983) concluded from her study that only moderate (rather than extremely low or high) degree of perceived social support was related to lower levels of emotional distress. The ability to return to gainful employment has also been linked to better psychosocial adaptation (Cobliner, 1977; Schonfield, 1972), perhaps because work carries with it additional economic and psychosocial benefits, such as better financial status, higher degree of independence, and higher self-concept. The third variable, daily hassles, has been only recently studied and has shown positive relationship to poorer level of psychosocial adjustment (Friedman et al., 1988).

CONCLUSION

The diagnosis of cancer triggers an overwhelming reaction of anxiety in the affected individual. Other reactions often observed and reported include denial, depression, and anger. Longitudinal studies of psychosocial adaptation to cancer have suggested that persons with cancer experience greater degrees of psychological distress over a period of approximately one year postdiagnosis than do those in comparison groups consisting of noncancer postsurgery persons or individuals without impairments.

The literature on coping strategies adopted by persons with cancer indicates that (1) denial is a rather common mechanism used by persons with cancer to ward off anxiety and it may be effective in reducing initial psychological distress; (2) active coping strategies such as cognitive, behavioral, and fighting spirit strategies appear to be associated with better psychosocial adaptation among persons with cancer; and (3) escape-avoidance coping strategies have been found to relate to poorer adaptation and feelings of not being in control of the course of cancer.

A large number of variables have been investigated as predictors of psychosocial adaptation to cancer. Among the more consistent findings are those that have reported the following: (1) age of persons has been generally found to be positively linked to better adaptation to cancer; (2) the individual's degree of physical impairment and extent of surgery have been generally found to relate to poorer emotional adaptation; (3) among the personality characteristics examined, passive and pessimistic attitudes, neuroticism, blaming others, and lacking belief in one's ability to gain control over the disease have all been linked to poorer psychosocial adaptation; and (4) perceptions of social and family support have been strongly associated with psychosocial adaptation to the diagnosis of cancer.

Although the recent accumulation of data on characteristics associated with psychosocial adaptation to cancer is encouraging, one major concern that should be addressed by future researchers is the lack of consistency in formulating and measuring the concept of adaptation to cancer. Adaptation has been variously defined in terms of (1) low emotional distress or degree of experienced stress; (2) fewer life concerns; (3) better problem resolution; (4) better use of coping strategies; (5) fewer health concerns or symptoms (eg, lack of physical discomfort); and (6) increased activity level (eg, number or types of activities engaged in). To complicate matters further, scores from disparate psychological measures have been used to operationally define this construct. This mixture of affective, cognitive, behavioral, physical, and medical correlates of psychosocial adaptation can confound the results obtained from these studies and interfere with efforts to compare findings across studies.

REFERENCES

Achterberg, J., & Lawlis, G. F. (1977). Psychological factors and blood chemistries as disease outcome predictors for cancer patients. *Multivariate Experimental Clinical Research, 3,* 107–122.

Achterberg, J., & Lawlis, G. F. (1979). A canonical analysis of blood chemistry variables related to psychological measures of cancer patients. *Multivariate Experimental Clinical Research, 4,* 1–10.

American Cancer Society. (1991). *Cancer facts and figures—1991.* Atlanta, GA: Author.

Bahnson, M. B., & Bahnson, C. B. (1969). Ego defenses in cancer patients. *Annals of the New York Academy of Sciences, 164,* 546–559.

Berkow, R. (Ed.). (1992). *The Merck manual of diagnosis and therapy* (16th ed.). Rahway, NJ: Merck Research Laboratories.

Billings, A. G., & Moos, R. H. (1981). The role of coping responses and social resources in attenuating the stress of life events. *Journal of Behavioral Medicine, 4*, 139–157.

Bloom, J. R. (1982). Social support, accommodation to stress, and adjustment to breast cancer. *Social Science and Medicine, 16*, 1329–1338.

Bukberg, J., Penman, D., & Holland, J. C. (1984). Depression in hospitalized cancer patients. *Psychosomatic Medicine, 46*, 199–212.

Burgess, C., Morris, T., & Pettingale, K. W. (1988). Psychological response to cancer diagnosis. II. Evidence for coping styles. *Journal of Psychosomatic Research, 32*, 263–272.

Carey, R. G. (1974). Emotional adjustment in terminal patients: A quantitative approach. *Journal of Counseling Psychology, 21*, 433–439.

Cassileth, B. R., Lusk, E. J., Huter, R., Strouse, T. B., & Brown, L. L. (1984). Concordance of depression and anxiety in patients with cancer. *Psychological Reports, 54*, 588–590.

Cobb, B. (1973). Cancer: Psychosocial factors. In J. F. Garrett & E. S. Levine (Eds.), *Rehabilitation practices with the physically disabled* (pp. 177–208). New York: Columbia University Press.

Cobliner, W. G. (1977). Psychosocial factors in gynecological or breast malignancies. *Hospital Physician, 10*, 38–40.

Craig, T. J., & Abeloff, M. D. (1974). Psychiatric symptomatology among hospitalized cancer patients. *American Journal of Psychiatry, 131*, 1323–1327.

Davis, R. K., Quinlan, D. M., McKegney, F. P., & Kimball, C. P. (1973). Organic factors and psychological adjustment in advanced cancer patients. *Psychosomatic Medicine, 35*, 464–471.

Derogatis, L. R., Abeloff, M. D., & Melisaratos, N. (1979). Psychological coping mechanisms and survival time in metastatic breast cancer. *Journal of the American Medical Association, 242*, 1504–1509.

Derogatis, L. R., Morrow, G. R., Fetting, J., Penman, D., Piasetsky, S., & Schmale, A. M. (1983). The prevalence of psychiatric disorders among cancer patients. *Journal of the American Medical Association, 249*, 751–757.

Dunham, C. S. (1978). Cancer. In R. M. Goldenson (Ed.), *Disability and rehabilitation handbook* (pp. 305–317). New York: McGraw-Hill.

Dunkel-Schetter, C., Feinstein, L. G., Taylor, S. E., & Falke, R. L. (1992). Patterns of coping with cancer. *Health Psychology, 11*, 79–87.

Ell, K., Nishimoto, R., Mantell, J., & Hamovitch, M. (1992). Coping with cancer: A comparison of older and younger patients. *Journal of Gerontological Social Work, 19*, 3–27.

Ell, K., Nishimoto, R., Morvay, T., Mantell, J., & Hamovitch, M. (1989). A longitudinal analysis of psychological adaptation among survivors of cancer. *Cancer, 63*, 406–413.

Elmayan, M. M. (1992). Cancer. In M. G. Brodwin, F. Tellez, & S. K. Brodwin (Eds.), *Medical, psychosocial and vocational aspects of disability* (pp. 233–249). Athens, GA: Elliott & Fitzpatrick.

Falvo, D. R. (1991). *Medical and psychosocial aspects of chronic illness and disability.* Gaithersburg, MD: Aspen.

Feifel, H., Strack, S., & Nagy, V. T. (1987a). Coping strategies and associated features of medically ill patients. *Psychosomatic Medicine, 49*, 616–625.

Feifel, H., Strack, S., & Nagy, V. T. (1987b). Degree of life-threat and differential use of coping modes. *Journal of Psychosomatic Research, 31*, 91–99.

Felton. B. J., Ravenson, T. A., & Hinrichsen, G. A. (1984). Stress and coping in the explanation of psychological adjustment among chronically ill adults. *Social Science and Medicine, 18*, 889–898.

Fobair, P., & Mages, N. L. (1981). Psychosocial morbidity among cancer patient survivors. In P. Ahmed (Ed.), *Living and dying with cancer* (pp. 285–308). New York: Elsevier.

Folkman, S., Lazarus, R. S., Dunkel-Schetter, C., DeLongis, A., & Gruen, R. J. (1986). Dynamics of a stressful encounter: Cognitive appraisal, coping, and encounter outcomes. *Journal of Personality and Social Psychology, 50*, 992–1003.

Francis, G. M. (1969). Cancer: The emotional component. *American Journal of Nursing, 69*, 1677–1681.

Freidenbergs, I., Gordon, W., Hibbard, M., Levine, L., Wolf, C., & Diller, L. (1981–1982). Psychosocial aspects of living with cancer: A review of the literature. *International Journal of Psychiatry in Medicine, 11*, 303–329.

Freidenbergs, I., & Kaplan. E. (1993). Cancer. In M. G. Eisenberg, R. L. Glueckauf, & H. H. Zaretsky (Eds.), *Medical aspects of disability* (pp. 105–118). New York: Springer.

Friedman, L. C., Baer, P. E., Lewy, A., Lane, M., & Smith, F. E. (1988). Predictors of psychosocial adjustment to breast cancer. *Journal of Psychosocial Oncology, 6*(1), 75–94.

Friedman, L. C., Nelson, D. V., Baer, P. E., Lane, M., & Smith, F. E. (1990). Adjustment to breast cancer: A replication study. *Journal of Psychosocial Oncology, 8*, 27–40.

Ganz, P. A., Schag, C. C., & Heinrich, R. L. (1985). The psychosocial impact of cancer on the elderly: A comparison with younger patients. *Journal of the American Geriatric Society, 33*, 429–435.

Glanz, K., & Lerman, C. (1992). Psychosocial impact of breast cancer: A critical review. *Annals of Behavioral Medicine, 14*, 203–212.

Gotay, C. C. (1984). The experience of cancer during early and advanced stages: The views of patients and their mates. *Social Science and Medicine, 18*, 605–613.

Gotay, C. C. (1985). Why me? Attributions and adjustment by cancer patients and their mates at two stages in the disease process. *Social Science and Medicine, 20*, 825–831.

Gottesman, D., & Lewis, M. C. (1982). Differences in crisis reactions among cancer and surgery patients. *Journal of Consulting and Clinical Psychology, 50*, 381–388.

Gottschalk. L. A. (1982). Manual of uses and applications of the Gottschalk-Gleser verbal behavior scales. *Research Communications in Psychology, Psychiatry and Behavior, 7*, 273.

Gottschalk, L. A., & Hoigaard-Martin, J. (1986). The emotional impact of mastectomy. *Psychiatry Research, 17*, 153–167.

Grassi, L., & Molinari, S. (1988). Pattern of emotional control and psychological reactions to breast cancer: A preliminary report. *Psychological Reports, 62*, 727–732.

Greer, S., Morris, T., & Pettingale, K. W. (1979). Psychological response to breast cancer. *Lancet, 2*, 785–787.

Gullo, S. V., Cherico, D. J., & Shadick, R. (1974). Suggested stages and response styles in life-threatening illness: A focus on the cancer patient. In B. Schoenberg, A. C. Carr, A. H. Kutscher, D. Peretz, & I. K. Goldberg (Eds.), *Anticipatory grief* (pp. 53–78). New York: Columbia University Press.

Healey, J. E., & Zislis, J. M. (1981). Cancers. In W. C. Stolov & M. R. Clowers (Eds.), *Handbook of severe disability* (pp. 363–376). Washington, DC: U. S. Department of Education.

Heim, E., Augustiny, K. F., Blaser, A., Burki, C., Kuhne, D., & Rothenbuhler, M. (1987). Coping with breast cancer—A longitudinal prospective study. *Psychotherapy and Psychosomatics, 48*, 44–59.

Hilton, B. A. (1989). The relationship of uncertainty, control, commitment, and threat of recurrence to coping strategies used by women diagnosed with breast cancer. *Journal of Behavioral Medicine*, *12*, 39–54.

Holmberg, L., Omne-Ponten, M., Burns, T., Adami, H. O., & Bergstrom, R. (1989). Psychosocial adjustment after mastectomy and breast-conserving treatment. *Cancer*, *64*, 969–974.

Irvine, D., Brown, B., Crooks, D., Roberts, J., & Browne, G. (1991). Psychosocial adjustment in women with breast cancer. *Cancer*, *67*, 1097–1117.

Jamison, K. R., Wellisch, D. K., & Pasnau, R. O. (1978). Psychosocial aspects of mastectomy. I. The woman's perspective. *American Journal of Psychiatry*, *134*, 432–436.

Jenkins, P. L., Linington, A., & Whittaker, J. A. (1991). A retrospective study of psychosocial morbidity in bone marrow transplant recipients. *Psychosomatics*, *32*, 65–71.

Jenkins, P. L., May, V. E., & Hughes, L. E. (1991). Psychological morbidity associated with local recurrence of breast cancer. *International Journal of Psychiatry in Medicine*, *21*, 149–155.

Keyes, K., Bisno, B., Richardson, J., & Marston, A. (1987). Age differences in coping, behavioral dysfunction and depression following colostomy surgery. *The Gerontologist*, *27*, 182–184.

Kneier, A. W., & Temoshok, L. (1984). Repressive coping reactions in patients with malignant melanoma as compared to cardiovascular disease patients. *Journal of Psychosomatic Research*, *28*, 145–155.

Koenig, R., Levin, S. M., & Brennan, M. J. (1967). The emotional status of cancer patients as measured by a psychological test. *Journal of Chronic Diseases*, *20*, 923–930.

Krouse, H. J., & Krouse, J. H. (1982). Cancer as crisis: The critical elements of adjustment. *Nursing Research*, *31*, 96–101.

Kübler-Ross, E. (1969). *On death and dying*. New York: Macmillan.

Lerman, C., Rimer, B., Blumberg, B., Christinzio, S., Engstrom, P. F., MacElwee, N., O'Connor, K., & Seay, J. (1990). Effects of coping style and relaxation on cancer chemotherapy side effects and emotional responses. *Cancer Nursing*, *13*, 308–315.

Levine, J., & Zigler, E. (1975). Denial and self-image in stroke, lung cancer, and heart disease patients. *Journal of Consulting and Clinical Psychology*, *43*, 751–757.

Lewis, F. M., & Bloom, J. R. (1978–1979). Psychosocial adjustment to breast cancer: A review of selected literature. *International Journal of Psychiatry in Medicine*, *9*, 1–17.

Lewis, M., Gottesman, D., & Gutstein, S. (1979). The course and duration of crisis. *Journal of Consulting and Clinical Psychology*, *47*, 128–134.

Lowery, B. J., Jacobsen, B. S., & DuCette, J. (1993). Causal attribution control and adjustment to breast cancer. *Journal of Psychosocial Oncology*, *10*, 37–53.

Maguire, P. (1975). The psychological and social consequences of breast cancer. *Nursing Mirror*, *140*, 54–57.

Malec, J., Wolberg, W., Romsaas, E., Trump, D., & Tanner, M. (1988). Millon Clinical Multiaxial Inventory (MCMI) findings among breast cancer clinic patients after initial evaluation and at 4- or 8-month follow-up. *Journal of Clinical Psychology*, *44*, 175–180.

Manuel, G. M., Roth, S., Keefe, F. J., & Brantley, B. A. (1987). Coping with cancer. *Journal of Human Stress*, *13*, 149–158.

Marks, G., Richardson, J. L., Graham, J. W., & Levine, A. (1986). Role of health locus of control beliefs and expectation of treatment efficacy in adjustment to cancer. *Journal of Personality and Social Psychology*, *51*, 443–450.

Mastrovito, R. C. (1974). Cancer: Awareness and denial. *Clinical Bulletin*, *4*, 142–146.

McNair, D. M., Lorr, M., & Droppleman, L. F. (1971). *EITS manual for the Profile of Mood States.* San Diego, CA: Educational and Industrial Testing Service.

Mendelsohn, G. A. (1990). Psychosocial adaptation to illness by women with breast cancer and women with cancer at other sites. *Journal of Psychosocial Oncology, 8,* 1–25.

Meyerowitz, B. E. (1980). Psychosocial correlates of breast cancer and its treatments. *Psychological Bulletin, 87,* 108–131.

Meyerowitz, B. E. (1983). Postmastectomy coping strategies and quality of life. *Health Psychology, 2,* 117–132.

Morris, T., Blake, S., & Buckley, M. (1985). Development of a method for rating cognitive responses to a diagnosis of cancer. *Social Science and Medicine, 20,* 795–802.

Morris, T., Greer, H. S., & White, P. (1977). Psychological and social adjustment to mastectomy: A two-year follow-up study. *Cancer, 40,* 2381–2387.

Nelson, D. V., Friedman, L. C., Baer, P. E., Lane, M., & Smith. F. E. (1989). Attitudes to cancer: Psychometric properties of fighting spirit and denial. *Journal of Behavioral Medicine, 12,* 341–355.

Nelson, D. V., Friedman, L. C., Baer, P. E., Lane, M., & Smith, F. E. (1994). Subtypes of psychosocial adjustment to breast cancer. *Journal of Behavioral Medicine, 17,* 127–141.

Northouse, L. L. (1988). Social support in patients' and husbands' adjustment to breast cancer. *Nursing Research, 37,* 91–95.

O'Malley, J. E., Koocher, G., Foster, D., & Slavin, L. (1979). Psychiatric sequelae of surviving childhood cancer. *American Journal of Orthopsychiatry, 49,* 608–616.

Peck, A. (1972). Emotional reactions to having cancer. *American Journal of Roentgenology, Radium Therapy and Nuclear Medicine, 114,* 591–599.

Pettingale, K. W., Burgess, C., & Greer, S. (1988). Psychological response to cancer diagnosis. I. Correlations with prognostic variables. *Journal of Psychosomatic Research, 32,* 255–261.

Plumb, M. M., & Holland, J. (1977). Comparative studies of psychological function in patients with advanced cancer. I. Self-reported depressive symptoms. *Psychosomatic Medicine, 39,* 264–276.

Plumb, M. M., & Holland, J. (1981). Comparative studies of psychological function in patients with advanced cancer. II. Interviewer-rated current and past psychological symptoms. *Psychosomatic Medicine, 43,* 243–254.

Psychological Aspects of Breast Cancer Study Group. (1987). Psychological response to mastectomy: A prospective comparison study. *Cancer, 59,* 189–196.

Quinn, M. E., Fontana, A. F., & Reznikoff, M. (1986). Psychological distress in reaction to lung cancer as a function of spousal support and coping strategy. *Journal of Psychosocial Oncology, 4,* 79–90.

Sanger, C. K., & Reznikoff, M. (1981). A comparison of the psychological effects of breast-saving procedures with the modified radical mastectomy. *Cancer, 48,* 2341–2346.

Schonfield, J. (1972). Psychological factors related to delayed return to an earlier life-style in successfully treated cancer patients. *Journal of Psychosomatic Research, 16,* 41–46.

Sobel, H. J., & Worden, J. W. (1979). The MMPI as a predictor of psychosocial adaptation to cancer. *Journal of Consulting and Clinical Psychology, 47,* 716–724.

Stam, H. J., Bultz, B. D., & Pittman, C. A. (1986). Psychosocial problems and interventions in a referred sample of cancer patients. *Psychosomatic Medicine, 48,* 539–548.

Stanton, A. L., & Snider, P. R. (1993). Coping with a breast cancer diagnosis: A prospective study. *Health Psychology, 12,* 126–133.

Taylor, S. E., Lichtman, R. R., & Wood, J. V. (1984). Attributions, beliefs about control, and adjustment to breast cancer. *Journal of Personality and Social Psychology, 46,* 489–502.

Taylor, S. E., Lichtman, R. R., Wood, J. V., Bluming, A. Z., Dosik, G. M., & Leibowitz, R. L. (1985). Illness-related and treatment-related factors in psychological adjustment to breast cancer. *Cancer, 55,* 2506–2513.

Timko, C., & Janoff-Bulman, R. (1985). Attributions, vulnerability, and psychological adjustment: The case of breast cancer. *Health Psychology, 4,* 521–544.

Veit, C. T., & Ware, J. E. (1983). The structure of psychological distress and well-being in general populations. *Journal of Consulting and Clinical Psychology, 51,* 730–742.

Vinokur, A. D., Threatt, B. A., Caplan, R. D., & Zimmerman, B. L. (1989). Physical and psychosocial functioning and adjustment to breast cancer. *Cancer, 63,* 394–405.

Vinokur, A. D., Threatt, B. A., Vinokur-Kaplan, D., & Satariano, W. A. (1990). The process of recovery from breast cancer for younger and older patients. *Cancer, 65,* 1242–1254.

Watson, M., Greer, S., Blake, S., & Shrapnell, K. (1984). Reaction to a diagnosis of breast cancer: Relationship between denial, delay and rates of psychological morbidity. *Cancer, 53,* 2008–2012.

Watson, M., Greer, S., Pruyn, J., & Van Den Borne, B. (1990). Locus of control and adjustment to cancer. *Psychological Reports, 66,* 39–48.

Watson, M., Greer, S., Rowden, L., Gorman, C., Robertson, B., Bliss, J. M., & Tunmore, R. (1991). Relationships between emotional control, adjustment to cancer and depression and anxiety in breast cancer patients. *Psychological Medicine, 21,* 51–57.

Weisman, A. D., & Worden, J. W. (1976–1977). The existential plight in cancer: Significance of the first 100 days. *International Journal of Psychiatry in Medicine, 7,* 1–15.

Wolberg, W. H., Romsaas, E. P., Tanner, M. A., & Malec, J. F. (1989). Psychosexual adaptation to breast cancer surgery. *Cancer, 63,* 1645–1655.

Worden, J. W., & Sobel, H. J. (1978). Ego strength and psychosocial adaptation to cancer. *Psychosomatic Medicine, 40,* 585–592.

CHAPTER 9

Diabetes Mellitus

DESCRIPTION

Diabetes mellitus is a chronic syndrome characterized by abnormal elevations of blood glucose (hyperglycemia) resulting from impairment in insulin secretion (Berkow, 1992; Hornichter, 1992). Diabetic symptoms include (1) polyuria (excessive urination), (2) polydipsia (excessive thirst), (3) polyphagia (excessive hunger), (4) fatigue, (5) weakness, (6) weight loss, (7) numbness in the hands and feet, and (8) blurred vision (De Stefano et al., 1990; Hornichter, 1992; Turk & Speers, 1983). Approximately 10 to 12 million Americans are affected by diabetes mellitus (American Diabetes Association, 1983). It is estimated that between 3.1% and 4.6% of the US population between the ages of 20 and 75 years has been diagnosed with diabetes mellitus but that others with the disease remain undiagnosed (Hornichter, 1992).

The two primary types of diabetes mellitus are the following:

1. Insulin-dependent diabetes mellitus (diabetes mellitus type I, formerly known as juvenile onset type). Insulin-dependent diabetes mellitus, typically developing during childhood or adolescence, results from selective destruction of most or all of the insulin-secreting beta cells of the islets of Langerhans located in the pancreas. Insulin-dependent diabetes mellitus accounts for approximately 10% of all diabetes mellitus cases, and its control necessitates continuous insulin treatment (Berkow, 1992; Hornichter, 1992).

2. Non-insulin-dependent diabetes mellitus (diabetes mellitus type II, formerly known as adult or maturity onset type). Non-insulin-dependent diabetes mellitus, accounting for about 90% of all diabetes mellitus cases, typically develops in individuals over 35 to 40 years of age and is more prevalent among women, blacks, and obese people. In non-insulin-depen-

dent diabetes mellitus, capacity for insulin secretion is maintained in most individuals, but insulin production is inadequate in response to glucose (Berkow, 1992; Hornichter, 1992).

Diabetes mellitus is the seventh leading cause of death in the United States (De Stefano et al., 1990). Although the cause of diabetes mellitus is unknown, several factors have been implicated and include (1) heredity, (2) viral infections, (3) autoimmunity, (4) psychological stress, and (5) prolonged obesity (Falvo, 1991; Turk & Speers, 1983). The latter two factors appear to affect only the development of non-insulin-dependent diabetes mellitus.

Complications resulting from diabetes mellitus generally involve (1) retinopathy (that may lead to blindness), (2) peripheral neuropathy (mainly sensory loss in extremities), (3) nephropathy (kidney failure), (4) infections (that may lead to gangrene), (5) foot ulcers, (6) arteriosclerosis ("hardening of the arteries") of both major (coronary) and small (peripheral) arteries that may result in myocardial infarction and cerebrovascular accident, (7) sexual impotence (in males), and (8) diabetic ketoacidosis (when the body begins to metabolize its own reservoirs of fats and proteins for energy maintenance). The last complication may also result in hypoglycemic coma, unconsciousness, and even death. Finally, complications associated with insulin treatment may indicate insulin reaction (hypoglycemia or low plasma glucose level) that includes adrenergic (eg, sweating, fainting, nervousness) and central nervous system symptoms (eg, confusion, visual problems, seizures; Berkow, 1992; Falvo, 1991; Hornichter, 1992).

PSYCHOSOCIAL ADAPTATION TO DIABETES MELLITUS

The onset and chronic course of diabetes mellitus have been associated with increased anxiety, depressive mood, social withdrawal, rebelliousness, insecurity, and denial among children and adults (Gath, Smith, & Baum, 1980; Koski, 1969; Rovet, Ehrlich, & Hoppe, 1987; Sanders, Mills, Martin, & Horne, 1975; Swift, Seidman, & Stein, 1967). Common fears expressed by persons with diabetes mellitus and their relatives typically include (1) fear of uncertain future and physical deterioration, (2) concerns about insulin reaction, (3) fear of medical complications, (4) worries regarding sexual performance, (5) concerns related to professional and other life goals, and (6) fears of early death (Denolin, Appelboom-Fondu, Lemiere, & Dorchy, 1982; Hamburg & Inoff, 1983; Rovet et al., 1987).

On the basis of anecdotal clinical observations, early researchers implied the existence of a "diabetic personality." These claims, however, were later dismissed as a myth by other researchers who reviewed the extensive literature on personality characteristics of youngsters and adults with diabetes mellitus since the 1930s (Dunn & Turtle, 1981; Fisher, Delamater, Bertelson, & Kirkley, 1982; Johnson, 1980; Lustman, Amado, & Wetzel, 1983). These researchers argued that in the majority of studies reviewed, no differences were found between individuals with diabetes mellitus and individuals without diabetes mellitus on most measured personality traits. Furthermore many of the differences that had surfaced could have been attributed to (1) methodological problems, including sampling, matching, and experimenter or rater biases; and (2) the use of many unreliable and invalid measures, including overreliance on unstructured interviews, clinical judgment, and often unspecified diagnostic criteria.

Several clinical accounts exist that imply that anxiety, depression, social isolation, and possible mood swings may be more prevalent among individuals with diabetes mellitus than in the general population but not more so than in individuals with other chronic diseases (Denolin et al., 1982; Dunn & Turtle, 1981; Johnson, 1980; Wilkinson, 1981). Some of these symptoms, however, may be developmentally related (eg, exacerbated during adolescence) or may mimic symptoms associated with hyperglycemia or hypoglycemia (eg, irritability, psychomotor retardation, confusion, fatigue, dizziness, trembling). In addition, psychogenic causation theories (ie, the view that certain personality or family attributes and disturbances predispose one to develop diabetes mellitus) are often confounded in somatopsychological research. Support for these contentions in the research literature concerning the impact of diabetes mellitus on psychosocial adaptation will be reviewed throughout this chapter.

Only sporadic attempts have been made to explore phases of psychosocial adaptation to the onset of diabetes mellitus among children and adolescents. Isenberg and Barnett (1965) and Jacobson and Hauser (1983) have suggested the following three-phase model:

1. *Onset period*. During this period of emotional upheaval, persons with diabetes mellitus and their family experience a crisislike situation. Initial feelings of shock, disbelief, and lack of emotional acceptance, especially among parents, are consistently reported. These reactions are typically followed by gradual acceptance of reality with concomitant feelings of anxiety, acute grief, especially about the loss of a child, and guilt and self-blame (see also Koski, 1969).

2. *General illness course*. This period normally ranges from approximately the second year post-diagnosis to the onset of chronic complications and evolves around daily management of one's diabetic status. During this time activities focus on following an appropriate diet, injecting insulin, and coping with potential insulin reactions. During adolescence, typical struggles of individuation from parental values and seeking a balance between dependence and independence are often magnified and may take an unex-

pected course because of greater anxiety and confusion over future medical implications (eg, sexual impotence, blindness, infections).

3. *Complications period.* During this last phase chronic complications ensue, requiring new medical and psychosocial adjustments. For some these complications shatter any previous hopes of having a typical future, leading to feelings of betrayal, anger, and depression. For others, the complications reawaken earlier fears and lead to feelings of intense anxiety.

Empirical studies of diabetes mellitus typically address one of two issues, namely, the prevalence of psychiatric disturbances among samples of persons with diabetes mellitus and comparisons of personality attributes and emotional reactions between individuals with diabetes mellitus and control groups (eg, samples from the general population, samples of persons with other chronic illnesses). In one of the earliest reported comprehensive studies, Swift et al. (1967) concluded that based on psychiatric interviews of children with diabetes mellitus and control group children and data obtained from a variety of objective, projective, and cognitive psychological tests, the sample of children with diabetes mellitus, as compared to controls, manifested more psychiatric and behavioral symptoms, including dependence-independence imbalance, less adequate self-concept, greater anxiety, more hostility, and poorer social and home adjustment. Other research results have lent partial support to the Swift et al. (1967) findings. Gath et al. (1980) reported that 18% of their sample of children with diabetes mellitus was recognized as having psychiatric disorders, mainly of neurotic and conduct behavior types. Grey and coworkers (Grey, Cameron, & Thurber, 1991; Grey, Genel, & Tamborlane, 1980) concluded that both anxiety and depression were common responses in their sample of adolescents with diabetes mellitus. Furthermore scores from a general interview-based psychosocial adjustment scale with parents classified 55% of their children with diabetes mellitus as manifesting moderate to severe psychosocial maladjustment.

Kovacs et al. (1985) reported that in their sample of children with diabetes mellitus, 36% were diagnosed as having psychiatric disorders. These diagnoses, however, were seen mainly as adjustment disorders associated with the stress of having developed the disease.

Several studies used the parent-rated Child Behavior Check List to explore adjustment disorders among children with diabetes mellitus. Lavigne, Traisman, Marr, and Chasnoff (1982) reported that male but not female children with diabetes mellitus were more likely to manifest affective symptoms than were control children, particularly in the area of symptom internalization (ie, tendencies of schizoid and obsessive-compulsive nature) and to a lesser extent in symptom externalization (ie, aggression). More recently Rovet et al. (1987) reached similar conclusions in their study of children with diabetes mellitus. In comparison to their siblings, children with diabetes mellitus in their sample had elevated scores on both the internalizing and externalizing scales of the Child Behavior Check List. This was particularly evident for boys with diabetes mellitus onset after four years of age. The majority of the late-onset boys had profiles resembling those of "schizoid" children (ie, anxious, fearful, shy). Both late- and early-onset boys also scored lower, but not significantly so, on the Piers-Harris Children's Self-Concept Scale than their siblings. Similarly, on the Goodenough-Harris Drawing test, late-onset boys drew more defective human figures than girls with diabetes mellitus and siblings without diabetes mellitus, suggesting an impairment in body image development.

Finally, the results of studies of ego development among children and adolescents with diabetes mellitus have suggested that (1) youngsters with diabetes mellitus were at lower levels of ego development (using Loevinger's Sentence Completion Test) than control group youngsters but at higher levels than young persons with psychiatric disorders; (2) girls with diabetes mellitus were at higher levels of ego development than boys; (3) self-esteem was more impaired among adolescents with diabetes mellitus who were at the lower levels of ego development; and (4) adolescents with diabetes mellitus used more suppression in comparison to adolescents with psychiatric disorders and adolescents without diabetes mellitus (Hauser, Jacobson, Noam, & Powers, 1983; Hauser et al., 1979; Jacobson, Beardslee, et al., 1986).

Three studies of the prevalence of psychiatric disorders among adults with diabetes mellitus provided useful information. Mason (1985), in a sample of 91 outpatients with diabetes mellitus (mean age 55 years), concluded from clinical interviews and hospital records that mental illness, mainly of severe depression type, was a prominent feature in from 14% to 23% of the sample. Overreliance on hospital records and unstructured interviews, however, renders these findings highly suspect.

Lustman, Griffith, Clouse, and Cryer (1986), studying a group of 114 individuals with diabetes mellitus (mean age 40 years) using the National Institute of Mental Health (NIMH) Diagnostic Interview Schedule and DSM—III criteria, reported that 71% had a history of at least one psychiatric disorder. Most commonly diagnosed disorders included general anxiety (41%), major depression episode (32.5%), simple phobia (26%), and dysthymic disorder (17.5%). These rates are approximately six to seven times greater than rates of psychiatric disorders in the general population. Individuals with poor metabolic (glucose) control had significantly higher rates of psychiatric disorders than those with good control. Popkin, Callies, Lentz, Colon, and Sutherland (1988) investigated the prevalence of psychiatric disorder among 75 individuals with diabetes mellitus (mean age 31 years) awaiting pancreas transplantation. Lifetime prevalence of at least one psychiatric disorder as identified by the Diagnostic Interview Schedule was

51%. Most common disorders included generalized anxiety disorder (32%), phobic disorder (25%), and major depression (24%). These inclusive lifetime rates were significantly higher than those reported for a comparison group of first-degree relatives (35%) and the general population (33%).

Tebbi, Bromberg, Sills, Cukierman, and Piedmonte (1990) sought to investigate the general well-being and vocational adjustment of young adults (mean age 24 years) with diabetes mellitus. In comparison to a control group, participants with diabetes mellitus reported more worries and fears about their health, were more depressed, experienced more difficulties in performing their jobs, and were more functionally limited in their range of activity participation.

In contrast to the results of these studies reporting increased risk of psychiatric disturbances, a growing body of research suggests that no, or only minor, differences exist between persons with and without diabetes mellitus in psychosocial and psychiatric symptomatology. Among the studies that have failed to find differences between samples of individuals with diabetes mellitus and either general population norms or samples of controls are those that have investigated these dependent variables:

1. General psychopathology as measured by the Minnesota Multiphasic Personality Inventory clinical scales, except depression (Murawski, Chazan, Balodimos, & Ryan, 1970)
2. Self-esteem (Hanson et al., 1990; Hauser et al., 1979; Jacobson, Hauser, et al., 1986; Kovacs, Brent, Steinberg, Paulauskas, & Reid, 1986; Saucier, 1984; Simonds, Goldstein, Walker, & Rawlings, 1981; Sullivan, 1978)
3. Depression (Kovacs et al., 1986; Littlefield, Rodin, Murray, & Craven, 1990; Mazze, Lucido, & Shamoon, 1984; Niemcryk, Speers, Travis, & Gary, 1990; Surridge et al., 1984)
4. Anxiety (Kovacs et al., 1986; Mazze et al., 1984; McCraw & Tuma, 1977; Niemcryk et al., 1990)
5. Behavioral symptomatology, using the Child Behavior Check List (Jacobson et al., 1986b; Wertlieb, Hauser, & Jacobson, 1986)
6. Interpersonal conflicts (Simonds, 1977)
7. Frequency of psychiatric disorders (Simonds, 1976–1977; Simonds, 1977)
8. Psychological adjustment using the Symptom Check List—90-Revised and the Psychosocial Adjustment to Illness Scale (Wysocki, Hough, Ward, & Green, 1992)
9. Physical and psychosocial impairment using the Sickness Impact Profile (Littlefield et al., 1990)
10. Attitudes and feelings toward the disease, using the Diabetic Adjustment Scale (Jacobson et al., 1986b)

11. Quality of life, using the Mooney Problem Checklist (Mazze et al., 1984)
12. Impaired body image, using the Rorschach (McCraw & Tuma, 1977).

In a similar vein Kovacs et al. (1990) concluded from their six-year longitudinal study that the positive psychological well-being of their sample of children with insulin-dependent diabetes mellitus was evidenced by their average range of scores on measures of self-esteem, anxiety, and depression, thus underscoring "the emotional resiliency of diabetic children" (p. 629).

The results of these studies and two recent large-scale investigations by Wilkinson and coworkers (Wilkinson et al., 1987; Wilkinson et al., 1988) using the General Health Questionnaire, the Clinical Interview Schedule, and the ICD-9 psychiatric diagnostic system estimate the prevalence of psychiatric disorders among samples of adolescents and adults with diabetes mellitus to range from approximately 18% to 24%, with females outnumbering males by a ratio of 2:1. These figures are similar to those found in samples of hospital-based medical patients. As discussed previously, depression and anxiety were found to be the most commonly reported psychosocial disorders.

Only one study was found that followed youth with insulin-dependent diabetes mellitus longitudinally. Kovacs and coworkers (Kovacs et al., 1986; Kovacs et al., 1990) assessed the psychosocial adjustment of school-aged children for a period of six years. Major findings included (1) the children's self-ratings of depression decreased for the first three years and then showed moderate degrees of elevation; (2) anxiety showed dramatic decrease during the first two years and, after a three-year plateau, increased unexpectedly during the sixth year (especially among girls); and (3) self-esteem scores increased during the first three years and then reached a plateau. The authors concluded from these findings that despite the uneven impact of disease duration on these children, as a group they demonstrated remarkable emotional resiliency and satisfactory psychosocial well-being.

CHARACTERISTICS ASSOCIATED WITH ADAPTATION TO DIABETES MELLITUS

An ample body of empirical research exists on the relationships between adaptation to diabetes mellitus and sociodemographic, disability-related, psychosocial, and environmental variables. Two of the most frequently investigated sociodemographic variables have been sex and age. Most available research suggests that whereas boys demonstrate more adjustment and behavioral problems, girls report more anxiety and poorer body image (Hamburg & Inoff, 1983; Rovet et al., 1987; Ryan & Morrow, 1986). Sex differences may, however, show differential interaction effects with age of onset (Ryan & Morrow, 1986) and personality attributes such as locus of control (Hamburg & Inoff, 1983). Research on age at onset of diabetes mellitus appears to support strongly the conclusion that children whose diagnosis was made at a later age demonstrate more psychosocial adjustment problems, lower acceptance, more negative self-esteem, and elevated behavioral problems than children with an early age of diagnosis (Allen, Tennen, McGrade, Affleck, & Ratzan, 1983; Andersson & Ekdahl, 1992; Grey et al., 1991; Rovet et al., 1987). Metabolic control and adherence to treatment (ie, compliance with diet and metabolic monitoring) also appear to worsen with increased age (Grey et al., 1991; Hanson et al., 1989; Jacobson et al., 1987; Swift et al., 1967).

Two additional sociodemographic variables that have been less thoroughly investigated, socioeconomic status and education, suggest that a positive relationship exists between higher levels of socioeconomic status and education and general psychosocial adaptation and control of diabetes mellitus (Hanson, DeGuire, Schinkel, Henggeler, & Burghen, 1992; Kovacs et al., 1985; Kvam & Lyons, 1991).

Although several disease-related variables have been studied to investigate their relationship to psychosocial adaptation to diabetes mellitus, the majority of studies have yielded inconsistent findings. Duration of disease was found by most researchers to be unrelated to reports of psychosocial adaptation (Brown, Kaslow, Sansbury, Meacham, & Culler, 1991; Ryan & Morrow, 1986; Sullivan, 1979; White, Richter, & Fry, 1992), although it might be curvilinearly related to adherence and metabolic control and further confounded by chronological age, that is, adolescents and adults and those with longer duration of diabetes mellitus have shown better adherence than younger adults and those with shorter disease duration (Eaton et al., 1992; Hanson et al., 1989).

Degree of control of disease has also shown no consistent relationship to psychosocial measures. Whereas limited research results suggest that poor disease control is associated with elevated depression and increased psychiatric problems (Dupuis, Jones, & Peterson, 1980; Gath et al., 1980), other researchers have found no relationship between degree of disease control and measures of psychosocial adjustment (Brown et al., 1991; Ryan & Morrow, 1986). Finally, only limited empirical support has been found to suggest that degree of severity of diabetes mellitus or increased complications resulting from it are linked to higher psychiatric morbidity (Littlefield et al., 1990; White et al., 1992; Wilkinson et al., 1988).

Numerous personality attributes and psychosocial characteristics have been investigated as predictors of adaptation to diabetes mellitus. Personality attributes most frequently studied include (1) locus of control, (2) self-concept or self-esteem (measures of self-concept have been conceptualized as both predictor and outcome variables in the study of psychosocial adaptation to chronic illness and disability), (3) degree of independence, (4) social competence, and (5) coping mode.

Studies of the relationship between locus of control and psychosocial adaptation to diabetes mellitus indicate that persons with internal locus of control (ie, those attributing responsibility for health maintenance and other life events to themselves) tend to (1) be less depressed (Close, Davies, Price, & Goodyer, 1986); (2) demonstrate better emotional adjustment (Dunn, Smartt, Beeney, & Turtle, 1986; Jacobson et al., 1986b); and (3) have better adherence and metabolic control (Brown et al., 1991; Eaton et al., 1992; Peyrot & McMurry, 1985; Schlenk & Hart, 1984) than those with external locus of control. It is noteworthy that in the Peyrot and McMurry (1985) study, analyses of the data suggested that a possible curvilinear relationship may exist between health locus of control and metabolic control in that either high externality or internality may be associated with poor glucose control.

Research on measures of self-concept typically indicates that the more positive one's self-concept the better one's psychosocial adjustment to diabetes mellitus, especially among children (Grey et al., 1980; Jacobson et al., 1986b; Swift et al., 1967). A similar association was generally reported between positive self-concept and measures of compliance and metabolic control (Anderson, Miller, Auslander, & Santiago, 1981; Jacobson et al., 1987). Kovacs et al. (1990), in their longitudinal study, failed to detect any relationship between self-esteem and metabolic control over a six-year period.

The relationships between measures of independence, self-efficacy, social competence, and adaptation to diabetes mellitus have been investigated only sporadically. The limited data available, however, suggest that successful psychosocial adjustment (including more positive self-esteem) may be related to higher degrees of independence (Grey et al., 1980) and better handling of dependence-independence conflicts among adolescent girls (Sullivan, 1979). Similarly, successful adjustment and better adherence and metabolic control appear to be related to self-efficacy (Wysocki et al., 1992), perceived competence (Jacobson et al., 1986b), and social competence (Hanson, Henggeler, & Burghen, 1987b; Jacobson et al., 1987). Social competence may act as a buffering variable, such that under high stressful situations, high (but not low) social competence defuses the link often found between stress and poor metabolic control (Hanson et al., 1987b).

A final psychosocial variable to be discussed that has received increased attention in the literature is that of coping style. Research on coping with the stress of living with chronic diseases and disabilities has emphasized the more stable properties of the individual and the psychosocial and physical environments (Pollock, 1989). Results from the studies reviewed on the role of coping modes in psychosocial adaptation to diabetes mellitus and in maintaining metabolic control are inconsistent. Whereas the results of some research suggest that increased use of coping in general (ie, using both active and avoidance modes of coping) is associated with poor metabolic control (Delamater, Kurtz, Bubb, White, & Santiago, 1987; Frenzel, McCaul, Glasgow, & Schafer, 1988), other research results have indicated that (1) persons with diabetes mellitus who use more constructive or mature coping modes (eg, problem solving, seeking professional support, being committed or persistent) show better adherence to a medical regimen and better metabolic control than persons with diabetes mellitus using nonconstructive coping modes (eg, denial, wishful thinking, avoidance, fantasy; Delamater et al., 1987; Grey et al., 1991; Hanson et al., 1989; Jacobson et al., 1990; Koski, 1969; Peyrot & McMurry, 1985); and (2) persons using more active, problem-focused coping strategies demonstrate more successful psychosocial adaptation and better general well-being than those with more passive, avoidance, fatalistic, and palliative modes (Grey et al., 1991; Kvam & Lyons, 1991; White et al., 1992).

In an exemplary study of 61 children and adolescents with insulin-dependent diabetes mellitus, psychosocial measures were obtained from both the youngsters and their parents over a four-year period (Jacobson, Hauser, Lavori et al., 1990). Measures of the child's adjustment included (1) self-reported behavioral problems, adaptation to diabetes mellitus, self-esteem, and perceived competence; (2) parent-reported behavioral problems and competence; (3) three measures of coping (locus of control, ego defenses, and adaptive strengths); and (4) adherence to diabetic regimen. A series of multiple regression analyses with degree of adherence over the four-year follow-up period as the criterion variable demonstrated that after controlling for the effect of sociodemographic variables (age at time of diagnosis was significantly related to adherence), both psychosocial adjustment (a composite score of all self- and parent-reported measures) and coping (ego defense level derived from semistructured clinical interviews) were significantly associated with adherence over the four-year follow-up period.

Somatopsychosocial characteristics most commonly investigated as to their relationships to adaptation to diabetes mellitus include (1) anxiety, (2) depression, (3) anger and hostility, and (4) perceived stress. Research on the relationship between anxiety and metabolic control suggests that, in general, increased levels of anxiety are associated with poorer metabolic control, although the directionality of this association has not been fully explored (Karlsson, Holmes, & Lang, 1988; Mazze et al., 1984; Niemcryk et al., 1990; Peyrot & McMurry, 1985; Turkat, 1982). Similarly, increased depression has been found to be associated with lower adherence to therapeutic regimen (Eaton et al., 1992) and poorer metabolic control (Karlsson et al., 1988; Mazze et al., 1984). Feelings of anger, hostility, and interpersonal conflicts have also been linked to poorer metabolic control (Karlsson et al., 1988; Peyrot & McMurry, 1985; Simonds, 1976–1977).

The findings of these studies strongly suggest that psychiatric symptomatology and poor general psychosocial adaptation are linked to poor regimen adherence and poor diabetic control (Jacobson, Adler, Wolfsdorf, Anderson, & Derby, 1990; Karlsson et al., 1988; Wysocki et al., 1992).

The relationship of perceived stress to metabolic control has been extensively investigated. Stress is alternatively regarded as a psychodynamic concomitant of chronic disease and as an environmental antecedent to it. The ensuing relationships between stress and diabetes mellitus are, therefore, complex, as each may influence the other directly or indirectly (Delamater et al., 1987; Fisher et al., 1982). Stress, for example, may impede adherence to therapeutic regimen, thus interfering with metabolic control. On the other hand, chronic poor-glucose control might have a negative impact upon general functioning, thus lowering body resistance to both internal and external stresses (Fisher et al., 1982). Positive relationships between increased levels of stress (eg, daily hassles, negative life events) and poor metabolic control have been reported consistently in the literature (Barglow, Hatcher, Edidin, & Sloan-Rossiter, 1984; Chase & Jackson, 1981; Frenzel et al., 1988; Hanson, Henggeler, & Burghen, 1987a; Hanson et al., 1987b; Johnson & Rosenbloom, 1982; Wysocki et al., 1992).

Among the environmental variables investigated, family relationships, levels of family cohesion, parental support, and emotional climate at home have been extensively addressed. Theoretical and clinical work has consistently suggested the existence of both rejection and neglect as well as guilt and overprotection among parents of poorly controlled children with diabetes mellitus (Jacobson & Hauser, 1983; Koski, 1969; Minuchin et al., 1975). Minuchin et al. (1975), for instance, observed higher levels of enmeshment in their family conflicts among children with poorly controlled diabetes mellitus. Furthermore these families were also marked by overprotectiveness, extreme rigidity, overindulgence, control, perfectionism, and poor ability to resolve problems.

Empirical research consistently substantiated that in families of youth with diabetes mellitus, high level of disengagement (poor cohesion) and high degree of enmeshment (exaggerated cohesion) are linked to both poor adherence and metabolic control (Anderson et al., 1981; Cederblad, Helgesson, Larsson, & Ludvigsson, 1982; Eaton et al., 1992) and to poor psychosocial adaptation, including behavioral problems, depression, and use of avoidance coping style (Grey et al., 1980; Hanson et al., 1989; Lawler, Volk, Viviani, & Mengel, 1990; Wertlieb et al., 1986). In a similar vein, positive family climate, as evidenced by high levels of adaptability, flexibility, encouragement of independence and personal growth, communication patterns, and support, was consistently associated with both successful adherence and metabolic control (Eaton et al., 1992; Hanson et al., 1992; Hanson et al., 1987a; Marrero, Lau, Golden, Kershnar, & Myers, 1982; Schlenk & Hart, 1984; Wysocki et al., 1992) and psychosocial adaptation or higher self-esteem (Hauser, Jacobson, Wertlieb, Brink, & Wentworth, 1985; Kvam & Lyons, 1991; Sullivan, 1979; White et al., 1992). Finally, better peer relationships in children with diabetes mellitus were found to be associated with high self-esteem and better psychosocial adaptation (Grey et al., 1980; Sullivan, 1979). In adults with diabetes mellitus, major social problems were found to be associated with higher psychiatric symptomatology (Wilkinson et al., 1988).

In a well-conceptualized and well-carried-out study, Hanson et al. (1992) sought to investigate whether general family relationships (ie, parents' perceptions of marital satisfaction; family affection, cohesion, adaptability, and conflict) and diabetes mellitus specific family relationships (ie, the family's specific behaviors relative to diabetes mellitus) relate to the youth's illness-specific psychosocial adaptation (ie, acceptance of illness), general psychosocial adaptation (ie, self-esteem, social competence, behavioral problems), and health outcomes (ie, adherence to treatment, metabolic control). Participants included 95 youth with insulin-dependent diabetes mellitus and their parents. Results obtained from a series of multiple regression analyses suggested that both illness-specific and general family relations (family adaptability) contributed significantly to dietary adherence after sociodemographic variables were controlled for and that both illness-specific (high illness support) and general family relations (family affection) significantly predicted participants' general psychosocial adaptation.

CONCLUSION

A review of the clinical and empirical literature on diabetes mellitus suggests that considerable inconsistency exists as to nature, frequency, and severity of psychosocial reactions among children, adolescents, and adults with the disease. This is due, in part, to the large number of measures used as outcome criteria for both physiological (eg, metabolic control, measured as glycosylated hemoglobin or HgbA1c; adherence to therapeutic regimen, measured as compliance with insulin injections; compliance with diet; glucose monitoring; development of complications) and psychosocial adaptation. Among the latter can be found (1) several measures of self-concept and self-esteem; (2) numerous measures of psychiatric symptoms (eg, anxiety, depression) obtained from a large number of self-rated, parent-rated, and clinical interview sources (eg, Minnesota Multiphasic Personality Inventory, Symptom Check List—90-Revised, Psychosocial Adjustment to Illness Scale, Rorschach); (3) measures of parent- and teacher-rated behavioral problems (eg, the Child Behavior Check List, the Rutter Behavioral Scale); (4) measures of social adaptation and functioning (eg, the Child and Adolescent Adjustment Profile); and (5) measures of illness-specific adaptation (eg, the Diabetic Adjustment Scale).

Despite these discrepancies in measures of psychosocial outcomes, several tentative conclusions may be warranted. First, the frequency of depression and anxiety (among girls) and behavioral problems (among boys) appears to be higher among children, and possibly also among adolescents and adults with diabetes mellitus, as compared to the general population, although these frequencies appear to be comparable to those reported in other populations of persons with chronic illnesses. Second, early formulations of a "diabetic personality" have failed to be supported following more recent empirical investigations. Third, age at onset of diabetes mellitus is associated with both physiological (eg, metabolic control) and psychosocial (eg, self-esteem) adaptation, such that the earlier the age of diagnosis, the better are these types of adaptation. Fourth, individuals with internal locus of control and those with positive self-concept seem to show better physiological and psychosocial adaptation than do persons with external locus of control and those with more negative self-esteem. Fifth, increased levels of stress, anxiety, and depression are associated with poorer adherence and metabolic control among youngsters with diabetes mellitus. Finally, family cohesion and parental support are strongly linked to measures of both psychosocial and physiological adaptation.

REFERENCES

Allen, D. H., Tennen, H., McGrade, B. J., Affleck, G., & Ratzan, S. (1983). Parent and child perceptions of the management of juvenile diabetes. *Journal of Pediatric Psychology, 8*, 129–141.

American Diabetes Association. (1983). *Diabetes: The disease*. McLean, VA: Author.

Anderson, B., Miller, J. P., Auslander, W., & Santiago, J. (1981). Family characteristics of diabetic adolescents: Relationship to insulin control. *Diabetes Care, 4*, 586–594.

Andersson, S. I., & Ekdahl, C. (1992). Self-appraisal and coping in out-patients with chronic disease. *Scandinavian Journal of Psychology, 33*, 289–300.

Barglow, P., Hatcher, R., Edidin, D. V., & Sloan-Rossiter, D. (1984). Stress and metabolic control in diabetes: Psychosomatic evidence and evaluation of methods. *Psychosomatic Medicine, 46*, 127–144.

Berkow, R. (Ed.). (1992). *The Merck manual of diagnosis and therapy* (16th ed.). Rahway, NJ: Merck Research Laboratories.

Brown, R. T., Kaslow, N. J., Sansbury, L., Meacham, L., & Culler, F. L. (1991). Internalizing and externalizing symptoms and attributional style in youth with diabetes. *Journal of the American Academy of Child and Adolescent Psychiatry, 30*, 921–925.

Cederblad, M., Helgesson, M., Larsson, Y., & Ludvigsson, J. (1982). Family structure and diabetes in children. *Pediatric and Adolescent Endocrinology, 10*, 94–98.

Chase, H. P., & Jackson, G. G. (1981). Stress and sugar control in children with insulin-dependent diabetes mellitus. *Journal of Pediatrics, 98*, 1011–1013.

Close, H., Davies, A. G., Price, D. A., & Goodyer, I. M. (1986). Emotional difficulties in diabetes mellitus. *Archives of Disease in Childhood, 61*, 337–340.

De Stefano, F., Dougherty, B. L., Ford, E. S., German, R. R., Newman, J. M., & Olson, D. R. (1990). *Diabetes surveillance. 1980–1987.* Washington, DC: U. S. Department of Health and Human Services.

Delamater, A. M., Kurtz, S. M., Bubb, J., White, N. H., & Santiago, J. V. (1987). Stress and coping in relation to metabolic control of adolescents with type 1 diabetes. *Developmental and Behavioral Pediatrics, 8,* 136–140.

Denolin, F., Appelboom-Fondu, J., Lemiere, B., & Dorchy, H. (1982). Psychological problems of diabetic adolescents: Long-term follow-up. *Pediatric and Adolescent Endocrinology, 10,* 21–24.

Dunn, S. M., Smartt, H. H., Beeney, L. J., & Turtle, J. R. (1986). Measurement of emotional adjustment in diabetic patients: Validity and reliability of ATT39. *Diabetes Care, 9,* 480–489.

Dunn, S. M., & Turtle, J. R. (1981). The myth of the diabetic personality. *Diabetes Care, 4,* 640–646.

Dupuis, A., Jones, R. L., & Peterson, C. M. (1980). Psychological effects of blood glucose self-monitoring in diabetic patients. *Psychosomatics, 21,* 981–991.

Eaton, W. W., Mengel, M., Mengel, L., Larson, D., Campbell, R., & Montague, R. B. (1992). Psychosocial and psychopathologic influences on management and control of insulin-dependent diabetes. *International Journal of Psychiatry in Medicine, 22,* 105–117.

Falvo, D. R. (1991). *Medical and psychosocial aspects of chronic illness and disability.* Gaithersburg, MD: Aspen.

Fisher, E. B., Delamater, A. M., Bertelson, A. D., & Kirkley, B. G. (1982). Psychological factors in diabetes and its treatment. *Journal of Consulting and Clinical Psychology, 50,* 993–1003.

Frenzel, M. P., McCaul, K. D., Glasgow, R. E., & Schafer, L. C. (1988). The relationship of stress and coping to regimen adherence and glycemic control of diabetes. *Journal of Social and Clinical Psychology, 6,* 77–87.

Gath, A., Smith, M. A., & Baum, J. D. (1980). Emotional, behavioural, and educational disorders in diabetic children. *Archives of Disease in Childhood, 55,* 371–375.

Grey, M., Cameron, M. E., & Thurber, F. W. (1991). Coping and adaptation in children with diabetes. *Nursing Research, 40,* 144–149.

Grey, M. J., Genel, M., & Tamborlane, W. V. (1980). Psychosocial adjustment of latency-aged diabetics: Determinants and relationship to control. *Pediatrics, 65,* 69–73.

Hamburg, B. A., & Inoff, G. E. (1983). Coping with predictable crises of diabetes. *Diabetes Care, 6,* 409–415.

Hanson, C. L., DeGuire, M. J., Schinkel, A. M., Henggeler, S. W., & Burghen, G. A. (1992). Comparing social learning and family systems correlates of adaptation in youths with IDDM. *Journal of Pediatric Psychology, 17,* 555–572.

Hanson, C. L., Harris, M. A., Relyea, G., Cigrang, J. A., Carle, D. L., & Burghen, G. A. (1989). Coping styles in youths with insulin-dependent diabetes mellitus. *Journal of Consulting and Clinical Psychology, 57,* 644–651.

Hanson, C. L., Henggeler, S. W., & Burghen, G. A. (1987a). Model of associations between psychosocial variables and health-outcome measures of adolescents with IDDM. *Diabetes Care, 10,* 752–758.

Hanson, C. L., Henggeler, S. W., & Burghen, G. A. (1987b). Social competence and parental support as mediators of the link between stress and metabolic control in adolescents with insulin-dependent diabetes mellitus. *Journal of Consulting and Clinical Psychology, 55,* 529–533.

Hanson, C. L., Rodrigue, J. R., Henggeler, S. W., Harris, M. A., Klesges, R. C., & Carle, L. (1990). The perceived self-competence of adolescents with insulin-dependent diabetes mellitus: Deficit or strength? *Journal of Pediatric Psychology, 15,* 605–618.

Hauser, S. T., Jacobson, A. M., Noam, G., & Powers, S. (1983). Ego development and self-image complexity in early adolescence. *Archives of General Psychiatry, 40*, 325–332.

Hauser, S. T., Jacobson, A. M., Wertlieb, D., Brink, S., & Wentworth, S. (1985). The contribution of family environment to perceived competence and illness adjustment in diabetic acutely ill adolescents. *Family Relations, 34*, 99–108.

Hauser, S. T., Pollets, D., Turner, B. L., Jacobson, A., Powers, S., & Noam, G. (1979). Ego development and self-esteem in diabetic adolescents. *Diabetes Care, 2*, 465–471.

Hornichter, R. D. (1992). Diabetes mellitus. In M. G. Brodwin, F. Tellez, & S. K. Brodwin (Eds.), *Medical, psychosocial and vocational aspects of disability* (pp. 285–296). Athens, GA: Elliott & Fitzpatrick.

Isenberg, P. L., & Barnett, D. M. (1965). Psychological problems in diabetes mellitus. *Medical Clinics of North America, 49*, 1125–1136.

Jacobson, A. M., Adler, A. G., Wolfsdorf, J. I., Anderson, B., & Derby, L. (1990). Psychological characteristics of adults with IDDM. *Diabetes Care, 13*, 375–381.

Jacobson, A. M., Beardslee, W., Hauser, S. T., Noam, G. G., Powers, S. I., Houlihan, J., & Rider, E. (1986). Evaluating ego defense mechanisms using clinical interviews: An empirical study of adolescent diabetic and psychiatric. *Journal of Adolescence, 9*, 303–319.

Jacobson, A. M., & Hauser, S. T. (1983). Behavioral and psychological aspects of diabetes. In M. Ellenberg & H. Rifkin (Eds.), *Diabetes mellitus: Theory and practice* (3rd. ed.) (pp. 1037–1052). New York: Medical Examination Publishing Co.

Jacobson, A. M., Hauser, S. T., Lavori, P., Wolfsdorf, J. I., Herskowitz, R. D., Milley, J. E., Bliss, R., Gelfand, E., Wertlieb, D., & Stein, J. (1990). Adherence among children and adolescents with insulin-dependent diabetes mellitus over a four-year longitudinal follow-up: I. The influence of patient coping and adjustment. *Journal of Pediatric Psychology, 15*, 511–526.

Jacobson, A. M., Hauser, S. T., Wertlieb, D., Wolfsdorf, J. I., Orleans, J., & Vieyra, M. (1986). Psychological adjustment of children with recently diagnosed diabetes mellitus. *Diabetes Care, 9*, 323–329.

Jacobson, A. M., Hauser, S. T., Wolfsdorf, J. I., Houlihan, J., Milley, J. E., Herskowitz, G., Wertlieb, D., & Watt, E. (1987). Psychologic predictors of compliance in children with recent onset of diabetes mellitus. *Journal of Pediatrics, 110*, 805–811.

Johnson, S. B. (1980). Psychosocial factors in juvenile diabetes: A review. *Journal of Behavioral Medicine, 3*, 95–116.

Johnson, S. B., & Rosenbloom, A. L. (1982). Behavioral aspects of diabetes mellitus in childhood and adolescence. *Psychiatric Clinics of North America, 5*, 357–369.

Karlsson, J. A., Holmes, C. S., & Lang, R. (1988). Psychosocial aspects of disease duration and control in young adults with type I diabetes. *Journal of Clinical Epidemiology, 41*, 435–440.

Koski, M. L. (1969). The coping processes in childhood diabetes. *Acta Paediatrica Scandinavica, 1–198 (Suppl.)*, 56.

Kovacs, M., Brent, D., Steinberg, T. F., Paulauskas, S., & Reid, J. (1986). Children's self-reports of psychologic adjustment and coping strategies during first year of insulin-dependent diabetes mellitus. *Diabetes Care, 9*, 472–479.

Kovacs, M., Feinberg, T. L., Paulauskas, S., Finkelstein, R., Pollock, M., & Crouse-Novak, M. (1985). Initial coping responses and psychosocial characteristics of children with insulin-dependent diabetes mellitus. *Journal of Pediatrics, 106*, 827–834.

Kovacs, M., Iyengar, S., Goldston, D., Stewart, J., Obrosky, D. S., & Marsh, J. (1990). Psychological functioning of children with insulin-dependent diabetes mellitus: A longitudinal study. *Journal of Pediatric Psychology, 15*, 619–632.

Kvam, S. H., & Lyons, J. S. (1991). Assessment of coping strategies, social support, and general health status in individuals with diabetes mellitus. *Psychological Reports, 68*, 623–632.

Lavigne, J. V., Traisman, H. S., Marr, T. J., & Chasnoff, l. J. (1982). Parental perceptions of the psychological adjustment of children with diabetes and their siblings. *Diabetes Care, 5*, 420–426.

Lawler, M. K., Volk, R. J., Viviani, N., & Mengel, M. B. (1990). Individual and family factors impacting diabetes control in the adolescent: A preliminary study. *Maternal Child Nursing Journal, 19*, 331–345.

Littlefield, C. H., Rodin, G. M., Murray, M. A., & Craven, J. L. (1990). Influence of functional impairment and social support on depressive symptoms in persons with diabetes. *Health Psychology, 9*, 737–749.

Lustman. P. J., Amado, H., & Wetzel. R. D. (1983). Depression in diabetics: A critical appraisal. *Comprehensive Psychiatry, 24*, 65–74.

Lustman, P. J., Griffith, L. S., Clouse, R. E., & Cryer, P. E. (1986). Psychiatric illness in diabetes mellitus. *Journal of Nervous and Mental Disease, 174*, 736–742.

Marrero, D. G., Lau, N., Golden, M. P., Kershnar, A., & Myers, G. C. (1982). Family dynamics in adolescent diabetes mellitus: Parental behavior and metabolic control. *Pediatric and Adolescent Endocrinology, 10*, 77–82.

Mason, C. (1985). The production and effects of uncertainty with special reference to diabetes mellitus. *Social Science and Medicine, 21*, 1329–1334.

Mazze, R. S., Lucido, D., & Shamoon, H. (1984). Psychological and social correlates of glycemic control. *Diabetes Care, 7*, 360–366.

McCraw, R. K., & Tuma, J. M. (1977). Rorschach content categories of juvenile diabetics. *Psychological Reports, 40*, 818.

Minuchin, S., Baker, L., Rosman, B., Liebman, R., Milman, L., & Todd, T. (1975). A conceptual model of psychosomatic illness in children. *Archives of General Psychiatry, 32*, 1031–1038.

Murawski, B. I., Chazan, B. I., Balodimos, M. C., & Ryan, J. R. (1970). Personality patterns in patients with diabetes mellitus of long duration. *Diabetes, 19*, 259–263.

Niemcryk, S. J., Speers, M. A., Travis, L. B., & Gary, H. E. (1990). Psychosocial correlates of hemoglobin Alc in young adults with type I diabetes. *Journal of Psychosomatic Research, 34*, 617–627.

Peyrot, M., & McMurry, J. F. (1985). Psychosocial factors in diabetes control: Adjustment of insulin-treated adults. *Psychosomatic Medicine, 47*, 542–557.

Pollock, S. E. (1989). Adaptive responses to diabetes mellitus. *Western Journal of Nursing Research, 11*, 265–275.

Popkin, M. K., Callies, A. L., Lentz, R. D., Colon, E. A., & Sutherland, D. E. (1988). Prevalence of major depression, simple phobia, and other psychiatric disorders in patients with long-standing type I diabetes mellitus. *Archives to General Psychiatry, 45*, 64–68.

Rovet, J., Ehrlich, R., & Hoppe, M. (1987). Behaviour problems in children with diabetes as a function of sex and age of onset of disease. *Journal of Child Psychology and Psychiatry, 28*, 477–491.

Ryan, C. M., & Morrow, L. A. (1986). Self-esteem in diabetic adolescents: Relationship between age at onset and gender. *Journal of Consulting and Clinical Psychology, 54*, 730–731.

Sanders, K., Mills, J., Martin, F. I. R., & Horne, D. J. (1975). Emotional attitudes in adult insulin-dependent diabetics. *Journal of Psychosomatic Research, 19*, 241–246.

Saucier, C. P. (1984). Self-concept and self-care management in school-age children with diabetes. *Pediatric Nursing, 10*, 135–138.

Schlenk, E. A., & Hart, L. K. (1984). Relationship between health locus of control, health value, and social support and compliance of persons with diabetes mellitus. *Diabetes Care*, *7*, 566–574.

Simonds, J. F. (1976–1977). Psychiatric status of diabetic youth in good and poor control. *International Journal of Psychiatry in Medicine*, *7*, 133–151.

Simonds, J. F. (1977). Psychiatric status of diabetic youth matched with a control group. *Diabetes*, *26*, 921–925.

Simonds, J. F., Goldstein, D., Walker, R., & Rawlings, S. (1981). The relationship between psychological factors and blood glucose regulation in insulin-dependent diabetic adolescents. *Diabetes Care*, *4*, 610–615.

Sullivan, B. J. (1978). Self-esteem and depression in adolescent diabetic girls. *Diabetes Care*, *1*, 18–22.

Sullivan, B. J. (1979). Adjustment in diabetic adolescent girls: II. Adjustment, self-esteem, and depression in diabetic adolescent girls. *Psychosomatic Medicine*, *41*, 127–128.

Surridge, D. H., Williams-Erdahl, D. L., Lawson, J. S., Donald, M. W., Monga, T. H., Bird, C. E., & Letemendia, F. T. J. (1984). Psychiatric aspects of diabetes mellitus. *British Journal of Psychiatry*, *145*, 269–276.

Swift, C. R., Seidman, F., & Stein, H. (1967). Adjustment problems in juvenile diabetes. *Psychosomatic Medicine*, *29*, 555–571.

Tebbi, C. K., Bromberg, C., Sills, I., Cukierman, J., & Piedmonte, M. (1990). Vocational adjustment and general well-being of young adults with IDDM. *Diabetes Care*, *13*, 98–103.

Turk, D. C., & Speers, M. A. (1983). Diabetes mellitus: A cognitive-functional analysis of stress. In T. G. Burish & L. A. Bradley (Eds.), *Coping with chronic disease: Research and applications* (pp. 191–217). New York: Academic Press.

Turkat, I. D. (1982). Glycosylated hemoglobin levels in anxious and nonanxious diabetic patients. *Psychosomatics*, *23*, 1056–1057.

Wertlieb, D., Hauser, S. T., & Jacobson, A. M. (1986). Adaptation to diabetes: Behavior symptoms and family context. *Journal of Pediatric Psychology*, *11*, 463–479.

White, N. E., Richter, J. M., & Fry, C. (1992). Coping, social support, and adaptation to chronic illness. *Western Journal of Nursing Research*, *14*, 211–224.

Wilkinson, D. G. (1981). Psychiatric aspects of diabetes mellitus. *British Journal of Psychiatry*, *138*, 1–9.

Wilkinson, G., Borsey, D. Q., Leslie, P., Newton, R. W., Lind, C., & Ballinger, C. B. (1987). Psychiatric disorder in patients with insulin-dependent diabetes mellitus attending a general hospital clinic: (i) two-stage screening and (ii) detection by physicians. *Psychological Medicine*, *17*, 515–517.

Wilkinson, G., Borsey, D. Q., Leslie, P., Newton, R. W., Lind, C., & Ballinger, C. B. (1988). Psychiatric morbidity and social problems in patients with insulin-dependent diabetes mellitus. *British Journal of Psychiatry*, *153*, 38–43.

Wysocki, T., Hough, B. S., Ward, K. M., & Green, L. B. (1992). Diabetes mellitus in the transition to adulthood: Adjustment, self-care, and health status. *Developmental and Behavioral Pediatrics*, *13*, 194–201.

CHAPTER 10

Rheumatoid Arthritis

DESCRIPTION

Rheumatoid arthritis is one of a family of more than 100 noninfectious and noncontagious arthritic diseases characterized by joint (arthron) inflammation (itis) (Shlotzhauer & McGuire, 1993). Earlier this disease was called rheumatism, a term derived from the Greeks, who thought that inflammation and swelling of the joints was due to the flow of bad humors (reuma; Brewerton, 1992). In the mid-19th century it was discovered that human cells travel to the site of inflammation in the body, but it was not until near the end of that century that this process was understood as a response of the body's immune system. The body generates specialized cells (antibodies) that attempt to fight the infection or injury by devouring foreign substances (antigens) that have invaded the body at the site of inflammation. Typically this process is self-limiting; the inflammation subsides as the antigens are destroyed and homeostasis of the body is restored. In some cases, however, this process does not stop, and inappropriate or excessive formation of antibodies leads to illness. Rheumatoid arthritis is one such autoimmune disorder in which a disruption in the immune system leads to an inability of the body to distinguish natural body tissues from foreign cells and the body begins to destroy itself (Pigg, Driscoll, & Caniff, 1985). There are two broad categories in this family of arthritic diseases (Brewerton, 1992; Kantrowitz, 1991; Pigg et al., 1985; Samuels & Samuels, 1991).

Inflammatory arthritis begins in the synovium, a membrane that encapsulates the joint and secretes a fluid that lubricates it. Swelling may be the result of excess synovial fluid or due to the enlargement of the synovium itself. The inflammation then spreads to surrounding tissue, potentially destroying cartilage, supporting tissue, and bone. The cause of this chronic and systemic (many joints in the body are affected) disease is unknown and there is no cure. Inflam-

225

mation typically begins in the small joints of the wrists, hands, and feet, progressing gradually to the knees, elbows, shoulders, hips, ankles, and spine. Symptoms include pain, swelling, stiffness, warmth, and loss of function. Associated symptoms may include fever, weight loss, anemia, and fatigue.

Inflammatory arthritis is a progressive, destructive disease process that may eventually involve vital organs (eg, lymph system, lungs, eyes) in some individuals. Although many individuals may experience spontaneous remission with no recurrence of symptoms, the course of the disease is typically highly variable and unpredictable. The individual with inflammatory arthritis may experience periods of gradual or rapid symptom exacerbations and remissions, similar to multiple sclerosis. Approximately 1% of the population is affected, a rate that increases with age. Three times as many females as males are affected. The onset of symptoms is typically between ages 30 and 50 years.

The primary subtype of inflammatory arthritis is rheumatoid arthritis. Other major subtypes include systemic lupus erythematosus (a highly unpredictable autoimmune disease appearing most frequently in the connective tissue of females younger than 40 years of age), ankylosing spondylitis (a genetic disease affecting the spine and appearing generally in males between the ages of 18 and 35 years), and gout (a metabolic disorder that results in the deposit of uric acid crystals in a single joint). Reactive arthritis refers to inflammation of one or more joints due to infections elsewhere in the body. The infection may be attributable to parasites, bacteria, viruses, or fungus or may be associated with acquired immune deficiency syndrome (AIDS), Lyme disease, hepatitis, or rubella.

Degenerative joint disease, also called osteoarthritis, is the most common form of arthritic disease, affecting more than 16 million Americans. Nearly all people experience some osteoarthritic symptoms as they age. Its name is somewhat misleading, as it is characterized by deterioration of the joints between bones (osteo) as a result of wear and tear or injury. The cartilage softens, cracks, flakes, splits, loses elasticity, and may be destroyed. As normal tissues degrade, inappropriate matter is deposited in their place, reducing and deforming the joint space. The bone itself may become exposed, and excess body tissue may form at the margins (bone spurs or osteophyte formations). Inflammation in this type of arthritis is not a necessary component but rather is secondary to the joint deterioration. The affected joint is typically localized in the knees, fingers, or hips and may be significantly and permanently deformed (arthrosis). Symptoms include pain, stiffness, muscle spasms, loss of range of motion, warmth, and swelling.

Degenerative arthritis may be the result of a birth injury or congenital defect (eg, dislocated hip), obesity, poor posture, physical stress, trauma, aging, or other forms of arthritis or may be attributable to persistent exposure to infection, toxins, or cold. Evidence is accumulating that some people may be genetically predisposed to degenerative arthritis (Brewerton, 1992; Pigg et al., 1985).

Arthritis affects more than 100 million people worldwide and more than 36 million in the United States in all ethnic groups, all geographic locations, and all levels of society (Brewerton, 1992; Samuels & Samuels, 1991). The social and economic consequences of arthritis are immense. It is the single biggest disease cause of loss of work time.

PSYCHOSOCIAL ADAPTATION TO RHEUMATOID ARTHRITIS

The scientific investigation of emotional and psychological characteristics among persons with rheumatoid arthritis dates at least from the work of Jones (1909). In the earliest investigations, emotional factors associated with significant life events (eg, surgery, pregnancy, death of a loved one, sexual problems in marriage) were thought to be agents triggering the onset of disease symptoms. An example of this line of investigation is the research of King and Cobb (1958) who interviewed a total of 1,323 individuals from among a random probability sample of 7,132 residents of Pittsburgh in 1951. They reported that of the 200 individuals who were found to be positive for rheumatoid arthritis, the primary sociodemographic characteristics were low income, low education, and high divorce rate. From these data they speculated that stressful environmental and psychological events may precipitate rheumatoid arthritis.

A somewhat more recent study attempted to contribute insight in this domain. Henoch, Batson, and Baum (1978) collected interview data from a total of 88 families of children with juvenile rheumatoid arthritis and compared them to random samples of 2,952 children in the same geographic area. Three times as many of the children with rheumatoid arthritis had been adopted, and the rate of marital problems in the intact families of children with rheumatoid arthritis was more than twice as great as that for the families of the children with no impairments. This investigation could not determine whether the children's rheumatoid arthritis was precipitated by family stress or whether the chronic illness had caused disruptions in the families that were manifest in the characteristics noted.

Meyerowitz (1966) proposed three testable hypotheses to guide investigations of the association between psychological, emotional, and social factors and arthritic disease onset. The hypotheses are as follows:

1. Specificity (prediagnosis) hypothesis—an identifiable constellation of psychological characteristics of the individual are present prior to the appearance of the symptoms of rheumatoid arthritis that serve as precipitating or causative agents in the onset of rheumatoid arthritis.
2. Disease-onset (paridiagnosis) hypothesis—a significant temporal association can be found between the occurrence of certain types of stressful life experiences and psychological states and the onset of the symptoms of rheumatoid arthritis.

3. Disease-course (postdiagnosis) hypothesis—identifiable psychological responses are observable in persons diagnosed with rheumatoid arthritis and these responses may influence the course of the disease and the individuals' subsequent adaptation to it.

Both Hoffman (1974) and Zeitlin (1977) reviewed the research literature up to the early 1970s that related to Meyerowitz's three hypotheses. After critiquing the early research for significant methodological shortcomings (eg, use of projective measures, poor control of intervening variables, lack of comparison groups) and noting the immense problems in designing research to adequately test these hypotheses, both reviewers concluded that the first hypothesis was clearly unfounded.

The evidence at that time for the second hypothesis was scant—both reviewers noted the reliance on biased retrospective reports of persons with rheumatoid arthritis and their parents or spouses—but generally unfavorable. For example, Mindham, Bagshaw, James, and Swannell (1981) found that neither affective symptoms nor psychiatric complications in a sample of 28 persons with rheumatoid arthritis were related in any specific way to the onset of specific rheumatoid arthritis symptoms or symptom groups, even in the most severely affected individuals.

Zeitlin (1977) noted that stress and psychological factors may play some role as one of a set of multicausal triggers (other factors might include genetic, autoimmune response to infection, and environmental agents) in the onset of some symptoms, but lamented the lack of longitudinal and predictive research on this hypothesis. Later researchers (Parker et al., 1993; Varni & Jay, 1984) refer to the multicausal triggers mentioned by Zeitlin (1977) as biopsychosocial factors, a term coined by Engel (1977), that is, the manifestation of a chronic illness is not just related to biological factors but is inextricably intertwined with psychological and social factors that occur both prior to and subsequent to the onset of the illness. We must concur with both Hoffman (1974) and Zeitlin (1977), who concluded that the third of Meyerowitz's hypotheses is the most parsimonious given the research results available to date. The review of the literature in this chapter focuses primarily on the research evidence for this hypothesis.

Frequent attempts were made by psychosomatic medical researchers to discover a universal "rheumatic personality" profile (Cleveland & Fisher, 1954; Johnson, Shapiro, & Alexander, 1947; Moos, 1964; Moos & Solomon, 1964; Polley, Swenson, & Steinhilber, 1970). This research typically relied upon data from self-report instruments such as the Minnesota Multiphasic Personality Inventory (Bourestom & Howard, 1965; Nalven & O'Brien, 1964) or from projective techniques such as the Thematic Apperception Test (Mueller, Lefkovits, Bryant, & Marshall, 1961). It was frequently reported that persons with rheumatoid arthritis were depressed, self-sacrificing, inhibited, shy, masochistic, rigid, conforming, unable to express themselves freely, and prone to fantasies about their disability. One particular personality trait that for a time was thought to be especially characteristic of persons with rheumatoid arthritis was contained or repressed hostility (Cleveland & Fisher, 1954; Cobb, 1959; King, 1955; Mueller et al., 1961), especially among females (Bourestom & Howard, 1965). It was hypothesized that as a consequence of the physical restrictions and the disruption of typical social, sexual, and vocational pursuits, the individual with rheumatoid arthritis tended to evade frustrating situations. Unable or unwilling to express feelings of frustration and dissatisfaction, these individuals tend to suppress or repress these feelings, only to have them emerge as aggression or hostility under stressful situations.

Although certain psychosocial reactions (ie, depression, anger, anxiety) are commonly expressed by persons with rheumatoid arthritis, they are by no means universal personality traits (Cleveland, Reitman, & Brewer, 1965; Nalven & O'Brien, 1964; Spergel, Ehrlich, & Glass, 1978; Ward, 1971). As Moos (1964) and others (Anderson, Bradley, Young, McDaniel, & Wise, 1985; Baum, 1982; Bradley, 1985; Genest, 1983; Smith, 1979) have aptly pointed out, any evidence in support of the so-called "rheumatic personality" was obtained from investigations that (1) differed in the definition and measurement of personality characteristics, (2) classified independent variables as both cause and effect of the disease, (3) used unsound retrospective self-reports or projective instruments to measure dependent variables that focused on negative personality traits, (4) included heterogeneous nonrandom samples or self-selected hospital patients, (5) failed to take into account intervening variables, (6) included either no or inadequate comparison groups, (7) differed in the diagnostic criteria used to define rheumatoid arthritis, and (8) relied on cross-sectional rather than longitudinal research designs. For example, more than 50% of the articles reviewed by Baum (1982) used special measures to define the dependent variables that were specially devised for the study and used by no other researcher. An additional 36% used projective devices (eg, Rorschach, Thematic Apperception Test) to operationalize psychosocial adaptation. Baum noted that in the articles reviewed, rheumatoid arthritis was not clearly defined and samples were typically nonrandom and often biased (eg, male patients in Veterans Administration hospitals). Confounding factors were not separated, with the result that psychosocial reactions manifested by persons with rheumatoid arthritis might have been reactions to chronic pain and not to the disease itself.

The consequences of rheumatoid arthritis include physical disability, decreased strength and stamina, chronic pain, dependency upon others and upon technology to compensate for the deterioration of functional abilities, disturbance of sleep patterns, prolonged medical treatment, substantial time devoted to treatment, and economic losses due to reduced earnings or loss of employment. In addition, this chronic disease can significantly disrupt the individual's lifestyle by altering involvement with valued life activities. These consequences will be typically expressed in such psychosocial domains as self-esteem, life satisfaction, social activities, family functioning, work satisfaction, sexual functioning, capacity to cope, locus of control, and changes in body image. Similar to research conducted with persons with other chronic illness (eg, epilepsy, multiple sclerosis), the complex interplay of physical, psychosocial, and situational factors leads to extensive interindividual variability in psychosocial adaptation to rheumatoid arthritis (Anderson et al., 1985; Baum, 1982; Iverson, 1995; Parker et al., 1993; Robinson, Kirk, & Frye, 1971; Young, 1992).

Until recently empirical data concerning psychosocial adaptation of persons with rheumatoid arthritis were derived from clinical case reports, personal life histories, anecdotal records, retrospective self-report questionnaire data of dubious psychometric adequacy, or data obtained from interviews with parents, spouses, or family members (Baker, 1981; Baker, 1982; Blake, Maisiak, Brown, & Kaplan, 1986; King & Cobb, 1958; Scotch & Geiger, 1962; Smith, 1979). Based upon clinical experience and anecdotal records, Krutzer (1984) suggested that a series of reactions is commonly evinced by persons with rheumatoid arthritis. The individual's first reaction is typified by shock at the diagnosis of the disease, followed by disbelief and denial to protect one's self-esteem. A period of anxiety and depression typically begins after the individual grasps the reality of his or her situation. This period may also be characterized by excess fear, despondency, disinterest, withdrawal, hopelessness, sadness, and grief. If the symptoms of the disease flare or its consequences worsen, anger and hostility may be expressed, and these reactions may exacerbate the individual's pain by increasing stress and tension. The anger may be inner or outer directed and may be a defense against depression and anxiety. Samuels and Samuels (1991) proposed a similar set of psychosocial reaction stages among persons with rheumatoid arthritis, but they failed to provide empirical evidence for their assertions.

The literature reviewed in the remainder of this section used generally sound research designs and serves as an initial step to providing an empirical database from which recommendations for intervention can be derived. It should be noted, however, that one or more of the criticisms outlined above applies to nearly all of these studies. (See also the general criticisms of this literature presented in Chapter 24.)

In an early comparison-group empirical study of general psychosocial reactions to rheumatoid arthritis, Crown and Crown (1973) administered the Middlesex Hospital Questionnaire to a nonrandom sample of persons in the early stages of rheumatoid arthritis as well as to comparison groups of hospital outpatients without disabilities and psychiatric hospital outpatients without disabilities in

England. Their results showed that the scores for the persons with rheumatoid arthritis were below those for the psychiatric hospital outpatients on all six scales of the questionnaire: free-floating anxiety, phobic anxiety, obsessionality, somatic anxiety, depression, and hysterical traits. The females with rheumatoid arthritis scored above the hospital outpatients without disabilities on the free-floating anxiety subscale, and the males with rheumatoid arthritis scored above the hospital outpatients without disabilities on the somatic anxiety subscale.

McAnarney, Pless, Satterwhite, and Friedman (1974) and Satterwhite (1978) reported the results of a large-scale study that compared a group of 42 children and adolescents with rheumatoid arthritis and a group of children without impairments. The groups were matched for age, sex, and socioeconomic status. Dependent variables included self-esteem, anxiety, global measures of emotional health (California Test of Personality, a human figure projective technique), and parent and teacher reports of behavior and school problems. Twice as many of the children with rheumatoid arthritis as the controls had been referred to a psychologist for school problems, three times as many were low achieving, and four times as many were experiencing significant school adjustment problems. According to parent evaluations, only 36% of the children with rheumatoid arthritis had no emotional problems, compared to 60% of the control children. The children with rheumatoid arthritis reported greater anxiety and more negative self-esteem than the comparison children. Other investigators have also found that persons with rheumatoid arthritis report more negative levels of self-esteem when compared to controls (Bradley, 1985; Earle et al., 1979).

Daniels, Moos, Billings, and Miller (1987) asked the mothers of a cross-sectional, nonrandom sample of children with juvenile rheumatoid arthritis to complete the Health and Daily Living Form. This instrument provides three scores: (a) an adjustment problem score derived from a set of questions in eight areas (anxiety, depression, nightmares, nail biting, mental or emotional problems, school problems, discipline problems, getting along with other children), (2) a physical problems score that concerns general health status (asthma, allergies, mobility impairments), and (3) a multiproblem index that is a weighted combination of the first two scores. In addition to the sample of 93 children with rheumatoid arthritis, a total of 72 of their siblings and a control group of 93 children without impairments were included in the investigation. Data were also collected on a set of family and sociodemographic variables. As expected, the children with rheumatoid arthritis scored significantly higher than the other two groups on the physical problems score. Both the children with rheumatoid arthritis and their siblings scored significantly higher than the control children on the adjustment problem scale. A total of 20% of the children with rheumatoid arthritis were found to exceed norms on the multiproblem index compared to 14% of the siblings and 5% of the children without impairments.

Several investigators have compared data on psychosocial reactions obtained from persons with rheumatoid arthritis to published norms. Robinson and colleagues (Robinson et al., 1971; Robinson, Kirk, Frye, & Robertson, 1972) administered the 16 Personality Factors test and the Eysenck Personality Inventory to groups of persons with rheumatoid arthritis and discovered that, compared to the norms for the instruments, they reported more anxiety, introversion, and depression. Gardiner (1980) analyzed data on the Eysenck Personality Inventory, the General Health Questionnaire, and the Zung Self-Rating Scale for Depression from a sample of postinpatient persons with rheumatoid arthritis and discovered that they scored above the norms for the general population on the Zung Self-Rating Scale for Depression and the General Health Questionnaire and scored higher than the norms on the neuroticism scale and lower on the extroversion scales of the Eysenck Personality Inventory. Vandik (1990) collected clinical data from 72 school-aged children with juvenile rheumatoid arthritis in Norway and found that 51% met the criteria for one or more psychiatric diagnoses of the DSM—III, including dysthymic disorder (19), separation anxiety disorder (8), major depression (3), compulsive disorder (2), overanxious disorder (2), oppositional disorder (3), and attention deficit hyperactive disorder (1). When scores on the Children's Global Assessment Scale were examined, it was found that 64% displayed mild psychiatric problems and 6% displayed moderate to severe psychiatric problems.

Cassileth et al. (1984), however, found no significant differences in self-reports of anxiety, depression, positive affect, emotional distress, loss of control, or global mental health as measured by the General Well-Being Schedule and the Mental Health Index between a sample of persons with rheumatoid arthritis and the instruments' norms for the general population. Similarly, in a study of children and adolescents with juvenile rheumatoid arthritis using the Profile of Mood States and the Child Behavior Check List (Daltroy et al., 1992), it was reported that the children did not differ significantly from published population norms on either of these scales. The researchers noted, however, that the mothers rated the children higher on the Child Behavior Check List internalizing scale (fearful, inhibited) than on the externalizing scale (aggressive, antisocial).

Ennett et al. (1991) argued that requiring a parent or teacher to judge the psychosocial adaptation of children with juvenile rheumatoid arthritis using instruments such as the Child Behavior Check List could yield nonpurposefully skewed data. In an attempt to collect data directly from the children, these researchers interviewed a sample of children between the ages of 7 and 13 years who had juvenile rheumatoid arthritis. Interview questions were designed to gather information on disease consequences (family activities, emotional impact, social functioning) and the children's self-perceptions of competence (eg, athletic abilities, physical attractiveness, social acceptance). The mothers of the children were also interviewed with a similar schedule of questions. Global disease severity was assessed from a review of the child's medical records. Positive correlations were found between the children's and the mothers' reports in all areas. The children's reports of disease consequences were positively related to their self-perceptions of competence even after disease severity was partialled out of the relationship. The children's outlooks on day-to-day experiences were significantly more positive than the mothers' inferences about their child's experiences. In addition, the mothers reported significantly greater impact of the children's disease on the family and less social acceptance than did the children.

Liang et al. (1984) studied psychiatric symptoms and psychosocial risk among a sample of 23 volunteers with rheumatoid arthritis and a sample of 76 volunteers with systemic lupus erythematosus. Both samples were predominantly white married females less than 50 years of age with mild forms of their respective diseases. Data were collected from the Minnesota Multiphasic Personality Inventory, the Health Locus of Control scale, and the Schedule of Recent Events. The individuals with rheumatoid arthritis reported that their biggest problem was mobility and their biggest fear was physical incapacity. The two groups reported similar locus of control with neither internal nor external predominating. Individuals with rheumatoid arthritis were found to be significantly at risk on the so-called neurotic triad of Minnesota Multiphasic Personality Inventory scales, namely, Hypochondriasis (35%), Depression (41%), and Hysteria (29%). The investigators interpreted these results as representing the "profound impact" of rheumatoid arthritis upon the psychosocial adaptation of the individuals in the sample.

Several investigations were discovered that attempted to follow up the psychosocial status of individuals with rheumatoid arthritis identified in earlier investigations. Hill, Herstein, and Walters (1974), for example, interviewed a group of 58 persons with rheumatoid arthritis in Canada who were among a group of 185 diagnosed as early as 1954. It was reported that the individuals in the sample had achieved limited educational success compared to the general population. This was attributed to prolonged absences from school due to pain or medical treatment, and the public policy of the period that excluded children with mobility problems from public education. Employment history and social relationships of the individuals studied were similar to those for the general population. Miller, Spitz, Simpson, and Williams (1982) collected questionnaire data from a total of 121 individuals over age 18 years who had been identified and treated in a specialty clinic as children between 1955 and 1978. The individuals reported that they were functioning well socially, with adaptation somewhat but not significantly lower for females than for males in the sample. No significant differences were found when the sample was compared to the norm for the population on variables of schooling, work status, or income.

A small number of investigations have concerned specific psychosocial reactions to rheumatoid arthritis. Several early clinical investigations provided evidence suggesting an increased risk of expressions of anxiety among persons with rheumatoid arthritis (Anderson et al., 1985; Bradley, 1985; Crown, Crown, & Fleming, 1974; Robinson et al., 1971; Robinson et al., 1972). Patrick, Morgan, and Charlton (1986) reported that approximately one third of the individuals with rheumatoid arthritis who were surveyed in London reported experiencing depression. Studies of persons with rheumatoid arthritis using the Minnesota Multiphasic Personality Inventory have noted elevated scores in the so-called neurotic triad of Hypochondriasis, Depression, and Hysteria scales (Baum, 1982; Liang et al., 1984; Nalven & O'Brien, 1964; Polley et al., 1970). It has been pointed out, however, that (1) dysphoria is not unique to persons with rheumatoid arthritis and is common in persons experiencing chronic, painful, and disabling diseases; and (2) many of the items on self-report measures of depression are confounded with the clinical manifestations of the disease itself (eg, questions concerning fatigue, sleep disturbances, or pain).

Elevated levels of depression, as measured by instruments such as the Beck Depression Inventory or the Zung Self-Rating Scale for Depression and other clinical psychiatric instruments (eg, Eysenck Personality Inventory, 16 Personality Factors test), are frequently observed in persons with rheumatoid arthritis (Bourestom & Howard, 1965; Bradley, 1985; Brown, Wallston, & Nicassio, 1989; Rimón, 1974; Rimón, Belmaker, & Ebstein, 1977; Robinson et al., 1971; Robinson et al., 1972). Goodenow, Reisine, and Grady (1990), for example, reported that 23% of their sample of 194 females with rheumatoid arthritis were above the cutoff point for depression, as measured by the Center for Epidemiologic Studies Depression Scale. DeForge, Sobal, and Krick (1989) administered the General Well-Being Schedule, the Zung Self-Rating Scale for Depression, and the Center for Epidemiologic Studies Depression Scale to a sample of 86 older individuals (mean age 71 years, range 60 to 89 years) with osteoarthritis living in two senior centers. Results revealed that depression was inversely related to perceptions of health, physical activity, independence in activities of daily living, and general well-being. Depression was not found to be related to age or to degree of self-reported pain. Chandarana, Eals, Steingart, Bellamy, and Allen (1987) administered by mail the General Health Questionnaire and the Hospital Anxiety and Depression Scale to a sample of persons with rheumatoid arthritis. A total of 32% of the respondents were identified as psychiatric cases by the General Health Questionnaire. The Hospital Anxiety and Depression Scale identified 21% of the respondents as anxious and 19% as depressed.

In a comparison group study, Earle et al. (Earle et al., 1979) discovered that their nonrandom sample of 50 persons with rheumatoid arthritis reported higher levels of depression and meaninglessness of life and lower self-esteem than did a comparison group of 72 nonpatients selected at random from the phone book. Zaphiropoulos and Burry (1974) collected data on depression using the Beck Depression Inventory from a sample of 50 persons with rheumatoid arthritis and 32 others suffering from a variety of painful noninflammatory disorders of loco- motion (eg, lower back pain). A total of 46% of those with rheumatoid arthritis scored in the range of mild to moderate depression, and 16% scored in the range of moderate to severe depression, whereas only 19% and 6% of the comparison sample fell into these two categories, respectively.

The study of coping by persons with rheumatoid arthritis has been a fruitful area of research. Early investigations noted that the individual's overall ability to cope with the stressful consequences of rheumatoid arthritis was inversely related to disease severity and chronicity and to the rapidity of progression of the disease (Moos & Solomon, 1964). More recent investigations have sought to determine whether the type of coping strategy that a person with rheumatoid arthritis uses in response to various stressful situations is related to specific aspects of his or her psychosocial adaptation (Manne & Zautra, 1992). For example, Beckham, Keefe, Caldwell, and Roodman (1991) administered the Coping Strategies Question- naire, three measures of psychosocial adaptation (ie, the Beck Depression Inven- tory, the Arthritis Impact Measurement Scales, and the Daily Hassles Scale), and a measure of disability status to a nonrandom sample of 65 predominately white, female, middle-class outpatients with rheumatoid arthritis. The data from the Coping Strategies Questionnaire were factor analyzed to yield two factor scores: Coping Attempts and Pain Control and Rational Thinking. It was discovered that the Pain Control and Rational Thinking score was inversely related to percep- tions of pain, self-reported psychological risk, and physical disability status, con- trolling for sociodemographic characteristics and disease-related variables. This result was similar to that reported by Brown, Nicassio, and Wallston (1989) and confirmed in a related investigation (Keefe et al., 1987) involving a sample of 52 individuals with rheumatoid arthritis who had undergone knee replacement sur- gery. In addition, it was discovered that neither factor score was significantly related to the individual's age, chronicity, obesity, or sex. The question remains, however, whether successful coping with pain is the cause of better psychosocial adjustment or whether better psychosocial adjustment is the cause of the individ- ual's perception of the effectiveness of successfully coping with pain.

Long and Sangster (1993) predicted that coping served as a mediating variable in understanding the relationships among disease severity, age, and pain and psy- chosocial adaptation in persons with rheumatoid arthritis. A self-selected nonran- dom sample of 215 predominantly white and older (mean age 62 years) persons in Canada with rheumatoid arthritis ($n = 107$) or osteoarthritis ($n = 108$) com- pleted the Ways of Coping Questionnaire, the Arthritis Impact Measurement Scales, the Brief Symptom Inventory, and the Life Orientation Test (a measure of optimism and pessimism). For the individuals with rheumatoid arthritis, pessimistic expectations played a larger role in psychosocial adaptation than did physical disability. For the individuals with osteoarthritis, pain and physical disabilities had a greater influence on psychosocial adaptation than did pessimistic expectations. Those with more optimistic expectations among both groups of persons were found to select problem-solving coping strategies more often, whereas those with more pessimistic expectations were found to select wishful-thinking coping strategies more often. Problem-solving coping did not predict psychosocial adaptation for either group, but wishful-thinking coping was related to poorer overall adaptation.

In a series of reports, Manne and Zautra (1989a; 1989b) investigated whether the reactions of significant others (unhelpful and critical remarks expressing rejection or avoidance or supportive and helpful remarks expressing acceptance and problem-solving orientation) led persons with rheumatoid arthritis to select a coping strategy that, in turn, increased or decreased their psychosocial adaptation. A nonrandom sample of 103 predominantly white and well-educated female volunteers completed a battery of instruments measuring coping, mental health (eg, self-blame, psychological distress), spousal relationships, and disease-related variables. In addition, interviews elicited supportive or critical remarks from the spouse without a disability. As predicted, negative reactions of the spouse were associated with the selection of wishful-thinking coping strategies and increased risk for psychosocial maladaptation, whereas positive reactions of the spouse were associated with information-seeking and cognitive-restructuring coping strategies and increased psychosocial well-being. It should be noted, however, that the types and valences of the spouses' remarks elicited in these interviews may have been biased by social-desirability responding, limiting the generalizability of these findings.

The psychosocial functioning of persons with rheumatoid arthritis has occasionally been related to that of persons diagnosed with other chronic diseases to identify similarities and differences. The effects of chronic illness on the psychosocial adaptation (anxiety, self-esteem, health locus of control) of 168 adolescents with chronic illnesses (cancer, cardiologic disorders, diabetes mellitus, cystic fibrosis, nephrology, and rheumatoid arthritis) was compared to that of 349 children without impairments who were of approximately the same age and distribution of sex and race (Kellerman, Zeltzer, Ellenberg, Dash, & Rigler, 1980). No differences were discovered between the children without impairments and the children with chronic illnesses on the measures of anxiety or self-esteem, but the latter were found to be more external than the former. The children with rheumatoid arthritis were found to be the most external of the children with chronic illnesses.

Cassileth et al. (1984), decrying researchers' "parochial inclination to view the psychosocial problems of each illness as unique" (p. 506), undertook a comprehensive investigation of the psychosocial adaptation of outpatient samples of individuals with rheumatoid arthritis ($n = 84$), clinical depression ($n = 100$), diabetes mellitus ($n = 199$), cancer ($n = 193$), renal disease ($n = 60$), and dermatological disorders ($n = 122$). The dependent variables were scores on the self-report General Well-Being Schedule and the six subscales of the Mental Health Index. Except for the individuals with clinical depression, no differences were found among the illness groups on measures of anxiety, depression, positive affect, emotional distress, loss of control, or global mental health. These results were replicated in additional analyses, with age and sex controlled and for males and females separately. The researchers interpreted these results as support for their contention that there are no illness-specific emotional reactions or enduring personality characteristics.

Felton and colleagues (Felton & Ravenson, 1984; Felton, Ravenson, & Hinrichsen, 1984; Ravenson & Felton, 1989) compared four groups of persons with chronic illnesses (cancer, rheumatoid arthritis, hypertension, and diabetes mellitus) on a variety of psychosocial adaptation measures, including coping, acceptance of illness, self-efficacy in life situations, affective balance, and self-esteem. Persons with rheumatoid arthritis and cancer (less controllable chronic illnesses) reported more illness-related problems, more negative self-esteem, and less positive affect and acceptance of illness than did persons with hypertension and diabetes mellitus (more controllable chronic illnesses). The relationship between coping and adaptation was not influenced by the type of chronic illness, with information-seeking coping linked to positive psychosocial adaptation and wish-fulfilling fantasy coping linked to negative psychosocial adaptation, as measured by affect, self-esteem, and acceptance of illness.

Pollock (1990) studied psychosocial adaptation in a sample of 60 individuals with adult-onset chronic illnesses: 20 individuals with rheumatoid arthritis, 20 individuals with diabetes mellitus, and 20 individuals with hypertension. In addition to physiological measures of health status, each respondent was asked to complete the Health-Related Hardiness Scale (an instrument developed by the author) and the Psychosocial Adjustment to Illness Scale. The hardiness and psychosocial adjustment scores were found to be significantly correlated for the total group, but not within the group of persons with rheumatoid arthritis. In a later investigation, Pollock, Christian, and Sands (1990) compared scores on the Mental Health Index for a sample of 211 individuals with chronic illnesses: 20% were individuals with rheumatoid arthritis, 59% were individuals with multiple sclerosis, and 21% were individuals with hypertension. The investigators found no significant differences in the psychosocial adaptation scores of the three groups.

In an effort to collect data that could lead to increased specificity and efficacy of therapeutic interventions, Devins et al. (1993) compared a sample of 110 persons with rheumatoid arthritis to samples of 94 persons with multiple sclerosis and 101 persons with end-stage renal disease. The Illness Intrusiveness Rating Scale was used to collect individuals' self-reports of the extent that their disease interfered with activities in 13 life domains (eg, sports and recreation, marital relationships, self-expression). On an overall measure, the persons with multiple sclerosis reported significantly more illness intrusiveness that did either the persons with end-stage renal disease or the persons with rheumatoid arthritis, who did not differ statistically from one another. The researchers did observe different patterns across 8 of the 13 life domains, with the persons with rheumatoid arthritis rating their disease more intrusive in domains related to physical activities and activities of daily living.

CHARACTERISTICS ASSOCIATED WITH ADAPTATION TO RHEUMATOID ARTHRITIS

The research literature has been consistent in reporting no significant relationship between sex of the individual and psychosocial adaptation to rheumatoid arthritis (Daltroy et al., 1992; Earle et al., 1979; Ennett et al., 1991). Daniels et al. (1987) found no relationship between age at onset of rheumatoid arthritis symptoms and psychosocial adaptation as measured by a parent report questionnaire in a sample of 93 children with rheumatoid arthritis. A similar result was reported by Miller et al. (1982) in their follow-up study of 121 young adults with rheumatoid arthritis. Earle et al. (1979) found that higher socioeconomic status, as measured by a combination of occupation and education, was related to higher scores on a specially designed inventory consisting of five self-report scales measuring psychosocial adaptation and that greater income was positively related to the two scales measuring self-esteem and work satisfaction. Pow (1987) also reported a relationship between socioeconomic status and psychosocial adaptation.

Empirical evidence concerning the possible links between psychiatric sequelae and disease pathophysiology in persons with rheumatoid arthritis is limited (Brewerton, 1992; Iverson, 1995; Ling, Perry, & Tsaung, 1981). The evidence concerning the relationship of age and psychosocial adaptation to rheumatoid arthritis is equivocal. Daltroy et al. (1992), Ennett et al. (1991), Kellerman et al. (1980) reported no significant relationship between age and various indices of psychosocial adaptation in samples of children and adolescents with juvenile rheumatoid arthritis, and Gardiner (1980) and Zaphiropoulos and Burry (1974) found no relationship between these two variables in adults with rheumatoid arthritis. Several studies have reported that decreasing psychosocial adaptation to rheumatoid arthritis (increased risk for anxiety and depression, decreased ability to cope) was related to increased age (Anderson et al., 1985; Baum, 1982; Chandarana et al., 1987; DeForge et al., 1989). On the other hand, Cassileth et al. (1984), Long and Sangster (1993), and Pow (1987) reported improved indices of mental health and better psychosocial adaptation among samples of persons of increasing age with rheumatoid arthritis. These latter findings might reflect either better coping skills of the older individuals or their decreasing expectations for functional independence.

The evidence concerning the relationship of chronicity and psychosocial adaptation to rheumatoid arthritis is also equivocal. In their reviews of the literature concerning rheumatoid arthritis, Anderson et al. (1985) and Baum (1982) discovered that increasing chronicity was related to increasing psychosocial risk (increased reactions of anxiety and depression, decreased ability to cope). Daniels et al. (1987) also found a negative relationship between chronicity of rheumatoid arthritis symptoms and psychosocial adaptation as measured by a parent report questionnaire in a sample of 93 children with rheumatoid arthritis. In contrast, Cassileth et al. (1984) found that, among a sample of 84 persons with rheumatoid arthritis, those with shorter chronicity of disease were more depressed, more anxious, and reported generally poorer overall mental health. A similar result was reported by Kellerman et al. (1980). No significant relationship between chronicity and psychosocial adaptation, however, was found in samples of persons with rheumatoid arthritis in other studies (Chandarana et al., 1987; Daltroy et al., 1992; Felton & Ravenson, 1984; Gardiner, 1980; Miller et al., 1982; Pollock et al., 1990; Ward, 1971; Zaphiropoulos & Burry, 1974).

Increasing psychosocial risk in persons with rheumatoid arthritis (ie, increased feelings of life meaninglessness, decreased ability to cope, decreased self-esteem, increased externality, and increased reactions of anxiety, denial, and depression) has been related to increasing disease severity as measured by indices such as pain, symptom activity, clinical disease aspects, and functional impairment. Hill et al. (1974) found that individuals with the more severe cases of rheumatoid arthritis in their sample reported more marital and sexual problems, more limited educational and vocational success, and more impact on social and leisure activities. Daniels et al. (1987) found a negative relationship between severity of rheumatoid arthritis symptoms and psychosocial adaptation as measured by a parent report questionnaire in a sample of 93 children with rheumatoid arthritis. Timko, Stovel, Moos, and Miller (1992a) found that children with moderate to severe forms of juvenile rheumatoid arthritis were reported by their parents to manifest more psychological problems as measured by the Health and Daily Living Form. A number of other investigations have reported similar associations (Anderson et al., 1985; Baum, 1982; Brown, Wallston, & Nicassio, 1989; Burckhardt, 1985; Chandarana et al., 1987; Earle et al., 1979;

Hawley & Wolfe, 1988; Manne & Zautra, 1989a; Mindham et al., 1981; Parker et al., 1988; Pow, 1987; Ravenson & Felton, 1989).

In comparison, DeForge et al. (1989) reported no relationship between self-reports of pain and measures of depression and general well-being in a sample of older individuals with rheumatoid arthritis. Thompson, Varni, and Hanson (1987) found no relationship between the self-reports of pain of children with juvenile rheumatoid arthritis and their mothers' reports of behavior problems as measured by the Child Behavior Check List. Ivey, Brewer, and Giannini (1981) compared children with mild and severe forms of juvenile rheumatoid arthritis and discovered no differences in anxiety, as measured by the Children's Manifest Anxiety Scale, or in self-concept, as measured by the Piers-Harris Self-Concept Scale. In a study conducted in the Netherlands (Wekking, Vingerhoets, van Dam, Nossant, & Swaak, 1991), no relationship was found between a set of disease indices and psychosocial adaptation as measured by the Arthritis Impact Measurement Scales. Eberhardt, Larsson, and Nived (1993) collected longitudinal data over two years on a set of disease-related variables, together with scores on the Health Assessment Questionnaire and the Symptom Check List—90, from a sample of 89 consecutive outpatients with rheumatoid arthritis. No significant relationships were found between the measures of psychosocial adaptation and any of the disease-related variables. In addition, there were no changes in the psychosocial adaptation of the sample observed over the study period. Bradbury (1989) found no relationship between disease severity and quality of life as measured by the Arthritis Impact Measurement Scales in a nonrandom sample of 41 males with rheumatoid arthritis. Similarly, Crown and Crown (1973), Daltroy et al. (1992), Gardiner (1980), and Kellerman et al. (1980) found no relationship between disease activity and psychosocial adaptation.

Researchers have studied the relationships of psychosocial adaptation to various combinations of a number of other variables, including locus of control, attitude toward illness, self-esteem, social and emotional supports, learned helplessness, perceptions of control, perceptions of competence, and family characteristics. For example, Burckhardt (1985) hypothesized that quality of life reports of persons with rheumatoid arthritis would be related to a set of sociodemographic variables, including age, pain severity, sex, severity of impairment, socioeconomic status, and social network characteristics. In addition, it was hypothesized that a second set of four variables would serve as mediators of these relationships: (1) perceptions of support, (2) attitude toward illness, (3) self-esteem, and (4) locus of control. Data were collected from a consecutive series of 94 individuals with rheumatoid arthritis and analyzed with path and multiple regression analyses. A total of 46% of the variation in quality of life was accounted for in the multiple regression, with all four of the mediator variables found to be significant predictors.

Bradbury (1989) used a cross-sectional design and a nonrandom sample of 41 males with rheumatoid arthritis to investigate the relationship between adaptation, as measured by the Arthritis Impact Measurement Scales, and a set of independent variables that included the Health Locus of Control scale, an adjective checklist to measure attitude toward illness, and self-reports of perceived social supports. Results indicated that among the individuals in the sample, psychosocial adaptation was inversely related to favorable attitude toward illness and to internal locus of control but was not related to perceived social supports.

This last finding is not consistent with the results of other investigations of social support. Goodenow, et al. (1990) discovered that a measure of social support was a significant predictor of psychosocial adaptation in persons with rheumatoid arthritis as measured by the Health Assessment Questionnaire with physical functioning controlled. In an investigation of the relationship between depression and perceptions of emotional support (Brown et al., 1989), a nonrandom clinic sample of persons with rheumatoid arthritis was studied at the time of diagnosis of the disease and then again at three and six months postdiagnosis. Perception of emotional support was found to be a significant predictor of depression at each time, with depression especially elevated for those individuals reporting the greatest dissatisfaction with emotional supports, controlling for sociodemographic characteristics. These researchers noted a possible reciprocal causal path between depression and perception of emotional support, suggesting a self-fulfilling downward spiral.

The findings of a large-scale survey of 583 persons with physical disabilities in London (Patrick, Morgan, & Charlton, 1986), of whom 50% were persons with rheumatoid arthritis, serve to clarify the relationship between social and emotional support and psychosocial adjustment. Respondents were asked to describe their social activities (eg, club memberships, frequency of out-of-home trips) and their experiences of emotional intimacy (eg, number of people in whom they confided). They were also asked to recollect and list significant life events in the preceding 12 months. Both degree of social support and emotional intimacy were found to be positively related to psychosocial adjustment, as measured by the Sickness Impact Profile, but only among those respondents who reported significant adverse life events. The researchers interpreted this finding as support for the hypothesis that social and emotional support serves to buffer the life stresses experienced by persons with rheumatoid arthritis (eg, deteriorating health status, impaired mobility, decreased physical capacities).

Bradley (1985) suggested that because of the uncontrollable and unpredictable nature of the course of arthritic disease, learned helplessness may be an important explanatory construct in understanding the psychosocial adaptation of persons with rheumatoid arthritis. To this end, Callahan and colleagues (Callahan, Brooks, & Pincus, 1988; Engle, Callahan, Pincus, & Hochberg, 1990) have offered the Rheumatology Attitudes Index as a specialized measure of learned helplessness among persons with rheumatoid arthritis. The 15 items of this self-report summated rating scale purport to operationalize learned helplessness as manifest in three areas: (1) motivation deficits (eg, reduced efforts with activities of daily living), (2) cognitive deficits (eg, decreased coping behaviors), and (3) emotional deficits (eg, increased anxiety and depression, decreased self-esteem). Callahan et al. (1988) collected data from persons with rheumatoid arthritis being treated at specialty clinics and in private practices (no comparison groups were included). A significant but low relationship was found between their measure of learned helplessness and self-reports of difficulty performing activities of daily living, but predicted relationships to measures of age, chronicity, and severity of impairments were not confirmed by the data. In a subsequent study (Engle et al., 1990), analyses of Rheumatology Attitudes Index data from a nonrandom sample of persons with systemic lupus erythematosus revealed a partial correlation of 0.63 with total scores on the Psychosocial Adjustment to Illness Scale (with age, chronicity, and education partialled out of the correlation). The value of a similar partial correlation with the Psychological Distress subscale of the Psychosocial Adjustment to Illness Scale was reported to be only 0.30. These results suggest that only between 9% and 40% of the variation in psychosocial adaptation is accounted for by learned helplessness. However, available psychometric data raise questions about the psychometric adequacy of this instrument. A coefficient alpha reliability value of 0.68 in the Callahan et al. (1988) study suggests that the questionnaire may not be a reliable measure of the construct in persons with rheumatoid arthritis.

Affleck, Tennen, Pfeiffer, and Fifield (1987) have explored the relationships between psychosocial adaptation to rheumatoid arthritis and several unique psychological characteristics. In an investigation of the relationship between adaptation and the individual's perception of control over the course, consequences, and treatment of the disease (Affleck et al., 1987), a nonrandom sample of 92 persons with rheumatoid arthritis were interviewed in their homes. Data were obtained on a set of sociodemographic variables, illness-related variables (eg, symptom activity, functional impairment, disease severity), coping, and psychosocial adaptation (as measured by the Health Assessment Questionnaire, Profile of Mood States, and Global Adjustment to Illness Scale). The researchers also collected data on the interviewees' perceptions of control of the disease course and day-to-day symptoms, as well as participation in and perceptions of control over the treatment they were receiving. Increased psychosocial adaptation was found to be related to increased participation in and perceived personal control over treatment. This result was found to be more pronounced as the severity of symptoms increased but was unrelated to the individual's age, sex, education, occupation, income, functional impairment, or disease severity. In confirmation of this result,

Schiaffino and Revenson (1992) found increased depression and psychosocial risk among those in their sample of individuals with rheumatoid arthritis who reported the lowest level of perceived control over life events.

Comparison of disease activity was the subject of a later study by Affleck and colleagues (Affleck, Tennen, Pfeiffer, & Fifield, 1988). A consecutive series of persons receiving treatment at a rheumatology clinic were asked to provide data on illness-related variables and to complete several measures of psychosocial adaptation. They were then interviewed to determine how they viewed their disease symptoms with reference to the "average arthritis patient." Statements obtained from the respondents were then categorized into either upward (better than) or downward (worse than) comparisons of disease activity (eg, amount of pain), functional status (eg, ability to perform activities of daily living), and psychosocial adjustment (eg, coping). It was discovered that those individuals expressing more favorable comparisons of disease activity and adjustment reported better psychosocial adaptation, but no relationship was found between comparisons of functional status and adaptation to rheumatoid arthritis.

A similar line of inquiry was pursued by Blalock and colleagues (Blalock, Afifi, DeVellis, Holt, & DeVellis, 1990; Blalock, DeVellis, & DeVellis, 1989; Blalock et al., 1992; DeVellis, Blalock, Hahn, DeVellis, & Hockbaum, 1988), who investigated whether psychosocial adaptation among persons with rheumatoid arthritis was related to the extent and types of social comparisons they made to other persons. It was predicted that when asked to evaluate their own functional abilities, persons with rheumatoid arthritis would compare themselves with others whom they considered less able in order to enhance or restore their perception of their own well-being (eg, as a coping mechanism). Blalock et al. (1990), supplementing data obtained in an earlier study (DeVellis et al., 1988), interviewed persons with rheumatoid arthritis concerning their social comparisons to others with and without the disease. Adaptation was measured by the General Well-Being Scale and the Arthritis Impact Measurement Scales. Although individuals who emphasized similarities between themselves and others with no impairments tended to be better adapted, psychosocial adaptation was not related to whether or not the individual made social comparisons. Contrary to expectations, among those who made social comparisons, adaptation was not related to the number of comparisons made, the directions of the comparisons, or the health of the target comparison person.

In an extension of this research, Blalock et al. (1989) collected data on a variety of adjustment measures from a nonrandom sample of white females with rheumatoid arthritis. The respondents were asked to evaluate their perceived abilities and their satisfaction with their abilities in four areas: (1) writing, (2) buttoning, (3) shoe tying, and (4) locking doors. They were also asked to make evaluative comparisons to others with and without rheumatoid arthritis on three dimensions: (1) performance difficulty, (2) desired performance, and (3) relative ability. As predicted, respondents tended to make downward comparisons of themselves to others with rheumatoid arthritis; that is, they tended to compare their abilities, even if they were not very good, to the abilities of others whom they considered to be worse off than they were. Those expressing greater satisfaction with their abilities tended to report less depression, higher self-esteem, greater life satisfaction, and more positive affect. Social comparisons were not, however, significant predictors of psychosocial adaptation when perceived ability and satisfaction with ability were partialled out.

Blalock et al. (1992) subsequently hypothesized that the relationship between satisfaction with abilities and psychosocial adaptation would be stronger in those individuals who viewed the abilities they were being asked to evaluate as more important to them. Data were collected by mailed questionnaires and follow-up telephone interviews from a nonrandom sample of persons with rheumatoid arthritis who had been diagnosed within the preceding 12 months. A set of measures of psychosocial adaptation was subjected to a principal components analysis to derive a composite score for each individual. A second set of disease-related measures was similarly analyzed to yield a single composite score. Respondents were asked to evaluate their satisfaction with their abilities in three areas: (1) household activities, (2) leisure activities, and (3) pain management. Respondents' ratings of the perceived importance of each of these activities were used to construct high and low importance groups. Hierarchical regression analyses were performed with the composite psychosocial adaptation score as the dependent variable and the following order of the independent variables: a set of seven sociodemographic variables, the disease-related composite score, the satisfaction ratings, and the interactions of these variables. For the two importance groups combined, better psychosocial adaptation was found to be associated with less functional disability and greater perceived satisfaction with abilities. In the low-importance group, the relationship between satisfaction with abilities and adaptation was nonsignificant, whereas this relationship was significant in the high-importance group. In other words, reported psychosocial distress was found to be more closely related to dissatisfaction with one's abilities than to one's abilities per se, but this relationship was true only among those respondents who viewed the abilities being evaluated as important for them.

Other researchers have investigated constructs similar to perceptions of disease control and comparisons of disease activity and abilities. Schiaffino and Revenson (1992), for example, asked a sample of persons with rheumatoid arthritis to rate their self-efficacy (perceived ability to accomplish desirable goals) and to report the extent of their agreement that their disease was a permanent and global personal attribute. Respondents were also administered the Arthritis Impact Measurement Scales and the Center for Epidemiologic Studies Depression Scale to measure psychosocial adaptation. It was discovered that those respondents with the lowest self-efficacy and greatest personal attribution of global disability reported the greatest depression and were at the greatest psychosocial risk.

Smith and colleagues (Smith, Dobbins, & Wallston, 1991; Smith & Wallston, 1992) investigated the construct of perceived competence (one's view of one's ability to interact effectively with the environment), a construct that they argued was related to coping and to self-efficacy. Smith et al. (1991) hypothesized that those persons with rheumatoid arthritis who report positive perceptions of competence, controlling for disease-related variables, would report positive psychosocial adaptation. Furthermore they predicted that this relationship should be mediated by the respondent's locus of control, mastery, coping, and perceptions of social support. A nonrandom sample of persons with rheumatoid arthritis were asked by mail to provide data on work status, perceived social supports, and pain and to complete measures of perceived competence, locus of control, depression, and life satisfaction. The results of path analyses provided support for the researchers' hypotheses. In a subsequent investigation, Smith and Wallston (1992) confirmed that the individual's coping strategy and perceived adequacy of social supports buffered the relationship between perceptions of competence and psychosocial adaptation.

Finally, study of the characteristics of the families of children with rheumatoid arthritis and the relationships of these characteristics to psychosocial adaptation of the children has yielded intriguing results. Timko and colleagues (Timko, Baumgartner, Moos, & Miller, 1993; Timko et al., 1992a; Timko, Stovel, Moos, & Miller, 1992b) conducted a longitudinal investigation of psychosocial adaptation among children with juvenile rheumatoid arthritis and found that at the time of the first testing, the children's scores on a set of school and social adjustment variables were negatively related to a set of family (eg, stress, lack of cohesion) and parent (eg, depression, drinking problems) variables. Analyses of similar data from the children and their parents one year later (time two of the investigation) confirmed this finding. In addition, analyses revealed that psychosocial adaptation of the children at time one was a strong predictor of psychosocial adaptation at time two. The researchers noted that the effects of juvenile rheumatoid arthritis uncovered in this longitudinal investigation were manifest primarily in the areas of physical activities and social functioning of the children.

Varni and colleagues (Varni, Wilcox, & Hanson, 1988; Varni, Wilcox, Hanson, & Brik, 1988) collected data on family characteristics, disease activity, and psychosocial adaptation (as measured by the parent-report Child Behavior Check List) from a nonrandom sample of 23 children with juvenile rheumatoid arthritis and their families. Although family support was found to be a significant predictor of the children's psychosocial adaptation, the children with juvenile rheumatoid arthritis were not exhibiting significant maladjustment when the data were compared to the Child Behavior Check List norms. Finally, Daniels et al. (1987) studied a sample of 93 children with juvenile rheumatoid arthritis and found no significant relationship between a set of family variables (eg, father's occupation, education of the parents, family size, marriage stability, ethnicity, family stress, parents' psychosocial adaptation) and psychosocial adaptation of the children as measured by a parent report questionnaire. They did report that parental depression and family stress tended to be negatively related to psychosocial adaptation in the children, but the result failed to reach statistical significance.

CONCLUSION

Psychosocial adaptation to rheumatoid arthritis is a complex phenomenon that demands theoretically and methodologically sophisticated multivariate research investigations. Regrettably very few of the studies reviewed for this chapter have these characteristics. Keeping in mind the methodological shortcomings of the research literature, several tentative conclusions can be presented.

First, the complex interplay of physical, psychological, and situational factors leads to extensive interindividual variability in psychosocial adaptation to rheumatoid arthritis expressed as changes in self-esteem, life satisfaction, social activities, academic achievement, family functioning, work satisfaction, sexual functioning, coping capacity, locus of control, body image, and reactions such as shock, depression, anxiety, and anger. The rates of depression, anxiety, and denial among both children and adults with rheumatoid arthritis are higher than those observed in comparable samples of persons without disability.

Second, psychosocial adaptation of persons with rheumatoid arthritis is similar to that for persons with other types of chronic illnesses. As expected, persons with rheumatoid arthritis are found to be at particular risk in areas related to perceptions of physical abilities, mobility, vocational success, occupational satisfaction, and competence in activities of daily living. Evidence reveals that there are no arthritis-specific emotional reactions or enduring personality characteristics.

Third, the type of coping strategy a person with rheumatoid arthritis selects in response to various stressful situations is related to specific aspects of his or her psychosocial adaptation. Research has consistently revealed that the selection of passive, emotion-focused, or wish-fulfilling coping strategies is associated with psychosocial distress, as measured by more negative self-esteem, increased depression, and increased externality. The question remains, however, whether selecting active and problem-focused coping strategies is the cause of the individual's better psychosocial adaptation or whether better psychosocial adaptation is the cause of the individual's selection of what researchers classify as effective coping strategies. Coping, however, should probably be viewed as a mediating variable between disease-related (eg, pain, symptom severity, functional impairment), sociodemographic (eg, income, education), and situational (eg, social and family support) variables and psychosocial adaptation. Because the course of rheumatoid arthritis varies over time, the coping process may be recursive, that is, increased stress associated with symptom exacerbation may temporarily overwhelm the individual's coping ability, leading to additional stress and symptom intensification. There is clearly a need for well-controlled prospective longitudinal investigation (Manne & Zautra, 1992). Clay, Wood, Frank, Hagglund, and Johnson (1995) have recently proposed the use of an innovative statistical methodology called growth modeling that could serve to identify underlying recursive processes evident in longitudinal data.

Fourth, study of the relationships between psychosocial adaptation and age, chronicity, and severity have yielded inconsistent results. It might be expected that older individuals who have experienced rheumatoid arthritis symptoms longer would experience greater psychosocial distress, but these associations are not always uncovered in the research evidence. Although increasing psychosocial distress has been related to most indices of increasing disease severity, the relationship to pain, a complex phenomenon, is not at all clear. Research is needed that controls the influence of moderating variables, such as coping behaviors, social and spousal supports, perceptions of impairment, and self-efficacy. Moreover, pain may be highly variable with increasing age, chronicity, and disease symptom exacerbation, suggesting the need for longitudinal research designs.

Fifth, perceptions of emotional and social support, perceptions of disease control, self-efficacy, favorable comparisons of disease activity, and favorable social comparisons of valued abilities and activities have been found to be significant predictors of a variety of measures of psychosocial adaptation. Future longitudinal research should attend to the contributions of these variables to positive manifestations of psychosocial adaptation in persons with rheumatoid arthritis.

REFERENCES

Affleck, G., Tennen, H., Pfeiffer, C., & Fifield, J. (1987). Appraisals of control and predictability in adapting to a chronic disease. *Journal of Personality and Social Psychology, 53*, 273–279.

Affleck, G., Tennen, H., Pfeiffer, C., & Fifield, J. (1988). Social comparisons in rheumatoid arthritis: Accuracy and adaptational significance. *Journal of Social and Clinical Psychology, 6*, 219–234.

Anderson, K. O., Bradley, L. A., Young, L. D., McDaniel, L. K., & Wise, C. M. (1985). Rheumatoid arthritis: Review of psychological factors related to etiology, effects, and treatment. *Psychological Bulletin, 98*, 358–387.

Baker, G. H. B. (1981). Psychological management. *Clinics in rheumatoid arthritis, 7*, 455–464.

Baker, G. H. B. (1982). Life events before the onset of rheumatoid arthritis. *Psychotherapy and Psychosomatics*, 38, 173–177.

Baum, J. (1982). A review of the psychological aspects of rheumatoid arthritis. *Seminars in Arthritis and Rheumatism*, 11, 352–361.

Beckham, J. C., Keefe, F. J., Caldwell, D. S., & Roodman, A. A. (1991). Pain coping strategies in rheumatoid arthritis: Relationships to pain, disability, depression, and daily hassles. *Behavior Therapy*, 22, 113–124.

Blake, D. J., Maisiak, R., Brown, S., & Kaplan, A. (1986). Acceptance by arthritis patients of clinical inquiry into their sexual adjustment. *Psychosomatics*, 27, 576–579.

Blalock, S. J., Afifi, R. A., DeVellis, B. M. E., Holt, K., & DeVellis, R. F. (1990). Adjustment to rheumatoid arthritis: The role of social comparison processes. *Health Psychology*, 9, 266–284.

Blalock, S. J., DeVellis, B. M. E., & DeVellis, R. E. (1989). Social comparison among individuals with rheumatoid arthritis. *Journal of Applied Social Psychology*, 19, 665–680.

Blalock, S. J., DeVellis, B. M. E., DeVellis, R. F., Giorgino, K. B., Sauter, S. V. H., Jordan, J. M., Keefe, F. J., & Mutran, E. J. (1992). Psychological well-being among people with recently diagnosed rheumatoid arthritis. *Arthritis and Rheumatism*, 35, 1267–1272.

Bourestom, N. C., & Howard, M. T. (1965). Personality characteristics of three disability groups. *Archives of Physical Medicine and Rehabilitation*, 46, 626–632.

Bradbury, V. L. (1989). The quality of life in a male population suffering from arthritis. *Rehabilitation Nursing*, 14, 187–190.

Bradley, L. A. (1985). Psychological aspects of arthritis. *Bulletin of the Rheumatic Diseases*, 35(4), 1–12.

Brewerton, D. (1992). *All about arthritis: Past, present, future.* Cambridge, MA: Harvard University Press.

Brown, G. K., Nicassio, P. M., & Wallston, K. A. (1989). Pain coping strategies and depression in rheumatoid arthritis. *Journal of Consulting and Clinical Psychology*, 57, 652–657.

Brown, G. K., Wallston, K. A., & Nicassio, P. M. (1989). Social support and depression in rheumatoid arthritis: A one-year prospective study. *Journal of Applied Social Psychology*, 19, 1164–1181.

Burckhardt, C. S. (1985). The impact of arthritis on quality of life. *Nursing Research*, 34, 11–16.

Callahan, L. F., Brooks, R. H., & Pincus, T. (1988). Further analysis of learned helplessness in rheumatoid arthritis using a "Rheumatology Attitudes Index." *Journal of Rheumatology*, 15, 418–426.

Cassileth, B. R., Lusk, E. J., Strouse, T. B., Miller, D. S., Brown, L. L., Cross, P. A., & Tenaglia, A. N. (1984). Psychosocial status in chronic illness: A comparative analysis of six diagnostic groups. *New England Journal of Medicine*, 311(8), 506–511.

Chandarana, P. C., Eals, M., Steingart, A. B., Bellamy, N., & Allen, S. (1987). The detection of psychiatric morbidity and associated factors in patients with rheumatoid arthritis. *Canadian Journal of Psychiatry*, 32, 356–361.

Clay, D. L., Wood, P. K., Frank, R. G., Hagglund, K. J., & Johnson, J. C. (1995). Examining systematic differences in adaptation to chronic illness: A growth modeling approach. *Rehabilitation Psychology*, 40, 61–70.

Cleveland, S. E., & Fisher, S. (1954). Behavior and unconscious fantasies of patients with rheumatoid arthritis. *Psychosomatic Medicine*, 16, 327–333.

Cleveland, S. E., Reitman, E. E., & Brewer, E. J. J. (1965). Psychological factors in juvenile rheumatoid arthritis. *Arthritis and Rheumatism, 8,* 1152–1158.

Cobb, S. (1959). Contained hostility in rheumatoid arthritis. *Arthritis and Rheumatism, 2,* 419–426.

Crown, S., & Crown, J. M. (1973). Personality in early rheumatoid disease. *Journal of Psychosomatic Research, 17,* 189–196.

Crown, S., Crown, J. M., & Fleming, A. (1974). Aspects of the psychology of rheumatoid disease. *Rheumatology Rehabilitation, 13,* 167–168.

Daltroy, L. H., Larson, M. G., Eaton, H. M., Partridge, A. J., Pless, I. B., Rogers, M. P., & Liang, M. H. (1992). Psychosocial adjustment in juvenile arthritis. *Journal of Pediatric Psychology, 17,* 277–289.

Daniels, D., Moos, R. H., Billings, A. G., & Miller, J. J. I. (1987). Psychosocial risk and resistance factors among children with chronic illness, healthy siblings, and healthy controls. *Journal of Abnormal Child Psychology, 15,* 295–308.

DeForge, B. R., Sobal, J., & Krick, J. P. (1989). Relation of perceived health with psychological variables in elderly osteoarthritis patients. *Psychological Reports, 64,* 147–156.

DeVellis, B. M. E., Blalock, S. J., Hahn, P. M., DeVellis, R. F., & Hockbaum, G. M. (1988). Evaluation of a problem-solving intervention for patients with arthritis. *Patient Education and Counseling, 11,* 29–42.

Devins, G. M., Edworthy, S. M., Seland, T. P., Klein, G. M., Paul, L. C., & Mandin, H. (1993). Differences in illness intrusiveness across rheumatoid arthritis, end-stage renal disease, and multiple sclerosis. *Journal of Nervous and Mental Diseases, 181,* 377–381.

Earle, J. R., Perricone, P. J., Maultsby, D. M., Perricone, N., Turner, R. A., & Davis, J. (1979). Psychosocial adjustment of rheumatoid arthritis patients from two alternative treatment settings. *Journal of Rheumatology, 6,* 80–87.

Eberhardt, K., & Larsson, B.-M. Nived, K. (1993). Psychological reactions in patients with early rheumatoid arthritis. *Patient Education and Counseling, 20,* 93–100.

Engel, G. L. (1977). The need for a new medical model: A challenge for biomedicine. *Science, 196,* 129–136.

Engle, E. W., Callahan, L. F., Pincus, T., & Hochberg, M. S. (1990). Learned helplessness in systemic lupus erythematosus: Analysis using the Rheumatology Attitudes Index. *Arthritis and Rheumatism, 33,* 281–286.

Ennett, S. T., DeVellis, B. M., Earp, J. A., Kredich, D., Warren, R. W., & Wilhelm, C. L. (1991). Disease experience and psychosocial adjustment in children with juvenile rheumatoid arthritis: Children's versus mothers' reports. *Journal of Pediatric Psychology, 16,* 557–568.

Felton, B. J., & Ravenson, T. A. (1984). Coping with chronic illness: A study of illness controllability and the influence of coping strategies on psychological adjustment. *Journal of Consulting and Clinical Psychology, 52,* 343–353.

Felton, B. J., Ravenson, T. A., & Hinrichsen, G. A. (1984). Stress and coping in the explanation of psychological adjustment among chronically ill adults. *Social Science and Medicine, 18,* 889–898.

Gardiner, B. M. (1980). Psychological aspects of rheumatoid arthritis. *Psychological Medicine, 10,* 159–163.

Genest, M. (1983). Coping with rheumatoid arthritis. *Canadian Journal of Behavioural Sciences, 15,* 392–408.

Goodenow, C., Reisine, S. T., & Grady, K. E. (1990). Quality of social support and associated social and psychological functioning in women with rheumatoid arthritis. *Health Psychology*, *9*, 266–284.

Hawley, D. J., & Wolfe, F. (1988). Anxiety and depression in patients with rheumatoid arthritis: A prospective study of 400 patients. *Journal of Rheumatology*, *15*, 932–941.

Henoch, M. J., Batson, J. W., & Baum, J. (1978). Psychosocial factors in juvenile rheumatoid arthritis. *Arthritis and Rheumatism*, *21*, 229–233.

Hill, R. H., Herstein, A., & Walters, K. (1974). Juvenile rheumatoid arthritis: Follow-up into adulthood—medical, sexual and social status. *Canadian Medical Association Journal*, *114*, 790–796.

Hoffman, A. L. (1974). Psychological factors associated with rheumatoid arthritis. *Nursing Research*, *23*, 218–234.

Iverson, G. L. (1995). The need for psychological services for persons with systemic lupus erythematosus. *Rehabilitation Psychology*, *40*, 39–49.

Ivey, J., Brewer, E. J., & Giannini, E. H. (1981). Psychosocial functioning in children with juvenile rheumatoid arthritis (JRA). *Arthritis and Rheumatism*, *24*, S100.

Johnson, A., Shapiro, L., & Alexander, F. (1947). Preliminary report on a psychosomatic study of rheumatic arthritis. *Psychosomatic Medicine*, *9*, 295–399.

Jones, R. L. (1909). *Arthritis deformans*. New York: Wood.

Kantrowitz, F. G. (1991). *Taking control of arthritis*. New York: Harper-Collins.

Keefe, F. J., Caldwell, D. S., Queen, K. T., Gil, K. M., Martinez, S., Crisson, J. E., Ogden, W., & Numley, J. (1987). Pain coping strategies in osteoarthritis patients. *Journal of Consulting and Clinical Psychology*, *55*, 208–212.

Kellerman, J., Zeltzer, L., Ellenberg, L., Dash, J., & Rigler, D. (1980). Psychological effects of illness in adolescence. I. Anxiety, self-esteem, and perception of control. *Journal of Pediatrics*, *97*, 126–131.

King, S. H. (1955). Psychosocial factors associated with rheumatoid arthritis. *Journal of Chronic Diseases*, *8*, 287–302.

King, S. H., & Cobb, S. (1958). Psychosocial factors in the epidemiology of rheumatoid arthritis. *Journal of Chronic Diseases*, *7*, 466–475.

Krutzer, P. (1984). Living with and adjusting to arthritis. *Nursing Clinics of North America*, *19*, 629–636.

Liang, M. H., Rogers, M., Larson, M., Eaton, H. M., Murowski, B. J., Taylor, J. E., Swafford, J., & Schur, P. H. (1984). The psychosocial impact of systemic lupus erythematosus and rheumatoid arthritis. *Arthritis and Rheumatism*, *27*, 13–19.

Ling, M. H. M., Perry, P. J., & Tsaung, M. T. (1981). Side effects of corticosteroid therapy: Psychiatric aspects. *Archives of General Psychiatry*, *38*, 471–477.

Long, B. C., & Sangster, J. A. (1993). Dispositional optimism/pessimism and coping strategies: Predictors of psychosocial adjustment of rheumatoid and osteoarthritis patients. *Journal of Applied Social Psychology*, *23*, 1069–1091.

Manne, S. L., & Zautra, A. J. (1989a). Couples coping with chronic illness: Women with rheumatoid arthritis and their healthy husbands. *Journal of Behavioral Medicine*, *13*, 327–342.

Manne, S. L., & Zautra, A. J. (1989b). Spouse criticism and support: Their association with coping and psychological adjustment among women with rheumatoid arthritis. *Journal of Personal and Social Psychology*, *56*, 608–617.

Manne, S. L., & Zautra, A. J. (1992). Coping with arthritis: Current status and critique. *Arthritis and Rheumatism*, *35*, 1273–1280.

McAnarney, E. R., Pless, I. B., Satterwhite, B., & Freidman, S. B. (1974). Psychological problems of children with chronic juvenile arthritis. *Pediatrics, 53*, 523–528.

Meyerowitz, S. (1966). The continuing investigation of psychosocial variables in rheumatoid arthritis. In A. G. Hill (Ed.), *Modern trends in rheumatology* (2nd ed.) (pp. 92–105). New York: Appleton-Century-Crofts.

Miller, J. J., Spitz, P. W., Simpson, U., & Williams, G. F. (1982). The social function of young adults who had arthritis in childhood. *Journal of Pediatrics, 100*, 378–382.

Mindham, R. H. S., Bagshaw, A., James, S. A., & Swannell, A. J. (1981). Factors associated with the appearance of psychiatric symptoms in rheumatoid arthritis. *Journal of Psychosomatic Medicine, 25*, 429–535.

Moos, R. H. (1964). Personality factors associated with rheumatoid arthritis: A review. *Journal of Chronic Diseases, 17*, 541–555.

Moos, R. H., & Solomon, G. F. (1964). Personality correlates of the rapidity of progression of rheumatoid arthritis. *Annals of Rheumatoid Diseases, 23*, 145–151.

Mueller, A. D., Lefkovits, A. M., Bryant, J. E., & Marshall, M. L. (1961). Some psychosocial factors in patients with rheumatoid arthritis. *Arthritis and Rheumatism, 4*, 275–286.

Nalven, F. B., & O'Brien, J. F. (1964). Personality patterns of rheumatoid arthritic patients. *Arthritis and Rheumatism, 7*, 19–29.

Parker, J. C., Bradley, L. A., DeVellis, R. M., Gerber, L. H., Holman, H. R., Keefe, F. J., Laurence, T. S., Liang, M. H., Lorig, K. R., Nicassio, P. M., Revenson, T. A., Rogers, M. P., Wallston, K. A., Wilson, M. G., & Wolfe, F. (1993). Biopsychosocial contributions to the management of arthritis disability. *Arthritis and Rheumatism, 36*, 885–889.

Parker, J. C., Frank, R., Beck, N., Finan, M., Walker, S., Hewett, J. E., Broster, C., Smarr, K., Smith, E., & Kay, D. (1988). Pain in rheumatoid arthritis: Relationship to demographic, medical, and psychological factors. *Journal of Rheumatology, 15*, 433–437.

Patrick, D. L., Morgan, M., & Charlton, J. R. H. (1986). Psychosocial support and change in the health status of physically disabled people. *Social Science and Medicine, 22*, 1347–1354.

Pigg, J. S., Driscoll, P. W., & Caniff, R. (1985). *Rheumatology nursing: A problem-oriented approach.* New York: John Wiley & Sons.

Polley, H. F., Swenson, W. M., & Steinhilber, R. M. (1970). Personality characteristics of patients with rheumatoid arthritis. *Psychosomatics, 11*, 45–49.

Pollock, S. E., Christian, B. J., & Sands, D. (1990). Responses to chronic illness: Analysis of psychological and physiological adaptation. *Nursing Research, 39*, 300–304.

Pow, J. M. (1987). The role of psychological influences in rheumatoid arthritis. *Journal of Psychosomatic Research, 31*, 223–229.

Ravenson, T. A., & Felton, B. J. (1989). Disability and coping as predictors of psychological adjustment to rheumatoid arthritis. *Journal of Consulting and Clinical Psychology, 57*, 344–348.

Rimón, R. (1974). Depression in rheumatoid arthritis. *Annals of Clinical Research, 6*, 171–175.

Rimón, R., Belmaker, R. H., & Ebstein, R. (1977). Psychosomatic aspects of juvenile rheumatoid arthritis. *Scandinavian Journal of Rheumatology, 6*, 1–10.

Robinson, H., Kirk, R. F. J., & Frye, R. L. (1971). A psychological study of rheumatoid arthritis and selected controls. *Journal of Chronic Diseases, 23*, 791–801.

Robinson, H., Kirk, R. F. J., Frye, R. L., & Robertson, J. A. (1972). A psychological study of patients with rheumatoid arthritis and other painful diseases. *Journal of Psychosomatic Research, 16*, 53–56.

Samuels, M., & Samuels, N. (1991). *Arthritis: How to work with your doctor and take charge of your health*. New York: Summit Books.

Satterwhite, B. B. (1978). Impact of chronic illness on child and family: An overview based on five surveys with implications for management. *International Journal of Rehabilitation Research, 1*, 7–17.

Schiaffino, K. M., & Revenson, T. A. (1992). The role of perceived self-efficacy, perceived control, and causal attributions in adaptation to rheumatoid arthritis: Distinguishing mediator for moderator effects. *Personality and Social Psychology Bulletin, 18*, 709–718.

Scotch, N. A., & Geiger, H. J. (1962). The epidemiology of rheumatoid arthritis: A review with special attention to social factors. *Journal of Chronic Diseases, 15*, 1037–1067.

Shlotzhauer, T. L., & McGuire, J. L. (1993). *Living with rheumatoid arthritis*. Baltimore: Johns Hopkins University Press.

Smith, C. A., Dobbins, C. J., & Wallston, K. A. (1991). The mediational role of perceived competence in psychological adjustment to rheumatoid arthritis. *Journal of Applied Social Psychology, 21*, 1218–1247.

Smith, C. A., & Wallston, K. A. (1992). Adaptation in patients with chronic rheumatoid arthritis: Application of a general model. *Health Psychology, 11*, 151–162.

Smith, L. L. (1979). Helping to manage the emotional effects of arthritis. *Health and Social Work, 4*(3), 134–150.

Spergel, P., Ehrlich, G. E., & Glass, D. (1978). The rheumatoid arthritic personality: A psychodiagnostic myth. *Psychosomatics, 19*, 79–86.

Thompson, R. L., Varni, J. W., & Hanson, V. (1987). Comprehensive assessment of pain in juvenile rheumatoid arthritis: An empirical model. *Journal of Pediatrics, 12*, 241–255.

Timko, C., Baumgartner, M., Moos, R. H., & Miller, J. J. I. (1993). Parental risk and resistance factors among children with juvenile rheumatic disease: A four-year predictive study. *Journal of Behavioral Medicine, 16*, 571–586.

Timko, C., Stovel, K. W., Moos, R. H., & Miller, J. J. I. (1992a). Adaptation to juvenile rheumatic disease: A controlled evaluation of functional disability with a one-year follow-up. *Health Psychology, 11*, 67–76.

Timko, C., Stovel, K. W., Moos, R. H., & Miller, J. J. I. (1992b). A longitudinal study of risk and resistance factors among children with juvenile rheumatic disease. *Journal of Clinical Child Psychology, 21*, 132–142.

Vandik, I. H. (1990). Mental health and psychosocial functioning in children with recent onset of rheumatic disease. *Journal of Child Psychology and Psychiatry, 31*, 961–971.

Varni, J. W. & Jay, S. M. (1984). Biobehavioral factors in juvenile rheumatoid arthritis: Implications for research and practice. *Clinical Psychology Review, 4*, 543–560.

Varni, J. W., Wilcox, K. T., & Hanson, V. (1988). Mediating effects of family social support on child psychological adjustment in juvenile rheumatoid arthritis. *Health Psychology, 7*, 421–431.

Varni, J. W., Wilcox, K. T., Hanson, V., & Brik, R. (1988). Chronic musculoskeletal pain and functional status in juvenile rheumatoid arthritis: An empirical model. *Pain, 32*, 1–7.

Ward, D. J. (1971). Rheumatoid arthritis and personality: A controlled study. *British Medical Journal, 2*, 297–299.

Wekking, E. M., Vingerhoets, A. J. J. M., van Dam, A. P., Nossant, J. C., & Swaak, A. J. J. G. (1991). Daily stressors and systemic lupus erythematosus: A longitudinal analysis—First findings. *Psychotherapy and Psychosomatics, 55*, 108–113.

Young, L. D. (1992). Psychological factors in rheumatoid arthritis. *Journal of Consulting and Clinical Psychology, 60,* 619–627.

Zaphiropoulos, G., & Burry, H. C. (1974). Depression in rheumatoid disease. *Annals of Rheumatoid Diseases, 33,* 132–135.

Zeitlin, D. J. (1977). Psychological issues in the management of rheumatoid arthritis. *Psychosomatics, 18,* 7–14.

Psychosocial Adaptation to Sensory Impairments

Part III of this book presented reviews of the research literature on psychosocial adaptation to three disease-related disorders: cancer, diabetes mellitus, and rheumatoid arthritis. In Part IV we provide reviews of the research literature on psychosocial adaptation to two sensory impairments: Chapter 11—blindness and visual impairments, and Chapter 12—deafness and hearing impairments.

These two sensory impairments share the following features: they (1) can be caused by a variety of agents, including genetic transmission, birth defects, traumatic accidents, and slowly progressing disease and aging processes, with the last class of agents the most common; (2) mainly involve a single functional limitation but may affect a second functional domain (eg, mobility among persons with visual impairments or communication among persons with hearing impairments); (3) are normally irreversible and slowly progressive; (4) pose no threat to the person's life or physical functioning; and (5) are essentially invisible, although the use of special devices (eg, walking cane, hearing aid) may render the impairments visible under certain circumstances.

Each of these reviews in Part IV will follow the same format as those in Parts II and III. We begin each chapter with a brief description of the sensory impairment, including a synopsis of available information on incidence and prevalence, causal factors, signs and symptoms, complications, course, and prognosis. This is followed by a review of the research literature on psychosocial adaptation to the impairment, focusing on the research conducted in the last 15 years. The third section of each chapter summarizes the available information on characteristics associated with psychosocial adaptation to the impairment. This section is organized into three areas: (1) sociodemographic characteristics (eg, age at time of injury or disease onset, chronicity, sex, educational level, socioeconomic status), (2) personality factors (eg, premorbid personality, ego strength, attribution of blame, perception of disability, locus of control), and (3) impairment-related variables (eg, neuropathology, severity of impairment, type of treatment). If it is available, information on environmental factors (eg, degree of family or peer support, level of independence, modifiability of the work environment) that are thought to be related to psychosocial adaptation to the impairment is also included. Each chapter ends with a presentation of tentative conclusions concerning psychosocial adaptation to the impairment derived from the findings reported in the literature reviewed.

CHAPTER 11
===

Blindness and Visual Impairments

DESCRIPTION

Blindness exerts a profound effect on one's life. The consequences of adventitious loss of sight include radical changes in a person's psychosocial, vocational, recreational, and environmental pursuits (Falvo, 1991; Heller, Flohr, & Zegans, 1987). It also results in a major blow to one's body image and self-concept (Delafield, 1976; Dover, 1959). It is estimated that almost 2 million Americans are legally blind and that approximately 12 million Americans have some form of visual impairment. Of these, two thirds are over the age of 65 years, and only 10% are below the age of 45 years (Kirchner & Lowman, 1978; Panek, 1992).

Among the many causes of blindness and other forms of visual impairment, the most common include (1) diabetic retinopathy, which results in approximately 5,000 new cases of blindness in the United States each year (Flom, 1992); (2) glaucoma (intraocular pressure in the eye); (3) cataracts (lens opacity) that are mainly associated with aging; (4) macular degeneration (central retina pathology), also associated mainly with older individuals; (5) retinitis pigmentosa (a bilateral, progressive eye disease affecting the retina's peripheral pigmentary layer); and (6) corneal diseases and traumas (Panek, 1992; Rosenthal & Cole, 1993).

PSYCHOSOCIAL ADAPTATION TO BLINDNESS AND VISUAL IMPAIRMENTS

There is a paucity of empirical research concerning psychosocial adaptation to sudden or progressive blindness. Most of the available information is contained in theoretical or clinical narratives often confined to individual case studies (Blank, 1957; Bornstein, 1977; Dover, 1959; Fitzgerald, 1970). The importance of vision in early personality development and later adult life has been emphasized by psychoanalysts. In one of the earliest efforts to analyze the role of sight in understanding personality structure, Blank (1957) maintained that personality disturbance in persons with visual impairments could often be traced to the unconscious significance of (1) the eye as a sexual organ; (2) the eye as a hostile, destructive organ; and (3) blindness as a punishment for sin (ie, castration).

Traditional psychodynamic models of psychosocial adaptation to blindness emphasized the importance of concepts such as loss, mourning, and grief. They also suggested that these experiences (eg, loss, grief) can be typically understood as evolving through various psychological stages (Carroll, 1961; Cholden, 1958; Parkes, 1972). Early clinical studies of acquired blindness (Blank, 1957; Cholden, 1954; Perlman & Routh, 1980) suggested that typical reaction to this traumatic event was composed of three major phases: (1) shock, (2) depression, and (3) recovery. During the shock phase the recently blinded person is unable to think or feel. This cognitive-affective anesthesia serves as a protective shield to the self (Dale, 1992). The shock reaction is followed by emergence of negative affect—depression—often equated with a state of mourning (Lepri, 1992). The individual grieves the loss of sight with accompanying feelings of helplessness, hopelessness, and self-blame. Finally, upon reaching the recovery or adaptation phase, the individual gradually resumes typical activities characterized by attempts at reestablishing interpersonal relations, engaging in daily problem-solving activities, and accepting blindness as a permanent condition.

A similar model of adaptation to visual impairment was suggested by Allen (1990), based on intensive work with six adults with a visual impairment over a course of one year. Allen (1990) divided the adaptation process into three distinct, dynamic phases. These hypothesized phases were (1) preimpact phase, in which the person was not fully aware of the gradual vision loss or, in the case of sudden loss, of the seriousness and permanency of the loss; (2) impact phase, which included realization of the visual loss with its concomitant reactions of depression, anger, insecurity, self-devaluation, and social withdrawal; and (3) learning to live with the impairment, a phase that reflected acceptance of the condition and its permanency, learning new ways of adapting to it, being able to carry out most typical activities independently, and viewing the future as a challenge to be overcome.

It is of interest that none of the clinical models of reaction to blindness and visual impairment pays much attention to the reaction of denial in the adaptation process. Although the existence of denial was recognized by other clinicians (Bauman, 1959; Dale, 1992; Freedman, 1965; Schulz, 1977; Silver, Boon, & Stones, 1983; Wright, 1983), they, too, failed to attribute major significance to its role in psychosocial adaptation to blindness and visual impairment. Dover (1959), in discussing the dynamics of the adaptation process to acquired blindness, recognized the importance of denial as a defense to ward off anxiety. She asserted that denial was frequently manifested through a search for new medical discoveries and magical treatments. Furthermore she distinguished between an active form of denial (eg, seeking a magical cure) and a passive form in which the individual who is recently blind appears only superficially to accept the condition and makes no attempt to actively adjust to the environment. Schulz (1977) distinguished between denial of the severity of the condition and denial of the affective content or meaning of the visual loss, viewing the latter as interfering with the process of adaptation.

Until very recently empirical studies of specific psychosocial reactions to blindness and visual impairment were rarely encountered in the literature. Fitzgerald (1970) interviewed persons in Great Britain whose course of visual loss ranged from sudden to slowly progressive. Initial reactions to blindness were assessed from the author's informal and semistructured interviews with these volunteer participants. He reported that over 85% of the individuals in the sample recalled experiencing depressive affect immediately after the onset of blindness, while 65% still experienced depression at least three months postonset. Similarly, experiencing the anxiety reaction also diminished over time, from 75% of the sample immediately following onset of blindness to 45% of the sample three months or more postonset. A similar trend of diminution was noted for the reaction of anger (a reduction from 60% to 30%).

On the basis of his clinical observations and interviews, Fitzgerald (1970) suggested that four distinct but partially overlapping phases of adaptation to blindness occurred: (1) disbelief (ie, shock); (2) denial or protest; (3) depression, often including other distressing reactions such as anxiety, anger, and suspiciousness; and (4) recovery or resolution (ie, successful adaptation). In a follow-up study of the same sample, Fitzgerald, Ebert, and Chambers (1987) reported that 50% of the participants were still depressed and 55% were still anxious more than 15 years later. Anger was also experienced by almost 35% of the participants in the follow-up study.

In two recent studies Leinhaas and Hedstrom (1994) and Teitelbaum, Davidson, Gravetter, Taub, and Teitelbaum (1994) sought to assess more directly depression among persons with a visual impairment. Leinhaas and Hedstrom (1994), based on their clinical work, concluded that the two most common types of emotional distress among persons with a visual impairment are depression and adjustment disorder. The researchers failed, however, to provide any empirical data to support these conclusions. Teitelbaum et al. (1994), on the other hand, in a sample of 87 older male veterans with a visual impairment (mean age = 71.3 years), found that although the mean Beck Depression Inventory score for the sample was within the average range, the scores ranged widely, indicating that several of the participants exhibited a severe degree of depression.

CHARACTERISTICS ASSOCIATED WITH ADAPTATION TO BLINDNESS AND VISUAL IMPAIRMENTS

In one of the few reports concerning the association between demographic, personality, and environmental characteristics and adaptation to blindness, Bauman (1954) divided over 400 persons from community agencies serving persons who were blind into three groups based on their perceived level of adaptation. Group 1 (the well-adjusted group, 37% of total sample) included those individuals who (a) were self-supporting, (b) were mostly mobile, (c) maintained satisfactory home and community activities, and (d) had a successful work history. The individuals in Group 2 (the partially adjusted group, 34% of total sample) were similar in most characteristics to the first group but demonstrated no successful work history. Group 3 (the maladjusted group, 29% of total sample) was composed of those individuals who (a) were not self-supporting, (b) were mobility-dependent on others, (c) had engaged in only limited home and community activities, and (d) had no recorded work history. All participants were interviewed extensively to determine their visual, medical, personal, social, educational, and vocational histories. In addition, a comprehensive test battery was administered to measure participants' intelligence, manual dexterity, emotional status, and vocational performance. Results indicated that, in general, participants from Group 1 scored higher than those from Group 3 on measures of intelligence, manual dexterity, emotional stability, and realistic acceptance of blindness. They also attained higher educational levels than participants from Group 3. No differences were found between these two groups on degree of vision loss, health indices, or level of social interaction. In a follow-up study 14 years later, Bauman and Yoder (1966) successfully located and interviewed 92% of the participants in the original sample and concluded that, on the whole, the same characteristics first found to be associated with adaptation to blindness still retained their discriminating power.

Zarlock (1961) sought to investigate the relationship between adaptation to blindness and other psychosocial variables in a controlled study of 52 individuals with blindness, half of whom were rated as being socially adjusted, and 25 individuals without a disability matched on several demographic variables (eg, age, intelligence, socioeconomic status, religious affiliation). Participants' scores on a Social Adjustment to Blindness Scale were found to correlate positively and significantly with scores on Barron's Ego Strength Scale and on the Fitting Attitudes towards Blindness Scale and negatively and significantly with scores on Taylor's Manifest Anxiety Scale, the California F Scale (measuring authoritarianism), and two specifically designed scales to measure attitudes towards medicine and religion. The last two scales may be regarded as measures of unrealistic hope or denial. The well-adjusted participants who were blind scored lower than their poorly adjusted counterparts on the attitudes towards medicine and religion scales (ie, less frequently denying their condition).

Lukoff and Whiteman (1962) also investigated the relationship between demographic and personality variables and adaptation to blindness. The latter was empirically defined as demonstrating successful behaviors in the areas of employment, independent traveling, and independence in eating and shopping. Nearly 500 persons served by the New York Commission for the Blind, considered representative of the total register of persons who are legally blind in that state, agreed to participate in the study. The following variables were found to be associated with higher levels of adaptation: (1) higher educational achievement, (2) earlier onset of blindness, (3) being a member of the white race, (4) better residual vision, (5) younger age, and (6) greater intelligence. The results of the study, however, must be interpreted with caution due to the lack of a control group, unsophisticated statistical treatment of the data, and a definition of adaptation that relied almost exclusively on community independent living.

Joffe and Bast (1978) studied ego functioning in 101 men who were blind using the California Psychological Inventory and extensive structured interviews. Two variables, in combination, were used to indicate adaptation or accommodation to blindness: occupational status (ie, employed versus unemployed) and mobility (ie, having good versus poor travel abilities). The authors found that although no differences were found between the employed and unemployed groups on such measures as educational level, age, and degree of vision, several psychological attributes (ie, measures of defense and coping) did discriminate between the groups. In contrast to nonaccommodators (those who were unemployed and had poor mobility skills), accommodators showed more extensive use of coping strategies (ie, mature, adaptive, flexible, purposive, present-oriented, reality-based behaviors) that included objectivity, intellectualization, suppression, and tolerance of ambiguity. Nonaccommodators, on the other hand, tended to rely more on defensive maneuvers (ie, immature, nonadaptive, rigid, past-oriented, and irrational processes) that included projection, regression, fantasy, displacement, rationalization, and use of doubt.

More recently Fitzgerald et al. (1987) conducted a follow-up study with 47 British volunteer participants who were blind in an attempt to predict successful adaptation, defined by combined depression-distress level and the use of coping skills, from four groups of variables (ie, demographics, health, vision, and mobility skills). The best predictors of depression-distress included (1) having a poor health history, (2) having less residual vision, (3) being unable to live independently, and (4) being unemployed. The best predictors of coping ability included (1) early acceptance of blindness, (2) early learning of blind skills, and (3) having a better predisability work history.

The link between degree of vision loss and psychosocial adaptation to blindness has yielded mixed results. Whereas most researchers have found a positive association between better residual vision and such measures as successful adaptation and lower depression (Fitzgerald et al., 1987; Lukoff & Whiteman, 1962; Wulsin, Jacobson, & Rand, 1991), others failed to detect such relationship (Teitelbaum et al., 1994). In the Wulsin et al. (1991) study, with a sample of 31 persons with a visual impairment having proliferative diabetic retinopathy, significant negative correlations were found between degree of visual loss and three separate measures of psychosocial functioning, including the Psychosocial Adjustment to Illness Scale, the Symptom Check List—90-Revised, and the Ways of Coping Checklist-Revised. In each case, and on three separate assessment periods (at first vitreous hemorrhage, at four months, and at eight months), worsened vision was associated with poorer psychosocial adjustment, increased psychological symptoms, and increased use of emotion-focused coping modes. Limited data also suggest that variables such as access to social support (Oppegard, Hansson, Morgan, Indart, Crutcher, & Hampton, 1984) and having better general health (Teitelbaum et al., 1994) may be associated with lower levels of depression among persons with a visual impairment.

In a series of investigations, Dodds and colleagues (Dodds, Bailey, Pearson, & Yates, 1991; Dodds, Ferguson, Ng, Flannigan, Hawes, & Yates, 1994; Dodds, Flannigan, & Ng, 1993) sought to investigate longitudinally the concept of adaptation to loss of sight. They conceptualized adjustment to vision loss as comprising general health, anxiety, depression, self-esteem, self-efficacy, locus of control, acceptance of disability, attitudes toward blindness, and attributional style. They then searched for specific existing measures to tap each of these domains, followed by the development of the Nottingham Adjustment Scale, a 55-item, factor analytic-derived questionnaire purporting to measure adjustment to blindness (Dodds et al., 1991; Dodds et al., 1993). According to the authors, successful adaptation to vision loss is characterized by (1) low levels of anxiety and depression, (2) high levels of self-esteem and self-efficacy; (3) a high sense of personal responsibility for recovery, (4) a positive attitude toward visual impairment; and (5) acceptance of one's own visual disability. The authors asserted that these indicators of successful adaptation to vision loss were indeed reported, following a 10-week period of a rehabilitation experience, in a study involving over 100 persons with visual impairments. The findings lent support to the notion that adaptation is indeed a multidimensional concept, and that the process of adaptation to loss and disability reflects changes in both negative (eg, decreased feelings of depression and anxiety) and positive (eg, improved self-concept, increased feelings of mastery and self-control) experiences. Following a series of structural modeling analyses the authors concluded that (1) attributional style exerts a direct effect on internal self-worth (a latent factor perceived to reflect a positive view of one's internalized self), which is a linear combination of anxiety, depression, and self-esteem (manifest variables); (2) acceptance of vision loss exerts a direct effect on self-as-agent (a latent factor), reflecting a belief in one's ability to control future goals and tasks, which is a linear combination of self-efficacy and locus of control (manifest variables); and (3) a direct link exists between self-as-agent (as measured by self-efficacy and locus of control) and internal self-worth (as measured by anxiety, depression, and self-esteem), further supporting existing research that suggests that as individuals gain control of their recovery, the less depressed and anxious they become and the more they gain a sense of personal worth (Ferguson, Dodds, Craig, Flannigan, & Yates, 1994).

CONCLUSION

The literature on adaptation to blindness and visual impairment comprises relatively few empirical studies. Many of the earlier studies are marred by methodological flaws (eg, small samples, inconsistent definition of adaptation, inadequate statistical analyses). Findings from the literature on adaptation to blindness and visual loss are therefore tentative and await further investigation. The following conclusions, however, are suggested: (1) depression following vision loss and blindness appears to be a widespread phenomenon; (2) successful psychosocial adaptation to visual impairment may be facilitated by higher intellectual and educational levels; (3) greater degree of visual loss has been frequently found to be associated with increased feelings of depression and poorer psychosocial adaptation; and (4) acceptance of vision loss, feelings of self-efficacy, and the belief in one's ability to control future events are associated with higher self-worth.

REFERENCES

Allen, M. (1990). Adjusting to visual impairment. *Journal of Ophthalmic Nursing & Technology, 9,* 47–51.

Bauman, M. K. (1954). *Adjustment to blindness.* Harrisburg, PA: State Council for the Blind.

Bauman, M. K. (1959). The initial psychological reaction to blindness. *New Outlook for the Blind, 53,* 165–169.

Bauman, M. K., & Yoder, P. (1966). *Adjustment to blindness re-viewed.* Harrisburg, PA: State Council for the Blind.

Blank, H. R. (1957). Psychoanalysis and blindness. *Psychoanalytic Quarterly, 26,* 1–24.

Bornstein, M. (1977). Analysis of a congenitally blind musician. *Psychoanalytic Quarterly, 46,* 23–37.

Carroll, T. J. (1961). *Blindness: What it is, what it does and how to live with it.* Boston: Little, Brown.

Cholden, L. (1954). Some psychiatric problems in the rehabilitation of the blind. *Bulletin of the Menninger Clinic, 18*, 107–112.

Cholden, L. (1958). *A psychiatrist works with blindness.* New York: American Foundation for the Blind.

Dale, B. (1992). Issues in traumatic blindness. *Journal of Visual Impairment and Blindness, 86*, 140–143.

Delafield, G. L. (1976). Adjustment to blindness. *New Outlook for the Blind, 70*, 64–68.

Dodds, A. G., Bailey, P., Pearson, A., & Yates, L. (1991). Psychological factors in acquired visual impairment: The development of a scale of adjustment. *Journal of Visual Impairment and Blindness, 85*, 306–310.

Dodds, A. G., Ferguson, E., Ng, L., Flannigan, H., Hawes, G., & Yates, L. (1994). The concept of adjustment: A structural model. *Journal of Visual Impairment and Blindness, 88*, 487–497.

Dodds, A. G., Flannigan, H., & Ng, L. (1993). The Nottingham Adjustment Scale: A validation study. *International Journal of Rehabilitation Research, 16*, 177–184.

Dover, F. T. (1959). Readjustment to the onset of blindness. *Social Casework, 40*, 334–338.

Falvo, D. R. (1991). *Medical and psychosocial aspects of chronic illness and disability.* Gaithersburg, MD: Aspen.

Ferguson, E., Dodds, A., Craig, D., Flannigan, H., & Yates, L. (1994). The changing face of adjustment to sight: A longitudinal evaluation of rehabilitation. *Journal of Social Behavior and Personality, 9*, 287–306.

Fitzgerald, R. G. (1970). Reactions to blindness: An exploratory study of adults with recent loss of sight. *Archives of General Psychiatry, 22*, 370–379.

Fitzgerald, R. G., Ebert, J. N., & Chambers, M. (1987). Reactions to blindness: A four-year follow-up study. *Perceptual and Motor Skills, 64*, 363–378.

Flom, R. (1992). Low vision management of the diabetic patient. *Problems in Optometry, 4*, 2–3.

Freedman, S. (1965). Reactions to blindness. *New Outlook for the Blind, 59*, 344–346.

Heller, B. W., Flohr, L. M., & Zegans, L. S. (Eds.). (1987). *Psychosocial interventions with sensorially disabled persons.* New York: Grune & Stratton.

Joffe, P. E., & Bast, B. A. (1978). Coping and defense in relation to accommodation among a sample of blind men. *Journal of Nervous and Mental Disease, 166*, 537–552.

Kirchner, C., & Lowman, C. (1978). Sources of variation in the estimated prevalence of visual loss. *Journal of Visual Impairment and Blindness, 72*, 329–333.

Leinhaas, M. M., & Hedstrom, N. J. (1994). Low vision: How to assess and treat its emotional impact. *Geriatrics, 49*, 53–56.

Lepri, B. P. (1992, March). *The psychosocial aspects of vision impairment in the elderly.* Paper presented at the meeting of the AACD National Convention, Baltimore.

Lukoff, I. F., & Whiteman, M. (1962). Intervening variables and adjustment: An empirical demonstration. *Social Work, 7*, 92–102.

Oppegard, K., Hansson, R. O., Morgan, T., Indart, M., Crutcher, M., & Hampton, P. (1984). Sensory loss, family support, and adjustment among the elderly. *Journal of Social Psychology, 123*, 291–292.

Panek, W. C. (1992). Visual disabilities. In M. G. Brodwin, F. Tellez, & S. K. Brodwin (Eds.), *Medical, psychosocial and vocational aspects of disability* (pp. 217–230). Athens, GA: Elliott & Fitzpatrick.

Parkes, C. M. (1972). *Bereavement studies of grief in adult life.* London: Tavistock.

Perlman, J. L., & Routh, D. K. (1980). Stigmatizing effects of a child's wheelchair in successive and simultaneous interactions. *Journal of Pediatric Psychology, 5*, 43–55.

Rosenthal, B. P., & Cole, R. G. (1993). Visual impairments. In M. G. Eisenberg, R. L. Glueckauf, & H. H. Zaretsky (Eds.), *Medical aspects of disability* (pp. 391–401). New York: Springer.

Schulz, P. J. (1977). Reaction to the loss of sight. In J. T. Pearlman, G. L. Adams, & S. H. Sloan (Eds.), *Psychiatric problems in ophthalmology* (pp. 38–67). Springfield, IL: C C Thomas.

Silver, R. L., Boon, C., & Stones, M. H. (1983). Searching for meaning in misfortune: Making sense of incest. *Journal of Social Issues, 39*, 81–102.

Teitelbaum, L. M., Davidson, P. W., Gravetter, F. J., Taub, H. A., & Teitelbaum, C. S. (1994). The relation of vision loss to depression in older veterans. *Journal of Visual Impairment and Blindness, 88*, 253–257.

Wright, B. A. (1983). *Physical disability—A psychosocial approach* (2nd ed.). New York: Harper & Row.

Wulsin, L. R., Jacobson, A. M., & Rand, L. I. (1991). Psychosocial correlates of mild visual loss. *Psychosomatic Medicine, 53*, 109–117.

Zarlock, S. P. (1961). Magical thinking and associated psychological reactions to blindness. *Journal of Consulting Psychology, 25*, 155–159.

CHAPTER 12

Deafness and Hearing Impairments

DESCRIPTION

A hearing impairment is defined to be any loss of hearing, of which deafness is the most severe form (Falvo, 1991). An individual who is deaf is functionally unable to process linguistic information for the typical purposes of life. If the deafness is present at birth, the individual is classified as congenitally deaf; if the deafness begins after birth, the individual is classified as adventitiously deaf or as deafened. Individuals who are adventitiously deaf prior to the onset of language are classified as prelingually deaf; if the deafness occurs before the individual enters the workforce, he or she is classified as prevocationally deaf. Those individuals whose sense of hearing, although impaired, is functional and who can process linguistic information with or without a hearing aid are classified as hard of hearing.

Although precise data concerning the prevalence of hearing impairments are difficult to obtain, it is estimated that nearly 30 million Americans have some level of hearing impairment, making it the most common form of physical disability in the United States. Approximately 0.1% of these individuals are deaf (Danek & Seidman, 1992; Kerman-Lerner & Hauck, 1993). Among school-aged children 5% are hearing impaired, and one tenth of those (0.5%) are so significantly impaired as to require special educational and related services. Congenital hearing impairments, which may account for as many as one third of all cases, are present in approximately 1 of every 1,000 live births (Danek & Seidman, 1992) and may be due to genetic (eg, Ushers' syndrome), prenatal (eg, rubella), or perinatal (eg, anoxia) factors. Postnatal hearing impairment can be attributed to the effects of untreated childhood diseases (eg, recurrent ear infections or otitis media), trauma (eg, concussion, drug toxins, noise exposure), degenerative conditions (eg, otosclerosis), new growths (eg, tumors), and physical deterioration of the hearing mechanism with age (a condition known as presbycusis). The prevalence of hearing impairment increases dramatically with age, with reported prevalence rates of 23% for persons between 65 and 75 years and 40% for those persons over 75 years of age (Danek & Seidman, 1992).

PSYCHOSOCIAL ADAPTATION TO DEAFNESS AND HEARING IMPAIRMENTS

Because a hearing impairment has a profound effect upon the individual's ability to communicate and because communication is essential for daily interactions that contribute to the development of emotional maturity and vocational competence, a hearing impairment may exert a profound effect upon the psychosocial functioning of the individual (Cartledge, Paul, Jackson, & Cochran, 1991; Holt, 1979; Misiaszek et al., 1985; Nash & Castle, 1980; Spear, 1984; Thomas, 1984). A child with a hearing impairment experiences a restricted range and qualitatively different interpersonal interactions that interfere with typical personality development and fail to support the development of social skills (Cooper, 1976; Ostby & Thomas, 1984). Parents may be overprotective or rejecting, peer interactions may be minimal, and close friendships with peers without hearing impairments may be difficult for the child to establish. In addition, as Luetke-Stahlman (1995) and others have pointed out, some degree of professional intervention will typically be required to compensate for effects of the loss of hearing on the child's communication and academic abilities. But because it is difficult to identify a hearing impairment in a very young child, and because the manifestations of a hearing impairment may be mistaken for other impairments (eg, mental retardation, behavior disorders), this essential intervention may not be provided during critical periods of the child's development.

Postlingual adventitious deafness, especially if it occurs after adolescence, disrupts established patterns of communication and behavior. Consequently, the person who is postlingually deaf experiences different and more intense psychosocial reactions than the person who is prelingually deaf (David & Trehub, 1989; Kerman-Lerner & Hauck, 1993). The person who is postlingually deaf must learn to cope with the permanent loss of an important sense on which he or she previously depended, as well as the ability to interact orally with friends and family. In this regard, the process of psychosocial adaptation to disability among persons who are postlingually adventitiously deaf is thought to parallel that of others who face difficult and stressful life situations and catastrophic losses (Demorest & Erdman, 1989; Falvo, 1991; Rosen, 1979; Thomas, 1984). Reactions may include (1) anxiety about the inability to maintain independence or the progressive nature of the impairment, (2) depression at the memories of cherished sounds that are now lost, (3) internalized anger at the loss of previously enjoyable activities and the difficulty of performing what were once easy life tasks, (4) externalized hostility toward others who individuals believe are talking about them, and (5) withdrawal from orally loaded social situations due to fears that others may reject them as being inattentive or stupid. Because the loss of hearing constitutes a significant injury to the individual's self-esteem, denial of impairment is also a commonly observed reaction. The individual's negative psychosocial reactions and attitudes may be compounded (eg, depression at the sudden loss of communication may lead to isolation that, in turn, elevates feeling of despair) and may become a contributing cause of unsuccessful adaptation to the hearing impairment (eg, denial may lead to refusal to seek speech and language interventions or to wear a hearing aid).

Throughout history, deafness has constituted a significant social stigma (Myklebust, 1960a; Ostby & Thomas, 1984). An often repeated aphorism with little scientific justification is that the ability to communicate is the distinguishing characteristic of humans. Until the early decades of this century, society acted as if it understood this to mean that anyone with a communication difficulty was subhuman and should be excluded from the community. Among the earliest scientific attempts to study the process of psychosocial adaptation to deafness and hearing impairments was a psychiatric review by Menninger (1924). An increase of clinical interest in this topic occurred just after World War II (Ingalls, 1946; Knapp, 1948; Zeckel, 1950), due in part to an increase in rehabilitation programs made available to veterans and the opportunities for research with this population that these programs afforded.

The most widely cited of the early work on the so-called psychology of deafness is the research by Myklebust (1960b; 1964; 1966) in which he studied the emotional adaptation of persons with hearing impairments using the Minnesota Multiphasic Personality Inventory. Myklebust compared the personality profiles of individuals with hearing impairments who were members of a self-help advocacy group in Chicago with the profiles of individuals with deafness who were residents of Gallaudet College. He discovered that both groups of individuals manifested significant psychosocial maladaptation, but that the individuals with deafness were more maladapted than the individuals with hearing impairments. Scores for both groups on the schizophrenia scale were above the norms for the general population. Low scores on the social introversion scale led Myklebust to interpret this finding as a manifestation of the psychological and social isolation associated with sensory deprivation rather than as evidence of psychiatric illness. Contrary to expectations, Myklebust failed to find any difference from the norms on the paranoia scale for either group in his investigation. He reported that males were less well adjusted than were females and that the earlier the onset and the more severe the impairment, the more maladjustment was apparent in the data.

It must be noted that the samples included in Myklebust's studies were not at all typical of the population of persons with hearing impairments. Moreover the Minnesota Multiphasic Personality Inventory was not normed for use with persons with hearing impairments. In addition to the probable language difficulties, a number of the items on the instrument confound sensory loss with psychopathology (eg, "I am quite often not in on the gossip and talk of the group that I belong to"). Despite these limitations and psychometric flaws, the Minnesota Multiphasic Personality Inventory continues to be used to investigate psychological characteristics of persons with hearing impairments (for example Knutson & Lansing, 1990). Researchers who have reviewed the literature after Mylkebust's studies have concluded that there is no evidence to support the existence of a unique "psychology of deafness" or a "deaf personality" (Feinstein & Lytle, 1987; Thomas, 1984).

Psychological characteristics of persons with hearing impairments that have been reported by clinicians have included egocentricity, despondency, overdependence, social withdrawal, disturbances of body image, submissiveness, rigidity, and introversion; expressing feelings of loss, hopelessness, social inadequacy, lack of empathy, and inferiority; demonstrating poor decision making and errors in social perception; displaying aggression and temper tantrums; verbalizing persecutory ideas and hostility; and raging against fate. Cooper (1976), for example, reported that individuals who are congenitally deaf typically display impulsive and aggressive behaviors, with low but elevated incidence of depression and obsessional symptoms. The prevalence of schizophrenia among individuals with deafness, however, was found not to differ from the prevalence in the general population. Individuals classified as hard-of-hearing were reported to display behaviors of inattention, irresponsibility, irritability, and tactlessness.

Misiaszek et al. (1985), from their review of the clinical literature, argued that audition and communication are essential for the development of identity and for the control of affect and drives. As a result, a hearing impairment should affect these ego functions and the individual's interactions with the external world. Impulsiveness, aggressiveness, egocentricity, rigidity, and lack of empathy should be resultant personality manifestations observed by others. Other writers have theorized that, because the sensory deprivation of a hearing impairment inhibits communication, it restricts and distorts the emotional content of interpersonal interchanges and leads to social isolation and social immaturity (Ives, 1969; Koetitz, 1976; Meadow, 1980; Watson, Henggeler & and Whelan, 1990). These effects are thought to be heightened during the transition period from adolescence to young adulthood (Nash & Castle, 1980).

The most striking finding of our review of the empirical literature concerning psychosocial adaptation to disability among persons with hearing impairments is the paucity of evidence in support of these theoretical contentions. And even this meager research base is flawed. As noted by others who have reviewed this literature (Hummel & Schirmer, 1984; Thomas, 1984), the small number of studies located (1) did not use consistent definitions of psychosocial adaptation; (2) generally failed to account for the confounding of such variables as age at onset, severity of impairment, educational experience, or linguistic environment of the home; (3) included biased and nonrepresentative samples; and (4) used instruments that were either constructed by the researchers for the investigation or were not validated for use with persons with hearing impairments.

The results of a small number of investigations provide some support for the contentions presented in the clinical and case study literature that persons with hearing impairments are at increased risk for psychosocial maladaptation. Meadow and Trybus (1979) reported that 8% to 10% of children and adolescents with hearing impairments have significant emotional and behavior problems, and that the prevalence of serious emotional problems was three to six times greater than in the population of persons without hearing impairments. Mahapatra (1974) used a self-report descriptive questionnaire to supplement a clinical interview protocol in a study of psychiatric illness in persons with acquired hearing loss. A total of 49 persons between the ages of 15 and 65 years who were consecutive admits to the otolaryngology (ear-nose-throat) wards of London hospitals for treatment of deafness due to otosclerosis were included in this study. The clinical data led to the diagnosis of depression in 35% of these individuals; an additional 10% of these individuals were diagnosed with paranoia; and one person was diagnosed with acute anxiety.

Freeman, Malkin, and Hastings (1975) studied a nonrandom sample of 120 Canadian children and adolescents aged 5 to 15 years with severe and profound prelingual hearing impairments who were living at home. A second group of 120 children without hearing impairments were matched to the target children by age, sex, and residence area. The dependent variables included parents' ratings of their children's social and emotional behaviors and of their communication skills. The children with hearing impairments were rated as more restless, possessive, dependent, fussy, and disobedient. In addition, they were rated as more likely to destroy the belongings of others and to steal things. Of the children with hearing impairments, 43% were reported to play little or not at all with their nonsibling peers versus only 11% of the children without hearing impairments. Based upon these ratings, 23% of the children with hearing impairments were classified as manifesting moderate to severe psychiatric disorders.

Powers, Elliott, Fairbank, and Monaghan (1988) designed a study to determine the prevalence of learning disabilities and the risk of psychosocial maladaptation among children with severe and profound hearing loss. All 27 students between the ages of 5 and 12 years at a residential school for persons who are deaf who were not otherwise impaired were rated by their classroom teacher, a speech-language pathologist, and the school principal on 5-point scales concerning speech abilities, signing abilities, learning problems, and behavior problems. A total of 26% of the students were identified as having significant learning problems, and 11% were rated as having significant emotional problems by one or more of the three raters. Of the seven students identified by these raters as having learning problems, three were similarly identified using the norms of the Pupil Rating Scale—Revised (Myklebust, 1981). Using the Social-Emotional Assessment Inventory for Deaf and Hearing-Impaired Students, 41% of the students were identified as in need of an intervention program for significant social and emotional problems.

Klansek-Kyllo and Rose (1985) compared a group of children and adolescents aged $4\frac{1}{2}$ to 16 years with severe and profound hearing impairments to a group of controls without hearing impairments on the Scales of Independent Behaviors, a parent-report rating scale of adaptive behaviors in home, school, and community environments. Significant differences appeared on the scales measuring language and communication behaviors, as well as on the scales measuring social interactions, use of money, and home-school orientation (a measure of preferred environment). The researchers attributed the last two of these differences to a lack of opportunity and to overprotection by the parents of the children with hearing impairments. No significant differences were noted on any of the scales measuring motor skills, activities of daily living, or community living skills.

Finally, Murphy and Newlon (1987) use a mailed questionnaire to study a group of 170 students with hearing impairments at eight colleges nationwide. This nonrandom sample included 76 college students with mild to moderate hearing impairments and 94 college students with deafness. The primary dependent variable was the self-report UCLA Loneliness Scale (Russell, Peplau, & Cutrona, 1980). The means for both groups exceeded the published norms for persons without hearing impairments, but contrary to expectations there was no difference in mean loneliness scores between the two groups. It was also noted that those students with hearing impairments who scored the highest on the loneliness scale also reported the least satisfactory peer relationships and felt the least comfortable with both oral and sign language communication.

In contrast to these results, a number of investigations have found that persons with hearing impairments do not differ substantially from persons without hearing impairments on a variety of variables measuring aspects of psychosocial adaptation to disability. Farrugia and Austin (1980), for example, undertook an investigation of the social and emotional adaptation of four samples of individuals—50 residential school students who were deaf, 50 public school students who were deaf, 50 public school students who were hearing impaired, and 50 public school students without hearing impairments. Teacher rating data were obtained with the Social-Emotional Assessment Inventory (Meadow, Karchmer, Petersen,

& Rudner, 1980). The most striking finding was that the mean ratings for the students in all four groups were above 3 on the 5-point scales, indicating that no psychosocial adaptation problems were present in these groups. In a study of a sample of 20 adolescents attending the Montreal Oral School for the Deaf (MacLean & Becker, 1979), data were collected from a specially designed rating instrument that purported to measure personal, educational, social, and total adjustment. The ratings were made by the school's psychologist following an interview with the child and his or her teachers and a review of all school records. Only one of the students was rated as below average on overall psychosocial adjustment, personal adjustment, and social adjustment. One additional student was rated as below average on personal adjustment, and only one student was rated as below average on educational adjustment.

An investigation of the effects of hearing loss on the psychosocial adaptation of 40 children aged 5 to 18 years with prelingual hearing impairments who were attending clinics at the University of Iowa (Davis, Elfenbein, Schum, & Bentler, 1986) yielded inconsistent results. In addition to a set of sociodemographic variables (eg, age, severity of hearing loss), parent-report data were collected using the Child Behavior Check List, and the children and adolescents were asked to respond to the Missouri Children's Picture Series, a set of drawings of people engaging in various activities that the respondent is asked to sort into groups. The respondents' sortings were interpreted to mean that although they were above the norms on the dimensions of aggression and somatization, they did not differ from the norms on the dimensions of conformity, maturity, inhibition, activity level, disturbance of sleep, and male-female confusion. Based upon the parent reports, the children were rated below the norms on scales measuring social and school adjustment and above the norms for the scales measuring externalizing behavior problems (eg, overactivity, acting out). The ratings did not differ from the published norms for the scales measuring internalizing behavior problems (eg, withdrawal, anxiety, depression).

Knutson and Lansing (1990) administered a battery of instruments to a total of 27 individuals with adventitious hearing impairments who were consecutive referrals to a clinical practice specializing in cochlea implants. The instrument included the Communication Profile for the Hearing Impaired, the Beck Depression Inventory (Beck, 1978), the UCLA Loneliness Scale (Russell et al., 1980), the Social Anxiety and Distress Scale (Watson & Friend, 1969), the Rathus Assertiveness Scale (Rathus, 1982), and the Depression, Paranoia, and Social Introversion scales of the Minnesota Multiphasic Personality Inventory. Results revealed wide intraindividual and interindividual variability in scores among individuals in the sample. The Minnesota Multiphasic Personality Inventory mean scale scores were more than one standard deviation above the norms, suggesting more problems in these three areas than among individuals without impairments. In contrast the Beck Depression Inventory scores, the Social Anxiety and Distress Scale scores, the Rathus Assertiveness Scale scores, and the UCLA Loneliness Scale scores were all within the norms for the general population. It must be pointed out, however, that the individuals in this self-selected sample were not representative of the population of persons with deafness and hearing impairments because of their willingness to undergo cochlea implant surgery in an attempt to recover their hearing.

Prior, Glazner, Sanson, and Debelle (1988) compared a group of 26 Australian children aged two to five years with moderate to severe hearing impairments with children without hearing impairments matched on age, sex, and socioeconomic status using the Child Temperament Questionnaire (Thomas & Chess, 1977) and the Preschool Behaviours Checklist (Behar & Stringfield, 1974). Contrary to the researchers' expectations, the children with hearing impairments were found to be more adaptable in temperament and less distractible than their peers without hearing impairments. The teachers did rate the children with hearing impairments as somewhat more anxious and more behaviorally maladapted than the control children, but no such differences between the two groups appeared in the parent rating data. In addition, temperament did not contribute significantly to the prediction of the ratings of behavioral adjustment in the children with hearing impairments.

Additional support for the successful psychosocial adaptation of persons with hearing impairments comes from a set of four investigations reported by Raymond and Matson (1989). The social skills of groups of adolescents aged 13 to 17 years with severe and profound hearing impairments were studied and it was found that all the adolescents were within appropriate ranges above the norms for adolescents without hearing impairments. In addition, none among a set of sociodemographic variables that included age, chronicity, degree of hearing impairment, or sex was a significant predictor of social skills as measured by teacher ratings. The researchers concluded that hearing impairment does not influence the acquisition and development of social skills.

Only a single study was found that attempted to compare the psychosocial adaptation of children with hearing impairments and children with other chronic illnesses and impairments (Tavormina, Kastner, Slater, & Watt, 1976). In this study a battery of instruments measuring various psychosocial characteristics was administered to children and adolescents aged 5 to 19 years with diabetes, asthma, cystic fibrosis, and hearing impairments. The children with hearing impairments were reported to be somewhat below the norms for children without hearing impairments on the measure of self-concept, but their scores did not differ significantly from the norms for a measure of locus of control and for an inventory measuring general personality characteristics (eg, neuroticism, extroversion, aggression). When comparisons were made among the groups of children with the various chronic illnesses and impairments, the children with hearing impairments were found to be more external, alienated, and aggressive, and less conforming and less mature than the children in the other groups. When the entire data set was reviewed, the researchers concluded that the children with hearing impairments were more similar to than different from children with chronic illnesses and impairments.

CHARACTERISTICS ASSOCIATED WITH ADAPTATION TO DEAFNESS AND HEARING IMPAIRMENTS

The clinical literature discussed at the beginning of the previous section would lead to the conclusion that an individual's ability to adapt to a hearing impairment will vary with the severity and chronicity of the impairment, and with the age, age at onset, and education of the individual (David & Trehub, 1989; Goetzinger & Proul, 1975; Koetitz, 1976; Nash & Castle, 1980; Thomas, 1984). The evidence for these contentions from the empirical research literature, however, is far from convincing. In addition to instrumentation weaknesses, much of the available data in this area were collected from biased and nonrepresentative samples. In particular, most of the studies include individuals who are self-selected participants in auditory rehabilitation programs, candidates for specialized surgical procedures, or individuals seeking medical treatments for specific disorders that contribute to hearing impairments (eg, tinnitus, otosclerosis). We will return to these methodological concerns and a number of others in Chapter 24, when we present a general discussion and recommendations for research in this area.

With regard to severity, Hallberg and Carlsson (1991) found that severity of hearing loss was related to self-perception of psychosocial maladaptation. Based upon parental reports, Watson et al. (1990) found that children with greater hearing loss were more likely to display behavior problems. On the other hand, Mahapatra (1974), Davis et al. (1986), Freeman et al. (1975), and Murphy and Newlon (1987) reported no relationships between severity of hearing impairment and a variety of characteristics measuring psychosocial adaptation (eg, loneliness, self-esteem, emotional behavior problems, social skills) in diverse samples of persons with hearing impairments.

In a study of 45 children and adolescents with hearing impairments in a residential school in India (Agrawal & Kaur, 1985), it was reported that anxiety and overall adjustment, as measured by scales developed and normed in India, were directly related to both age at onset and chronicity of impairment. Mahapatra (1974) reported no relationship between chronicity of hearing impairment and psychiatric morbidity in individuals with hearing impairments. Meadow and Dyssegaard (1983a; 1983b) discovered that older children with a hearing impairment were more socially adapted than younger children with a hearing impairment, but there were no differences by age on scales measuring self-image or emotional adaptation. Hallberg and Carlsson (1991) found that older age and greater educational attainment were related to self-perceptions of psychosocial adaptation. Based upon parental reports, Watson et al. (1990) found that older children were more likely to display behavior problems. In contrast, Murphy and Newlon (1987) found that age was not related to scores on a measure of loneliness in a sample composed of college students with hearing impairments, and Davis et al. (1986) reported that psychosocial adaptation was not related to age in a sample of children with hearing impairments.

Knutson and Lansing (1990) found, as predicted, that the use of ineffective communication strategies as measured by the Communication Profile for the Hearing Impaired was related to increased loneliness, increased depression, and increased social anxiety and distress in a nonrandom sample of adults with acquired hearing impairments. Similarly, Hallberg and Carlsson (1991) found that the use of ineffective communication behaviors was related to respondents' self-perceptions of psychosocial maladaptation.

To determine whether the presence of an impairment in addition to a hearing impairment is a significant psychosocial risk factor, Meadow (1984) collected teacher informant data using the Social-Emotional Assessment Inventory for Deaf and Hearing-Impaired Students for a total of 262 children aged three to six years in public preschools and kindergartens. Of this total, 79 were children with a hearing impairment and no other impairment who were matched by age and sex with children without an impairment, and 52 were children with a hearing impairment and another type of impairment (eg, visual impairment, mental retardation, cerebral palsy, learning disability) who were similarly matched to children without a hearing impairment but with the same type of other impairment. The children with a hearing impairment and no other impairment did not differ from their peers without any impairment on four scales measuring social and emotional adaptation. Compared to these two groups of children, the children with multiple handicaps, with and without a hearing impairment, scored lower on the scales measuring sociable communicative behaviors and higher on the scales measuring impulsive dominating behaviors and anxious compulsive behaviors. The children with multiple handicaps with a hearing impairment scored lower than the children in the other three groups on the scales measuring developmental social and emotional lags.

Early and appropriate educational experiences are essential to the intellectual, social, and vocational development of all children. As a result the type of educational experiences provided to the child with a hearing impairment is a variable that has received some attention by researchers. Until the middle 1970s, most children with hearing impairments were educated in segregated day or residential special schools. Since 1975, the public schools have become responsible for serving this population of children, and the preferred setting is presumed to be integrated programs in typical schools. Studies of the efficacy of this public policy also provide information on the relationship between educational setting and the psychosocial adaptation of children with hearing impairments.

Early case studies and descriptive reports suggested that residential schools for persons who are deaf isolated the child from his or her family and peers, and the resultant experiential deprivation limited the child's social and emotional development (Delgado, 1982; Evans, 1975; Feinstein & Lytle, 1987; Misiaszek et al., 1985). Meadow (1984), for example, estimated that the prevalence of social and emotional maladaptation in children with hearing impairments who were educated in residential schools for persons who are deaf ranged from 10% to 20%. Other investigations have failed to uncover the negative effects of residential school placement (see, for example, Yachnik, 1986) and have suggested that these segregated settings may have advantages over public day settings in the areas of communication skills training, meaningful peer relationships, leadership experiences, and athletic activities (Delgado, 1982; Misiaszek et al., 1985). It has been argued, moreover, that integration in public day schools might place the child at psychosocial risk due to the negative attitudes of teachers and peer ostracism.

In their attempt to resolve this controversy, Lytle, Feinstein, and Jonas (1987) collected data from all new secondary students entering the federally funded model residential school for persons who are deaf operated at Gallaudet College. Of a total of 80 adolescents for whom data were available, 18 had previously been educated in a residential school for persons who are deaf, 24 in a special day school for persons who are deaf, 21 in public school settings using a total communication approach, and 17 in public school settings using an oral-only approach. The Social-Emotional Assessment Inventory for Deaf and Hearing-Impaired Students was completed by the parents of each child. Results revealed that previous educational setting was related to referrals for mental health and counseling services during the first year at the Gallaudet secondary program. Students educated in both types of public school settings were referred or sought assistance more than were students educated in the special schools for persons who are deaf. Among the students educated in the two types of public school settings, those in the oral-only setting were referred or sought assistance more often. Although low scores on the psychosocial adaptation measure were related to an increased likelihood of referral among all the students, these scores did not differ by the students' previous educational settings. The authors cautioned that their results might reflect intense and temporary psychosocial manifestations of culture shock by the students new to a residential school setting and might not persist longitudinally.

278 PSYCHOSOCIAL ADAPTATION TO CHRONIC ILLNESS AND DISABILITY

Farrugia and Austin (1980) compared samples of public school students who were deaf, public school students who were hearing impaired, residential school students who were deaf, and public school students with no hearing impairment using teacher rating data obtained with the Social-Emotional Assessment Inventory for Deaf and Hearing-Impaired Students. The public school students who were deaf were rated significantly below the students in the other three groups on the scales measuring self-image, social adjustment, and emotional adjustment. In addition, the public school students who were hearing impaired were rated significantly below their peers in the residential school and those with no hearing impairments on the scale measuring self-esteem. The investigators interpreted these results to mean that students with hearing impairments are socially isolated and rejected by their hearing peers in public school environments. This isolation and rejection in turn restrict social and emotional development and prolong immature behaviors.

Evidence favoring integrated public school programs over segregated special programs is available from a study by Sarfaty and Katz (1978) who administered the Tennessee Self-Concept Scale to a group of 48 eighth and ninth grade Israeli students aged 14 and 15 years with moderate to severe hearing impairments. Of the total, 21 were in special day schools, 13 were in special classes in typical schools, and 14 were in regular classes in typical schools. When compared to self-concept profiles of 257 peers without hearing impairments, it was found that all three groups of children with hearing impairments were significantly disadvantaged. The self-concept scores of the children with hearing impairments in the special classes exceeded those for the children with hearing impairments in the regular classes whose scores exceeded those for the children with hearing impairments in the special day schools.

The findings of a more recent investigation of this question (Cartledge et al., 1991) contribute to rather than eliminate the confusion in this area. A total of 76 adolescents with moderate to profound hearing impairments and average intelligence were assessed by their teachers using the Social-Emotional Assessment Inventory for Deaf and Hearing-Impaired Students. The students were also rated by their teachers using the Social Skills Rating Scale—Teacher Form (Gresham & Elliott, 1990). Rated were 64 behaviors organized into three domains: namely, compliance, cooperation, and social initiation. Of the total sample, 37 students were living in a residential school for persons who are deaf, 21 were living at home and attending a self-contained special class in a public school that used a total communication approach, and the remaining 18 were living at home and attending a self-contained special class in a public school that used an oral communication approach. The results of a multivariate analysis of variance revealed no significant differences in any of the means for the students in the three educational settings.

An environmental variable that is unique to the two types of disabilities in this part of the book is the congruence between the visual and hearing ability of the child and his or her parents. More than 90% of children with congenital hearing impairments are born into families in which neither parent has a hearing impairment (Danek & Seidman, 1992). It is thought that these children may be linguistically and socially isolated from their parents and may not have opportunities for typical early childhood experiences that support emotional growth and the development of intellectual and social skills (Watson et al., 1990). The parents' denial of the child's disability and anxieties associated with raising a difficult child may lead them to be less responsive, more controlling, and overprotective, characteristics that may contribute to the child's psychosocial maladaption (Ostby & Thomas, 1984; Watson et al., 1990).

The results of several early investigations did reveal that children with deafness raised by parents with deafness scored significantly higher on a number of social skill and social maturity measures than did children with deafness raised by parents without deafness (Delgado, 1982; Meadow, 1968). Meadow (1968), for example, found that children with deafness raised by parents with deafness scored higher on a measure of self-image and their social behaviors and self-confidence were rated higher by knowledgeable informants (eg, teachers) than were children with deafness raised by parents without deafness. These two groups of children did not differ on measures of communication skills and language development. It was speculated that the child with deafness adapts to the loss of hearing earlier and easier in a family in which deafness is a common characteristic than does the child with deafness in a family in which the lack of hearing constitutes a barrier to communication.

More recently, Yachnik (1986) screened 217 volunteer college students at Gallaudet College and California State University—Northridge using as criteria for participation (1) intact family, (2) prelingual deafness, and (3) same communication mode used by child and parents. A total of 28 students who were deaf and whose parents were deaf and a total of 28 students who were deaf and whose parents were not deaf were administered the Self-Description Questionnaire (Marsh & O'Neill, 1984), an instrument that purports to measure 13 dimensions of self-concept. Yachnik compared the scores on nine dimensions (four academic, three social, two physical) and the global scores for the two groups and discovered four significant differences: that the students who were deaf and whose parents were deaf scored higher on the global and the three social scales than did the students who were deaf and whose parents were not deaf.

The psychosocial environment for the person with a hearing impairment is created in large part by the attitudes and behaviors of immediate family members, especially parents. Supportive, understanding, and cooperative family members can assist individuals to cope with and accept their impairment (Demorest & Erdman, 1989). A small number of investigations have provided preliminary evidence in support of these contentions.

Watson et al. (1990), for example, collected data from 75 children with hearing impairments and their parents on a battery of measures, including the Child Behavior Check List, the Symptom Check List—90-Revised, the Family Adaptation and Cohesion Evaluation Scales, and the Revised Behavior Problem Checklist. With a set of sociodemographic variables (eg, sex, age, race, socioeconomic status, degree of hearing loss, communication mode) partialled out, it was discovered that the child's behavioral and social competence was directly related to family cohesion and inversely related to parental stress, family stress, and parental adaptation to the child's impairment. Although this study contributes important information on the relationship of family support to psychosocial adaptation in children with hearing impairments, several limitations must be noted. First, none of the measures of adaptation has been validated for use with persons with a hearing impairment. Second, the partial correlation and regression results reported can only suggest links among the variables and cannot explicate causal relationships. Third, the sample was nonrandom and cross-sectional, so it may have been possible that those families that were the most or least well adjusted declined to participate in the study. Finally, the measures of the children's behavior were all based upon parental reports that may have been biased.

Data concerning family support and psychosocial adaptation in older persons with hearing impairments were provided by Oppegard et al. (1984) who studied a group of 102 adults aged 60 to 92 years who were living independently in the community. Dependent measures included the Beck Depression Inventory, the Manifest Anxiety Scale, and self-reports of family support. It was discovered that among those reporting low levels of family support, level of hearing impairment was positively related to the measures of anxiety and depression, but no such relationship was found among those reporting high levels of family support. These results were interpreted to mean that family support acts as a stress buffer for older persons with hearing impairments.

The last characteristic associated with psychosocial adaptation to be considered is coping. Two investigations were located that sought to determine whether coping mode was a useful predictor of social and emotional competence in persons with hearing impairments. Hallberg and Carlsson (1991) randomly selected from among individuals seen at an audiology clinic in Sweden a sample of 71 individuals between the ages of 40 and 60 years. A total of 62 persons provided data for the investigation. An open-ended interview concerning the individual's use of coping strategies in demanding auditory situations was supplemented with responses to Swedish translations of the Hearing Measurement Scale (Noble & Atherley, 1970), a measure of hearing loss and reactions to hearing loss, and the Communication Profile for the Hearing Impaired. Qualitative analyses of the interview data led to the definition of two broad categories of coping strategies: controlling the social scene (eg, striving to maintain interaction, structuring the communication) or avoiding the social scene (eg, avoiding or minimizing communication; see also Hallberg & Barrenäs, 1995). The independent variables in a multiple regression analysis predicting self-perception of psychosocial maladaptation included severity and chronicity of tinnitus symptoms, hearing aid use, coping strategy, sex, age, marital status, years of education, communication behaviors (eg, avoiding communication, signing ability), and the severity, type and duration of hearing loss. Four of these predictors contributed significantly to the explanation of the variance in the dependent variable. In decreasing order of magnitude, these predictors were ineffective communication behaviors, severity of hearing loss, controlling coping strategy, and decreasing years of education.

Finally, Kluwin, Blennerhassett, and Sweet (1990) studied a nonrandom sample of 324 high school students with hearing impairments in public school classes in the United States and Canada. To measure psychosocial adaptation, the students were rated by their teachers using the Social-Emotional Assessment Inventory for Deaf and Hearing-Impaired Students. The coping strategy instrument used was a modified version of the Adolescent Coping Orientation for Problem Experiences (Patterson & McCubbin, 1987), a 54-item self-report rating scale that purports to measure 12 dimensions of coping in stressful situations: namely, ventilating feelings, seeking diversions, developing self-reliance, developing social support, solving family problems, avoiding problems, seeking spiritual support, investing in close friends, seeking professional support, engaging in demanding acts, being humorous, and relaxing. The original instrument was modified to reduce semantic complexity and a signed version was developed for videotape presentation in an attempt to control for the effects of differences in reading abilities. Contrary to predictions, there were no significant correlations between scores on any scale measuring psychosocial adaptation and any of the coping dimension scales (coefficient alpha values ranged from 0.41 to 0.71). It might also be argued that the modifications of a coping instrument developed for use with adolescents without impairments did not yield a valid instrument for the measurement of these constructs among persons with hearing impairments.

CONCLUSION

As we pointed out in Chapter 11 in our discussion of psychosocial adaptation to disability among individuals with blindness and visual impairments, individuals with deafness and hearing impairments constitute a heterogeneous group and the psychosocial adaptation to disability varies substantially both within and among these individuals. Nevertheless several general conclusions can be derived from the literature reviewed in this chapter, the first of which is that the empirical data fail to confirm the commonly expressed hypothesis that persons with hearing impairments are at significantly increased risk for emotional and social maladaptation. Although some individuals with hearing impairments are certainly at increased psychosocial risk due to parenting that restricts crucial developmental experiences, poor early educational experiences, and the stigmatizing attitudes and discriminatory behaviors of others, the majority of individuals appear to function quite ably as adults in society.

The following tentative conclusions are offered based upon this review of the literature: (1) children and adolescents with prelingual deafness are somewhat more likely than are children without hearing impairments to display a range of social behaviors and emotional reactions, especially in school settings, that could impede psychosocial adaptation (eg, withdrawal, loneliness, restlessness, acting out, impulsiveness, aggressiveness); (2) the prevalence of depression, anger, and anxiety among persons with adventitious postlingual deafness is somewhat higher than expected in the general population; (3) increased risk of psychosocial maladaptation is not a necessary concomitant of severe, early onset, and long-lasting hearing impairment, but it may be associated with poor communication abilities, the presence of additional disabilities, and poor educational experiences in segregated school settings; (4) children with deafness raised by parents with deafness appear to be better adapted than children with deafness raised by parents without deafness; (5) regardless of the presence or absence of deafness in the parents, a supportive family environment is conducive to psychosocial adaptation of persons with hearing impairments; and (6) the use of assertive and problem-focused coping strategies may support psychosocial adaptation among adults with hearing impairments, but no conclusion can be reached concerning the relationship of coping and psychosocial adaptation in children and adolescents with hearing impairments.

There is clearly a need for additional investigations of the psychosocial adaptation to disability in persons with hearing impairments and the sociodemographic, disability-related, personality, and environmental characteristics that predict successful adaptation. There is a unique difficulty collecting valid empirical data on psychosocial adaptation to deafness and hearing impairment that deserves mention. Traditional measurement methods rely upon extensive verbal interchange with the examiner or considerable reading skills, both of which may be significantly disrupted in persons with hearing impairments. The use of interpreters may overcome the communication difficulty, but it also introduces a confounding variable as the interpreter must be able to detect the subtle, qualitative, and emotion-laden content of the respondent's nonverbal responses to the examiner's questions. A number of the studies on psychosocial adaptation to disability that we reviewed may be criticized for using instruments that have not been validated for and may be inappropriate for use with persons with hearing impairments.

REFERENCES

Agrawal, R., & Kaur, J. (1985). Anxiety and adjustment levels among the visually and hearing impaired and their relationships to locus of control, cognitive, social, and biographical variables. *Journal of Psychology, 119*, 265–269.

Beck, A. T. (1978). *Depression inventory.* Philadelphia: Center for Cognitive Therapy.

Behar, L., & Stringfield, S. A. (1974). Behavior rating scale for the preschool child. *Developmental Psychology, 10*, 601–610.

Cartledge, G., Paul, P. V., Jackson, D., & Cochran, L. L. (1991). Teachers' perceptions of the social skills of adolescents with hearing impairments in residential and public school settings. *Remedial and Special Education, 12*(2), 34–39, 47.

Cooper, A. F. (1976). Deafness and psychiatric illness. *British Journal of Psychiatry, 129*, 216–226.

Danek, M. M., & Seidman, M. D. (1992). Hearing disabilities. In M. G. Brodwin, F. A. Tellez, & S. K. Brodwin (Eds.), *Medical, psychosocial, and vocational aspects of disability* (pp. 195–215). Athens, GA: Elliott & Fitzpatrick.

David, M., & Trehub, S. E. (1989). Perspectives on deafened adults. *American Annals of the Deaf, 134*, 200–204.

Davis, J. H., Elfenbein, J., Schum, R., & Bentler, R. A. (1986). Effects of mild and moderate hearing impairments on language, educational, and psychosocial behavior of children. *Journal of Speech and Hearing Disorders, 51*, 53–62.

Delgado, G. L. (1982). Beyond the norm—Social maturity and deafness. *American Annals of the Deaf, 127*, 356–360.

Demorest, M. E., & Erdman, S. E. (1989). Relationships among behavioral, environmental, and affective communication variables: A canonical analysis of the CPHI. *Journal of Speech and Hearing Disorders, 54*, 180–188.

Evans, D. A. (1975). Experiential deprivation: Unresolved factor in the impoverished socialization of deaf school children in residence. *American Annals of the Deaf, 120*, 545–552.

Falvo, D. R. (1991). *Medical and psychosocial aspects of chronic illness and disability.* Gaithersburg, MD: Aspen.

Farrugia, D., & Austin, G. F. (1980). A study of social-emotional adjustment patterns of hearing-impaired students in different educational settings. *American Annals of the Deaf, 125*, 535–541.

Feinstein, C. B., & Lytle, R. (1987). Observations from clinical work with high school aged, deaf adolescents attending a residential school. *Adolescent Psychiatry, 14*, 461–477.

Freeman, R. F., Malkin, S. F., & Hastings, J. D. (1975). Psychosocial problems of deaf children and their families: A comparative study. *American Annals of the Deaf, 120*, 391–405.

Goetzinger, C. P., & Proul, G. O. N. (1975). The impact of hearing impairment upon the psychological development of children. *Journal of Auditory Research, 15*, 1–60.

Gresham, F., & Elliott, S. (1990). *Social skills rating system manual.* Circle Pines, MN: American Guidance Services.

Hallberg, L. R.-M., & Barrenäs, M.-L. (1995). Coping with noise-induced hearing loss: Experiences from the perspective of middle-aged male victims. *British Journal of Audiology, 29*, 219–230.

Hallberg, L. R.-M., & Carlsson, S. G. (1991). Hearing impairment, coping and perceived hearing handicap in middle-aged subjects with acquired hearing loss. *British Journal of Audiology, 25*, 323–330.

Holt, K. S. (1979). Assessment of handicap in childhood. *Child: Care, Health and Development, 5,* 151–162.

Hummel. J. W., & Schirmer, B. E. (1984). Review of research and description of programs for the social development of hearing impaired students. *Volta Review, 86,* 259–266.

Ingalls, G. S. (1946). Some psychiatric observations on patients with hearing defect. *Occupational Therapy and Rehabilitation, 25,* 62–66.

Ives, L. A. (1969). Development of personality and emotional-social adjustment in deaf and partially hearing children. *Public Health, 83,* 78–88.

Kerman-Lerner, P., & Hauck, K. (1993). Speech, language, and hearing disorders. In M. G. Eisenberg, R. L. Glueckauf, & H. H. Zaretsky (Eds.), *Medical aspects of disability: A handbook for the rehabilitation professional* (pp. 208–230). New York: Springer.

Klansek-Kyllo, V., & Rose, S. (1985). Using the Scale of Independent Behaviors with hearing-impaired students. *American Annals of the Deaf, 130,* 533–537.

Kluwin, T., Blennerhassett, L., & Sweet, C. (1990). The revision of an instrument to measure the capacity of hearing-impaired adolescents to cope. *Volta Review, 92,* 283–291.

Knapp, P. H. (1948). Emotional aspects of hearing loss. *Psychosomatic Medicine, 10,* 203–222.

Knutson, J. F., & Lansing, C. R. (1990). The relationship between communication problems and psychological difficulties in persons with profound acquired hearing loss. *Journal of Speech and Hearing Disorders, 55,* 656–664.

Koetitz, L. E. (1976). Cognitive and psycho-social development in deaf children: A review of the literature. *Education and Training in Mental Retardation, 11,* 66–72.

Luetke-Stahlman, B. (1995). Social interaction: Assessment and intervention with regard to students who are deaf. *American Annals of the Deaf, 140,* 295–303.

Lytle, R. R., Feinstein, C., & Jonas, B. (1987). Social and emotional adjustment in deaf adolescents after transfer to a residential school for the deaf. *Journal of the American Academy of Child and Adolescent Psychology, 26,* 237–241.

MacLean, G., & Becker, S. (1979). Studies of the psychosocial adjustment of the hearing-impaired: I. Adolescents and their families, A pilot study. *Canadian Journal of Psychiatry, 24,* 744–748.

Mahapatra, S. B. (1974). Psychiatric and psychosomatic illness in the deaf. *British Journal of Psychiatry, 125,* 450–451.

Marsh, H., & O'Neill, R. (1984). The Self-Description Questionnaire III: The validity of multidimensional self-concept ratings of late adolescents. *Journal of Educational Measurement, 21,* 153–174.

Meadow, K. P. (1968). Toward a developmental understanding of deafness. *Journal of Rehabilitation of the Deaf, 2,* 1–18.

Meadow, K. P. (1980). *Deafness and child development.* Berkeley, CA: University of California Press.

Meadow, K. P. (1984). Social adjustment of preschool children: Deaf and hearing, with and without other handicaps. *Topics in Early Childhood Special Education, 3*(4), 27–40.

Meadow, K. P., & Dyssegaard, B. (1983a). Social-emotional adjustment of deaf students. Teachers' ratings of deaf children: An American-Danish comparison. *International Journal of Rehabilitation Research, 6,* 345–348.

Meadow, K. P., & Dyssegaard, B. (1983b). Teachers' ratings of deaf children: An American-Danish comparison. *American Annals of the Deaf, 128,* 900–908.

Meadow, K. P., Karchmer, M. A., Petersen, L. M., & Rudner, L. (1980). *Meadow/Kendall Social-Emotional Assessment Inventory for Deaf Students: Manual.* Washington, DC: Gallaudet College, Pre-College Programs.

Meadow, K. P., & Trybus, R. J. (1979). *Hearing and hearing impairment.* New York: Grune & Stratton.

Menninger, K. A. (1924). The mental effect of deafness. *Psychoanalytical Review, 11,* 144–155.

Misiaszek, J., Dooling, J., Gieseke, M., Melman, H., Misiaszek, J. G., & Jorgensen, K. (1985). Diagnostic considerations in deaf patients. *Comprehensive Psychiatry, 26,* 513–521.

Murphy, J. S., & Newlon, B. J. (1987). Loneliness and the mainstreamed hearing impaired college student. *American Annals of the Deaf, 132,* 21–25.

Myklebust, H. R. (1960a). The psychological effects of deafness. *American Annals of the Deaf, 105,* 372–385.

Myklebust, H. R. (1960b). *The psychology of deafness: Sensory deprivation, learning, and adjustment.* New York: Grune & Stratton.

Myklebust, H. R. (1964). *The psychology of deafness: Sensory deprivation, learning, and adjustment* (2nd ed.). New York: Grune & Stratton.

Myklebust, H. R. (1966). *The psychology of deafness: Sensory deprivation, learning, and adjustment* (3rd ed.). New York: Grune & Stratton.

Myklebust, H. R. (1981). *The Pupil Rating Scale Revised: Screening for learning disabilities.* New York: Grune & Stratton.

Nash, K. R., & Castle, N. E. (1980). Special problems of deaf adolescents and young adults. *Exceptional Educational Quarterly, 1*(2), 99–106.

Noble, W. G., & Atherley, G. R. C. (1970). The Hearing Measurement Scale: A questionnaire for the assessment of auditory disability. *Journal of Auditory Research, 10,* 229–250.

Oppegard, K., Hansson, R. O., Morgan, T., Indart, M., Crutcher, M., & Hampton, P. (1984). Sensory loss, family support, and adjustment among the elderly. *Journal of Social Psychology, 123,* 291–292.

Ostby, S., & Thomas, K. R. (1984). Deafness and hearing impairment: A review and proposal. *Journal of Applied Rehabilitation Counseling, 15*(2), 7–11.

Patterson, J. M., & McCubbin, H. I. (1987). *Family assessment intervention for research and practice.* Madison, WI: University of Wisconsin Press.

Powers, A., Elliott, R., Fairbank, D., & Monaghan, C. (1988). The dilemma of identifying hearing disabled and hearing impaired students. *Volta Review, 90,* 209–218.

Prior, M. R., Glazner, J., Sanson, A., & Debelle, G. (1988). Research note: Temperament and behavioural adjustment in hearing impaired children. *Journal of Child Psychology and Psychiatry, 29,* 209–216.

Rathus, D. (1982). A 30-item schedule for assessing assertive behavior. *Behavior Therapy, 4,* 398–406.

Raymond, K. L., & Matson, J. L. (1989). Social skills in the hearing impaired. *Journal of Clinical Child Psychology, 18,* 247–258.

Rosen, J. K. (1979). Psychological and social aspects of the evaluation of acquired hearing impairment. *Audiology, 18,* 238–252.

Russell, D., Peplau, L. A., & Cutrona, C. E. (1980). The revised UCLA Loneliness Scale: Concurrent and discriminant validity evidence. *Journal of Personality and Social Psychology, 39,* 472–480.

Sarfaty, L., & Katz, S. (1978). The self-concept and adjustment patterns of hearing-impaired pupils in different school settings. *American Annals of the Deaf, 123,* 438–441.

Spear, J. H. (1984). On the road again: A mental health map to the mainstreamed hearing impaired. *Volta Review, 86*(Suppl. 5), 3–15.

Tavormina, J. B., Kastner, L. S., Slater, P. M., & Watt, S. L. (1976). Chronically ill children: A psychologically and emotionally deviant population? *Journal of Abnormal Child Psychology, 4,* 99–110.

Thomas, A., & Chess, S. (1977). *Temperament and development.* New York: Brunner/Mazel.

Thomas, A. J. (1984). Acquired deafness and mental health. *British Journal of Medical Psychology, 54,* 219–229.

Watson, D., & Friend, R. (1969). Measurement of social-evaluative anxiety. *Journal of Consulting and Clinical Psychology, 33,* 448–457.

Watson, S. M., Henggeler, S. W., & Whelan, J. P. (1990). Family functioning and the social adaptation of hearing-impaired youths. *Journal of Abnormal Child Psychology, 18,* 143–163.

Yachnik, M. (1986). Self-esteem in deaf adolescents. *American Annals of the Deaf, 131,* 305–310.

Zeckel, A. (1950). Psychopathological aspects of deafness. *Journal of Nervous and Mental Diseases, 112,* 322–346.

Psychosocial Adaptation to Neurological and Neuromuscular Disabilities

Part IV of this book presented reviews of the research literature on psychosocial adaptation to two sensory impairments: (1) blindness and visual impairments and (2) deafness and hearing impairments. In Part V we provide reviews of the research literature on psychosocial adaptation to nine neurological and neuromuscular disabilities: (1) Chapter 13—epilepsy, (2) Chapter 14—multiple sclerosis, (3) Chapter 15—cerebral palsy, (4) Chapter 16—amyotrophic lateral sclerosis, (5) Chapter 17—muscular dystrophy, (6) Chapter 18—myasthenia gravis, (7) Chapter 19—neurofibromatosis, (8) Chapter 20—Parkinson's disease, and (9) Chapter 21—spina bifida.

These nine neurological and neuromuscular disabilities share certain similarities. They (1) are irreversible; (2) are either visible (eg, cerebral palsy, spina bifida) or become visible at later stages (eg, amyotrophic lateral sclerosis, Parkinson's disease), with the exception of interictal periods in epilepsy; and (3) involve a wide range of functional limitations, particularly as several of these conditions progress, that include mobility, communication, manipulation, consciousness, fatigue, endurance, and, in certain cases, cognitive limitations. Other features, however, differentiate among these disabilities. These include (1) type of etiology, ranging from birth trauma or congenital condition (eg, cerebral palsy, spina bifida) to late-life progressive disease process (eg, Parkinson's disease, myasthenia gravis); (2) type and pace of onset, ranging from stable (eg, most types of epilepsy) to variable or fluctuating (eg, multiple sclerosis) to progressive or deteriorating (eg, Parkinson's disease, most types of muscular dystrophy); (4) lethality, ranging from low probability (eg, most types of epilepsy, neurofibromatosis) to high probability (eg, amyotrophic lateral sclerosis, myasthenia gravis); and (5) degree of cognitive involvement, ranging from minimal (eg, neurofibromatosis, amyotrophic lateral sclerosis) to moderate or even marked (eg, certain types of cerebral palsy).

Each of these reviews in Part V will follow the same format as those in Parts II, III, and IV. We begin each chapter with a brief description of the disability, including a synopsis of available information on incidence and prevalence, causal factors, signs and symptoms, complications, course, and prognosis. This is followed by a review of the research literature on psychosocial adaptation to the disability, focusing on the research conducted in the last 15 years. The third section of each chapter summarizes the available information on characteristics associated with psychosocial adaptation to the disability. This section is organized into three areas: (1) sociodemographic characteristics (eg, age at time of injury or disease onset, chronicity, sex, educational level, socioeconomic status), (2) personality factors (eg, premorbid personality, ego strength, attribution of blame, perception of disability, locus of control), and (3) disability-related variables (eg, neuropathology, severity of impairment, type of treatment). If it is available, information on environmental factors (eg, degree of family or peer support, level of independence, modifiability of the work environment) that are thought to be related to psychosocial adaptation to the disability is also provided. Each chapter ends with a presentation of tentative conclusions concerning psychosocial adaptation to the disability derived from the findings reported in the literature reviewed.

CHAPTER 13

Epilepsy

DESCRIPTION

Epilepsy is one of the oldest known and the most common of the chronic neurological disorders, with an incidence generally agreed to be from 1% to 2% of the total US population (Epilepsy Foundation of America, 1975; Hauser & Hesdorffer, 1990; Ward, Fraser, & Troupin, 1981). Approximately 100,000 new cases are diagnosed each year (Hauser & Hesdorffer, 1990), with 75% of those occurring before age 13 years and 30% before age 3 years (Sands & Minters, 1977). Epilepsy is not a unitary condition. "The epilepsies" is a more correct term for that set of disorders in which a recurrent seizure pattern is present and unrelated to any coincident causal agent, such as drug reaction or brain infection. A seizure is a brief alteration or loss of consciousness, with or without motor manifestations, due to sudden and excessive nerve cell discharge originating in one area of the brain (the focus). The type of seizure pattern is determined by the focus and by the extent, pattern, and rapidity of spread to surrounding areas of the brain (Hermann, Desai, & Whitman, 1988).

The cause of the disorder is clear in only 40% of the cases (Hermann et al., 1988). Genetic factors are suspected in some forms of epilepsy commonly experienced by children, while head injury is the leading cause of neurological damage leading to epilepsy in young adults (Ward, Penry, & Purpura, 1983). Any agent that damages the brain (eg, anoxia, birth injuries, febrile convulsions, toxins, tumors, severe allergies, infections, stroke, vascular diseases, trauma) is a potential causal agent for a recurrent seizure pattern and hence the diagnosis of epilepsy (Engel, 1982; Fraser, 1993; Lechtenberg, 1985).

PSYCHOSOCIAL ADAPTATION TO EPILEPSY

Most experts (Chadwick, 1990; Dell, 1986; Dodrill, 1983; Goldin & Margolin, 1975; Hartshorn & Byers, 1992; Kaplan & Wyler, 1983; Lechtenberg, 1984;

Lechtenberg, 1985; Livingston, 1977; Scott, 1978; Seidenberg & Berent, 1992; Tarter, 1972; Tizard, 1962; Wright, 1975) agree that problems of psychosocial adaptation to chronic illness and disability among persons with epilepsy are formidable, often more so than the medical difficulties persons with epilepsy may face. The individual with epilepsy is confronted with numerous unresolved problems. Unless the convulsive disorder is secondary to another disability (eg, stroke or head trauma), the individual with epilepsy is not otherwise impaired. Consequently he or she feels like a person without a chronic illness at times and at other times feels like a person with a chronic illness. He or she faces questions such as: "Because epilepsy is a brain disorder, am I physically or mentally ill? Because epilepsy has no cure, what is the prognosis for my becoming seizure free? Can a low threshold for abnormal electrical discharge in the brain be genetically transmitted to my offspring? If a seizure occurs in a social or work situation, how will people react?" The stress associated with the anticipation of seizures or the concealment of the disorder can lead to feelings of embarrassment, shame, guilt, and, finally, social isolation. In a recent review of the literature on adaptation problems among persons with epilepsy (Levin, Banks, & Berg, 1988), it was argued that an understanding of the individual's emotional and psychosocial reactions to the disorder may lead to more effective clinical treatment and the selection of appropriate intervention strategies designed to teach coping skills.

While some researchers have presented evidence to suggest that the psychosocial problems of persons with some forms of epilepsy may be manifestations attributable to underlying neuropathology (Austin, Smith, Risinger, & McNelis, 1994; Bear, Freeman, & Greenberg, 1984; Beran & Flanagan, 1987; Brown, McGowan, & Reynolds, 1986; Himmelhoch, 1984), most theorists and advocates have searched for or supported a basis for these adaptation difficulties most clearly explicated by the stigma-of-epilepsy model (Arangio, 1975; Bagley, 1972; Dell, 1986; Hauck, 1972; Jacoby, 1992; Livingston, 1977; Ryan, Kempner, & Emlen, 1980; Scrambler & Hopkins, 1990; Wiley, 1974).

Stigma theory has been used to explain the behavior, perceptions, beliefs, and development of the psychosocial self of various groups of stigmatized persons or those with characteristics that others see as negative, unfavorable, or unacceptable (Westbrook, Bauman, & Shinnar, 1992). The more visible, disruptive, or disturbing the characteristics of the group are, the more potent is the stigma that other persons attach to the group and the more likely this stigma will contribute to the psychosocial maladaptation of individuals in the group. For persons with epilepsy, this stigma consists of deeply discrediting attributes, such as a propensity to crime and violence, sexual deviance, inheritability, insanity, and mental incompetence. This leads to the denial of common benefits (eg, a driver's license or life insurance), restrictions on typical life experiences (eg, eugenic marriage laws or exclusion from school), and limitations on opportunities that lead to independence (eg, housing or employment discrimination). Persons with epilepsy internalize the rejection and devaluation by society, leading them to express negative and nonadaptive reactions, such as denial, anxiety, depression, lowered self-esteem, hostility, and maladaptive behaviors such as dependency, rigidity, anger, and aggression. These reactions and behaviors confirm the prejudices and misconceptions of persons without epilepsy and reinforce discriminatory attitudes and behaviors. The stigma of epilepsy becomes a self-perpetuating vicious cycle similar to the stigma cycle associated with other differences among people based on characteristics such as race, religion, or physical attractiveness (Ajzen & Fishbein, 1980; Goffman, 1963).

In attempting to account for the attribution of discrediting characteristics and the devaluation and rejection of persons with epilepsy, researchers and theorists have focused on (1) parental reaction patterns ranging from overprotectiveness and infantilization to anger, resentment, and rejection (Austin, McBride, & Davis, 1984; Hartlage & Green, 1972; Hermann et al., 1988; Hoare, 1986; Leonard, 1984; Long & Moore, 1979; Terdal, 1981); (2) the perceptions and practices of professionals, such as physicians, teachers, and other health, rehabilitation, and education providers (Antonak & Rankin, 1982; Bagley, 1972; Beran & Beran, 1983; Beran, Jennings, & Read, 1981; Dreisbach, Ballard, Russo, & Schain, 1982; Hackney & Taylor, 1976; Holdsworth & Whitmore, 1974; Martin, 1974; Mason, Fenton, & Jamieson, 1990; Merkens, Perrin, Perrin, & Gerrity, 1989; Stude, 1973); and (3) the attitudes of the general society, particularly peers and employers (Caveness & Gallup, 1980; Caveness, Merritt, & Gallup, 1974; Collings, 1990; Dorenbaum, Cappelli, Keene, & McGrath, 1985; Gade & Toutges, 1983; Holmes & McWilliams, 1981; Sands & Zalkind, 1972; Wright, 1975). Although data reveal national and regional differences, misconceptions, stigmatizing perceptions, and negative attitudes have been found in diverse samples in countries throughout the world (Awaritefe, Lange, & Awaritefe, 1985; Canger & Cornaggia, 1985; Gallhofer, 1984; Gutteling, Seydel, & Wiegman, 1986; Hauck, 1972; Irie et al., 1993; Lai et al., 1990; Livanainen, Uutela, & Vilkkumaa, 1980; Räder, Ritter, & Schwibbe, 1986; Remschmidt, 1973), lending support to the universal nature of the stigma of epilepsy.

Although Carter (1947) noted nearly 50 years ago that individuals' reactions to their epilepsy should be taken into account in developing comprehensive treatment plans, no studies were located in the medical, psychiatric, or psychological literature that have studied adaptation to epilepsy as a set of distinct psychosocial reactions, and no articles or research studies were located that conceptualized adaptation as a process of change in reactions to epilepsy that can be ordered hierarchically and temporally. The literature examined subsumed adaptation within the domain of psychopathology in persons with epilepsy or focused on discrete psychosocial reactions evinced by persons with epilepsy.

Serious scientific investigations* of the association between epilepsy and psychopathological disorders have been a concern of theorists and researchers since the middle of this century (Whitman & Hermann, 1986a). Early attempts to elucidate a universal personality associated with epilepsy (Bridge, 1947; Landisberg, 1947) resulted in generalizations in the medical and psychological literature classifying people with epilepsy into one of two types (Bagley, 1972): (1) those who were combative, stubborn, constantly complaining, and perseverative; and (2) those who were dull witted, introverted, shy, and withdrawn. These characterizations, derived from impressionistic case studies or from research using small and nonrepresentative samples of individuals with epilepsy living in institutions, led physicians and policy makers to champion programs to further segregate and control individuals with epilepsy. Tizard (1962) reviewed this evidence and concluded that the existence of the "epileptic personality" was insupportable. What, if anything, these researchers were observing was an "institutional personality" reflecting predictable psychological reactions to social isolation and environmental deprivation.

The ample empirical literature on the association between psychopathology and epilepsy since 1962 has most recently been reviewed by Hermann and Whitman (1984; 1992). These authors concluded that, despite persistent and substantial methodological difficulties limiting conclusions from the literature, persons with epilepsy appear more likely than the general population to be at increased risk for psychopathology. (Although Hermann and Whitman focused on persons with temporal lobe epilepsy, they also reviewed and commented upon the literature concerning persons with epilepsy generally.) A small number of researchers have conducted controlled investigations of the prevalence of psychopathology in persons with epilepsy using data from clinical instruments such as the Minnesota Multiphasic Personality Inventory (Dodrill, 1986; Hermann, Schwartz, Karnes, & Vahdat, 1980; Kløve & Doehring, 1962; Matthews & Kløve, 1968), the California Psychological Inventory (Naugle & Rodgers, 1992), or the General Health Questionnaire (Hermann, Whitman, Wyler, Anton, & Vanderzwagg, 1990; Kogeorgos, Fonagy, & Scott, 1982). Most studies of the personality of persons with epilepsy, however, have relied on medical record reviews, anecdotal data in clinical case reports, and retrospective information derived from psychiatric interviews, rating scales, and self-report questionnaires (Beit-Jones & Kapust,

---

*Specifically excluded from this review are the historically interesting but pseudoscientific reports and hysterical panegyrics of eugenicists such as Barr, Laughlin, Mott, and Lombroso, who atavistically connected epilepsy with criminality and immorality (Temkin, 1971) and extolled the virtues of involuntary sterilization for the solution of social problems during the Eugenics Period (Antonak, 1988).

1986; Broughton, Creberman, & Roberts, 1984; Brown et al., 1986; Carter, 1947; Chaplin, Floyd, & Lasso, 1993; Danesi, 1984; DeHass, 1962; Livingston, 1977; Matthews, Barabas, & Ferrari, 1982; Mattsson, 1972; Olsson & Campenhausen, 1993; Ozuma, 1979; Remschmidt, 1973; Richardson & Friedman, 1974; Robertson & Trimble, 1983; Ryan et al., 1980; Standage & Fenton, 1975; Ward & Bower, 1978). The criticism common to these subjective studies is that they are susceptible to (1) sampling biases in the selection of cases, and (2) experimenter bias during both the collection and the interpretation of the data. Seldom have control groups been included in these studies. Interviewers or evaluators unaware of the purposes of the research have rarely been used to investigate the adaptation of individuals with epilepsy, and consensual agreement is seldom reported.

Specific indices of psychopathology that have been investigated include affective disorders such as clinical depression (Robertson, 1989; Robertson & Trimble, 1983), aggression (Hermann, Schwartz, Whitman, & Karnes, 1980; Pincus, 1980; Rodin, 1973), neuroses (Goldstein, Seidenberg, & Peterson, 1990), psychoses (Hermann, Schwartz, Whitman, & Karnes, 1981; Parnas & Korsgaard, 1982), sexual dysfunction (Blumer & Walker, 1967; Ellison, 1982), and suicide (Hawton, Fagg, & Marsack, 1980; Matthews & Barabas, 1981). To date, the findings of these studies have obfuscated the connections between epilepsy and psychopathology. For example, depression has been frequently studied (McNamara, 1991; Mendez, Cummings, & Benson, 1986; Pazzaglia & Frank-Pazzaglia, 1976; Scott, 1978), in part because it is commonly the basis for psychiatric hospitalization of persons with epilepsy. The prevalence of psychosocial maladaptation in persons with epilepsy will be overestimated in clinical series undertaken in specialty clinics or in tertiary care facilities.

Following their exhaustive reviews of the considerable literature in this area, Robertson and colleagues (Robertson, 1989; Robertson & Trimble, 1983) stated that, although ictally related (seizure-related) depression had been noted as early as 1861, and studied intensely since the 1950s, there was still no clear understanding of whether depression in persons with epilepsy is a periictal (during seizures) manifestation of a neurobiological impairment or an interictal (between seizures) psychological manifestation of a chronic neurological disorder. Similarly the relationships between sexual dysfunction or psychosis and epilepsy are unclear, and the presumed increased incidence of aggression in persons with epilepsy has not been supported in controlled objective investigations (Whitman, King, & Cohen, 1986).

Hermann and colleagues (Hermann et al., 1988; Hermann & Whitman, 1984; Hermann & Whitman, 1986; Hermann & Whitman, 1992), echoing the earlier views of Scott (1978), have suggested that psychopathology and personality studies of individuals with epilepsy have generally failed to separate the influence of confounding variables, many of which are known to be associated with psychopathology in the general population. They posit three sets of etiologic factor groupings to conceptualize the relationships between psychopathology and epilepsy and the variables known or presumed to mediate these relationships. The etiologic factor groupings are as follows:

1. *Neuroepilepsy factors*, in which the psychopathology is a function of a central nervous system disorder that is related to the diagnosis of epilepsy. Variables of interest here are seizure cause, type, frequency, and severity; age at onset and chronicity of disability; electroencephalogram (EEG) features; neuropsychological status; and cerebral metabolism (ie, abnormalities in the concentrations of neurotransmitters and neurohormones).

2. *Psychosocial factors*, viewing psychopathology as a manifestation of stress, stigma, and discrimination. Among the variables in this domain are fear of seizures, learned helplessness, locus of control, perceived stigma, enacted stigma (discrimination), adaptation to epilepsy, and socioeconomic status.

3. *Medication factors*, stressing the risk of behavioral aberrations as side effects of antiepileptic drugs. Variables to study include the number, type, and dosage of antiepileptic drugs and associated physiological characteristics such as cerebral metabolism and serum levels of folic acid.

Many psychosocial reactions to epilepsy have been reported in the literature, including aggressiveness, anger, apprehension, anxiety, belligerence, deepened emotionality, demandingness, denial, dependency, depression, emotional lability, euphoria, fear, frustration, helplessness, hopelessness, hostility, humorlessness, hypermoralism, inferiority, insecurity, invalidism, irritability, low drive, low self-esteem, moodiness, neuroticism, rejection, resignation, sadness, shock, withdrawal, and worry. Most studies of these psychosocial reactions have relied on anecdotal and retrospective data derived from interviews and clinical case reports, relative reports of behavior changes of persons with epilepsy, or the self-reports of persons with epilepsy using behavioral or symptom checklists of dubious psychometric quality. Although objective data concerning the prevalence of these psychosocial reactions, independent of psychopathology, have become available in the last two decades, concerns over methodological weaknesses of these few studies limit the generalizability of their findings.

Beran and his colleagues (Beran & Flanagan, 1985; Beran & Flanagan, 1987; Beran & Reed, 1980; Flanagan & Beran, 1985) have for several years used survey research methods and a specially designed self-report questionnaire to collect data on a variety of social and personality characteristics from nonrandom samples of persons with epilepsy in Australia. When the respondents were asked to rate themselves against the general public, they indicated that emotional problems and mood swings were more of an attribute of persons with epilepsy than of persons without epilepsy, but no other characteristics (eg, aggression, intelligence, productivity, ambition) achieved significant differences in attribution.

Researchers using the Washington Psychosocial Seizure Inventory have reported psychosocial adaptation problems among samples of persons with epilepsy (Beran & Flanagan, 1985; Dodrill, 1986; Dodrill, Beyer, Diamond, Dubinsky, & Geary, 1984; Tan, 1986). Similar findings using the WPSI in other language forms (see Chapter 3) have been reported for samples of individuals with epilepsy in the United States, Canada, Chile, France, Japan, and Germany (Alvarado et al., 1992; Dodrill, Beier, et al., 1984; Wang, Nakashima, & Takahashi, 1993). Beran and Flanagan (1985) analyzed data from 94 Australian individuals who completed the Washington Psychosocial Seizure Inventory, reporting that 51% were experiencing global psychosocial adaptation problems. Arnston, Droge, Norton, and Murray (1986) reported on analyses of data obtained from a nonrepresentative nationwide sample of 357 of approximately 3,000 persons with epilepsy who responded to a 29-page questionnaire that included items concerning the reactions of depression and anxiety. A total of 24% of their respondents cited emotional problems as the single greatest problem they experienced because of their epilepsy; 39% reported symptoms of anxiety; and 25% reported symptoms of depression. A more recent study reported that 72% of 116 persons with epilepsy who were being seen as outpatients at a hospital in Chile were experiencing significant problems of overall psychosocial adaptation (Alvarado et al., 1992).

A group of 35 children with epilepsy and their parents in England were included among a volunteer sample of 273 children and their parents in a study of psychosocial adaptation to chronic health impairments conducted by Eiser, Havermans, Pancer, and Eiser (1992). Parents were asked to complete the Child and Adolescent Adjustment Profile, a questionnaire concerning their child's hostility, dependency, withdrawal, productivity, and peer relations. The investigators also included questions to study the variables of rule following, frustration, and tolerance. A principal components analysis yielded six factors: (1) frustration/hostility, (2) dependency, (3) rule following, (4) peer relations, (5) work, and (6) withdrawal. The children with epilepsy were found to be particularly at risk on the first, fourth, and fifth of these factors. Overall psychosocial adaptation was found to decrease with increasing age of the children in the sample, a relationship that was particularly pronounced for the dependency and rule-following factors. The question remains, though, whether these results are accurate representations of the child's psychosocial adaptation or manifestations of the interaction of the parents' changing perceptions and their child's behaviors. For example, parents may be willing to accept greater dependency and difficulties in rule-following violations in younger children but not in older children.

Several studies conducted recently have attempted to broaden the investigation of psychosocial adaptation to epilepsy through the inclusion of the construct of quality of life as a multidimensional dependent variable (Devinsky & Cramer, 1993; Hartshorn & Byers, 1992; Jacoby, 1992). Jacoby (1992), for example, suggested that, in addition to studying specific reactions to a chronic illness, such as epilepsy, researchers should study the individual's multidimensional affective response to his or her total life situation. This would include the study of functioning in physical, social, psychological, and vocational domains. As part of a larger study in the United Kingdom of the consequences of the early withdrawal of antiepileptic drugs, Jacoby (1992) collected data from 468 individuals with epilepsy whose seizures were well controlled two years after their entry into a clinical trial. A self-report questionnaire was constructed that operationalized quality of life with the variables health, positive affect, self-esteem, mastery (including marriage and vocational status), and stigma. Results indicated that 86% of the sample did not feel stigmatized and 56% reported positive affect. The marriage rate among individuals in the sample was slightly lower than in the general population, but the employment rate was comparable to the population as a whole. Those individuals in the sample who expressed the most concern about their epilepsy were those with the least well-controlled seizures, and they also scored lowest on the positive affect, mastery, and self-esteem variables and highest on the variables measuring anxiety, stigma, emotional distress, and isolation. Jacoby (1992) concluded that the way persons with epilepsy react to the disorder is related in complex ways to how they perceive the social, personal, and vocational consequences of their experiences. These perceptions, in turn, influence the coping strategies they use and the psychosocial reactions that are consequently observed by the researcher.

The psychosocial adaptation of individuals with epilepsy has occasionally been related to adaptation of individuals diagnosed with other chronic neurological disorders and health impairments. This research has been undertaken, in part, to explore the view that psychosocial reactions to chronic illness, especially in children, are not unique to a specific illness but rather are manifestations of processes that underlie reactions to all illnesses (Eiser et al., 1992; Howe, Feinstein, Reiss, Molock, & Berger, 1993; Stein & Jessup, 1982). Such a "general factors" model would suggest that increased risks to psychosocial adaptation would be common across all chronic illnesses. The assumption, presumably, is if it can be shown that individuals with epilepsy evince problems of adaptation similar to those evinced by persons with other chronic impairments, then clinicians may increase rehabilitation success by selecting from intervention strategies validated for other populations. A review of this research revealed that the comparison groups have included amyotropic lateral sclerosis (Schiffer & Babigian, 1984), asthma (Austin et al., 1994), closed-head injury (Beran & Flanagan, 1987), diabetes mellitus (Matthews et al., 1982), mental retardation (Deb & Hunter, 1991a; Deb & Hunter, 1991b; Deb & Hunter, 1991c), multiple sclerosis (Schiffer & Babigian, 1984; Tan, 1986), narcolepsy/cataplexy (Broughton et al., 1984), and mixed neurological impairments (Howe et al., 1993; Kogeorgos et al., 1982).

Tan (1986), for example, compared psychosocial adaptation as measured by the Washington Psychosocial Seizure Inventory of three groups: (1) adults with epilepsy, (2) adults with multiple sclerosis, and (3) adult volunteers without impairments who were from a church organization. The Washington Psychosocial Seizure Inventory was modified for the individuals with multiple sclerosis by changing the words "epilepsy" and "seizures" to "multiple sclerosis" and "attacks" and for the individuals without impairments by deleting 30 items on seizures, epilepsy, and medication. Although the modifications to the Washington Psychosocial Seizure Inventory raise serious questions regarding the validity of the resultant data for the measurement of psychosocial adaptation in persons with multiple sclerosis, it is of interest to note that individuals in both groups of individuals with neurological impairments scored lower on the scale of emotional adaptation compared with the individuals without impairments and that the items most frequently checked by those in both groups of individuals with neurological impairments referred to the psychosocial reactions of anxiety, anger, denial, and depression.

Analyzing data from four measured emotional reactions, Matthews et al. (1982) discovered that among 7- to 12-year-olds matched for age, family status, sex, socioeconomic status, and intelligence, children with epilepsy were more likely to view life events as beyond their control, to express greater anxiety, and to report a more negative self-concept than either children with diabetes or children without impairments. Beran and Flanagan (1987) reported a higher incidence of psychosocial maladaptation as measured by the Washington Psychosocial Seizure Inventory among their sample of Australian individuals with closed-head injury compared with a sample with idiopathic epilepsy, attributing this difference to brain pathology.

A cross-sectional study by Austin et al. (1994) compared measurements of a set of 15 quality-of-life variables between nonrandom samples of 136 children with epilepsy and 133 children with asthma. The children ranged in age from 8 to 12 years and all had been diagnosed at least one year prior to their inclusion in the study. Multivariate analyses of the data, controlling for chronicity, revealed that the children with epilepsy experienced more problems on the social, school, and psychological domain variables included in the set, whereas the children with asthma experienced more problems on the physical domain variables. The authors, while recognizing the need for longitudinal investigation and the inclusion of a comparison group of children without chronic health impairment, suggested that these differences in quality of life may be reflections of the neuropathology present in the children with epilepsy.

Kogeorgos et al. (1982) compared psychosocial adaptation of a group of 66 persons with epilepsy with a heterogeneous sample of 50 individuals with chronic neurological impairments (including multiple sclerosis, muscular dystrophy, poliomyelitis, and myasthenia gravis) and 50 persons without impairments using the General Health Questionnaire. They discovered that 46% of the persons with epilepsy were evaluated as having probable psychiatric problems compared with only 28% of the individuals with general neurological impairments and 22% of the individuals with no impairments. Broughton et al. (1984), on the other hand, reported a similarity of self-reported psychosocial adaptation characteristics between their samples of individuals in Ottawa, Canada, with epilepsy and narcolepsy/cataplexy, although they did find pronounced psychosocial problems reported by individuals in both of these samples when compared with a sample of individuals without impairments.

Similar to the cautions expressed previously, the generalizability of the results of these comparative investigations may be limited by sampling bias (ie, studying persons who have been hospitalized for psychiatric complaints), small sample sizes, confounding of sample characteristics (ie, the presence of psychiatric history in members of research samples obtained from outpatient clinics), and instrumentation weaknesses (ie, using a nonvalidated self-report measure or an instrument validated for populations other than persons with epilepsy). For example, in a well-designed study comparing individuals with multiple sclerosis, hypertension, and rheumatoid arthritis (Pollock, Christian, & Sands, 1990), no differences were found in measures of psychosocial adaptation, suggesting that similar elements composed the process of adaptation for the three groups.

CHARACTERISTICS ASSOCIATED WITH ADAPTATION TO EPILEPSY

The psychosocial adaptation reactions manifest by the individual with epilepsy are a result of the dynamic interplay of complex factors involving the person on the one hand (eg, extent of neurological damage, age at onset, chronicity, seizure type and frequency, antiepileptic drug effects) and the environment in which the person functions on the other hand (eg, lifestyle restrictions, discrimination, parental reactions, societal attitudes). Only a few studies have investigated specifically the epilepsy-related, demographic, experiential, and situational characteristics associated with and predicting these adaptation reactions, and several of these have reported contradictory findings.

Although Broughton et al. (1984) found no relationship between age and psychosocial maladaptation patterns in their sample of 60 individuals in Ottawa, the data from another study in Ottawa (Dorenbaum et al., 1985) suggested that a complex curvilinear relationship between these two variables may be more accurate, with increased risk of psychosocial maladaptation among adolescents. Regarding age at onset, Hermann, Schwartz, Karnes, & Vahdat (1980) reported no clear relationship to Minnesota Multiphasic Personality Inventory personality profiles, a result similar to that found by Kogeorgos et al. (1982) using the General Health Questionnaire. The results of other investigations, however, have shown age at onset of epilepsy to be inversely related to psychosocial distress (Hoare & Kerley, 1991), psychiatric problems (Scott, 1978), and neuropsychological indices of maladaptation (Dodrill & Matthews, 1992). Taken together, these results suggest a possible curvilinear relationship between psychosocial adaptation problems and age at onset of epilepsy, with the risk greatest in adolescent onset of epilepsy.

The data concerning the relationship of chronicity of disability and psychosocial adaptation among persons with epilepsy are particularly confusing. Chronicity was found not to be related to self-reported psychosocial adaptation in a study by Broughton et al. (1984), but Deb and Hunter (1991a; 1991b; 1991c) reported increased incidence of aggression, irritability, self-injury, and destructiveness among those with the longest history of epilepsy among samples of persons with mental retardation. Hoare and Kerley (1991) reported increased psychosocial distress with increasing chronicity among a nonrandom sample of children with epilepsy who were aged 5 to 15 years seen at a specialty clinic in Scotland. Both of these last two studies used nonrandom samples of individuals in the United Kingdom selected from special and atypical populations. In contrast, Collings (1990) discovered that chronicity was related inversely to an overall measure of psychosocial well-being in a nonrandom sample of 392 individuals in Great Britain. Dodrill and Mathews (1992) have pointed out that inconsistent results such as these may be accounted for by the failure of the researchers to take into account both the severity and the frequency of seizures (lack of seizure control) among the individuals studied.

Collings (1990) also reported that well-being was inversely related to employment status and living status among adults with epilepsy (ie, those who were married and living in the community reported greater degree of well-being than those who were single and living alone or with their parents). It must be noted, however, that Collings' global measure was derived from a principal components analysis of six indices of psychosocial functioning and general health that presupposed adaptation could be represented on a linear continuum. Moreover analyses of these data involved univariate nonparametric measures of association that could not possibly separate confounded multivariate influences of the demographic and experiential variables.

With regard to epilepsy-related variables, it has been consistently reported that psychosocial adaptation problems increase with increasing frequency of seizures (Arnston et al., 1986; Collings, 1990; Dodrill, 1986; Hartlage & Green, 1972). A similar result was found with increased severity of seizures in studies by Collings (1990), Deb and Hunter (1991a), Hoare and Kerley (1991), and Arnston et al. (1986), but a lack of relationship was reported in a study by Flanagan and Beran (1985). Dodrill and Matthews (1992) note, however, that seizure frequency and intensity can fluctuate considerably in persons with epilepsy, so that careful tests of the relationships of these variables to psychosocial adaptation are difficult to carry out. Seizure type has also not shown a consistent relationship to psychosocial adaptation (Brown et al., 1986; Hermann et al., 1980; Kløve & Matthews, 1966), although it has been suggested (Dodrill & Matthews, 1992; Hermann & Whitman, 1984) that seizure type is one of a combination of epilepsy-related variables that contribute to increased psychological risk.

In a comprehensive study of predictors of psychopathology as measured by the General Health Questionnaire (Hermann et al., 1990), data from 102 individuals referred to an inpatient hospital monitoring unit were collected on five neurologic variables (ie, age at onset, chronicity, seizure type, number of seizures, and etiology), eight psychosocial variables (ie, stigma, personal limitations, adjustment to seizures, vocational status, financial status, life event changes, social support, and locus of control), four demographic variables (ie, age, sex, educational level, and IQ), and two variables concerning medications (ie, monopharmacy versus polypharmacy and barbiturate prescription). Although only 23% of the variance in General Health Questionnaire scores could be accounted for by the total set of predictors, the best predictors of psychopathology were found to be life event changes, adjustment to seizures (as measured by the Washington Psychosocial Seizure Inventory), and financial status.

The need to analyze data from multiple predictors to separate the confounding influences of variables that may limit the generalizability of research is illustrated by a recent study (Trostle, Hauser, & Sharbrough, 1989). When Washington Psychosocial Seizure Inventory data obtained from a nonrandom sample of 112 persons with epilepsy living in the community were compared to previously published data from clinic and state school samples, it was discovered that the community sample reported the fewest adaptation problems. This suggests that the biasing influence of demographic and experiential characteristics of samples must be accounted for even when analyzing so-called objective data. Similar cautions have been expressed for two decades by other researchers investigating psychosocial reactions and personality characteristics of persons with epilepsy (Beran & Flanagan, 1987; Kogeorgos et al., 1982; Ozuma, 1979; Robertson & Trimble, 1983; Scott, 1978; Zielinski, 1972).

CONCLUSION

The lack of consistency in methods used to diagnose epilepsy and to measure psychosocial adaptation and the differences in criteria used to define and classify epilepsy-related variables make it difficult to compare the results of studies conducted by different researchers at different times in different settings, leading to seemingly contradictory results. As Hermann and Whitman (1984) astutely pointed out, sample selection biases limit generalization from studies of *patients* with epilepsy to *persons* with epilepsy in the general population. The absence of comparison groups composed of individuals with different seizure types or of adequate control groups of persons with neurological and chronic health impairments and persons without impairments limits the internal validity of those studies investigating psychosocial adaptation with empirical measures, that is, maladaptive psychosocial reactions cannot be unequivocally attributed to epilepsy without evidence that these reactions are not accounted for by situational or demographic characteristics of the samples studied. The power of even well-designed investigations to detect true subtle differences in patterns of psychosocial adaptation to epilepsy has undoubtedly been diminished by these biases.

Despite these weaknesses, several tentative conclusions may be warranted from this review of the research concerning the psychosocial adaptation to chronic illness and disability among individuals with epilepsy. First, persons with epilepsy as a group appear more likely than the general population to be at increased risk for psychopathology. It is not possible, however, to predict with acceptable accuracy those individuals who are likely to manifest specific maladaptive psychosocial reactions. Depression, although commonly the basis for psychiatric hospitalization of persons with epilepsy, is not universally experienced. Similarly, due to the absence of population-based studies of persons with and without epilepsy, the relationships between sexual dysfunction, aggression, or psychosis and epilepsy remain unclear. The reported increased incidences of these types of personality disorders among persons with epilepsy are thought to overstate the true relationships (Hauser & Hesdorffer, 1990; Whitman & Hermann, 1986b).

Second, preliminary data—of dubious quality—suggest that while children with epilepsy may manifest psychosocial reactions that are uniquely related to their neurological impairment, they nevertheless display an overall profile of reactions similar to all individuals who experience chronic illnesses (Eiser et al., 1992; Howe et al., 1993; Stein & Jessup, 1982). Medical treatment and medication regimens increase the child's feelings of dependency, isolate the child from peers, and restrict typical activities that are essential for development. Parental stress related to the costs of treatment, the child's educational experience, and the future autonomy of the child contribute to reactions of anxiety and denial. It is not possible at this time to make any statement, definitive or tentative, about the commonality of psychosocial reaction patterns between adults with epilepsy and adults with other types of chronic illnesses due to the lack of data.

Third, psychosocial adaptation to epilepsy appears to have a complex curvilinear relationship with age of the individual, with increased risk of psychosocial maladaptation among adolescents and reduced risk among children and adults. The same conclusion appears to apply to the relationship between psychosocial adaptation and age at onset of epilepsy. Although the data are contradictory, preliminary indications seem to suggest that psychosocial well-being is inversely related to chronicity of impairment. Moreover, maladaptation is related to lack of social support, unemployment, and dependent living and financial status, although the available research often fails to distinguish between the independent and the dependent variables. Finally, with regard to impairment-related variables, it has been consistently reported that psychosocial adaptation problems increase with increasing frequency and severity of seizures but do not appear to be predictably related to seizure type.

Hermann and Whitman (1984) cautioned that "assessment of the interictal (ie, between seizure) psychological state of individuals with epilepsy has historically been an enterprise long on speculation, theory, and surmise" (p. 451). Hermann and colleagues (Hermann et al., 1988; Hermann & Whitman, 1984; Hermann & Whitman, 1986; Hermann & Whitman, 1992) have lamented the paucity of objective investigations of psychosocial adaptation to epilepsy and the failure of the studies they reviewed to take into account or to control the confounding effects of mediating variables, such as seizure type and frequency, impairment chronicity, age at onset, cerebral metabolism, and antiepileptic drug effects. Sophisticated data-analytic techniques (eg, discriminant function analysis, canonical correlation) are available that permit the researcher to explore the reciprocal relationships among predetermined sets of these variables and their combined influences on adaptation to epilepsy. Data-reduction techniques (eg, multidimensional scaling, principal components analysis) are also available to construct psychometrically sound multidimensional measures of psychosocial adaptation. Notable attempts to use these statistical techniques are the multivariate studies of Hermann et al. (1990), Austin et al. (1994), Eiser et al. (1992), and Kogeorgos et al. (1982). There is clearly a need to extend these research efforts.

REFERENCES

Ajzen, I., & Fishbein, M. (1980). *Understanding attitudes and predicting social behavior.* Englewood Cliffs, NJ: Prentice Hall.

Alvarado, L., Ivanovic-Zuvic, F., Candia, X., Méndez, M., Ibarra, X., & Alarcón, J. (1992). Psychosocial evaluation of adults with epilepsy in Chile. *Epilepsia, 33,* 651–656.

Antonak, R. F. (1988). A history of the provision of services to people who are mentally retarded. In S. N. Calculator & J. Bedrosian (Eds.), *Communication assessment and intervention strategies for developmentally disabled adults* (pp. 9–44). San Diego, CA: College Hill Press.

Antonak, R. F., & Rankin, P. (1982). Measurement and analysis of knowledge and attitudes toward epilepsy and persons with epilepsy. *Social Science and Medicine, 16*, 1591–1593.

Arangio, A. J. (1975). *Behind the stigma of epilepsy*. Washington, DC: Epilepsy Foundation of America.

Arnston, P., Droge, D., Norton, R., & Murray, E. (1986). The perceived psychosocial consequences of having epilepsy. In S. Whitman & B. P. Hermann (Eds.), *Psychopathology in epilepsy: Social dimensions* (pp. 143–161). New York: Oxford University Press.

Austin, J. K., McBride, A. B., & Davis, H. W. (1984). Parental attitude and adjustment to childhood epilepsy. *Nursing Research, 33*, 92–96.

Austin, J. K., Smith, M. S., Risinger, M. W., & McNelis, A. M. (1994). Childhood epilepsy and asthma: Comparison of quality of life. *Epilepsia, 35*, 608–615.

Awaritefe, A., Lange, A. C., & Awaritefe, M. (1985). Epilepsy and psychosis: A comparison of societal attitudes. *Epilepsia, 26*, 1–9.

Bagley, C. (1972). Social prejudice and the adjustment of people with epilepsy. *Epilepsia, 13*, 33–45.

Bear, D., Freeman, R., & Greenberg, M. (1984). Behavioral alterations in patients with temporal lobe epilepsy. In D. Blumer (Ed.), *Psychiatric aspects of epilepsy* (pp. 197–227). Washington, DC: American Psychiatric Press.

Beit-Jones, M. S., & Kapust, L. R. (1986). Temporal lobe epilepsy: Social and psychological considerations. *Social Work in Health Care, 11*(2), 17–33.

Beran, R. G., & Beran, T. (1983). A survey of doctors in Sydney, Australia: Perspectives and practices regarding epilepsy and those affected by it. *Epilepsia, 24*, 79–104.

Beran, R. G., & Flanagan, P. J. (1985). Examination of the problems confronting those with epilepsy. *Clinical and Experimental Neurology, 21*, 183–188.

Beran, R. G., & Flanagan, P. J. (1987). Psychosocial sequelae of epilepsy: The role of associated cerebral pathology. *Epilepsia, 28*, 107–110.

Beran, R. G., Jennings, V. R., & Read, T. (1981). Doctors' perspectives of epilepsy. *Epilepsia, 22*, 397–406.

Beran, R. G., & Reed, T. (1980). Patient perspectives of epilepsy. *Clinical and Experimental Neurology, 17*, 69–74.

Blumer, D., & Walker, A. E. (1967). Sexual behavior in temporal lobe epilepsy. *Journal of Neurology, Neurosurgery, and Psychiatry, 16*, 37–43.

Bridge, E. M. (1947). Emotional disturbance in epileptic children. *The Nervous Child, 6*, 11–21.

Broughton, R. J., Creberman, A., & Roberts, J. (1984). Comparison of the psychosocial effects of epilepsy and narcolepsy/cataplexy: A controlled study. *Epilepsia, 25*, 423–433.

Brown, S. W., McGowan, M. F. L., & Reynolds, E. H. (1986). The influence of seizure type and medication on psychiatric symptoms in epileptic patients. *British Journal of Psychiatry, 148*, 300–304.

Canger, R., & Cornaggia, C. (1985). Public attitudes toward epilepsy in Italy: Results of a survey and comparison with U.S.A. and West German data. *Epilepsia, 26*, 221–226.

Carter, J. D. (1947). Children's expressed attitudes toward their epilepsy. *The Nervous Child, 6*, 34–37.

Caveness, W., & Gallup, G. (1980). A survey of public attitudes toward epilepsy in 1979 with an indication of trends over the past thirty years. *Epilepsia, 21*, 509–518.

Caveness, W. F., Merritt, H. H., & Gallup, G. H. J. (1974). A survey of public attitudes toward epilepsy in 1974 with an indication of trends over the past twenty-five years. *Epilepsia, 15*, 523–528.

Chadwick, D. (Ed.). (1990). *Quality of life and quality of care in epilepsy.* Oxford, England: Royal Society of Medicine Services.

Chaplin, J. E., Floyd, M., & Lasso, R. Y. (1993). Early psychosocial adjustment and the experience of epilepsy: Findings from a general practice survey. *International Journal of Rehabilitation Research, 16,* 316–318.

Collings, J. A. (1990). Psychosocial well-being and epilepsy: An empirical study. *Epilepsia, 31,* 418–426.

Danesi, M. A. (1984). Patient perspectives on epilepsy in a developing country. *Epilepsia, 25,* 184–190.

Deb, S., & Hunter, D. (1991a). Psychopathology of people with mental handicaps and epilepsy I. Maladaptive behaviour. *British Journal of Psychiatry, 159,* 822–826.

Deb, S., & Hunter, D. (1991b). Psychopathology of people with mental handicaps and epilepsy II: Psychiatric illness. *British Journal of Psychiatry, 159,* 826–830.

Deb, S., & Hunter, D. (1991c). Psychopathology of people with mental handicaps and epilepsy III: Personality disorder. *British Journal of Psychiatry, 159,* 830–834.

DeHass, A. M. L. (1962). Social aspects of epilepsy. *Epilepsia, 3,* 44–55.

Dell, J. L. (1986). Social dimensions of epilepsy: Stigma and response. In S. Whitman & B. P. Hermann (Eds.), *Psychopathology in epilepsy: Social dimensions* (pp. 185–210). New York: Oxford University Press.

Devinsky, O., & Cramer, J. A. (Eds.). (1993). Assessing quality of life in epilepsy: Development of a new inventory. *Epilepsy, 34*(Suppl. 4), S1–S44.

Dodrill, C. (1983). Psychosocial characteristics of epileptic patients. In A. Ward, J. Penry, & D. Purpura (Eds.), *Epilepsy* (pp. 341–353). New York: Raven Press.

Dodrill, C. B. (1986). Correlates of generalized tonic-clonic seizures with intellectual, neuropsychological, emotional, and social function in patients with epilepsy. *Epilepsia, 27,* 399–411.

Dodrill, C. B., Beier, R., Kasparick, M., Tacke, I., Tacke, U., & Tan, S.-Y. (1984). Psychosocial problems in adults with epilepsy: Comparison of findings from four countries. *Epilepsia, 25,* 176–183.

Dodrill, C. B., Beyer, D. N., Diamond, M. B., Dubinsky, B. L., & Geary, B. B. (1984). Psychosocial problems among adults with epilepsy. *Epilepsia, 25,* 168–175.

Dodrill, C. B., & Matthews, C. G. (1992). The role of neuropsychology in the assessment and treatment of persons with epilepsy. *American Psychologist, 47,* 1139–1142.

Dorenbaum, D., Cappelli, M., Keene, D., & McGrath, P. J. (1985). Use of a child behavior checklist in the psychosocial assessment of children with epilepsy. *Clinical Pediatrics, 24,* 634–637.

Dreisbach, M., Ballard, M., Russo, D. L., & Schain, R. J. (1982). Educational intervention for children with epilepsy: A challenge for collaborative service delivery. *Journal of Special Education, 16,* 111–121.

Eiser, C., Havermans, T., Pancer, M., & Eiser, J. R. (1992). Adjustment to chronic disease in relation to age and gender: Mothers' and fathers' reports of their childrens' behavior. *Journal of Pediatric Psychology, 17,* 261–275.

Ellison, J. (1982). Alterations of sexual behavior in temporal lobe epilepsy. *Psychosomatics, 23,* 499–509.

Engel, J. (1982). Recent developments in the diagnosis and therapy of epilepsy. *Annals of Internal Medicine, 9,* 554–598.

Epilepsy Foundation of America. (1975). *Basic statistics on the epilepsies.* Philadelphia: Davis.

Flanagan, P. J., & Beran, R. G. (1985). A simple and validated tool for the clinician to assess psychosocial status when conducting anticonvulsant drug trials. *Clinical and Experimental Neurology*, *21*, 189–194.

Fraser, R. T. (1993). Epilepsy. In M. G. Eisenberg, R. L. Glueckart, & H. H. Zaretsky (Eds.), *Medical aspects of disability: A handbook for the rehabilitation professional* (pp. 192–207). New York: Springer.

Gade, E., & Toutges, G. (1983). Employers' attitudes toward hiring epileptics: Implications for job placement. *Rehabilitation Counseling Bulletin, 26*, 353–356.

Gallhofer, B. (1984). Epilepsy and its prejudice: Teachers' knowledge and opinions: Are they a response to psychopathological phenomena? *Psychopathology, 17*, 187–212.

Goffman, E. (1963). *Stigma: Notes on the management of spoiled identity.* Englewood Cliffs, NJ: Prentice Hall.

Goldin, G. J., & Margolin, R. J. (1975). The psychosocial aspects of epilepsy. In G. N. Wright (Ed.), *Epilepsy rehabilitation* (pp. 66–80). Boston: Little, Brown.

Goldstein, J., Seidenberg, M., & Peterson, R. (1990). Fear of seizures and behavioral functioning in adults with epilepsy. *Journal of Epilepsy, 3*, 101–106.

Gutteling, J. M., Seydel, E. R., & Wiegman, O. (1986). Previous experiences with epilepsy and effectiveness of information to change public perceptions of epilepsy. *Epilepsia, 27*, 739–745.

Hackney, A., & Taylor, D. C. (1976). A teachers' questionnaire description of epileptic children. *Epilepsia, 17*, 275–281.

Hartlage, L. C., & Green, J. B. (1972). The relation of parental attitudes to academic and social achievement in epileptic children. *Epilepsia, 13*, 21–26.

Hartshorn, J. C., & Byers, V. L. (1992). Impact of epilepsy on quality of life. *Journal of Neuroscience Nursing, 24*, 24–30.

Hauck, G. (1972). Sociological aspects of epilepsy research. *Epilepsia, 13*, 79–85.

Hauser, W. A., & Hesdorffer, D. C. (1990). *Epilepsy: Frequency, causes and consequences.* New York: Demos.

Hawton, K., Fagg, J., & Marsack, P. (1980). Association between epilepsy and attempted suicide. *Journal of Neurology, Neurosurgery, and Psychiatry, 43*, 168–170.

Hermann, B. P., Desai, B. T., & Whitman, S. (1988). Epilepsy. In V. B. Van Hasselt, P. S. Strain, & M. Hersen (Eds.), *Handbook of developmental and physical disabilities* (pp. 247–270). New York: Pergamon Press.

Hermann, B. P., Schwartz, M. S., Karnes, W. E., & Vahdat, P. (1980). Psychopathology in epilepsy: Relationship of seizure type to age at onset. *Epilepsia, 21*, 15–23.

Hermann, B. P., Schwartz, M. S., Whitman, S., & Karnes, W. E. (1980). Aggression and epilepsy: Seizure type comparisons and high risk variables. *Epilepsia, 21*, 691–699.

Hermann, B. P., Schwartz, M. S., Whitman, S., & Karnes, W. E. (1981). Psychosis and epilepsy: Seizure type comparisons and high risk variables. *Journal of Clinical Psychology, 37*, 714–721.

Hermann, B. P., & Whitman, S. (1984). Behavioral and personality correlates of epilepsy: A review, methodological critique and conceptual model. *Psychological Bulletin, 95*, 451–497.

Hermann, B. P., & Whitman, S. (1986). Psychopathology in epilepsy: A multietiologic model. In S. Whitman & B. P. Hermann (Eds.), *Psychopathology in epilepsy: Social dimensions* (pp. 5–37). New York: Oxford University Press.

Hermann, B. P., & Whitman, S. (1992). Psychopathology in epilepsy: The role of psychology in altering paradigms of research, treatment, and prevention. *American Psychologist, 47*, 1134–1138.

Hermann, B. P., Whitman, S., Wyler, A. R., Anton, M. T., & Vanderzwagg, R. (1990). Psychosocial predictors of psychopathology in epilepsy. *British Journal of Psychiatry, 156,* 98–105.

Himmelhoch, J. M. (1984). Major mood disorders related to epileptic changes. In D. Blumer (Ed.), *Psychiatric aspects of epilepsy* (pp. 271–294). Washington, DC: American Psychiatric Press.

Hoare, P. (1986). Adults' attitudes to children with epilepsy: The use of a visual analogue scale questionnaire. *Journal of Psychosomatic Research, 30,* 471–479.

Hoare, P., & Kerley, S. (1991). Psychosocial adjustment of children with chronic epilepsy and their families. *Developmental Medicine and Child Neurology, 33,* 201–215.

Holdsworth, L., & Whitmore, K. (1974). A study of children with epilepsy attending ordinary schools. II: Information and attitudes held by their teachers. *Developmental Medicine and Child Neurology, 16,* 759–765.

Holmes, D. A., & McWilliams, J. M. (1981). Employers' attitudes toward hiring epileptics. *Journal of Rehabilitation, 20,* 21.

Howe, G. W., Feinstein, C., Reiss, D., Molock, S., & Berger, K. (1993). Adolescent adjustment to chronic physical disorders—I. Comparing neurological and non-neurological conditions. *Journal of Child Psychology and Psychiatry, 34,* 1153–1173.

Irie, H., Uchino, A., Kondoh, M., Utsugi, Y., Hirabayashi, N., Takahashi, T., Oana, Y., & Shimizu, M. (1993). Psychosocial problems in patients with seizure-free periods more than 3 years by using the WPSI. *Japanese Journal of Psychiatry and Neurology, 47,* 361–362.

Jacoby, A. (1992). Epilepsy and the quality of everyday life: Findings from a study of people with well-controlled epilepsy. *Social Science and Medicine, 34,* 657–666.

Kaplan, B. J., & Wyler, A. R. (1983). Coping with epilepsy. In T. G. Burish & L. A. Bradley (Eds.), *Coping with chronic disease* (pp. 259–284). New York: Academic Press.

Kløve, H., & Doehring, H. (1962). MMPI in epileptic groups with differential etiology. *Journal of Clinical Psychology, 18,* 149–153.

Kløve, H., & Matthews, C. G. (1966). Psychometric and adaptive abilities in epilepsy with differential etiology. *Epilepsia, 7,* 330–338.

Kogeorgos, J., Fonagy, P., & Scott, D. F. (1982). Psychiatric symptom patterns of chronic epileptics attending a neurological clinic: A controlled investigation. *British Journal of Psychiatry, 140,* 236–243.

Lai, C.-W., Huang, X., Lai, Y.-H., Zhang, Z., Liu, G., & Yang, M.-Z. (1990). Survey of public awareness, understanding, and attitudes toward epilepsy in Henan Province, China. *Epilepsia, 31,* 182–187.

Landisberg, S. (1947). A personality study of institutionalized epileptics. *American Journal of Mental Deficiency, 52,* 16–22.

Lechtenberg, R. (1984). *Epilepsy and the family.* Cambridge, MA: Harvard University Press.

Lechtenberg, R. (1985). *The diagnosis and treatment of epilepsy.* New York: Macmillan.

Leonard, B. J. (1984). The adolescent with epilepsy. In R. W. Blum (Ed.), *Chronic illness and disabilities in childhood and adolescence* (pp. 239–263). New York: Grune & Stratton.

Levin, R., Banks, S., & Berg, B. (1988). Psychosocial dimensions of epilepsy: A review of the literature. *Epilepsia, 29,* 805–816.

Livanainen, M., Uutela, A., & Vilkkumaa, I. (1980). Public awareness and attitudes toward epilepsy in Finland. *Epilepsia, 21,* 413–423.

Livingston, S. (1977). Psychosocial aspects of epilepsy. *Journal of Clinical Child Psychology, 6,* 6–10.

Long, C. G., & Moore, J. R. (1979). Parental expectations for their epileptic children. *Journal of Child Psychology and Psychiatry, 20,* 299–312.

Martin, J. (1974). Attitudes toward epileptic students in a city high school. *Journal of School Health, 44,* 144–145.

Mason, G., Fenton, G. W., & Jamieson, M. (1990). Teaching medical students about epilepsy. *Epilepsia, 31,* 95–100.

Matthews, C. G., & Kløve, H. (1968). MMPI performances in major motor, psychomotor, and mixed seizure classifications of known and unknown etiology. *Epilepsia, 9,* 43–53.

Matthews, W. S., & Barabas, G. (1981). Suicide and epilepsy: A review of the literature. *Psychosomatics, 22,* 515–524.

Matthews, W. S., Barabas, G., & Ferrari, M. (1982). Emotional concomitants of childhood epilepsy. *Epilepsia, 23,* 671–681.

Mattsson, A. (1972). Long-term physical illness in childhood: A challenge to psychosocial adaptation. *Pediatrics, 5,* 801–811.

McNamara, M. E. (1991). Psychological factors affecting neurological conditions: Depression and stroke, multiple sclerosis, Parkinson's disease, and epilepsy. *Psychosomatics, 32,* 255–267.

Mendez, M. F., Cummings, J. L., & Benson, D. F. (1986). Depression in epilepsy: Significance and phenomenology. *Archives of Neurology, 43,* 766–770.

Merkens, M. J., Perrin, E. C., Perrin, J. M., & Gerrity, P. S (1989). The awareness of primary physicians of the psychosocial adjustment of children with chronic illness. *Journal of Developmental and Behavioral Pediatrics, 10,* 1–6.

Naugle, R. I., & Rodgers, D. A. (1992). Personality inventory responses of males with medically intractable seizures. *Journal of Personality Assessment, 59,* 500–514.

Olsson, I., & Campenhausen, G. (1993). Social adjustment in young adults with absence seizures. *Epilepsia, 34,* 846–851.

Ozuma, J. (1979). Psychosocial aspects of epilepsy. *Journal of Neurosurgical Nursing, 11,* 242–246.

Parnas, J., & Korsgaard, S. (1982). Epilepsy and psychosis. *Acta Psychiatrica Scandinavica, 66,* 89–99.

Pazzaglia, P., & Frank-Pazzaglia, L. (1976). Record in grade school of pupils with epilepsy: An epidemiological study. *Epilepsia, 17,* 361–366.

Pincus, J. H. (1980). Can violence be a manifestation of epilepsy? *Neurology, 30,* 304–307.

Pollock, S. E., Christian, B. J., & Sands, D. (1990). Responses to chronic illness: Analysis of psychological and physiological adaptation. *Nursing Research, 39,* 300–304.

Räder, K., Ritter, G., & Schwibbe, M. H. (1986). Epilepsy and prejudice: The dimensionality of stereotypes toward epileptics. *International Journal of Rehabilitation Research, 9,* 325–334.

Remschmidt, H. (1973). Psychological studies of patients with epilepsy and popular prejudice. *Epilepsia, 14,* 347–356.

Richardson, D. W., & Friedman, S. B. (1974). Psychosocial problems of the adolescent patient with epilepsy. *Clinical Pediatrics, 13,* 121–126.

Robertson, M. M. (1989). The organic contribution to depressive illness in patients with epilepsy. *Journal of Epilepsy, 2,* 189–230.

Robertson, M. M., & Trimble, M. R. (1983). Depressive illness in patients with epilepsy: A review. *Epilepsia, 24*(Suppl. 2), S109–S116.

Rodin, E. A. (1973). Psychomotor epilepsy and aggressive behavior. *Archives of General Psychiatry, 28,* 210–213.

Ryan, R., Kempner, K., & Emlen, A. (1980). The stigma of epilepsy as a self-concept. *Epilepsia, 21*, 433–444.

Sands, H., & Minters, F. C. (1977). *The epilepsy fact book.* Philadelphia: F. A. Davis.

Sands, H., & Zalkind, S. S. (1972). Effects of an educational campaign to change employer attitudes toward hiring epileptics. *Epilepsia, 13*, 87–96.

Schiffer, R. B., & Babigian, H. M. (1984). Behavioral disorders in multiple sclerosis, temporal lobe epilepsy, and amyotrophic lateral sclerosis. *Archives of Neurology, 41*, 1067–1069.

Scott, D. F. (1978). Psychiatric aspects of epilepsy. *British Journal of Psychiatry, 132*, 417–430.

Scrambler, G., & Hopkins, A. (1990). Generating a model of epilepsy stigma: The role of qualitative analysis. *Social Science and Medicine, 30*, 1187–1194.

Seidenberg, M., & Berent, S. (1992). Childhood epilepsy and the role of psychology. *American Psychologist, 47*, 1130–1133.

Standage, K. F., & Fenton, G. W. (1975). Psychiatric symptom profiles of patients with epilepsy: A controlled investigation. *Psychological Medicine, 5*, 152–160.

Stein, R. E. K., & Jessup, D. J. (1982). A noncategorical approach to chronic childhood illness. *Public Health Reports, 97*, 354–362.

Stude, E. (1973). Evaluation of short-term training for rehabilitation counselors: Effectiveness of an institute on epilepsy. *Rehabilitation Counseling Bulletin, 16*, 146–154.

Tan, S.-Y. (1986). Psychosocial functioning of adult epileptic and MS patients and adult normal controls on the WPSI. *Journal of Clinical Psychology, 42*, 528–534.

Tarter, R. F. (1972). Intellectual and adaptive functioning in epilepsy: A review of 50 years of research. *Diseases of the Nervous System, 33*, 763–770.

Temkin, O. (1971). *The falling sickness: A history of epilepsy from the Greeks to the beginnings of modern neurology* (2nd ed.). Baltimore: Johns Hopkins University Press.

Terdal, L. G. (1981). Epilepsy. In J. I. Lindemann (Ed.), *Psychological and behavioral aspects of physical disability* (pp. 147–178). New York: Plenum Press.

Tizard, B. (1962). The personality of epileptics: A discussion of the evidence. *Psychological Bulletin, 59*, 196–210.

Trostle, J. A., Hauser, W. A., & Sharbrough, F. W. (1989). Psychologic and social adjustment to epilepsy in Rochester, Minnesota. *Neurology, 39*, 633–637.

Wang, Y., Nakashima, K., & Takahashi, T. (1993). The application of the WPSI to epilepsy patients. *Japanese Journal of Psychiatry and Neurology, 47*, 537–539.

Ward, A., Penry, J., & Purpura, D. (Eds.). (1983). *Epilepsy.* New York: Raven Press.

Ward, A. A., Jr., Fraser, R. T., & Troupin, A. S. (1981). Epilepsy. In W. C. Stolov & M. R. Clowers (Eds.), *Handbook of severe disability* (pp. 155–167). Washington, DC: U. S. Department of Education, Rehabilitation Services Administration.

Ward, F., & Bower, B. D. (1978). A study of certain social aspects of epilepsy in childhood. *Developmental Medicine and Child Neurology, 20*(Suppl. 39), 1–63.

Westbrook, L. E., Bauman, L. J., & Shinnar, S. (1992). Applying stigma theory to epilepsy: A test of a conceptual model. *Journal of Pediatric Psychology, 17*, 633–649.

Whitman, S., & Hermann, B. P. (1986a). Introduction. In S. Whitman & B. P. Hermann (Eds.), *Psychopathology in epilepsy: Social dimensions* (pp. viii–xviii). New York: Oxford University Press.

Whitman, S., & Hermann, B. P. (Eds.). (1986b). *Psychopathology in epilepsy: Social dimensions.* New York: Oxford University Press.

Whitman, S., King, L. N., & Cohen, R. L. (1986). Epilepsy and violence: A scientific and social analysis. In S. Whinnan & B. P. Hermann (Eds.), *Psychopathology in epilepsy: Social dimensions* (pp. 284–302). New York: Oxford University Press.

Wiley, L. (1974). The stigma of epilepsy. *Nursing Research, 4*(1), 36–45.

Wright, G. N. (1975). Rehabilitation and the problem of epilepsy. In G. N. Wright (Ed.), *Epilepsy rehabilitation* (pp. 1–7). Boston: Little, Brown.

Zielinski, J. J. (1972). Social prognosis in epilepsy. *Epilepsia, 13*, 133–140.

CHAPTER 14

Multiple Sclerosis

DESCRIPTION

Multiple sclerosis, a chronic, progressive, demyelinating disease with onset commonly between ages 20 and 40 years, is the most common acquired neurological disease in young adults in North America and Europe, with a reported incidence in the United States varying from 30 to 100 per 100,000 persons (Falvo, 1991; Kraft, 1981; Scheinberg & Holland, 1987; Smith & Scheinberg, 1990). Two to three females are afflicted for every male. The disease is five times more common in temperate latitudes than in the tropics (Matthews, 1993).

Although the first medical description of the disease was published in England in 1838 (Stenager, 1991), the cause remains unknown. It is thought to be an autoimmune disease in which the myelin (the covering of the nerve fibers) is treated as foreign by the body's defenses and is attacked, resulting in lesions (scar tissue or plaques) that delay or block the passage of nerve impulses. This leads to an array of symptoms varying from person to person, depending upon which parts of the brain and spinal cord are affected, and within the person from time to time. Symptoms can include numbness, impaired mobility, paralysis, hand tremors, spasticity, fatigue, vertigo, problems in bladder control, sexual dysfunction, difficult communication, cognitive deterioration, emotional lability, and visual impairments (eg, double vision, eye muscle jerking, blurred vision, problems of depth perception). The rate of progression of the disease is unpredictable (Matthews, 1993). The person typically experiences cyclical periods of new or worsening symptoms (exacerbations) lasting two to three weeks alternating with periods of symptom stability or decrement (remissions). While in most individuals the period between exacerbations may extend to five years, as many as 10% of individuals with the disease exhibit continuous progression of symptoms without remission.

There is currently no reliable method to make an antemortem diagnosis of multiple sclerosis. The neurologist arrives at the diagnosis by the gradual elimination of other possible neurological diseases, a process that may take from several months to several years in extreme cases. Tests that may be performed to provide confirmatory data include analysis of cerebrospinal fluid obtained from lumbar puncture, tracing patterns of evoked electrical activity of the brain, computerized tomographic scanning, and magnetic resonance imaging.

There is no cure for multiple sclerosis, nor are there preventive measures, but treatments are available that offer symptomatic relief (Falvo, 1991; Matthews, 1993; Smith & Scheinberg, 1990). Drugs can be used to alleviate inflammation, to suppress the immune system, and to treat pain, depression, incontinence, and spasticity. Physical therapy can increase mobility and prevent disuse atrophy of the muscles. Multiple sclerosis itself is not fatal, but the individual may die from the general hazards associated with advanced chronic diseases such as infections, pulmonary embolism, complications of pathological fractures, or pneumonia.

PSYCHOSOCIAL ADAPTATION TO MULTIPLE SCLEROSIS

The psychological consequences of the progressive disabilities associated with multiple sclerosis have been a concern of researchers since the 1850s (McDonald, 1983; Stenager, 1991). It was not until the 1950s, however, that serious scientific study was directed to the psychosocial adaptation of persons with the disease. Frequent attempts were made to discover a universal personality profile among persons with multiple sclerosis (Duval, 1984; Harrower & Kraus, 1951; Lemere, 1966; Riklan, Levita, & Diller, 1961) using data from instruments such as the Minnesota Multiphasic Personality Inventory (Bourestom & Howard, 1965; Canter, 1951; Davis, Osborne, Siemens, & Brown, 1971; Gilberstadt & Farkas, 1961; Halligan & Reznikoff, 1985; Ivnik, 1978; Peyser, Edwards, & Poser, 1980; Peyser, Edwards, Poser, & Filskov, 1980; Shontz, 1955). The outcome of this line of investigation was doomed to failure (Devins & Seland, 1987; McIvor, Riklan, & Reznikoff, 1984). Similar to research with persons with other chronic illness (eg, epilepsy, arthritis), it was discovered that the complex interplay of physical, psychological, and situational factors leads to extensive interindividual variability in personality characteristics. Although certain psychosocial reactions (ie, depression, anxiety) are commonly expressed by persons with multiple sclerosis, they are by no means universal personality traits.

Most studies of psychosocial adaptation of persons with multiple sclerosis have relied on clinical case reports, personal histories, anecdotal records, or retrospective self-report data obtained from mail surveys of dubious psychometric adequacy or from interviews with persons with multiple sclerosis and their families (Baldwin, 1952; Baretz & Stephenson, 1981; Burnfield & Burnfield, 1978;

Kinley, 1980; Langworthy, 1950; Lemere, 1966; Mei-Tal, Meyerowitz, & Engel, 1970; Philippopoulos, Wittkower, & Cousineau, 1958; Power, 1985; Schneitzer, 1978; Shontz, 1956; Sugar & Nadell, 1948; Surridge, 1969; Tarbell, 1980; Walsh & Walsh, 1987). Many reactions to multiple sclerosis have been reported in this literature, including aggressiveness, anger, apprehension, anxiety, denial, dependency, emotional lability, euphoria, helplessness, hopelessness, hostility, irritability, low drive, resignation, and shock. The most commonly studied psychosocial reaction has been depression (Baldwin, 1952; Baretz & Stephenson, 1981; Dalos, Rabins, Brooks, & O'Donnell, 1983; Handron, 1993; McNamara, 1991; Millefiorini et al., 1992; Minden, Orav, & Reich, 1987; Philippopoulos et al., 1958; Rabins et al., 1986; Rao et al., 1991; Schiffer, 1987; Schiffer & Babigian, 1984; Schiffer, Rudick, & Herndon, 1983; Schiffer, Wineman, & Weitkamp, 1986; Surridge, 1969; Whitlock & Siskind, 1980). An increased risk for the diagnosis of depressive disorder, based on behavioral indices, has been a consistent finding of this research. The contribution of depression to the onset and progress of the neurological disease, however, remains speculative.

One question that has been the subject of considerable inquiry among researchers is whether affective disorders, such as depression, and intellectual impairments in persons with multiple sclerosis are psychosocial reactions to the progressive, unpredictable, and chronic nature of the disease or are clinical manifestations of neurobiological impairments attributable to the disease process itself (Devins & Seland, 1987; Garland & Zis, 1991; LaRocca, 1984; Mahler, 1992; Millefiorini et al., 1992). It should be noted that a third position is also possible, namely, that both the disease and the affective disorder are the result of some common causal agent, such as a genetic defect. Research investigating these possible relationships is difficult to conduct due to the confounding of sociodemographic (eg, disease chronicity, age at onset of symptoms) and disease-related variables (eg, the effects of psychoactive drug treatment), sampling biases, measurement problems, and the complexity and expense of obtaining neurophysiological data. The results of several studies will be presented to illustrate the type of research that has been undertaken to investigate this question.

Arias Bal, Vázquez-Barquero, Peña, Miro, and Berciano (1991), for example, collected data on a set of neurological, sociodemographic, and disability-related variables from a consecutive series of 50 persons being treated for multiple sclerosis in Spain. These variables were related to psychiatric status as measured by the Clinical Interview Schedule, a semistructured interview protocol. A total of 54% of the individuals in their sample were found to score above the Clinical Interview Schedule cutoff score for psychiatric morbidity, with females outnumbering males by more than 3 to 1. Depression was the most frequently diagnosed psychiatric condition (22% of the sample), followed by anxiety (12%). Although the clinical manifestations were not sufficient to lead to a psychiatric diagnosis, other symptoms revealed by the Clinical Interview Schedule were affective lability (30%) and irritability (20%).

Millefiorini et al. (1992) undertook to investigate the relationships among depression, cognitive impairment, functional disability, and brain pathology in a study of 100 consecutive persons with multiple sclerosis who were being seen at a specialty clinic in Italy. Depression was diagnosed by DSM—III-R criteria using a combination of indices present in the person's responses to a clinical interview and the results of the Minnesota Multiphasic Personality Inventory. In addition, each person was tested with a comprehensive neuropsychological battery and with the Kurtzke (1961) disability scale, and their brains were scanned using magnetic resonance imaging. These researchers reported that the diagnosis of depression in their sample was directly related to the severity of disability and disease symptoms, but they were unable to find a consistent relationship between depression and specific imaging indices. Although they concluded that depression was predominantly a reactive disorder rather than an organic disorder, they did stipulate that the type of imaging procedures they used could not determine if the depression was due to neurophysiological changes related to the disease rather than to the extent and location of lesions.

Inconclusive findings such as these concerning depression in persons with multiple sclerosis led Schubert and Foliart (1993) to undertake a metaanalysis of the results of six research investigations that compared the risk for depression in persons with the disease and in persons without the disease (Dalos et al., 1983; Minden et al., 1987; Rabins et al., 1986; Schiffer et al., 1983; Surridge, 1969; Whitlock & Siskind, 1980). Three of these studies reported increased risk and three of these studies reported no increase risk. The results of the metaanalysis revealed that compared to persons without the disease, persons with multiple sclerosis were at a statistically significant risk for depression. This study, however, was unable to determine whether the depression was reactive or organic.

From their review of this array of research literature concerning depression in persons with multiple sclerosis, Garland and Zis (1991) concluded that the available data were not sufficient to validate any of the three positions (ie, organic, reactive, or common causal factor). In particular, they noted:

• The risk of major depressive episodes in persons with multiple sclerosis is greater than for persons with other noncentral nervous system neurological disorders. This increased risk of psychopathology suggests that affective disorders may be the result of structural lesions, in support of the organic position.
• Research data suggest that the presence of depressive symptoms in persons with multiple sclerosis is associated with increased severity of disability (ie, exacerbations) and the reduction or lack of social supports. These associa-

tions are commonly seen in research with samples of individuals experiencing other chronic illnesses, lending support to the reactive position.

- Insufficient data are available to link the presence of both multiple sclerosis and affective disorders to a common causal (eg, genetic) factor.

Two other areas of inquiry into psychosocial adaptation that have received attention in recent years are the rate of suicide and the selection of a coping strategy by persons with multiple sclerosis. An investigation of suicide in Denmark between 1953 and 1985 among persons with multiple sclerosis reported that the rate was nearly twice as high as the rate for the general population (Stenager et al., 1992). Greater risk of suicide was associated with males, individuals with symptom onset before age 30 years, individuals diagnosed with the disease before age 40 years, and individuals within the first five years after confirmation of the diagnosis. Eklund and MacDonald (1991) collected questionnaire data from a nonrandom sample of 125 persons with multiple sclerosis. A total of 13% of their sample reported experiencing suicidal ideation.

Investigations of coping among persons with disabilities typically are based upon Lazarus and Folkman's (1984) theoretical formulation that distinguishes emotion-focused coping (ie, strategies to regulate feelings) from problem-focused coping (ie, strategies to alter stressful situations). For example, Wineman, Durand, and Steiner (1994) hypothesized that persons with a chronic illness who experienced considerable uncertainty in their lives (such as the unpredictable course of multiple sclerosis) would be more likely to select an emotion-focused coping strategy. A nonrandom sample of persons with multiple sclerosis responded to a battery of measures, including the Mishel Uncertainty in Illness Scale, the Ways of Coping Questionnaire, and the Profile of Mood States. As predicted, individuals who expressed the highest level of illness uncertainty were more likely to select emotion-focused coping strategies. Their analyses revealed, however, that coping strategy selection was not a significant predictor of emotional well-being in their sample. This lack of a relationship may have been an artifact of sampling bias or of the operational definition of psychosocial adaptation in this study.

Eklund and MacDonald (1991) obtained questionnaire data from a sample of 125 persons with multiple sclerosis who responded to a mail survey sent to all members of a regional Multiple Sclerosis Society chapter. They discovered that those individuals expressing the highest scores on a measure of anger, fear, and depression also reported the lowest self-esteem and that they selected the least well-adapted coping strategies. It was noted, however, that the majority of the respondents in their sample were within published norms on the personality and self-esteem measures.

In a study of the relationship of coping, as measured by the Jalowiec Coping Scale, and stressors among 20 persons being treated for multiple sclerosis who were hospitalized for exacerbation of symptoms, Buelow (1991) discovered that the use of a fatalistic coping strategy was related to reported expressions of uncertainty about the future and that expression of depression was directly related to the use of an emotion-focused coping strategy. Similarly, Warren, Warren, and Cockerill (1991) reported that among 95 pairs of consecutive persons being treated for multiple sclerosis seen at a special clinic in Canada and matched for age and sex but differing in the presence of symptom exacerbations, those experiencing exacerbations tended to use more emotion-focused coping and less problem-focused coping strategies.

Handron (1993) has argued that whereas some would view emotion-focused coping strategies as primitive and immature and their selection as an indication of lack of psychosocial adaption, others (Folkman & Lazarus, 1988; Kübler-Ross, 1969) would suggest that selecting these strategies may serve a protective function for the individual. For example, denial of illness, an emotion-focused attempt to disavow the threatening implications of disease exacerbations, may be beneficial to the individual as a diversional strategy that temporarily hides an unpleasant reality while allowing the individual to maintain awareness of the seriousness of the disease.

Only one investigation was located that conceptualized reactions to multiple sclerosis as phases of a hierarchical adaptation process. Starting with Kübler-Ross's (1969) model of reactions to death and dying and using data from mail surveys and follow-up interviews of persons with multiple sclerosis, Matson and Brooks (1977) proposed an adaptation model consisting of four temporally ordered phases: (1) denial, (2) resistance, (3) affirmation, and (4) integration. The authors acknowledged that progress toward integration may be slow, and a person with multiple sclerosis may move back and forth on the adaptation continuum because of transient circumstances, such as exacerbation of the symptoms and stressful life events. Brooks and Matson (1982) obtained additional mail survey and interview data seven years later from individuals of the original sample. Unfortunately they operationalized adaptation as a unidimensional variable and did not provide any empirical data to test their model.

The psychosocial functioning of persons with multiple sclerosis has occasionally been related to that of persons diagnosed with other neurological disorders and chronic diseases to identify similarities and differences. Comparison groups have included persons with amyotrophic lateral sclerosis (Schiffer & Babigian, 1984), cardiac disease (Stuifbergen, 1988; Wassem, 1987), diabetes (Stuifbergen, 1988), end-stage renal disease (Devins, Edworthy, et al., 1993), epilepsy (Schiffer & Babigian, 1984; Tan, 1986), hypertension (Pollock, Christian, & Sands, 1990), muscular dystrophy (Surridge, 1969), Parkinson's disease (Harrower & Kraus, 1951; Riklan et al., 1961), poliomyelitis (Harrower & Kraus, 1951), rheumatoid arthritis (Bourestom & Howard, 1965; Devins, Edworthy, et al., 1993; Pollock et al., 1990; Stuifbergen, 1988; Wassem, 1987), spinal cord injury (Bourestrom &

Howard, 1965; Dalos et al., 1983; Wineman et al., 1994), and traumatic brain injury (Gilberstadt & Farkas, 1961). Tan (1986), for example, compared psychosocial adaptation of three groups: (1) adults with epilepsy, (2) adults with multiple sclerosis, and (3) adult volunteers without impairments who were from a church organization. Individuals in both of the chronic illness groups scored low on a scale of emotional adaptation in comparison with individuals without impairments, with the items most frequently checked relating to anxiety, anger, denial, and depression.

Devins, Edworthy, et al. (1993) undertook to test a model that linked illness-induced lifestyle disruptions with risk of psychosocial distress. They theorized that interference with valued activities and interests will decrease the individual's access to positive life experiences and decrease his or her feelings of personal control over outcomes in important life domains. They compared 110 persons with rheumatoid arthritis, 94 persons with multiple sclerosis, and 101 person with end-stage renal disease on a specially designed Illness Intrusiveness Ratings Scale, a self-report measure that purports to measure disease impact in 13 life domains: (1) health, (2) diet, (3) work, (4) active recreation, (5) passive recreation, (6) financial situation, (7) relationships with spouse, (8) sex life, (9) family relationships, (10) other social relationships, (11) self-expression, (12) religious expression, and (13) community and civic involvement. On the overall measure, persons with multiple sclerosis reported significantly more illness intrusiveness than did persons with rheumatoid arthritis or with end-stage renal disease. The authors related this difference to the unpredictability of the course of multiple sclerosis and to the difficulty of diagnosis and the variability of symptoms.

Other findings of this line of research suggest that, compared with persons with other chronic diseases and physical disabilities, persons with multiple sclerosis (1) express extreme variability in their reactions to the disease (Dalos et al., 1983), and (2) express more intense depressive reactions (Gilberstadt & Farkas, 1961; LaRocca, 1984; Schiffer & Babigian, 1984; Surridge, 1969), but (3) do not appear to differ in the types of coping strategies selected (Wineman et al., 1994). A recent study by Pollock et al. (1990), however, raised the issue that comparative investigations may be flawed by sampling bias, confounding of sample characteristics and measures of reactions, and instrumentation weaknesses. In a well-designed study, they found no differences in their measures of psychological adaptation among groups of persons with multiple sclerosis, hypertension, and rheumatoid arthritis, suggesting to them that the process of adaptation was similar for the three groups.

CHARACTERISTICS ASSOCIATED WITH ADAPTATION TO MULTIPLE SCLEROSIS

A number of investigators have analyzed data on the relationships among sociodemographic, personality, and disease-related variables and psychosocial reaction to multiple sclerosis (Berrios & Quemada, 1990; Braham, Houser, Cline,

& Poser, 1975; McIvor et al., 1984; Pavlou & Counte, 1982; Power, 1985; Schiffer & Babigian, 1984; Schiffer et al., 1986; Whitlock & Siskind, 1980; Wineman, 1990). McIvor et al. (1984), for example, related depression to a set of variables (eg, age, chronicity and severity of disability, family and peer support, remission status) and found that persons in their sample who were older and more disabled were more depressed, and those who were in remission were less depressed. Their finding that loss of social support was a factor in depression was confirmed by the results of a study by Wineman (1990), who discovered that adaptation to multiple sclerosis was directly related to the person's perceptions of support and inversely related to perceptions of nonsupport and functional disability. Wassem (1991) collected data from interviews with a random sample of 100 Multiple Sclerosis Society members in Ohio and reported that those with the most severe symptoms were more external on a measure of locus of control. Arias Bal et al. (1991) discovered that psychiatric morbidity in their sample of 50 persons being treated for multiple sclerosis was more common in females than in males and that symptoms of depression, anxiety, and affective lability increased with increasing age and increasing severity of disability.

Devins, Seland, Klein, Edworthy, and Saary (1993) collected data on a battery of instruments measuring disease-related variables (eg, severity, chronicity, fatigue, presence of exacerbations), sociodemographic characteristics (eg, age, sex), personality variables (eg, illness intrusiveness, feelings of personal control), and psychosocial adaptation. Their analyses revealed that psychosocial risk was related to decreased feelings of personal control, increased symptom severity, and increased illness intrusiveness, even after controlling for disease-related and sociodemographic variables. Pavlou and Counte's (1982) analyses of data on attitudes, stereotypic beliefs, and knowledge about multiple sclerosis showed that the best predictor of all three dependent measures was the person's educational level, with age the next most important for predicting knowledge and beliefs and the number of hospitalizations for exacerbations the next most important predictor. Wassem (1992), from analyses of data from a nonrandom sample of 62 persons with multiple sclerosis, reported that 72% of the variance in scores on the Bell Disability Scale of Adjustment was accounted for by a combination of a measure of disability severity (Kurtzke's Disability Status Scale) and a measure of confidence in performing self-care and disease management activities. Similar studies (Stenager, Knudsen, & Jensem, 1991; Zeldow & Pavlou, 1984; Zeldow & Pavlou, 1988) have confirmed that degree of physical disability and psychosocial adaptation are inversely related.

Another variable thought to influence the adaptation and rehabilitation potential of persons with multiple sclerosis is self-appraisal of the functional limitations associated with the disease. Differences between a person's perception and the perceptions of others (ie, spouse, family members, clinicians) are hypothe-

sized to lead to marital stress, family conflict, low level of participation in rehabilitation programs, and poor vocational adjustment. This suggests that
rehabilitation goals and intervention strategies should vary with the person's
appraisal of disability and that counseling goals for the family should include an
assessment of the spouse's and children's perceptions of the disease and associated disabilities (Crawford & McIvor, 1985; Power, 1984). Power's (1985) in-
depth interviews of persons with multiple sclerosis and their families revealed
that fewer than half the family units were making a successful adaptive response
to the diagnosis of multiple sclerosis (ie, reporting acceptance of the diagnosis
and demonstrating adaptation to symptoms and functional limitations of the disease). Among the reactions expressed by the family units considered to be maladaptive were shock and confusion over the initial diagnosis, denial of the
diagnosis, anger over the presence of the disease, anxiety and insecurity over the
future course of the disease, and hopelessness. When the family's and person's
perceptions and expectations did not coincide, family stress and tension resulted.
Spouses felt trapped, overwhelmed, and resentful and frequently displayed disruptive behavior (eg, excessive drinking and fighting). These findings were confirmed in a later study of the impact of spouses' perceptions of illness on family
functioning among persons with multiple sclerosis (Stuifbergen, 1988).

Perception of illness uncertainty (eg, concerning symptoms, diagnosis, prognosis, treatment, and future status) is a variable related to disability appraisal.
Wineman, O'Brien, Nealon, and Kaskel (1993), for example, investigated
whether congruence in the perception of uncertainty between well spouses and
spouses with multiple sclerosis influenced feelings of well-being and family satisfaction. Analyses of their data from 61 persons being treated for multiple sclerosis (27 males and 34 females) and their well spouses (mean years married = 30,
range 1 to 56 years) revealed that while illness uncertainty was a significant predictor of mood and family satisfaction in the spouse with multiple sclerosis, congruence of perception of illness uncertainty was not a significant predictor of
either dependent variable in the spouse with multiple sclerosis.

Few researchers have conceptualized the reactions of persons with multiple
sclerosis as phases of an overall process of adaptation to this chronic illness and
the disabilities associated with it. Stewart and Sullivan (1982) argued that reactions during the prediagnosis period should be distinguished from reactions during the postdiagnosis period but provided no empirical data to support their
contention. Wassem (1987) proposed a model to predict adaptation to disease
(including multiple sclerosis) based on Bandura's social learning theory but operationalized adaptation with a unidimensional measure. Noting that the consequences of multiple sclerosis included changes in economic (eg, loss of
employment, cost of care), social (eg, changes in family integration, reduction in
social contacts and recreational activities), and psychological (eg, loss of sexual

potency, changes in body image, loss of self-esteem) circumstances, Marks (1990) proposed a model in which adaptation to multiple sclerosis was thought to be related to seven variables classified in one of three dimensions (illness-related, environmental, and personality characteristics). The analyses of data obtained, however, did not constitute a reasonable test of this model because all the variables were conceptualized as unidimensional, and the relationships among them were investigated using simple linear bivariate correlation analyses.

CONCLUSION

Experts agree that the response to rehabilitation opportunities of the person with multiple sclerosis will be limited if he or she has not made a successful adaptation to the disease and its subsequent disabilities (Chodoff, 1959; Devins & Seland, 1987; Marks, 1990; Marsh, Ellison, & Strite, 1983; Power, 1985; Zeldow & Pavlou, 1984). More effective clinical management and improved long-term rehabilitation planning are possible if the clinician can determine the person's emotional and psychosocial reactions to the disease and can select an appropriate intervention strategy designed to teach coping skills.

Previous reviews of the research concerning psychosocial adaptation to multiple sclerosis have isolated significant problems that have limited the usefulness of the information collected. Among these concerns, to be discussed in detail in Chapter 24, are (1) sample selection bias (eg, the use of hospitalized persons, nonrepresentative samples of self-selected persons, nonrandom volunteer samples), (2) the use of unreliable retrospective self-report data obtained from mail surveys or from interviews with persons with multiple sclerosis and their families, (3) the absence of adequate comparison groups, (4) observer bias inherent in subjective measurements of reactions, (5) the lack of psychometrically sound instruments to operationalize the concept of adaptation, (6) the failure to conceptualize psychosocial adaptation to chronic illness and disability as a multidimensional process, and (7) the confounding of demographic, illness-related, and situational variables with measures of reactions to disability.

Because of these methodological weaknesses, only a small number of tentative conclusions can be made from this review of the research concerning the psychosocial adaptation to chronic illness and disability among individuals with multiple sclerosis. First, persons with multiple sclerosis must confront and attempt to cope with profound stresses, including the unknown cause of the disease, variability of symptoms, ambiguity of diagnosis, unpredictability of exacerbations and remissions, lack of a cure, and the reactions of other persons to visible symptoms, such as spasticity or ataxia. Persons with multiple sclerosis manifest extensive interindividual variability in psychosocial reactions to the complex interplay of these physical, psychological, and situational factors. Although certain psychosocial reactions (ie, depression, anxiety) are commonly expressed by persons with multiple sclerosis, similar to persons with other chronic illness (eg, epilepsy, arthritis), there is no universal personality profile associated with multiple sclerosis.

Second, an increased risk for the diagnosis of affective disorders (eg, depression, anxiety, denial), based on behavioral indices, has been a consistent finding reported in the research literature. Insufficient data are available at present to answer several important questions about this risk: Does depression contribute to the onset and progress of the disease? Are affective disorders (1) psychosocial reactions to the progressive, unpredictable, and chronic nature of the disease; (2) clinical manifestations of neurobiological impairments attributable to the disease process; or (3) are both the disease and the affective disorders the result of some common causal agent, such as a genetic defect?

Third, compared to persons with other chronic diseases and physical disabilities, persons with multiple sclerosis express both greater variability and more intensity in their psychosocial reactions to the disease but do not appear to differ in the types of coping strategies selected. Fourth, individuals with multiple sclerosis are more likely to select emotion-focused than problem-focused coping strategies. Research suggests that the selection of emotion-focused coping strategies is related to (1) high level of illness uncertainty; (2) manifesting the psychosocial reactions of anger, fear, denial, and depression; (3) more negative self-esteem; and (4) the presence of symptom exacerbations. Finally, research concerning characteristics associated with psychosocial adaptation in persons with multiple sclerosis suggests that adaptation is (1) directly related to symptom remission, feelings of personal control, and social and family support; and (2) inversely related to age, severity of functional disability, symptom exacerbation, loss of social support, and perceptions of illness intrusiveness and of illness uncertainty.

An illustration of the difficulties encountered by researchers who study psychosocial adaptation to multiple sclerosis is the question of whether it is related to chronicity of disability. Results of research using samples of persons with impairments other than multiple sclerosis have indicated that adaptation increases with increasing chronicity, yet studies have consistently reported the lack of a linear relationship between chronicity and adaptation in a variety of samples using a variety of measures (Larsen, 1990; Maybury & Brewin, 1984; McIvor et al., 1984; Pavlou & Counte, 1982; Pollock et al., 1990; Rabins et al., 1986; Zeldow & Pavlou, 1984). A plausible explanation for this unexpected finding may be found by examining the results of the investigations by Matson and Brooks (1977) and by Brooks and Matson (1982). In particular, the relationship between these two variables may more correctly be viewed as curvilinear.

As predicted in the model of Stewart and Sullivan (1982), nonadaptive reactions of anxiety, irritability, and depression are common during the period when symptoms of multiple sclerosis are first apparent. With diagnosis a brief period of acceptance occurs because of the reduction of uncertainty and associated stress, the increased support from the person's family, the person's realization that death is not imminent, and the initiation of therapeutic symptom treatment. This period is followed, however, by a period of pronounced and prolonged disintegration, with the reappearance of the reactions of depression, irritability, anger, and hostility. Regressions to earlier phases of the hypothesized adaptation process are predictable from the renewed life crises associated with unexpected exacerbations of physical symptoms and the resultant imposition of disability. Depending on the course of the disease and a variety of situational variables, some persons with multiple sclerosis may gradually evince acceptance of and successful adjustment to the disease. Other persons with multiple sclerosis may continually cycle through a sequence of nonadaptive and quasi-adaptive reactions consequent to repeated cycles of exacerbations and remissions. The failure of research investigating the relationship between chronicity and psychosocial adaptation to demonstrate the predicted linear relationship is understandable under these circumstances. A hypothesized, complex, curvilinear relationship between chronicity and adaptation cannot be tested with univariate statistical analyses of data obtained using unidimensional instruments with small and nonrepresentative samples in cross-sectional research.

REFERENCES

Arias Bal, M. A., Vázquez-Barquero, J. L., Peña, C., Miro, J., & Berciano, J. A. (1991). Psychiatric aspects of multiple sclerosis. *Acta Psychiatrica Scandinavica, 83,* 292–296.

Baldwin, M. V. (1952). A clinico-experimental investigation into the psychologic aspects of multiple sclerosis. *Journal of Nervous and Mental Diseases, 115,* 299–342.

Baretz, R. M., & Stephenson, G. R. (1981). Emotional responses to multiple sclerosis. *Psychosomatics, 22,* 117–127.

Berrios, G. E., & Quemada, J. I. (1990). Depressive illness in multiple sclerosis: Clinical and theoretical aspects of the association. *British Journal of Psychiatry, 156,* 10–16.

Bourestom, N. C., & Howard, M. T. (1965). Personality characteristics of three disability groups. *Archives of Physical Medicine and Rehabilitation, 46,* 626–632.

Braham, S., Houser, H. B., Cline, A., & Poser, M. (1975). Evaluation of the social needs of nonhospitalized chronically ill persons. *Journal of Chronic Diseases, 28,* 401–419.

Brooks, N. A., & Matson, R. R. (1982). Social-psychological adjustment to multiple sclerosis. *Social Science and Medicine, 16,* 2129–2135.

Buelow, J. M. (1991). A correlational study of disabilities, stressors, and coping methods in victims of multiple sclerosis. *Journal of Neurosurgical Nursing, 23,* 247–252.

Burnfield, A., & Burnfield, P. (1978). Common psychological problems in multiple sclerosis. *British Medical Journal, 1,* 1193–1194.

Canter, A. H. (1951). MMPI profiles in multiple sclerosis. *Journal of Consulting Psychology, 15,* 253–256.

Chodoff, P. (1959). Adjustment to disability: Some observations on patients with multiple sclerosis. *Journal of Chronic Diseases, 9,* 653–670.

Crawford, J. D., & McIvor, G. P. (1985). Group psychotherapy: Benefits in multiple sclerosis. *Archives of Physical Medicine and Rehabilitation, 66,* 810–823.

Dalos, N. P., Rabins, P. V., Brooks, B. R., & O'Donnell, P. (1983). Disease activity and emotional state in multiple sclerosis. *Annals of Neurology, 13,* 573–577.

Davis, L. J., Osborne, D., Siemens, P. J., & Brown, J. R. (1971). MMPI correlates with disability in multiple sclerosis. *Psychological Reports, 28,* 700–702.

Devins, G. M., Edworthy, S. M., Seland, T. P., Klein, G. M., Paul, L. C., & Mandin, H. (1993). Differences in illness intrusiveness across rheumatoid arthritis, end-stage renal disease, and multiple sclerosis. *Journal of Nervous and Mental Diseases, 181,* 377–381.

Devins, G. M., & Seland, T. P. (1987). Emotional impact of multiple sclerosis: Recent findings and suggestions for future research. *Psychological Bulletin, 101,* 363–375.

Devins, G. M., Seland, T. P., Klein, G. M., Edworthy, S. M., & Saary, M. J. (1993). Stability and determinants of psychosocial well-being in multiple sclerosis. *Rehabilitation Psychology, 38,* 11–26.

Duval, M. L. (1984). Psychosocial metaphors of physical distress among MS patients. *Social Science and Medicine, 19,* 635–638.

Eklund, V.-A., & MacDonald, M. L. (1991). Descriptions of persons with multiple sclerosis, with an emphasis on what is needed from psychologists. *Professional Psychology: Research and Practice, 22,* 277–284.

Falvo, D. R. (1991). *Medical and psychosocial aspects of chronic illness and disability.* Gaithersburg, MD: Aspen.

Folkman, S., & Lazarus, R. S. (1988). Coping as a mediator of emotion. *Journal of Personality and Social Psychology, 54,* 466–475.

Garland, F. J., & Zis, A. P. (1991). Multiple sclerosis and affective disorders. *Canadian Journal of Psychiatry, 36,* 112–117.

Gilberstadt, H., & Farkas, E. (1961). Another look at MMPI profile types in multiple sclerosis. *Journal of Consulting Psychology, 25,* 440–444.

Halligan, F. R., & Reznikoff, M. (1985). Personality factors and change with multiple sclerosis. *Journal of Consulting and Clinical Psychology, 53,* 547–548.

Handron, D. S. (1993). Denial and serious chronic illness—A personal perspective. *Perspectives in Psychiatric Care, 29*(1), 29–33.

Harrower, M. R., & Kraus, J. (1951). Psychological studies on patients with multiple sclerosis. *Archives of Neurology and Psychiatry, 66,* 44–57.

Ivnik, R. J. (1978). Neuropsychological stability in multiple sclerosis. *Journal of Consulting and Clinical Psychology, 46,* 913–923.

Kinley, A. E. (1980). MS: From shock to acceptance. *American Journal of Nursing, 74,* 71–73.

Kraft, G. H. (1981). Multiple sclerosis. In W. C. Stolov & M. R. Clowers (Eds.), *Handbook of severe disability* (pp. 111–118). Washington, DC: U. S. Department of Education, Rehabilitation Services Administration.

Kübler-Ross, E. (1969). *On death and dying.* New York: Macmillan.

Kurtzke, J. F. (1961). On the evaluation of disability in multiple sclerosis. *Neurology, 11,* 686–694.

Langworthy, O. R. (1950). A survey of the maladjustment problems in multiple sclerosis and the possibilities of psychotherapy. *Research Publications. Association for Research in Nervous and Mental Diseases, 28*, 598–611.

LaRocca, N. G. (1984). Psychosocial factors in multiple sclerosis and the role of stress. *Annals of the New York Academy of Sciences, 436*, 435–442.

Larsen, P. D. (1990). Psychosocial adjustment in multiple sclerosis. *Rehabilitation Nursing, 15*, 242–246.

Lazarus, R. S., & Folkman, S. (1984). *Stress, appraisal, and coping.* New York: Springer.

Lemere, F. (1966). Psychiatric disorders in multiple sclerosis. *American Journal of Psychiatry, 122*(Suppl. 12), 55–57.

Mahler, M. E. (1992). Behavioral manifestations associated with multiple sclerosis. *Psychiatric Clinics of North America, 15*, 427–438.

Marks, S. F. (1990). Nursing assessment of positive adjustment for individuals with multiple sclerosis. *Rehabilitation Nursing, 15*, 147–151.

Marsh, G. G., Ellison, G. W., & Strite, C. (1983). Psychosocial and vocational rehabilitation approaches of multiple sclerosis. *Annual Review of Rehabilitation, 3*, 242–267.

Matson, R., & Brooks, N. (1977). Adjusting to multiple sclerosis: An exploratory study. *Social Science and Medicine, 11*, 245–250.

Matthews, S. (1993). *Multiple sclerosis: The facts* (3rd ed.). New York: Oxford University Press.

Maybury, C. P., & Brewin, C. R. (1984). Social relationships, knowledge and adjustment to multiple sclerosis. *Journal of Neurology, Neurosurgery, and Psychiatry, 47*, 372–376.

McDonald, W. I. (1983). Attitudes to the treatment of multiple sclerosis. *Archives of Neurology, 40*, 667–670.

McIvor, G. P., Riklan, M., & Reznikoff, M. (1984). Depression in multiple sclerosis as a function of length and severity of illness, age, remissions, and perceived social support. *Journal of Clinical Psychology, 40*, 1028–1033.

McNamara, M. E. (1991). Psychological factors affecting neurological conditions: Depression and stroke, multiple sclerosis, Parkinson's disease, and epilepsy. *Psychosomatics, 32*, 255–267.

Mei-Tal, V., Meyerowitz, S., & Engel, G. L. (1970). The role of psychological process in a somatic disorder: Multiple sclerosis. *Psychosomatic Medicine, 32*, 67–86.

Millefiorini, E., Padovani, A., Pozzilli, C., Loriedo, C., Bastianello, S., Buttinelli, C., DiPiero, V., & Fieschi, C. (1992). Depression in the early phase of MS: Influence of functional disability, cognitive impairment and brain abnormalities. *Acta Neurologica Scandinavica, 86*, 354–358.

Minden, S. L., Orav, J., & Reich, P. (1987). Depression in multiple sclerosis. *General Hospital Psychiatry, 9*, 426–434.

Pavlou, M., & Counte, M. (1982). Aspects of coping in multiple sclerosis. *Rehabilitation Counseling Bulletin, 25*, 138–145.

Peyser, J. M., Edwards, K. R., & Poser, C. M. (1980). Psychological profiles in patients with multiple sclerosis: A preliminary investigation. *Archives of Neurology, 37*, 437–440.

Peyser, J. M., Edwards, K. R., Poser, C. M., & Filskov, S. B. (1980). Cognitive function in patients with multiple sclerosis. *Archives of Neurology, 37*, 577–579.

Philippopoulos, G. S., Wittkower, E. D., & Cousineau, A. (1958). The etiologic significance of emotional factors in onset and exacerbation of multiple sclerosis. *Psychosomatic Medicine, 20*, 458–474.

Pollock, S. E., Christian, B. J., & Sands, D. (1990). Responses to chronic illness: Analysis of psychological and physiological adaptation. *Nursing Research, 39*, 300–304.

Power, P. (1984). Adolescent reaction to parental neurological illness: Coping and intervention strategies. *Pediatric Social Work, 3*(2), 45–52.

Power, P. W. (1985). Family coping behavior in chronic illness: A rehabilitation perspective. *Rehabilitation Literature, 46*, 78–83.

Rabins, P. V., Brooks, B. R., O'Donnell, P., Pearlson, G. D., Moberg, P., Jubelt, B., Coyle, P., Dalos, N., & Folstein, M. F. (1986). Structured brain correlates of emotional disorders in multiple sclerosis. *Brain, 109*, 585–597.

Rao, S. M., Leo, G. L., Ellington, L., Nauertz, T., Bernardin, L., & Unverzagt, F. (1991). Cognitive dysfunction in multiple sclerosis: II. Impact on employment and social functioning. *Neurology, 41*, 692–696.

Riklan, M., Levita, E., & Diller, L. (1961). Psychologic studies in neurologic disease—A review: Parkinson's disease and multiple sclerosis. *Journal of the American Geriatrics Society, 9*, 857–867.

Scheinberg, L., & Holland, N. (1987). *Multiple sclerosis: A guide for patients and families* (2nd ed.). New York: Raven Press.

Schiffer, R. B. (1987). The spectrum of depression in multiple sclerosis. *Archives of Neurology, 44*, 596–599.

Schiffer, R. B., & Babigian, H. M. (1984). Behavioral disorders in multiple sclerosis, temporal lobe epilepsy, and amyotrophic lateral sclerosis. *Archives of Neurology, 41*, 1067–1069.

Schiffer, R. B., Rudick, R. A., & Herndon, R. M. (1983). Psychologic aspects of multiple sclerosis. *New York State Journal of Medicine, 83*, 312–316.

Schiffer, R. B., Wineman, N. M., & Weitkamp, L. R. (1986). Association between bipolar affective disorder and multiple sclerosis. *American Journal of Psychiatry, 143*, 94–95.

Schneitzer, L. (1978). Rehabilitation of patients with multiple sclerosis. *Archives of Physical Medicine and Rehabilitation, 59*, 430–437.

Schubert, D. S. P., & Foliart, R. H. (1993). Increased depression in multiple sclerosis patients: A metaanalysis. *Psychosomatics, 34*, 124–130.

Shontz, F. C. (1955). MMPI responses of patients with multiple sclerosis. *Journal of Consulting Psychology, 19*, 74.

Shontz, F. C. (1956). Some psychological problems of patients with multiple sclerosis. *Archives of Physical Medicine and Rehabilitation, 37*, 218–220.

Smith, C., & Scheinberg, L. (1990). Symptomatic treatment and rehabilitation in multiple sclerosis. In S. D. Cook (Ed.), *Handbook of multiple sclerosis* (pp. 327–349). New York: Marcel Dekker.

Stenager, E. (1991). Historical and psychiatric aspects of multiple sclerosis. *Acta Psychiatrica Scandinavica, 84*, 398.

Stenager, E., Knudsen, L., & Jensem, K. (1991). Multiple sclerosis: The impact of physical impairment and cognitive dysfunction on social and sparetime activities. *Psychotherapy and Psychosomatics, 56*, 123–128.

Stenager, E. N., Stenager, E., Koch-Henriksen, M., Brønnum-Hansen, H., Hyllested, K., Jensem, K., & Bille-Brake, U. (1992). Suicide and multiple sclerosis: An epidemiological investigation. *Journal of Neurology, Neurosurgery, and Psychiatry, 55*, 542–545.

Stewart, D. C., & Sullivan, T. J. (1982). Illness behavior and the sick role in chronic disease: The case of multiple sclerosis. *Social Science and Medicine, 16*, 1397–1404.

Stuifbergen, A. K. (1988). *Chronic physical illness and family functioning: An analysis of the impact of spouses' perceptions of severity of illness and consensus between spouses on dimensions of family functioning.* Unpublished doctoral dissertation, University of Texas at Austin, Austin, TX.

Sugar, C., & Nadell, R. (1948). Mental symptoms in multiple sclerosis. *Journal of Nervous and Mental Diseases, 98,* 267–280.

Surridge, D. H. (1969). An investigation into some psychiatric aspects of multiple sclerosis. *British Journal of Psychiatry, 115,* 749–764.

Tan, S.-Y. (1986). Psychosocial functioning of adult epileptic and MS patients and adult normal controls on the WPSI. *Journal of Clinical Psychology, 42,* 528–534.

Tarbell, D. J. (1980). Coping with multiple sclerosis: Strange encounters of the demyelinating kind. *Journal of Applied Rehabilitation Counseling, 11,* 177–182.

Walsh, P. A., & Walsh, A. (1987). Self-esteem and disease adaptation among multiple sclerosis patients. *Journal of Social Psychology, 127,* 669–671.

Warren, S., Warren, K. G., & Cockerill, R. (1991). Emotional stress coping in multiple sclerosis (MS) exacerbation. *Journal of Psychosomatic Research, 35,* 37–47.

Wassem, R. (1991). A test of the relationship between health locus of control and the course of multiple sclerosis. *Rehabilitation Nursing, 16,* 189–193.

Wassem, R. (1992). Self-efficacy as a predictor of adjustment to multiple sclerosis. *Journal of Neuroscience Nursing, 24,* 224–229.

Wassem, R. A. (1987). A test of Bandura's social learning theory: Predicting adjustment to chronic physical disability. (Doctoral dissertation, Indiana University School of Nursing, 1987). *Doctoral dissertation* (University Microfilms No. PUZ8820239).

Whitlock, F. A., & Siskind, M. M. (1980). Depression as a major symptom of multiple sclerosis. *Journal of Neurology, Neurosurgery, and Psychiatry, 43,* 861–865.

Wineman, N. M. (1990). Adaptation to multiple sclerosis: The role of social support, functional disability, and perceived uncertainty. *Nursing Research, 39,* 294–299.

Wineman, N. M., Durand, E. J., & Steiner, R. P. (1994). A comparative analysis of coping behaviors in persons with multiple sclerosis or a spinal cord injury. *Research in Nursing and Health, 17,* 185–194.

Wineman, N. M., O'Brien, R. A., Nealon, N. R., & Kashel, B. (1993). Congruence in uncertainty between individuals with multiple sclerosis and their spouses. *Journal of Neuroscience Nursing, 25,* 356–361.

Zeldow, P. B., & Pavlou, M. (1984). Physical disability, life stress, and psychosocial adjustment in multiple sclerosis. *Journal of Nervous and Mental Diseases, 172,* 80–84.

Zeldow, P. B., & Pavlou, M. (1988). Physical and psychosocial functioning in multiple sclerosis: Descriptions, correlations, and a tentative typology. *British Journal of Medical Psychology, 61,* 185–195.

CHAPTER 15

Cerebral Palsy

DESCRIPTION

Although there are references to "palsy" in the Old Testament, "palsies of cerebral origin" were first described clinically in 1843 by William J. Little and became known as Little's Disease. The term cerebral palsy (literally "brain weakness") was coined by William Osler, a professor of surgery at Johns Hopkins University, in his work with a group of residents with physical impairments at the Elwyn Institute in Pennsylvania. Cerebral palsy is a generic term referring to a family of impairments of muscle tone (eg, spasticity, rigidity), muscle control (eg, writhing or jerky movements, twitching, quivering), or locomotion (eg, impairment of posture, balance, walking) resulting from permanent and nonprogressive defects or lesions of the immature brain (Bax, 1964; Falvo, 1991). Although the neurological impairment is primary, individuals with cerebral palsy typically manifest secondary disabilities, varying with the location, severity, and extent of the brain injury; the development of the brain and the body; and the treatment the individual receives (Easton & Halpern, 1981; Kohn, 1990). Secondary disabilities may include sensory disorders, seizures, cognitive impairment, medical complications (eg, heart defects, asthma, dental abnormalities), and speech and language disabilities (Gold, 1993; Robinson, 1973).

The incidence of cerebral palsy in the United States is estimated to range from 1 to 4 per 1,000 live births, with approximately 9,000 new cases identified each year and a prevalence of nearly 1 million affected individuals. A large number of causal agents—essentially anything that can result in brain injury—have been identified and can be classified as either hereditary (less than 5% of cases; microcephaly, sickle cell disease), prenatal (45% of cases; rubella, Rh hemolytic disease, maternal diabetes), perinatal (30% of cases; placental pathology, anoxia, birth injury, low birth weight), or neonatal (20% of cases; trauma, hemorrhage, encephalitis, respiratory distress, toxemia, malnutrition). The overall birth rate of babies with severe congenital brain injuries later leading to a classification as cerebral palsy is dropping, but advances over the past three decades in neurosurgical and neonatal intensive care of these babies, combined with a rehabilitation philosophy espousing early, comprehensive, and vigorous therapy, have increased the likelihood of survival for individuals with significant functional disabilities, most of whom are living and being served in community settings (Blum, Resnick, Nelson, & St. Germaine, 1991; Gold, 1993; Hirose & Ueda, 1990).

PSYCHOSOCIAL ADAPTATION TO CEREBRAL PALSY

Researchers and theorists have argued for more than 40 years that individuals with cerebral palsy are predisposed to negative psychosocial reactions to their physical disabilities (Cruickshank, 1952; Freeman, 1970; Gething, 1985; Hourcade & Parette, 1984; Jureidini, 1988; Rose, 1984). Psychosocial reactions of people with cerebral palsy are thought to range on a continuum, from shyness, apathy, and withdrawal; through denial, anxiety, and passive dependency; to demandingness, hostility, aggressiveness, and anger. These reactions, in turn, limit positive interactions with others and may lead to loss of self-esteem, distorted self-concept, and further isolation. Explanations that are most frequently advanced in this literature include the following:

- Physical limitations of the infant with cerebral palsy quantitatively and qualitatively reduce opportunities to explore and master the environment.
- The toddler with cerebral palsy may internalize parental reactions of depression, anxiety, and irritability as feelings of inferiority and rejection.
- Parental overprotection out of concern for the child's well-being prolongs dependency and restricts access to important but risky experiences that are essential to the development of adaptive coping strategies.
- Confrontations with the typical consequences of behavior prevent the child from learning to express anger and disappointment in acceptable ways.
- Parental pressure to achieve encourages behaviors in some children that are viewed by others as rude, aggressive, or hostile. In other children, pressure engenders feelings of inadequacy that are manifest as passivity, shyness, or withdrawal.
- Frequent and often painful physical and medical treatments (eg, surgery, fitting prostheses, physical therapy), combined with health care environments that may not be supportive of the individual's independence, produce stresses that contribute to feelings of vulnerability, apprehension, and anxiety about rehabilitation services.

- Segregated or restrictive education programs do not provide important socializing experiences.
- Stereotyped negative attitudes of others engender feelings of inferiority, self-consciousness, and rejection that may be incorporated into the individual's self-image.
- The adolescent with cerebral palsy has limited opportunities to participate in sports, clubs, and social activities, isolating the individual from his or her peers.
- Physical appearance becomes more important to the adolescent, sexual drives are largely unfulfilled, and the demands of adulthood loom large.
- Diminished mobility hinders access to recreational resources and limits involvement in the social world.
- Architectural and transportation barriers restrict employment and independent living opportunities for adults with cerebral palsy.

Support for these contentions has been derived from a variety of sources, including ethnographic case summaries of individuals with cerebral palsy (Bursztajn, Gutheil, Warren, & Brodsky, 1986; McCraig & Frank, 1991; Richardson, 1972); insights from clinical or personal experience (Freeman, 1970; Jureidini, 1988; Rappaport, 1961; Richardson, 1963; Richardson, Hastorf, & Dornbusch, 1964); responses to semistructured interview questions or to projective devices (Cruickshank, 1952; Cullinan & Riklan, 1979; Resnick & Hutton, 1987; Romanova, 1983; Sherrill, Hinson, Gench, Kennedy, & Low, 1990; Stensman, 1989; Weinberg & Williams, 1978); analyses of data from informants, typically the mother or teacher of young persons with cerebral palsy (Breslau, 1983; Breslau, 1985; Breslau & Marshall, 1985); or extrapolations of research findings concerning psychosocial adaptation of individuals to other neurological impairments, particularly traumatic brain injury (Mattsson, 1972; Minde, 1978).

In one of the earliest case-controlled investigations of psychosocial adaptation of persons with cerebral palsy, Cruickshank (1952) collected the responses to a sentence completion projective device of 264 junior and senior high school students with physical disabilities and 264 peers matched for age and sex. Among the students with disabilities, 40 had cerebral palsy. The scoring of the responses suggested that the children with physical disabilities as a group were more insecure and anxious concerning their social position, felt greater dissatisfaction with society, tended to withdraw from social situations, had fewer typical adolescent interests, engaged in more fantasy ideation, and were generally psychosocially immature.

The results of a number of surveys have reported a higher than expected risk for psychosocial and psychiatric distress among persons with cerebral palsy. Glick (1953) found that 57% of a nonrandom sample of 150 adults with cerebral palsy seeking job assistance at a rehabilitation center displayed emotional problems considered significant impediments to job placement. Storrow and Jones (1960), using subjective criteria of dubious reliability, found that 48% of a nonrandom sample of adolescents and young adults with cerebral palsy at a vocational training center manifested symptoms of functional psychiatric illness and that in 34% of the sample the symptoms would justify a psychiatric diagnosis. Perrin, Ramsey, and Sandler (1987) collected informant data from the teachers and parents of children aged 5 to 16 years, 47 of whom had various orthopaedic impairments including cerebral palsy. The ratings of the school and social competence of the children with orthopaedic impairments were significantly below those for a comparison group of children without disabilities.

The results of several large-scale surveys in which children with cerebral palsy have been included among samples of children with orthopaedic and chronic health impairments suggest an increased risk of poor psychosocial adaptation. In a study conducted in Cleveland (Breslau, 1983; Breslau, 1985), 304 children aged 6 to 18 years with physical disabilities, of whom 98 had cerebral palsy and 78 were multiply impaired, were identified from the case records of two hospitals and four clinics. Data were also collected from siblings without disabilities of nearly two thirds of the children with disabilities and from a random probability sample of 360 children without disabilities of the same ages. The mothers of the children in all groups served as informants using the Psychiatric Screening Inventory to measure risk for psychiatric problems in seven areas: (1) self-destructive tendencies, (2) mentation problems, (3) conflict with parents, (4) regressive anxiety, (5) fighting, (6) delinquency, and (7) isolation. Analyses of the data revealed that the scores for the children with cerebral palsy exceeded the scores for the children without disabilities (ie, indicated more psychosocial morbidity) on a composite of the seven scales and on the scales measuring risk of mentation problems, conflict with parents, regressive anxiety, and isolation. When compared to their siblings, the children with cerebral palsy were found to be significantly different on the scales measuring mentation problems, delinquency, and isolation, but not significantly different on the composite measure.

The children with and without disabilities were divided into groups representing level of severity of psychiatric problems using the composite Psychiatric Screening Inventory (PSI) score. A total of 30% of the children with cerebral palsy were reported to be at risk for severe psychiatric problems. When the profiles of the 83 children with disabilities and the 39 children without disabilities who exceeded the cutoff for severe problems were compared, it was revealed that the children with disabilities were at highest risk for mentation problems and isolation and the children without disabilities were at highest risk for fighting and delinquency. Among the children with disabilities, level of cognitive functioning (as measured by intelligence quotient (IQ) score) and adaptive behavior (as measured by activities of daily living skill score) were found to account for the differences in mentation problem scores but not for the differences in isolation scores. The mothers of 82 of the children with cerebral palsy completed the PSI a second time an average of five years after the first occasion (Breslau & Marshall, 1985). There were no significant changes in any of the scale scores for the children with cerebral palsy, an observation that led the authors to a pessimistic view of the psychiatric prognosis for these children.

The mothers of a nonrandom sample of 270 children between the ages of 4 and 16 years with six types of chronic physical disabilities, including 19 children who had cerebral palsy, completed the Child Behavior Check List, an inventory of psychosocial behavior in three areas: (1) internalized behavior problems, (2) externalized behavior problems, and (3) social competence (Wallander, Varni, Babani, Banis, & Wilcox, 1988). As a group, these children's scores corresponded to the 75th percentile rank for internalized behavior problems, the 69th percentile rank for externalized behavior problems, and the 12th percentile rank for social competence. The children with cerebral palsy were reported at greatest risk in the area of social competence as their scores on this scale were significantly lower than the scores for any of the other groups of children with disabilities who did not differ on this scale.

In another set of studies (Wallander, Varni, Babani, Banis, De Haan, et al., 1989; Wallander, Varni, Babani, De Haan, et al., 1989), Child Behavior Check List data for 27 children aged 6 to 11 years with cerebral palsy revealed that the scores on the internalized and externalized behavior problems scales corresponded to the 84th and 82nd percentile ranks, respectively, but the social competence scores corresponded only to the 4th percentile rank. And yet another set of studies (Wallander & Varni, 1989; Wallander, Varni, Babani, Banis, & Wilcox, 1989) analyzed Child Behavior Check List data for a sample of 17 children with cerebral palsy among a group of 153 children aged 4 to 16 years with five different chronic illnesses and disabilities. The scores for the children with disabilities (there were no significant differences among the five groups of children with disabilities) on the internalized and externalized behavior problems scales corresponded to the 75th and 65th percentile ranks, respectively.

Findings concerning increased risk for psychosocial distress among persons with cerebral palsy have been reported in investigations conducted in countries other than the United States. As part of a follow-up study of 34 of an original group of 41 children with cerebral palsy who attended a private school for children with physical disabilities in Montréal, Minde (1978) collected parent and teacher report data using a checklist of symptoms of psychosocial distress. A total of 18% of the children were diagnosed with either a conduct or a neurotic disorder. In a large-scale follow-up survey using national registry and hospital records concerning 12,058 individuals born in northern Finland in 1966

(Mailanen & Rantakallio, 1988), a total of 445 individuals with disabilities, including epilepsy, cerebral palsy, and mental retardation, were identified. Psychiatric disorders were found to be nine times more frequent among those with disabilities (47 of 445 or 105.6 per 1,000) than among those without disabilities (167 of 11,023 or 15.1 per 1,000). Another study in Finland (Kokkonen, Saukkonen, Timonen, Serlo, & Kinnunen, 1991) compared the social outcomes of a group of 52 individuals aged 19 to 26 years with physical disabilities, 48 of whom were diagnosed with cerebral palsy, with a random sample of 209 controls of roughly the same age and sex distributions and born in the same geographical area. Only 16% of those with cerebral palsy completed secondary school, 58% were living at home with their parents, 88% were single, and 37% were competitively employed. The percentages for these four characteristics for the individuals without disabilities were 51%, 35%, 64%, and 56%, respectively. A total of 11% of the individuals with cerebral palsy reported that loneliness was a "major problem."

Anderson (1979), in Great Britain, interviewed nonrandom samples of 89 adolescents with cerebral palsy and 30 adolescents with spina bifida who were over the age of 15 years together with controls matched for age and sex. Two thirds of the adolescents with disabilities were attending special schools; 21% were classified as mildly disabled; 36% as moderately disabled; and 43% as severely disabled. Among those with disabilities, 33% were judged to have marked psychological problems and 19% to have borderline psychological problems. Psychosocial reactions most commonly reported were depression, low self-confidence, fear of new situations and of meeting new people (especially peers of the opposite sex), and anxiety about the future, particularly about employment and marriage. Only 21% of the students with disabilities rated their out-of-school social life as satisfying versus 94% of the control students; only 20% reported they dated a student of the opposite sex, even though most were interested in doing so, compared with 73% of the control students.

Several attempts to investigate empirically the psychosocial adaptation to disability among persons with cerebral palsy have been reported in the literature. Eggland (1973) hypothesized that individuals with disabilities who manifest external locus of control will view their disability as a greater threat than will individuals with disabilities who manifest internal locus of control and as a result will have greater difficulty adjusting to their disability and less success in habilitation efforts. Locus of control of a group of 20 children with cerebral palsy in grades one and four who were attending a special public school for children with physical disabilities was compared with locus of control of a group of 82 children without disabilities in these same two grades in the same school system. It was found that the children with cerebral palsy at both grades were more external than the children without disabilities and that no sex differences existed among the children with cerebral palsy. Eggland concluded that efforts should be made to change the locus of control of children with cerebral palsy from external to internal in order to increase the likelihood of adaptation to their disability and the success of psychosocial habilitation efforts.

In a study of children attending ordinary schools in Scotland (O'Moore, 1980), the psychosocial adaptation characteristics of a group of 38 children with physical disabilities, 58% of whom had cerebral palsy, was compared with those of a group of children without disabilities matched for sex, age, IQ, family composition, socioeconomic status, and home circumstances. The children with cerebral palsy, whose ages ranged from 9 to 12 years, all had average intelligence, vision, and hearing. Analyses of data from a battery of instruments (ie, California Test of Personality, Junior Eysenck Personality Scale, Bristol Social Adjustment Guides, and a social acceptance test measuring appearance, popularity in school, and rejection by peers) indicated that the children with physical disabilities as a group scored lower than the children without disabilities on social acceptance, social adaptation, and self-concept. In addition, significant correlations were found between social acceptance scores and scores representing perception of personal worth, feelings of belonging, and composite emotional adaptation.

Blum et al. (1991) collected data on the Beck Depression Inventory, the Offer Self-Image Questionnaire for Adolescents, and the Rosenberg Self-Esteem Inventory from a group of 60 adolescents and young adults with cerebral palsy whose ages ranged from 12 to 22 years. A total of 50% of the sample used a wheelchair and 90% lived at home. Although 98% of the sample reported being treated well by their parents, 33% reported that their parents treated them as infants sometimes, and 25% reported that they were overprotected by their parents. A noticeable absence of self-reports of conflicts with parents that are typical for adolescents and young adults without disabilities was interpreted as an indication of closeness to parents that might impair autonomy and delay independence. Self-reports of activities revealed a generally restricted social life, especially with regard to dating, but 77% of the sample hoped to someday marry and have children.

King, Shultz, Steel, Gilpin, and Cathers (1993) designed a study to investigate the hypothesis that how adolescents with physical disabilities value and view themselves should be significant predictors of psychosocial adaptation to their disabilities. A total of 53 male and female individuals aged 14 to 18 years with average intelligence, 28 of whom had cerebral palsy, completed a battery of instruments measuring self-efficacy, attitudes toward physical disabilities, personal values, and interpersonal style. As predicted, the responses of the adolescents in this study were significantly below published norms on the variables measuring self-perceptions of romantic appeal, scholastic competence, social acceptance, independence, and persistence.

In contrast to these findings of increased risk for psychosocial maladaptation among individuals with cerebral palsy are the results of a small number of empirical studies. Banham (1973), for example, reported no significant differences in the social and emotional adaptation, as measured by a set of scales developed for this investigation, of a group of 37 children with cerebral palsy attending a specialized preschool program at Duke University (age range 18 to 60 months, mean IQ = 73) and a group of 47 children without disabilities matched for age and sex. Andrews, Platt, Quinn, and Nielson (1977) collected data on the work, social, and psychological adaptation of a nonrandom sample of 50 males with cerebral palsy ranging in age from 17 to 55 years (mean = 28 years) and in IQ from 62 to 118 (mean = 83), all of whom were attending a specialized vocational center in Australia. Scores on the General Health Questionnaire, the measure of psychological adaptation, did not differ significantly from the General Health Questionnaire norms for the general population. In a comparison of a group of 15 children aged 4 to 8 years with cerebral palsy and a group of children without disabilities matched for age, sex, ethnicity, IQ, and socioeconomic status (Teplin, Howard, & O'Connor, 1981), it was reported that teachers rated the children with cerebral palsy significantly below their peers without disabilities on the Coopersmith Behavior Rating Form, but there was no difference in self-concept scores between the two groups, as measured by the Purdue Self-Concept Scale for Preschool Children.

Magill and Hurlbut (1986), arguing that one's physical self-evaluation is an important determinant of one's self-esteem, especially during adolescence, compared scores on the Tennessee Self-Concept Scale of a group of 11 male and 11 female adolescents, aged 13 to 18 years, with cerebral palsy with a group of adolescents without disabilities matched for age and sex. Five of the males and five of the females with cerebral palsy were judged to be mildly impaired, four of each were judged to be moderately impaired, and two of each to be severely impaired (requiring a wheelchair). The researchers discovered no significant differences between the adolescents with and without disabilities on either the total Tennessee Self-Concept Scale score or on any of the seven subscales. Magill-Evans and Restall (1991) completed a follow-up seven years later of a total of 39 of the original sample of individuals with cerebral palsy plus their matched peers without disabilities. An increase in the mean self-concept scores from the original to the follow-up study suggested that as adults, individuals with cerebral palsy have a wider choice of environments available to them and experience more positive interpersonal interactions that contribute to a more adapted and positive self-appraisal.

A review of the medical, psychiatric, and psychological literature on psychosocial adaptation to cerebral palsy revealed no studies that conceptualized psychosocial adaptation to cerebral palsy as a set of distinct reactions or as a process of change in reactions that can be ordered hierarchically and temporally.

CHARACTERISTICS ASSOCIATED WITH ADAPTATION TO CEREBRAL PALSY

A few studies were located that attempted to identify characteristics that are associated with or predict psychosocial adaptation to cerebral palsy. These characteristics can be divided into two categories: sociodemographic characteristics (eg, sex, age, self-care skills, mobility, personality attributes, family status variables, intelligence) and neurologically related variables (eg, site of brain lesion, extent of brain damage, presence of a convulsive disorder, associated sensory disabilities).

Results concerning sex differences in psychosocial adaptation have been conflicting. A survey of 445 individuals with disabilities, including epilepsy, cerebral palsy, and mental retardation (Mailanen & Rantakallio, 1988), reported no sex differences in the prevalence of psychiatric disorders. O'Moore (1980) found no sex differences in social acceptance of children aged 9 to 12 years. Similarly Wallander and colleagues (Wallander & Varni, 1989; Wallander, Varni, Babani, Banis, & Wilcox, 1989) found no significant associations between sex and informant reports of behavior problems or social competence of children with cerebral palsy.

In another investigation by Wallander and colleagues (Wallander, Hubert, & Varni, 1988), however, the analyses of data collected from the mothers of children with cerebral palsy on the Child Behavior Check List and the Dimensions of Temperament Survey showed that, contrary to expectations, males were rated higher on somatic complaints and lower on depression and aggression than females, while the females in the sample were rated higher on hyperactivity, schizoid/obsessive behavior, and cruelty and lower on depression. Other studies also reported significant but not consistent sex differences. For example, females among a nonrandom sample of 47 children aged 5 to 16 years who had various orthopaedic impairments, including cerebral palsy, were rated higher by informants on social and school competence and emotional adaptation than were males (Perrin et al., 1987). On the other hand, Magill and Hurlbut (1986) reported that among 22 adolescents, aged 13 to 18 years, with cerebral palsy the 11 females scored significantly below the 11 males on the subscales of the Tennessee Self-Concept Scale measuring physical self-esteem and social self-esteem. These inconsistent differences may be attributable to the confounding of age and other personality variables with sex in these studies, that is, the importance of physical ability, attractiveness, self-esteem, acceptance, and social participation may vary with developmental stage differently for females than for males, yielding different results concerning the relationship of sex and psychosocial adaptation.

For the same reason (ie, confounding of other variables) the results of investigations of the relationship of age to psychosocial adaptation are also contradictory: several studies have reported a direct relationship (Banham, 1973; Östring & Nieminen, 1982), whereas another has reported an inverse relationship (Susset, Vobecky, & Black, 1979), and still others have reported no relationship between age and psychosocial adaptation (Perrin et al., 1987; Wallander & Varni, 1989; Wallander, Varni, Babani, Banis, & Wilcox, 1989).

The presence and severity of secondary disabilities have been linked to psychosocial adaptation in persons with cerebral palsy in several investigations. For example, Susset, Vobecky, and Black (1979) collected extensive data from 506 individuals, aged 6 to 75 years, with chronic physical disabilities, including 79 persons with cerebral palsy who received services at a large rehabilitation facility in Québec. Data were combined to yield two composite indices, one representing physical adaptation (eg, mobility, self-care, independence) and the other representing psychosocial adaptation (eg, employment, communication, social contacts). Among the individuals with cerebral palsy, the correlation between these two indices was +0.52.

The relationship between adaptation to cerebral palsy and secondary cognitive disability, as measured by intelligence, is fairly clear. Östring and Nieminen (1982) found that among a group of 30 children aged 9 to 13 years with cerebral palsy who were attending a special school in Finland, children who were more intelligent were better adjusted as measured by a set of projective devices (eg, the Rorschach, Children's Seashore House Picture Test). Children with cerebral palsy who had the lowest IQ scores were found to be rated lowest by their mothers on the social competence scale of the Child Behavior Check List (Wallander, Varni, Babani, Banis, De Haan, et al., 1989; Wallander, Varni, Babani, De Haan, et al., 1989). Banham, (1973) reported that among a group of 37 infants with cerebral palsy (age range 18 to 60 months, mean IQ = 73) attending a specialized preschool program at Duke University, scores on measures of social and emotional adaptation increased with increasing IQ.

The associations among several family and environmental variables and adaptation to cerebral palsy have also been studied. Blum et al. (1991) reported that among a group of 60 individuals with cerebral palsy whose ages ranged from 12 to 22 years, those who reported being overprotected by their parents scored significantly lower on measures of happiness, self-esteem, and perceived popularity and scored significantly higher on measures of self-consciousness and anxiety. Other variables that have been found to be positively associated with psychosocial adaptation include living at home as opposed to in a nursing home or hospital (Susset et al., 1979); having opportunities for play and educational interactions with children without disabilities (Minde, 1978); and family income, family cohesion, and maternal education (Wallander & Varni, 1989; Wallander et al., 1989).

Among the personality attributes thought to be linked to successful adaptation to cerebral palsy are positive self-concept (Hourcade & Parette, 1984; King et al., 1993; Östring & Nieminen, 1982); realistic self-assessment of disability (Resnick & Hutton, 1987; Susset et al., 1979; Weinberg, 1976); positive outlook on life (Gething, 1985; Susset et al., 1979); internal locus of control (Eggland, 1973); perceptions of personal worth (O'Moore, 1980); and a combination of cognitive and behavioral coping strategies (Minde, 1978; Rose, 1984).

There is a notable lack of confirmatory evidence for the hypothesized relationship between central nervous system pathology and emotional and behavioral alteration in persons with cerebral palsy. Outcome variables that are thought to be directly related to brain injury but for which confirmatory data are not as yet available include hypersensitivity or hyposensitivity, anosognosia (a decreased awareness of physical or cognitive dysfunction evidenced by a failure to self-monitor), attention deficit, and low frustration tolerance (Hourcade & Parette, 1984; McGlynn & Schacter, 1989; Rosenbloom, 1971).

Andrews et al. (1977) reported that psychological adaptation was not related to level of disability in persons with cerebral palsy, and Cullinan and Riklan (1979) found no significant difference in Minnesota Multiphasic Personality Inventory profiles among 37 young adults with cerebral palsy separated into mild, moderate, and severe levels of physical disability. Magill-Evans and Restall (1991) found no relationship between severity of disability and a measure of self-esteem in a group of 19 young adults with cerebral palsy, a finding similar to that of Resnick and Hutton (1987). Using parent reports to assess risk for psychiatric problems in seven areas (ie, self-destructive tendencies, mentation problems, conflict with parents, regressive anxiety, fighting, delinquency, and isolation), Breslau (1983) and Breslau and Marshall (1985) found that scores for a group of children with cerebral palsy and a group of children with cystic fibrosis (a nonneurological chronic health impairment) exceeded the scores for a comparison group of children without disabilities but that the children with cystic fibrosis were found to be at less risk of psychiatric problems than were the children with cerebral palsy. The authors interpreted these results to mean that children with cerebral palsy are at increased risk for psychiatric problems that are reactive in nature and are not just neurologically based.

In comparison, Scherzer, Ilson, Miké, and Iandoli (1973) found that among a sample of 123 children with cerebral palsy who had attended a specialized treatment and habilitation preschool program, those with the least disabling conditions were most likely to be rated highest on social adaptation and emotional maturity by their teachers. Other researchers reporting negative relationships between severity of impairment and psychosocial adaptation include Anderson (1979) and O'Moore (1980).

CONCLUSION

Children with cerebral palsy, as a group, are at risk for significant problems of overall psychosocial adaptation due to limitations that reduce opportunities to explore and master the environment during infancy and to limitations of educational, recreational, and social opportunities during early childhood. These limitations are related to the child's primary physical impairments, as well as secondary cognitive and communicative impairments, parental and peer reactions, restrictive educational programs, environmental barriers, and low expectations and stereotyped negative attitudes of teachers, medical personnel, and the general public. Support for these contentions has been derived from a variety of sources, including ethnographic case summaries of individuals with cerebral palsy, insights from clinical or personal experience, responses of persons with cerebral palsy to semistructured interview questions or to projective devices, reports of informants (typically the child's mother or teacher), and analyses of data from a small number of empirical investigations.

Among the reactions in which this increased risk is evident are anxiety (especially in novel social situations), immaturity, withdrawal and isolation, and internalized anger. External locus of control, distorted body image, and lowered self-concept are also more prevalent among children with cerebral palsy than among their peers without disabilities. As children with cerebral palsy mature to adolescents and young adults, increased psychosocial risk begins to be expressed in areas related to educational achievement, social competence, dating and sexual behavior, vocational potential, and independence. In addition, psychosocial reactions of depression, anxiety, and externalized anger become more prevalent, as well as lowered self-confidence and self-evaluation. Data from investigations of adults are quite limited but suggest that as adults, individuals with cerebral palsy have a wider choice of environments available to them and experience more positive interpersonal interactions that contribute to a more adapted and positive self-appraisal. Areas of increased risk among adults with cerebral palsy center on vocational success, marriage, and independence.

The few studies that were located concerning the relationships among characteristics associated with cerebral palsy and psychosocial adaptation have generally failed to separate the influence of confounding variables (eg, medication effects, chronicity of impairment), many of which are known to be associated with psychopathology in the general population. Limited support is available for the following tentative conclusions:

- The presence and severity of functional limitations (eg, cognitive, mobility, or communicative impairments) are generally associated with increased expressions of psychosocial maladaptation in children with cerebral palsy. This relationship is somewhat more pronounced among adolescents and is much less pronounced or absent among adults.
- Family variables such as stability, cohesion, income, and realistic parental expectations are associated with positive psychosocial adaptation, as is the presence of social supports for adults with cerebral palsy.
- The relationships among the location, extent, and severity of central nervous system pathology and psychosocial adaptation are unclear at present. Studies that have attempted to relate pathology and personality distortions among individuals with cerebral palsy have yielded contradictory results. The recent availability of sophisticated brain imaging technology should increase the ability of researchers to clarify these important relationships.

Similar to the cautions expressed in previous chapters, the generalizability of the results of the literature reviewed is limited by sampling biases (ie, studying children receiving treatment at specialty clinics or adults who have been hospitalized for psychiatric complaints), small sample sizes, confounding of sample characteristics, and instrumentation weaknesses (ie, using informant reports, nonvalidated self-report measures, or instruments validated for populations other than persons with cerebral palsy). The ways in which persons with cerebral palsy react to their disability are related in complex ways to their developmental, familial, social, personal, and vocational experiences and to how they perceive the consequences of these experiences. These perceptions, in turn, influence the coping strategies they use and the psychosocial reactions that are consequently manifest.

REFERENCES

Anderson, E. (1979). The psychological and social adjustment of adolescents with cerebral palsy or spina bifida and hydrocephalus. *International Journal of Rehabilitation Research, 2*, 245–247.

Andrews, G., Platt, L. J., Quinn, P. T., & Nielson, P. D. (1977). An assessment of the status of adults with cerebral palsy. *Developmental Medicine and Child Neurology, 19*, 803–810.

Banham, K. M. (1973). Social and emotional adjustment of retarded CP infants. *Exceptional Children, 40*, 107.

Bax, M. C. O. (1964). Terminology and classification of cerebral palsy. *Developmental Medicine and Child Neurology, 6*, 295.

Blum, R. W., Resnick, M. D., Nelson, R., & St. Germaine, A. (1991). Family and peer issues among adolescents with spina bifida and cerebral palsy. *Pediatrics, 88*, 280–285.

Breslau, N. (1983). The psychological study of chronically ill and disabled children: Are healthy siblings appropriate controls? *Journal of Abnormal Child Psychology, 11*, 379–391.

Breslau, N. (1985). Psychiatric disorders in children with physical disabilities. *Journal of the American Academy of Child Psychiatry, 24,* 87–94.

Breslau, N., & Marshall, I. A. (1985). Psychological disturbance in children with physical disabilities: Continuity and change in a 5-year followup. *Journal of Abnormal Child Psychology, 13,* 199–216.

Bursztajn, H., Gutheil, T. G., Warren, M. J., & Brodsky, A. (1986). Depression, self-love, time, and the "right" to suicide. *General Hospital Psychiatry, 8,* 91–95.

Cruickshank, W. M. (1952). A study of the relation of physical disability to social adjustment. *American Journal of Occupational Therapy, 6,* 100–109.

Cullinan, T. F., & Riklan, M. (1979). MMPI characteristics associated with cerebral palsy and dystonia musculorum deformans. *Perceptual and Motor Skills, 48,* 1003–1007.

Easton, J. K. M., & Halpern, D. (1981). Cerebral palsy. In W. C. Stolov & M. R. Clowers (Eds.), *Handbook of severe disability* (pp. 137–154). Washington, DC: U. S. Department of Education, Rehabilitation Services Administration.

Eggland, E. T. (1973). Locus of control and children with cerebral palsy. *Nursing Research, 22,* 329–333.

Falvo, D. R. (1991). *Medical and psychosocial aspects of chronic illness and disability.* Gaithersburg, MD: Aspen.

Freeman, R. D. (1970). Psychiatric problems in adolescents with cerebral palsy. *Developmental Medicine and Child Neurology, 12,* 64–70.

Gething, L. (1985). Perceptions of disability of persons with cerebral palsy, their close relatives, and able bodied persons. *Social Science and Medicine, 6,* 561–565.

Glick, S. (1953). Survey of the adult cerebral palsied population. *Cerebral Palsy Review, 14,* 9–18.

Gold, J. T. (1993). Pediatric disorders: Cerebral palsy and spina bifida. In M. G. Eisenberg, R. L. Glueckart, & H. H. Zaretsky (Eds.), *Medical aspects of disability: A handbook for the rehabilitation professional* (pp. 281–306). New York: Springer.

Hirose, T., & Ueda, R. (1990). Long-term follow-up study of cerebral palsy children and coping behavior of parents. *Journal of Advanced Nursing, 15,* 762–770.

Hourcade, J., & Parette, H. P., Jr. (1984). Cerebral palsy and emotional disturbance: A review and implications for intervention. *Journal of Rehabilitation, 50*(3), 55–60.

Jureidini, J. (1988). Psychotherapeutic implications of severe physical disability. *American Journal of Psychotherapy, 42,* 297–307.

King, G. A., Shultz, I. Z., Steel, K., Gilpin, M., & Cathers, T. (1993). Self-evaluation and self-concept of adolescents with physical disabilities. *American Journal of Occupational Therapy, 47,* 132–140.

Kohn, J. G. (1990). Issues in the management of children with spastic cerebral palsy. *Pediatrician, 17,* 230–236.

Kokkonen, J., Saukkonen, A.-L., Timonen, E., Serlo, W., & Kinnunen, P. (1991). Social outcome of handicapped children as adults. *Developmental Medicine and Child Neurology, 33,* 1095–1100.

Magill, J., & Hurlbut, N. (1986). The self-esteem of adolescents with cerebral palsy. *American Journal of Occupational Therapy, 40,* 402–407.

Magill-Evans, J. E., & Restall, G. (1991). Self-esteem of persons with cerebral palsy: From adolescence to adulthood. *American Journal of Occupational Therapy, 45,* 819–825.

Mailanen, I., & Rantakallio, P. (1988). The single parent family and the child's mental health. *Social Science and Medicine, 27,* 181–186.

Mattsson, A. (1972). Long-term physical illness in childhood: A challenge to psychosocial adaptation. *Pediatrics, 5,* 801–811.

McCraig, M., & Frank, G. (1991). The able self: Adaptive patterns and choices in independent living for a person with cerebral palsy. *American Journal of Occupational Therapy, 45,* 224–234.

McGlynn, S. M., & Schacter, D. L. (1989). Unawareness of deficits in neuropsychological syndromes. *Journal of Clinical and Experimental Neuropsychology, 11,* 143–205.

Minde, K. K. (1978). Coping styles of 34 adolescents with cerebral palsy. *American Journal of Psychiatry, 135,* 1344–1349.

O'Moore, M. (1980). Social acceptance of the physically handicapped child in the ordinary school. *Child: Care, Health and Development, 6,* 317–337.

Östring, H., & Nieminen, S. (1982). Concept of self and the attitude of school age CP children towards their handicap. *International Journal of Rehabilitation Research, 5,* 235–237.

Perrin, E. C., Ramsey, B. K., & Sandler, H. M. (1987). Competent kids: Children and adolescents with a chronic illness. *Child: Care, Health and Development, 13,* 13–32.

Rappaport, S. R. (1961). Behavior disorder and ego development in a brain-injured child. *The Psychoanalytic Study of the Child, 16,* 423–501.

Resnick, M. D., & Hutton, L. (1987). Resiliency among physically disabled adolescents. *Psychiatric Annals, 17,* 796–800.

Richardson, S. A. (1963). Some social psychological consequences of handicapping. *Pediatrics, 32,* 291–297.

Richardson, S. A. (1972). People with cerebral palsy talk for themselves. *Developmental Medicine and Child Neurology, 14,* 524–535.

Richardson, S. A., Hastorf, A. H., & Dornbusch, S. M. (1964). Effects of physical disability on a child's description of himself. *Child Development, 35,* 893–907.

Robinson, R. O. (1973). The frequency of other handicaps in children with cerebral palsy. *Developmental Medicine and Child Neurology, 15,* 305–316.

Romanova, O. L. (1983). An experimental psychological study of the personality traits of patients with physical defects. *Soviet Neurology and Psychiatry, 16*(1), 29–36.

Rose, M. H. (1984). The concepts of coping and vulnerability as applied to children with chronic conditions. *Issues in Comprehensive Pediatric Nursing, 7,* 177–186.

Rosenbloom, L. (1971). The contribution of motor behavior to child development. *Physiotherapy, 57,* 159–162.

Scherzer, A. L., Ilson, J. B., Miké, V., & Iandoli, M. (1973). Educational and social development among intensively treated young patients having cerebral palsy. *Archives of Physical Medicine and Rehabilitation, 54,* 478–484.

Sherrill, C., Hinson, M., Gench, B., Kennedy, S. O., & Low, L. (1990). Self-concepts of disabled youth athletes. *Perceptual and Motor Skills, 70,* 1093–1098.

Stensman, R. (1989). Body image among 22 persons with acquired and congenital severe mobility impairment. *Paraplegia, 17,* 27–35.

Storrow, H. A., & Jones, M. H. (1960). Management of emotional barriers to rehabilitation in cerebral palsied adults. *Archives of Physical Medicine and Rehabilitation, 41,* 570–574.

Susset, V., Vobecky, J., & Black, R. (1979). Disability outcome and self-assessment of disabled persons: An analysis of 506 cases. *Archives of Physical Medicine and Rehabilitation, 60,* 50–56.

Teplin, S. W., Howard, J. A., & O'Connor, M. J. (1981). Self-concept of young children with cerebral palsy. *Developmental Medicine and Child Neurology, 23,* 730–738.

Wallander, J. L., Hubert, N. C., & Varni, J. W. (1988). Child and maternal temperament characteristics, goodness-of-fit, and adjustment in physically handicapped children. *Journal of Clinical Child Psychology, 17*, 336–344.

Wallander, J. L., & Varni, J. W. (1989). Social support and adjustment in chronically ill and handicapped children. *American Journal of Community Psychology, 17*, 185–201.

Wallander, J. L., Varni, J. W., Babani, L., Banis, H. T., De Haan, C. B., & Wilcox, K. T. (1989). Disability parameters, chronic strain, and adaptation of physically handicapped children and their mothers. *Journal of Pediatric Psychology, 14*, 23–42.

Wallander, J. L., Varni, J. W., Babani, L., Banis, H. T., & Wilcox, K. T. (1988). Children with chronic physical disorders: Maternal reports of their psychological adjustment. *Journal of Pediatric Psychology, 13*, 197–212.

Wallander, J. L., Varni, J. W., Babani, L., Banis, H. T., & Wilcox, K. T. (1989). Family resources as resistance factors for psychological maladjustment in chronically ill and handicapped children. *Journal of Pediatric Psychology, 14*, 157–173.

Wallander, J. L., Varni, J. W., Babani, L., De Haan, C. B., Wilcox, K. T., & Banis, H. T. (1989). The social environment and the adaptation of mothers of physically handicapped children. *Journal of Pediatric Psychology, 14*, 371–387.

Weinberg, N. (1976). Social stereotyping of the physically handicapped. *Rehabilitation Psychology, 23*, 115–124.

Weinberg, N., & Williams, J. (1978). How the physically disabled perceive their disabilities. *Journal of Rehabilitation, 44*(3), 31–33.

CHAPTER 16

Amyotrophic Lateral Sclerosis

DESCRIPTION

Amyotrophic lateral sclerosis (also known as "Lou Gehrig's disease") is a rapidly progressive motor neuron disease of unknown etiology that now affects approximately 35,000 Americans. It is characterized by degeneration of various nerves and nerve nuclei along the voluntary motor pathways of the central nervous system (CNS), namely, the cerebral cortex, brainstem, and spinal cord. These damaged sections of the corticospinal tracts (lateral columns of the spinal cord) are then replaced by scar tissue, producing lesions known as plaques, similar to those found in other types of sclerosis (Berkow, 1992; Corcoran, 1981; Ilan & Friedmann, 1993).

Amyotrophic lateral sclerosis is a chronic disease of middle to late adult life. Most affected individuals range in age from 40 to 70 years (Ilan & Friedmann, 1993; Lindemann & Stanger, 1981). Approximately 50% of affected individuals die within 3 years of disease onset, and an additional 10% survive between 3 and 10 years (Berkow, 1992). The prevalence of the disease in the United States is estimated to range from three to seven cases per 100,000 persons, with males affected three times as often as females (Lindemann & Stanger, 1981; Merritt, 1989).

Symptom type, extent, and severity vary with the location of the neurons first attacked and the rapidity of disease progression. The primary symptoms of amyotrophic lateral sclerosis include (1) weakness, (2) fatigue, (3) involuntary muscle twitching or wormlike writhing movements, (4) loss of strength in the extremities due to denervation atrophy leading to gait and hand manipulation abnormalities, (5) dysarthria and dysphagia (impaired speech and swallowing), (6) pain, and (7) respiratory muscle weakness leading to breathing problems and eventually to death. Sensation is not typically impaired, and vision, hearing, and cognitive functioning usually remain intact (Corcoran, 1981; Hunter, Robinson, & Neilson, 1993; Ilan & Friedmann, 1993; Lindemann & Stanger, 1981; Montgomery & Erickson, 1987; Newrick & Langton-Hewer, 1984).

PSYCHOSOCIAL ADAPTATION TO AMYOTROPHIC LATERAL SCLEROSIS

A review of the clinical literature suggests that depressive reactions typically occur as neuromuscular diseases progress (Leach & Delfiner, 1989; Lindemann & Stanger, 1981). Case study reports indicate that individuals with amyotrophic lateral sclerosis demonstrate reactions of grief, despair, and depression and that these reactions are attributable to loss of health and fear of dying (Kim, 1989; Stone, 1987). Kelemen (1983) concluded that among persons with amyotrophic lateral sclerosis, psychosocial reactions to diagnosis typically include (1) intellectualization (eg, attempting to gain knowledge and become fully informed about the details of the disease), (2) religiosity (eg, seeking religion as a solution to the uncertainty of the disease onset), and (3) regression (eg, demonstrating regressive behaviors that reflect depression, anger, resentment, passivity, stubbornness, and dependence). These reports often describe the person with amyotrophic lateral sclerosis as a prisoner in his or her body who becomes painfully aware of the rapidly progressive deterioration of the physical body and impending death. Interviews with individuals and their families often reveal that the most prominent themes of concern include (1) loss of mobility, (2) feelings of helplessness and powerlessness, (3) fears of becoming totally dependent on others, and (4) loss of friends and becoming socially isolated (Leach & Delfiner, 1989; Sebring & Moglia, 1987).

Empirical investigations of psychosocial reactions to amyotrophic lateral sclerosis, however, have been infrequent and do not always confirm these clinical impressions. In one of the earliest attempts to investigate how individuals with amyotrophic lateral sclerosis reacted to their disease, Brown and Mueller (1970) administered a battery of psychological tests, including Rotter's Internal-External Locus of Control Scale, the Multiple Affect Adjective Check List, and the Minnesota Multiphasic Personality Inventory, to 10 individuals with amyotrophic lateral sclerosis. In addition, all 10 individuals were subjected to an extensive psychiatric interview. As compared to test scores available for other groups (eg, adolescents without disabilities, college students, individuals with various psychiatric conditions, individuals with renal disease, individuals with cancer), the individuals with amyotrophic lateral sclerosis showed (1) a high degree of internality (ie, belief in personal control of life events), (2) no significantly different profiles on the Multiple Affect Adjective Check List (ie, degrees of anxiety, depression, and hostility) when compared to individuals with other diseases or college students, and (3) a tendency toward moderate elevation of the Minnesota Multiphasic Personality Inventory's "neurotic triad" scales (ie, Hypochondriasis, Depression, and Conversion Hysteria). Based on these results and data obtained from the personal interviews, the authors concluded that the individuals with amyotrophic lateral sclerosis resorted to both active mastery of their behavior and environment and the exclusion of dysphoric mood from awareness. The latter was interpreted further as indicative of the use of denial or isolation of negative affect by the individuals.

In an attempt to replicate the findings of this study with a larger sample, Houpt, Gould, and Norris (1977) administered Rotter's scale, the Multiple Affect Adjective Check List, the Beck Depression Inventory, and the Tennessee Self-Concept Scale to 40 consecutive hospital inpatients with amyotrophic lateral sclerosis. A semistructured interview was also conducted to assess depression and denial. Unlike the Brown and Mueller (1970) study, Houpt et al. (1977) reported that internality may be curvilinearly related to length of disability (chronicity, or time since diagnosis), that is, individuals whose chronicity was less than one year or more than two years showed less internality (ie, they relied more on physicians' advice, existential fatalism, or religious faith) than did individuals whose chronicity was between one and two years. In addition, it was found that (1) 70% of the individuals in their sample did not demonstrate denial of affect; (2) individuals with amyotrophic lateral sclerosis did not differ significantly in their scores on the Multiple Affect Adjective Check List from individuals in Brown and Mueller's (1970) sample; and (3) 35% of their sample were at least moderately depressed on the Beck Depression Inventory, a finding that is comparable to percentages reported in other medical populations. It appears, contrary to the results of Brown and Mueller (1970), that negative affectivity was evident in this sample and that internality and denial did not appear to be overrepresented among their sample.

Gould (1980) reported similar results in a follow-up study of the survivors of the original sample in the Houpt et al. (1977) investigation and included additional consecutively admitted hospital patients with amyotrophic lateral sclerosis in a larger sample of 65 individuals. Gould speculated that manifestations of denial might have been attributable to the operation of partial denial, where reality was not denied or ignored but rather redefined. In a study of the frequency of anxiety and depression, as measured by the Hospital Anxiety and Depression Scale, among persons with amyotrophic lateral sclerosis, Earll, Johnston, and Mitchell (1993) concluded that of their sample of 50 respondents, 26% and 12% exceeded the cut-off points for anxiety and depression, respectively. Results suggestive of denial were also reported by Schiffer and Babigian (1984), who reviewed hospital-based medical records of 124 individuals with amyotrophic lateral sclerosis and found that only 6 had sought psychiatric assistance. This finding, however, may be misleading in as much as the remaining individuals may have sought psychological help elsewhere.

In a more recent investigation, Montgomery and Erickson (1987) studied the Minnesota Multiphasic Personality Inventory profiles of a group of 38 young individuals with amyotrophic lateral sclerosis (mean age = 46 years). Eighteen (47%) of the individuals had a profile of scores on the clinical scales of Depression, Psychasthenia, and Schizophrenia, that suggested psychological maladaptation. This profile is thought to be characteristic of individuals who experience considerable emotional distress manifested as depression, tenseness, nervousness, impaired concentration, guilt, alienation, and impaired social skills (Graham, 1987). When studying the relationship of psychosocial distress to chronicity of amyotrophic lateral sclerosis, Montgomery and Erickson (1987) noted increased distress and ego impairment with the progression of the disease. These findings may be not be generalizable, however, as the researchers failed to account for the advance of medical symptoms in the individuals studied, some of which are reflected by items interspersed throughout the scales of the Minnesota Multiphasic Personality Inventory.

Ferro, Riefolo, Nesci, and Mazza (1987), after reviewing the limited number of empirical studies relating to psychosocial adaptation to amyotrophic lateral sclerosis, suggested that (1) denial and isolation are, indeed, the main defense mechanisms used by persons with this disease; (2) individuals with amyotrophic lateral sclerosis may fluctuate between an internal and external locus of control because of the medical instructions involved and change in treatment programs reflected in the adoption of conflicting fatalistic and religious views; and (3) anxiety and depression, when experienced, are linked to fears of limited mobility, loss of functional abilities, and death.

CHARACTERISTICS ASSOCIATED WITH ADAPTATION TO AMYOTROPHIC LATERAL SCLEROSIS

Only a meager number of investigations have attempted to explore the association between psychosocial adaptation to amyotrophic lateral sclerosis and certain sociodemographic, personality, or disease-related variables. Researchers have typically reported that no relationship appears to exist between amyotrophic lateral sclerosis and cognitive dysfunction, perceptual distortion, memory loss, or dementia (Brown & Mueller, 1970; Hudson, 1981; Montgomery & Erickson, 1987). Brown and Mueller (1970) found no relationship between Minnesota Multiphasic Personality Inventory scores and chronicity of the disease or degree of functional impairment. Similar findings were reported by Gould (1980), who found no relationship between psychopathological reactions and severity of illness or age of the individual.

Montgomery and Erickson (1987) investigated various sociodemographic and disease-related variables as predictors of psychological distress among individuals with amyotrophic lateral sclerosis. The level of psychological distress was assessed by scores on the three Minnesota Multiphasic Personality Inventory clinical scales reflecting maladaptation (ie, Depression, Psychasthenia, and Schizophrenia). The results of a series of multiple regression analyses revealed no association between depression and any disease-related measure. Scores on the Psychasthenia and Schizophrenia scales, in contrast, were associated with degree of both upper motor neuron involvement and pulmonary dysfunction. Persons with respiratory dysfunction, in particular, showed greater somatic preoccupation, anxiety, despair, alienation, and confusion. Earll et al. (1993) also failed to find any relationship between two disease-related variables (ie, number of symptoms and overall objective symptom severity) and measures of psychosocial adaptation (eg, anxiety, depression, well-being). However, self-perception of one's condition as serious was found to be associated with poorer psychosocial outcomes.

In a study of 181 persons with amyotrophic lateral sclerosis, Hunter et al. (1993) sought to investigate the relationships between several sociodemographic variables, functional involvement (eg, degree of self-care and mobility), and psychological well-being (the 12-item General Health Questionnaire). Results indicated that although no significant differences were found between men and women or among various age groups on the General Health Questionnaire, a significant trend was evident for psychological distress to increase with higher levels of functional impairment. Furthermore psychological distress was reported at all stages of the disease but was higher at earlier stages (2 to 5 years) than at later stages (6 to 11 years) of disease duration.

Peters, Swenson, and Mulder (1978) reviewed Minnesota Multiphasic Personality Inventory profiles of 38 individuals with amyotrophic lateral sclerosis (mean age 54 years, range 33 to 75 years) in an attempt to establish the existence of a characteristic personality profile. When compared to the profiles of a large group of individuals from a general medical practice, no statistically significant differences were found in any of the Minnesota Multiphasic Personality Inventory scales for the females with amyotrophic lateral sclerosis. Males with amyotrophic lateral sclerosis, in contrast, scored slightly higher than did the males in the general medical practice sample on the Hypochondriasis, Depression, Conversion Hysteria, and Schizophrenia scales. Nevertheless, no unique personality profile typical of individuals with amyotrophic lateral sclerosis emerged from these data. These results replicated the results reported by Brown and Mueller (1970), who found no specific personality profile among their small sample of individuals with amyotrophic lateral sclerosis.

Schwartz, Devine, Schechter, and Bender (1990) investigated the types of psychosocial coping mechanisms selected by persons with amyotrophic lateral sclerosis and persons with myasthenia gravis, another type of neuromuscular disorder. The individuals with amyotrophic lateral sclerosis were older (61.9 versus 53.6 years), predominantly male (53% versus 32%), and had a shorter chronicity of disease (2.8 versus 10.4 years) than the individuals with myasthenia gravis. Degree of illness severity, however, was comparable between the groups. Compared to the individuals with myasthenia gravis, the individuals with amyotrophic lateral sclerosis used less active cognitive coping (ie, attempts at managing and appraising event stressfulness) but more active behavioral coping (ie, behavioral attempts at dealing directly with the problem). Both groups of individuals, however, tended to focus directly on illness-related problems. It may be speculated that individuals with amyotrophic lateral sclerosis, in contrast to individuals with myasthenia gravis and other neuromuscular disorders that are not immediately life threatening, may use defense mechanisms (eg, denial, isolation) and coping strategies (eg, active behavioral mastery of the environment) precisely because of their conscious or unconscious efforts to ward off anxiety and despair associated with the imminent loss of control over their bodies and their impending deaths.

In another study seeking to investigate coping modes among individuals with amyotrophic lateral sclerosis, Earll et al. (1993) used a cross-sectional research design to obtain psychological data from a sample of 50 persons and their caregivers. Assessment of coping modes was obtained through semistructured interviews, while psychosocial outcomes were measured by the Hospital Anxiety and Depression Scale (Zigmond & Snaith, 1983), the Bradburn Well-Being: Affect Balance Scale (Bradburn, 1969), and the Rosenberg Self-Esteem Scale (Rosenberg, 1965). Most respondents appeared to cope with their difficulties by using problem-focused or cognitive-focused response modes. No relationships, however, were found between coping modes and ranking of disease seriousness, causal attributions of condition onset, or measures of anxiety, depression, and well-being.

Lastly, McDonnald, Wiedenfeld, Hillel, Carpenter, and Walter (1994) investigated the relationship between psychological status following diagnosis and survival among 144 persons with amyotrophic lateral sclerosis. Results indicated that psychological status, as measured by a composite of scores on seven separate psychological measures (eg, measures of hopelessness, depression, stress, anger, and health locus of control) was significantly predictive of respondent mortality. Persons who obtained higher psychological scores (ie, manifested lower psychological distress) had longer survival time, during the study period, than persons who scored lower on the combined psychological status index.

CONCLUSION

The limited clinical and empirical literature on psychosocial adaptation to amyotrophic lateral sclerosis indicates that people who have this disease often report feelings of helplessness, powerlessness, and increased dependency on others as the disease progresses. Moderate levels of depression appear to be experienced by approximately one third of this population. It has been argued that denial may be the defense mechanism used most frequently by persons with this disease.

No consistent relationships were found between measures of psychosocial adaptation to amyotrophic lateral sclerosis (eg, depression, anxiety) and sociodemographic or disease-related variables. Likewise, the limited data on the association of coping modes and measures of psychosocial adaptation do not support any consistent relationship between the two sets of variables.

Even these limited conclusions must be considered tentative given the quality of the research from which they are derived. Most of the studies reviewed relied on data obtained from anecdotal and clinical reports, from informants, or from small and nonrandom samples of persons with amyotrophic lateral sclerosis. Seldom did researchers control for the confounding of psychosocial reactions with sample characteristics (especially disease-related medical symptoms and functional limitations), and researchers often neglected to consider the premorbid status of the individual (eg, personality attributes, family support) when studying psychosocial distress. Finally, there is a conspicuous lack of research using longitudinal designs to trace temporal changes in psychosocial adaptation to the disease.

REFERENCES

Berkow, R. (Ed.). (1992). *The Merck manual of diagnosis and therapy* (16th ed.). Rahway, NJ: Merck Research Laboratories.

Bradburn, N. M. (1969). *The structure of psychological well-being.* New York: Hawthorne.

Brown, W. A., & Mueller, P. S. (1970). Psychological function in individuals with amyotrophic lateral sclerosis. *Psychosomatic Medicine, 32,* 141–152.

Corcoran, P. J. (1981). Neuromuscular diseases. In W. C. Stolov & M. R. Clowers (Eds.), *Handbook of severe disability* (pp. 83–100). Washington, DC: U. S. Department of Education, Rehabilitation Services Administration.

Earll, L., Johnston, M., & Mitchell, E. (1993). Coping with motor neurone disease—An analysis using self-regulation theory. *Palliative Medicine, 9*(Suppl. 2), 21–30.

Ferro, F. M., Riefolo, G., Nesci, D. A., & Mazza, S. (1987). Psychodynamic aspects in patients with amyotrophic lateral sclerosis. *Advances in Experimental and Medical Biology, 209,* 313–316.

Gould, B. S. (1980). Psychiatric aspects. In D. W. Mulder (Ed.), *The diagnosis and treatment of amyotrophic lateral sclerosis* (pp. 157–166). Boston: Houghton Mifflin.

Graham, J. R. (1987). *The MMPI: A practical guide* (2nd ed.). New York: Oxford University Press.

Houpt, J. L., Gould, B. S., & Norris, F. H. (1977). Psychological characteristics of patients with amyotrophic lateral sclerosis. *Psychosomatic Medicine, 39,* 299–303.

Hudson, A. J. (1981). Amyotrophic lateral sclerosis and its association with dementia, Parkinsonism and other neurological disorders: A review. *Brain, 104*, 217–247.

Hunter, M. D., Robinson, I. C., & Neilson, S. (1993). The functional and psychological status of patients with amyotrophic lateral sclerosis: Some implications for rehabilitation. *Disability and Rehabilitation, 15*, 119–126.

Ilan, H., & Friedmann, L. W. (1993). Neuromuscular disorders. In M. G. Eisenberg, R. L. Glueckauf, & H. H. Zaretsky (Eds.), *Medical aspects of disability* (pp. 243–255). New York: Springer.

Kelemen, J. (1983). Coping with amyotrophic lateral sclerosis. In L. I. Charash, S. G. Wolf, A. H. Kutscher, R. E. Lovelace, & M. S. Hale (Eds.), *Psychosocial aspects of muscular dystrophy and allied diseases* (pp. 148–158). Springfield, IL: C C Thomas.

Kim, T. S. (1989). Hope as a mode of coping in amyotrophic lateral sclerosis. *Journal of Neuroscience Nursing, 21*, 342–347.

Leach, C. F., & Delfiner, J. S. (1989). Approaches to loss and bereavement in amyotrophic lateral sclerosis. In S. C. Klagsbrun (Ed.), *Preventive psychiatry: Early intervention and situational crisis management* (pp. 201–211). Philadelphia: Charles Press.

Lindemann, J. E., & Stanger, M. E. (1981). Progressive muscular disorders. In J. E. Lindemann (Ed.), *Psychological and behavioral aspects of physical disability* (pp. 273–300). New York: Plenum Press.

McDonnald, E. R., Wiedenfeld, S. A., Hillel, A., Carpenter, C. L., & Walter, R. A. (1994). Survival in amyotrophic lateral sclerosis. *Archives of Neurology, 51*, 17–23.

Merritt, H. (1989). *A textbook of neurology* (3rd ed.). Philadelphia: Lea & Febiger.

Montgomery, G. K., & Erickson, L. M. (1987). Neuropsychological perspectives in amyotrophic lateral sclerosis. *Neurologic Clinics of North America, 5*, 61–81.

Newrick, P. G., & Langton-Hewer, R. (1984). Motor neurone disease: Can we do better? A study of 42 patients. *British Medical Journal, 289*, 539–542.

Peters, P. K., Swenson, W. M., & Mulder, D. W. (1978). Is there a characteristic personality profile in amyotrophic lateral sclerosis? *Archives of Neurology, 35*, 321–322.

Rosenberg, M. (1965). *Society and the adolescent self-image.* Princeton, NJ: Princeton University Press.

Schiffer, R. B., & Babigian, H. M. (1984). Behavioral disorders in multiple sclerosis, temporal lobe epilepsy, and amyotrophic lateral sclerosis. *Archives of Neurology, 41*, 1067–1069.

Schwartz, L. B., Devine, P. A., Schechter, C. B., & Bender, A. N. (1990). Psychosocial aspects of neuromuscular disorders: Impact of illness on life style. *Loss, Grief and Care, 4*(3), 3–21.

Sebring, D. L., & Moglia, P. (1987). Amyotrophic lateral sclerosis: Psychosocial interventions for patients and their families. *Health and Social Work, 12*, 113–120.

Stone, N. (1987). Amyotrophic lateral sclerosis: A challenge for constant adaptation. *Journal of Neuroscience Nursing, 19*, 166–173.

Zigmond, A. S., & Snaith, R. P. (1983). The Hospital Anxiety and Depression Scale. *Acta Psychiatrica Scandinavica, 67*, 361–370.

CHAPTER 17

Muscular Dystrophy

DESCRIPTION

Muscular dystrophy is a term pertaining to a group of inherited, early onset, and progressive neuromuscular disorders (Berkow, 1992; Corcoran, 1981; Emery, 1994; Ilan & Friedmann, 1993; Lindemann & Stanger, 1981; Swash & Oxburg, 1991). There are four common types of muscular dystrophy.

1. *Duchenne dystrophy* is an x-linked recessive disorder that occurs only in boys with signs and symptoms usually manifest between three and seven years of age. Approximately 85% of all muscular dystrophy cases are of the Duchenne dystrophy type with prevalence rates estimated at 1.9 to 4.0 per 100,000 individuals. The disorder is caused by a deficiency of the muscle protein dystrophin. Symptoms typically include diminished ambulation leading to wheelchair use by early adolescence; gradually increasing limitations on eating, dressing, and personal hygiene; and steadily falling respiratory ability resulting in death usually by the age of 20 years. Intellectual development may also be arrested, resulting in an average IQ approximately one standard deviation below the general population mean.

2. *Becker muscular dystrophy* is also an x-linked recessive genetic disorder but one presenting a slower progression, less severe clinical symptomatology, and longer life span for the affected individual. Onset is usually in the teens, and over 90% of people with Becker muscular dystrophy live beyond the age of 20 years and often survive into middle age and beyond.

3. *Facioscapulohumeral muscular dystrophy* is an autosomal dominant form of muscular dystrophy that may be inherited from either parent and is characterized by weakness of the facial muscles and shoulder girdles. Speech may be affected if facial weakness is marked. The onset of symptoms is typically between ages 7 and 20 years, with severe incapacity typically not reached until age 40 years. Life expectancy is close to average.

4. *Myotonic muscular dystrophy* is a relatively rare autosomal dominant form of the disorder that combines both myotonia (ie, delayed relaxation or stiffness of muscles following voluntary contraction) and dystrophic muscular weakness. This form of the disorder affects more males than females. Onset can vary from birth (congenital form) to adulthood. Many organs and systems are eventually involved (eg, cardiac muscle, endocrine system), with distal muscles (eg, the hands) affected first. Death typically occurs in severely affected individuals when they are in their 50s.

PSYCHOSOCIAL ADAPTATION TO MUSCULAR DYSTROPHY

Muscular dystrophy, in its various clinical forms, is a neuromuscular disorder that first appears in childhood. The disorder typically affects ambulation and, in its most severe form (Duchenne dystrophy), progresses to involve other neuromuscular systems, resulting in an early death. It is not surprising, therefore, that most clinical reports view persons with muscular dystrophy as experiencing depression, especially when a wheelchair is required for ambulation (Lindemann & Stanger, 1981; Pierpont, LeRoy, & Baldinger, 1984). Other psychosocial reactions often noted in the literature (Emery, 1994; Goldfarb & Shapiro, 1990; Ilan & Friedmann, 1993; Lindemann & Stanger, 1981; Lovelace, 1983; Lubowe, 1989) include (1) dependency (at times directly related to parental overprotection) and passivity, (2) social isolation (due to negative attitudes of peers and shame about a disfigured body), (3) negative body image and self-concept (as a consequence of the child's internalization of society's negative perceptions), (4) feelings of helplessness (because of increased dependency on parents and others), (5) anxiety over impending death, and (6) anger and aggressive behavior directed toward parents and peers. The richness of these clinical data stands in sharp contrast to the dearth of empirical studies on psychosocial adaptation to muscular dystrophy. Furthermore most of the existing empirical studies focus on only one form of muscular dystrophy, namely, myotonic muscular dystrophy.

Studies of depression as a reaction to the diagnosis and progressive symptoms of muscular dystrophy have been reported most frequently in the literature on this disorder. Brumback and associates (Brumback, 1987; Brumback & Carlson, 1983; Brumback & Wilson, 1984), in their studies of persons with myotonic muscular dystrophy, concluded that over 50% of the individuals in their samples manifested a high degree of affective symptoms, most notably feelings of depression (eg, dysphoria, fatigue, lack of interest or pleasure in daily activities) as indicated by elevated scores on the Depression scale of the Minnesota Multiphasic Personality Inventory. Furthermore these researchers found that the severity of these affective symptoms was independent of the degree of neuromuscular involvement. Depression in persons with myotonic muscular dystrophy has been frequently found as a concomitant reaction with other cognitive and affective manifestations, as evidenced by elevated scores on the Schizophrenia and Hypochondriasis scales of the Minnesota Multiphasic Personality Inventory (Bird, Follett, & Griep, 1983; Brumback, 1987; Brumback & Wilson, 1984; Franzese et al., 1991; Glantz, Garron, Wright, & Siegel, 1986). These latter reactions suggest experiences of apprehension, tension, confusion, anhedonia, blunted affect, somatic complaints, and feelings of worthlessness (Duckworth & Anderson, 1986; Graham, 1987). Franzese et al. (1991) documented the existence of affectivity among a group of 28 individuals with myotonic muscular dystrophy, of whom 50% demonstrated "borderline depression" and 53% showed borderline to pathological levels of external irritability.

Emotional adjustment among boys (ages 3 to 13 years) with Duchenne muscular dystrophy was investigated by Leibowitz and Dubowitz (1983). Based on responses to the parent and teacher forms of the Rutter Behavior Questionnaire, these researchers found that (1) 37% of the children were found to demonstrate some emotional disturbance, as reported by their teachers, with antisocial tendencies (53%) and neurotic behaviors (31%) being the primary disorders; and (2) 33% of the children were found to exhibit emotional disturbances, as reported by their parents, with neurotic (61%) and antisocial (39%) behaviors being the primary disorders. In a later study Thompson, Zeman, Fanurik, and Sirotkin-Roses (1992) reported that among children with Duchenne muscular dystrophy (ages 4 to 14 years), 89% were classified as exhibiting behavior problems as measured by the parent-reported Missouri Children's Behavior Checklist (Sines, Pauker, Sines, & Owen, 1969). Most of these problems (37%) were reported to be of the internalizing behavior profile pattern.

Only three studies were located in which persons with muscular dystrophy were compared psychologically to other groups of respondents. Harper (1983) investigated Minnesota Multiphasic Personality Inventory psychological profiles of 15 adolescents with Duchenne muscular dystrophy and 29 male adolescents with nonprogressive congenital and traumatic orthopaedic disabilities. Adolescents in the latter group scored significantly higher on the Psychopathic Deviate and Hypomania scales, while those with Duchenne muscular dystrophy scored significantly higher on the Social Introversion scale. Adolescents with Duchenne muscular dystrophy demonstrated a 0 (Social Introversion)—5 (Masculinity-Femininity)—2 (Depression) configuration on the Minnesota Multiphasic Personality Inventory, suggesting an "inhibited, socially sensitive, passive male who is reporting long-standing feelings of dissatisfaction and hopelessness" (Harper, 1983, p. 863).

Glantz et al. (1986) compared scores on the Minnesota Multiphasic Personality Inventory and other psychological measures of a group of 15 persons with myotonic muscular dystrophy to the scores of persons having other chronic diseases, including spinal diseases ($n = 33$), chronic asthma ($n = 25$), and multiple sclerosis ($n = 15$). Persons with myotonic muscular dystrophy scored significantly higher than their counterparts on the Minnesota Multiphasic Personality Inventory scales of Hypochondriasis, Depression, and Schizophrenia, suggesting a unique pattern of psychosocial reactions among persons with myotonic muscular dystrophy. In the third study Duveneck, Portwood, Wicks, and Lieberman (1986), using a battery of psychological tests, compared 27 persons with myotonic muscular dystrophy to groups of 17 persons with spinal cord injury, 11 persons with limb-girdle syndrome (a progressive neuromuscular disease), and 27 individuals without disabilities. Results showed that the group of persons with myotonic muscular dystrophy scored significantly higher than both the persons without disabilities and the persons with spinal cord injuries on the Minnesota Multiphasic Personality Inventory Depression scale and on the Depression Test of the Institute for Personality and Ability Testing. Persons with myotonic muscular dystrophy also showed lower levels of positive mental health compared to the same two groups as suggested by lower scores on the Minnesota Multiphasic Personality Inventory Ego Strength scale and the Well-Being scale of the California Psychological Inventory. No differences were found on any of the measures between persons with myotonic muscular dystrophy and persons with limb-girdle syndrome.

The limited empirical data on psychosocial adaptation to myotonic muscular dystrophy suggest that depression is a rather strong accompaniment of the disorder. It is not clear, however, if depression is directly associated with myotonic muscular dystrophy because of abnormal biochemical processes unique to the disorder or if depression is a secondary reaction to the chronic, progressive condition (Brumback & Wilson, 1984). No reliable data are available on the nature, frequency, and severity of depression among persons with other forms of muscular dystrophy (eg, Becker, Duchenne).

Only one study was located that investigated the selection of coping modes among persons with muscular dystrophy. Ahlstrom and Sjoden (1994) modified two cancer-specific self-assessment questionnaires (ie, the Reaction to the Diagnosis of Cancer Questionnaire and the Mental Assessment of Cancer Scale) in an effort to investigate coping modes in a sample of 60 Swedish persons (age range 16 to 64 years) with various forms of muscular dystrophy. Additional data were obtained by a semistructured interview that focused on such issues as (1) reactions to initial diagnosis, (2) methods used to get through the day, (3) methods used to readjust to present difficulties, and (4) possible changes in personal values. Coping modes adopted by this sample included (1) avoidance/denial (18%), (2) fighting spirit (18%), (3) helplessness/hopelessness (18%), (4) fatalism (12%), (5) stoic acceptance (9%), (6) anxious preoccupation (5%), (7) future uncertainty (2%), and (8) a residual group of coping strategies that included, among others, anticipation of physical deterioration, creation of new life values, minimization or lowering of expectations, establishment of control over everyday life, and secretiveness due to shame. No attempt was made to relate the use of any of these coping modes with sociodemographic, disease-related, personality, or environmental variables.

CHARACTERISTICS ASSOCIATED WITH ADAPTATION TO MUSCULAR DYSTROPHY

The data on enduring cognitive and personality characteristics of persons with muscular dystrophy are limited. Conflicting findings exist as to the cognitive deterioration among persons with muscular dystrophy. Whereas some researchers have concluded that mental retardation is much more prevalent among persons with muscular dystrophy (Calderon, 1966; Dodge, Gamstorp, Byers, & Russell, 1965), other researchers found no differences between the mean IQ levels of persons with muscular dystrophy and of the general population (Franzese et al., 1991; Portwood, Wicks, Lieberman, & Fowler, 1984). Limited data suggest that a positive association exists between low performance on cognitive and learning tests and increased emotional disturbance among boys with Duchenne muscular dystrophy (Leibowitz & Dubowitz, 1983).

Data on more general personality changes among persons with muscular dystrophy are also inconclusive. Rather common but largely anecdotal reports of such changes suggest that psychopathology is a cardinal feature of myotonic muscular dystrophy (Ambrosini & Nurnberg, 1979: Bundy, 1982; Glantz et al., 1986) and Duchenne muscular dystrophy (Leibowitz & Dubowitz, 1981). Bird and colleagues (1983) also reported, based on participants' Minnesota Multiphasic Personality Inventory scores and clinical interviews, that 32% of their sample of 29 persons with myotonic muscular dystrophy demonstrated prominent personality abnormalities. These severe psychopathological symptoms were more common among persons with advanced physical conditions and lower cognitive ability, suggesting that more extensive brain abnormalities and severe neuromuscular conditions may be linked to more serious personality changes among persons with myotonic muscular dystrophy. Harper (1983) found no relationship between scores on the Minnesota Multiphasic Personality Inventory scales and physical stage ratings among adolescents with Duchenne muscular dystrophy, although social withdrawal and general stress were found to be associated with rapidity of disease progression. In a similar vein, Ville, Ravaud, Marchal, Paicheler, and Fardeau (1992) failed to observe any relationship between a measure of self-esteem and measures of both subjective and objective degrees of disablement among persons with facioscapulohumeral muscular dystrophy. Further analyses, however, suggested that when these individuals experience difficulties with social and occupational integration, the disease may be associated with a devalued self-esteem.

Finally, in a study seeking to explore the association between parental stress level, coping modes, family functioning, and behavioral problems in children with Duchenne muscular dystrophy, Thompson et al. (1992) concluded that (1) parental distress, as measured by the Global Severity Index of the Symptom Checklist—90-Revised, accounted for a significant proportion of the variance in the child's internalizing and externalizing behavior problems; (2) high parental use of palliative coping (eg, emotion-focused, avoidance, self-blame), relative to use of adaptive coping (eg, problem-focused, seeking information, seeking social support) modes, was associated with poor adjustment of children; and (3) high level of family conflict was linked to externalizing behavior problems among the children.

CONCLUSION

The literature on muscular dystrophy indicates that depression and anxiety are rather common reactions among children and adolescents who face the lifelong prospect of living with this disease or who are facing an early death (in Duchenne dystrophy). Behavioral problems that include both externalized and internalized forms of anger and aggressiveness have also been reported by teachers and parents, especially among youngsters with Duchenne dystrophy.

Conflicting data exist concerning the occurrence of mental impairment among persons with muscular dystrophy, although limited findings suggest a possible relationship between poor performance on cognitive tasks and increased emotional problems among youngsters with Duchenne muscular dystrophy. The scarce data on the relationships between sociodemographic variables, disease-related indices, personality attributes, and psychosocial adaptation among children, adolescents, or adults with muscular dystrophy do not at present support definitive conclusions.

The research on psychosocial adaptation among children and adults with muscular dystrophy is also marred by methodological concerns raised in previous chapters in this section. (See Chapter 24 for a complete presentation of these issues.) These concerns include sampling biases (eg, using nonrandom samples with limited description of the participants' sociodemographic characteristics), small sample sizes, lack of longitudinal designs to detect changes of psychosocial adaptation across time, narrowness of the reactions studied (measuring mainly depression), instrumentation weakness (eg, adapting instruments validated for populations other than persons with muscular dystrophy), confounding sample characteristics (eg, chronological age, degree of cognitive impairment, severity of functional limitations) with psychosocial adaptation, and using almost exclusively univariate statistical procedures to untangle the complex and rich data generated by the process of adaptation to muscular dystrophy.

REFERENCES

Ahlstrom, G., & Sjoden, P. O. (1994). Assessment of coping with muscular dystrophy: A methodological evaluation. *Journal of Advanced Nursing, 20,* 314–323.

Ambrosini, P., & Nurnberg, H. G. (1979). Psychopathology: A primary feature of myotonic dystrophy. *Psychosomatics, 20,* 393–399.

Berkow, R. (Ed.). (1992). *The Merck manual of diagnosis and therapy* (16th ed.). Rahway, NJ: Merck Research Laboratories.

Bird, T. D., Follett, C., & Griep, E. (1983). Cognitive and personality function in myotonic muscular dystrophy. *Journal of Neurology, Neurosurgery, and Psychiatry, 46,* 971–980.

Brumback, R. A. (1987). Disturbed personality and psychosocial adjustment in myotonic dystrophy. *Psychological Reports, 60,* 783–796.

Brumback, R. A., & Carlson, K. M. (1983). The depression of myotonic dystrophy: Response to imipramine. *Journal of Neurology, Neurosurgery, and Psychiatry, 46,* 587–588.

Brumback, R. A., & Wilson, H. (1984). Cognitive and personality function in myotonic muscular dystrophy. *Journal of Neurology, Neurosurgery, and Psychiatry, 47,* 888–889.

Bundy, S. (1982). Clinical evidence for heterogeneity in myotonic dystrophy. *Journal of Medical Genetics, 19,* 341–348.

Calderon, R. (1966). Myotonic dystrophy: A neglected cause of mental retardation. *Journal of Pediatrics, 68,* 423–431.

Corcoran, P. J. (1981). Neuromuscular diseases. In W. C. Stolov & M. R. Clowers (Eds.), *Handbook of severe disability* (pp. 83–100). Washington, DC: U. S. Department of Education, Rehabilitation Services Administration.

Dodge, P. R., Gamstorp, I., Byers, R. R., & Russell, P. (1965). Myotonic dystrophy in infancy and childhood. *Pediatrics, 35,* 3–19.

Duckworth, J., & Anderson, W. P. (1986). *MMPI interpretation manual for counselors and clinicians* (3rd ed.). Muncie, IN: Accelerated Development.

Duveneck, M. J., Portwood, M. M., Wicks, J. J., & Lieberman, J. S. (1986). Depression in myotonic muscular dystrophy. *Archives of Physical Medicine and Rehabilitation, 67,* 875–877.

Emery, A. E. H. (1994). *Muscular dystrophy: The facts.* New York: Oxford University Press.

Franzese, A., Antonini, G., Iannelli, M., Leard, M. G., Spada, S., & Vichi, R. (1991). Intellectual functions and personality in subjects with noncongenital myotonic muscular dystrophy. *Psychological Reports, 68,* 723–732.

Glantz, R., Garron, D., Wright, R., & Siegel, I. (1986). Personality changes and brain magnetic resonance imaging in myotonic dystrophy. *Muscle and Nerve, 9*(Suppl.), 198.

Goldfarb, L. P., & Shapiro, H. K. (1990). Psychosocial aspects of Charcot-Marie-Tooth disease in childhood. *Loss, Grief and Care, 9*(3–4), 109–124.

Graham, J. R. (1987). *The MMPI: A practical guide* (2nd ed.). New York: Oxford University Press.

Harper, D. C. (1983). Personality correlates and degree of impairment in male adolescents with progressive and nonprogressive physical disorders. *Journal of Clinical Psychology, 39,* 859–867.

Ilan, H., & Friedmann, L. W. (1993). Neuromuscular disorders. In M. G. Eisenberg, R. L. Glueckauf, & H. H. Zaretsky (Eds.), *Medical aspects of disability* (pp. 243–255). New York: Springer.

Leibowitz, D., & Dubowitz, V. (1981). Intellect and behavior in Duchenne muscular dystrophy. *Developmental Medicine and Child Neurology, 23*, 577–590.

Leibowitz, D., & Dubowitz, V. (1983). Emotional adjustment and behavior in Duchenne muscular dystrophy. In L. I. Charash, S. G. Wolf, A. H. Kutscher, R. E. Lovelace, & M. S. Hale (Eds.), *Psychosocial aspects of muscular dystrophy and allied diseases* (pp. 12–18). Springfield, IL: C C Thomas.

Lindemann, J. E., & Stanger, M. E. (1981). Progressive muscular disorders. In J. E. Lindemann (Ed.), *Psychological and behavioral aspects of physical disability* (pp. 273–300). New York: Plenum Press.

Lovelace, R. E. (1983). Psychosocial aspects of Duchenne and myotonic muscular dystrophy compared with Charcot-Marie-Tooth syndrome. In L. I. Charash, S. G. Wolf, A. H. Kutscher, R. E. Lovelace, & M. S. Hale (Eds.), *Psychosocial aspects of muscular dystrophy and allied diseases* (pp. 4–11). Springfield, IL: C C Thomas.

Lubowe, S. (1989). Suffering and its amelioration in the genetic disease muscular dystrophy: A comprehensive psychosocial view. *Loss, Grief and Care, 3*(3–4), 87–104.

Pierpont, M. E., LeRoy, B. S., & Baldinger, S. R. (1984). Genetic disorders. In R. W. Blum (Ed.), *Chronic illness and disabilities in childhood and adolescence* (pp. 347–373). New York: Grune & Stratton.

Portwood, M. M., Wicks, J. J., Lieberman, J. S., & Fowler, W. M. (1984). Psychometric evaluation in myotonic muscular dystrophy. *Archives of Physical Medicine and Rehabilitation, 65*, 533–536.

Sines, J., Pauker, J., Sines, L., & Owen, D. R. (1969). Identification of clinically relevant dimensions of children's behavior. *Journal of Consulting and Clinical Psychology, 33*, 728–734.

Swash, M., & Oxburg, J. (1991). *Clinical neurology.* New York: Churchill Livingstone.

Thompson, R. J., Zeman, J. L., Fanurik, D., & Sirotkin-Roses, M. (1992). The role of parent stress and coping and family functioning in parent and child adjustment to Duchenne muscular dystrophy. *Journal of Clinical Psychology, 48*, 11–19.

Ville, I., Ravaud, J. F., Marchal, F., Paicheler, H., & Fardeau, M. (1992). Social identity and the international classification of handicaps. *Disability and Rehabilitation, 14*, 168–175.

CHAPTER 18

Myasthenia Gravis

DESCRIPTION

Myasthenia gravis is a generally progressive disease caused by an autoimmune attack on the acetylcholine receptors of the postsynaptic neuromuscular junction. Consequent impairments in neuromuscular transmission result in muscle weakness and fatigue (Berkow, 1992). Because the eyes, face, throat, and limbs are most commonly affected, the individual with myasthenia gravis typically manifests diplopia (double vision), ptosis (drooping eyelids), blank facial expression, difficulty chewing and swallowing, dysarthria (inability to articulate words properly), and voice disorders such as hoarseness and hypernasality (Lindemann & Stanger, 1981; McQuillen, 1978). Approximately 10% of persons with myasthenia gravis develop life-threatening respiratory muscle complications, known as myasthenia crisis (Berkow, 1992).

It is estimated that 1 to 2 per 20,000 individuals experiences the disease, with 2 to 5 new cases per 100,000 persons diagnosed annually. Myasthenia gravis is more prevalent in women than in men (by a ratio of 3 to 2). The disease may develop suddenly or gradually, with considerable variability in its expression between individuals and within an individual from day to day. Similar to multiple sclerosis, symptom-free periods typically alternate with periods of exacerbation of the symptoms. The greatest number of women manifests symptoms between 20 and 30 years of age, while for most men symptom onset is delayed to between 50 and 70 years of age (Berkow, 1992; Goldenson, 1978; Lindemann & Stanger, 1981).

PSYCHOSOCIAL ADAPTATION TO MYASTHENIA GRAVIS

A wide range of psychosocial reactions to myasthenia gravis has been noted in the literature. Depression has been reported in over 50% of persons with myasthenia gravis (Doering, Henze, & Schussler, 1993). Other difficulties in adaptation to the disease include increased dependency needs and anxiety (MacKenzie, Martin, & Howard, 1969; Paradis, Friedman, Lazar, & Kula, 1993; Schwartz & Cahill, 1971). In a clinical study of 26 persons with myasthenia gravis, Sneddon (1980) reported that the reactions of anger, frustration, anxiety, and depression were common. Other interpersonal reactions included embarrassment, feeling threatened in social contacts, and withdrawal from others.

In an empirical study, Cordess, Folstein, and Drachman (1983) investigated the prevalence of psychosocial disorders among a group of 52 persons with myasthenia gravis and compared it to that of persons with peripheral nerve disorders of polymyositis matched for sociodemographic characteristics and degree of severity. Individuals in the samples were assessed with the General Health Questionnaire and the Present State Examination. Percentages of persons with psychosocial distress as measured by the General Health Questionnaire (ie, scores of 5 or higher) did not differ between the two study groups (20% and 25%, for the myasthenia gravis and comparison group, respectively). The Present State Examination scores for the myasthenia gravis group were consistent with the profiles of so-called simple depression and general anxiety.

In a later study Tennant, Wilby, and Nicholson (1986) compared 31 Australian individuals with myasthenia gravis on a range of psychosocial correlates (ie, state and trait anxiety, anger, depression, affect suppression) with a matched group of individuals without disabilities. The individuals with myasthenia gravis, as a group, (1) had a significantly greater mean trait anxiety score, (2) were more likely to suppress affect (anger, depression, and state anxiety), and (3) had a greater, but not significantly different, score on a scale measuring depression. Magni and associates (1988) studied the prevalence of psychiatric disturbances among 74 Italian individuals with myasthenia gravis. Using criteria adopted from the DSM—III, they concluded that 51% of their sample demonstrated some form of psychiatric condition. The most common diagnoses included adjustment, affective, and personality disorders. The prevalence of psychiatric disorders was higher among persons with a more severe clinical status.

Paradis et al. (1993) assessed the frequency of anxiety disorders among a sample of 20 individuals with myasthenia gravis and compared it to that of 12 individuals with polymyositis. A total of 43% of the combined neuromuscular diseases group was diagnosed with an anxiety disorder following administration of the DSM—III-R–based Anxiety Disorders Interview Schedule-Revised (DiNardo & Barlow, 1988). The only difference between the two study groups was that 40% of the individuals with myasthenia gravis were diagnosed with panic disorder—agoraphobia—compared to only 7% in the polymyositis group. On the Symptom Checklist—90-Revised, the two groups differed on the clinical scales measuring anxiety and paranoid ideation, as well as on the Global Severity

Index. In all instances persons with myasthenia gravis scored higher (ie, showed increased psychological distress) than persons with polymyositis. The authors attributed these differences to the uncertainty of symptoms among individuals in the former group, their sense of loss of control, and their fear of respiratory crisis.

In a recent study of psychosocial coping mechanisms among a group of 44 German individuals with myasthenia gravis (Doering et al., 1993), it was found that persons with myasthenia gravis adopted a variety of coping styles, including passive cooperation, acceptance, stoicism, altruism, and distraction. The selection of these coping styles was apparently independent of the severity of symptoms. The researchers concluded that levels of self-reported trait anxiety and depression in this sample were generally within average limits despite having 41% of the persons with myasthenia gravis diagnosed with psychiatric disorders according to the International Classification of Diseases. The researchers attributed the lower levels of affective turmoil among the individuals they studied to the coping strategies employed (eg, use of calm and accepting attitudes).

In a study comparing differences in coping styles of individuals with amyotrophic lateral sclerosis and with myasthenia gravis, Schwartz, Devine, Schechter, and Bender (1991) found that persons with myasthenia gravis scored significantly lower on active behavioral coping than their counterparts with amyotrophic lateral sclerosis but higher, though not significantly so, on active cognitive coping. Both groups of individuals demonstrated a high degree of problem-focused coping when dealing with their illnesses. The researchers suggested that these findings may be partially due to the realization among the individuals with myasthenia gravis that no treatment is available for their disorder and, therefore, that their behavioral attempts to cope with it are futile.

CHARACTERISTICS ASSOCIATED WITH ADAPTATION TO MYASTHENIA GRAVIS

A literature search focused on characteristics associated with psychosocial adaptation to myasthenia gravis uncovered only limited information. Lindemann and Stanger (1981) concluded from their review of the literature that no unique myasthenia gravis personality profile exists. This conclusion was supported in a recent study (Doering et al., 1993) in which it was found that persons with myasthenia gravis engaged in a wide range of behavioral, cognitive, and affective coping methods following the initial diagnosis of the disorder. Another line of research centers on the role of life events in predisposing one to, and aggravating the course of, myasthenia gravis, but this research has yielded conflicting results. Whereas some evidence suggests that the occurrence of certain stressful life events is related to the course and outcome of myasthenia gravis (Chafetz, 1966; MacKenzie et al., 1969), other reports refute this finding (Magni et al., 1989).

The study by Schwartz et al. (1991), discussed previously, explored five psychosocial variables in persons with myasthenia gravis: (1) life satisfactions, (2) health locus of control, (3) psychosocial well-being, (4) public and body image, and (5) quality of life. In comparison to the persons with amyotrophic lateral sclerosis (a terminal illness), the individuals with myasthenia gravis scored significantly higher on the perceived health and social activity subscales of the life satisfactions measure. They also scored higher than persons with amyotrophic lateral sclerosis on the internal locus of control, psychosocial functioning, and quality of life indices and showed more positive body and public images. The researchers suggested that their findings may be attributed to the more severe physical and psychosocial changes that accompany amyotrophic lateral sclerosis. Unfortunately, without a comparison group of individuals without disabilities or a control group with a sudden onset impairment, these results provide little useful information on the attributes associated with psychosocial adaptation to myasthenia gravis.

Finally, in the Cordess et al. (1983) and Paradis et al. (1993) studies, no significant relationships were found between scores on the General Health Questionnaire or diagnosis of anxiety and the severity, duration, treatment response, or course of myasthenia gravis.

CONCLUSION

The scarce literature on psychosocial adaptation to myasthenia gravis does not allow firm conclusions on the prevalence and nature of specific reactions to this disorder. Depression and anxiety have been reported to be common reactions among persons with myasthenia gravis (rates range from 20% to 50%). These percentages, however, do not appear to differ from those reported in other groups of persons with neuromuscular or chronic health disorders. At the present, no data are available to demonstrate any association between psychosocial adaptation to myasthenia gravis and disease-related manifestations (eg, severity, duration, progression). Likewise, no data are available to link reactions to the disorder with sociodemographic variables or premorbid personality characteristics.

The research literature reviewed in this chapter, similar to the research efforts associated with the study of psychosocial adaptation to other disabilities and chronic illnesses, has a number of methodological limitations, most prominent of which are small sample sizes, the absence of adequate comparison groups, failure to conceptualize psychosocial adaptation to the disease as a complex multidimensional process (especially since myasthenia gravis is noted for its periods of symptom exacerbation and remission), and confounding of disease-related and sociodemographic variables with measures of psychosocial reactions to the disease.

REFERENCES

Berkow, R. (Ed.). (1992). *The Merck manual of diagnosis and therapy* (16th ed.). Rahway, NJ: Merck Research Laboratories.

Chafetz, M. E. (1966). Psychological disturbances in myasthenia gravis. *Annals of the New York Academy of Sciences, 135*, 424–427.

Cordess, C., Folstein, M. F., & Drachman, D. B. (1983). Quantitative psychiatric assessment of patients with myasthenia gravis. *Journal of Psychiatric Treatment and Evaluation, 5*, 381–384.

DiNardo, P. A., & Barlow, D. H. (1988). *Anxiety Disorders Interview Schedule-Revised (ADIS-R)*. Albany, NY: State University of New York at Albany, Phobia and Anxiety Disorders Clinic.

Doering, S., Henze, T., & Schussler, G. (1993). Coping with myasthenia gravis and implications for psychotherapy. *Archives of Neurology, 50*, 617–620.

Goldenson, R. M. (Ed.). (1978). *Disability and rehabilitation handbook*. New York: McGraw-Hill.

Lindemann, J. E., & Stanger, M. E. (1981). Progressive muscular disorders. In J. E. Lindemann (Ed.), *Psychological and behavioral aspects of physical disability* (pp. 273–300). New York: Plenum Press.

MacKenzie, K. R., Martin, M. J., & Howard, F. M. (1969). Myasthenia gravis: Psychiatric concomitants. *Canadian Medical Association Journal, 100*, 988–991.

Magni, G., Micaglio, G., Ceccato, M. B., Lalli, R., Bejato, L., & Angelini, C. (1989). The role of life events in the myasthenia gravis outcome: A one-year longitudinal study. *Acta Neurologica Scandinavica, 79*, 288–291.

Magni, G., Micaglio, G., Lalli, R., Bejato, L., Candeago, M. R., Merskey, H., & Angelini, C. (1988). Psychiatric disturbances associated with myasthenia gravis. *Acta Psychiatrica Scandinavica, 77*, 443–445.

McQuillen, M. P. (1978). Myasthenia gravis. In R. M. Goldenson (Ed.), *Disability and rehabilitation handbook* (pp. 486–489). New York: McGraw-Hill.

Paradis, C. M., Friedman, S., Lazar, R. M., & Kula, R. W. (1993). Anxiety disorders in a neuromuscular clinic. *American Journal of Psychiatry, 150*, 1102–1104.

Schwartz, L. G., Devine, P. A., Schechter, C. B., & Bender, A. N. (1991). Impact of illness on lifestyle. *Loss, Grief and Care, 4*(3), 3–21.

Schwartz, M. L., & Cahill, R. (1971). Psychopathology associated with myasthenia gravis and its treatment by psychotherapeutically oriented group. *Journal of Chronic Diseases, 24*, 543–552.

Sneddon, J. (1980). Myasthenia gravis: A study of social, medical and emotional problems in 26 patients. *Lancet, 1*, 526–528.

Tennant, C., Wilby, J., & Nicholson, G. A. (1986). Psychological correlates of myasthenia gravis: A brief report. *Journal of Psychosomatic Research, 30*, 575–580.

CHAPTER 19

Neurofibromatosis

DESCRIPTION

Neurofibromatosis was first described in 1793 by Telesius von Tilenau of Leipzig, but it was Frederick Daniel von Recklinghausen, a German pathologist, who first recognized neurofibromatosis as a distinct clinical disorder and who gave the disorder his name in 1882 (Riccardi, 1981; Rosner, 1990). Although thought to be a hereditary disorder as early as 1900, this was not confirmed until 1918. Approximately half of the cases of neurofibromatosis are inherited as an autosomal dominant genetic disorder—one expressed when one defective gene of a pair of genes on one of the autosomes (nonsex) chromosomes is received from a parent (Simpson, 1984). The other half of the cases occur in families with no history of the disorder as a noninherited genetic condition due to spontaneous mutation of a gene soon after fertilization of the egg (Abuelo, 1991).

Neurofibromatosis is more correctly viewed as a family of neurocutaneous disorders (ie, involving the neurological system and the skin) with eight distinct categories or types identified to date. The incidence is reported to be 1 per 3,000 to 4,000 live births, making neurofibromatosis as common as cystic fibrosis and Down's syndrome and nearly twice as common as muscular dystrophy. There are more than 100,000 affected individuals in the United States and more than 1 million worldwide, with no differences in incidence attributable to sex, socioeconomic status, racial and ethnic group, or geographic location (Riccardi, 1987; Riccardi & Mulvihill, 1981; Rosner, 1990). The most common Type I (previously known as von Recklinghausen's disease) has been mapped to a defect in a gene carried by chromosome 17. A less common Type II, called central or acoustic neurofibromatosis, has been mapped to a defect in a gene carried by chromosome 22. There is presently no laboratory test to diagnose neurofibromatosis, although a prenatal diagnostic test using genetic markers is a possibility in the near future (Berkow, 1992; Carey, 1992).

Symptoms are typically first evident by childhood or adolescence and tend to be progressive. Neurofibromatosis is characterized by highly variable expressivity in that the type and severity of clinical manifestations shown by persons with the disorder can vary considerably (Nativio & Belz, 1990; Pierpont, LeRoy, & Baldinger, 1984; Pueschel & Goldstein, 1991; Spaepen, Borghgraef, & Fryns, 1992). The café-au-lait spot, an irregularly shaped patch of light brown color, is the characteristic skin lesion present all over the body in nearly 95% of affected individuals. Freckling in the armpits and groin is also common. Multiple neurofibromas (cutaneous and subcutaneous benign tumors of nerve tissue and surrounding fibrous tissues) are present in approximately one third of affected individuals but seldom appear before age 10 years. The neurofibromas may be found anywhere on and in the body, may be small or large, may increase in size and number throughout the individual's life, and may become malignant (Rosner, 1990; Simpson, 1984).

Mental retardation and attention-deficit hyperactive disorder occur more frequently in children with neurofibromatosis than in the general population (Eliason, 1986; Stine & Adams, 1989). Less common symptoms may include hearing loss, visual impairments, hypertension, seizures, and headaches (Mouridsen, Andersen, Sorensen, & Rich, 1992; Varnhagen et al., 1988). Intraspinal and intracranial tumors may lead to severe skeletal deformities and pain. The report (and later play and movie) of the sensational case of John Merrick, whose neurofibromatosis was manifest as elephantiasis of the face and torso, contributed the stigmatizing label of "elephant man's disease." Although not a fatal disorder, neurofibromatosis-related deaths may occur in late childhood to middle adulthood due to intracranial and spinal cord tumors. Surgery may be appropriate in some cases for cosmetic and functional relief (Rosner, 1990).

PSYCHOSOCIAL ADAPTATION TO NEUROFIBROMATOSIS

In addition to the symptoms and physical stigmata of neurofibromatosis, the individual experiences significant developmental and learning problems (approximately 10% are classified as mentally retarded; Spaepen et al., 1992), especially as the individual approaches adolescence. These consequences place individuals with neurofibromatosis at significant risk for psychosocial distress. Although increased attention of biomedical researchers to the study of the cause and treatment of neurofibromatosis began in the 1970s and continues to the present, this is not true of psychosocial research. The literature on psychosocial reactions to neurofibromatosis is scant and composed almost entirely of anecdotal reports and clinical case studies (Anderson, 1992; Buschman, 1988; Roback, Kirshner, & Roback, 1981–1982; Snell, 1983).

Based upon clinical (and personal) experience and a review of published case studies, Messner and colleagues (Messner, Gardner, & Messner, 1985; Messner, Messner, & Lewis, 1985; Messner & Smith, 1986) have provided insights into the process of psychosocial adaptation to neurofibromatosis. The individual with neurofibromatosis, similar to the individual with multiple sclerosis or rheumatoid arthritis, lives with fear and uncertainty concerning the variable and uncertain progression of the disorder. It would, therefore, not be unreasonable to expect persons with neurofibromatosis to manifest the reactions of depression, apprehension, despair, anxiety, and irritability. If the individual becomes cosmetically disfigured, then he or she may experience a distorted self-perception and loss of self-esteem and may report feelings of isolation, hopelessness, and resignation. Moreover, negative reactions of others to the disfigurement and the ridicule of classmates, peers, and coworkers may lead, on the one hand, to social isolation and reactions of withdrawal, despair, and hopelessness due to the loss or alteration of a previously typical lifestyle. On the other hand, the individual may react with hostility and aggression against the stigmatizing reactions of others. Psychosocial reactions to neurofibromatosis may also be magnified as the onset of symptoms and confirmation of diagnosis may be delayed until late childhood and adolescence, difficult periods for adjustment even in persons without impairments.

A review of this case and clinical literature uncovered a curious collection of clinical lore that was frequently repeated, almost word for word, in various sources (see, for example, Messner, Gardner, & Messner, 1985), namely, that persons with neurofibromatosis are generally even tempered, compliant, gentle, longing for acceptance, and not embittered by their misfortune. We were unable, however, to find the basis for or the original source of these claims. They are strangely similar to those concerning persons with Down's syndrome that were common in the 1950s, put forward by well-intentioned but misguided advocates seeking the provision of community-based services, claims now known to be not only inaccurate but also stigmatizing.

Although "common sense" suggests that persons with neurofibromatosis have an increased risk for affective disorders (Riccardi, 1987) and that they should manifest a diversity of emotional and psychosocial reactions due to the variability and progression of the clinical symptoms, there are extremely limited empirical data to support these contentions. A comprehensive search of the medical, psychiatric, psychological, and sociobehavioral literature databases located only two studies (Spaepen et al., 1992; Varnhagen et al., 1988) in which psychosocial adaptation to neurofibromatosis was investigated empirically. One additional investigation (Moore, Ater, Needle, Slopis, & Copeland, 1994) reported on the neuropsychological profiles of children with neurofibromatosis and compared them to groups of children with a brain tumor with or without neurofibromatosis.

Furthermore we found no longitudinal or cross-sectional studies of persons with neurofibromatosis that traced psychosocial reactions from the onset of symptoms, and no studies relating psychosocial functioning of persons with neurofibromatosis to that of persons diagnosed with other neurological disorders and chronic diseases.

Moore et al. (1994) found that for a volunteer group of 65 children with neurofibromatosis only seen at a university medical center, the mean full-scale IQ was 93. Approximately 6% of the sample scored in the range used to define mental retardation. The mean score for the children on the Academic Achievement scale of the Wide Range Achievement Test was more than 1 standard deviation below the population mean. When combined with the intelligence quotient (IQ) test scores, more than 30% of the sample met the criteria for definition of learning disability. The children scored below average but within the norms for the population on measures of language, memory, visual-spatial skills, motor skills, and attention and above average but within the norms for the population on a measure of distractibility. The authors concluded that in comparison with age norms, the children with neurofibromatosis in their sample were at increased risk for cognitive deficits that would typically be manifested in school as learning disabilities.

In one of the studies located, Varnhagen and associates (Varnhagen et al., 1988) assessed 16 Canadian schoolchildren with neurofibromatosis (ages ranged from 4 to 18 years) and 9 unaffected siblings using the Eysenck Personality Questionnaire and the Profile of Mood States. On the Eysenck Personality Questionnaire, no statistically significant differences were found between the groups on any of the three scales—psychoticism (P), extroversion (E), and neuroticism (N). Although similar to the norms for their ages, the children with more severe symptoms of neurofibromatosis tended to score higher on the P and N scales than did children with less severe symptoms, and both of these groups tended to score higher than the group of unaffected siblings. Finally, on the Profile of Mood States, no statistically significant differences were found between the two groups, with the exception of elevated aggression scale scores among the children with neurofibromatosis. Nonsignificant differences between the two groups suggested higher levels of tension-anxiety and confusion among the children with neurofibromatosis. It was noted by the researchers that, similar to the Eysenck Personality Questionnaire results, the responses for all of the children were similar to the norms for their ages.

In the second study Spaepen et al. (1992) studied a nonrandom sample of 19 persons ranging in age from 5 to 15 years with neurofibromatosis who were being treated at a university clinic in Belgium. Interviews with the parents of the children suggested that shock, guilt, and anger were commonly manifest initial reactions. A Belgian version of the Child Behavior Check List was administered to the parents of 15 of the children in the sample. Because of missing data, the social competence subscale results were not reported. A total of eight behavior problems were found to exceed the cutoff scores in this order of frequency: (1) hyperactive, (2) anxious, (3) social withdrawal, (4) immature, (5) aggressive, (6) obsessive-compulsive, (7) somatic complaints, and (8) uncommunicative. The investigators concluded that these preliminary findings suggest an increased risk for behavior problems in children with neurofibromatosis that warrants additional investigation.

CHARACTERISTICS ASSOCIATED WITH ADAPTATION TO NEUROFIBROMATOSIS

A limited number of studies have provided meager information on the cognitive, affective, or behavioral correlates of this disorder. Attributes periodically suggested in the case reports include blunted affect, attention deficit, and mild learning disability (Anderson, 1992; Eliason, 1986; Spaepen et al., 1992). Survey data of dubious quality have supported estimates of a concomitant seizure disorder among persons with neurofibromatosis that range from 3% to 12% (Riccardi, 1987). Several recent investigations have explored the relationship between intellectual ability in persons with neurofibromatosis and specific neural characteristics as revealed through magnetic resonance imaging (Ferner, Chaudhuri, Bingham, Cox, & Hughes, 1993; North et al., 1994), but the results to date have been equivocal.

Estimates of the percentage of affected individuals for whom intellectual ability is at least mildly compromised range between 2% and 50% (Frank-Stromborg, 1992; Riccardi, 1982; Riccardi, 1987). Eliason (1986) obtained data on a battery of neuropsychological measures from a sample of 23 children between the ages of 6 and 13 years who were receiving follow-up medical care in a university medical center. Based upon the mean full-scale IQ scores, the children were functioning in the average range, with only one child falling into the range of mild mental retardation. Mean verbal IQ scores significantly exceeded mean nonverbal IQ scores, with 74% of the children differing by 15 or more IQ points. The results of the study by Varnhagen and associates (Varnhagen et al., 1988), discussed previously, confirm these findings. Statistically significant differences on the Weschler scales were noted between the unaffected children and the children with neurofibromatosis on both verbal and full-scale IQ (the children with neurofibromatosis scored, on the average, 14 to 19 points lower). The scores for the children with neurofibromatosis, however, fell within the low-average range of intelligence and did not support a diagnosis of mental retardation. Spaepen et al. (1992) found that 3 of the 19 children in their study scored below 70 on the Wechsler Intelligence Scale for Children (WISC) or Wechsler Preschool and Primary Scale of Intelligence (WPPSI) full-scale score. Subscale analyses for these individuals suggested difficulties in visual-perceptual organization, attention, memory, and fine motor skills.

The neuropsychological data in the Eliason (1986) study were used to classify the children into three broad cognitive disability subtypes: (1) visual-perceptual, (2) language, and (3) mixed. The percentages in these three groups for the children with neurofibromatosis were 56%, 30%, and 4%, as compared with percentages of 6%, 28%, and 62% for a sample of 297 children of the same ages diagnosed with learning disabilities. Eliason speculated that this unusually high percentage of visual-perceptual problems had important consequences for psychosocial adaptation, as research in the field of learning disabilities has linked these types of problems with the defining characteristics of hyperactivity— impulsivity and social imperception (ie, the inability to perceive and interpret social cues in the environment). Spaepen et al. (1992) also reported that their sample of 19 children with neurofibromatosis showed significant impairments in the areas of visual-perception and auditory discrimination and to a lesser extent in the areas of memory and attention. They suggested that these characteristics are similar to those observed in children with brain damage and average intelligence and point to possible intervention strategies.

Several reviews of case reports have revealed a disproportionate co-occurrence of neurofibromatosis and behavior disorders (Cole & Myer, 1978; Riccardi, 1982). More recent research has found a similar link between neurofibromatosis and childhood autism (Gillberg & Forsell, 1984; Mouridsen et al., 1992). The exact basis for the co-occurrence of neurofibromatosis and either cognitive or behavioral disorders is unknown, but it is suspected that both are related to structural brain or neurochemical abnormalities associated with neurofibromatosis (Abuelo, 1991).

CONCLUSION

The literature on psychosocial reactions to neurofibromatosis is scant and composed almost entirely of anecdotal reports and clinical case studies. A comprehensive search of the medical, psychiatric, psychological, and sociobehavioral literature databases located only a small number of investigations of psychosocial adaptation to neurofibromatosis and only a limited number of studies of the cognitive, affective, or behavioral correlates of this disorder. A curious collection of clinical lore has appeared frequently in various sources, repeated almost word for word. We were unable, however, to find the basis for or the original source of these claims. It is premature to attempt to provide conclusions concerning the psychosocial adaptation of persons with neurofibromatosis based on such a meager literature base.

REFERENCES

Abuelo, D. N. (1991). Genetic disorders. In J. L. Matson & J. A. Mulick (Eds.), *Handbook of mental retardation* (2nd ed.) (pp. 97–114). New York: Pergamon Press.

Anderson, B. W. (1992). (Letter to the editor). *American Journal of Psychiatry, 149,* 148–149.

Berkow, R. (Ed.). (1992). *The Merck manual of diagnosis and therapy* (16th ed.). Rahway, NJ: Merck Research Laboratories.

Buschman, P. R. (1988). Pediatric orthopedics: Dealing with loss and chronic sorrow. *Loss, Grief and Care, 2*(3–4), 39–44.

Carey, J. C. (1992). Health supervision and anticipatory guidance for children with genetic disorders (including specific recommendations for Trisomy 21, Trisomy 18 and neurofibromatosis). *Pediatric Clinics of North America, 39,* 25–53.

Cole, W. G., & Myer, N. A. (1978). Neurofibromatosis in childhood. *Australian and New Zealand Journal of Surgery, 48,* 360–365.

Eliason, M. J. (1986). Neurofibromatosis: Implications for learning and behavior. *Journal of Developmental and Behavioral Pediatrics, 7,* 175–179.

Ferner, R. E., Chaudhuri, R., Bingham, J., Cox, T., & Hughes, R. A. C. (1993). MRI in neurofibromatosis I. The nature and evolution of increased intensity T2 weighted lesions and their relationship to intellectual impairment. *Journal of Neurology, Neurosurgery, and Psychiatry, 56,* 492–545.

Frank-Stromborg, M. (1992). Neurofibromatosis. *Seminars in Oncology Nursing, 8,* 265–271.

Gillberg, C., & Forsell, C. (1984). Childhood psychosis and neurofibromatosis—More than a coincidence? *Journal of Autism and Developmental Disorders, 14,* 1–8.

Messner, R. L., Gardner, S., & Messner, M. R. (1985). Neurofibromatosis—an international enigma: A framework for nursing. *Cancer Nursing, 8,* 314–322.

Messner, R. L., Messner, M. R., & Lewis, S. J. (1985). Neurofibromatosis: A familial and family disorder. *Journal of Neurosurgical Nursing, 17,* 221–229.

Messner, R. L., & Smith, M. N. (1986). Neurofibromatosis: Relinquishing the masks; A quest for quality of life. *Journal of Advanced Nursing, 11,* 459–464.

Moore, B. D., Ater, J. L., Needle, M. N., Slopis, J., & Copeland, D. R. (1994). Neuropsychological profile of children with neurofibromatosis, brain tumor, or both. *Journal of Child Neurology, 9,* 368–377.

Mouridsen, S. E., Andersen, L. B., Sorensen, S. A., & Rich, B. (1992). Neurofibromatosis in infantile autism and other types of childhood psychoses. *Acta Paedopsychiatrica, 55,* 15–18.

Nativio, D. G., & Belz, C. (1990). Childhood neurofibromatosis. *Pediatric Nursing, 16,* 575–580.

North, K., Joy, P., Yuille, D., Cocks, N., Mobbs, E., Hutchins, P., McHugh, K., & deSilva, M. (1994). Specific learning disability in children with neurofibromatosis type I: Significance of MRI abnormalities. *Neurology, 44,* 878–883.

Pierpont, M. E., LeRoy, B. S., & Baldinger, S. R. (1984). Genetic disorders. In R. W. Blum (Ed.), *Chronic illness and disabilities in childhood and adolescence* (pp. 347–373). New York: Grune & Stratton.

Pueschel, S. M., & Goldstein, A. (1991). Genetic counseling. In J. L. Matson & J. A. Mulick (Eds.), *Handbook of mental retardation* (2nd ed.) (pp. 279–291). New York: Pergamon Press.

Riccardi, V. M. (1981). VonRecklinghausen's neurofibromatosis. *New England Journal of Medicine, 305,* 1617–1626.

Riccardi, V. M. (1982). The multiple forms of neurofibromatosis. *Pediatric Review*, *3*, 293–298.

Riccardi, V. M. (1987). Neurofibromatosis. *Nursing Clinics of North America*, *5*, 337–349.

Riccardi, V. M., & Mulvihill, J. J. (Eds.). (1981). *Advances in neurology, Vol. 29: Neurofibromatosis.* New York: Raven Press.

Roback, H. B., Kirshner, H., & Roback, E. (1981–1982). Physical self-concept changes in a mildly facially disfigured neurofibromatosis patient following communication skill training. *International Journal of Psychiatry in Medicine*, *11*, 137–143.

Rosner, J. (1990). Clinical review of neurofibromatosis. *Journal of the American Optometric Association*, *61*, 613–618.

Simpson, J. M. (1984). Neurological disorders with autosomal dominant transmission. *Journal of Neurosurgical Nursing*, *16*, 262–269.

Snell, S. C. (1983). Case study of a patient with neurofibromatosis. *Journal of Neurosurgical Nursing*, *15*, 19–21.

Spaepen, A., Borghgraef, M., & Fryns, J.-P. (1992). Von Recklinghausen-neurofibromatosis: A study of the psychological profile. In G. Evers-Kiebooms, J.-P. Fryns, J.-J. Cassiman, & H. Van den Berghe (Eds.), *Psychosocial aspects of genetic counseling* (pp. 85–91). New York: John Wiley & Sons.

Stine, S., & Adams, W. (1989). Learning problems in neurofibromatosis patients. *Clinical Orthopedics*, *245*, 43–48.

Varnhagen, C. K., Lewin, S., Das, J. P., Bowen, P., Ma, K., & Klimek, M. (1988). Neurofibromatosis and psychological process. *Journal of Developmental and Behavioral Pediatrics*, *9*, 257–265.

CHAPTER 20

━━━━━━

Parkinson's Disease

CHARACTERISTICS

Parkinson's disease, also known as paralysis agitans or "shaking palsy," is an idiopathic, degenerative disorder of the central nervous system, most notable for its late age at onset and slow progression of symptoms (Berkow, 1992; Corcoran, 1981; Cummings, 1992; Dakof & Mendelsohn, 1986; Duvoisin, 1984; Ilan & Friedmann, 1993). The major symptoms include slowness and poverty of movement (bradykinesia), muscle rigidity, tremor and shaking of limbs, postural instability, and fatigue. The cause is unknown, but there is a slight familial tendency in patterns of occurrence. Etiologically the disorder stems from the loss of neurons in the substantia nigra, the basal ganglia, and in other brainstem dopaminergic cell groups, leading to depletion of the neurotransmitter dopamine in these regions. This finding led to the successful treatment of the disorder with the drug levodopa (l-dopa).

Age at onset is typically between 50 and 70 years, with approximately 1% to 2% of the world population in this age group affected by the disorder (Duvoisin, 1984; Ilan & Friedmann, 1993). Although the disorder does not cause death, an increased risk of morbidity in persons with Parkinson's disease is associated with complications of inactivity, including poor nutrition and pneumonia. The following characteristics are common as Parkinson's disease progresses (Corcoran, 1981; Cummings, 1992; Dakof & Mendelsohn, 1986; Ilan & Friedmann, 1993; Longstreth, Nelson, Linde, & Munoz, 1992): (1) self-care activities require more time, (2) communication becomes more difficult because of slowness of speech and writing, (3) dependency on others increases, (4) intellectual functioning (eg, decision making, memory, judgment) gradually deteriorates, (5) withdrawal from interpersonal relations increases, and (6) depression and anxiety intensify.

PSYCHOSOCIAL ADAPTATION TO PARKINSON'S DISEASE

Although numerous clinical and empirical investigations have studied the occurrence and nature of depression among persons with Parkinson's disease, little research has been directed at exploring other psychosocial reactions to this disorder (eg, anxiety, denial, anger). This is surprising given speculations that anxiety may be a more common symptom in Parkinson's disease than either depression or cognitive impairment (Brown & MacCarthy, 1990; Ellgring et al., 1993; Lauterbach & Duvoisin, 1991; MacMahon & Fletcher, 1989).

Reports of depression among persons with Parkinson's disease, based on samples ranging in size from 26 to 802 persons, suggest that between 3% and 90% of this population are clinically depressed (Cummings, 1992; Dakof & Mendelsohn, 1986: Gotham, Brown, & Marsden, 1986; Hantz, Caradoc-Davies, Caradoc-Davies, Wheatherall, & Dixon, 1994; Huber, Friedenberg, Paulson, Shuttleworth, & Christy, 1990; Mayeux, Stern, Rosen, & Leventhal, 1981), with the average of these prevalence figures approximately 40% to 50% (Mayeux, 1990; Mayeux, Williams, Stern, & Côte, 1984). The large discrepancy in these percentages is due to several factors, including (1) the use of different definitions of the dependent variable (eg, major depression versus dysthymic disorder) and diagnostic criteria for assessing it (eg, various editions of the DSM and International Classification of Diseases), (2) the use of diverse assessment procedures ranging from self-reports (eg, the Depression scale of the Minnesota Multiphasic Personality Inventory or the Beck Depression Inventory) to clinical assessment methods (eg, Hamilton Rating Scale for Depression or DSM-based clinical diagnosis), (3) biases in the selection of samples (eg, nonrandom samples, sampling only inpatient or outpatient groups), (4) differential attention by researchers to the various physical symptoms of Parkinson's disease that mimic depression, and (5) the use of judges or raters of different clinical experience, levels of professional training, and educational backgrounds.

Despite these discrepant findings, several tentative conclusions emerge from the literature on depression in persons with Parkinson's disease.

- In the few studies using age-matched contrast or comparison groups (eg, persons with other progressive neuromuscular diseases, persons with disabilities of sudden and traumatic onset, persons without disabilities), persons with Parkinson's disease consistently demonstrated higher scores on a variety of depression measures (Cummings, 1992; Dakof & Mendelsohn, 1986; Ehmann, Beninger, Gawel, & Riopelle, 1990a; Gotham et al., 1986; Mayeux et al., 1981; Mayeux et al., 1986; Menza & Mark, 1994; Robins, 1976; Santamaria, Tolosa, & Valles, 1986).

- Age at onset of Parkinson's disease is apparently unrelated to degree of depression (Cummings, 1992; Dakof & Mendelsohn, 1986; Gotham et al., 1986; Mayeux et al., 1984).
- Data are inconsistent concerning the relationship between chronicity of Parkinson's disease (ie, time since initial diagnosis) and severity of depression. Whereas some researchers conclude that no consistent relationship has been documented (Cummings, 1992; Dakof & Mendelsohn, 1986; Mayeux et al., 1981; Mayeux et al., 1984; Starkstein, Preziosi, Bolduc, & Robinson, 1990), others maintain there is a possible connection relating increased disease chronicity to increased depression (Bielauskas & Glantz, 1989; Ehmann et al., 1990a; Menza & Mark, 1994). Unfortunately no empirically sound longitudinal studies have been undertaken to explore potential linear or nonlinear patterns linking chronicity of Parkinson's disease and depressive symptomatology.
- The data concerning the relationship between disease severity (eg, motoric symptoms of tremor, rigidity, and slowness of movement) and depression are inconsistent (Cummings, 1992; Dakof & Mendelsohn, 1986; Ehmann et al., 1990a; Gotham et al., 1986; Huber et al., 1990; Robins, 1976). A weak but often significant relationship has been reported between level of depression and degree of functional deterioration as measured by activities of daily living skills performance (Cummings, 1992; Ehmann et al., 1990a; Gotham et al., 1986; Menza & Mark, 1994; Starkstein, Robinson, Leiguarda, & Preziosi, 1993).
- A possible link also appears to exist between severity of depression and degree of cognitive impairment, as measured by the Mini-Mental State Examination (Folstein, Folstein, & McHugh, 1975) or dementia in Parkinson's disease (Cummings, 1992; Dakof & Mendelsohn, 1986; Mayeux et al., 1981; Menza & Mark, 1994; Santamaria et al., 1986; Starkstein, Preziosi, et al., 1989; Starkstein et al., 1993; Taylor, Saint-Cyr, Lang, & Kenny, 1986). There is speculation that such a link may reflect the effect of pathological changes in dopaminergic cells that enervate the frontal cortex (Starkstein, Preziosi, et al., 1989; Starkstein et al., 1993).

The high prevalence of self-reported and clinically observed depression among persons with Parkinson's disease has prompted researchers to suggest several models of causation.

- A *biochemical or organically based model* suggests that the etiology of depression is intrinsic to the disease process itself (ie, linked to increased degeneration of dopaminergic or serotonergic neurotransmitter activity).
- Proponents of a *reactive model* argue that evidence exists to directly link the reaction of depression and other affective changes to the progressively

disabling condition associated with Parkinson's disease (Mayeux, 1990). Mayeux and colleagues (1984) reported that in their sample of consecutive persons with Parkinson's disease, 28% met DSM—III criteria for major depressive disorder whereas 14% met the criteria for dysthymic disorder. Based on these findings they suggested the possible existence of two separate types of depressive disorder among persons with Parkinson's disease: one associated with profound dysphoric affective change and the second with more insidious onset and moderate degree of severity.

• An *interactive model* combines the first two models and views depression as a result of both specific biochemical changes and psychosocial factors (Bielauskas & Glantz, 1989; Dakof & Mendelsohn, 1986; Ehmann et al., 1990a; Menza & Mark, 1994; Taylor et al., 1986).

Unfortunately extant research does not offer clear support for any of these three models. Whereas some studies have suggested that lower levels of dopamine and serotonin among persons with Parkinson's disease are indeed associated with increased degree of depression (Mayeux et al., 1986; Sano et al., 1989), others have found that increased level of disability or functional limitations is often correlated with increased level of depression (Ehmann et al., 1990a; Gotham et al., 1986).

The thorny issue of the clinical similarity between the symptoms of Parkinson's disease and those of depression (eg, slowness of movement, slowness of mental functioning, stooped posture, weight loss, sleeping difficulties, blank facial expression) has been addressed by several researchers. Levin, Llabre, and Weiner (1988) used a test battery that included the Beck Depression Inventory and the Premorbid Pessimism and Future Despair subscales of the Millon Behavioral Health Inventory with a group of 119 persons with Parkinson's disease. They concluded from their findings that persons with Parkinson's disease showed significantly more depression on all measures when compared to a control group composed of spouses and volunteers without impairments. These differences were maintained even after the somatic items on the Beck Depression Inventory were removed, suggesting that depression in persons with Parkinson's disease is not a somatic artifact.

Similar findings were also reported by Ehmann et al. (1990a) in a study in which 45 persons with Parkinson's disease scored significantly higher on both a cognitive-affective and a somatic subscale of the Beck Depression Inventory than a control group of persons with other disabilities (ie, osteoarthritis, amyotrophic lateral sclerosis, Charcot-Marie-tooth disease, and muscular dystrophy) matched for age and sex. This finding suggested to these researchers a possible connection between mood changes (ie, increased depression) and specific deficiencies in dopamine production in persons with Parkinson's disease. In a related study (Ehmann, Beninger, Gawel, & Riopelle, 1990b) these researchers also found that the persons with Parkinson's disease used generally fewer coping strategies (cognitive, behavioral, and avoidance), as measured by the Billings and Moos' Coping Questionnaire, than did persons with other chronic impairments in a control group, further suggesting differential reactions of coping with depression and with other affective changes among persons with Parkinson's disease.

Finally, Huber et al. (1990) found that when compared to a contrast group of spouses without impairments, a sample of 103 persons with Parkinson's disease scored significantly higher on the total Beck Depression Inventory. These researchers then grouped the items of the Beck Depression Inventory into four subscales representing mood, self-reproach, vegetative symptoms, and somatic complaint. On further analysis it was found that only the somatic complaint and mood subscales were likely to differentiate the two groups. Furthermore, whereas scores on the vegetative symptoms and somatic complaint subscales showed a tendency to increase with disease severity, scores on the mood and self-reproach subscales did not.

In an effort to explore further the nature of depression in persons with Parkinson's disease, Starkstein and associates (Starkstein, Berthier, Bolduc, Preziosi, & Robinson, 1989; Starkstein, Preziosi, et al., 1989; Starkstein, Preziosi, Bolduc, et al., 1990; Starkstein, Preziosi, Forrester, & Robinson, 1990) studied various correlates of depression as they relate to early onset (before age 55 years) versus late onset (after age 55 years) of Parkinson's disease. Among their conclusions were these: (1) depression was higher on both the Hamilton Rating Scale for Depression and the Beck Depression Inventory for the early onset group than for the late onset group, even when disease chronicity was controlled for; (2) in the early onset group, chronicity and cognitive impairment accounted for significant proportions of the variance in depression scores, but in the late onset group only impairments in activities of daily living skills contributed significantly to the explanation of variation in the depression scores; and (3) depression scores were significantly higher at the very early and the late stages of the disease, as compared to the middle stages. According to these researchers, the differential manifestations of depression during progression of Parkinson's disease may suggest shifting areas of hemisphere involvement or increasing levels of brain dysfunction.

Follow-up studies of persons with Parkinson's disease are scarce. Starkstein and his colleagues (Starkstein, Bolduc, Mayberg, Preziosi, & Robinson, 1990; Starkstein, Mayberg, Leiguarda, Preziosi, & Robinson, 1992) sought to investigate the prevalence and severity of cognitive impairment and depression among persons with Parkinson's disease one to four years after an initial examination and to explore the relationships of these variables with earlier obtained medical and psychiatric indices. Among their findings were the following: (1) individuals who were initially diagnosed as depressed had significantly more severe levels of tremor, rigidity, and akinesia during follow-up; (2) individuals with major depression showed a significantly greater decline in activities of daily living and faster progression of illness when compared to those with no depression; (3) when compared to nondepressed individuals, depressed individuals also showed significantly higher levels of cognitive impairment and a greater degree of decline in cognitive ability during follow-up. Based on these findings the authors have reintroduced the notion that two forms of Parkinson's disease may indeed exist. The first form is associated with major depression and rapid functional and cognitive decline, while the second is linked to no, or only minor, affective changes and a gradual deterioration of cognitive and functional abilities.

As discussed, the prevalence and nature of anxiety among persons with Parkinson's disease have been only rarely and only recently investigated (see, for example, Lauterbach & Duvoisin, 1991; Starkstein et al., 1993; Stein, Heuser, Juncos, & Uhde, 1990). Findings generally suggest that the prevalence of anxiety disorders among samples of individuals with Parkinson's disease ranges from 38% (Stein et al., 1990) to 52% (Starkstein et al., 1993) when using self-report and clinician-rated measures. The findings of other studies suggest that (1) persons with Parkinson's disease experience more anxiety than controls with osteoarthritis (Menza & Mark, 1994) and (2) a significant association exists between depression and anxiety in persons with Parkinson's disease (Starkstein et al., 1993).

CHARACTERISTICS ASSOCIATED WITH ADAPTATION TO PARKINSON'S DISEASE

In contrast to the abundance of data available on depression reactions to the onset of Parkinson's disease, surprisingly little information can be found on other characteristics associated with psychosocial adaptation to the disease. MacCarthy and Brown (1989) investigated the relationships between a group of physical and medical variables (eg, duration of disease, stage of disease, functional impairment), intervening variables (eg, coping style, social support, perceived control, self-esteem), and various aspects of psychosocial adaptation to Parkinson's disease. Outcome measures of psychosocial adaptation included (1) depression, as measured by the Beck Depression Inventory; (2) well-being, as measured by the Bradburn Positive Affect Scale; and (3) acceptance of illness, as measured by the Acceptance of Sick Role scale. Among the authors' main findings were the following: (1) functional impairment, more negative self-esteem, and maladaptive coping (ie, acting out and distraction) were the best predictors of level of depression; (2) functional impairment and maladaptive coping were the best predictors of acceptance of illness; (3) higher self-esteem, adaptive coping (ie, problem solving, reorientation, and distancing), and amount of instrumental social support were the best predictors of positive well-being; (4) duration of illness was related to acceptance of illness and self-esteem; and (5) zero-order correlations between ratings of stage of disease progression and measures of depression and well-being were marginal, but ratings of stage of disease progression were significantly associated with acceptance of illness.

Brown and MacCarthy (1990) concluded from a study on longitudinal variations in activities of daily living and self-reported depression of persons with Parkinson's disease, "permanently" nondepressed persons were the least disabled in activities of daily living skills performance, whereas "permanently" depressed persons were the most severely disabled. These researchers suggested that the longitudinal association between disability level and depression is complex and nonlinear. They further suggested that whereas increase in the severity of disability is linked to increase in dysphoric and pessimistic aspects of depression, severity of disability may not be related to other depressive aspects (eg, guilt, self-blame).

Only one study was found that investigated different patterns of psychosocial adaptation to Parkinson's disease. Dakof and Mendelsohn (1986), using cluster analysis of data obtained from persons diagnosed with Parkinson's disease using a battery of psychological tests (ie, clinical interview, the Mini-Mental State Exam, the Symptom Check List—90-Revised), discovered four clusters of persons that they named (1) sanguine and socially engaged (40% of participants); (2) depressed, anxious, and worried (28% of participants); (3) depressed, powerless, and misunderstood (15% of participants); and (4) passive, resigned, and having flat affect (17% of participants). A high degree of depression appeared to be a concomitant of the second and third clusters. Persons in the third cluster, and to a lesser degree in the second and fourth clusters, showed more motoric impairment, as compared to those in the first cluster. The researchers concluded that these findings showed considerable variation in how persons with Parkinson's disease adapt to the unpredictable progression of the disease. Unfortunately no other studies were found that investigated the types of coping or adaptation styles manifested by persons with Parkinson's disease.

More recently, Menza and Mark (1994) speculated that the personality traits of novelty seeking and harm avoidance, hypothesized to be related to dopaminergic pleasure and reward and to serotonergic systems, respectively, could predict the occurrence of depression among persons with Parkinson's disease. Results showed that harm avoidance, a personality pattern associated with the serotonergic behavioral inhibition system, was indeed strongly related to level of self-reported depression.

CONCLUSION

A growing body of research indicates that depression and, to a lesser degree, anxiety are frequently experienced psychosocial reactions among people with Parkinson's disease. Estimates of the incidence of these reactions in the population, however, tend to vary widely due to differing definitions and methods of measuring these reactions, inadequate sampling procedures, and inconsistent attention paid to the overlap between the physical symptoms associated with the disease and generic signs of depression. Despite these limitations, several tentative conclusions emerge from the current psychosocial literature on Parkinson's disease.

First, when compared to control groups of people with other physically disabling conditions or persons without disabilities, persons with Parkinson's disease report greater levels of depression. Second, no consistent relationships have been established between duration or severity of Parkinson's disease and severity of depression. Third, depression in persons with Parkinson's disease has been linked to functional impairment as indicated by activities of daily living performance. Fourth, no relationship appears to exist between sociodemographic variables (eg, age, sex, ethnic background) and the nature or severity of depression.

Several researchers have recently suggested that more than one form of Parkinson's disease may exist. These forms may be distinguishable by the following etiologic factors and clinical features: (1) the existence of major depression versus no or only minor depression; (2) biochemical or endogenous versus reactive or exogenous depression; (3) early versus late age of disease onset; and (4) rapid versus gradual functional and cognitive decline. Research on the possible existence of more than one form of Parkinson's disease is only in its infancy but will certainly have a major impact on the investigation of the etiology, progression, nature, and severity of psychosocial reactions to the disease.

REFERENCES

Berkow, R. (Ed.). (1992). *The Merck manual of diagnosis and therapy* (16th ed.). Rahway, NJ: Merck Research Laboratories.

Bielauskas, L. A., & Glantz, R. H. (1989). Depression type in Parkinson's disease. *Journal of Clinical and Experimental Neuropsychology, 11*, 597–604.

Brown, R. G., & MacCarthy, B. (1990). Psychiatric morbidity in patients with Parkinson's disease. *Psychological Medicine, 20*, 77–87.

Corcoran, P. J. (1981). Neuromuscular diseases. In W. C. Stolov & M. R. Clowers (Eds.), *Handbook of severe disability* (pp. 83–100). Washington, DC: U. S. Department of Education, Rehabilitation Services Administration.

Cummings, J. L. (1992). Depression and Parkinson's disease: A review. *The American Journal of Psychiatry, 149*, 443–454.

Dakof, G. A., & Mendelsohn, G. A. (1986). Patterns of adaptation to Parkinson's disease. *Health Psychology, 8,* 355–372.

Duvoisin, R. C. (1984). *Parkinson's disease: A guide for patient and family* (2nd ed.). New York: Raven Press.

Ehmann, T. S., Beninger, R. J., Gawel, M. J., & Riopelle, R. J. (1990a). Coping, social support, and depressive symptoms in Parkinson's disease. *Journal of Geriatric Psychiatry and Neurology, 3,* 85–90.

Ehmann, T. S., Beninger, R. J., Gawel, M. J., & Riopelle, R. J. (1990b). Depressive symptoms in Parkinson's disease: A comparison with disabled control subjects. *Journal of Geriatric Psychiatry and Neurology, 3,* 3–9.

Ellgring, H., Seiler, S., Perleth, B., Frings, W., Gasser, T., & Oertel, W. (1993). Psychosocial aspects of Parkinson's disease. *Neurology, 43*(Suppl. 6), S41–S44.

Folstein, M. F., Folstein, S. E., & McHugh, P. R. (1975). "Mini-mental state": A practical method for grading the cognitive state of patients for the clinician. *Journal of Psychiatric Research, 12,* 189–198.

Gotham, A. M., Brown, R. G., & Marsden, C. D. (1986). Depression in Parkinson's disease: A quantitative and qualitative analysis. *Journal of Neurology, Neurosurgery, and Psychiatry, 49,* 381–389.

Hantz, P., Caradoc-Davies, G., Caradoc-Davies, T., Wheatherall, M., & Dixon, G. (1994). Depression in Parkinson's disease. *American Journal of Psychiatry, 151,* 1010–1014.

Huber, S. J., Friedenberg, D. L., Paulson, G. W., Shuttleworth, E. C., & Christy, J. A. (1990). A pattern of depressive symptoms varies with progression of Parkinson's disease. *Journal of Neurology, Neurosurgery, and Psychiatry, 53,* 275–278.

Ilan, H., & Friedmann, L. W. (1993). Neuromuscular disorders. In M. G. Eisenberg, R. L. Glueckauf, & H. H. Zaretsky (Eds.), *Medical aspects of disability* (pp. 243–255). New York: Springer.

Lauterbach, E. C., & Duvoisin, R. C. (1991). Anxiety disorders in familial Parkinsonism. *American Journal of Psychiatry, 148,* 274.

Levin, B. E., Llabre, M. M., & Weiner, W. J. (1988). Parkinson's disease and depression: Psychometric properties of the Beck Depression Inventory. *Journal of Neurology, Neurosurgery, and Psychiatry, 51,* 1401–1404.

Longstreth, W. T., Nelson, L., Linde, M., & Munoz, D. (1992). Utility of the sickness impact profile in Parkinson's disease. *Journal of Geriatric Psychiatry and Neurology, 5,* 142–148.

MacCarthy, B., & Brown, R. (1989). Psychosocial factors in Parkinson's disease. *British Journal of Clinical Psychology, 28,* 41–52.

MacMahon, D. G., & Fletcher, P. J. (1989). Psychiatric aspects of Parkinson's disease. *British Medical Journal, 299,* 388–389.

Mayeux, R. (1990). Depression in the patient with Parkinson's disease. *Journal of Clinical Psychiatry, 51*(Suppl.), 20–23.

Mayeux, R., Stern, Y., Rosen, J., & Leventhal, J. (1981). Depression, intellectual impairment, and Parkinson's disease. *Neurology, 31,* 645–650.

Mayeux, R., Stern, Y., Williams, J. B., Cote, L., Frantz, A., & Dyrenfurth, I. (1986). Clinical and biochemical features of depression in Parkinson's disease. *American Journal of Psychiatry, 143,* 756–759.

Mayeux, R., Williams, J. B., Stern, Y., & Côte, L. (1984). Depression and Parkinson's disease. *Advances in Neurology, 40,* 241–250.

Menza, M. A., & Mark, M. H. (1994). Parkinson's disease and depression: The relationship to disability and personality. *Journal of Neuropsychiatry and Clinical Neuroscience*, *6*, 165–169.

Robins, A. H. (1976). Depression in patients with Parkinsonism. *British Journal of Psychiatry*, *128*, 141–145.

Sano, M., Stern, Y., Williams, J., Cote, L., Rosenstein, R., & Mayeux, R. (1989). Coexisting dementia and depression in Parkinson's disease. *Archives of Neurology* (46), 1284–1286.

Santamaria, J., Tolosa, E., & Valles, A. (1986). Parkinson's disease with depression: A possible subgroup of idiopathic parkinsonism. *Neurology*, *36*, 1130–1133.

Starkstein, S. E., Berthier, M. L., Bolduc, P. L., Preziosi, T. J., & Robinson, R. G. (1989). Depression in patients with early versus late onset of Parkinson's disease. *Neurology*, *39*, 1441–1445.

Starkstein, S. E., Bolduc, P. L., Mayberg, H. S., Preziosi, T. J., & Robinson, R. G. (1990). Cognitive impairments and depression in Parkinson's disease: A follow up study. *Journal of Neurology, Neurosurgery, and Psychiatry*, *53*, 597–602.

Starkstein, S. E., Mayberg, H. S., Leiguarda, R., Preziosi, T. J., & Robinson, R. G. (1992). A prospective longitudinal study of depression, cognitive decline, and physical impairments in patients with Parkinson's disease. *Journal of Neurology, Neurosurgery, and Psychiatry*, *55*, 377–382.

Starkstein, S. E., Preziosi, T. J., Berthier, M. L., Bolduc, P. L., Mayberg, H. S., & Robinson, R. G. (1989). Depression and cognitive impairment in Parkinson's disease. *Brain*, *112*, 1141–1153.

Starkstein, S. E., Preziosi, T. J., Bolduc, P. L., & Robinson, R. G. (1990). Depression in Parkinson's disease. *Journal of Nervous and Mental Disease*, *178*, 27–31.

Starkstein, S. E., Preziosi, T. J., Forrester, A. W., & Robinson, R. G. (1990). Specificity of affective and autonomic symptoms of depression in Parkinson's disease. *Journal of Neurology, Neurosurgery, and Psychiatry*, *53*, 869–873.

Starkstein, S. E., Robinson, R. G., Leiguarda, R., & Preziosi, T. J. (1993). Anxiety and depression in Parkinson's disease. *Behavioural Neurology*, *6*, 151–154.

Stein, M. B., Heuser, I. J., Juncos, J. L., & Uhde, T. W. (1990). Anxiety disorders in patients with Parkinson's disease. *American Journal of Psychiatry*, *147*, 217–220.

Taylor, A. E., Saint-Cyr, J. A., Lang, A. E., & Kenny, F. T. (1986). Parkinson's disease and depression. *Brain*, *109*, 279–292.

CHAPTER 21

Spina Bifida

DESCRIPTION

Spina bifida (literally "two-part spine") is the name associated with a group of congenital spinal column disorders in which one or more of the vertebral arches fail to close during development of the embryo (Menolascino & Egger, 1978). Although the defect may occur anywhere and on any surface of the spinal column, it is most common for it to occur on the anterior surface in the lumbar region. If a herniated sac is present (spina bifida cystica), it may contain fluid (a meningocele), spinal cord material (a myelocele), or both (a meningomyelocele). The absence of herniation with underlying spinal cord defect is called spina bifida occulta, a condition associated with no or only mild symptoms. Spina bifida is typically one of several anomalies present in individuals with multiple impairments.

The incidence of spina bifida occulta is estimated to range from 5% to as much as 25% of the general population, although the incidence of the more complex cystica forms is reported to be from 0.4 to 4 per 1,000 live births (Menolascino & Egger, 1978). Incidence figures appear to vary with different populations and races (Kleinberg, 1982) and appear to be dropping with the arrival of prenatal diagnosis using serum or amniotic fluid a-fetoprotein screening (Abuelo, 1991). Epidemiological data suggest that spina bifida is related to increased maternal age, maternal diet, maternal malnutrition, and teratogenic factors in the intrauterine environment such as drugs, alcohol, and radiation. Although the cause is unknown, most experts subscribe to the view of polygenic expression modified by environmental factors (Liptak et al., 1988).

The manifestations of the disability depend upon the type, location, and severity of the spinal cord defect. Because the lumbar region is the common site of the lesion, trunk and lower extremity paralysis or muscle weakness, impaired sensation of touch and pain below the lesion, and bowel and bladder dysfunction are frequent. If the canal transporting the cerebrospinal fluid is involved, hydrocephaly will be present, leading to associated impairment of mental ability and a diagnosis of mental retardation. Untreated spina bifida leads to death within the first year in as many as 75% of cases and to severe disability in 60% of those surviving the first year (Laurence & Tew, 1967). Various neurosurgical treatments to reduce spinal column damage and treat the hernia to reduce nursing problems and prevent secondary impairments are available, depending upon a careful assessment of various personality-related and disability-related variables. Survival rates for children born with spina bifida are close to 90% (Kleinberg, 1982; Leonard & Freeman, 1981), although ethical controversy surrounds the aggressive treatment of newborns with the most severe impairments (Cohen, 1987; Sassaman, 1991).

PSYCHOSOCIAL ADAPTATION TO SPINA BIFIDA

Researchers and theorists (Hayden, Davenport, & Campbell, 1979; Lavigne, Nonal, & McLore, 1988; Liptak et al., 1988; Murch & Cohen, 1989; Wallander, Varni, Babani, Banis, De Haan, et al., 1989) have argued that individuals with spina bifida, similar to others with physical disabilities, are predisposed to manifest negative psychosocial reactions to their physical disability ranging on a continuum from withdrawal to anxiety to demandingness to anger. These maladaptive behaviors limit positive interactions with others and lead to decreased self-esteem, more negative self-concept, and further isolation. The individual experiences a self-perpetuating negative spiral of social failure and psychosocial maladaptation. Support for these contentions, however, has been based primarily on insights from clinical case summaries, observational studies of social behaviors, the verbal responses of adolescents and young adults with spina bifida to semistructured interview questions, personal case histories written by persons with spina bifida (Fosdal, 1992), or the analyses of questionnaire data from informants, typically the mothers of individuals with spina bifida.

Gerber (1973), for example, presented case studies of four women in late adolescence seeking psychotherapy, each of whom had successful surgery in early childhood to correct a spinal column defect. Gerber noted that all four women expressed feelings of depression, anxiety at the prospect of living independently, and a special fear of sexual functioning because of their visible surgical scars. Kolin, Scherzer, New, and Garfield (1971) conducted medical and psychiatric evaluations of a group of 13 children with spina bifida who were aged 7 to 11 years and reported that the children expressed moderate to intense anxiety regarding their disability (not empirically operationalized), that denial was infrequent (no data were provided), and that only 3 of the 13 children were considered clinically depressed (not empirically operationalized).

Tin and Teasdale (1985) observed the social behaviors of a nonrandom sample of eight children with spina bifida who were aged 5 to 7 years on a playground in an integrated school in Australia. These observations were compared with observations of a group of children without disabilities who were matched for age, sex, socioeconomic status, and intellectual ability. The children with spina bifida were observed to have fewer playground interactions, to interact with fewer persons, to spend more time alone, and to be less active participants in group social activities. The peers of these children initiated fewer interactions with them than with the children without disabilities. It must be noted, however, that the interactions of five of the children with spina bifida were restricted by limited mobility; three used a wheelchair and two used a pair of crutches.

McAndrew (1979) interviewed 35 Australian individuals with spina bifida who were between the ages of 14 and 26 years. Three individuals reported that they had no close friends, and nine reported only infrequent social contacts with other individuals without impairments. Nearly 65% reported that they felt depressed at least once a month. McAndrew noted frequent reports of the interviewees that their disability was hard to cope with and accept and that they frequently felt disheartened, embarrassed, and uncomfortable. When asked to consider their future, many of those interviewed (no percentages were provided) predicted that they would have problems making and keeping friends, finding marriage partners, and finding employment. On the other hand, none of those interviewed admitted suicidal ideas in the preceding year, 50% said they were rarely or never bored, and 67% said they were rarely or never lonely.

Anderson (1979) interviewed nonrandom samples of 89 adolescents with cerebral palsy and 30 adolescents with spina bifida who were over age 15 years and attending school in Great Britain, together with age- and sex-matched controls. Among the adolescents with disabilities, 33% were judged to have marked and 19% to have borderline psychological problems, with the highest rates found for the females with spina bifida (no data provided). Reactions most commonly reported were depression, low self-confidence, fear of new situations and of meeting new people (especially peers of the opposite sex), and anxiety about their future. Only 21% of the students with disabilities rated their social life out of school as satisfactory versus 94% of the control students. Compared with 73% of the controls, only 20% reported they went out with a student of the opposite sex even though most were interested in doing so.

Dorner (1976; 1977) interviewed in London a nonrandom sample of 46 adolescents (mean age of 16 years) with spina bifida. A total of 85% of those interviewed reported feeling depressed sometimes. This reaction was more commonly reported by females than by males and was more closely associated with feelings of social isolation than with severity of spina bifida symptoms. More than 25% of the adolescents in this sample reported having suicidal ideas. A majority expressed worry about their future, especially about living independently, finding employment, and getting married and having children. Similar observations concerning adolescents with spina bifida were reported by Blum (1983) based upon clinical impressions. Blum noted that adolescent males were more concerned than females with issues concerning sexuality and that adolescent females were more likely than males to express suicidal ideation. No empirical data were provided to support these observations, however. Clinical interview and behavioral observation data were collected from a nonrandom sample of 59 children with spina bifida being treated at a specialty clinic in Milan, Italy (Redaelli et al., 1992). Mental disturbances were reported to be present in 34% of the sample. The study, however, failed to provide operational definitions for the independent variables, and no indication of the measure of psychosocial adaptation was reported.

In a large-scale study conducted in Cleveland (Breslau, 1983; 1985), 304 children with physical disabilities who were aged 6 to 18 years were identified from the case records of two hospitals and four clinics. Of the total sample, 65 children had cystic fibrosis, 98 had cerebral palsy, 63 had spina bifida, and 78 were multiply impaired. A total of 206 children with disabilities were identified who had siblings without disabilities. In addition to the siblings, data were collected from a random probability sample of 360 age-matched children without impairments who were from the city. The mothers of the children in both groups served as informants for the Psychiatric Screening Inventory, measuring risk for psychiatric problems in seven areas: (1) self-destructive tendencies, (2) mentation problems, (3) conflict with parents, (4) regressive anxiety, (5) fighting, (6) delinquency, and (7) isolation. Analyses of the data revealed that the scores for the children with spina bifida exceeded those for the children without disabilities on a composite of the seven scales as well as on the scales measuring risk of mentation problems and isolation. When compared to their siblings, the children with spina bifida were found to be significantly different on the scales measuring mentation problems, fighting, delinquency, and isolation but not significantly different on the composite measure. The authors interpreted these results to mean that children with spina bifida are at risk for psychiatric problems that are reactive disturbances and are not neurologically based. The children with and without disabilities were divided into groups representing level of severity of psychiatric problems using the composite Psychiatric Screening Inventory score. When the profiles of the 83 children with disabilities and the 39 children without impairments who exceeded the cutoff for severe problems were compared, it was revealed that the children with disabilities were at highest risk for mentation problems and isolation and the children without impairments were at highest risk for fighting and delinquency. Among the children with disabilities, level of cognitive functioning (as measured by intelligence quotient (IQ) score) and adaptive behavior (as measured by activities of daily living skills score) were found to account for the differences in mentation problem scores but not for the differences in isolation scores. A total of 27% of the children with spina bifida were reported to be at risk for severe psychiatric problems.

The mothers of 255 of the children with physical disabilities (56 with cystic fibrosis, 50 with spina bifida, 82 with cerebral palsy, and 67 with multiple disabilities) completed the Psychiatric Screening Inventory a second time an average of five years after the first occasion (Breslau & Marshall, 1985). The only significant change from occasion 1 to occasion 2 was a decrease in the regressive anxiety scale score for the total sample of children with disabilities. There were no significant differences from occasion 1 to occasion 2 on any of the scale scores for the children with spina bifida. These results led the authors to a pessimistic view of the psychiatric prognosis for the children with physical disabilities.

The mothers of a nonrandom sample of 270 children with disabilities who were between the ages of 4 and 16 years who attended a clinic completed the Child Behavior Check List, an inventory of psychosocial behavior in three areas: (1) internalized behavior problems, (2) externalized behavior problems, and (3) social competence (Wallander, Varni, Babani, Banis, & Wilcox, 1988). Of the total sample, 80 children had juvenile diabetes, 77 children had spina bifida, 40 children had hemophilia, 30 children were chronically obese, 24 children had juvenile rheumatoid arthritis, and 19 children had cerebral palsy. As a group these children's scores corresponded to the 75th percentile rank for internalized behavior problems, the 69th percentile rank for externalized behavior problems, and the 12th percentile rank for social competence. Child Behavior Check List data comparing a subsample of 23 children with spina bifida and 27 children with cerebral palsy (Wallander, Varni, Babani, Banis, De Haan, et al., 1989; Wallander, Varni, Babani, De Haan, et al., 1989) revealed that the children in the two groups did not differ on either internalized or externalized behavior problems, with scores corresponding to the 84th and 82nd percentile ranks, respectively. The children with spina bifida were, however, rated as more socially competent than the children with cerebral palsy, although the combined group of 50 children attained scores corresponding only to the fourth percentile rank on social competence.

Three reports were found that failed to support the predicted impairment of psychosocial adaptation of individuals with spina bifida. Halliwell and Spain (1977) asked teachers to complete the Rutter Behavior Scale for 58 children with spina bifida and 47 children without impairments born in London between 1967 and 1969. No significant differences between the two groups of children were discovered, nor did the teachers report that the children with spina bifida were less well liked or had fewer friends. It must be pointed out, however, that the children were not a random sample nor were the teachers unaware of the purpose of the investigation. In fact, the presence of these children in public (ordinary) schools in London in 1977 suggests that they must have been well adjusted and well behaved.

Rinck, Berg, and Hafeman (1989) pointed out the conflicting information on the incidence of depression in individuals with spina bifida. They discovered these rates: (1) a rate similar to age- and sex-matched peers without impairments (Hayden et al., 1979); (2) 23% of a sample (Kolin et al., 1971); (3) 65% of a sample, with no suicidal ideas in the preceding year (McAndrew, 1979); and (4) 85% of a sample, with 25% admitting suicidal ideas in the past (Dorner, 1976). Rinck et al. (1989) interviewed the parents of 38 adolescents between 10 and 20 years of age and discovered that 74% considered their child to be happy and outgoing, 18% considered their child to be shy and withdrawn, and only 8% considered their child to be angry or depressed.

Finally, Barakat and Linney (1992) tested a multidimensional ecological model that sought to link psychosocial adaptation in children with physical disabilities to measures of the child's disability, parental reactions, social support, parent–child interactions, and parental adaptation. Data were collected on a battery of measures from the parents of 29 children with spina bifida and from the parents of 28 children with no disabilities who were matched for age, sex, race, socioeconomic status, and family composition. Videotapes of parent–child interactions in unstructured play situations were also examined and analyzed. Although the children with spina bifida scored lower on the measures of mental ability and adaptive behavior, no significant differences were found on the dependent variables measuring the child's psychosocial adaptation to disability. For both groups adaptation was found to be directly related to the presence of adequate social supports and to maternal adaptation.

Only a meager number of attempts have been reported in the literature to investigate psychosocial adaptation to disability using empirical data collected directly from samples of persons with spina bifida. Kazak and Clark (1986) found that 56 children with spina bifida scored significantly below a group of 53 age- and sex-matched children without impairments on the total Piers-Harris Self-Concept Scale as well as the subscales of anxiety, popularity, and happiness. In a pair of investigations (Campbell, Hayden, & Davenport, 1977; Hayden et al., 1979), a self-selected group of 20 adolescents with spina bifida who were aged 10 to 19 years and a group of age- and sex-matched adolescents without impairments were administered scales measuring various aspects of personality and adaptation to disability. In addition, both the individuals with spina bifida and their parents were interviewed using a semistructured protocol. In comparison with the controls, the group of adolescents with spina bifida was found to have a more negative self-concept, self-esteem, body image, and self image and also to have had fewer friends. They also interacted less frequently with their peers and expressed greater self-criticism and greater anxiety about success in school and about meeting new people. No differences between the two groups of adolescents were found, however, on the scales measuring depression or expression of anger.

Tew and Laurence (1985) examined an unselected consecutive series of 10-year-old children with spina bifida in South Wales and compared the psychosocial and school adjustment of these 55 individuals with that of a group of 52 children without impairments matched for sex, age, place of residence, and socioeconomic status. The children with spina bifida were found to express greater feeling of personal inferiority to their peers; to exhibit greater social maladaptation in interactions with their peers, parents, and siblings; and to engage more frequently in daydreaming. No differences were found, however, in the school adjustment of the two groups of children based upon teacher-reported interview data.

In contrast to these findings indicating a risk of psychosocial maladaptation among individuals with spina bifida are the results of five studies. Spaulding and Morgan (1986) compared 19 children with spina bifida who were between the ages of 5 and 15 years with 19 age- and sex-matched children without impairments on a variety of variables, including the child's behavior as rated by his or her parents and the child's self-concept and own ratings of his or her behavior. Analyses of these data revealed no difference between the two groups on any variable. Lord, Varzos, Behrman, Wicks, and Wicks (1990) administered the UCLA Loneliness Scale to 31 adolescents with spina bifida who were aged 12 to 19 years and attending regular schools and asked their parents to complete the Personality Inventory for Children. The adolescents were found to be below the norms for their age peers on the Personality Inventory for Children social skills scale and the loneliness measure, but they did not differ on the Personality Inventory for Children scales measuring overall adaptation or delinquency.

Blum, Resnick, Nelson, and St. Germaine (1991) collected data on self-report measures from a group of 102 adolescents and young adults (age range 12 to 22 years) with spina bifida. Nearly two thirds used a wheelchair, 74% had been treated for hydrocephalus, and 91% lived at home. When asked to rate themselves in comparison to their peers, 60% selected "pretty much the same," 32% selected "a little different," and 8% selected "very different." Self-reports of activities revealed a generally restricted social life, especially with regard to dating, but 64% of the sample hoped to someday marry and have children. Monson (1992) collected data on autonomy, coping, and self-esteem from 22 adolescents with spina bifida who were aged 12 to 18 years and from adolescents without impairments matched for age and sex. The results of a multivariate analysis of variance indicated no significant difference between the vector of dependent variables for the two groups.

Finally, Cartright and colleagues (Cartright, Joseph, & Grenier, 1993) obtained data by mail using the Offer Self-Image Questionnaire from a self-selected sample of 50 persons with spina bifida in Louisiana aged 11 to 21 years. The questionnaire consists of 130 items that purport to measure 11 dimensions of self-image. These dimensions are then scored to represent the five composite "selfs": (1) psychological self, (2) social self, (3) sexual self, (4) family self, and (5) coping self. When compared to published norms for samples of persons without spina bifida, the overall profiles of the sample of persons with spina bifida did not differ significantly. In fact, the persons with spina bifida scored above the norms on 6 of the 11 dimensions of self-image. The only composite self for which the results were significantly below average was the sexual self.

A review of the medical, psychiatric, or psychological literature on psychosocial adaptation to spina bifida revealed a finding similar to that concerning epilepsy. No studies were located that conceptualized adaptation to spina bifida as a set of distinct psychosocial reactions or as a process of change in reactions that can be ordered hierarchically and temporally.

CHARACTERISTICS ASSOCIATED WITH ADAPTATION TO SPINA BIFIDA

Only a few studies were located that attempted to identify characteristics that are associated with or predict psychosocial adaptation to disability among individuals with spina bifida. The variable predicted to be most closely associated with adaptation is the severity of disability associated with the physical disability (Anderson, 1979; McAndrew, 1979). Children with spina bifida and cerebral palsy who had the lowest IQ scores and the lowest adaptive behavior scores were found to be rated lowest by their mothers on the social competence scale of the Child Behavior Check List (Wallander, Varni, Babani, Banis, De Haan, et al., 1989; Wallander, Varni, Babani, De Haan, et al., 1989). Redaelli et al. (1992) observed that among their nonrandom sample of 59 children with spina bifida in Italy, indices of mental disturbance and psychosocial maladaptation were more frequently discovered among those children who were older and among those with neurophysiological complications (eg, hydrocephalus), weak family support systems, and repeated and prolonged hospitalization.

When adaptation is operationalized as vocational success, then the results of a study by Evans, Hickman, and Carter (1974) support this contention. These authors interviewed 195 of 586 individuals with spina bifida born in London between 1940 and 1953. Of the 47 males with no residual disability, 45 were employed and 1 was a full-time student; of 49 females with no residual impairment, 47 were employed. In contrast, only 23 of 47 males and 35 of 59 females with a disability were employed. In general, the more severe the disability (ie, impaired mobility and frequent incontinence), the less likely the individual was to be working.

The results of other studies, however, raise doubts about this predicted association. In an early study (Kolin et al., 1971), 13 children with spina bifida were classified into three disability categories (mild, moderate, severe) based on clinical judgment and into three psychosocial adaptation categories (good, fair, and poor) based on a composite judgment of self-care, school performance, mental ability, and social competence. The authors did not, however, analyze the association of these two variables statistically. Our analysis revealed that there was no statistically significant association between level of disability and level of psychosocial adaptation, chi^2 (4) = 5.60, p = 0.23. Tew and Laurence (1976) collected data on the number of times a group of 43 children with spina bifida who were aged 8 to 10 years were admitted to the hospital, as well as the length of stay in the hospital and the number of surgeries they had. These variables were not found to be related to the children's emotional adaptation in school as reported by their teachers. Cartright et al. (1993) found no statistically significant relationships between severity of disability and 11 dimensions of self-image in a sample of 50 adolescents and young adults with spina bifida. In addition, no significant relationship was reported between age and self-image for the females in the sample. For the males, however, older individuals scored higher on the dimensions measuring vocational goals and family relations, while younger individuals scored higher on the dimensions measuring body image and social relations.

In another study, Child Behavior Check List data were collected (Wallander, Feldman, & Varni, 1989) from the mothers of 61 children with spina bifida who had a mean age of nine years. Data were also collected on a set of six disability variables (ie, lesion level, number of surgeries for a cerebrospinal fluid shunt, number of surgeries for skin ulcers below the waist, total number of surgeries, ambulation status, bladder function), and a composite disability index for each individual was derived. The sample was divided into three groups by degree of disability: high, medium, and low. No significant differences were found between the groups on any of the three Child Behavior Check List scale scores, suggesting to the authors that adaptation of children with spina bifida (as reported by their mothers) was not related to overall level of disability.

Among the personality attributes thought to be linked to successful adaptation to spina bifida are temperament and coping ability. Lavigne et al. (1988) found that among 34 children with spina bifida aged three to eight years, the best predictors of psychosocial adaptation (as measured by Child Behavior Check List scores completed by the mothers) were the child's self-coping score on the Zeitlin Coping Inventory and temperament as reported in an interview with the mothers. In another investigation, data were collected from the mothers of children with spina bifida and cerebral palsy on behavior problems, as measured by the Child Behavior Check List, and temperament, as measured by the Dimensions of Temperament Survey (Wallander, Hubert, & Varni, 1988). A significant association between these two variables was found for the total sample. When analyzed by sex, these data revealed that contrary to expectations, the males in the sample were rated highest on somatic complaints and lowest on depression and aggression, while the females in the sample were rated highest on hyperactivity, schizoid/obsessive behavior, and cruelty, and lowest on depression.

Two environmental variables, quality of life experiences and family support, have been linked to better adaptation to disability among persons with spina bifida. Murch and Cohen (1989) collected data by mail from a nonrandom sample of 53 adolescents with spina bifida who were aged 12 to 18 years who attended a clinic for chronically ill children. The questionnaire included measures of positive and negative life experiences, family environment, anxiety, depression, and self-esteem. Those individuals who reported experiencing the most negative life experiences also reported the highest levels of anxiety and depression and the lowest levels of self-esteem. The adolescent's adaptation was positively related to family climate and support. In a sample of 153 children with various physical disabilities who were aged 4 to 16 years, 17 of whom had spina bifida (Wallander & Varni, 1989; Wallander, Varni, Babani, Banis, & Wilcox, 1989), it was found that family cohesion and organization and maternal education were negatively related to both internalized and externalized behavior problems of the children. These variables, as well as family income, were positively related to the children's ratings of social competence.

CONCLUSION

It has been argued that individuals with spina bifida, similar to others with physical disabilities, are predisposed to manifest negative psychosocial reactions to their physical disability ranging on a continuum from withdrawal to anxiety to demandingness to anger (Hayden et al., 1979; Wallander, Varni, Babani, Banis, De Haan, & Wilcox, et al., 1989). Support for these contentions from the results of well-designed and well-controlled empirical investigations, however, has been limited. Based upon the literature reviewed in this chapter, several tentative conclusions can be stated.

Analyses of informant data, primarily those data provided by mothers using instruments such as the Child Behavior Check List or the Psychiatric Screening Inventory, suggest that children with spina bifida may be at increased risk for reactive problems of psychosocial adaptation. The areas of greatest concern generally are reported to include the reactions of anxiety, depression, withdrawal, and anger. Other domains of potential difficulty include increased feelings of isolation, more negative self-esteem, and avoidance of social situations. It must be pointed out, however, that the majority of these studies use data from self-selected samples of mothers and children attending specialty clinics, do not include comparison groups of children without impairments, and do not attempt to control for the confounding effects of sociodemographic or disability-related factors. In addition, biases are introduced in that the informants (and the researchers) are not unaware of the purposes of the investigation.

Several additional conclusions can be stated based upon the results of a small number of investigations of the psychosocial adaptation to disability using empirical data collected directly from samples of persons with spina bifida. Children and adolescents with spina bifida generally score lower than their peers without impairments on indices measuring social skills, vocational potential, independence, body image, and self-concept and the psychosocial reactions of anger, anxiety, and depression. No conclusion can be stated for young adults and adults with spina bifida due to the lack of empirical evidence.

With regard to characteristics associated with psychosocial adaptation to spina bifida, conclusions can be stated that are similar to those reached in the chapters concerning other physical and chronic health disabilities. Among those individuals with spina bifida, psychosocial risk is greatest for those who (1) have associated neurophysiological disabilities (eg, hydrocephalus) or secondary impairment (eg, incontinence); (2) experience complex, painful, prolonged, and repeated medical treatments; (3) are adolescents (ie, a curvilinear relationship between age and psychosocial adaptation); and (4) live in difficult family situations (eg, poverty, divorced parents, mother with a mental disorder). There is clearly a need for more research in this area, and that research should start with the premise that disability-related, sociodemographic, personality, and social characteristics interact in complex ways to influence psychosocial adaptation. The conflicting reports on the existence, degree, and duration of depression and anxiety among persons with spina bifida may be attributed, in part, to differential involvement of variables from each of the four proposed classes.

REFERENCES

Abuelo, D. N. (1991). Genetic disorders. In J. L. Matson & J. A. Mulick (Eds.), *Handbook of mental retardation* (2nd ed.) (pp. 97–114). New York: Pergamon Press.

Anderson, E. (1979). The psychological and social adjustment of adolescents with cerebral palsy or spina bifida and hydrocephalus. *International Journal of Rehabilitation Research, 2*, 245–247.

Barakat, L. P., & Linney, J. A. (1992). Children with physical handicaps and their mothers: The interrelation of social support, maternal adjustment, and child adjustment. *Journal of Pediatric Psychology, 17*, 725–739.

Blum, R. W. (1983). The adolescent with spina bifida. *Clinical Pediatrics, 22*, 331–335.

Blum, R. W., Resnick, M. D., Nelson, R., & St. Germaine, A. (1991). Family and peer issues among adolescents with spina bifida and cerebral palsy. *Pediatrics, 88*, 280–285.

Breslau, N. (1983). The psychological study of chronically ill and disabled children: Are healthy siblings appropriate controls? *Journal of Abnormal Child Psychology, 11*, 379–391.

Breslau, N. (1985). Psychiatric disorders in children with physical disabilities. *Journal of the American Academy of Child Psychiatry, 24*, 87–94.

Breslau, N., & Marshall, I. A. (1985). Psychological disturbance in children with physical disabilities: Continuity and change in a 5-year followup. *Journal of Abnormal Child Psychology, 13*, 199–216.

Campbell, M. M., Hayden, P. W., & Davenport, S. L. H. (1977). Psychological adjustment of adolescents with myelodysplasia. *Journal of Youth and Adolescence, 6*, 397–407.

Cartright, D. B., Joseph, A. S., & Grenier, C. E. (1993). A self-image profile analysis of spina bifida adolescents in Louisiana. *Journal of the Louisiana State Medical Society, 145*, 394–396, 399–402.

Cohen, L. (1987). Euthanasia of handicapped newborns. In J. A. Mulick & R. F. Antonak (Eds.), *Transitions in mental retardation: Vol. 2. Issues in therapeutic intervention* (pp. 213–230). Norwood, NJ: Ablex Publishing Corporation.

Dorner, S. (1976). Adolescents with spina bifida: How they see their situation. *Archives of Diseases in Childhood, 51*, 439–444.

Dorner, S. (1977). Problems of teenagers. *Physiotherapy, 63*, 190–192.

Evans, K., Hickman, V., & Carter, C. O. (1974). Handicap and social status of adults with spina bifida cystica. *British Journal of Preventive and Social Medicine, 28*, 85–92.

Fosdal, M. O. (1992). Living with spina bifida. *Journal of Neuroscience Nursing, 24*, 286–289.

Gerber, L. A. (1973). Issues in the psychology of patients with previous successful spina bifida surgery. *Psychiatric Quarterly, 47*, 117–123.

Halliwell, M. D., & Spain, B. (1977). Spina bifida children in ordinary schools. *Child: Care, Health and Development, 3*, 389–405.

Hayden, P. W., Davenport, S. L. H., & Campbell, M. M. (1979). Adolescents with myelodysplasia: Impact of physical disability on emotional maturation. *Pediatrics, 64*, 53–59.

Kazak, A. E., & Clark, M. W. (1986). Stress in families of children with myelomeningocele. *Developmental Medicine and Child Neurology, 28*, 220–228.

Kleinberg, S. B. (1982). *Educating the chronically ill child.* Rockville, MD: Aspen.

Kolin, I. S., Scherzer, A. L., New, B., & Garfield, M. (1971). Studies of the school-age child with meningomyelocele: Social and emotional adaptation. *Journal of Pediatrics, 78*, 1013–1019.

Laurence, K. M., & Tew, B. J. (1967). Follow-up of 65 survivors from the 425 cases of spina bifida born in South Wales between 1956 and 1962. *Developmental Medicine and Child Neurology, 9*(Suppl. 13), 1–31.

Lavigne, J. V., Nonal, D., & McLore, D. G. (1988). Temperament, coping, and psychological adjustment in young children with myelomeningocele. *Journal of Pediatric Psychology, 13*, 363–378.

Leonard, C. O., & Freeman, J. M. (1981). Spina bifida: A new disease. *Pediatrics, 68*, 136–137.

Liptak, G. S., Bloss, J. W., Briskin, H., Campbell, J. E., Hebert, E. B., & Revell, G. M. (1988). The management of children with spinal dysfunction. *Journal of Child Neurology, 3*, 3–20.

Lord, J., Varzos, N., Behrman, B., Wicks, J., & Wicks, D. (1990). Implications of mainstream classrooms for adolescents with spina bifida. *Developmental Medicine and Child Neurology, 32*, 20–29.

McAndrew, I. (1979). Adolescents and young people with spina bifida. *Developmental Medicine and Child Neurology, 21*, 619–629.

Menolascino, F. J., & Egger, M. L. (1978). *Medical dimensions of mental retardation.* Lincoln, NE: University of Nebraska Press.

Monson, R. B. (1992). Autonomy, coping, and self-care agency in healthy adolescents and in adolescents with spina bifida. *Journal of Pediatric Nursing, 7*, 9–13.

Murch, R. L., & Cohen, L. H. (1989). Relationship among life stress, perceived family environment, and the psychological distress of spina bifida adolescents. *Journal of Pediatric Psychology, 14*, 193–214.

Redaelli, T., Cassinis, A., Cosignani, F., Conti, B., Onofri, M. P., & Dall'Aqua, A. (1992). Interdisciplinary treatment of spina bifida children. *Paraplegia, 30*, 683–689.

Rinck, C., Berg, J., & Hafeman, C. (1989). The adolescent with myelomeningocele: A review of parent experiences and expectations. *Adolescence, 24*, 699–710.

Sassaman, E. A. (1991). Ethical considerations in medical treatment. In J. L. Matson & J. A. Mulick (Eds.), *Handbook of mental retardation* (2nd ed.) (pp. 327–335). New York: Pergamon Press.

Spaulding, B. R., & Morgan, S. B. (1986). Spina bifida children and their parents: A population prone to family dysfunction? *Journal of Pediatric Psychology, 11*, 359–374.

Tew, B. J., & Laurence, K. M. (1976). The effects of admission to hospital and surgery on children with spina bifida. *Developmental Medicine and Child Neurology, 18*(Suppl. 37), 119–125.

Tew, B. J., & Laurence, K. M. (1985). Possible personality problems among 10-year-old spina bifida children. *Child: Care, Health and Development, 11*, 375–390.

Tin, L. G., & Teasdale, G. R. (1985). An observational study of the social adjustment of spina bifida children in integrated settings. *British Journal of Educational Psychology, 55*, 81–83.

Wallander, J. L., Feldman, W. S., & Varni, J. W. (1989). Physical status and psychosocial adjustment in children with spina bifida. *Journal of Pediatric Psychology, 14*, 89–102.

Wallander, J. L., Hubert, N. C., & Varni, J. W. (1988). Child and maternal temperament characteristics, goodness-of-fit, and adjustment in physically handicapped children. *Journal of Clinical Child Psychology, 17*, 336–344.

Wallander, J. L., & Varni, J. W. (1989). Social support and adjustment in chronically ill and handicapped children. *American Journal of Community Psychology, 17*, 185–201.

Wallander, J. L., Varni, J. W., Babani, L., Banis, H. T., De Haan, C. B., & Wilcox, K. T. (1989). Disability parameters, chronic strain, and adaptation of physically handicapped children and their mothers. *Journal of Pediatric Psychology, 14*, 23–42.

Wallander, J. L., Varni, J. W., Babani, L., Banis, H. T., & Wilcox, K. T. (1988). Children with chronic physical disorders: Maternal reports of their psychological adjustment. *Journal of Pediatric Psychology, 13*, 197–212.

Wallander, J. L., Varni, J. W., Babani, L., Banis, H. T., & Wilcox, K. T. (1989). Family resources as resistance factors for psychological maladjustment in chronically ill and handicapped children. *Journal of Pediatric Psychology, 14*, 157–173.

Wallander, J. L., Varni, J. W., Babani, L., De Haan, C. B., Wilcox, K. T., & Banis, H. T. (1989). The social environment and the adaptation of mothers of physically handicapped children. *Journal of Pediatric Psychology, 14*, 371–387.

PART VI

Applications and Research Recommendations

Part VI provides an opportunity for us to reflect upon the findings reported in our reviews of the research literature on psychosocial adaptation to the 18 chronic illnesses and disabilities presented in Parts II, III, IV, and V. Our goal for the first chapter in this part is to provide the clinician with insights into the application of the research findings presented in Chapters 4 to 21 to counseling interventions. Our goal for the second chapter is to provide the theoretician with a framework for conceptualizing research to study psychosocial adaptation to chronic illness and disability. Our goal for the third and last chapter in the book is to provide the researcher with recommendations for improving the quality of future research in this domain of inquiry.

Chapter 22 summarizes the considerable literature concerned with models for counseling persons with chronic illnesses and disabilities. These models are divided into four general domains: (1) theory-driven approaches, (2) psychosocial phase-specific interventions, (3) clinical approaches, and (4) empirical investigations. For each domain examples are provided of intervention strategies designed to reduce clients' maladaptive psychosocial reactions, teach them appropriate coping skills and problem-solving methods, and provide them with emotional, cognitive, and behavioral supports during the process of adaptation. The chapter concludes with an examination of the small but growing number of well-designed empirical studies to assess the effectiveness of various psychosocial interventions with people with a chronic illness or disability.

Despite considerable disagreement among clinicians and researchers as to the nature and process of adaptation to chronic illness and disability, it is generally agreed that changes in self-representation are observed following the "crisislike" situation that the onset of a chronic illness or disability constitutes in the lives of affected individuals. Chapter 23 begins with a review of ecological models of adaptation to the onset of life crises and transition that have been proposed by

397

researchers and clinicians. Building upon these models and insights gained from the reviews of the research literature in the chapters in Parts II, III, IV, and V, a conceptual framework for the study of psychosocial adaptation to chronic illness and disability is proposed. To successfully investigate the nature, process, and outcomes of psychosocial adaptation to chronic illness and disability, four broad classes of variables must be considered. These classes of variables and their interactions are illustrated with examples from the research literature. The chapter concludes with an overview of recently introduced statistical methods that can assist the theoretician who wishes to undertake research to validate the proposed conceptual framework.

The tentative nature of the meager conclusions concerning psychosocial adaptation to chronic illness and disability that we presented at the ends of Chapters 4 to 21 is due primarily to the considerable number of significant research problems that limit the usefulness and generalizability of the available information. Chapter 24 presents a summary of these significant problems organized in list format into five areas: (1) research conceptualization, (2) study design, (3) sampling, (4) measurement, and (5) data analysis. We propose, when possible, modest recommendations to overcome or circumvent these problems in future research investigations.

CHAPTER 22

Counseling Intervention Strategies

This chapter will review the literature on counseling intervention strategies designed to nurture the psychosocial adaptation of persons with chronic illnesses and disabilities. For the purposes of this review, this literature will be divided into four general domains.

1. *Theory-driven approaches* typically focus on the potential merit or heuristic applications of widely used therapeutic orientations or conceptual formulations to persons with physical disabilities. Examples include the application of Freudian, Adlerian, person-centered, Gestalt, rational-emotive, and behavioral theories and approaches.

2. *Psychosocial phase-specific interventions* attempt to match one or more interventions with specific reactions or experiences thought to characterize a hypothesized phase of psychosocial adaptation. Examples include confronting an individual's denial behaviors or reinforcing an individual's interpersonal contacts to combat depression.

3. *Clinical approaches* are direct applications of therapeutic interventions to specific groups of persons with a physical disability, such as persons who have survived cancer, a myocardial infarction, or a spinal cord injury. Therapeutic outcomes in these clinical studies, however, are seldom assessed empirically. Conclusions concerning the success of the treatment are typically garnered through subjective clinical impressions of the therapist, client, or group members.

4. *Empirical investigations* seek to assess the impact of various psychosocial treatments or therapeutic interventions upon the clients using well-designed research approaches. Empirical investigations use control or comparison groups together with samples of persons with disabilities and psychometrically sound measures of psychosocial, behavioral, or functional outcomes.

THEORY-DRIVEN APPROACHES

Reviews of applications of traditional counseling and psychotherapeutic theories and strategies to persons with disabilities have become increasingly popular in the disability literature during the past 25 years (Cook, 1992; English, 1971; Livneh, 1986a; Livneh & Sherwood, 1991; Shontz, 1978). Core concepts from a particular personality or psychotherapeutic theory are normally examined, and their usefulness for either understanding the process of adaptation to chronic illness and disability or to counseling the individual with a disability is assessed. For example, psychoanalytically based psychodynamic therapeutic interventions (Freudian and Neo-Freudian) are characterized by assisting persons with a physical disability or chronic illness to gain insight into the impact of the disability or disease on their present conflicts, anxieties, and vulnerabilities (Rodin, Craven, & Littlefield, 1991). Issues to be confronted might include (1) the role of the ego's defense mechanisms (eg, regression, rationalization, projection, denial) in minimizing anxiety yet preventing acceptance of the permanence of the disability; (2) the impact of the loss of physical integrity and chronic disease on body image, attitudes toward self and others, and the reawakening of childhood fears and conflicts such as castration anxiety and narcissism (Cubbage & Thomas, 1989; Grzesiak & Hicok, 1994; McDaniel, 1976; Wright, 1983); and (3) the parallelism between the loss of a body part or function and earlier losses (eg, death of parents or other love objects) and the ensuing feelings of sadness, grief, and mourning.

Rodin et al. (1991) advocated a three-phase psychodynamic approach to the treatment of depression in persons with a chronic illness. The phases included (1) facilitation of grief and mourning, where clients are afforded the opportunity to express feelings of bereavement; (2) provision of meaning, where clients discuss personal meaning of disease and disability as determined by the nature and severity of impairment, premorbid personality attributes and belief system, life stage, and prior life experiences; and (3) achievement of a sense of mastery over impairment-related feelings.

Individual (ie, Adlerian) therapy has an overriding goal of assisting individuals to develop a social, useful, and productive lifestyle. It has been advocated to help persons with a disability to progress from a noncoping status (ie, felt inferiority) to a coping status (ie, overcoming inferiority) (Rule, 1987). Furthermore, the professional helper focuses on how the client's lifestyle perceptions (eg, the personal meaning attached by the client to the disability) are contributing to (through compensation) or undermining (through despair and retreat) the acceptance of and adaptation to the disability (Rule, 1984).

Another example may be borrowed from Gestalt therapy. The central Gestalt principles of holistic integration, self-awareness, and assuming personal responsibility may be applied through role-playing exercises. For example, in "the game of unfinished business," the client is invited to complete unfinished life situations stemming from the onset of a disabling condition and gain awareness of the resultant feeling (Coven, 1977). Additional Gestalt therapy applications might include (1) games of dialogue, where the client is given the opportunity to gain awareness of personal polarizations by carrying on a dialogue between conflicting components of the self (eg, "able" versus "disabled" components of self, independent versus dependent parts); and (2) exercises of reversals, where the client is asked to assume the role opposite of his or her overt behavior, thus exposing the client to denied or avoided experiences and attributes and forcing confrontation with them (Allen, 1985).

The traditional person-centered (ie, Rogerian) approach to counseling persons with a physical disability is limited in its scope (see, for example, Cook, 1987; See, 1985). Some of its potential merits for the client include (1) clarification of feelings triggered by the onset of the physically disabling condition, (2) gaining insight into the impact of the disability upon self-concept and gradual acknowledgment of the discrepancy created between the current situation and future hopes and aspirations (ie, real self versus ideal self), and (3) reaching better understanding of those salutary inner resources and strengths that steer the client toward eventual acceptance of the disability and successfully coping with its ramifications.

Ellis' rational emotive therapy provides another example for applying therapeutic principles when working with persons with a physical disability. Here clients' irrational ideas and beliefs regarding the perceived impact of disability upon their lives (eg, feelings of depression and decreased self-esteem) are directly confronted and challenged (Ostby, 1985). Disabilities are viewed as noxious events experienced by the individual. Proponents of rational emotive therapy seek to teach persons with a disability ways to examine the situation rationally and to prevent them from overcatastrophizing their conditions, thereby setting in motion a chain of self-defeating, irrational, and dysfunctional perceptions and beliefs regarding their remaining abilities and skills. In a similar vein, proponents of Beck's cognitive therapy view depression in persons with a chronic illness or disability as characterized by negative views of the self, the environment, and the future (Rodin, 1973; Rodin et al., 1991). Recommended interventions include (1) didactic techniques to teach the client about the cognitions underlying depression, (2) self-monitoring and behavioral techniques to provide the client with experiences of mastery and pleasure (eg, cognitive rehearsal, self-reliance training, role-playing, and diversion activities including physical exercises and social contact), and (3) semantic techniques to challenge negative cognitions and affirm alternative, adaptive, and rational responses and cognitions.

Behavioral therapy seeks to eliminate maladaptive behaviors resulting from a disability (eg, avoiding anxiety-provoking situations, acting aggressively toward others) and to replace them with adaptive and socially appropriate behaviors through individually tailored procedures based on operant conditioning, classical conditioning, modeling, or other learning principles. Maladaptive behaviors are normally minimized or extinguished by the withdrawal of those reinforcers that sustain them (eg, paying excessive attention to pain behaviors, rewarding dependent behaviors). These maladaptive behaviors are then replaced by disability-appropriate behaviors (eg, ensuring the client's participation in physical therapy and exercise regimen, rewarding mastery of independent living skills) and maintained through behavior rehearsal and role-playing techniques. Persons with disabilities are further trained in acquiring self-assertiveness and self-affirmation skills to ease their ability to express successfully their needs, wishes, thoughts, and feelings (Marshak & Seligman, 1993; Wright, 1983).

Finally, the somatopsychological approach of Dembo, Leviton, and Wright (1956) and Wright (1980; 1983) asserts that behavior is the end product of a unique interaction between the person's internal (or psychological) processes and external (or environmental) conditions. In the context of disability, functional limitations and social prejudice are perceived to interact and place the person with a disability into a subordinate status in which goals frequently become inaccessible. Wright (1983) recommended a fourfold intervention approach to counseling persons with disabilities. These interventions are directed at (1) enlarging the scope of values (assisting the client in realizing values other than those directly affected by the disability), (2) subordinating physique (seeking to minimize the significance of those values that rely heavily on the performance of physical tasks and accomplishments), (3) containing disability effects (curtailing the spread of disability-related limitations into those life domains not affected by the disability), and (4) transforming comparative status values into asset values (initiating a shift from other-comparison to self-comparison, where intrinsic positive qualities of the client are emphasized). To facilitate these general interactions, clients typically role play difficult situations in group settings, experience real-life situations with a successful role model who is a person with a disability, and experience real-life situations with other novices who also have disabilities. Furthermore, clients are helped to negotiate environmental barriers—both physical and attitudinal—through (1) person-centered methods, such as skill training and teaching personal responsibility for behavior; and (2) environment-oriented methods, such as modifying employers' negative attitudes and removing architectural and transportation barriers (Wright, 1980).

Despite the proliferation of these and other psychotherapeutic approaches to working with persons with chronic illnesses and physical disabilities, it must be emphasized that these approaches do not differ in any conceptual or substantive mode from counseling individuals without disabilities (Grzesiak & Hicok, 1994; Livneh & Sherwood, 1991).

PSYCHOSOCIAL PHASE-SPECIFIC INTERVENTIONS

Discussed in this second general domain are psychotherapeutic interventions directly aimed at each hypothesized phase of psychosocial reactions evoked during the process of adaptation to chronic illness and disability (Dunn, 1975; Livneh, 1986a; Livneh & Sherwood, 1991; Singleton, 1985).

As we have suggested previously (see Chapter 1), a large number of clinicians argue for the existence of observable phases of psychosocial adaptation to the onset of a chronic illness of a physically disabling condition. The more commonly described phases include shock, anxiety, denial, depression, internalized anger, externalized hostility, and, lastly, acknowledgment and "final" adjustment. Despite the lack of convincing empirical support for the existence of temporal ordering of these clinically observed phases, the heuristic value of these reactions in the study of psychosocial adaptation to illness or disability is evident. Accordingly several writers have suggested an eclectic approach to counseling persons with a disability that relies on linking specific counseling strategies with clinically observed psychosocial reactions. As a rule strategies viewed as more supportive and affective-insightful in nature (eg, Rogerian therapy, Gestalt therapy) appear to be more useful in earlier phases of the adaptation process, while those perceived as more confrontational and cognitive-behavioral-action oriented (eg, rational emotive therapy, behavioral therapy) appear to be more profitable in the later phases (Dunn, 1975; Halligan, 1983; Hohmann, 1975; Kerr & Thompson, 1972; Livneh, 1986b; Marshak & Seligman, 1993; Walters, 1981; Weller & Miller, 1977).

For instance, during the earliest experienced reactions following the onset of the disability or symptoms of the chronic illness (ie, shock and anxiety) clinicians may consider providing the client with physical and emotional support and reassurance or performing muscle relaxation and breathing exercises to calm the client. During this initial impact period the clinician also attempts to communicate frequently with the client regarding his or her present situation, provides the client with careful explanations of ongoing treatment procedures, and, when possible, briefly outlines for the client what to expect next.

If a client appears to deny the extent or duration of his or her disability and if the clinician determines that this denial is harmful to the client's well-being, the therapeutic intervention may entail (1) providing the client with accurate and relevant information on the future implications of the disability so as to dispel any fears and misconceptions associated with it; (2) carefully confronting the client through observations of any inconsistencies and discrepancies between client overt behaviors, nonverbal messages, and existing conditions; (3) heightening client self-awareness, especially concerning inconsistencies in the affective and behavioral domains, through Gestalt therapy techniques; (4) reinforcing behaviors and physical activities incompatible with denial; (5) introducing a person with a similar disability who serves as a role model for achieving success; (6) asking the client to project (ie, channel fantasies) into the future and incorporate problems into his or her life, thus allowing the client to distance the self from pressing present concerns; (7) setting short-term goals and specific time limits, thus avoiding wrestling with future implications of the disability; and (8) enlisting family members and friends to provide support and feedback to client.

For clients who manifest lengthy periods of depressive affect that often includes feelings of internalized anger, self-blame, and guilt, recommended intervention strategies may include (1) reinforcing the client's strengths and assets by rewarding positive self-statements; (2) breaking down problems perceived by the client to be overwhelming into smaller and more manageable issues; (3) setting concrete, short-term, and limited goals that assure the client of successful outcomes; (4) interrupting and challenging the client's illogical beliefs that lead to feelings of hopelessness and despair; (5) encouraging the client to express feelings of frustration, grief, loss, guilt, and shame; (6) reinforcing interpersonal contacts and social skills acquisition (eg, self-assertiveness) for withdrawn clients; (7) teaching the client ways to release feelings of bitterness and pent-up anger in a socially appropriate manner; and (8) engaging the client, when appropriate, in physical (eg, recreational and sports) activities.

Clients who engage in verbally or physically aggressive behaviors may benefit from an intervention focusing on (1) teaching the expression of anger in a socially sanctioned manner; (2) training self-relaxation to defuse feelings of frustration and bitterness; (3) preparing a contract to gradually decrease acting-out behaviors while discussing the merits of assuming personal and social responsibility for actions; (4) role-playing anger-causing situations (eg, Gestalt therapy techniques) to assist the client in becoming aware of inner conflicts, predisability unfinished business, and underdeveloped needs and wishes; (5) adopting behavioral modification techniques to reduce maladaptive, aggressive behaviors (eg, aversive conditioning, negative reinforcement) and to teach adaptive, socially appropriate behaviors; and (6) expressing anger and frustration through artistic endeavors (eg, painting, clay work, performing, writing).

Lastly, during the hypothesized final phase of reintegration (ie, acknowledgment and adjustment), the person with a disability may be assisted through the adoption of a wide range of psychological, social, vocational, educational, and recreational pursuits. Intervention strategies might include (1) exploring and clarifying new values; (2) initiating new interests and hobbies; (3) encouraging the use of humor, especially when confronting frustrating situations; (4) teaching problem-solving and decision-making skills; (5) teaching self-management strategies through self-reinforcement procedures; (6) encouraging the client to expand his or her social network; (7) teaching prevocational and vocational skills; (8) teaching and practicing job-acquisition skills, job-placement skills, and job-maintenance skills; (9) encouraging participation in self-help support groups mainly as a role model for individuals who are recently disabled; and (10) continuously reinforcing and rewarding adaptive, community-based activities on the part of the person with a disability.

CLINICAL APPROACHES

Strategic clinical interventions for persons with various types of chronic illnesses and disabilities typically have the therapeutic goal of providing clients (and their families) with emotional, cognitive, and behavioral support and with adaptive coping skills throughout the process of rehabilitation. Useful psychosocial intervention strategies for persons with physical disabilities have included the following:

- Assisting the client in dealing with the personal meaning of the disability. This approach borrows heavily from grief counseling, where issues such as loss, suffering, and acceptance of altered physique (ie, body image) or reduced physical functioning are aired. The client is given permission and is even encouraged to ventilate feelings (ie, cathartic release) associated with the disability and is gradually assisted in integrating the meaning and reality of the loss (Dailey, 1979; Lindemann, 1981).
- Using cognitive-behavioral therapy methods to interrupt the client's irrational beliefs, such as those associated with upholding the disability (and loss in general) as a state of general helplessness, hopelessness, failure, and dependency (Freeman, 1987; Sweetland, 1990; Turk, 1979).
- Teaching the client appropriate coping skills required to function successfully in the community. These skills, in general, instill in the client who is recently disabled a sense of personal mastery (ie, self-efficacy) and may include, for instance, assertiveness skills (Brackett, Condon, Kindelan, & Bassett, 1984) social (interpersonal) skills (Turk, 1979), decision-making skills, and problem-solving skills (Telch & Telch, 1985).
- Providing clients with accurate information on their medical conditions and the status and probable future functional implications of these conditions (ie, client education; Razin, 1982). This approach is useful in reducing initial levels of anxiety and counteracting the detrimental effects of chronic denial (Ganz, 1988; Telch & Telch, 1985).
- Offering supportive group therapy in which participants are afforded the opportunity to share their fears, concerns, and needs (Livneh & Pullo, 1992;

Telch & Telch, 1985) and to gain approval and social support from the remaining group members. Four general group modalities appear to dominate the field. These include (1) educational groups, where information on the physical condition, its treatment, and lifestyle implications is provided; (2) psychotherapeutic groups, where the focus is placed on ventilating and sharing feelings and concerns, and gaining self-understanding; (3) coping skills training groups, in which group members are trained to cope with their disability and its ramifications by acquiring specific cognitive and behavioral skills; and (4) social support groups, in which members provide mutual support to each other and create a climate for exchanging ideas and problem-solving methods. Group approaches have been used with persons with a variety of disabilities and chronic illnesses, including persons with an amputation (Rogers, MacBride, Whylie, & Freeman, 1978–1979), persons with epilepsy (Dansereau, 1963), persons with multiple sclerosis (Larcombe & Wilson, 1984; Welch & Steven, 1979), individuals with spinal cord injury (Banik & Mendelson, 1978; Mann, 1977), persons with cancer (Bothwell & Eisenberg, 1986; Spiegel, 1985–1986; Spiegel & Yalom, 1978), survivors of myocardial infarction (Hackett, 1978; Horlick, Cameron, Firor, Bhalerao, & Baltzan, 1984; Mone, 1970; Subramanian & Ell, 1989), survivors of a stroke (Singler, 1975), persons who are blind (Gold, 1993; Goldman, 1970; Manaster, 1971), persons with rheumatoid arthritis (Shearn & Fireman, 1985; Strauss et al., 1986), and women with disabilities (Kriegsman & Celotta, 1981). Interested readers may wish to consult the highly informative reviews of group therapies with persons with a physical disability that have been provided by Lasky and Dell Orto (1979), Roback (1984), and Seligman (1982).

In addition to these general approaches, several disability-specific interventions have been suggested, such as (1) dealing with sexuality and body image changes in clients with a spinal cord injury (Dailey, 1979; Eisenberg, 1984); (2) modifying Type A behavior patterns in clients who sustained myocardial infarction through stress management, relaxation training, and cognitive self-control (Razin, 1982; Razin, 1984); and (3) assisting clients with cancer to control pain, nausea, and vomiting through deep muscle relaxation and guided imagery (Telch & Telch, 1985).

Eisenberg (1984) described a structured, short-term counseling and sex education program for persons with a spinal cord injury. Each session lasted for approximately 60 to 90 minutes, and group members included both males and females. Sexual partners of the participants were included when possible. The eight-session experience comprised the following phases: (1) introduction, where the format and content of the anticipated experiences are delineated and consent for participation is ensured; (2) film and discussion, where a film of a group discussion (on sexual experience) including persons with a spinal cord injury and their partners is presented and is aimed to reduce anxiety and demonstrate group interaction; (3) male sexual response, where the male reproductive system and the impact of a spinal cord injury on it are reviewed; (4) sex as part of the total relationship, where other factors and issues (eg, communication) that might interfere with successful sexual adjustment are examined; (5) female sexual response, where the female reproductive system is reviewed, as well as alternative satisfactory sexual experiences; (6) techniques for preparation, relaxation, and arousal, where the advantages and disadvantages of specific techniques for reaching sexual satisfaction (eg, massage, use of vibrators, fantasy, prosthetic devices) are discussed; (7) marriage, divorce, and children, where information on artificial insemination, adoption, foster child placement, and causes for marital success and failure are reviewed; and (8) film and discussion, where an explicit film depicting sexual activity between a quadriplegic male and his girlfriend is viewed, followed by group discussion. Eisenberg (1984) argued that such a time-limited group counseling model enables participants of both sexes to (a) learn how to develop and maintain positive self-concept, (b) learn how to efficiently use nonimpaired physical functions, and (c) develop those social skills necessary for successful coping with the disability and its psychosocial impact.

Several comprehensive psychosocial intervention models described in the literature merit attention. Meyerowitz, Heinrich, and Schag (1983) described a three-phase competency-based coping model for persons with cancer composed of (1) a problem-specification phase, in which daily stressors are identified, including the various cognitions, feelings, and situations with which the client must cope (eg, physical discomfort, psychological distress, family problems, sexual difficulties, disruption of recreational activities, job-related problems); (2) a response enumeration phase, in which the range and type of responses given to each problem area are determined with a goal of developing a comprehensive list of all available coping strategies to be used for each specified problem; and (3) a response evaluation phase in which the relative efficacy of each response for decreasing the problem is determined (an adaptive coping strategy is regarded as one that decreases emotional distress, achieves a specific goal, and reduces the problematic nature of the situation).

A second model (Kaufman & Micha, 1987) seeks to provide an integrated psychotherapeutic system for persons with cancer who have a good prognosis. It is composed of three therapeutic approaches—individual, family, and group—and an educational component. The individual therapy is further divided into (1) a crisis intervention segment in which clients are encouraged to ventilate their feelings, explore their current situation in the context of past events, interact constructively with their environment, and focus on specific issues; and (2) a psychodynamic segment that focuses on issues such as guilt, denial, dependency, loss of power, and abandonment. The family and group psychotherapeutic components, as the terms imply, focus on communication and structural modes within these systems, including (1) motivating the family to become involved in the therapeutic process; (2) helping the spouse and other members to accept the reality of the disease; (3) assisting family members to ventilate their feelings of anxiety, sadness, and anger; (4) teaching family members how to provide the person with cancer with supportive coping strategies; (5) building group cohesiveness so that feelings of isolation and abandonment can be minimized; and (6) showing group members the importance of shared experiences, feelings, and fears of pain, uncertainty, and death.

The educational component of this model is geared toward (1) clarifying the medical condition, its treatment, and the associated functional implications; (2) reducing anxiety through relaxation techniques, self-hypnosis, or biofeedback; (3) supporting medical compliance; (4) using visual imaging to gain a sense of mastery and competence in combating cancer; (5) teaching the client about appropriate lifestyle, dietary, and exercise regimens; and (6) referring the client to self-help groups. Obviously components of these and similar comprehensive intervention programs can be readily applied to other life-threatening, chronic illnesses or disabling conditions, such as myocardial infarction, spinal cord injury, traumatic brain injury, diabetes, and neuromuscular disorders.

Among the applications of therapeutic interventions to children with physical disabilities, the model advocated by Atala and Carter (1992) may be of particular interest to most readers. The authors describe a multimodal "coping and psychotherapy" intervention with children undergoing limb amputation. Components of this model include (1) play intervention, using dolls and puppets to allow the child to become less defensive, more open to receiving information, and willing to ventilate feelings of anxiety, sadness, and rage; (2) filmed modeling, where the youngster views a film of a child undergoing a similar medical procedure, thus minimizing surgery-related anxiety; (3) emotive imagery and relaxation, which include techniques of progressive relaxation, breathing exercises, hypnosis, fantasizing, and distraction techniques to reduce anxiety-triggering situations; and (4) mastery and behavioral rehearsal techniques, where the child may be instructed to administer specific medical procedures and actively teach coping skills to a doll or a puppet. The authors argued that their proposed model provides young pediatric clients with useful nonverbal and metaphorical clinical tools to gain information, decrease surgery-associated anxiety, and increase mastery and coping skills.

Numerous group-based clinical approaches have also been advocated in the literature. Among the many educational, psychotherapeutic, coping-skills training, and social support group approaches, the structured group treatment model of Subramanian and Ell (1989) with survivors of myocardial infarction is worth noting. These authors proposed a treatment strategy, based on a cognitive-behavioral approach, that directly addresses the needs of low socioeconomic status, minority group members who have sustained myocardial infarction. The goals of the proposed model include the following: (1) providing participants with information about their disability, the recovery process, availability of community resources, and management of various life stressors; and (2) increasing participants' coping skills so that they can mobilize support systems and better manage stressful situations. Group treatment strategies are primarily psychoeducational and include (1) teaching problem-solving skills to increase levels of self-control and self-efficacy; (2) assertiveness training, using behavioral rehearsal, to assist participants in anticipating behaviors in difficult or stressful situations; and (3) teaching cognitive skills to become aware of dysfunctional thinking patterns and to develop constructive thinking patterns to manage feelings. Examples of these strategies include learning how to directly ask physicians and other medical personnel questions about required changes in lifestyle (strategy 2) and confronting the faulty belief that exercise will trigger another heart attack (strategy 3).

To implement the model, Subramanian and Ell (1989) suggested a four-session sequence composed of two inpatient and two outpatient group sessions that typically extends over an 8- to 10-week period. Specific objectives for sessions 1 and 2 include (1) providing rationale for therapy, (2) providing accurate information about causes of heart attacks and dispelling misconceptions about the disease, (3) developing group cohesiveness, (4) identifying participants' sources of stress, and (5) presenting and practicing problem-solving skills. Objectives for outpatient sessions 3 and 4 include (a) reviewing prior material, (b) prioritizing participants' present sources of stress, (c) continuing problem-solving work via the use of behavioral rehearsal, and (d) practicing constructive (eg, realistic, coping-based) thinking and its relation to management of maladaptive emotions (eg, depression, guilt, fear of dying). The authors asserted that their unique program was likely to result in participants' experiencing decreased stress levels, strengthening their social support network, enhancing feelings of personal control, developing problem-solving skills, and ultimately achieving a better overall adaptation.

EMPIRICAL INVESTIGATIONS

The number of well-designed empirical investigations to assess the effectiveness of various psychosocial interventions with persons with a chronic illness or disability is surprisingly small, despite the growing number of intervention efforts. In general the types of interventions that have been investigated to document their impact upon clients include behavioral, supportive, educational, group, and mixed approaches. In this part of the chapter the nature and main features of several examples of empirical investigations will be outlined.

Langosch et al. (1982) studied the effectiveness of a behavior-based therapeutic approach with persons with coronary heart disease. Three groups were compared. The two experimental groups received either stress management or relaxation training, while the control group received routine medical care only. The authors reported that significant but modest improvement occurred among the clients in both treatment groups, as compared to those in the control group, on self-report measures of assertiveness and reduced social anxiety. Brown and Munford (1983–1984) also studied a behavioral intervention applied to postmyocardial infarction clients. The therapy consisted of muscle relaxation, imagery-based desensitization, stress and anger management, and cognitive restructuring. On the basis of pretreatment and posttreatment comparisons, the authors concluded that the behavioral intervention was effective in increasing adaptive function, facilitating return to premorbid activity levels, and decreasing symptoms of depression. These improvements were maintained at three- and nine-month follow-ups. The lack of a comparison group that did not receive any special counseling intervention precludes any definitive conclusion concerning the efficacy of the intervention.

Linn, Linn, and Harris (1982) investigated the effect of supportive psychosocial counseling on the quality of life, functional status, and survival rate among individuals with end-stage cancer. The therapeutic approach used with the experimental group consisted of reducing denial, increasing feelings of control over the environment, using "life review" to emphasize personal accomplishments, developing a sense of meaning of life, and improving self-esteem. The control group received typical medical treatment only. Results indicated that clients in the counseling intervention group improved significantly, as compared to their counterparts in the control group, on measures of quality of life (eg, decreased depression, improved life satisfaction, increased self-esteem) within a three-month period. Functional status and survival rate, however, showed no posttreatment differences between the two groups.

Cognitive-behavioral interventions have also been shown to be useful with persons with a myocardial infarction who manifest Type A behaviors. Shapiro, Friedman, and Piaget (1991), for example, compared the effects of a cognitive-behavioral plus coronary counseling intervention program with that of cardiac counseling only program. Individuals in the experimental group reported significantly higher overall level of satisfaction and higher congruence between real and ideal selves than clients in the control group two years posttreatment. They also demonstrated a psychologically healthier control profile (eg, positive assertiveness) than did individuals in the control group.

Oldenberg, Perkins, and Andrews (1985) investigated the relative efficacy of two hospital-based psychosocial treatment modalities—education and counseling—as compared to routine medical care for improving the physical and psychosocial functioning of individuals who survived a heart attack. Clients in the education group received standardized information on heart disease and its treatment, coronary risk factors, and sexual functioning. They also received relaxation training. Clients in the counseling group received, in addition to the same information component used in the education group, 6 to 10 counseling sessions focusing on anxieties and fears they encountered and strategies to lower coronary risks upon discharge from the hospital. Outcome measures consisted of a battery of health and psychosocial instruments that included measures of marital dissatisfaction, hostility, anxiety, general health, attitudes toward illness, cardiac symptoms, and frequency of physical activity. Results indicated that both treatment groups, as compared to a routine care group, performed significantly better on measures of psychological adaptation (eg, reduced anxiety, decreased Type A behavior) and lifestyle functioning (eg, reduced cigarette smoking, decreased work overload) at 3, 6, and 12 months posttreatment. Participants also reported experiencing fewer symptoms related to heart disease. Individuals in the counseling group sustained these improvements at the final one-year postintervention follow-up at higher levels than did individuals in the education-only and routine care groups.

Bradley et al. (1987) investigated the efficacy of two psychosocial treatments to decrease levels of anxiety and depression, alleviate pain behaviors, reduce disease activity, and increase activity level among clients with rheumatoid arthritis. The first treatment group (biofeedback-assisted, cognitive-behavioral group) received five sessions of individual thermal biofeedback training to increase peripheral skin temperature at painful joints. Group members also participated in 10 group meetings with family members or close friends that focused on education, relaxation, behavioral goal setting, and use of self-rewards. Participants in the second treatment group (structured-group social-support therapy group) received 15 sessions of structured social support that included group meetings with family members or close friends. The meetings focused on education, discussion of coping modes, and encouragement to improve coping modes. A control group included individuals whose intervention consisted of medical treatment only. Outcome measures included indices of self-reported trait anxiety and depression, ratings of pain intensity, perceptions of health locus of control, and scores on the Arthritis Helplessness Index (Nicassio, Wallston, Callahan, Herbert, & Pincus, 1985). Behavioral variables included frequency of seven pain behaviors (eg, grimacing, sighing) during specified activities. Finally, physiological measures consisted of changes in participants' peripheral skin temperature level at painful joints, grip strength, and number of tender joints. Results of this study indicated that at posttreatment (1) clients in the cognitive-behavioral treatment group exhibited significantly less pain behaviors and reported lower pain intensity than did clients in the other two groups; (2) clients in the cognitive-behavioral treatment group also produced significantly lower scores on the physiological measure and on ratings of disease activity as compared to clients in the other groups; and (3) clients in the cognitive-behavioral treatment group and clients in the structured-group social support therapy group reported lower ratings of trait anxiety and depression, as compared to the no-treatment control group. The last finding was also true at a six-month follow-up. The investigators proposed that the salutary effects of relaxation training and the social support program were the most important factors in reducing the pain behavior, disease activity, and emotional distress of the individuals in the treatment groups.

Thompson and Meddis (1990) compared the effectiveness of an in-hospital combined counseling and education treatment with that of a routine care only group for persons with a myocardial infarction. Clients in the treatment group were provided with four 30-minute sessions that focused on (1) standardized education on the nature of myocardial infarction, its management, coronary risk factors and techniques to modify them, and the impact of myocardial infarction on clients' sexual, social, vocational, and recreational activities; and (2) supportive counseling focused upon ventilation of feelings associated with the heart attack, interpretation of thoughts and feelings, encouragement to act on the environment, and learning how to troubleshoot immediate problems. Dependent variables included measures of anxiety, depression, and general health. Clients in the treatment group reported significantly lower levels of anxiety and depression, as compared to clients in the control group, both immediately after treatment and at a six-month follow-up. Lowered anxiety was particularly evident in the clients' general health, ability to resume work and leisure activities, and relations with their spouses.

In an innovative study, Connor (1992) sought to examine the effect of psychosocial intervention on denial among persons who were terminally ill with cancer. The intervention component consisted of clarifying to clients how their interpersonal world had been changed by the advent of the life-threatening disease. The purpose of such an intervention was "to create an opportunity for the patient to explore and to gain insight into his or her own coping processes" (p. 6). Specific issues addressed included (1) most difficult aspects of having cancer, (2) belief in recovery from cancer, (3) effect of disease on family and friends, and (4) any positive things that have come out of having cancer. Measures included the Reversal Scale of the Defense Mechanism Inventory (Gleser & Ihilevich, 1969) and the Death Anxiety Scale (McMordie, 1979). Research results indicated that following psychosocial intervention, interpersonal deniers in the experimental group reported significantly lower scores on the Defense Mechanism Inventory Reversal Scale. Clients in the control group, in contrast, reported higher denial scores on the posttest. Neither the group main effect nor the group-by-occasion interaction effect reached statistical significance for the death anxiety measure, although the occasion effect was significantly lower for both groups. Connor argued that in this study, denial, as used by clients who are terminally ill, can be modified by carefully designed psychosocial intervention. Moreover, the finding that denial increased among clients in the control group suggested that in the absence of appropriate intervention, denial and overall defensiveness may gradually rise and possibly interfere with medical treatment.

In a well-designed study, Gordon et al. (1980) compared psychosocial functioning among clients with cancer who received a multifaceted psychosocial intervention program with that of clients with similar sociodemographic and medical background in a control group who received education services only. The intervention modalities used with the therapeutic group included (1) an educational component that focused on providing clients with information on cancer, its treatment, associated side effects, and hospital procedures, and on teaching relaxation techniques and identifying emotional reactions to cancer; (2) a counseling component in which clients were encouraged to ventilate feelings, were offered support and reassurance, were helped with clarifying feelings and thoughts, were encouraged to exert more control over their environment, and were assisted in exploring past and present situations; and (3) an environmental component that focused on service referral to other health care facilities. Outcome measures included a comprehensive interview schedule that assessed degree of functioning in 13 life domains, including, among others, physical discomfort, housework, vocational activities, family and social concerns, affect, and body image. In addition, a battery of psychosocial tests was administered that included measures of quality of life, anxiety, psychiatric impairment, health locus of control, and activities of daily living. From analyses of their data, the researchers concluded that the experimental psychosocial intervention effectively alleviated some of the psychosocial problems reported by clients. Moreover clients in the treatment group experienced a more rapid decrease in their symptoms (ie, depression, anxiety, hostility) and reached a more realistic outlook on life. Finally, a larger percentage of the treatment group clients, as compared to their control counterparts, returned to work and showed more active use of their time.

Group therapy interventions with clients having various disabilities have also been investigated empirically. Miller, Wolfe, and Spiegel (1975), for example, assessed the benefits of a short-term group therapy program on knowledge of medical facts and self-concept of hospital inpatients with a spinal cord injury. The treatment group was provided with information on spinal cord injury and related functional involvement. Participants' ensuing experiences and feelings were also discussed. As compared to the members of a comparison group (no data were provided on the preintervention comparability of the two groups), members of the treatment group showed greater gains in their factual knowledge of spinal cord injury and a higher self-concept. Crawford and McIvor (1985) investigated the psychological benefits from group psychotherapy for clients hospitalized with multiple sclerosis. Three groups were created by random assignment: (1) an insight-oriented group that focused upon verbalizing and confronting conflicts; (2) a current events group, in which discussion of daily news was the primary vehicle of intervention; and (3) a control group receiving no special counseling treatment. Outcomes included measures of depression, anxiety, locus of control, and self-concept. Results indicated that after 50 group sessions, the individuals in the insight-oriented group were significantly less depressed than were individuals in either of the other two groups. Moreover, individuals in both therapy groups were significantly more internally oriented (ie, assumed a more self-directed, personally controlled course of treatment) than were individuals in the comparison group. No posttreatment differences among the groups were detected on the measures of anxiety or self-esteem.

Investigation of the effectiveness of group therapy modalities with persons with cancer and myocardial infarction has become increasingly popular among researchers in the past decade. Results suggest that supportive and educational group therapies for persons with cancer are beneficial for (1) increasing understanding of the disease, (2) improving self-concept, (3) decreasing mood disturbances, and (4) increasing coping in medical situations (Cain, Kohorn, Quinlan, Latimer, & Schwartz, 1986; Ferlic, Goldman, & Kennedy, 1979; Heinrich & Schag, 1985; Spiegel, Bloom, & Yalom, 1981; Spiegel & Yalom, 1978). In a well-designed study, Telch and Telch (1986) compared the relative efficacy of two treatments—a coping skills group and a supportive therapy group—on clients' adaptation to cancer. Members of the coping skills group were trained in relaxation and stress management, assertiveness, cognitive restructuring, problem solving, activity planning, and affective management. The members of the supportive therapy group collectively shared feelings, problems, and concerns. Outcome measures included questions regarding medical concerns, family and social relationships, daily living problems, and psychosocial adjustment difficulties. In addition, standard measures of mood states (eg, anxiety, depression, anger) and perceived self-efficacy were included. Results attested to the superiority of the training received by the members of the coping skills group over the training in the supportive therapy group and a no-treatment control group for (1) reducing depression, anxiety, and anger; (2) increasing satisfaction with work-related and social activities; and (3) improving coping with medical procedures.

Further support for the superiority of behavior-oriented, coping skills training programs over supportive discussion group interventions with persons with cancer was provided in a study conducted by Cunningham and Tocco (1989). They

found the former approach to have a greater impact on reducing group participants' anxiety and depression, as measured by both the Symptom Check List—
90-Revised and the Profile of Mood States. Additional benefits associated with
the coping skills training included improved sleep patterns, increased energy,
reduced pain, and improved interpersonal communication. Fawzy et al. (1990)
investigated the effect of brief, multifaceted, structured group therapy on levels
of psychological distress and coping ability of persons with a malignant melanoma. The group intervention consisted of providing members with medical and
health education, disease-related problem-solving skill training, stress management, and psychological support. Outcomes included measures of affective
states, coping style, psychosocial adjustment to illness, and quality of life. As
compared to persons in a routine cancer treatment control group, clients in the
therapeutic group demonstrated upon treatment completion (1) lower mood disturbance, depression, confusion, and fatigue; (2) higher degrees of vigor and
activity; and (3) greater use of cognitive-behavioral coping strategies. These differences were also maintained at a six-month follow-up.

Reports of group psychotherapy with clients with a myocardial infarction have
also supported the usefulness of this approach for reducing depression, anxiety,
social alienation, and days hospitalized and for increasing rates of survival and
return to work (Gruen, 1975; Ibrahim et al., 1974; Rahe, O'Neil, Hagan, &
Arthur, 1975; Rahe, Ward, & Hayes, 1979). Findings also suggested that among
postmyocardial infarction clients, group psychosocial interventions may be useful in reducing coronary risk factors (Mitsibounas, Tsouna-Hadjis, Rotas, & Sideris, 1992). It appears, then, that the provision of group-based therapeutic
intervention consisting of medical and psychosocial advice, support, and guidance fosters participants' self-insight and teaches how lifestyle affects coronary
condition and future survival (see also Stern, 1984).

Despite the reported success of group therapy modalities with clients with a
myocardial infarction, Horlick et al. (1984) failed to detect any differences in
their measures of psychological (eg, depression, anxiety), behavioral (eg, smoking), or occupational (eg, return to work) functioning between outpatients with a
myocardial infarction who were exposed to an educational discussion group
treatment and members of a control group. It should be noted that the therapeutic
group experience consisted of only six sessions focusing on educational and
medical aspects of myocardial infarction (ie, cognitive issues were emphasized at
the expense of affective issues).

In summation, the results of recent empirical investigations of the effectiveness of individual and group intervention strategies with persons with disabilities
(in particular those with myocardial infarction and cancer) suggest that these
interventions are capable of (1) reducing mood disturbance, especially levels of
depression and anxiety; (2) improving social functioning; (3) reducing behavioral

risk factors, such as smoking and Type A behaviors; and (4) improving occupational attendance. Readers seeking other reviews of empirical investigations of psychosocial interventions with persons with cancer should consult the works of Watson (1983) and Trijsburg, Van Knippenberg, and Rijpma (1992). Mumford, Schlesinger, and Glass (1982) provided a similar review of research focusing on clients with a myocardial infarction, whereas Trieschmann (1988) focused on clients with a spinal cord injury.

CONCLUSION

This chapter reviewed the literature on counseling intervention strategies designed to nurture the psychosocial adaptation of persons with chronic illnesses and disabilities. This literature was organized into four broad categories. First, theoretical formulations that focus on the potential merit or heuristic value associated with applying generic counseling interventions to working with persons with a physical disability were described. The core concepts, therapeutic rationale, goals, and intervention processes of these theory-driven approaches (ie, psychoanalytically based psychodynamic, Adlerian, Gestalt, Rogerian, rational-emotive, cognitive-behavioral, and somatopsychological approaches) were outlined and examples of each were provided.

Second, psychosocial phase-specific psychotherapeutic interventions were described and illustrated. These interventions attempt to link recommended therapeutic techniques with hypothesized phases that are experienced during the psychosocial adaptation process (eg, shock, anxiety, denial, depression, internalized anger, externalized hostility, acknowledgment, adjustment). Third, clinical approaches that describe applications of therapeutic interventions to persons with disabilities were summarized. These investigations are typically nonempirical and focus on describing the application of a wide range of therapeutic interventions to specific groups of persons with a disability, such as persons who have survived cancer, heart disease, and spinal cord injury. The goals are to provide clients (and their families) with emotional, cognitive, and behavioral support and with adaptive coping skills throughout the process of rehabilitation. Several disability-specific (ie, spinal cord injury, myocardial infarction) therapeutic interventions were also described in this section.

Finally, examples of empirical investigations that seek to assess the efficacy of various psychosocial treatments or therapeutic interventions using well-designed research approaches were presented. These outcome-oriented investigations pay careful attention to the use of appropriate control groups, psychometrically sound measures, and sophisticated methods for the statistical analyses of data. The goal of this type of research is to document the effect of individual and group therapeutic modalities upon the psychosocial, behavioral, or functional adaptation of persons with chronic illnesses and disabilities.

The onset of a chronic illness or physical disability constitutes a "crisislike" situation in the lives of the affected individuals. Despite considerable disagreement among clinicians and researchers, psychosocial adaptation to chronic illness or disability is thought to be a gradual unfolding process comprising phases of reactions. Chapter 23 will present and review several models of this process of adaptation to life crises, major life transitions, and chronic illnesses and disabilities that have been proposed in the literature. Four primary classes of variables identified from this review will be outlined. This will be followed by a conceptual framework for theoreticians, clinicians, and researchers who seek to further investigate the processes and outcomes of psychosocial adaptation to chronic illness and disability. The chapter will conclude with a brief introduction to several powerful statistical methods for the analyses of data needed to validate this conceptual framework.

REFERENCES

Allen, H. A. (1985). The Gestalt perspective. *Journal of Applied Rehabilitation Counseling, 16*(3), 21–25.

Atala, K. D., & Carter, B. D. (1992). Pediatric limb amputation: Aspects of coping and psychotherapeutic intervention. *Child Psychiatry and Human Development, 23*, 117–130.

Banik, S. N., & Mendelson, M. A. (1978). Group psychotherapy with a paraplegic group, with an emphasis on specific problems of sexuality. *International Journal of Group Psychotherapy, 28*, 123–128.

Bothwell, M., & Eisenberg, C. (1986). Planned collectivity: An entity that works for cardiac patients. *Social Work with Groups, 8*, 69–79.

Brackett, T. O., Condon, N., Kindelan, K. M., & Bassett, L. (1984). The emotional care of a person with a spinal cord injury. *Journal of the American Medical Association, 252*, 793–795.

Bradley, L. A., Young, L. D., Anderson, K. O., Turner, R. A., Agudelo, C. A., & McDaniel, L. K. (1987). Effects of psychological therapy on pain behavior of rheumatoid arthritis patients: Treatment outcome and six-month follow-up. *Arthritis and Rheumatism, 30*, 1105–1114.

Brown, M. A., & Munford, A. (1983–1984). Rehabilitation of post MI depression and psychological invalidism: A pilot study. *International Journal of Psychiatry in Medicine, 13*, 291–297.

Cain, E. N., Kohorn, E. I., Quinlan, D. M., Latimer, K., & Schwartz, P. E. (1986). Psychosocial benefits of a cancer support group. *Cancer, 57*, 183–189.

Connor, S. R. (1992). Denial in terminal illness: To intervene or not to intervene. *The Hospice Journal, 8*(4), 1–15.

Cook, D. (1987). Psychosocial impact of disability. In R. M. Parker (Ed.), *Rehabilitation counseling: Basics and beyond* (pp. 97–120). Austin, TX: Pro-Ed.

Cook, D. (1992). Psychosocial impact of disability. In R. M. Parker & E. M. Szymarski (Eds.), *Rehabilitation counseling: Basics and beyond* (2nd ed.) (pp. 249–272). Austin, TX: Pro-Ed.

Coven, A. B. (1977). The Gestalt approach to rehabilitation counseling. *Rehabilitation Counseling Bulletin, 20*, 167–174.

Crawford, J. D., & McIvor, G. P. (1985). Group psychotherapy: Benefits in multiple sclerosis. *Archives of Physical Medicine and Rehabilitation, 66*, 810–823.

Cubbage, M. E., & Thomas, K. R. (1989). Freud and disability. *Rehabilitation Psychology, 34*, 161–173.

Cunningham, A. J., & Tocco, E. K. (1989). A randomized trial of group psychoeducational therapy for cancer patients. *Patient Education and Counseling, 14*, 101–114.

Dailey, A. L. (1979). Spinal cord injured college students: Counseling and guidance approaches. *Journal of College Student Personnel, 20*, 341–347.

Dansereau, R. A. (1963). Group counseling for epileptics. *Rehabilitation Literature, 24*, 172–176.

Dembo, T., Leviton, G. L., & Wright, B. A. (1956). Adjustment to misfortune—A problem of social-psychological rehabilitation. *Artificial Limbs, 3*(2), 4–62.

Dunn, M. E. (1975). Psychological intervention in a spinal cord injury center: An introduction. *Rehabilitation Psychology, 22*, 165–178.

Eisenberg, M. G. (1984). Spinal cord injuries. In H. B. Roback (Ed.), *Helping patients and their families cope with medical problems* (pp. 107–129). San Francisco: Jossey-Bass.

English, R. W. (1971). The application of personality theory to explain psychological reactions to physical disability. *Rehabilitation Research and Practice Review, 3*, 35–47.

Fawzy, F. I., Cousins, N., Fawzy, N. W., Kemeny, M. E., Elashoff, R., & Morton, D. (1990). A structured psychiatric intervention for cancer patients. *Archives of General Psychiatry, 47*, 720–725.

Ferlic, M., Goldman, A., & Kennedy, B. J. (1979). Group counseling in adult patients with advanced cancer. *Cancer, 43*, 760–766.

Freeman, R. D. (1987). Psychosocial interventions with visually impaired adolescents and adults. In B. W. Heller, L. M. Flohr, & L. S. Zegans (Eds.), *Psychosocial interventions with sensorially disabled persons* (pp. 153–166). New York: Grune & Stratton.

Ganz, P. A. (1988). Patient education as a moderator of psychological distress. *Journal of Psychosocial Oncology, 6*, 181–197.

Gleser, G. C., & Ihilevich, D. (1969). An objective instrument for measuring defense mechanisms. *Journal of Consulting and Clinical Psychology, 33*, 51–60.

Gold, J. T. (1993). Pediatric disorders: Cerebral palsy and spina bifida. In M. G. Eisenberg, R. L. Glueckart, & H. H. Zaretsky (Eds.), *Medical aspects of disability: A handbook for the rehabilitation professional* (pp. 281–306). New York: Springer.

Goldman, H. (1970). The use of encounter microlabs with a group of visually handicapped rehabilitation clients. *New Outlook for the Blind, 64*, 219–226.

Gordon, W. A., Freidenbergs, I., Diller, L., Hibbard, M., Wolf, C., & Levine, L. (1980). The efficacy of psychosocial intervention with cancer patients. *Journal of Consulting and Clinical Psychology, 48*, 743–759.

Gruen, W. (1975). Effects of brief psychotherapy during the hospitalization period on the recovery process in heart attacks. *Journal of Consulting and Clinical Psychology, 43*, 223–232.

Grzesiak, R. C., & Hicok, D. A. (1994). A brief history of psychotherapy and physical disability. *American Journal of Psychotherapy, 48*, 240–250.

Hackett, T. P. (1978). The use of groups in the rehabilitation of the postcoronary patient. *Advances in Cardiology, 24*, 127–135.

Halligan, F. G. (1983). Reactive depression and chronic illness: Counseling patients and their families. *Personnel and Guidance Journal, 61*, 401–406.

Heinrich, R. L., & Schag, C. C. (1985). Stress and activity management: Group treatment for cancer patients and spouses. *Journal of Consulting and Clinical Psychology, 53*, 439–446.

Hohmann, G. W. (1975). Psychological aspects of treatment and rehabilitation of the spinal cord injured person. *Clinical Orthopedics, 112*, 81–88.

Horlick, L., Cameron, R., Firor, W., Bhalerao, U., & Baltzan, R. (1984). The effects of education and group discussion in the post myocardial infarction patient. *Journal of Psychosomatic Research, 28*, 485–492.

Ibrahim, M. A., Feldman, J. G., Sultz, H. A., Staiman, M. G., Young, L. J., & Dean, D. (1974). Management after myocardial infarction: A controlled trial of the effect of group psychotherapy. *International Journal of Psychiatry in Medicine, 5*, 253–268.

Kaufman, E., & Micha, V. G. (1987). A model for psychotherapy with the good-prognosis cancer patient. *Psychosomatics, 28*, 540–548.

Kerr, W. G., & Thompson, M. A. (1972). Acceptance of disability of sudden onset in paraplegia. *Paraplegia, 10*, 94–102.

Kriegsman, K. H., & Celotta, B. (1981). Creative coping: A program of group counseling for women with physical disabilities. *Journal of Rehabilitation, 47*, 36–39.

Langosch, W., Seer, P., Brodner, G., Kallinke, D., Kulick, B., & Heim, F. (1982). Behavior therapy with coronary heart disease patients: Results of a comparative study. *Journal of Psychosomatic Research, 26*, 475–484.

Larcombe, N. A., & Wilson, P. H. (1984). An evaluation of cognitive-behavior therapy for depression in patients with multiple sclerosis. *British Journal of Psychiatry, 145*, 366–371.

Lasky, R. G., & Dell Orto, A. E. (Eds.). (1979). *Group counseling and physical disability: A rehabilitation and health care perspective.* North Scituate, MA: Duxbury.

Lindemann, J. I. (Ed.). (1981). *Psychological and behavioral aspects of physical disability.* New York: Plenum Press.

Linn, M. W., Linn, B. S., & Harris, R. (1982). Effects of counseling for late stage cancer patients. *Cancer, 49*, 1048–1055.

Livneh, H. (1986a). A unified approach to existing models of adaptation to disability—I. A model of adaptation. *Journal of Applied Rehabilitation Counseling, 17*(1), 5–16, 56.

Livneh, H. (1986b). A unified approach to existing models of adaptation to disability—II. Intervention strategies. *Journal of Applied Rehabilitation Counseling, 17*(2), 6–10.

Livneh, H., & Pullo, R. (1992). Group counseling for people with physical disabilities. In D. Capuzzi & D. Gross (Eds.), *Group counseling: Strategies for the 1990s* (pp. 141–163). Denver, CO: Love.

Livneh, H., & Sherwood, A. (1991). Application of personality theories and counseling strategies to clients with physical disabilities. *Journal of Counseling and Development, 69*, 525–538.

Manaster, A. (1971). The theragnostic group in a rehabilitation center for visually handicapped persons. *New Outlook for the Blind, 65*, 262–264.

Mann, A. H. (1977). Psychiatric morbidity and hostility in hypertension. *Psychological Medicine, 7*, 653–659.

Marshak, L. E., & Seligman, M. (1993). *Counseling persons with physical disabilities: Theoretical and clinical perspectives.* Austin, TX: Pro-Ed.

McDaniel, J. W. (1976). *Physical disability and human behavior* (2nd ed.). New York: Pergamon Press.

McMordie, W. R. (1979). Improving measurement of death anxiety. *Psychological Reports, 44*, 957–980.

Meyerowitz, B. E., Heinrich, R. L., & Schag, C. C. (1983). A competency-based approach to coping with cancer. In: T. G. Burish & L. A. Bradley (Eds.), *Coping with chronic disease: Reasearch and applications* (pp. 137–158). New York: Academic Press.

Miller, D. K., Wolfe, M., & Spiegel, M. H. (1975). Therapeutic groups for patients with spinal cord injuries. *Archives of Physical Medicine and Rehabilitation, 56*, 130–135.

Mitsibounas, D. N., Tsouna-Hadjis, E. D., Rotas, V. R., & Sideris, D. A. (1992). Effects of group psychosocial intervention on coronary risk factors. *Psychotherapy and Psychosomatics, 58*, 97–102.

Mone, L. E. (1970). Short-term group psychotherapy with postcardiac patients. *International Journal of Group Psychotherapy, 20*, 99–108.

Mumford, E., Schlesinger, H., & Glass, G. (1982). The effects of psychological intervention on recovery from surgery and heart attacks: An analysis of the literature. *American Journal of Public Health, 72*, 141–151.

Nicassio, P. M., Wallston, K. A., Callahan, L. F., Herbert, M., & Pincus, T. (1985). The measurement of helplessness in rheumatoid arthritis: The development of the Arthritis Helplessness index. *Journal of Rheumatology, 12*, 462–467.

Oldenberg, B., Perkins, R. J., & Andrews, G. (1985). Controlled trial of psychological intervention in myocardial infarction. *Journal of Consulting and Clinical Psychology, 53*, 852–859.

Ostby, S. S. (1985). A rational-emotive perspective. *Journal of Applied Rehabilitation Counseling, 16*(3), 30–33.

Rahe, R. H., O'Neil, T., Hagan, A., & Arthur, R. J. (1975). Brief group therapy following myocardial infarction: Eighteen-month follow-up of a controlled trial. *International Journal of Psychiatry in Medicine, 6*, 349–358.

Rahe, R. H., Ward, H. W., & Hayes, V. (1979). Brief group therapy in myocardial infarction rehabilitation: Three- to four-year follow-up of a controlled trial. *Psychosomatic Medicine, 41*, 229–242.

Razin, A. M. (1982). Psychosocial intervention in coronary artery disease: A review. *Psychosomatic Medicine, 44*, 363–387.

Razin, A. M. (1984). Coronary artery disease. In H. B. Roback (Ed.), *Helping patients and their families cope with medical problems* (pp. 216–250). San Francisco: Jossey-Bass.

Roback, H. B. (Ed.). (1984). *Helping patients and their families cope with medical problems.* San Francisco: Jossey-Bass.

Rodin, E. A. (1973). Psychomotor epilepsy and aggressive behavior. *Archives of General Psychiatry, 28*, 210–213.

Rodin, G., Craven, J., & Littlefield, C. (1991). *Depression in the medically ill: An integrated approach.* New York: Brunner/Mazel.

Rogers, J., MacBride, A., Whylie, B., & Freeman, S. J. (1978–1979). The use of groups in the rehabilitation of amputees. *International Journal of Psychiatry in Medicine, 8*, 243–255.

Rule, W. R. (1984). Lifestyle and adjustment to disability. In W. R. Rule (Ed.), *Lifestyle counseling for adjustment to disability* (pp. 15–33). Rockville, MD: Aspen.

Rule, W. R. (1987). Acceptance and adjustment to disability: An Adlerian orientation. In G. L. Gandy, E. D. Martin, & R. E. Hardy (Eds.), *Rehabilitation counseling and services: Profession and process* (pp. 219–233). Springfield, IL: C C Thomas.

See, J. D. (1985). Person-centered perspective. *Journal of Applied Rehabilitation Counseling, 16*(3), 15–20.

Seligman, M. (Ed.). (1982). *Group psychotherapy and counseling with special populations*. Baltimore: University Park Press.

Shapiro, D. H., Friedman, M., & Piaget, G. (1991). Changes in mode of control and self-control for post myocardial infarction patients evidencing Type A behavior: The effects of a cognitive/behavioral intervention and/or cardiac counseling. *International Journal of Psychosomatics, 38*(Special issue), 4–12.

Shearn, M. A., & Fireman, B. H. (1985). Stress management and mutual support groups in rheumatoid arthritis. *American Journal of Medicine, 78*, 771–775.

Shontz, F. C. (1978). Psychological adjustment to physical disability: Trends in theories. *Archives of Physical Medicine and Rehabilitation, 59*, 251–254.

Singler, J. K. (1975). Group work with hospitalized stroke patients. *Social Casework, 56*, 348–354.

Singleton, S. M. (1985). Crisis intervention with the spinal cord injured individual. *Emotional First Aid, 2*, 29–35.

Spiegel, D. (1985–1986). Psychosocial interventions with cancer patients. *Journal of Psychosocial Oncology, 3*, 83–95.

Spiegel, D., Bloom, J. R., & Yalom, I. (1981). Group support for patients with metastatic cancer: A randomized prospective outcome study. *Archives of General Psychiatry, 38*, 527–533.

Spiegel, D., & Yalom, I. D. (1978). A support group for dying patients. *International Journal of Group Psychotherapy, 28*, 233–245.

Stern, M. J. (1984). Psychosocial rehabilitation following myocardial infarction and coronary artery bypass surgery. In N. K. Wenger & H. K. Hellerstein (Eds.), *Rehabilitation of the coronary patient* (2nd ed.) (pp. 453–471). New York: John Wiley & Sons.

Strauss, G. D., Spiegel, J. S., Daniels, M., Spiegel, T., Landsverk, J., Roy-Byrne, P., Edelstein, C., & Ehlhardt, J. (1986). Group therapies for rheumatoid arthritis: A controlled study of two approaches. *Arthritis and Rheumatism, 29*, 1203–1209.

Subramanian, K., & Ell, K. O. (1989). Coping with a first heart attack: A group treatment model for low-income Anglo, Black, and Hispanic patients. *Social Work with Groups, 11*, 99–117.

Sweetland, J. D. (1990). Cognitive-behavioral therapy and physical disability. *Journal of Rational-Emotive and Cognitive Behavior Therapy, 8*, 71–78.

Telch, C. F., & Telch, M. J. (1985). Psychological approaches for enhancing coping among cancer patients: A review. *Clinical Psychology Review, 5*, 325–344.

Telch, C. F., & Telch, M. J. (1986). Group coping skills instruction and supportive group therapy for cancer patients: A comparison of strategies. *Journal of Consulting and Clinical Psychology, 54*, 802–808.

Thompson, D. R., & Meddis, R. (1990). A prospective evaluation of in-hospital counseling for first time myocardial infarction men. *Journal of Psychosomatic Research, 34*, 237–248.

Trieschmann, R. B. (Ed.). (1988). *Spinal cord injuries: Psychological, social, and vocational rehabilitation* (2nd ed.). New York: Demos.

Trijsburg, R. W., Van Knippenberg, F. C., & Rijpma, S. E. (1992). Effects of psychological treatment on cancer patients: A critical review. *Psychosomatic Medicine, 54*, 489–517.

Turk, D. C. (1979). Factors influencing the adaptive process with chronic illness: Implications for intervention. In I. G. Sarason & C. D. Spielberger (Eds.), *Stress and anxiety* (pp. 291–311). Washington, DC: Hemisphere.

Walters, J. (1981). Coping with a leg amputation. *American Journal of Nursing, 81*, 1349–1352.

Watson, M. (1983). Psychosocial intervention with cancer patients: A review. *Psychological Medicine*, *13*, 839–846.

Welch, G. J., & Steven, K. (1979). Group work intervention with a multiple sclerosis population. *Social Work with Groups*, *2*, 221–234.

Weller, D. J., & Miller, P. M. (1977). Emotional reactions of patient, family, and staff in acute-care period of spinal cord injury: Part I. *Social Work in Health Care*, *2*, 369–377.

Wright, B. A. (1980). Person and situation: Adjusting the rehabilitation focus. *Archives of Physical Medicine and Rehabilitation*, *61*, 59–64.

Wright, B. A. (1983). *Physical disability—A psychosocial approach* (2nd ed.). New York: Harper & Row.

CHAPTER 23

Conceptual Framework for the Study of Psychosocial Adaptation to Chronic Illness and Disability

INTRODUCTION

The onset of a chronic illness or physical disability constitutes a "crisislike" situation in the lives of affected individuals (Livneh, 1986a; Livneh & Antonak, 1990; Moos & Schaefer, 1984; Shontz, 1965; Siller, 1976; Wright, 1983). Despite considerable disagreement among clinicians and researchers about the nature, process, and outcomes of adaptation to chronic illness and disability, it is generally agreed that changes in self-representation (eg, sense of self, self-identity) are typically observed following the onset of a disability or the diagnosis of a chronic or life-threatening medical condition (Bury, 1982; Ville, Ravaud, Marchal, Paicheler, & Fardeau, 1992). The psychosocial experiences that contribute to these gradual changes in self-representation, however, are far from being agreed upon.

Much of the debate regarding psychosocial adaptation centers around the parallelism between the intrapersonal (ie, psychological) and interpersonal (ie, social) unfolding of the adaptation process (see, for example, Wright, 1983). Most theoreticians, clinicians, and researchers view the process of psychosocial adaptation as a unitary concept with psychological and social dimensions that are theoretically unique yet that share common clinical variance. The psychological dimension consists of reactions that are internally oriented, that is, they revolve around personal experiences and intense emotions such as anxiety, depression, and anger. The social dimension, however, is externally oriented, that is, it relates to experiences and activities at home, at work, and in the community at large.

Stated differently, the psychological phases of adaptation to chronic illness and disability typically constitute a process that culminates in greater personal openness to experience, improved self-esteem, heightened self-awareness, more acute sense of self, and, in general, acceptance of and successful coping with the aftermath of a traumatic personal loss. The social phases of adaptation to chronic illness and disability, on the other hand, are components of a process whose unfolding reflects a movement from strained relationships, social withdrawal, and interpersonal distancing (ie, behaviors manifested during anxiety and depression), to actions against others (ie, oppositional tendencies and hostile acts observed during experienced anger), and finally to collaboration with others (ie, acquisition of social skills, mutually satisfying social interactions, participation in familial, social, and vocational activities). A social adaptation process has been posited that unfolds parallel to the psychological adaptation process as the person with a chronic illness or disability moves from a state of dependency upon others to a state of independence and interdependence with others (Ben-Sira, 1981; Livneh, 1986b).

As we argued in Chapter 1, the concepts of adaptation and adjustment to chronic illness and disability share several common features and are often used interchangeably in the disability studies literature. Reviews of the seminal works of Shontz (1975), Roessler and Bolton (1978), and Wright and colleagues (Dembo, Leviton, & Wright, 1956; Wright, 1983), among others, suggest that adaptation to chronic illness and disability is a dynamic, gradually unfolding, and progressive process through which the individual strives to reach an optimal state of person-environment congruence referred to as adjustment. When successfully attained, a person operating at this level demonstrates (1) psychosocial equilibrium or reintegration; (2) awareness of remaining assets and existing functional limitations; (3) positive self-esteem, self-concept, and sense of personal mastery; (4) successful negotiation of the environment; and (5) active participation in social, vocational, and recreational activities (see, for example, Livneh, 1986a; Roessler & Bolton, 1978; Wright, 1983). In this conceptualization, adjustment is a theoretically optimal level of functioning constituting a distal (eg, advanced, positive, adaptive) phase, reaction, or experience within an overall psychosocial adaptation process following the onset of a chronic illness or disability.

However, not all persons with chronic illnesses and disabilities reach this optimal level of functioning. Accordingly several writers (see, for example, Livneh, 1986a; Rodin, Craven, & Littlefield, 1991; Wright, 1983) have suggested that psychosocial adaptation to chronic illness and disability may be conveniently conceptualized as a one-dimensional continuum ranging from failed adaptation (ie, maladaptive psychosocial functioning) to successful adaptation (ie, adaptive psychosocial functioning). The maladaptive pole of the continuum typically is characterized by the dominance of manifestations of earlier experienced psychosocial reactions (or phases or experiences), such as anxiety, depression, anger, and the correlates of these reactions, such as negative self-esteem, social withdrawal, and denial of the disability and its associated limitations, chronicity, and future implications. The adaptive pole of the continuum, in contrast, is characterized by the existence of reactions (or phases or experiences) that are indicative of a state of independence and interdependence, positive self-esteem, self-efficacy, personal mastery, and adaptive coping. As we outlined in Chapter 1, investigations of the patterns of coping with chronic illnesses and disabilities (see, for example, Dunkel-Schetter, Feinstein, Taylor, & Falke, 1992; Feifel, Strack, & Nagy, 1987a; Feifel, Strack, & Nagy, 1987b; Hanson, Buckelew, Hewett, & O'Neal, 1993) have revealed that a person's use of more active, directive, problem-focused, information-seeking, and social support-seeking coping modes is construed as both a precursor to and a general reflection of successful psychosocial adaptation to chronic illness and disability. In contrast, a person's use of more passive, nondirective, emotion-focused, self-blame, and avoidance-escape-resignation coping modes is typically regarded as both a predictor of and as a correlate of failed psychosocial adaptation to chronic illness and disability.

Before proceeding to review various ecological models of psychosocial adaptation to life crises, major life transitions, and chronic illnesses and disabilities, it will be helpful to present a brief summary of the major findings suggested by our reviews presented in Chapters 4 to 21. The 18 conditions considered in these chapters span a broad spectrum of medical impairments, including:

- conditions that are attributed to sudden onset (eg, spinal cord injury, amputation, traumatic brain injury) versus conditions that are slowly progressive (eg, multiple sclerosis, Parkinson's disease, neurofibromatosis);
- conditions that are generally present at birth or early infancy (eg, cerebral palsy, spina bifida) versus conditions that are first manifested in adulthood or old age (eg, amyotrophic lateral sclerosis, myasthenia gravis);
- conditions that are life threatening (eg, cancer, myocardial infarction) versus conditions that normally are not expected to pose a threat to the person's life (eg, epilepsy, blindness, deafness);
- conditions that involve one or two functional domains (eg, blindness, deafness) versus conditions that interfere with several functional domains (eg, traumatic brain injury, cerebral palsy);
- conditions that usually deteriorate over time (eg, multiple sclerosis, Parkinson's disease) versus conditions that are relatively stable over time (eg, cerebral palsy, epilepsy); and
- conditions that are highly visible (eg, spinal cord injury, cerebral palsy, muscular dystrophy) versus conditions that are not readily visible or only visible under special circumstances (eg, rheumatoid arthritis, epilepsy, deafness).

Findings reported in the clinical and empirical research literature on reactions or phases of psychosocial adaptation to chronic illnesses and disabilities suggest the following conclusions:

- Anxiety and depression are the most frequently investigated psychosocial reactions to chronic illness and disability. They are also the most commonly experienced reactions following the onset of a chronic illness or disability. Anger and denial also appear to be experienced periodically following the onset of various medical conditions. Research findings on the prevalence, manifestation, and duration of these two reactions, however, are inconclusive. Finally, the psychosocial reactions of acknowledgment, acceptance, and adjustment have been theoretically and empirically considered as inseparable and, as a result, interchangeable manifestations of an optimal, even if elusive, final phase of successful adaptation to chronic illness and disability.
- Self-reported or clinician-observed psychosocial reactions (eg, anxiety, depression, anger) are by no means unique to persons with chronic illnesses and disabling conditions, nor are these reactions qualitatively different from those manifested by persons without chronic illnesses and disabling conditions who experience major life crises. Research findings do, however, suggest a higher level of psychosocial distress in persons with chronic illnesses and disabling conditions, especially in the period immediately following the onset of a disability or the diagnosis of a chronic or life-threatening medical condition. For most persons with chronic illnesses and disabling conditions, this psychosocial distress appears to reflect a temporary state that, in most cases, diminishes with the passage of time.
- Empirical evidence has not substantiated a universal, progressive, phase-like, orderly sequence of predetermined psychosocial reactions to chronic illness and disability. Moreover, our reviews of the scant number of longitudinal research studies of psychosocial adaptation to the various chronic illnesses and disabling conditions uncovered no unequivocal evidence in support of universally experienced psychosocial reactions across disabling conditions or even within specific types of conditions. Support does appear to be accumulating for the existence of distinct psychosocial reactions (eg, anxiety, depression, acceptance) following the onset of a disability or the diagnosis of a severe or chronic life-threatening condition. In addition, accumulating evidence supports a weak but significant positive association between duration of chronic illness or disability and diverse clinical-behavioral indicators of improved psychosocial functioning (ie, decreased distress, positive self-concept, increased level of adaptation).
- There are numerous clinical and anecdotal reports in the literature suggesting that individuals with physically disabling conditions, and possibly even groups of persons with physically disabling conditions, experience distinct psychosocial reactions to their conditions. The onset, duration, and sequencing of these reactions are often interpreted by clinicians and theore-

ticians as supporting the existence of phases of psychosocial adaptation to chronic illness and disability.

The inconsistent research findings concerning the nature, variability, temporal sequencing, and clinical correlates of psychosocial reactions to chronic illnesses and disabilities in particular and to major life crises in general have spurred researchers and theoreticians to suggest multifaceted models of psychosocial adaptation. We will now present an overview of some of the more influential ecological models of adaptation.

ECOLOGICAL MODELS OF ADAPTATION TO LIFE CRISES, TRANSITIONS, AND DISABILITY

Several ecological models of adaptation to life crises, major life transitions, and chronic illnesses and disabilities have been proposed in the literature. Scofield, Pape, McCracken, and Maki (1980), in their ecological model of psychosocial adaptation to disability, dichotomized components of adaptation into those that focus on the person himself or herself and those that focus on the external environment. Each of these components was further subdivided into smaller units. The person-oriented components (which may include direct intervention strategies) incorporate approaches that alter both the individual's perceptions or frame of reference (eg, restoring perceptual modalities, managing pain) and approaches to modifying his or her response tendencies (eg, decreasing social withdrawal and avoidance, increasing self-advocacy). The environment-oriented approaches, on the other hand, incorporate procedures for altering environmental normative standards (eg, clarifying needs and assets, developing opportunities for employment and recreation) as well as modifying environmental response tendencies (eg, reducing the community's stigmatizing perceptions of people with disabilities, altering employers' biased behaviors).

Somewhat akin to Scofield et al.'s (1980) perspective, Coulton (1981), focusing on health care maintenance in a model of person-environment fit, suggested a typology of intervention strategies according to both the goal of intervention (ie, change in person or change in environment) and the primary target of intervention (ie, modification of the individual or modification of the environment). For example, when both goal and target involve the person, interventions include provision of prosthetic devices, counseling, and rehabilitation education. When the target shifts to the environment, interventions focus more on milieu treatment and behavior modification through environmental reinforcement contingencies. On the other hand, when both goal and target involve the environment, interventions are commonly targeted at physical, behavioral, and social-economic modifications of the environment (ie, home remodeling). When the focus shifts to the person, he or she is equipped or trained to modify that environment (eg, taught to build a ramp). More important, however, Coulton (1981) argued that the degree of congruence between the person and the environment—a congruence that is often fragmented following life crises and major changes—rests largely on a successful harmony between (1) the individual's needs, capabilities, and aspirations; and (2) the resources, demands, and opportunities available in the environment. A successful fit between the two is seen as positively affecting a person's physical health, mental health, and general feelings of well-being. These indices are generally regarded as reflective of successful adaptation to disability. Likewise, poor physical and mental health may negatively effect the degree of congruence between the individual and his or her environment.

Although other ecological models of psychosocial adaptation and intervention have been proposed in the literature (Hurst & McKinley, 1988; Sigelman, Vengroff, & Spanhel, 1979), Schlossberg's (1981) model of psychosocial adaptation to life transitions is often regarded as a milestone in the conceptualization of human adaptation to both anticipated and traumatic life transitions. In her model Schlossberg (1981) suggested that adaptation to transitions depends upon (1) the balance of the individual's available personal, social, and environmental resources and deficits; and (2) the differences between the pretransition and posttransition environments. Moreover, she argued that the process of adaptation may be conceived as mediated by three separate sets of factors.

1. *Characteristics inherent in the particular event or transition.* Included here are variables such as the change (gain or loss) in life roles, the effect experienced by the change, the source of change (internal or external), the timing of the life events (on time or off time), the onset of the change (gradual or sudden), and the duration of the anticipated change (permanent, temporary, or uncertain).

2. *Characteristics inherent in the pretransition and posttransition contexts or environments.* Included here are variables such as internal support systems (eg, family units, peer network), institutional supports (eg, occupational organizations, religious institutions), and physical settings (eg, climate, living arrangements, worksite).

3. *Characteristics of the transitioning individual.* Included in this category are those sociodemographic (eg, age, sex, ethnicity, socioeconomic status) and personality (eg, psychosocial competence, attitudes, value and belief system, prior experience with transitions) variables that are inherent in the person himself or herself.

Models similar to Schlossberg's (1981) have also been proposed in the disability literature. In one of the earliest and most influential models, Moos and Schaefer (1984) proposed that the psychosocial outcome of life crises is first determined by three sets of factors. These are (1) background and personal factors, such as age, sex, socioeconomic status, ego strength, cognitive and emotional maturity, self-confidence, belief system, and prior experience with illness and disability; (2) illness-related factors, such as type of symptoms, body part(s) affected, degree of pain, rapidity of onset, and illness progression; and (3) physical and social environment factors, including environmental physical features, human or social features, availability of social support, community support, and type of work setting. Each of these three sets of factors is further filtered through (1) cognitive appraisal (ie, perceived meaning of the illness or disability); (2) adaptive tasks (eg, dealing with pain, hospital environment, and health care staff); and (3) coping skills (ie, appraisal-focused, problem-focused, and emotion-focused types of coping).

In a similar model, Vash (1981) proposed that psychosocial reactions to disability are determined by three groups of factors. These are (1) factors associated with the nature of the disability itself, including time of onset, life stage, type of disability, impaired functions, severity and visibility of disability, degree of disability stability, and presence of pain; (2) personal factors, including sex, interests and values, available personal resources, and personality attributes; and (3) environmental factors, including both the immediate environment (eg, level of family acceptance, financial resources) and broader cultural context (eg, technology, enforceable laws to protect rights).

Rodin et al. (1991) argued that psychosocial responses to medical illnesses are highly dependent on factors such as personality, life stage, previous life experiences, emotional conflicts and vulnerabilities, and the social milieu of the person affected. They further argued that characteristics of the medical illness or disability interact with three sets of factors (ie, societal stigma, personality, and cognitive-affective appraisal) to form a personal meaning of the illness or disability. The highly emphasized personal meaning of illness or disability, in turn, leads to personal appraisal of coping strategies (eg, interpersonal, behavioral, affective). It is the individual's ability to appraise the situation and adopt a coping strategy that dictates if he or she will achieve successful adjustment (typified by a sense of mastery and positive self-esteem) or adaptive failure (characterized by symptoms of depression, anxiety, social withdrawal, and low self-esteem).

Models adopting similar concepts have also been proposed to explicate the process of psychosocial adaptation to specific illnesses and disabilities. Wiklund, Sanne, Vedin, and Wilhelmsson (1985), for example, summarized the available literature on psychosocial adaptation to myocardial infarction within a framework of crisis theory. More specifically, they suggested that psychosocial reactions to myocardial infarction are determined by factors such as (1) genetic and somatic factors (eg, the presence of angina pectoris, shortness of breath); (2) degree of perceived threat; (3) previous experience with crisis situations;

(4) available individual resources, including both psychological attributes (eg, emotional stability) and sociodemographic characteristics (eg, age, sex); and (5) social network (eg, family members, health care personnel, available social assistance). All these factors combine to determine the type of affective, cognitive, behavioral, and physiological reactions the individual manifests when confronting the medical crisis of myocardial infarction.

Waltz, Badura, Pfaff, and Schott (1988) posited a causal model of long-term adaptation to myocardial infarction. They reasoned that adaptation is first determined by several exo-genous and background variables including general health status, premorbid mental health, personality and behavioral patterns (eg, Type A personality), social class, and environmental conditions. These background variables continuously interact with the individual's cognitive assessment of the illness situation (seen as a long-term stress and adaptation process). The individual's level of success coping with myocardial infarction reflects the end product of this long-term process of adaptation.

Hilton (1989) proposed a conceptual framework for understanding adaptation to cancer. Based in part on Lazarus and Folkman's (1984) model of coping with psychological stress, Hilton proposed a multicomponent model that included (1) personal factors, such as belief system; that interact with (2) environmental or situational factors, such as uncertainty of situation; to provide the base for (3) cognitive reappraisal of the event's significance for the individual's well-being; and (4) assessment of coping modes to be used and availability of coping resources. As a result of these series of cognitive and situational appraisals, specific coping and behavioral strategies are adopted that lead to further reappraisal of the situation and eventually determine the degree of successful psychosocial adaptation to the disease.

Trieschmann (1988), in her discussion of the process of psychosocial adaptation to spinal cord injury, suggested that this process is determined by an interaction among three sets of variables, including (1) personality variables, such as style and method of coping with stress; (2) organic or biological variables, such as medical status and age; and (3) environmental variables, that include level of family support and socioeconomic status.

Finally Langer (1994), dealing more specifically with the psychosocial reaction of depression following the onset of a disability, implicated the following factors as central determinants of the degree and duration of depression: (1) future course (prognosis) of the condition (eg, stable or progressive, acute or chronic); (2) time since onset; (3) existence of pain or discomfort; (4) predisability personal affective and cognitive style; (5) prior experience with disability and loss in general (eg, type and availability of coping resources); (6) meaning of disability to the affected individual (eg, its symbolic nature); (7) meaning of the disability to others and to society at large; (8) available social resources; (9) influence of environmental factors (eg, financial status, accessibility, quality of life); and (10) current life stressors.

It becomes apparent from this cursory review of the leading models that four primary classes of variables have been implicated in understanding variations in the process of psychosocial adaptation. These broad classes include (1) variables associated with the disability itself, (2) variables associated with sociodemographic or organismic characteristics of the individual, (3) variables associated with personality and behavioral attributes of the individual, and (4) variables associated with the physical and social environment. The next section of this chapter outlines these four classes of variables and proposes a conceptual framework for theoreticians, clinicians, and researchers.

PROPOSED CONCEPTUAL FRAMEWORK

It is proposed that to successfully investigate the nature, process, and outcomes of psychosocial adaptation to chronic illness and disability, four broad classes of variables must be considered.

Class 1 variables are associated with the disability itself. Included here are those characteristics that are directly disability related, such as (1) cause of condition (eg, heredity, birth, trauma), (2) type of disability (eg, sensory, orthopaedic, cognitive), (3) type of onset (eg, sudden, gradual), (4) extent of condition (eg, temporary, uncertain, permanent), (5) degree of functional involvement, (6) body areas affected, (7) extent of brain and central nervous system involvement, (8) age at diagnosis, (9) age at symptom onset, (10) chronicity (at time of study), (11) stability of condition, (12) lethality (ie, terminal versus nonterminal condition), and (13) visibility (eg, aesthetic involvement).

Class 2 variables are associated with sociodemographic characteristics of the individual. These organismic variables include (1) sex and sex-role identification, (2) chronological age, (3) life or developmental stage, (4) ethnicity, (5) socioeconomic status, (6) state of general health, (7) level of education, (8) marital status, (9) occupational attainment and job history, and (10) existing vocational skills.

Class 3 variables are associated with personality attributes of the individual. Among the variables in this class are (1) coping strategies used (eg, problem-focused, appraisal-focused, emotion-focused); (2) defense mechanisms used (eg, projection, rationalization, repression); (3) perceived control, locus of control, and other attributional processes (ie, belief in the externality versus internality of events); (4) personal meaning of the condition; (5) attitudes toward health, sickness, and deviance; (6) personal values and beliefs (eg, political, religious); (7) self-concept and ego strength; (8) body image; (9) cognitive competence or intellectual ability; (10) acceptance of disability; (11) premorbid psychosocial adaptation; and (12) previous experience with crises of a similar nature (eg, life-threatening experience, death of a family member, severe bodily injury).

Specific elements of these three classes of disability-related and person-related variables interact with specific elements of the fourth class of variables. *Class 4 variables are associated with characteristics of the physical and social (external) environment.* These situational variables include (1) social support systems (eg, cohesion of family unit, network of friends and colleagues), (2) economic and institutional support (eg, community support groups, available medical care, political and religious groups, occupational organizations), (3) physical settings (eg, urban versus rural location, living arrangements, physical or architectural accessibility to community activities and workplace), (4) attitudinal barriers or supports (eg, stigma attached to the condition, media portrayal of the condition), and (5) encountered stress (ie, number, duration, and severity of stressful life events).

It is hypothesized that the degree and speed of psychosocial adaptation to chronic illnesses and disabling conditions are closely linked to the interactions among elements in these four classes of variables (see Figure 23–1). For example, two individuals with similar physical disabilities (ie, little variation among class 1 variables) could conceivably show widely differing patterns of psychosocial adaptation to their condition because of differing interactions among the variables in class 2 (eg, upper versus lower socioeconomic status), class 3 (eg, use of active versus use of passive coping modes), or class 4 (eg, social isolation versus close family network). Alternatively, two individuals with widely dissimilar physical conditions (eg, adult-onset blindness and Parkinson's disease) may exhibit similar psychosocial reactions to their disabilities. This may be attributed to their sharing similar age at onset, educational level, personal values, and environmental accessibility conditions.

Viewing psychosocial adaptation to chronic illness and disability with this conceptual framework may partially explain the discrepancy often reported in the type of symptoms, severity level, duration, and sequencing of specific reactions to disability. Put differently, the conflicting reports on phenomenological differences in the type, degree, and duration of depression and anxiety among people with neuromuscular and brain-related disabilities (eg, stroke and traumatic brain injury) may be attributed, in part, to differential involvement of variables from each of the four proposed classes (Cummings, 1992; Fedoroff et al., 1991; Hermann & Wallesch, 1993; Schlossberg, 1981). For example, depression associated with neuromuscular disorders may be triggered by (1) primary, organically induced factors that are directly related to neurochemical or structural alterations in the brain (ie, class 1 involvement); (2) secondary, psychoreactive factors (eg, life stage, coping strategies used) that result from inability to cope successfully with the resultant neuromuscular and functional deficits (ie, class 2 and 3

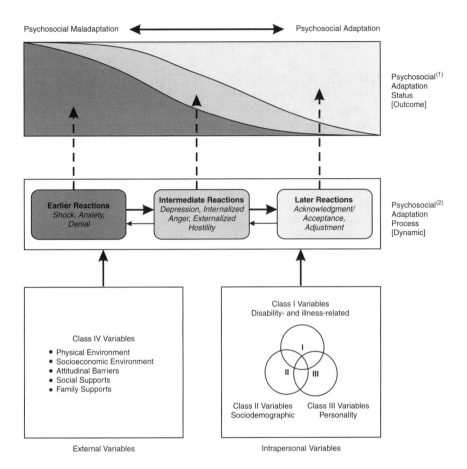

(1) Psychosocial adaptation status is an assessed outcome that ranges from unsuccessful or maladaptive functioning (dominance of earlier reactions such as anxiety, denial, depression, or anger) to successful or adaptive functioning (dominance of later reactions such as acknowledgment or acceptance, and behaviors reflecting adjustment such as those indicating positive self-esteem, adaptive coping, self-efficacy, and personal mastery)

(2) Psychosocial adaptation process can be viewed both *internally*, indicating a transition through psychosocial experiences and reactions in a phaselike process that is uniquely defined for each person, and *externally*, indicating a dynamic congruence or balance between the person's attributes, skills, and resources and environmental or community demands and requirements

Figure 23–1. A Model of Psychosocial Adaptation to Chronic Illness and Disability (CID)

involvement); or (3) tertiary, environmentally triggered factors (eg, societal attitudes, employment restrictions, architectural barriers) that reflect reactions to
limited life opportunities and an inability to adjust to sociooccupational role
changes (ie, class 2, 3, and 4 involvement).

Adopting this conceptual framework may be useful for researchers who seek
to investigate variation in psychosocial adaptation to chronic illnesses and disabilities. Among the types of research problems this framework addresses are
(1) qualitative and quantitative differences often observed in affective reactions
among persons with the same or similar physical disabilities; (2) differences in
sequence and duration of hypothesized phases of psychosocial adaptation to disabling conditions; and (3) differences in the effectiveness of treatment interventions (eg, psychotropic, psychotherapeutic, environmental) for the alleviation of
anxiety, depression, and other reactions to the onset of a chronic illness or disability.

GROWTH MODELING AND ADAPTATION TO CHRONIC ILLNESS AND DISABILITY

The conceptual framework and research suggestions outlined above may be
approached and further refined by use of a recently proposed paradigm known as
growth modeling (Clay, Wood, Frank, Hagglund, & Johnson, 1995; Harper,
1991; Willett, Ayoub, & Robinson, 1991). This paradigm rests on the assumption
that psychosocial adaptation to stressful and dysfunctional life events (eg,
chronic disease, disability, child abuse and neglect) changes over time. Moreover
it is assumed that these changes or periodic fluctuations in both positive (or adaptive) and negative (or maladaptive) directions differ appreciably among persons
with a chronic illness or disability. In other words, the process of adaptation is
characterized by wide-ranging individual variation. Consequently proponents of
this paradigm assert that the focus should be placed on within-group differences
rather than on the more traditional between-group differences, using longitudinal
research designs to investigate developmental trends in adaptation across the
lifespan (Harper, 1991).

The investigation of these adaptational trends, it is argued, must pay careful
attention to the functioning of children and adults with disabilities within their
physical and psychosocial environments. When investigating psychosocial adaptation to chronic childhood diseases using this developmental perspective,
Harper (1991) suggested recognizing the complex set of interactions among several illness- or disability-related (eg, visibility and appearance), sociodemographic (eg, chronological age, functional limitations), personality (eg, cognitive
level, maturity, and life experience), and situational (eg, peer social interactions,
family functioning) variables. Clay et al. (1995) examined individual differences

in psychosocial adaptation to chronic illness in two groups of children (ie, children with juvenile diabetes and children with juvenile rheumatoid arthritis) using the growth modeling paradigm.

The latent growth curve model (LGM), or CURVE model, is a recently introduced statistical methodology (McArdle & Epstein, 1987) that allows the researcher to analyze longitudinal data, incorporating notions borrowed from repeated measures ANOVA and latent variable (factor) analyses. CURVE models are "latent variable (factor) models that use means, variances, and covariances to create latent adjustment curves for each individual and for the group" (Clay et al., 1995, p. 63). Using the CURVE methodology a researcher creates a developmental structural equation model that incorporates data about both the group's mean and individual variations. CURVE models, accordingly, allow the researcher to evaluate competing assumptions, such as (1) there is no change in the level or variability of psychosocial adaptation over time; (2) changes in psychosocial adaptation over time are attributable to individual differences throughout the adaptation process; and (3) internal and external factors exert differential (and measurable) temporal influences and result in variations in psychosocial adaptation over time.

In their study Clay et al. (1995) obtained measures of psychosocial adaptation (ie, behavioral problems and emotional distress) from three samples of children: (1) those with juvenile diabetes mellitus, (2) those with juvenile rheumatoid arthritis, and (3) those without disabilities. Respondents included both the children and their mothers. Responses were obtained at four times: at diagnosis and at 6, 12, and 18 months postdiagnosis. Growth factor scores indicated a considerable amount of within-group variability in the process of psychosocial adaptation. Using a traditional between-groups analysis (ie, repeated measures ANOVA) failed to reveal these across-time differences. The results of additional analyses suggested that several variables measured at the time of initial diagnosis (eg, mother's state anger level, mother's feelings of cohesion, child's level of externalized anger, age of child) were found to be associated with variation in individual psychosocial adaptation growth factor scores over time and could therefore be conceptualized as factors indicative of psychosocial risk or resistance. These factors could, in turn, suggest effective interventions to prevent or to treat psychosocial distress.

CONCLUSION

A number of ecological models have been proposed in the literature to assist theoreticians, clinicians, and researchers in their study of the nature and process of psychosocial adaptation to chronic illness and disability. These models are often embedded within broader models that attempt to explain coping with fundamental life transitions and significant life crises. This chapter began with a review of a number of the more prominent of these models, both general models of adaptation and disability- or illness-specific models. The significant components of these models were presented and, when feasible, the typology of intervention strategies proposed by the model was discussed.

The ecological models reviewed were found to share certain conceptual and structural components. In particular they view the unfolding process of adaptation to the pivotal event (eg, disability onset, disease diagnosis) as composed of four primary classes of variables, including (1) variables associated with the disability itself (eg, nature of disabling condition, its chronicity, severity, visibility), (2) variables associated with sociodemographic or organismic characteristics of the individual (eg, sex, age, occupation), (3) variables associated with personality and behavioral attributes of the individual (eg, repertoire of coping strategies, self-concept, intellectual ability), and (4) variables associated with the physical and social environments (eg, family cohesiveness, living arrangements).

The interactions among elements in these four classes of variables, it is hypothesized, determine to a large extent the nature, degree, temporal sequencing, and pace of psychosocial adaptation to a chronic illness or disability. Furthermore, the nature of many of these variables and their unique and differential influences during the adaptation process can explain much of the within-group variation in psychosocial adaptation often observed among individuals with common disabling conditions.

The chapter concluded with the presentation of a recently proposed powerful analytic paradigm—the CURVE growth-modeling statistical methodology—that should be useful for clarifying the idiosyncratic nature of the process of psychosocial adaptation to chronic illness and disability. An example of the application of this methodology to the study of psychosocial adaptation among children with juvenile rheumatoid arthritis and juvenile diabetes mellitus was presented. From the results of research like this, it may be possible for the clinician to design and adjust a sequence of individually tailored treatment modalities to improve the coping abilities, the psychosocial adaptation, and, in the long run, the quality of life of persons with chronic illnesses and disabilities.

The speculative nature of the conclusions concerning psychosocial adaptation to chronic illness and disability, as we pointed out a number of times in our reviews of the literature for each of the 18 chronic illnesses and disabilities considered in Chapters 4 to 21, is due in part to the considerable number of research problems that limit the usefulness and generalizability of the available information. In Chapter 24, the last chapter of this book, we will present a summary of these significant problems organized into five areas: (1) research conceptualization, (2) study design, (3) sampling, (4) measurement, and (5) data analysis.

REFERENCES

Ben-Sira, Z. (1981). The structure of readjustment of the disabled: An additional perspective on rehabilitation. *Social Science and Medicine, 15,* 565–580.

Bury, M. (1982). Chronic illness as a biographical disruption. *Sociology of Health and Illness, 4,* 167–182.

Clay, D. L., Wood, P. K., Frank, R. G., Hagglund, K. J., & Johnson, J. C. (1995). Examining systematic differences in adaptation to chronic illness: A growth modeling approach. *Rehabilitation Psychology, 40,* 61–70.

Coulton, C. (1981). Person-environment fit as the focus in health care. *Social Work, 26,* 26–35.

Cummings, J. L. (1992). Depression and Parkinson's disease: A review. *The American Journal of Psychiatry, 149,* 443–454.

Dembo, T., Leviton, G. L., & Wright, B. A. (1956). Adjustment to misfortune—A problem of social-psychological rehabilitation. *Artificial Limbs, 3*(2), 4–62.

Dunkel-Schetter, C., Feinstein, L. G., Taylor, S. E., & Falke, R. L. (1992). Patterns of coping with cancer. *Health Psychology, 11,* 79–87.

Fedoroff, J. P., Lipsey, J. R., Starkstein, S. E., Forrester, A., Price, T. R., & Robinson, R. G. (1991). Phenomenological comparisons of major depression following stroke, myocardial infarction or spinal cord lesions. *Journal of Affective Disorders, 22,* 83–89.

Feifel, H., Strack, S., & Nagy, V. T. (1987a). Coping strategies and associated features of medically ill patients. *Psychosomatic Medicine, 49,* 616–625.

Feifel, H., Strack, S., & Nagy, V. T. (1987b). Degree of life-threat and differential use of coping modes. *Journal of Psychosomatic Research, 31,* 91–99.

Hanson, S., Buckelew, S. P., Hewett, J., & O'Neal, G. (1993). The relationship between coping and adjustment after spinal cord injury: A 5-year follow-up study. *Rehabilitation Psychology, 38,* 41–52.

Harper, D. C. (1991). Paradigms for investigating rehabilitation and adaptation to childhood disability and chronic illness. *Journal of Pediatric Psychology, 16,* 533–542.

Hermann, M., & Wallesch, C. W. (1993). Depressive changes in stroke patients. *Disability and Rehabilitation, 15,* 55–66.

Hilton, B. A. (1989). The relationship of uncertainty, control, commitment, and threat of recurrence to coping strategies used by women diagnosed with breast cancer. *Journal of Behavioral Medicine, 12,* 39–54.

Hurst, J. C., & McKinley, D. L. (1988). An ecological diagnostic classification plan. *Journal of Counseling and Development, 66,* 228–232.

Langer, K. G. (1994). Depression and denial in psychotherapy of persons with disabilities. *American Journal of Psychotherapy, 48,* 181–194.

Lazarus, R. S., & Folkman, S. (1984). *Stress, appraisal, and coping.* New York: Springer.

Livneh, H. (1986a). A unified approach to existing models of adaptation to disability—I. A model of adaptation. *Journal of Applied Rehabilitation Counseling, 17*(1), 5–16, 56.

Livneh, H. (1986b). A unified approach to existing models of adaptation to disability—II. Intervention strategies. *Journal of Applied Rehabilitation Counseling, 17*(2), 6–10.

Livneh, H., & Antonak, R. F. (1990). Reactions to disability: An empirical investigation of their nature and structure. *Journal of Applied Rehabilitation Counseling, 21*(4), 13–21.

McArdle, J. J., & Epstein, D. (1987). Latent growth curves within developmental structural equation models. *Child Development, 58*, 110–133.

Moos, R. H., & Schaefer, J. A. (1984). The crisis of physical illness. In R. H. Moos (Ed.), *Coping with physical illness. Vol. 2: New perspectives* (pp. 3–31). New York: Plenum Press.

Rodin, G., Craven, J., & Littlefield, C. (1991). *Depression in the medically ill: An integrated approach*. New York: Brunner/Mazel.

Roessler, R., & Bolton, B. (1978). *Psychosocial adjustment to disability*. Baltimore: University Park Press.

Schlossberg, N. K. (1981). A model for analyzing human adaptation to transition. *The Counseling Psychologist, 9*, 2–18.

Scofield, M. E., Pape, D. A., McCracken, N., & Maki, D. R. (1980). An ecological model for promoting acceptance of disability. *Journal of Applied Rehabilitation Counseling, 11*, 183–187.

Shontz, F. C. (1965). Reactions to crisis. *Volta Review, 67*, 364–370.

Shontz, F. C. (1975). *The psychological aspects of physical illness and disability*. New York: Macmillan.

Sigelman, C. K., Vengroff, L. P., & Spanhel, C. L. (1979). Disability and the concept of life functions. *Rehabilitation Counseling Bulletin, 23*, 103–113.

Siller, J. (1976). Psychological aspects of physical disability. In J. Meislin (Ed.), *Rehabilitation medicine and psychiatry* (pp. 455–484). Springfield, IL: C C Thomas.

Trieschmann, R. B. (Ed.). (1988). *Spinal cord injuries: Psychological, social, and vocational rehabilitation* (2nd ed.). New York: Demos.

Vash, C. L. (1981). *The psychology of disability*. New York: Springer.

Ville, I., Ravaud, J. F., Marchal, F., Paicheler, H., & Fardeau, M. (1992). Social identity and the international classification of handicaps. *Disability and Rehabilitation, 14*, 168–175.

Waltz, M., Badura, B., Pfaff, H., & Schott, T. (1988). Marriage and the psychological consequences of a heart attack: A longitudinal study of adaptation to chronic illness after 3 years. *Social Science and Medicine, 27*, 149–158.

Wiklund, I., Sanne, H., Vedin, A., & Wilhelmsson, C. (1985). Coping with myocardial infarction: A model with clinical applications, a literature review. *International Journal of Rehabilitation Medicine, 7*, 167–175.

Willett, J. B., Ayoub, C. C., & Robinson, D. (1991). Using growth modeling to examine systematic differences in growth: An example of change in the functioning of families at risk of maladaptive parenting, child abuse, or neglect. *Journal of Consulting and Clinical Psychology, 59*, 38–47.

Wright, B. A. (1983). *Physical disability—A psychosocial approach* (2nd ed.). New York: Harper & Row.

CHAPTER 24

Recommendations for Future Research

From the reviews of the literature for the 18 chronic illnesses and disabilities considered in Chapters 4 through 21, we were able to isolate a number of significant problems that limit the usefulness and generalizability of the available research information. In this last chapter of the book we present these problems, organized in list format into five areas: (1) research conceptualization, (2) study design, (3) sampling, (4) measurement, and (5) data analysis. In addition to a presentation of the problems we identified in each of these areas, we provide modest recommendations to overcome or circumvent them in future research concerned with psychosocial adaptation of persons with chronic illnesses and disabilities.

RESEARCH CONCEPTUALIZATION PROBLEMS

Significant problems related to the conceptualization of research investigating psychosocial adaptation to chronic illness and disability can be isolated, including the following.

Study the Positive Aspects of Psychosocial Adaptation

Researchers have tended to focus their attention on the negative aspects of psychosocial adaptation, including emotional distress, behavior problems, psychiatric disturbances, marital difficulties, and occupational failure (Wright, 1983). Despite the many negative experiences that beset the lives of persons with chronic illnesses or disabilities (many of which stem from negative societal attitudes and poor medical management), researchers should not adopt similar biased views. They should, whenever possible, examine the positive nature of the variables and characteristics associated with psychosocial adaptation (Wright, 1988).

Examine Within-Group Differences

The literature on psychosocial adaptation to chronic illness and disability has traditionally focused on between-group differences (ie, differences between groups of persons with various disorders and differences between persons with chronic illnesses or disabilities and persons without illnesses or disabilities). Frequently the perceptions and interpretations of the variables measured may differ significantly from those of the researcher, leading to erroneous conclusions (Wright, 1988). Moreover Wright (1988) cautioned that the researcher may tend to attribute differences in responses of the groups of individuals studied to the label that has been attached to them. Only recently have researchers recognized the need to address within-group differences (ie, differences among persons with a similar disorder). The importance of conducting within-group analyses cannot be overemphasized. These analyses allow researchers to examine the relations among illness- and disability-related variables, specific contextual features (eg, degree of stress, coping processes, extent of social networks), and psychosocial outcomes. Individuals who cope more effectively with disorder-triggered stress and reach a more adaptive status could be compared on these dimensions to persons with similar disorders who do not fare as well. Furthermore, understanding of long-term psychosocial adaptation requires a within-groups approach where persons with similar disorders are compared longitudinally with each other on such variables as coping strategies used or the type, sequence, and duration of psychosocial reactions experienced.

Reduce Method-Specific Error Variance

Outcome assessment in the literature on psychosocial adaptation to chronic illness and disability spans a wide range of physical, functional, psychological, social, occupational, attitudinal, and behavioral variables. In the absence of a consistent conceptual framework and an empirical approach to studying psychosocial adaptation, many of the findings reported in the literature cannot be compared to each other. Moreover, the plethora of assessment methods (eg, self-reports, informant reports, clinical judgments, nonstandardized objective measures, projective tests) further increases method-specific and error variances and reduces confidence in the accuracy and generalizability of the results of the investigation. Researchers should use only psychometrically sound measures that are valid assessments of psychosocial adaptation. Examples include unobtrusive observations of the behaviors and coping skills of persons with chronic illnesses and disabilities or informant-reported empirical ratings that are behaviorally anchored. It is also recommended that meta-analytic studies be undertaken to integrate the results of diverse investigations. If coherent and theoretically defensible collections of outcome constructs can be obtained, then psychometricians may be able to devise measures that do not capitalize on method-specific variance.

STUDY DESIGN PROBLEMS

Significant problems related to the design of research to answer questions related to psychosocial adaptation to chronic illness and disability can be isolated, including the following.

Carefully Define Psychosocial Adaptation

There has been a notable lack of consistency in the definition of psychosocial adaptation to chronic illness or disability. For instance, adaptation has been variously conceived as:

- degree of life satisfaction;
- vocational or avocational potential or productivity;
- performance of domestic skills or activities of daily living skills;
- absence of medical complications;
- coping style;
- degree of illness or disability acceptance as a unidimensional construct;
- emotional and psychological distress, as a multidimensional construct, often temporally ordered;
- degree of emotional distress as a unidimensional construct;
- presence of new and distressing physical and behavioral reactions to general health and mental status;
- presence of psychosomatic complaints;
- pathological dimensions of personality that influence the course of the illness or disability and the efficacy of treatment;
- impact on interpersonal relations, communication, and sexual behavior;
- psychological reactions that typically include shock, anxiety, depression, guilt, hostility, and denial; and
- degree of quality of life attained and maintained.

Consequently the results of different investigations may not be comparable, leading to seemingly contradictory results (eg, the lack of a clear relationship between psychosocial adaptation and age at onset or chronicity of illness or disability). It is recommended that researchers obtain behavioral indices of psychosocial reactions (eg, observable, low-inference data that can be cross-validated with relative ease by other researchers) rather than rely on the more typical use of constructs that require inference of psychological status (eg, dysphoria, discouragement, guilt). Researchers should also consider the use of the multimethod approach to data collection (eg, a combination of self-report questionnaire, clinical interview, behavioral observations, and informant data) to establish a multisource perspective and a broader definition of the concept of psychosocial adaptation.

As a step toward classifying empirical definitions and outcome measures of psychosocial adaptation to chronic illness or disability, the list of definitional constructs provided above can be conveniently collapsed into three broad categories.

1. Functional or performance-based status variables refer to the individual's ability to function in the community, including performance of activities of daily living, vocational productivity, avocational activities, and maintenance of social and familial relationships.

2. Quality-of-life status or subjective well-being and personal satisfaction variables commonly reflect degree of life satisfaction, level of disability or illness acceptance, level of emotional or psychological distress, and degree of quality of life attained and maintained.

3. Medical or symptomatic status that, although only infrequently and indirectly used in the literature as a criterion for psychosocial adaptation, may be useful in its capacity to capture such features as absence of medical complications or degree of medical stability, presence of new and distressing physical symptoms, and even survival, as opposed to death from complications of the condition.

Use Adequate Comparison Groups

The study of between-group variability requires comparison groups composed of individuals with different chronic illness or disability types or of control groups of persons with and without disorders. The absence of adequate comparison groups limits the internal validity of the studies using empirical measures. Low internal validity, in turn, precludes the identification of psychosocial profiles of class 1 variables (see Chapter 23) that are unique characteristics associated with a chronic illness or disability. Adaptation to chronic illness and disability should be investigated in comparative studies using carefully constructed comparison groups of various types. For example, the psychosocial adaptation of persons with cerebral palsy can be compared with that of persons with other neuromuscular disorders, individuals who sustained traumatic disabilities, and persons without disabilities who have been diagnosed with endogenous depression.

Investigate Extraneous Variable Confounding

The confounding of sociodemographic variables (eg, age, sex, socioeconomic status, living and marital status), experiential variables (eg, developmental stage, school and work experiences), disability- or illness-related variables (eg, underlying neuropathology, seizure frequency, length of coma, chronicity, drug side effects, remission and exacerbation of disease activity), and situational variables (eg, social support, accident history, learning problems, drug and alcohol abuse) with measures of affectivity, in particular depression and cognitive functioning, must be accounted for in any investigation attempting to attribute psychosocial reactions to an illness or disability. Data-analytic techniques (eg, discriminant function or canonical correlation analyses) can reveal the reciprocal relationships among predetermined sets of these variables and their influences on adaptation to chronic illness and disability, but the necessary data must first be collected by the researcher. Researchers planning to design strategies to eliminate psychosocial problems of adaptation of persons with a chronic illness or disability would ultimately benefit from these efforts.

Conduct Longitudinal Investigations

Investigations of the psychosocial reactions of persons with chronic illnesses and disabilities have typically involved the cross-sectional research approach. Data are obtained at one point in time from groups of persons with the same illness or disability but of different ages. The individuals are arranged into age groups by some predetermined criteria (eg, adolescents, young adults, adults, older adults) and the relationship of age to adaptation is investigated with regression techniques. Because the data collection is constrained to a short period, the problem of sample attrition that is a common weakness in longitudinal research is overcome. There are, however, limitations unique to cross-sectional research. Although the data-analytic procedures can validate a hypothesized reaction phase sequence, the timing of the onset or disappearance of specific adaptation reactions cannot be delineated with this approach. In addition, the individuals in the older samples may not be representative of the general population of persons with the illness or disability due to hospitalization, placement in specialized living environments, or death. There is a need for well-designed and well-executed investigations that involve the collection of comprehensive sets of data from diverse samples of individuals at different points in time. Although difficult and costly to implement (Magnusson, Bergman, Rudinger, & Törestad, 1991), longitudinal research designs are essential for studying the process of psychosocial adaptation to chronic illness and disability.

Reduce Confounding of the Sequencing of Medical Symptoms and Psychosocial Reactions

The cause-and-effect relationship between somatic symptoms and psychosocial reactions is often confounded. For example, anxiety and depression are frequently regarded as reactions following the onset of symptoms or the diagnosis of a disease, but as we pointed out in the review chapters, there are data that suggest that these and other affective changes (eg, anger, suppression of anger) may predispose an individual to a disease (eg, Parkinson's disease) or exacerbate the symptoms of a disorder (eg, multiple sclerosis, rheumatoid arthritis). These relationships and their interactive effects must be thoughtfully investigated. The literature on life events and adjustment suggests that researchers should focus on contemporary events, such as the onset of disability, and study their relations to psychosocial adaptation both prospectively and retrospectively. Retrospective data can be obtained by asking the individual to provide a history of previous events related to depression, anxiety, and other premorbid symptoms or by asking the individual's spouse or close family members to comment on these events. Models to investigate the temporal relationships among these variables can be built and tested using statistical methods such as path analysis and LISREL. For example, it might be possible to isolate among persons with chronic illnesses and disabilities who manifest maladaptive psychosocial reaction (ie, depression, anger, anxiety) two distinct groups: those with indications of affective disturbances prior to the onset of disability and those with no indications of affective disturbances prior to the onset of disability. The prospective study of the psychosocial adaptation of the individuals in these two groups could yield data that are relatively free of the confounding by the sequencing of medical symptoms.

Reduce Confounding of Disease-Specific Symptoms and Psychosocial Reactions

Specific disease- or disability-triggered symptoms are often confounded with psychosocial reactions to the disorder. For example, the assessment of depression and other psychiatric conditions in persons with spinal cord injury, multiple sclerosis, or Parkinson's disease are often complicated by overlapping manifestations of somatic (ie, physical sequelae) and reactive (ie, psychosocial) status. This is particularly true when the scales of the Minnesota Multiphasic Personality Inventory or the Beck Depression Inventory are used to assess reactions of depression, anxiety, hypochondriasis, and even psychotic tendencies in these groups of persons. Symptoms such as irritability, sleep disturbance, appetite loss, fatigue, weight loss, and worry about health may be direct somatic manifestations of disease progression or disability complications rather than reflections of psychosocial reactions to the onset of the disorder. There is a need for researchers to be careful when using the Minnesota Multiphasic Personality Inventory, the Beck Depression Inventory, and similar scales to assess psychosocial adaptation among these and other groups of individuals. Researchers should also study separate content groups of items (eg, vegetative, cognitive, and affective content items in the Depression scale of the Minnesota Multiphasic Personality Inventory and the Beck Depression Inventory) to ensure that depression and other presumed psychiatric reactions are not merely somatic artifacts of the disorder. Finally, researchers should use, whenever possible, correction procedures (eg, Kendall, Edinger, & Eberly, 1978; Rodevich & Wanlass, 1995) to attenuate potential biases toward persons with chronic illnesses and disabilities in the Minnesota Multiphasic Personality Inventory scales and items.

SAMPLING PROBLEMS

Significant problems related to sampling in research on psychosocial adaptation to chronic illness and disability can be isolated, including the following.

Reduce Sampling Biases

The reliance upon data from small samples and the introduction of sample selection biases (eg, the use of consecutive self-selected individuals or nonrepresentative volunteers) have undoubtedly reduced the power of even well-designed investigations to detect subtle differences in patterns of psychosocial adaptation to chronic illness and disability or to estimate the prevalence of variables related to adaptation. This in turn leads to what may appear to be inconclusive or contradictory research findings (eg, the presence of a relationship in one study and the absence of this relationship in another study). Statistical power analysis can tell the investigator the minimum number of participants necessary to achieve an acceptable level of power in experimental research (eg, the ability to detect relationships that may exist between variables or characteristics of interest). Different sampling techniques, such as multistage probability sampling, are available to circumvent some of the problems present if simple random sampling is not possible. Statistical investigation of the representativeness of a sample should also be reported to assist others to evaluate the generalizability of the results.

Limit Generalizations from Patients to Persons

As others have astutely pointed out (Hermann & Whitman, 1984; Hermann & Whitman, 1992), sample selection biases in research concerned with psychosocial adaptation to chronic illness or disability limit generalization from studies of *patients* with illnesses or disabilities to *persons* in the general population with illnesses or disabilities. Among these sampling biases are the preponderance of institutionalized or hospitalized individuals in research conducted prior to the mid-1960s. For example, a large number of studies of psychosocial reactions to spinal cord injury or rheumatoid arthritis involved the study of men in Veterans

Administration hospitals. More recently the majority of investigations of psychosocial adaptation to chronic illness and disability have been conducted at university research centers, comprehensive teaching hospitals, or specialized medical clinics. These types of centers, however, often treat motivated volunteer samples of persons who also have illness or disabilities that present more severe, complex, or intractable problems. Risk of psychosocial maladaptation may be misrepresented (either positively or negatively) in the data from studies conducted in these settings with these biased samples. Research needs to include samples of individuals from diverse settings, in particular those to which the researchers hope to generalize their results.

Reduce Mortality Threats to Experimental Validity

Attrition due to the elevated mortality rates associated with certain populations of persons with chronic illnesses and disabilities (eg, Duchenne muscular dystrophy, myocardial infarction, cancer, amyotrophic lateral sclerosis) significantly reduces the generalizability of research findings, especially longitudinal research. Attrition should be carefully reported and accounted for statistically prior to the interpretation of results. Trend studies (selecting different samples from a changing population at each data collection point) and cohort studies (selecting different samples from a constant population at each data collection point) can be used to attenuate the effects of sample attrition in panel studies (selecting a sample from the population at the start of the investigation and collecting data from this sample at each data collection point). Increasing size and diversity of the sample can also help to overcome the limitations due to attrition.

Lessen Sample Heterogeneity

The lack of consistency in methods used to define and diagnose specific illnesses and disabilities (eg, muscular dystrophy, rheumatoid arthritis, multiple sclerosis, epilepsy, traumatic brain injury), differences in criteria used to define and classify illness- and disability-related variables (eg, seizure type, severity, chronicity, age at onset, neurological status, length of coma), substantial heterogeneity among respondents (eg, in diagnostic status, course of illness, severity of disability, chronicity), and the clustering of respondents with diverse symptoms together as a single group (eg, not examining separately individuals with different cancer sites, disease stage, or type of medical treatment received) reduces the interpretability of research results. It has also been noted that studies of psychopathology associated with certain diseases (eg, multiple sclerosis) frequently included in their clinical samples persons suffering from other incorrectly diagnosed neurological diseases (McNamara, 1991). More careful sampling, the development of data-based diagnostic criteria, the use of sophisticated diagnostic procedures (eg, positron emission tomography (PET) scanners), and the use of multivariate statistical procedures can clarify the outcomes of research with heterogeneous populations and reduce the difficulty of comparing the results of studies conducted by different researchers at different times in different settings.

MEASUREMENT PROBLEMS

Significant problems related to the measurement of psychosocial adaptation to chronic illness and disability can be isolated, including the following.

Use Psychometrically Sound Instruments

When searching for a measure of psychosocial adaptation to a specific illness or disability, the researcher should select an instrument that operationalizes the construct in a fashion consistent with the way in which it is conceptualized by the researcher. The lack of psychometrically sound multidimensional instruments to measure psychosocial adaptation to most specific illnesses and disabilities continues to be a significant deficiency. While the instruments reviewed in Chapter 3 seem to represent reasonable first attempts, the absence of sound documentation regarding reliability and validity reduces the strength of our recommendations for the use of these instruments. The development and testing of the Arthritis Impact Measurement Scales provide an excellent model to researchers (and to students in tests and measurements courses) for the tedious, exacting, time-consuming, and often expensive psychometric work that must be undertaken to produce an instrument that will eliminate these deficiencies. If instruments that meet the researcher's theoretical needs are not available for a specific illness or disability, then he or she should consider a general measure that does, rather than settle for a specific measure that is theoretically or empirically unsatisfactory. Regardless of how the researcher defines the construct of psychosocial adaptation, it is necessary to select a psychometrically sound instrument to answer questions concerning the prescription and evaluation of intervention strategies for persons with diverse chronic illnesses and disabilities.

Use Multidimensional Instruments

The unidimensional conception of psychosocial adaptation to chronic illness and disability evident in most of the research reviewed in this book ignores the fact that psychosocial reactions experienced by persons with chronic illnesses and disabilities have multiple facets and that adaptation has multiple antecedents. This failure to conceptualize adaptation as a multidimensional construct may be attributable to both the lack of a multidimensional instrument to measure adaptation and to the lack of familiarity with multivariate statistical procedures to correctly analyze the obtained data. The recently introduced Reactions to Impairment and Disability Inventory may overcome the first of these deficiencies by furnishing researchers with a multidimensional measurement device that appears to possess promising psychometric qualities to explore this construct.

Use Previously Constructed Instruments

Researchers all too frequently construct their own measures of psychosocial adaptation to chronic illness and disability for a study and fail to provide psychometric documentation regarding the measure (eg, equality of units underlying interval scales, item homogeneity, scale reliability, factor structure, construct validity). Even well-designed and well-executed research will have limited value for theory building and theory testing if the data analyzed are substandard. Without assurances of the psychometric adequacy of the instrument, confidence in the accuracy and applicability of the conclusions drawn from research may be unjustified. The instruments reviewed in Chapters 2 and 3 should be carefully examined and used in research on psychosocial adaptation.

Revise, Update, and Revalidate Available Instruments

Instruments to measure psychosocial adaptation to chronic illness and disability have not been periodically refined and improved by their authors. Tremendous changes in society's responses to persons with chronic illnesses or disabilities have occurred in the past three decades, coupled with significant change in legislation and public policy concerning the provision of comprehensive medical, psychosocial, and vocational services. Even the language used to refer to people with chronic illnesses or disabilities has changed significantly. These changes point to a significant need to revise, update, and revalidate several of the older scales, such as the General Health Questionnaire, Acceptance of Disability scale, and Bell Disability Scale of Adjustment. An old instrument that is beyond theoretical, linguistic, and psychometric redemption should be withdrawn by its author(s). In other than this extreme case, we recommend that researchers refine previously published instruments and refrain from the creation of new ones. Two ways that researchers and practitioners can assist in this process are to report in their own research psychometric information from the analyses of their data and to communicate this information to the authors of the instrument. It is a difficult process to track down reports of the use of one's instrument worldwide even with the assistance of computerized searches of the medical and psychological literature. If intervention or treatment studies are located, it is most often true that the researchers failed to report basic psychometric information (eg, reliability estimates, distribution characteristics), in part, we suspect, because they failed to undertake these prerequisite analyses.

Avoid the Use of Modified Instruments

It is incorrect to assume that an existing instrument to measure psychosocial adaptation can be modified by replacing the original referent of the items with a new referent without affecting the reliability and validity of the modified instrument. The modified instrument is a new instrument, and new documentation regarding its psychometric adequacy must be obtained, as the evidence available regarding the original instrument no longer applies. The conclusions of research in which, for example, the referent *epilepsy* in the Washington Psychosocial Seizure Inventory items is changed to *diabetes* or the referent *arthritis* in the Arthritis Impact Measurement Scales items is changed to *cancer* must be suspect unless the researcher making such changes investigates and reports important psychometric indices. Journal editors must demand this information as part of the review process and reject those manuscripts that fail to provide it. Readers with minimal training in psychometrics cannot be expected to fulfill an editor's responsibility to discriminate defensible research conclusions from conclusions based upon the analyses of data from unacceptable modifications of sound instruments intended for other uses.

Use Language- and Culture-Specific Instruments

Instruments developed for use in one country (eg, the General Health Questionnaire, Glasgow Assessment Schedule) may not be valid measures of the construct of psychosocial adaptation in another country because adaptation is in large part a culture-specific social phenomenon. In addition, simple translation of the words on an instrument into another language for use with a subset of the population within a country, or in another country altogether, is not sufficient to guarantee translation of the concepts for another culture. Significant changes may need to be made that necessitate the revalidation of the instrument. For example, changing "It makes my blood boil to have someone talk about my physical impairment" from the Reactions to Impairment and Disability Inventory may require translating "makes my blood boil" into a concept that would shift the item from one measuring Externalized Hostility to one measuring Internalized Anger. The item "I show less affection" from the Sickness Impact Profile may not be translatable at all for use in a culture that teaches children to control outward displays of affection.

Report Psychometric Characteristics of Instruments

With the exception of those instruments with widespread appeal (and commercial potential), such as the Sickness Impact Profile, Psychosocial Adaptation to Illness Scale, and General Health Questionnaire, there are few sources of information on the psychometric adequacy and utility of instruments to measure psychosocial adaptation to chronic illness and disability. Few practitioners have easy access to the measurement journals and standard sources of test information known to university researchers. While several social psychology, applied rehabilitation, and illness- or disability-related professional journals will publish reports concerning the development of a new instrument, very few will even consider a manuscript reporting the results of an investigation of the psychometric characteristics of a previously published instrument. There is a need for a well-edited professional journal that provides an outlet for the publication of studies of this sort. An alternative would be a special regular section of an established disability studies, rehabilitation research, or medical research journal devoted to the publication of data concerning the psychometric characteristics of measures of psychosocial adaptation to chronic illness and disability.

Master Sophisticated Measurement Methods

Researchers need to use sophisticated measurement methods if they hope to answer complex questions about psychosocial adaptation to chronic illness and disability. The traditional unidimensional scaling methods that underlie instruments such as the Acceptance of Disability scale or the Acceptance of Loss scale impose several limitations on research results and subsequent interpretations. These include the inability of the methods to consider commonalities or differences that may exist in the process of adaptation to various illnesses and disabilities and the imposition of the researcher's a priori conceptions of the relevant dimensions and constructs of the adaptation domain. Techniques such as multidimensional scaling (Schmelkin, 1988), unfolding-theoretic analysis (Davison, 1977), ordering-theoretic analysis (Krus, Bart, & Airasian, 1975), latent variable analysis (Loehlin, 1987), meta-analysis (Glass, 1977), and cluster analysis (Kaufman & Rousseeuw, 1990) are available to help the researcher to overcome these limitations and permit the identification and exploration of the salient dimensions of the process of psychosocial adaptation.

Investigate Threats to Internal Validity

Reliance on retrospective self-report data using behavior or symptom checklists may introduce respondent reactivity threats (eg, denying certain reactions in order to preserve one's self-image, social desirability responding, purposefully reporting nonexistent reactions to gain sympathy) or the fortuitous confounding of unrelated personality attributes of the respondent (eg, responding similarly to all items on a scale even when the characteristics may not be present, responding positively or negatively to all items on a scale, choosing the most or least extreme response to every item) with substantive psychosocial adaptation content. These threats compromise the internal validity of an experimental investigation and decrease the interpretability and generalizability of the results of nonexperimental descriptive research. It is incumbent upon the developer of any instrument to measure and report the susceptibility of the instrument reviewed to the threats of these biasing influences. Similar analyses should be undertaken for the instruments reviewed in Chapters 2 and 3 for which these data are not yet available. Researchers should either control for these influences experimentally, use outcome measures that are known to be free of biases (eg, observations of behavior in natural environments), or measure and report the susceptibility of their measures to these biasing influences so that others can judge for themselves whether the researcher's conclusions are warranted.

Consider Unobtrusive Measures

We were unable to discover any research that collected data using an objective but unobtrusive indirect method to measure adaptation. Indirect methods yield responses that are not taken literally. Rather the respondent's performance on an objective task is thought to reveal latent psychosocial constructs that are interpreted as adaptation to a chronic illness or disability. Models for these novel and powerful methods are available in the literature concerning the measurement of attitudes (Dawes & Smith, 1985; Livneh & Antonak, 1994a; Livneh & Antonak, 1994b; Mueller, 1986). Among unobtrusive measures are (1) physiological measures, in which respondents are aware of being measured but are inactive participants in the measurement process; (2) disguised methods, in which respondents are purposefully deceived as to the true purpose of the measurement situation; and (3) behavioral observations in natural environments in which respondents are unaware that they are being observed or measured. The relative immunity of these methods from respondent reactivity, sensitization, and response style confounding and their imbeddedness in the broader psychosocial research context suggest that these methods may provide data free from biasing influences yet sensitive enough to respondents' personal experiences and subjective perceptions to answer important research questions (Antonak & Livneh, 1995; Livneh & Antonak, 1994a; Livneh & Antonak, 1994b).

Exercise Caution with Subjective Measures

Just as obtrusive measures introduce respondent biases that compromise the validity of an investigation, subjective measures of psychosocial adaptation (eg, projective techniques such as the Thematic Apperception Test, examination of clinical records, ratings based upon interviews, reports of informants who do not know the person well) introduce experimenter biases that may limit the validity and generalizability of the results. Investigators who use subjective measures should consider several means to control for or reduce these biasing factors: (1) using raters who are unaware of the purposes of the investigation or of the characteristics of the persons studied, (2) determining and reporting indices of interrater reliability, (3) reporting confirmatory objective data for a random subsample of research participants, (4) restricting generalizations to informant relationships and observation environments that are identical to those present in the data collection procedures, and (5) providing detailed and comprehensive descriptions of the data collection process so that the reader may judge the adequacy of the conclusions of the research.

DATA ANALYSIS PROBLEMS

Significant problems related to the analyses of the empirical data collected in research on psychosocial adaptation to chronic illness and disability can be isolated, including the following.

Statistically Eliminate Confounding

As mentioned previously, confounding of the variable of psychosocial adaptation (eg, response biasing or nonrandom sampling) was a common problem encountered in the research on psychosocial adaptation to chronic illness and disability reviewed for this book. For investigations in which confounding is present, statistical techniques such as analysis of covariance and multiple regression may be used to measure and partial out the effects of one or more underlying concomitant variables (eg, socioeconomic status, sex) on psychosocial adaptation.

Test Prerequisite Statistical Assumptions

It was quite common to find in investigations of psychosocial adaptation clear violations of the requisite assumptions for traditional parametric statistical tests of hypotheses. Seldom were samples randomly drawn; rarely did intervention studies randomly assign participants to groups; some measures did not yield independent data (ie, the Washington Psychosocial Seizure Inventory); data that were at best ordinal were analyzed as if they were interval; and almost never did we encounter tests of the normality of the distribution of data, the homogeneity of sample variances, the linearity of regressions, or the difference of correlation matrices from identity matrices. Although large samples and the selection of conservative probability levels for hypothesis testing assuaged some concerns, it was clear that alternative statistical analyses should have been used in many of the studies reviewed. For example, data should have been transformed to approximate a more normal distribution, nonlinearity of regression should have been dealt with by fitting a polynomial curve, and one of the large number of distribution-free statistical tests should have been selected to test associations among variables or differences among group means.

Master Sophisticated Analysis Methods

Researchers need to use sophisticated analysis methods if they hope to answer complex questions about psychosocial adaptation to chronic illness and disability. The traditional unidimensional analysis methods impose several limitations on research results and subsequent interpretations. These include the inability to consider commonalities or differences that may exist in the process of adaptation to various disabilities and the imposition of the researcher's a priori conceptions of the relevant dimensions and constructs of the adaptation domain. Techniques such as multidimensional scaling, unfolding-theoretic analysis, ordering-theoretic analysis, partial correlation, multiple discriminant analysis, principal factors analysis, multivariate analysis of variance, and linear structural relations modeling overcome these limitations and permit the exploration of the salient dimensions of the process of adaptation in a more realistic multidimensional framework.

CONCLUDING COMMENTS

Clinicians and researchers alike have demonstrated increased interest in the psychological and social reactions evinced by persons who experience traumatic or sudden-onset disabilities, disease-related health disorders, sensory impairments, and chronic neurological and neuromuscular disorders. To account for these reactions, theorists have posited the construct of psychosocial adaptation to chronic illness and disability. Viewed as a special case of coping with a traumatic life event, psychosocial adaptation is thought to entail the gradual process of assimilation of changes in the individual's body, body image, ego, self-concept, and person-environment interactions. Experts agree that the individual's response to rehabilitation opportunities will be limited if he or she has not made a successful adaptation to these changes. But there remain a number of unanswered questions in this domain of inquiry. How are persons with chronic illnesses and disabilities affected by their conditions? How do they cope with these imposed conditions? What disability- or illness-related, sociodemographic, personality, and environmental factors are linked to successful psychosocial adaptation? This book was written as an attempt to address these and other questions pertinent to the topic of psychosocial adaptation to chronic illness and disability.

Part I of the book consisted of three chapters. Chapter 1 began with an introduction to the construct of psychosocial adaptation to chronic illness and disability, including the definition of key terms, an exegesis of the relationships of the construct to related constructs (eg, coping), and a historical overview of research on the construct. The chapter continued with an examination of several theoretical models that have been propounded to account for the nature, structure, and temporal ordering of the psychosocial reactions that the process of psychosocial adaptation to chronic illness and disability comprises. Chapter 1 concluded with a discussion of the distinction between psychosocial adaptation associated with a chronic illness, such as multiple sclerosis, and psychosocial adaptation to disability associated with a traumatic event, such as a spinal cord injury.

The purpose of Chapters 2 and 3 was to address one of the more important methodological issues in the study of psychosocial adaptation to chronic illness and disability: namely, the selection of an instrument to operationalize the construct as a dependent variable in descriptive and experimental research. In these two chapters we provided information for clinicians and researchers in the fields of health and disability studies on the availability and suitability of 21 instruments for measuring psychosocial adaptation to chronic illness and disability. Chapter 2 presented reviews of 10 general measures of this construct organized into three categories: (1) measures of psychosocial adaptation to illness (five instruments), (2) unidimensional measures of psychosocial adaptation to disability (three instruments), and (3) multidimensional measures of psychosocial adaptation to disability (two instruments). Chapter 3 presented reviews of 11 instruments developed to investigate the psychosocial adaptation of individuals with eight specific chronic illnesses and disabilities: (1) cancer, (2) diabetes mellitus, (3) hearing impairment, (4) rheumatoid arthritis, (5) seizure disorders, (6) spinal cord injury, (7) traumatic brain injury, and (8) visual impairment.

In Parts II, III, IV, and V we provided reviews of the research literature on psychosocial adaptation to 18 specific chronic illnesses and disabilities. In particular, Part II concerned four traumatic or sudden-onset disabilities: Chapter 4—cardiovascular disorders, Chapter 5—spinal cord injury, Chapter 6—traumatic brain injury, and Chapter 7—amputation. Part III concerned three disease-related health disorders: Chapter 8—cancer, Chapter 9—diabetes mellitus, and Chapter 10—rheumatoid arthritis. Part IV concerned two sensory impairments: Chapter 11—blindness and visual impairments and Chapter 12—deafness and hearing impairments. Part V concerned nine neurological and neuromuscular disabilities: Chapter 13—epilepsy, Chapter 14—multiple sclerosis, Chapter 15—cerebral palsy, Chapter 16—amyotrophic lateral sclerosis, Chapter 17—muscular dystrophy, Chapter 18—myasthenia gravis, Chapter 19—neurofibromatosis, Chapter 20—Parkinson's disease, and Chapter 21—spina bifida.

For each of these chapters we began with a brief description of the chronic illness or disability, including a synopsis of available information on incidence and prevalence, causal factors, signs and symptoms, complications, course, and prognosis. This was followed by a review of the research literature on psychosocial adaptation to the chronic illness or disability, focusing on the research conducted in the last 15 to 20 years. The next section of each chapter summarized the available information on characteristics associated with psychosocial adaptation to the chronic illness or disability, organized into four areas: (1) sociodemographic characteristics (eg, age at time of injury or disease onset, chronicity, sex, educational level, socioeconomic status), (2) personality factors (eg, premorbid personality, ego strength, attribution of blame, perception of disability, locus of control), (3) illness- or disability-related variables (eg, neuropathology, severity of impairment, type of treatment), and, when available, (4) environmental variables (eg, social networks, family support or peer support, level of independence, modifiability of the work environment). Each chapter ended with a presentation of tentative conclusions concerning psychosocial adaptation to the chronic illness or disability derived from the findings reported in the literature reviewed.

Part VI provided us with an opportunity to reflect upon the findings reported in our reviews of the research literature in Chapters 4 to 21. Our goal for Chapter 22 was to provide the clinician with insights into the application of the research findings to therapeutic interventions. The chapter began with an overview of theoretical models that have been used to support clinical interventions. Examples were provided of intervention strategies designed to reduce clients' maladaptive psychosocial reactions, teach them appropriate coping skills and problem-solving methods, and provide them with emotional, cognitive, and behavioral supports during the process of adaptation. The chapter concluded with an examination of the small but growing number of well-designed empirical studies to assess the effectiveness of various psychosocial interventions with persons with chronic illnesses and disabilities.

Our goal for Chapter 23 was to provide the theoretician with a framework for conceptualizing the study of psychosocial adaptation to chronic illness and disability. The chapter began with a review of ecological models of psychosocial adaptation to the onset of life crises and transition that have been proposed by researchers and clinicians. Building upon these models and insights gained from the reviews of the research literature in the chapters in Parts II, III, IV, and V, a conceptual framework for the study of psychosocial adaptation to chronic illness and disability was proposed. We argued that to successfully investigate the nature and process of psychosocial adaptation to chronic illness and disability, four broad classes of variables must be considered. These classes of variables and their interactions were illustrated with examples from the research literature. The chapter provided examples of the application of this framework to both research and clinical practice for groups of persons with diverse chronic illnesses and disabilities.

Our goal for Chapter 24 was to provide the researcher with recommendations for improving the quality of future research in this domain of inquiry. On the basis of our reviews of the literature on psychosocial adaptation to the 18 chronic illnesses and disabilities considered in this book, we presented a listing of significant research problems that limit the usefulness and generalizability of the available information, together with recommendations for future research, organized into five areas: (1) research conceptualization, (2) study design, (3) sampling, (4) measurement, and (5) data analysis.

Psychosocial adaptation to chronic illness and disability is an ongoing process. It is a continuous effort to successfully cope with both personal loss—the loss of health; control; certain skills and abilities; familial, social, and vocational roles—and imposed environmental restrictions. It is therefore recommended that this developmental process be studied longitudinally with a set of sensitive and psychometrically sound instruments that operationalize adaptation as a disability-specific and, furthermore, person-specific unfolding hierarchical process consisting of a complex set of psychosocial reactions and experiences. It is our contention that results obtained from such research endeavors should lead to a better understanding of the individual's and his or her family's emotional experiences and psychosocial reactions and the characteristics associated with them.

In a similar vein we heed Beatrice Wright's (1983) insightful advice that persons with disabilities are not passive entities but are highly complex, active copers and that their disability constitutes only one aspect of their rich lives. Moreover the limitations imposed on persons with chronic illnesses and disabilities are not merely a reflection of their health, physical, or cognitive impairments but are equally a function of external barriers imposed by the physical and social-attitudinal environments.

Consequently rehabilitation efforts and related therapeutic strategies to help persons with chronic illnesses and disabilities to cope efficiently with their limitations must combine the teaching and mastery of personal coping and independent living skills as well as efforts to modify the restrictions imposed by the physical and social environments. Then and only then can the challenges triggered by the onset of a chronic illness or disability be fully appreciated, confronted, and successfully resolved.

REFERENCES

Antonak, R. F., & Livneh, H. (1995). Direct and indirect methods to measure attitudes toward persons with disabilities, with an exegesis of the error-choice method. *Rehabilitation Psychology, 40,* 3–24.

Davison, M. L. (1977). On a metric, unidimensional unfolding model for attitudinal and developmental data. *Psychometrika, 42,* 523–548.

Dawes, R. M., & Smith, T. L. (1985). Attitude and opinion measurement. In G. Lindzey & E. Aronson (Eds.), *The handbook of social psychology: Vol. 1. Theory and method* (3rd ed.) (pp. 509–566). New York: Random House.

Glass, G. V. (1977). Integrating findings: The meta-analysis of research. *Review of Research in Education, 5,* 351–379.

Hermann, B. P., & Whitman, S. (1984). Behavioral and personality correlates of epilepsy: A review, methodological critique and conceptual model. *Psychological Bulletin, 95,* 451–497.

Hermann, B. P., & Whitman, S. (1992). Psychopathology in epilepsy: The role of psychology in altering paradigms of research, treatment, and prevention. *American Psychologist, 47,* 1134–1138.

Kaufman, L., & Rousseeuw, P. J. (1990). *Finding groups in data: An introduction to cluster analysis.* New York: Wiley.

Kendall, P. C., Edinger, J., & Eberly, C. (1978). Taylor's MMPI correction factor for spinal cord injury: Empirical endorsement. *Journal of Consulting and Clinical Psychology, 46,* 370–371.

Krus, D. J., Bart, W. M., & Airasian, P. W. (1975). *Ordering theory and methods.* Los Angeles: Theta Press.

Livneh, H., & Antonak, R. F. (1994a). Indirect methods of attitude measurement. A reply to Linkowski and Yuker. *Rehabilitation Education, 8,* 144–148.

Livneh, H., & Antonak, R. F. (1994b). Indirect methods to measure attitudes toward persons with disabilities. *Rehabilitation Education, 8,* 103–137.

Loehlin, J. C. (1987). *Latent variable models: An introduction to factor, path, and structural analysis.* Hillsdale, NJ: Lawrence Erlbaum Associates.

Magnusson, D., Bergman, L. R., Rudinger, G., & Törestad, B. (Eds.). (1991). *Problems and methods in longitudinal research: Stability and change.* New York: Cambridge University Press.

McNamara, M. E. (1991). Psychological factors affecting neurological conditions: Depression and stroke, multiple sclerosis, Parkinson's disease, and epilepsy. *Psychosomatics, 32,* 255–267.

Mueller, D. J. (1986). *Measuring social attitudes: A handbook for researchers and practitioners.* New York: Teachers College Press.

Rodevich, M. A., & Wanlass, R. L. (1995). The moderating effect of spinal cord injury on MMPI-2 profiles: A clinically derived T-score correction procedure. *Rehabilitation Psychology, 40,* 181–190.

Schmelkin, L. P. (1988). Multidimensional scaling. In R. F. Antonak & H. Livneh, *The measurement of attitudes toward people with disabilities: Methods, psychometrics, and scales* (pp. 51–68). Springfield, IL: C C Thomas.

Wright, B. A. (1983). *Physical disability—A psychosocial approach* (2nd ed.). New York: Harper & Row.

Wright, B. A. (1988). Attitudes and the fundamental negative bias: Conditions and corrections. In H. Yuker (Ed.), *Attitudes toward persons with disabilities* (pp. 3–21). New York: Springer.

Index